Berlioz

———◆———

Berlioz

D. KERN HOLOMAN

HARVARD UNIVERSITY PRESS
Cambridge, Massachusetts
1989

Copyright © 1989 by D. Kern Holoman
All rights reserved
Printed in the United States of America
10 9 8 7 6 5 4 3 2 1

Publication of this book has been supported
through the generous provisions of the
Maurice and Lula Bradley Smith Memorial Fund

This book is printed on acid-free paper, and its binding
materials have been chosen for strength and durability.

Library of Congress Cataloging-in-Publication Data

Holoman, D. Kern, 1947–
Berlioz.

Bibliography: p.
Includes index.
1. Berlioz, Hector, 1803–1869. 2. Composers—France—
Biography. I. Title.
ML410.B5H58 1989   780'.92'4 [B]   88-35788
ISBN 0-674-06778-9 (alk. paper)

Designed by Gwen Frankfeldt

For Betty and Kate

Acknowledgments

$\mathcal{J}$t was a coincidence both pleasing and challenging that Hugh Macdonald, David Cairns, and I were all at work on Berlioz's biography at the same time. They have both been unfailingly generous in volunteering material whenever I needed it—I am especially grateful for Cairns's transcriptions of documents from Berlioz's youth—and in reading and correcting drafts of the manuscript and, in Cairns's case, the final proofs. (At a recent meeting of the three of us, in conjunction with French bicentennial festivities, we argued rambunctiously over such matters as how many pistols Berlioz owned and what was one of the street addresses of his cousin Alphonse Robert. This sort of thing has made, over the years, for an invariably bracing intellectual camaraderie, from which I am certain I profit most of all and for which no formal acknowledgment will quite suffice.) I am equally grateful to colleagues and friends who read the first complete manuscript and prepared detailed and useful responses; these were John M. Anderson, Peter Bloom, Pierre Citron, François Lesure, Jean-Michel Nectoux, Julian Rushton, Richard Swift (who offered, additionally, invaluable assistance with my analytical graphs), and my father, W. Kern Holoman.

The present volume is autobiographical in emphasizing Berlioz's affection for the orchestra and for orchestral conducting, and I have now to thank the members, past and present, of the UCD Symphony, University of California, Davis, for their prodigious efforts in mastering, season by season (though we still have *Faust* to go), Berlioz's great works, the better that we might all learn what goes on in them. A number of my students helped compile the documentation found at the close of the book, document and assemble the illustrations, and labor over the typescripts and xeroxes; these were Curtis Lasell, John Auch, Daniel Stowe, and Donna M. Di Grazia. Darin M. Wilson reduced many of the musical examples from full score.

I am lastingly indebted to Joshua Rifkin for inducing me to undertake the work; to Margaretta Fulton of Harvard University Press for seeing that I finished it; to Quica Ostrander, who copyedited the book and prepared the index; to the production staff at HUP; to David Budmen, who prepared the musical examples and coped, probably more than anyone else, with my legendary handwriting; and to Christina Acosta of the staff of *19th-Century Music,* who volunteered to do a last reading of the proofs.

It remains to acknowledge the assistance of my colleagues at the Davis campus of the University of California for their moral support, intellectual sustenance, and prodding; of Joseph Kerman of the Berkeley campus for much the same; of the Committee on Research of the Davis campus for grants to forward the work, and the Office of Academic Affairs for granting me leaves of absence to finish it; and of the staff of the Department of Music, notably Dorothyann R. Rohde and Patricia Flowers, for ceaseless running of errands, extra effort, good cheer, and above all maintaining the administrative and financial health of the department while I ignored it for weeks on end. For making my stays in Paris pleasant and profitable, I warmly thank Pierre Citron, François Lesure, Catherine Massip, Jean-Michel Nectoux, Nicole Wild, and Florence Abondance Getreau. For clarifying various other points I am grateful to Claude Abraham, Lucien Charmard-Bois of the Musée Berlioz at La Côte-St.-André, H. Robert Cohen, the staff of the Library of Congress, Philippe Dinkel of the Bibliothèque du Conservatoire, Geneva, Yvette Fédoroff, Walter Frisch, Lousie Goldberg of the Sibley Music Library, Eastman School of Music, Peter A. Ward Jones of the Bodleian Library, Oxford, Vera Brodsky Lawrence, R. Allen Lott, Ida Reed and the staff of the Music Library, University of North Carolina, Chapel Hill, Scott Rodrick, Susan T. Sommer of the New York Public Library, Cosette Thompson, R. Larry Todd, J. Rigbie Turner of the Pierpont Morgan Library, Simone Wallon, Ruzena Wood of the Cecil Hopkinson Berlioz Collection, National Library of Scotland, Edinburgh, Rebecca Willberg, and Robert Winter.

In the last stages of production, H. Robert Cohen and Richard Macnutt offered invaluable and timely assistance with the illustrations.

Nor could I have completed this work without the support of my family, who cheerfully did without me for one sojourn in France, and managed to live with me for another. This *Berlioz* is, most of all, for them.

D.K.H.
Davis, California

Contents

Berlioz

Chapter One

"The Real Berlioz"

*F*or three decades, beginning with the *Symphonie fantastique* in 1830, Berlioz's music was the most consistently fresh, exciting, and forthright being produced in Europe. The number of works is not especially large, but the number of musical issues they confront is great indeed. Their virility alone is enough to confirm Liszt's judgment, and Paganini's, that Berlioz was the true successor to Beethoven. Yet Berlioz's associates and immediate followers, except for a few devotees, could not fathom it.

Behind the music stood an enigmatic character, whose quick tongue and undeniably dramatic presence often overshadowed what was happening in his work. His irreverence before the altars of the musical establishment seldom went unnoticed and earned him, early on, his share of detractors. His own accounts of his adventures, even today, strike the reader as larger than life. The music embodies so much excitement at the surface—languages of the damned, and church bells, and purposeful violations of the rules— that it was easy enough to dismiss it as noisy and shallow stuff. The character who rooted himself so vividly in the imaginations of those who first tried to assess him was the Berlioz of the flaming red hair, the passionate rebel, *Jeune-France,* the prototypical Romantic.

A few progressives and some sympathetic disciples grasped the import of Berlioz's work: Schumann at the beginning, and later Rimsky-Korsakov and the other Russians; in Paris there were Saint-Saëns and a handful of lesser figures: Stephen Heller, Berthold Damcke, and Ernest Reyer. The early biographers, too, saw the many-sided genius of Berlioz, but were troubled by the sauciness of the man and his music; they had their hands full, anyway, sorting out the facts of his life story.

Ernest Legouvé, an early admirer and chronicler of his life, expressed the optimistic aspirations of the last century when he wrote simply that "it is the real Berlioz I would like to portray."[1] Whether it is possible to find "the real Berlioz" in a man of such diverse interests and such broad accomplishment, I cannot say. What is clear, from the evidence at hand, is that the search should be attempted once more.

*B*erlioz wanted most to be remembered for his all-encompassing love of art and for a commitment to high ideals that both dominates and unites his work as composer, conductor, and critic. His all but limitless energy was channeled toward an unyielding integrity of musical purpose. No composer writes more frequently of his devotion to the beautiful. Describing, in his twenties, a thwarted passion, he says proudly: "The love of my art, at least, I have still—that will never leave me." "There is a religion of beauty," he said later; "I subscribe to it." Expressions regarding his "love of beauty and truth" are ubiquitous.[2] No other composer can so often be found weeping quietly, after a concert of his work, over the beauty of what he has just heard, lost to music's dominion over the spirit.

"The real Berlioz" is a gentler, subtler individual than one encounters at the witches' sabbath, or on the Day of Judgment, or, for that matter, in much of the *Mémoires*. It is as easy for us to feel deep affection for him today, once we know his story, as it was for Liszt, Chopin, and the brothers Deschamps more than a century ago. His devoted friendships, of which there were many, almost invariably were based on mutual admiration for particular artists and their art. He admired women, especially mezzo-sopranos and such intelligent aristocrats as the Princess Carolyne Sayn-Wittgenstein and the Grand Duchess Elena Pavlovna of Russia, though he was not especially successful in any of his romantic attachments. His sense of humor was pronounced, as, for the most part, was the depth of his character. He had a healthy view of humankind's potential for victory and of its inevitable tribulations. At the height of his powers he was a wise man, who could look back with satisfaction on an adventurous youth and yet be comfortable with the responsibilities of celebrity. In one of Pierre Petit's 1863 photographs, for instance (see fig. 12.3), there is something of a nineteenth-century Gioconda: the hint of a grin, the suggestion at last of inner peace. The dominating feature of his personality was the fiery intelligence that controlled his actions, stirred his muse, and sustained his considerable ambition.

No artist's work is more autobiographical: his music confirms, for example, a deep patriotism and an equally profound (though, on the whole, agnostic) spiritualism, neither of which is particularly evident in other documents of his life. The ebullience of the Capulets' ball in *Roméo et Juliette* tells us a good deal about his spirit, as do the sultry longing of *Le Roi de Thulé* in the Faust settings and the shimmer of ancient Carthage in *Les Troyens*. We see him in the characters he created: Dido in *Les Troyens*, troubled in her personal life, but every inch a queen; Romeo, alone with his thoughts in the Capulets' garden; the brigand-vagabond Cellini, whose art was worth all his riches; and even the *cabaretier* of the same opera, cross and crotchety, but ever with a twinkle in his eye.

Berlioz was a keen observer of people and of the human condition. His early training in medicine contributed to the acuity of his assessments; his descriptions of his own physical conditions border on the clinical. In 1830, for example, he writes of a dental abscess at excruciating length. He revels in his descriptions of the crazed conductor Louis Jullien, noting especially the "blood passing through his carotid arteries." Indeed, his articulate characterizations breathe life into our own conceptions of Harriet Smithson, and Le Sueur, and Cherubini, and the eccentric Kapellmeister Guhr ("Sacré nom te Tieu!"). But there is more to his prose than astute observation: behind it is systematic and rational thought. Given the prevailing practices of nineteenth-century journalism, it is exceptionally honest, with an attractive way of inviting the public to share its author's innermost thoughts, as though letting one in on a private confidence.

One cannot be around orchestras for long without sensing why Berlioz especially admired fine orchestral players. There was inevitably excitement to be found in their midst, and they were the conservators, sine qua non, of the music he loved best. Berlioz was a natural at their head and more comfortable in the concert hall than at the opera house, where he had no control over the cumbersome traditions one would inevitably inherit. The discipline he brought to managing orchestral affairs and producing concerts was to benefit Parisian musical life at once and remains among his most significant legacies. His notions of the craft of conducting, moreover, came to be the very rules of the profession.

Like the other children of his time, Berlioz enjoyed the allures of life in Louis-Philippe's industrialized society and at the same time suffered the formidable costs in time, money, and health of European travel. The century's new technologies revolutionized his perceptions of time and space; his lifestyle, too, was improved by the railway, the telegraph, lithographic plates and mass-produced paper, gas lighting, electricity, photography, and, not least of all, modern orchestral instruments. Paris, where he established his practice, became so much a part of his life that despite its disappointments and perpetual uncertainties, he could never leave it without coming back.

In his creative world, Berlioz journeyed down the familiar path of imitation, aggressive experimentation, and arrival at a comfortable, detached classicism. But the works fall more naturally into four groups than into the conventional early, middle, and late periods. A few childhood compositions and the student years in Paris culminate in three works heralding the achievement of a personal style: *Huit Scènes de Faust, Neuf Mélodies,* and the *Symphonie fantastique.* After the offhand and, with one exception, insubstantial works from his sojourn in Italy, there follows the sparkling decade of *Harold en Italie,* the Requiem, *Benvenuto Cellini, Roméo et Juliette,* the *Nuits d'été,* and the *Grande Symphonie funèbre et triomphale.* The European travels of 1843 and later, though they caused at first a radical decline in new composition, led to a maturation nourished by Berlioz's international experience and culminating in *La Damnation de Faust*. His last works achieve a tranquil refinement appropriate to the close of one's career: this is the period of *L'Enfance du Christ, Les Troyens,* and *Béatrice et Bénédict*.

His compositional thought was born of the musical practice of provincial France, of the Parisian heritage of Gluck and the others, and in Beethoven and Shakespeare. He was essentially self-taught, helped along by a single didactic treatise, a shadowy ne'er-do-well, and an aging, sometimes doddering composition teacher, probably the nation's best. It is important to remember, as his story unfolds, how radically different these circumstances were from those that molded his German contemporaries Schumann and Mendelssohn and his friends Liszt and Chopin.

Public figures must learn to live with public misapprehension, but Berlioz suffered more than most from the effects of unduly cruel rumor. Periodicals reported that the Requiem needed four choruses, that a cathedral large enough for the Te Deum had yet to be built, and that *Les Troyens* set all twelve books of the *Aeneid*. It was stated as fact that *Cellini* had required twenty-nine general rehearsals; it was held that the *Journal des Débats* paid Berlioz 10,000 francs each year. He came to be resigned to the confusion, which was the result of perhaps a half-dozen passages in his work and one or two unusual events in his life. "My destiny," he came to realize, "is to be confined outside the road generally taken—despite myself."[3]

Although documents of Berlioz's life number many thousands of pages, some dilemmas and unanswered questions nevertheless remain. Berlioz's library and belongings have been dispersed and must be reconstructed in the mind's eye. There is no study where the master worked, few relics left to evoke his living conditions. What remains of his close and sometimes boisterous life with the musicians he loved is a room or two of party favors: a plaster bas-relief, a golden crown into every leaf of which is engraved the title of one of his great works, a few batons, and a guitar, which the museum attendant will tell you was broken by the young Berlioz in an access of spleen.

And one needs to come to terms with the unseemly side of Berlioz's character. It may be understandable that he lied about taking a private room when in fact he was lodging with a mistress: this was a simple effort to spare his family, particularly his aging father, from the sordid details of his domestic discontent. His practices of maintaining both a legal address and a different private address and collecting his personal mail from a forwarder were typical of many another liaison of the era. But the letters of his wife, Harriet, and their son, Louis, tell a sadder tale; it is hard to reconcile Louis's complaints to his aunt of hearing nothing at all from his father with Berlioz's pious testimony of regular correspondence. Louis Berlioz succeeds his mother as the central victim of this tragedy when, in childish hand and unpolished grammar, he writes: "Je ne sais où est mon Papa."

Each reader will have to decide for himself or herself how to juxtapose the Berlioz of the *Mémoires* and "the real Berlioz." One can proceed, at least, from the assumption that the book is, by and large, factual—so factual, indeed, that long stretches must have been based on a lost journal or on draft copies of the most important correspondence. But the stories of Estelle of the pink boots and the composer's passion for an Italian corpse have an aroma of sensational journalism, and I will argue that the prevailing tone of the *Mémoires,* one of misery and defeat, leaves an overall impression of Berlioz's life that is demonstrably false. His autobiography has come to be recognized as one of the most significant documents of the musical life of the nineteenth century. I agree with that assessment. Yet I cannot get over the feeling that it is an enigmatic self-portrait.

Berlioz's life and especially his works continue to intrigue us because his orientation to people, events, and artistic trends was so consistently out of step. His music often defies, and purposefully so, placement in any continuum of the nineteenth century's formal and harmonic practice. Explanations of its structure have a way of seeming simplistic next to the exalted analyses useful in approaching the music of the Viennese; nevertheless, it can be music of surpassing difficulty. People still react to his music in a way they do not so often do to that of Schumann or Mendelssohn, weeping, as Berlioz himself did, over passage after passage from his great works. Revisionism has shattered any number of myths about the life and left the magic of the music undiminished. From that alone I conclude that the old notion of Berlioz as a failure is the greatest myth of all.

Chapter Two

La Côte-St.-André
(1803–21)

The child born at 5:00 P.M. on Sunday, 11 December 1803, in the small village of La Côte-St.-André belonged to the first generation of a new century.[1] He and his contemporaries were to forge a new politics, a new industry, a new art. They would know Napoleon only as a legend.

The Berlioz family had been tanners in the valley of the river Isère since the seventeenth century. They had acquired money and reputation, and Berlioz's paternal grandfather, a lawyer and government official, had constructed a spacious, comfortable family home on a property at the edge of town. The child's maternal lineage, through the Marmion family, appears to have been no less eminent. Grandfather Nicolas Marmion, who stood as the baby's godfather, also had handsome properties. The two close uncles, Félix Marmion and Victor Berlioz, were educated and articulate.

Louis-Joseph Berlioz, the composer's father, was a physician who successfully defended his dissertation in Paris shortly after his first child was born. He was a creative and above all hardworking town doctor, an advocate of such progressive cures as hydrotherapy and acupuncture. In 1810 he won a competition sponsored by the ancient and honorable medical faculty at Montpellier; his treatise, entitled *Mémoires sur les maladies chroniques, les évacuations sanguines et l'acupuncture,* was published in 1816. In 1814 he was admitted as an associate member to the Medical Society of Paris. On these accomplishments might have been built a research career of national prominence, especially had Dr. Berlioz elected to practice in a metropolitan area. But he ignored the temptations of fame and fortune that later seduced his son and instead chose to lead a life of quiet respectability in his native region. His inherited property in the area was considerable, and his work there guaranteed a healthy, if not extravagant, income.

Widely read and of an intellectual bent, Dr. Berlioz was remembered to have been a generous, good man, particularly with regard to his concern for the poor. His afflictions included a certain melancholia and a confirmed

FIGURE 2.1 Louis-Joseph Berlioz.

political and intellectual skepticism. Despite the several standoffs between father and son during the harsh years of Berlioz's young manhood, the overall record is one of profound filial devotion.

The composer's mother, Marie-Antoinette-Joséphine, née Marmion, is an enigmatic character, in part because until recently only his *Mémoires* have had much to say of her personality.[2] She was apparently fretful and easily aroused to fits of temper, the parent from whom the boy inherited his more controversial attributes of character. But the evidence also suggests a loyal *mère de famille,* who sang her children lullabies and sentimental songs and imagined herself devoted beyond measure to their best interests.[3] She caused her son more heartache than he merited, but her notions of familial propriety were born more of provincial tradition than of any ill will. By the time her older children were facing the trials of adolescence, she had buried a son and a daughter. We meet her in the *Mémoires* at less than her best.

Louis-Hector, the couple's firstborn, was thus the offspring of a healthily mixed lineage. From his father's side came a rational and inquisitive frame of mind, given to doubting common stock; the vivid temper and depth of passion were surely maternal. But these latter traits, decidedly the more provocative side of his personality, were as essential to his commitment to art and his drive for success as all the discipline inherited from his father's outlook on life. Where heredity is concerned, in any case, the young Berlioz seems a far cry from the puny children born of exhausted loins that the Romantics came to describe as their generation.

La Côte-St.-André was, and remains, rural, perhaps somewhat primitive, doubtless a result of its distance from Lyon, some sixty-five kilometers to the northwest, and Grenoble, forty-eight kilometers to the southeast. Nestled in a ridge overlooking the wide plain of Bièvre, the village seems dwarfed by the surrounding geography, and thus the quieter, the more tranquil. The rich color of the landscape and the sensational view of fields and distant hills have captivated every disciple who has made the pilgrimage to Berlioz's birthplace. Italy is proximate; the Alps loom proudly at the eastern horizon. Berlioz cherished this countryside, and it surely has much to do with his superb powers to evoke majestic musical landscape. But after 1830 his visits there can be counted on the fingers of a hand.

The Berlioz home is a rambling town house on the main street, of two stories with an attic and any number of intermediate nooks and crannies, enveloping three sides of a courtyard. It is fashioned of masonry and stone. An entry hall leads up into the living area and down into a cellar, where it is said that the young composer held his chamber music sessions. The main dwelling rooms were on the first floor above the entry level; bedrooms and Dr. Berlioz's consulting room were in other parts of the house. The guides tell tourists that the smallest closet was Hector's room, but this is only surmise.

Additionally the family owned a farmhouse with orchards and vines at Le Chuzeau, a few kilometers east of town, and property in a hamlet near Grenoble called Les Jacques. Le Chuzeau is but a brief walk from the house in La Côte. There Mme Berlioz and her children would repair to enjoy the onset of spring and fall, to relax during the summer, and always to collect whatever was ripe or fresh. The value of these properties, inherited by Berlioz and his sisters, was to sustain the adult composer through more than a few of his many fiscal embarrassments.

He felt at home, too, in Grenoble, a cosmopolitan city through which flow the icy waters of the Isère as they rush from Mont-Cenis, high in the Alps, toward the Rhone. It was the seat of a fine faculty, with which the family had some dealings, and the home of cousins and later a beloved niece. The Marmion home lay nearby in Meylan, then just another of the picturesque villages overlooking Grenoble, now the suburban terminus of one of the tramways.

The child grew up with a sister three years younger than he, Marguerite-Anne-Louise, called by the family Nanci—or, as she herself preferred to spell it, Nancy. (Another sister, Louise-Julie-Virginie, died at eight years of age, when Berlioz was twelve; Louis-Jules lived three years, 1816–19.) The other surviving children were Adèle-Eugénie, born in 1814, and Prosper, born in 1820, a little more than a year before their elder brother departed for Paris. (The composer outlived them all, as he outlived both his wives and his only child.) Another well-loved member of the household was Monique Netty, the chambermaid and nurse.

Nanci and Adèle, the siblings who survived to maturity, are significant characters in the Berlioz biography, even as children. His fondness for his sisters evolved into a natural affection for women in general; he was always at ease in the company of women and quick to enjoy an affair of the heart. Nanci was the more straitlaced of the two, much taken with propriety and the social dignities incumbent on a gracious family. Adèle was the gentler and more naturally affectionate and for that reason offers posterity a somewhat less striking personality. Both became attractive women, married comfortably, and bore handsome children. They and their husbands became the executors of the Berlioz property in the Isère, seeing to the disposition of the estate and the protection of its employees once the parents had died and the children had all moved away. The male lineage, and therefore the name, was lost with the death of Berlioz's son, Louis.

Each member of the family was or grew to be literate and supportive of accomplishment in the liberal arts. They read widely and welcomed music as an important part of the household's interests. Both the immediate family and the relatives were gifted correspondents: they exchanged many-paged letters in which the usual gossipy fare was often couched in elevated conceits. (Berlioz became an expert at the one-sentence letter, but his epistles homeward were always lengthy.) In sum there was a congenial family atmosphere, considerable warmth, a well-developed sense of the good life.

The documents of life in La Côte-St.-André include, in addition to the composer's own recollections, various letters of the family, a journal kept by Nanci in her teenage years, some documents relating to the establishment of musical tuition in the town, and a journal kept by Dr. Berlioz, his *livre de raison* (book of accounts). Primary source for much of what we know of the family lineage, the *livre de raison* is an intriguing artifact, comprising a genealogy and history of the family, a biography of Berlioz's paternal grand-father, an autobiographical essay by Dr. Berlioz himself, and inventories of the family properties and library. A few musical manuscripts suggest something of the nature of music education in La Côte-St.-André and preserve some of Berlioz's earliest efforts at composition. There is little else: after Berlioz's death several of his childhood friends tried to recollect the early years, but without notable success. Yet the surviving evidence fits snugly together, with no long gaps and relatively few unanswerable questions, to suggest that the composer's upbringing was on the whole rather ordinary.

At some point, possibly when the lad was six years of age, he was sent to the local seminary for elementary education. How long he stayed remains a mystery. In any event, the education of so promising a child was reckoned by Dr. Berlioz to be the responsibility of the family, and thus he tutored his son in a course of study that relied heavily on the classics, supplemented by readings in other literatures, geography, and history. Dr. Berlioz's considerable library had been acquired and continued to grow through diligent inquiry to various dealers in Paris. It was up to date, in some respects rather voguish.

This free-style curriculum allowed Berlioz to develop his personal fancies, especially for books on travel and tales of yore. Together, father and son read the Greeks, Virgil, La Fontaine's *Fables, Paul et Virginie* (Bernardin de Saint-Pierre's saccharine tale of young love in the Indies, 1788). As his passion for music began to develop during his early teens, Berlioz devoured the composers' biographies in J. F. Michaud's *Biographie universelle,* a multivolume set which was arriving in annual fascicles. There was the assumption, though at first a subtle one, that the son would continue in his father's profession; thus the readings included, for example, a *Traité d'ostéologie* (by Alexander Monro, in French translation, 1759). The family kept abreast of politics and literary trends through a subscription to the Paris *Journal des Débats,* the newspaper that would eventually offer Berlioz the better part of his life's income.

Dr. Berlioz encouraged his son's new excitement about music by purchasing a flute and flute tutor and then some treatises on composition. He does not seem to have known or cared about buying printed music, however, and most of the music in the family library either postdates the arrival of the music masters in town or was sent from Paris, much later, by Berlioz himself.

The negative side of this education was that it lacked the discipline of conventional schooling. Berlioz was never to be comfortable in a classroom; he never learned to curb his natural passions in the presence of those—the majority—who failed to share his enthusiasms. But in terms of unbridling both the boy's imagination and his curiosity, Dr. Berlioz's tutelage worked so well as to cause the entire family, soon enough, some second thoughts.

The children's moral upbringing was the responsibility of Mme Berlioz. Mother and children were good Catholics, or at least avid ones; they attended daily mass and Sunday communion, and Berlioz regularly went for confession, he says, with nothing to confess. He was confirmed, in perhaps 1814 or 1815, at the nearby convent of the Visitation, where the girls went to convent school. As an adult, Berlioz came to disavow formal expressions of religion, but his memories of the church, its rituals, ceremonies, litanies, and processions, were vivid and often found expression in his music.

Among the other fond memories of his childhood were the late summer visits of the family to the home of their grandfather, Nicolas Marmion, in the village of Meylan. Here during the summer of 1815 they met the eighteen-year-old niece of a neighbor, a young woman named Estelle Dubœuf. Berlioz was smitten with the handsome girl: her hair, her good looks, and above all her pink boots. She was standing, he recalled, on a rock, her hand resting on the trunk of a cherry tree. She seemed the embodiment of Florian's *Estelle,* a pastoral romance that had shortly before spoken directly to his budding sexuality. They saw each other on and off for the next three years, once more in 1832, and again several times when both had grown old. It was to her that his thoughts turned during the darkest moments of 1848: by the time he first wrote of Estelle she was a vision of his childhood, mingled with memories of Latin and of the sounds of the flageolet, a mountain star, his *stella montis.*

To explain the Estelle incident is to try to rationalize Romanticism. They were the merest of acquaintances at the time; she became in his imagination more a literary conceit than an ordinary mortal. She happened along just as he discovered the ability of the heart to yearn. She knew nothing of it then, of course, and her reaction upon learning of his love half a century later was, at first, one of perplexed amusement.

The friends of his adolescence were, by and large, the young men from the prospering families of La Côte, among them three who also went to Paris to study: Charles Bert, Berlioz's cousin Alphonse Robert, and Antoine Charbonnel, later the town pharmacist. Berlioz shared his enthusiasm for music with two young men of more modest standing: Joseph Favre and Imbert *fils.* Favre played the clarinet in the town band and later became a shoemaker; the two stayed in close enough touch that Berlioz at some point gave him the autograph of an early musical project. (Favre lived long enough for his personal recollections to be of some value to the early biographers.) Imbert *fils* was the son of Berlioz's first music teacher, who will enter this narrative momentarily.

*I*t was soon after Berlioz delighted in finding a flageolet about the house that Dr. Berlioz bought him a true flute and Devienne's *Méthode de flute théorique et pratique* (Paris, 1795). By 1815–16 he had conceived the idea of notating his own music on paper. At first he probably tried to imitate the musical fare of the local religious institutions and the practices of the Alpine folk; then he was drawn to such of the excerpts from comic opera as had filtered into town, outdated by two decades or more, from Paris. He was trained in rhythm, he says, by the 4:00 A.M. cadence of Claude Ferlet, the blacksmith across the street whose merry pounding woke him up each morning.[4]

His growing interest in the techniques of composition was aided by two treatises that had made their way into the family library: Rameau's *Eléments de musique, développés et simplifiés par M. d'Alembert* (Paris, 1752) and Charles-Simon Catel's *Traité d'harmonie* (1802). The former was too complex for self-teaching, but the latter, more a simplified code of rules than any well-developed theory, proved accessible enough to serve the young man as a first tutor. Indeed, Catel's little booklet helped form several generations of aspiring composers, both in France and elsewhere (through translations into English, German, and Italian).

There had been a National Guard band in La Côte since 1805, supplied with both instruments and a director by a music dealer in Lyon. The first director was a M. Bouchmann, hesitant in French but accomplished on the woodwind instruments and violin. His band listed in its inventory piccolos, clarinets, horns, a bassoon, trumpets, a trombone, and basic percussion. Berlioz had been drawn increasingly into the activities of the band for some time. Local tradition has it that he was the percussion player, but he must surely have tried his hand at the woodwind instruments too.

When Bouchmann disappeared, the band carried on for a time by itself, but neither its accomplishments nor Berlioz's own fledgling efforts at composition and flute playing were enough to satiate the young man's growing appetites. In 1817 his father and other prominent townspeople joined together to bring a music master to town, securing the services of M. Imbert, second violinist in the pit orchestra of a Lyon theater. His contract reads as follows:

1. M. Imbert engages himself to give music lessons in voice and instruments to twelve students from the town, at a fee of eight francs [each] per month;
2. He will instruct the National Guard band, direct it, and rehearse it twice a week;
3. If some of the less fortunate musicians of the guard wish to have private lessons, he will provide these at a fee of five francs per month;
4. If these conditions are met, the community will furnish him lodging in the town house and will assure him the sum of 100 francs per month if the students from the town are unable to provide it;
5. The present conditions will last a year from this day, 20 May 1817.

> Buffevent [the mayor]
> Imbert[5]

Imbert arrived with his son, known to posterity only as Imbert *fils,* a boy about Berlioz's age who played the clarinet and French horn well. Imbert *père* also brought new music to town, notably the string quartets of Pleyel, attributed at the time to Haydn. It was doubtless he who advised Dr. Berlioz on the purchase of such music as was then added to the family library. Imbert was a kindly man and a successful teacher, and soon an active society of chamber musicians had begun to meet, under his tutelage, on Sundays after mass. To Berlioz these sessions were infinitely more interesting than the activities of the band, and increasingly his musical enthusiasm focused on the "local philharmonic society."

Having found a group of serious amateurs to share such *matinées* and *soirées,* Berlioz began to write chamber music for them: quartets, quintets, and arrangements of popular songs for the instrumentalists on hand. His first extended composition was a *potpourri concertant sur des thèmes italiens* for flute, horn, two violins, viola, and bass (that is, cello), written perhaps in early 1818. He himself played the flute, Imbert's son played the horn, and Imbert joined the amateurs in covering the strings parts.

Soon the music master had taught Berlioz all the composition he could, but in the other areas his appointment was found to be satisfactory enough for his contract to be extended by a year on 20 May 1818. This time the guarantors of the agreement included not only the mayor but Dr. Berlioz and the other prosperous Côtois as well. Late that summer, however, Imbert *fils* committed suicide, and the dejected father, having no further household and doubtless anxious to quit the locus of so unhappy an event, abruptly left town.

Berlioz applied himself in those succeeding months, with more than a hint of his future determination, to finding a publisher for his *potpourri.* A letter of 25 March 1819 proposes the work to the Parisian firm of Janet & Cotelle, and two weeks later a similar letter was penned to Ignaz Pleyel himself.[6] Both letters—they are probably the first preserved examples of his hand-writing—mention other compositions, suggesting that by the spring of 1819 Berlioz had composed a number of works, including the two quintets for flute and strings that he mentions in the *Mémoires.* There were no takers in Paris.

By the spring of 1819 a replacement had been found for Imbert, one F.-X. Dorant. His contract, dated 24 July, was entered into with four private citizens. Dorant agreed to give music lessons in voice and instruments; MM. Berlioz, Bert, Antoine Rocher, and Rocher *fils* promised to reimburse Dorant should the agreed fee of ten francs a month per student not be forthcoming from the anticipated eight pupils.[7]

Dorant was an Alsatian with a broader repertoire and a better command of instruments than Imbert had; he was, moreover, a relatively accomplished composer. Most important of all, Dorant played the guitar well and began to give Nanci Berlioz guitar lessons. Her brother was quick to master the new instrument himself, and thus he added to his accomplishments in percussion and flute skill on an instrument that could accompany the voice. Dorant helped him to arrange guitar accompaniments for operatic arias and then to fashion his first original songs. Berlioz's earliest preserved manuscript music is a setting of Pollet's *Fleuve du Tage*, left in one of Dorant's notebooks (fig. 2.2).

For one of these songs, possibly *Le Dépit de la bergère*, there was an interested publisher—interested at least until he received the following letter from La Côte:

> Sir:
> They told me you would make me suffer if I put myself in your hands. Alas! the prophecy has been fulfilled. I would have been reasonably satisfied with the terms I accepted (terms which, you will grant, I have no other reason to be pleased about) if you had carried them out punctually.
> I am still waiting for the second proof!!
> I have the honor to salute you,
>
> Hector Berlioz[8]

FIGURE 2.2 Berlioz's setting of J.-J.-B. Pollet's *Fleuve du Tage*. Notebook of F.-X. Dorant, Musée Berlioz, La Côte-St.-André.

Le Dépit de la bergère was indeed offered for sale by the Paris firm of Auguste Le Duc, perhaps as early as 1819. Stylistically it seems the least polished of Berlioz's early songs—perhaps it really is the earliest—with unwieldy voice-leading and harmonic progression. (Note, for example, in the first four measures of figure 2.3, the embarrassed chain of dominant sonorities between the opening D-major triad and the cadence in the fourth bar, and how the bass line lacks any consideration of voice leading. At A–A♯–B near the beginning of the last system, over C♯ in the bass, Berlioz leaves another good example of the drawbacks of self-teaching.) Two more sophisticated songs were entered, in his own hand, in one of Dorant's albums: an *Invocation à l'amitié*, with a refrain for three voices, and *L'Arabe jaloux*.[9] *L'Arabe jaloux*, in particular, demonstrates a beginning mastery of the late eighteenth-century *romance*. Its revised version, retitled *Le Maure jaloux* for publication, involves several complexities (for example, a Neapolitan chord) and relationships not found in the other two works. All three of the early romances suggest guitar accompaniment, though the published editions call for piano.

Berlioz tells of another original composition, *Je vais donc quitter pour jamais,* in which he first wrote the melody that was later adopted for the very beginning of the *Symphonie fantastique.* The song sets longing words of Florian and may be somehow related to the Estelle affair.

A manuscript *Recueil de romances* (Collection of ballads) for voices and guitar, settings of well-known operatic arias and *romances* of the day, completes the corpus of music from the La Côte period.[10] The songs, by Berton, Boieldieu, Dalayrac, Dellamaria, Martini, and the like, are the simplest of excerpts from the *opéras-comiques* staged in Paris during the late 1780s and 1790s. The youngest is from Boieldieu's *Petit Chaperon rouge* (Little Red Riding Hood, 1818), a charming ariette. The date of the notebook itself is uncertain; its overall appearance suggests a fair copy prepared for some Paris publisher. But the repertoire is surely that of La Côte-St.-André in the second decade of the century; Berlioz's original guitar accompaniments just as surely come from that time. This is the manuscript he later gave to Joseph Favre; it is now housed in the Berlioz museum at La Côte-St.-André.

*T*he arrival of Dorant, Berlioz's discovery of the guitar, and his reasonably successful first attempts at composition must have presented his parents with a dilemma. They had, after all, encouraged the children in their musical interests and had taken the lead in securing the services of qualified teachers for the community. It most likely dawned on them as early as 1820 or so that dreams of a composer's life were beginning to preoccupy their son. Polite society conceived any number of injunctions against careers in the theater, which in the provinces was imagined to include the practice of

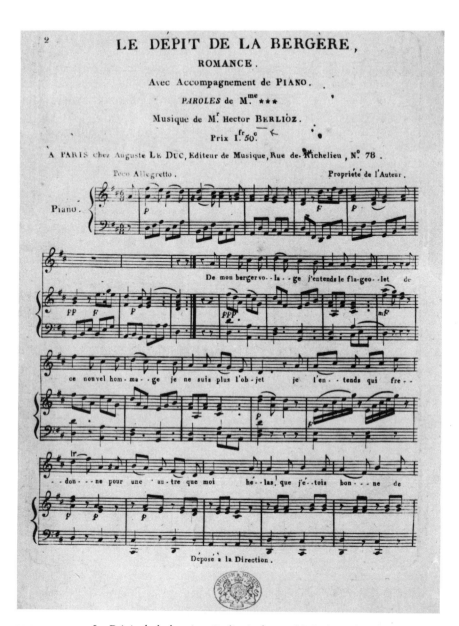

FIGURE 2.3 *Le Dépit de la bergère*, Berlioz's first published work. (Paris: Auguste Le Duc, [c. 1819])

music; moreover, the Berlioz family was mourning the death of another son, Louis-Jules, and surely concerned more than ever with matters of lineage. And so it was that the parents' insistence that their elder son enter a proper profession began to develop real momentum just as he was coming to quite the opposite conclusion. A collision was already inevitable; I think it a mark of Berlioz's shrewdness that he did not care to face the issue until after he had left home to see for himself what Paris had to offer.

There could have been no denying his accomplishments in music thus far. Within the confines of small-town musical life—there was, for example, no piano in La Côte—he had absorbed most of the rudiments of musical discipline. His experience with the band and the chamber players had led to a certain ease in writing for instrumental aggregations and experience in the production of live concerts. He could sight-sing without error and had already developed a splendid ear and a prodigious memory. He had discovered staff paper, music theory, and the rigors of publishing. He had learned a certain amount of serious repertoire; the sprightly idiom of the comic opera had become second nature to him. His compositional ideas were sound enough for him already to have produced a number of melodies that he later reused with great success.

Sometime early in 1821 it was agreed that he would go to Paris that autumn to study medicine. To that end, he was sent to Grenoble to stand for his baccalaureate. In this preliminary he was successful, and his degree of *Bachelier ès lettres* was duly conferred on 22 March 1821. That same spring, far away in St. Helena, Napoleon died.

On 26 October Berlioz went to the *mairie* to secure his passport for domestic travel. That document contains our first description of his appearance:

> 1 m., 63 cm. [5′ 4″] in height; blond hair and eyebrows; ordinary forehead; grey eyes; well-formed nose; medium mouth; beginnings of a beard; round chin; oval face; ruddy complexion; no distinguishing marks.[11]

He left for Paris at the end of the month in the company of his cousin Alphonse Robert, with whom he was to share lodgings. In his pockets, as he climbed into the coach, were the first 500 francs or so of the allowance that within a few months became the centerpiece of his struggle to achieve something approaching independence.

Chapter Three

The Latin Quarter and the Boulevards
(1821–30)

Since the Middle Ages, Paris has drawn to it the nation's best students, young people intent on careers in the law, medicine, and government, undaunted by the deprivations of urban life on modest stipends. They arrive naïve provincials, taken most of all with the eminence of the faculties that have drawn them there, but are quick to find more intriguing allures: diversions of the flesh, entertainments of the fancy, the seats of government and commerce, the great temples of art. In these, too, Paris has for centuries been—with remarkably few interruptions—the envy of Europe. A little older and much wiser, the city's students generally return home with their degrees to become leaders in business, or the professions, or local politics. But not a few discover in Paris an irresistible new life and elect to spend their careers in the hubbub of this most cosmopolitan of worlds.

Life in the French capital during the 1820s was, in comparison with the tumult of the previous three decades, outwardly tranquil, favoring the growth of diverse enterprises. Yet widespread discontent lurked just below the surface of this apparent stability. The throne of France had been restored to Louis XVIII following the Hundred Days of Napoleon's return in 1814, and the king, knowing well enough that legitimacy itself was no longer of much political consequence, was at first determined to create for his nation a modern, enlightened constitutional monarchy. That changed with the assassination of his nephew, the Duc de Berry, in February 1820. The very existence of a legitimate Bourbon monarchy seemed threatened: the duke was known to be the only member of the royal family capable of fathering an heir. (This he had done a few months before, unbeknownst to his murderer.) The government's swift, predictable reaction to this evidence of civil unrest was to clamp tight controls on the press and the Sorbonne and to institute repressive electoral policies favoring the titled landowners. Louis XVIII was succeeded in September 1824 by his brother, who became Charles X in a pompous coronation at Rheims, offending by this gesture and many subsequent ones some of the fundamental tenets of 1789. Popular unhappiness was compounded, as the decade progressed, by economic crisis: successive poor harvests resulted in rampant inflation, industrial recession, and the failure of banks.

Paris, at the center of all this, was curiously isolated from the sentiments of a nation where 85 percent of the populace lived in the provinces, their countrified lifestyles yet to be much affected by the economic and social revolutions of the century. Greater Paris numbered about 800,000 citizens when Berlioz arrived there.[1] To its timeless bustle had been added the noisy trappings of modern life: the streets were congested with horse-drawn vehicles, including new modes of public transportation. Steamboats plied the river, and an occasional steam-powered carriage was tried in town. Gas lighting gradually brought new nighttime vistas, radical changes on the stage, and more than a few terrible fires. Paris remained an obligatory stop for tourists, including musicians, who came from all over Europe to examine these wonders.

The look of the city was always undergoing change. Berlioz's five decades of residency there were a time of uninterrupted construction, from new residential quarters to pleasure palaces and railroad stations. Napoleon had initiated public works aimed at creating grand vistas with wide avenues and columned arcades; the bulk of Baron Haussmann's work—opening up the boulevards, rebuilding the slums, erecting four bridges and reconstructing three others, building a public market at Les Halles and a grand new opera house—took place while Berlioz lived in Paris. It may have been that one of Haussmann's goals, after the events of 1830 and 1848, was to reduce the possibility of further insurrection by the simple expedient of making barricades more difficult to erect. By and large, however, the modernization of Paris was part and parcel of industrial revolution.

*A*rriving in Paris in early November, Berlioz and his cousin took modest rooms on the Left Bank in the boarding house of a M. Drouault, at 104, rue St. Jacques.[2] Together they enrolled in the November session at the Faculty of Medicine and began to attend the anatomy course of the brilliant young surgeon Jean-Zuléma Amussat, still in his twenties. They heard lectures in related subjects as well—for instance, chemistry with Baron Thénard and physics with Gay-Lussac, whose experiments with electricity delighted Berlioz. Robert, the more enthusiastic of the two young men where things anatomical were concerned, purchased a cadaver and led Berlioz to the dissecting rooms of the Hospice de la Pitié to examine it. Berlioz fled—I shall not try to match his graphic description in the *Mémoires*[3]—from the horrors of the morgue; this event, which must have taken place within a few weeks of his arrival in Paris, was critical in dissuading him from medical study.

He attended classes in the liberal arts as well, including the history course of Charles de Lacretelle and lectures in literature offered by a poet and sometime librettist named François Andrieux. Berlioz soon discovered that his admiration for the technical prowess of the scientists could not compensate for his aversion to medicine, which he already found to be *une étude dégoûtante*. Yet the increasingly attractive notion of a career in arts and letters had to be measured against the almost certain opposition of his family. For the first several weeks in Paris, he was merely disoriented and confused, not least by the unfamiliar sensation of rank anonymity. His ruminations led to a period of introspection, self-doubt, and panic:

> I reflect that I know nothing, that I have everything to learn, that maybe Papa will be unhappy with me, that maybe . . . *Que sais-je moi*.[4]

It did not take long for the two young Côtois to be received into at least one elevated stratum of Parisian society, for they soon found themselves invited to cotillions and *soirées* given by relatives and friends of the family. The parties seemed not so different from those at home, except that there were sixty to dance, to "an orchestra of two violins and a flageolet," instead of sixteen, and one had to take care not to step on people's feet.[5] Berlioz's interest in these events gave way in a short time to boredom; gradually he turned for companionship to a circle of liberal young intellectuals, several of them from the Dauphiné. These were young men who could share what were becoming ever more passionate enthusiasms for poetry and music.

Soon after his arrival Berlioz ventured to the Opéra, in its new theater on the rue Le Peletier. Within a few weeks he had seen Salieri's *Les Danaïdes* and Méhul's *Stratonice* and a ballet based on Dalayrac's *Nina*. At the Opéra-Comique in the Salle Feydeau, dominated at the time by Boieldieu, he heard lesser but no less interesting fare. He was transported, as was a generation of operagoers, by Mme Branchu and Mlle Grassari, by Dérivis and Adolphe Nourrit; he saw spectacle and heard an enormity of sound that theretofore he could only have imagined; he watched the work of the brilliant new conductor at the Opéra, François-Antoine Habeneck. On 26 November, little more than three weeks after his arrival, he was able to fulfill one of the dreams of his childhood, for Gluck's *Iphigénie en Tauride* was offered. Simply seeing the posted announcement, he later wrote with some hyperbole, caused his nose to bleed: "My teeth began to chatter and my legs to shake: . . . *Iphi— Iphigénie en Tauride*."[6]

By mid-decade he was to discover Spontini's masterpiece *Olimpie* (1819), along with *La Vestale* (1807) and *Fernand Cortez* (1809). Not long afterward the accomplishments of both Spontini and Gluck were being eclipsed in Paris by the dawn of Rossini, Auber, and Meyerbeer; in another decade the eclipse was complete. But whatever the whim of the public, it was the great works of Gluck and Spontini, absorbed scene by scene, then bar by bar, that so broadened Berlioz's understanding of dramatic music in the early and middle

L'OPÉRA AVANT L'INCENDIE : FACADE SUR LA RUE LE PELETIER ET INTÉRIEUR DE LA SALLE. — Voir page 727.

FIGURE 3.1 The Opéra in the rue Le Peletier.

(Acad.^e Roy.^{le} de Musique)   Mme BRANCHU.   (Role de la Vestale.)
Opéra du même nom.

Toi que j'implore avec effroi
Redoutable Déesse
Sur la malheureuse Pictropie
Obtiens grace devant toi &.^c

FIGURE 3.2 Madame Branchu as Julia in Spontini's *La Vestale*.

1820s. They unveiled to him, in short, a new stylistic universe, the starting point for compositional efforts more substantial than the *romance* and *potpourri*.

*M*uch of this, but by no means all, Berlioz reports in what appear to have been weekly letters home. The family, having by now attached proud significance to a medical career for their obviously gifted son, must surely have harbored suspicions about even his earliest correspondence, with so little about medicine and so much gossip of politics and theatrical goings-on. The journals kept by his sister Nanci, then sixteen years old, offer tantalizing glimpses of their perceptions: they are concerned at his "distractions" and particularly troubled by letters in March and April 1822 describing, presumably as an eyewitness, an incident of street fighting. Alphonse Robert was reporting home, too, and their letters were compared. "Hector has written a very sad letter," Nanci notes, and goes on to suggest that Robert, too, was in some sort of trouble.[7]

Berlioz's clear disinterest in his studies became the main concern of a flurry of letters between members of the family. A visit to La Côte that spring by Alphonse Robert confirmed their suspicions. Berlioz's own return home in the autumn was made the more uncomfortable by Robert's having preceded him, but some understanding with his father—presumably an agreement that he would enroll for another year of medical study—was achieved, and Berlioz left for Paris again on 21 October 1822, with 500 francs of further subven-

FIGURE 3.3 Adolphe Nourrit.

tion.[8] He and his cousin then separated: Berlioz took lodgings at 71, rue St. Jacques, and Robert moved to 79, hôtel de Nantes.

In total, Berlioz pursued his medical studies, with some diligence, for just over a year. It was a broadening year at that, during which he cultivated a lifelong interest in technology—electricity in particular—and a habit of scientific observation and diagnostic analysis that was to serve him well. And it was not his fault, but rather the result of political unrest, that his studies were twice interrupted by long closures of the College of Medicine. He enrolled in his fifth term at the beginning of November 1822, but the faculty was dismissed on 18 November, not to return until the following April. Berlioz thereafter continued to follow those few lectures that attracted his interest, but was never to return to active study of medicine.

The late autumn of 1822 and the following winter months thus offered him leisure to pursue his interest in music, and it is then that his work in composition first began to develop real momentum. Trips to the opera were to be expected of genteel medical students; Berlioz's discovery that the library of the Conservatoire was open to the public is more telling testimony to the seriousness of his new purpose. He spent long afternoons learning the operatic masterpieces from scores in the library, poring over page after page and copying out his favorite passages. (Two manuscripts of excerpts from Gluck—the only great composer he so far knew much about—come from late 1822; at one point he writes "ne plus ultra de la musique."[9]) And there in the halls of the Conservatoire he encountered its colorful personnel: Luigi Cherubini, the institution's authoritarian new director, lurching about on his cane and prone to irascibility; Habeneck, himself and his students in a flush of excitement over their discovery of Beethoven's works; the Belgian savant François-Joseph Fétis, then a teacher of counterpoint, soon to be librarian of the Conservatoire and founder of the influential *Revue musicale;* Hottin, a prototypical porter and *garçon d'orchestre;* and, among the students, one Hyacinthe Gerono, flutist, cellist, and mediocre composer.

In early 1822 Berlioz had arranged publication of a *romance* from La Côte, *Le Maure jaloux,* and composed another, *Pleure pauvre Colette,* to a text by "Mr Bourgerie"—presumably Jean-Marc Bourgery, an acquaintance from the medical school. These were published in April 1822 by Mme Cuchet, surely at the composer's own expense; it may not be coincidence that this project was undertaken while Alphonse Robert was away and could not report the expenditure. Over the three months from December 1822 to February 1823, Berlioz published four more songs, this time with the publisher Boieldieu, *jeune.* At least one of these, *Amitié, reprends ton empire,* had also been composed in La Côte-St.-André. A second setting of a text by Bourgerie was titled *Canon libre à la quinte;* it was noted, punningly, in the press as follows:

A new canon has just appeared, but this will not lower the rents nor be trumpeted about in the papers. It is a canon for laughter: not fired, but sung.

We therefore engage musicians to buy . . . the canon of M. Bourgerie and Hector Berlioz, to judge for themselves if it rings well in the ear.[10]

The remaining two songs, *Le Montagnard exilé* and *Toi qui l'aimas, verse des pleurs*, were to texts by Albert Du Boys, a law student and poet who had become that sort of intimate friend Berlioz always had about to share his accesses of enthusiasm. Du Boys, whose father had been a deputy from the Isère, was soon to become an important contact for Berlioz, with a post in the office of the national director of Fine Arts. Berlioz's *romances* could have had little commercial success—the legal depository of printed music teems with such titles—but they did offer him direct experience with the music publishing trade, another branch of the profession in which during these years he learned to move adroitly.

The first Paris composition of any great length is a lost cantata, *Le Cheval arabe*, to a text of Millevoye. The cantata and a hastily prepared three-voice fugue in hand, Berlioz took it upon himself to meet the noted teacher of composition Jean-François Le Sueur and was probably introduced to him by Gerono late in 1822. Le Sueur must have been amused by the circumstances of the meeting and taken with the candidate's brash approach, but he was not impressed with the young man's technique. He sent Berlioz away for elementary harmony lessons with Gerono—who may have been Le Sueur's regular *répétiteur* (teaching assistant)—and promised to accept him as a private student later on. Berlioz mastered the rudiments straightaway, and by the end of 1822 or January 1823 at the latest, he was proud to style himself "élève de Mr Lesueur."[11]

*L*e Sueur was nearly sixty-three years old when he took Berlioz as a pupil. The triumphs of his career, *La Caverne* (1793) and *Ossian, ou Les Bardes* (1804), were long past. He had retired to more modest endeavors: his posts as composition teacher at the Conservatoire, which he held until his death, and as master of the music at the royal Tuileries Chapel, which he held until the dismantling of the chapel after the 1830 revolution. The rest of his time he spent filling notebook after notebook with vast and eccentric theoretical musings and a long history of music which was never published. Le Sueur's work as a teacher had considerable influence on the century, for his charges included, in addition to Berlioz, Gounod, Ambroise Thomas, Antoine Elwart, and Eugène-Prosper Prévost. Twelve of the *prix de Rome* winners between 1822 and 1839 were or had been his pupils.

Berlioz conceived a filial affection for Le Sueur and for the master's wife and three daughters. As a family they offered the resolute approval of his ambitions that his own could never manage. Le Sueur's circle of devoted young people included several whose successful careers later intersected with Berlioz's own: Théodore and Louis Schlösser, both composer-instrumental-

FIGURE 3.4 Jean-François Le Sueur.

ists; Stéphen de La Madelaine, novelist and essayist for the *Revue et Gazette musicale;* the violinist (and later violist) Chrétien Urhan; and the noted *amateur de musique* Victor Schœlcher. For all his connections with young people, however, Le Sueur was essentially untouched by the nascent Romanticism in his own country and altogether unaware of the great changes in music already under way in Germany. Berlioz came to be candid about his teacher's blind spots and the narrowness of his old age, but he remained a devoted disciple and conducted important performances of Le Sueur's music long after his teacher's death. It was Berlioz who induced Le Sueur to hear Beethoven's Fifth in April 1828; the master was exhilarated and perplexed by the work, ultimately declaring that "such music ought not to be written."[12]

Le Sueur was Berlioz's only important mentor, a good deal more influential in directing his early career than anyone else at the Conservatoire. They shared an unquenchable curiosity, an interest in theoretical issues, a love of antiquity, admiration for Gluck and Napoleon, and—most of all—a unanimity of thought on the lofty goals of dramatic music. Moreover, Le Sueur had been something of a radical in his own youth, fired from various posts for his unorthodox ideas, a veteran of highly publicized tiffs with Sacchini and Méhul. (It was Napoleon himself who saved Le Sueur's career.) When the rift with his family in La Côte-St.-André threw Berlioz into desperate circumstances, Le Sueur offered money—which was never accepted—and good advice, including the sensible admonition not to join the chorus of the Opéra. Berlioz aspired to what he saw as Le Sueur's intellectualism; he too wished someday to be considered a savant. Le Sueur's notions of "imitative" dramatic music—that is, a musical rhetoric dominated by references to nature and human passions—became the crux of Berlioz's own musical thought.

Le Sueur examined Berlioz's songs, corrected his exercises, monitored the progress of his longer compositions, and encouraged him in his new ideas. Berlioz profited especially from Sunday trips to the Tuileries palace to see Le Sueur conduct at the king's mass. Berlioz would stand with the orchestra as Charles X departed; then he and Le Sueur would walk along the river or through the gardens and talk about matters of art. Le Sueur surely recounted his own tireless efforts to arrange concerts of his works and regaled Berlioz with faulty but vivid accounts of the history of music. It may have been Le Sueur who dissuaded Berlioz from further ventures in publication and focused his attention on larger forms; indeed, both Berlioz's major compositions of the mid-1820s, the Mass and *Les Francs-Juges,* are Le Sueurian in subject and design. Le Sueur's "little oratorios," as Berlioz called them— *Rachel, Ruth et Noémi,* and *Ruth et Booz*—are sure precursors of *L'Enfance du Christ.*

Berlioz had been entertaining notions of abandoning medicine for the equally respectable study of law.[13] But the quiet tutelage of Le Sueur had its effect, and sometime during the winter the truth of the matter, with all its forbidding implications, dawned on him: he had already decided to become a composer. In mid-March 1823 he set out for La Côte-St.-André to discuss the situation with his parents.

The long and bitter struggle that ensued pitted the stubborn determination of a self-assured, often arrogant young adult against the fear of a conservative family both for their son's well-being and for their own reputation. It is easy enough to understand Berlioz's despair at the situation: ceaseless gossip about him passed between relatives who kept in remarkably close touch, yet no one from his immediate family ever bothered to go to Paris to investigate the circumstances there. The volatile atmosphere in La Côte-St.-André during that spring visit was made all the more trying by the eccentricities of his mother. There was, it turned out, little hope of talking the situation through to a satisfactory resolution. The parents were convinced that he was trading the assurance of a prosperous life for the vagaries and vulgarities of a theatrical career. This they considered—with some justification, in view of the prevailing repertoire of the popular stage: tightrope acts, melodramas, and much firing of pistols—tantamount to joining a circus.

One of the few relatives to remain reasonably calm during this first standoff was Berlioz's uncle Félix Marmion. An army officer of wide-ranging intellectual interests, he was well suited to his role as intermediary. The affection between uncle and nephew lasted for the better part of their lives, and Marmion was the only family member who ever heard more than an occasional composition of Berlioz—or, for that matter, any serious music at all. His strategy was to remain close to all the parties of the dispute. He doubted his nephew's powers of reason just once, as a result of the general disarray of relationships after Berlioz's marriage to Harriet in 1833, and the nephew seldom doubted his uncle's good intentions.

There is nevertheless a hint of impatience in Marmion's first epistle to La Côte concerning the situation in Paris, wherein he expresses the hope that the grim look on Dr. Berlioz's face, so changed after the long period of chagrin caused by young Hector's folly, would have a salutary effect when he came to visit. "If he is not open to paternal counsel," writes Uncle Félix, "he is a lost child." Later he conceived a more appropriate course of action: to counsel patience while an impetuous young man worked through his troubles. "It is a period of crisis," he writes, "which must be left to pass."[14]

An uneasy truce was thus reached that spring in La Côte, with the son promising to complete a bachelor's program during the next academic year. The sojourn did offer some leisure to visit friends and relatives, and in its quieter periods Berlioz settled on several ideas for future work. He left on 11 May 1823 to return to Paris; Dr. Berlioz's account book records a reduced allowance of 400 francs, intended to last for two months.[15]

*T*he logical first step for an ambitious composer in those days was to write an opera; for production at the Académie Royale de Musique, as the Opéra was called, was the only assured avenue to national prestige. Berlioz cockily approached François Andrieux, whose lectures he was still attending, for a suitable libretto. Andrieux declined with a charming letter, pleading advanced age: he was fit, he said, only for a Requiem mass. But he was intrigued enough by the proposition to pay an unannounced call on the composer's ménage that June to explain himself.

The search for a dramatic scenario and a libretto to set preoccupied Berlioz for much of the summer. Gerono proved to be his best connection, and he prepared a text for a little opera, *Estelle et Némorin*, based on Florian's *romance*. Berlioz composed the bulk of that work and an oratorio, *Le Passage de la mer rouge* (The crossing of the Red Sea), in the remaining months of the year and showed them to Le Sueur in early 1824. But his most forward-looking project was a dramatic scene for bass and orchestra called *Beverley, ou le Joueur*, based on a French adaptation of Edward Moore's *The Gamester*. Berlioz probably saw the play at the Odéon in February 1823 and composed "violent music" for one of its scenes later in the year or early the following spring. He hoped that the scene might be performed by Dérivis at a concert where the great actor Talma was scheduled to appear—possibly a benefit that in fact took place on 1 April 1824. All these works were eventually burned, doubtless because their best music had been reused in subsequent compositions.

Berlioz's quest over the years for libretti was not to be especially successful until he realized, with *La Damnation de Faust* of 1846, that only he could compose texts appropriate to his conception of dramatic music. During the

1820s he prevailed on most of his literarily inclined friends for libretti, always with disappointing results. One of these collaborators, however, became an intimate friend and lifelong correspondent. Humbert Ferrand, a law student at the time, was later a poet and travel writer whose works appeared under the pseudonym Georges Arandas. He supplied Berlioz with at least three texts for works finished in the mid-1820s, and together they embarked on several other projects. A well-born youth, Ferrand was unprepossessing of appearance (with "the profile of an old lady or more exactly of a nutcracker," wrote Nanci, in a dismissal she was later to regret)[16] and spoke in an unattractive voice marked by wild modulation of register. After returning in 1827 to his home in Belley, just east of Lyon, he for a time undertook frequent trips to Paris, where he and Berlioz would discuss their plans at length. He was the author of the *Scène héroïque grecque, Les Francs-Juges,* and an opera to have been called *Les Noces d'or d'Oberon et Titania.*

This friendship was one of the more unusual of Berlioz's many relationships constructed on a mutual love of art. He admired Ferrand as one who shared his essential beliefs and wrote of his "keen and lofty feeling for beauty, a religious respect for truth, and belief in the power and greatness of art." They found it easy to discuss poetry and music and to argue prosody and plot, and Ferrand was helpful in encouraging Berlioz's first journalistic efforts. Berlioz, however, found his friend's habitual lassitude unforgivable and more than once penned mildly insulting references to "insouciance combined with laziness, with which you are abundantly endowed."[17] Yet for decades Ferrand offered Berlioz a sympathetic ear, honored him for his art, and fortified him in times of despondency. He even tolerated Berlioz's rambling enthusiasm for Gluck and *Les Danaïdes* with apparent interest. For all that they addressed each other as *vous* during the thirty-odd years of their correspondence.

By now Berlioz could boast of a certain expertise in matters of the operatic repertoire, acquired by assiduous comparison of what he heard at the Opéra with what he saw in the scores at the Conservatoire. He could no longer tolerate public and official indifference to his idols and so began to attack these issues in inflammatory *polémiques musicales* for a journal called *Le Corsaire.* (They had been found too aggressive to appear in the more traditional newspaper, *La Quotidienne.*) The first of these, championing Spontini, Mozart, and Gluck, was published on 12 August 1823; the second, on the great singers, appeared on the following 11 January. The next day his thoughts were turned back to his predicament of career: he learned that he had passed the examination necessary for advanced professional work in law or medicine, thus earning the degree of *Bachelier ès sciences physiques.*

The next three years were to show just how ruthless a doubting family could be. In June 1824 Berlioz was back in La Côte-St.-André for the summer holidays, once again explaining himself. At first things were calm enough: Berlioz describes in a letter to Ferrand[18] that his father was sympathetic to the new profession and that even his mother was beginning to be reconciled to his return to Paris. At some point they made another deal, that Berlioz would work on his music for a year and then all the parties would reconsider the situation. Berlioz found time to make some progress on a mass commissioned by the Church of St.-Roch for performance the following fall and to revise his oratorio on the crossing of the Red Sea. There was the usual socializing with friends and relatives in nearby villages, but his thoughts were of Paris; he yearned for news of the Opéra and wrote his acquaintances there to learn of the latest developments.

To Le Sueur he wrote a vivid summary of his life in La Côte, a significant document that calls Le Sueur "father," reveals plans for the Mass, and describes the tensions in La Côte. It is the only letter from Berlioz to Le Sueur that has been preserved, and is among his best letters of the decade.

> Sir:
>
> For some time I have been tormented with the desire to write to you and have not dared to do so, restrained by a plethora of considerations that now seem to me each more ridiculous than the others. I feared bothering you with my letters, and that the desire to address you would not seem to you to spring from the filial love which a young man must naturally feel in corresponding with that sort of celebrated and rare personage who impresses his compatriots while honoring his country by his genius and knowledge. But I said to myself: this special man to whom I am yearning to write will perhaps find my letters less importunate if their substance is that art on which he exerts so much force. This great musician has had the grace to permit me to take lessons from him, and if ever the exceptional patience and kindness of a master and the gratitude and (dare I express it) filial love of his students have warranted the title of father, I am among his children.
>
> I was welcomed by my family as I expected, that is to say, with great warmth. I haven't had to suffer from my mother's unhappiness and useless remonstrances, which only make us more upset with each other. Papa, however, suggested that as a precaution I never talk about music in front of her. By contrast, I discuss it with him quite often. I have told him of the curious discoveries you have been kind enough to show me from your work on music of antiquity. I have not been able to persuade him that the ancients knew harmony: he is full of the ideas of Rousseau and other writers who have advanced the opposite opinion. But when I cited the Latin passage, I believe by Pliny the Elder, in which there are details on the way to accompany the voice and on the facility with which an orchestra can evoke passion by way of using rhythms different from the voices, he fell into confusion and said that he had nothing to reply to such an explanation. "However," he said to me, "I would want to have the work in my hands to be convinced."
>
> I have done nothing since I have been here, primarily because I have not been master of my time during the first weeks: the visits to receive and the visits to make, in a little town where everybody knows each other, absorbed me almost

completely. Then, when I wished to set about this Mass of which I have spoken, I remained so cold, so icy in reading the *Credo* and the *Kyrie* that, more than convinced that I would not be able to do anything tolerable in this frame of mind, I gave it up. I set about revising that oratorio on the *Passage de la mer rouge*, which I showed you seven or eight months ago and which I now find terribly confused in certain areas. I hope to be able to perform it at St.-Roch on my return, which will (I think) be during the first days of August.

While awaiting the pleasure of seeing you again, Monsieur, I have been charged by my father to convey his best regards and to relay his many thanks for the care you have lavished on me; do not doubt, sir, that I am full of them myself, and accept the assurance of my respectful greetings.

Your devoted servant and student:

Hector Berlioz

P.S.: Be so kind as to remember me to Mme and Mlles Lesueur, and to offer them my homage.[19]

Then suddenly in late July, Berlioz left for Paris, leaving behind in explanation only a letter. The usual barrage of correspondence broke out, notably with patient Uncle Félix. To Nanci, Marmion advised that they leave Berlioz to "keep dreaming of his unhappy passion"; then he assured his nephew of his own understanding. But this time the rupture was violent: Dr. Berlioz wrote that "the moment [of his departure] would never escape my memory." Berlioz tried a conciliatory tone, explaining that he had written his father "clearly and succinctly" about his career; he was sure it "would produce an effect"; Dr. Berlioz's "cruel sentences" had hurt him. Now they were arguing the same points again and again, and Berlioz was intractable. "I am led toward a magnificent career: one cannot describe a career in the arts with any other word," he writes, convinced of his potential for success. He has begun young; he has the experience and the other talents necessary to succeed; "I wish to leave on this earth some trace of my existence." To his father's argument that Le Sueur's training in and knowledge of ancient languages and mathematics were much broader, he responds that Le Sueur was a great musician before he became a learned one. "Nothing in the world will make me change," he says, signing his letter "your respectful and loving son."[20]

*T*he autumn of 1824 was devoted largely to his setting of the Mass text for soloists, chorus, and orchestra. In La Côte he had written of his despair over the icy Latin; now his imagination was kindled by an image that haunted him for another decade: the trumpets and timpani announcing last judgment of the quick and the dead. In 1824 the result was a rousing, extravagant *Et resurrexit*—the only movement from the Mass to escape destruction later on—with a couplet from the Dies irae inserted: "Tuba mirum spargens sonum / coget omnes ante thronum" (A mighty trumpet will drive mankind before the throne).[21]

Berlioz eventually dismantled the *Resurrexit* to reuse passages in his masterworks of 1836–37. The fanfare and first "Et iterum" appear in large measure unchanged at the moment of apocalypse in the Requiem (ex. 3.1a), and the next section, "Et iterum" and "Cujus regni non erit," was refurbished to conclude the Roman carnival scene in *Benvenuto Cellini* (ex. 3.1b). Other passages from the Mass undoubtedly met with similar recycling, and Berlioz's vision of Judgment Day reasserted itself over the years in several guises.

His affection for the world of opera, meanwhile, grew unchecked by conventional standards of propriety. After a performance of Rodolphe Kreutzer's *La Mort d'Abel,* for example, he writes the composer with wild abandon: "O génie! je succombe! je meurs! les larmes m'étouffent." "Ah! foutre!" he responds to news that Le Sueur's great *La Caverne* might be revived.[22] At an 1825 performance of Sacchini's *Œdipe à Colonne* he and another enthusiast wept openly in each other's arms and then exchanged addresses. And at the Odéon on 7 December 1824 and many nights thereafter, he reveled in the first genuinely Romantic music to reach his ear: the French version of Weber's *Der Freischütz,* adapted by the writer Castil-Blaze and entitled *Robin des bois.*

Robin des bois introduced Berlioz to what seems to have been the surprising idea that producers of opera felt free to cut, rearrange, and otherwise "mutilate" a masterpiece at will.[23] In fact this *castilblazade* is not so different from many another adaptation, including notably the French version of Mozart's *Die Zauberflöte, Les Mystères d'Isis,* by Ludwig Lachnith. The alterations amounted to some refittings of the vocal line, reorderings, and some cuts, notably in the Hermit Scene at the end. These things scarcely mattered to the public, who thronged to over a hundred performances of *Robin des bois* and were quick to buy the scores and dozens of salon arrangements that the music dealers obligingly, and promptly, published. But Berlioz had been led by his study of scores and his own predispositions to become a purist. Some months later he attacked Castil-Blaze, one of the most powerful figures of the French theater, for this and other travesties. For the rest of his life he was to be hostile to such men—Fétis among them—partly from an intellectual distaste for those who dared tamper with Gluck, Weber, and Beethoven, but partly from a visceral dislike of their very power.

Arrangements to produce the Mass were so far limited to the optimism of the curate of St.-Roch, a vague promise of support secured by Le Sueur from the conductor Valentino, and Berlioz's altogether naive assumption that his approach to Chateaubriand begging 1,200 francs—possibly 1,500—would meet with success. ("Please accept my regrets," wrote Chateaubriand well after the event; "they are very real.")[24] It was agreed that the student choir of St.-Roch would copy the parts and sing the work. A volunteer orchestra was called, and printed invitations were distributed:

You are invited to attend a MESSE EN GRANDE SYMPHONIE composed by M. H. BERLIOS, student of M. Lesueur, which will be celebrated at the parish church of Saint-Roch promptly at 9:30 on Tuesday, 28 December 1824, feastday of the Holy Innocents, patron saints of the children's choir of the same parish.[25]

The few players who showed up for the rehearsal on 27 December could make no headway in the mistake-ridden parts that the children had prepared, and the morrow's performance was canceled. The experience, though shattering at the time, was not without its profits. Berlioz had heard enough of the work to rewrite it sensibly, and Valentino, Habeneck's predecessor and colleague at both the Opéra and the Royal Chapel, agreed to conduct it when more favorable circumstances could be arranged. And Berlioz learned a good deal about producing a public event. For the rest of his career he relied on professionally copied parts and skilled musicians, no matter what the risk to his own purse.

His worst mistake was to write home of the aborted rehearsal in such terms that Nanci was led to infer that the family was "covered with shame and infamy."[26] On 24 February 1825 Berlioz's father severed the allowance—though he made Nanci write the letter—and thus reduced his son to supporting himself through innumerable loans and low-paying jobs, the beginnings of a general monetary distress that affected him until the end of the 1830s. Dr. Berlioz's seemingly bold stroke has the feel of a last-ditch, studiedly dramatic measure. He was prone to second thoughts over his sternest dicta, however, and there was but a single period, in late 1826, when Berlioz was actually left adrift in Paris for any length of time. Uncle Victor Berlioz helped ease the tension on this particular occasion; his nephew's reasoning, "that with the arts one can pay to society the tribute she expects of us," had been persuasive indeed.[27]

Humbert Ferrand, whose notion it had been to approach Chateaubriand for money, now offered a libretto based on a play they perhaps had seen at the Ambigu-Comique in 1823: *Les Francs-Juges, ou Les Tems de barbarie*, the work of one J.-H.-F. de Lamartelière. This tale of vigilante terror, mistaken identity, and romance—all set in the Black Forest—had real promise for an opera, and Berlioz was seduced by the tableaux of Bohemian shepherds and shepherdesses, the opportunity for distant horn calls, and the dark doings of the Francs-Juges in a castle dungeon. But Ferrand's libretto had its flaws, and the collaboration was aggravated by the composer's own preference for grand tableau over memorable aria—a preference easy to trace through his entire career. And Berlioz had not yet achieved the discipline to sustain his own interest or focus his so far minimal technique in a work of such length. At the beginning, however, *Les Francs-Juges* seemed an idea worthy of zestful labor, and the overture, finished last of all, became his first international success. *Les Francs-Juges* was Berlioz's major work for the better part of the next two years.

a. For the Requiem:

Resurrexit, mm. 76–82:

Requiem, movt. II, mm. 141–47:

Resurrexit, mm. 91–94:

Requiem, movt. II, mm. 163–66:

EXAMPLE 3.1 Reuses of the *Resurrexit.*

b. For *Benvenuto Cellini:*

Resurrexit, mm. 106–12:

Benvenuto Cellini, Roman carnival scene, mm. 687–93:

Resurrexit, mm. 168–74:

Benvenuto Cellini, Roman carnival scene, mm. 766–72:

EXAMPLE 3.1 *(continued)*

A plan to present the *Messe solennelle* in March at the church of Ste.-Geneviève, now the Panthéon, came to naught. But efforts to secure a performance backed by adequate funding and an appropriate level of artistry came to fruition when Augustin de Pons, a singer with family wealth and a predilection for Gluck equal to Berlioz's own, lent him 1,200 francs to hire the performers and rent the necessary equipment for another attempt at St.-Roch. At this juncture Berlioz sought the first of his many interviews with Viscount Sosthène de La Rochefoucauld, the director of Fine Arts, widely considered a risible figure and the frequent butt of journalistic barbs, but sympathetic to younger composers in a way that the old guard at the Conservatoire—Cherubini, Kreutzer, and Berton—could never manage. La Rochefoucauld was happy to authorize the performance, use of the Opéra chorus, an orchestra of professional musicians, Valentino as conductor, and Ferdinand Prévost as bass soloist—so long as the composer had the where-withal to pay the 150 performers. Berlioz himself had already recopied all the parts.

The Mass was thus offered to the public on Sunday, 10 July 1825, and this time it was an unchallenged success. The audience was respectable, the press well represented and favorably inclined, and the reaction of the musicians gratifying. Le Sueur, there with his wife and daughters, was proud: "You'll not be doctor or apothecary," he said, "but rather a great composer." What criticisms he had were saved for later. It was Mme Lebrun, colorful member of the Opéra chorus known for the saltiness of her language, who gave Berlioz his most memorable pat on the back—though my translation cannot do justice to the original:

> Damn, my boy: now there's an un-worm-eaten O *Salutaris,* and I defy those little bastards in the counterpoint classes at the Conservatoire to write a movement so tightly knit, so bloody religious.

Berlioz, uplifted by a performance as near perfect as one could have hoped, regained his confidence as a composer at one stroke. "Here," he wrote, "the first step well taken."[28]

But Fétis, who was there, later said, "Everyone came away shrugging his shoulders and saying that what he had heard was not music." Berlioz himself, in hindsight and with literary skills polished by experience, later wrote, "The devout old ladies, the woman who rented the chairs, the holy-water man, the vergers, and all the gapers of the quarter declaring themselves well satisfied, I had the simplicity to regard it a success."[29]

The success of the performance was painted in glowing colors by the students returning to La Côte-St.-André for their summer holidays. They swore "they had never seen a Mass have such an effect, nor make such a splash." But Berlioz would be singularly misled, wrote Nanci,[30] to think the splendid debut had disposed his family to let him carry on: her father was angry, and her mother did not dare admit that she was flattered. Berlioz was summoned home, and there ensued another round of negotiations, another provisional deal, and the extraordinary incident of his mother's curse and retreat to the country house at Le Chuzeau[31]—for all intents and purposes her last appearance in his biography.

He moved in the autumn from the Left Bank to the Cité, taking a Spartan *chambre de bonne* in the attic of a building at 27, rue de Harlay, on the quai des Orfèvres. He tried to sustain himself on a regimen of bread, fruit, and water, often taken beneath the Vert Galant, the statue of Henri IV on the Pont Neuf. There he devoured, in French translation, the *Irish Melodies* of Thomas Moore, and there he first set forth to master Walter Scott's series of Waverley novels. He met his literary friends at the theater or at cafés around town to discuss his finds. This circle now included Du Boys and Ferrand; for a short time Edouard Rocher, a chemistry student from a La Côte family still noted today for the excellent clear brandies it distills; Thomas Gounet, a government functionary of literary bent; and Stéphen de La Madelaine, the singer and essayist from Le Sueur's band of disciples. For pocket money he tutored students in guitar and elementary harmony.

After supplying the libretto for *Les Francs-Juges*, Ferrand had written a cantata called the *Scène héroïque grecque*. It was a timely piece: the Greek revolution against the Ottomans had been started in 1821 by followers of a clergyman—*un prêtre grec* appears in the cantata—and had become a civil war by 1824, reaching its climax in early 1826 with the intervention of the Egyptian pasha. Berlioz was attracted by the locale, of course, and the text reflected such political sentiments as he had so far conceived for himself. His setting is a long cantata—the longest of his preserved works before 1829–30—of four movements, with soloists, chorus, and a large orchestra with full brass and percussion, "music which on every page bore the stamp of Spontini's powerful influence."[32] The warriors' hymn and finale are noisy movements of much brass fanfare and intricate orchestral figuration, though otherwise there is nothing especially attractive to be found there. More charming is the opening air of the Greek warrior, "O mère des héros," in its broad tempo and chromatic wanderings suggestive of the later arias of Père Laurence in *Roméo et Juliette* and King Herod in *L'Enfance du Christ*. The loveliest movement is the prayer of Greek women, a tableau of almost breathtaking similarity in concept and brush stroke to the scene of the Trojan women three decades later (ex. 3.2). And in several respects the cantata is so similar to the later *prix de Rome* works as to seem a preliminary study for them. Like most of the other works of this period, it serves as a source for borrowing in later compositions.

We owe the preservation of the *Scène héroïque* to the same kind of chance that saved the *Resurrexit, Rob-Roy,* and *La Mort d'Orphée.* In 1828, after the first performance, Berlioz had a fair manuscript copy prepared and bound, with a contemporaneous lithograph of Greek warriors tipped in, and sent to Ferrand. What may be an original title page serves as the backing

Scène héroïque, mm. 5–13:

Les Troyens, no. 16, mm. 5–11:

Scène héroïque (con't.)

Les Troyens, no. 14 ("Puissante Cybèlle"), mm. 6–8:

EXAMPLE 3.2 *Prière* (movt. III) from the *Scène héroïque*, compared with the scene of the Trojan women, *Les Troyens*, act II.

for a pasted-over scribal title; at the top, in Berlioz's own hand, is a citation (in French) from Moore's *Irish Melodies:*

> Oh for the swords of former time!
> Oh for the men who bore them,
> When arm'd for Right, they stood sublime,
> And tyrants crouch'd before them.[33]

The *Scène héroïque* increased by one Berlioz's repertoire for future performance.

Before 1825 was done, Berlioz had penned yet another *polémique musicale* to *Le Corsaire,* this one an assault on Castil-Blaze. The essay, published 19 December 1825, includes these telling lines:

> Without having great mastery of literature, I have some in music which might be useful [here]: I know all of Gluck by heart; I can even remember the majority of the orchestration; I have copied most of these scores for study. In short, I think I know him as well as possible.[34]

Carl Maria von Weber, in transit to England for the production there of *Oberon,* arrived in Paris on 25 February 1826 for a brief stay, necessarily extended while the blacksmith repaired his carriage. He had meant to travel incognito, but once in Paris could not resist the temptation to call on the musical elite: Cherubini, Fétis, Auber, Catel, Berton, Rossini, and of course Le Sueur. Berlioz just missed him at Le Sueur's on the 26th, then spent the next few days trailing Weber's courtesy calls and trips to the theater. At Auber's *Emma* on the 26th, *Olimpie* on the 27th, and Boieldieu's *La Dame blanche* on the 28th, Berlioz tried vainly to catch a glimpse of his idol. It was his last chance: Weber died in England on 5 June.

Relying on Le Sueur and La Rochefoucauld for an introduction, Berlioz approached Kreutzer, who still conducted at the Opéra, with the hope that his *Scène héroïque* might be included in the traditional Holy Week *concerts spirituels.* An assistant to La Rochefoucauld had told Berlioz of a proposed new policy which might encourage the programming of works by younger composers on these and other concerts. But these maneuvers came to an abrupt resolution when Kreutzer declared that "the Opéra was not made for presenting the works of young people."[35] The same applied to a libretto by La Madelaine, *La Mort d'Hercule,* summarily rejected by the adjudicators. Berlioz could only hope, and he did so with a certain irrational optimism, that *Les Francs-Juges* would be received at the Odéon under the same program of support for new composers.

With these reverses of 1826 and following years came the growth of an arrogance on Berlioz's part that became more prominent as time went by. He resented the attitudes of the Old Guard composers, attributing to them an egotism that the successful use to keep others from success. He saw their reluctance to embrace his music as a selfish attempt to keep all the glory and financial rewards for themselves. Step by step, accordingly, he strained and then ruptured contacts that might otherwise have led to quicker national recognition of his talents.

In 1826 he undertook still another dramatic setting, a work for the Opéra-Comique based on Walter Scott and titled *Richard en Palestine.* The librettist, Léon Compaignon, was a part-time composer and self-proclaimed "student of Rossini" who lived in Chartres and traded his literary work for errands the composer would run for him in Paris. Berlioz's half of their correspondence is preserved intact. These dozen letters from 1826 and 1827 testify to his developing sense of good poetry, significant contributions to the libretto, and involvement in the issues of dramatic texts. He eventually saw that Compaignon could never manage and thus suggested enlisting "a friend," probably Stéphen de La Madelaine, to complete the work. Berlioz never began the music, though it may be from this period that another Walter Scott work, the *Waverley* overture, emerges. *Les Francs-Juges,* its second act nearly done, was encountering obstacles as well. Berlioz now doubted the suitability of that text, too, fearing that it treated situations of interest only to himself.

𝓔ach July since the year of Berlioz's birth, the Académie des Beaux-Arts of the French Institute had sponsored a competition for composers and other artists, leading to a *prix de Rome*. In general concept it was not unlike the dozens of other prize competitions of which French education was, and is, so fond. Winners of the Rome prize enjoyed instant celebrity, a cash stipend for five years, one or two years in Rome, and at least a putative sojourn in Germany, this last an opportunity many of the laureates seem to have declined. Winners most often secured comfortable positions for the remainder of their careers, though comparatively few of them achieved any international standing. And there were celebrated composers who never managed to win the prize at all: Saint-Saëns, for example, and most notably Ravel.

Any citizen could enter the competition, but in fact only the students favored by Le Sueur or Berton stood much chance of winning, for they, with Cherubini, were the most influential of the judges. The routine, gleefully described by Berlioz on any number of occasions, consisted of a preliminary test followed by the writing of a "fugue in strict style, a musical problem of surpassing uselessness and very difficult to solve."[36] Those candidates not eliminated at that stage were declared finalists and allowed to take residence at the Institute for nearly a month, there to write a cantata on a prescribed text. (Debussy's *L'Enfant prodigue* was a *prix de Rome* cantata.) A jury would meet to judge the works from readings with piano accompaniment, and the winning composition would be heard with its complete orchestration at a presentation ceremony in August or September.

Berlioz formally entered the competition in 1826[37] and progressed no further than the fugue. He would repeat the process four more times, inching closer toward the prize each year.

The immediate result in 1826 was that Le Sueur urged Berlioz to perfect his training by enrolling at the Conservatoire for formal study of counterpoint. Using a birth certificate obtained from La Côte-St.-André without his parents' knowledge, Berlioz enrolled for the first time in the autumn of 1826.

Augustin de Pons, who had lent Berlioz the funds to produce his Mass, now thought to write Dr. Berlioz for repayment of the money, worried, he said, about his friend's privations. (Berlioz, for his part, says he had already paid back half.) His father, who had also got wind of the failed *prix de Rome* attempt, began to repay the debt from Berlioz's allowance and reduced his monthly stipend to 50 francs. Berlioz responded by refusing to return to La Côte for a summer holiday, and thereupon commenced a methodical separation from his family. At first he considered moving to Brazil, where he imagined he might play the flute in a theater orchestra and the encouragement to young composers of his talent might be more substantial than in his own nation. The Brazilian consul, however, could offer no more than good wishes, and Berlioz could not even afford the post-coach to Le Havre, let alone the trans-Atlantic fare.

Nor could he afford, for other reasons, to leave Paris at all: there were the next year's *prix de Rome,* which Le Sueur had assured him would be his, and the promise of a production of *Les Francs-Juges* to be taken into account. So instead he joined Antoine Charbonnel, a pharmacy student from La Côte, in a bohemian housing arrangement. They took adjoining attic rooms on the Left Bank at 58, rue de la Harpe, where they began on 6 September to keep scrupulous accounts of their expenditures in an effort to live on a franc per person each day.[38] Mme Berlioz had sent 100 francs for housekeeping purposes, and this was spent on pots and pans, eight dinner plates, and two glasses. They dined on fruit and water, leeks, cheese, bread, and dressings. At the end of each month the diet was particularly rigorous: the entry for 29 September 1826 shows only a purchase of grapes, and the next day they spent 68 centimes on bread and salt. Berlioz writes that he can no longer afford to visit Compaignon in Chartres, and he begs another correspondent to remember the proper postage. Yet certain essentials of life could not be avoided: the accounts include reckonings for spurs, colored ribbons, and a cane, and he paid 110 francs for a piano.

Failing to find any employment as a flutist, he auditioned for the hack chorus of the new Théâtre des Nouveautés—the fine story of how he offered to sing, by heart, anything from the operatic repertoire is in chapter 12 of the *Mémoires*—and was offered a spot at a salary of 50 francs a month. Now he was actually involved with the vaudeville stage, a fact he kept from his parents for several years. Also in late 1826, with an eye to the future, he began to study Italian.

Act III of *Les Francs-Juges* was completed that fall, and the overture probably dates from October. There is virtually no documentation concerning the genesis of the *Waverley* overture. It can be from no earlier than 1825, when Berlioz discovered Walter Scott, and it was clearly done by February 1828, when Le Sueur asks a correspondent to consider Berlioz's overtures, in the plural, for performance.[39] It seems to be the last major work written before he knew of Beethoven, and though it shows a growing mastery of the orchestral instruments and some skill at sonata form, it does not match the *Francs-Juges* overture either in dramatic gesture or in melodic invention.

For months Berlioz had gone about his enterprises with prodigious energy; now he succumbed to several weeks of ill health, overtaxed by his various undertakings and probably weakened by his ill-advised diet. (To his family's chagrin, he refused to consult Alphonse Robert, who had by then established a medical practice.) When he recovered in late January 1827, he tried to make up for the lost time by buying an alarm clock, the better to be up by 7:00 or even 6:00 A.M. so as to have more daylight to copy the parts for

Les Francs-Juges, which he hoped the Odéon would soon be needing. He began to read the works of Fenimore Cooper and Lord Byron.

Berlioz writes comparatively little of his experience as an enrolled student at the Conservatoire, as though his studies were somehow secondary to his other pursuits. Perhaps counterpoint seemed dull. The violinist Eugène Sauzay, a colleague in Reicha's class, recalled writing countless four- and five-voiced fugues, vocal and instrumental, which he composed late at night, wrapped in his mother's fur coat, in a small room in the faubourg Montmartre. Sauzay saw that the class did not match Berlioz's temperament and suggests that it was of Berlioz that Cherubini observed: "It isn't that Monsieur doesn't like fugue; rather, fugue doesn't like him."[40]

Most of the students worshipped the formidable figures who taught there, notably Habeneck and Baillot. Sauzay is right to see these as the golden years of the Conservatoire, with professors of long experience, an excited new generation of young musicians, and talk of Beethoven in the air. The busy institution occupied a full city block, dominated by an enviable concert hall. Cherubini, the director, was by all accounts a caustic, tradition-bound authority, loath to bend the rules, whether administrative or compositional. Berlioz's descriptions of him in the *Mémoires* are rather less than fair, for they had relatively long periods during which they got along quite well. His obituary of Cherubini[41] is more to the point: there he confesses to have admired him and to have admired much of his music. Cherubini led the Conservatoire into the century of Romanticism with dignity.

Cherubini's notebooks in fact provide what little documentation there is of Berlioz's progress at the Conservatoire. In January of 1827 we find the first record of his attendance in Reicha's class:

> 29 January 1827. Berlioz, [age] 23. He has not been in the class long; we must wait [to assess him].

The record goes on:

> 12 July 1827. In Le Sueur's composition class. Berlioz, 23.8. He has imagination, but he is disorganized, and long-winded.

> 28 January 1828. In Reicha's counterpoint class. Berlioz, 24.1. His fugue is acceptable.

> 1 July 1828. In Le Sueur's composition class. Berlioz, 24.7. Not good.

> 4 July 1828. In Reicha's counterpoint class. Berlioz is excused [because he is in the *prix de Rome* competition].[42]

Berlioz had discontinued counterpoint by February 1829, and the last entry for him, on 30 June 1829, says merely that he is on leave to compete for the *prix de Rome*. In these same notebooks, we find the last mention of poor Gerono, enrolled since 1813: in July 1826, at age 28.6, his "education is terminated."

FIGURE 3.5 Luigi Cherubini.

For the *prix de Rome* competition of 1827, the preliminaries of which Berlioz passed with ease, the cantata was to be written on a text called *La Mort d'Orphée*. (Orpheus is torn limb from limb in a Bacchic orgy, transfixed by his vision of Eurydice.) Berlioz summarized the preliminaries in a letter to his sister:

> There were only four of us, and I was the only one to get what they call the *answer* correct—and that is the main object of the fugue. Another candidate, who already won the second prize last year, failed to get the answer correct but redeemed himself in part by some other feature he had introduced into his work. He was admitted to the competition. Thus only two of us actually have the right to continue; in fact we are four. The other two are students of Berton and were admitted over the strong objections of Cherubini and Le Sueur. Already you can see an example of how they judge at the Institute.[43]

Once *en loge,* the students went to hear the text dictated by a secretary and copied it as best they could, then returned to their cells for at least three weeks of work. Each evening they were allowed to receive friends in the courtyard from 6:00 until 9:00 P.M. and to glean news of the outside world, though a porter was stationed there to prevent indiscretions. The walls of the cells still show the graffiti of the bored candidates, including the 1856 fugue subject penciled there by Bizet.[44]

Berlioz's *La Mort d'Orphée* is a fine work, for which he had every reason to expect a prize. This was not to happen: the pianist Rifaut (shortly afterward named professor of accompaniment at the Conservatoire) floundered during the reading for reasons that remain unclear. Some suggest he was bitter at never having won the prize himself; others hold he was put up to it by Le Sueur's rival, Berton. The jury declared the work unplayable and asked Berlioz to withdraw it. According to the formal report, "The fourth cantata, not susceptible to performance with piano, was withdrawn from the competition by the author, with the consent of the Academy."[45]

Berlioz was not one to take lightly the declaration that his music was *inexécutable* and immediately set about planning a concert where it might be played. His disappointment was compounded by the news, which must have come in September, that *Les Francs-Juges* would not be done at the Odéon. Once again professional reverses compounded an already serious fatigue and led to another round of illness. He had enough sense, this time, to resign from the chorus of the Nouveautés before the new season. His financial status (and presumably his diet) had, however, improved somewhat: money from his father was in greater supply, and he seems to have had several paying pupils. He also sold arrangements and études for guitar to a publisher of such things. At some point during the winter he moved to more befitting rooms at 96, rue de Richelieu, across the street from Maurice Schlesinger's music shop and a few steps from the other great music publishing houses, the newspapers, the theaters, and the Conservatoire. Here he lived for the three years until his departure for Rome, and here he sought lodgings again when he returned.

*T*he annual return of Parisians from their summer holidays coincided that year with the arrival of a company of some two dozen English actors and actresses managed by a genial though ordinary actor named William Abbott. It was Abbott's announced purpose to satiate the French curiosity for Shakespeare. Other than that his arrangements were haphazard at best. A theater was not secured until the last minute, and the announced repertoire and personnel of the company changed weekly as its impresario tried to cover for his "not especially distinguished" troupe by arranging for short appearances by England's best actors: Edmund Kean, the younger Macready, and Charles Kemble. The season opened at the Théâtre de l'Odéon on 6 September, after a ceremony of national anthems and long-winded speeches, with Sheridan's *The Rivals*. A charming but otherwise unremarkable Irish actress named Harriet Smithson, then twenty-seven, had the role of Lydia Languish; her mother played Mrs. Malaprop. The evening was enough of a success to leave the press clamoring for the promised tragedies of Shakespeare.

The great Charles Kemble, when he arrived in Paris, fretted over the company's lack of a female star. He postponed his most famous role, Romeo, to await the arrival from England of a proper Juliet, Maria Foote. In the meantime, the "part of Ophelia was nothing, and could be given to Miss

I cannot chuse but weep, to think,
they should lay him in the cold ground!

Melle SMITHSON, Rôle d'Offélia dans Hamlet.

FIGURE 3.6
Miss Smithson in the role
of Ophelia in *Hamlet*.

Smithson." Her extraordinary entrance that 11 September, an apotheosis of grief and delirium, surprised her colleagues as profoundly as it captivated the intellectual aristocracy of France. She did not know what to make of it all: "My God, what are they saying? Do they like it— or hate it?" She began the evening, writes her biographer, as an "inconsequential walking-lady; . . . she completed it as a tragic actress of note."[46] She played without makeup, relying on the sound of her voice, the expression of her face, and especially her repertoire of gesture and mime. The writers remembered her "grace, abandon, and childlike naivety," and all report unanimous tears and applause.

Berlioz was there that night, along with Vigny, Dumas, Gautier, and a host of the other Romantics—none of whom he yet knew personally. It was not the first time Shakespeare had been seen in France, nor even the first time Shakespeare had been performed in France in English; Talma had played Hamlet, and Shakespeare was the idol of Nodier's salon at the Arsenal, the very birthplace of Romanticism in France. But Berlioz, like the writers, was in 1827 just on the verge of producing his most Romantic works. Shakespeare served as the model for the French brand of Romanticism; the English company sowed seeds whose full flower would soon be culled. Berlioz was just the right age, and at the perfect point in his artistic growth, for such a lightning bolt. Pierre Citron summarizes his discovery of Shakespeare and of Harriet Smithson as a "déclenchement de sa passion."[47]

Berlioz followed the rest of the season closely, at least until the company moved to the Salle Favart, and began to learn the plays from the pocket-sized editions on sale and from Letourneur's translation of 1776. The imagery and sound of some dozen various lines (not, by and large, the favorites of Anglophones) struck his ear, and these he committed to memory. Miss Smithson was now to be entrusted with the great roles, and she was leading lady in both *Romeo and Juliet* on 15 September—badly cut, and with the changes David Garrick's performances had by then made traditional—and *Othello* on the 18th; she also enjoyed considerable success in Nicolas Rowe's *Jane Shore*. Maria Foote eventually arrived in Paris to take the Shakespeare roles, but by then Parisians much preferred Harriet's interpretations. All this was Berlioz's first experience with tragedy of the nonclassical sort; he was overcome by Shakespeare's characterizations, his freedom from the Greek unities, and the force of the action onstage.

Romeo and Juliet was the climax of what Berlioz called "the supreme drama of my life." In that electric atmosphere on which all accounts agree, he conceived a poetic love for the Irish actress, an altogether distant romance, without even the hope of ever meeting her. It may well be true that he announced to his cronies at *Romeo and Juliet* that "that woman shall be my wife, and on this play I shall write my grandest symphony."[48]

FIGURE 3.7 Harriet Smithson.

FIGURE 3.8 Harriet
Smithson, c. 1827.

And both predictions came to pass. She would be his Ophelia, Desdemona,
and Juliet, the focus of a storybook tale both larger than life and at the same
time very much more human than anything in the fairytales. Delacroix and
Dumas were likewise smitten with the "angel of poetry"; she became the
Ophelia of many a painting and poem. She was the inspiration, in short, for
some of the most extraordinary imagery of Romanticism. In that regard
Berlioz was no different from the rest: to a generation of artists, she *was* the
secret of Shakespeare. "A whole society," wrote Jules Janin, "stirred to this
woman's magic."[49]

Of all this, there is no hint to his family. Indeed, there is but sparse
documentation of his goings and comings during these months. His
Paris friends, of course, already knew of his frame of mind. They saw him
making frequent use of his pass to the Odéon and teased him about his
headlong tumble. To Ferrand he only hints of the crisis: "For three months
I have been in the throes of a chagrin from which nothing can distract me.

My distaste for life is pushed to its limit."[50] Otherwise it was a private matter: there is no other first-person evidence of the last five months of 1827. By the end of the year Harriet had returned to England.

Thursday, 22 November 1827, was St. Cecilia's Day, for which occasion Berlioz had been able to arrange a second performance of his Mass, this time at the much larger church of St.-Eustache, an institution of well-established and celebrated musical practice. Berlioz conducted the modest orchestra and chorus he had inveigled from the Odéon theater. (The connection was doubtless with the young conductor there, Narcisse Girard; Berlioz's pass to the orchestra pit for the Shakespeare plays had surely come from Girard.) The Et resurrexit, now specifically designated a "tableau of the Last Judgment," caused him such excitement with its fanfare for fifteen brass instruments that he had to call for an interval afterward to sit down and regain his equilibrium. The public cannot have been large, as the area had been for two days the scene of riots over the parliamentary elections, leading to brutal police intervention and several deaths. But a few of the smaller papers covered the concert, and his admirers complimented him effusively.

On the heels of the Shakespeare season came the first performances of the new Société des Concerts du Conservatoire, an orchestra founded by Habeneck and his colleagues to promote modern symphonic music, especially the symphonies of Beethoven. (The main connections between the orchestra and the academy were that the director of the Conservatoire served as ex officio president of the administrative committee and that sociétaires had to be present or former affiliates of the institution.) The self-governing society of fifty-six strings, twenty-five winds, and a full chorus included the best players in the nation—the violinists Urhan and Artôt, the cellist Tajan-Rogé, the oboist Vogt, the trumpet player Dauvernay, the timpanist Schneitzoeffer, and so on—and these same players became Berlioz's first choices for his own concerts. Among the singers were several young people who went on to have significant careers at the Opéra. The regulations foresaw a series of six concerts beginning in January of each year, to take place in the 1,078-seat Salle du Conservatoire, also called the Menus-Plaisirs du Roi ("the king's little pleasantries" or "lesser dalliances"). To avoid conflict with the Opéra and other theaters, from whose orchestras the musicians were drawn, the concerts were to be presented on Sunday afternoons at 2:00 P.M. For all the musicians the income represented a salutary addition to their relatively modest stipends as theater players and studio teachers; moreover the society soon accrued a substantial pension fund.

The inaugural concert, on 9 March 1828, featured the first performance in France of the *Eroica* Symphony. Habeneck, who after several years of study was now a rabid proponent of Beethoven, went on to lead his orchestra through the entire orchestral repertoire of the master they had begun to call the Colossus of Bonn. By the end of the first season, his musicians had played

FIGURE 3.9
François-Antoine Habeneck.
He conducts with a violin bow
and holds a violin part.

Beethoven's Third and Fifth Symphonies, the Third Piano Concerto, the Violin Concerto, and numerous other works. The Sixth and Seventh Symphonies were offered early the next year. On 27 March 1831, while Berlioz was in Rome, they gave the first Paris performance of the Ninth Symphony. These were the militant years of the Société des Concerts, as Sauzay called them, when at nearly every concert they offered a new masterwork to the delight of a grateful public. The players were "gay and insouciant, believing in Beethoven alone." "We rehearsed three times a week, from 9:00 until noon, sometimes even 1:00, without lunch, without heat, in a damp and cold room . . . We were, if not martyrs to art, at least valiant and diligent artists."[51]

Berlioz had already heard bits and pieces of Beethoven—a reading at the Odéon, for example, and one of the symphonies and an overture at the Institute's award ceremony in 1827. He can have been no less aware of the Beethoven fever at the Conservatoire than he had been of Shakespeare the previous September. Yet there is little indication that he had much grasp of Beethoven's magnitude before hearing the performances of the Société des Concerts. Then the hefty dose, coming on top of the other upheavals of his artistic consciousness, electrified him. He became a disciple of the Société des Concerts, for decades its most influential reviewer. At the same time he started to research Beethoven's life and works, though at first his knowledge consisted mostly in the shopworn anecdotes. For some weeks he alludes to Beethoven in nearly every letter.

The Société des Concerts did in fact permanently alter the fabric of concertgoing in Paris; in some measure it broke the dominion of the theater in general, and of imported Italian opera in particular, over French musical life. Habeneck, for instance, is said to have had little interest in his duties at the Opéra after the Société was founded. The musicians were pleased to capture center stage from sopranos and tenors. Other concert series fed on the success of the Société: Chélard's Athénée Musical of 1829 and after, for example, and Fétis's four Concerts Historiques of 1832–33. By midcentury there were even rival orchestras, including Berlioz's own Société Philharmonique of 1850–51 and Seghers's Société Ste.-Cécile of 1849–56. In the next decades the concert series of Jules Pasdeloup and then Edouard Colonne and Charles Lamoureux were all to thrive.

Berlioz had been refining ideas for a public concert of his own since *Orphée* had been declared unplayable. Studying the Société des Concerts, he saw how to go about staging such an event, and he began to settle on plans for a performance in May. It would be on a Sunday at 2:00 P.M., preferably the first Sunday after the Conservatoire season was done, in the commodious Salle des Concerts. Now he had useful contacts in the world of orchestral musicians, and friends from the Nouveautés, Odéon, Opéra, and Conservatoire would willingly assist. And he had a repertoire: two new overtures, *Orphée*, excerpts from *Les Francs-Juges,* and the *Scène héroïque* of 1826. He would need sixteen-hour workdays to copy the parts and guarantee their correctness, but that could be done, even if it meant losing the income from his guitar students. Berlioz exaggerated only mildly when he declared that no artist in France had ever attempted such a concert.

In April, but a few weeks after the first of the Conservatoire concerts, he approached the minister La Rochefoucauld to ask for permission to use the hall. The deputy from the Isère brought political pressure to bear, and at length Berlioz's concert was tentatively scheduled for 18 May. Cherubini would have none of it, proffering a formidable list of lame objections: it was the week of Ascension and Pentecost; Berlioz could not possibly match the accomplishments of the splendid season just drawing to a close; the Conservatoire's teaching schedule had been interrupted enough by the new series; the weather was too nice. (Throughout Berlioz's career the weather was of great influence on the promise for success of Sunday afternoon events. It should not be too cold and wet, for that meant an uncomfortable trudge through the mud, nor should it be pleasant enough to lure the public to the Champs de Mars or the fountains at Versailles to take the sun. That left a few weeks in November and March as the only ideal time for afternoon concerts, and in fact Berlioz usually tried to offer his season between All Saints' Day and Christmas week.)

Berlioz's description in the *Mémoires* of the impediments thrown before him is solidly confirmed by a good deal of official correspondence with the office of Fine Arts and the Conservatoire. One cannot help admiring him as he so adroitly outflanks Cherubini in diplomacy, or remain unmoved by his arguments. "I have already overcome the main obstacles," he writes with growing vexation. "Everything is ready: soloists, chorus, and orchestra; . . . Must it be that by the ill will of M. Cherubini I shall have given my time and all my leisure for a month and a half, along with 400 francs for copying, just to garner repugnance and discouragement?"[52] La Rochefoucauld's first reaction to these unlikely lines of battle was to collapse in tears of mirth; then he overruled Cherubini on 13 May.

This news reached Berlioz the next day, too late to convene the necessary rehearsals, so the concert was delayed until 26 May, a holiday Monday, at 2:30 P.M. In the interim, he borrowed 150 francs from his father to prepay the hall and covered another 200 francs of expenses with a loan from Charles Bert, an old friend from La Côte, now a medical student. Cherubini, reconciled to the inevitable, authorized the Conservatoire's voice students to act as a chorus. Meanwhile, Berlioz released a letter to the press, printed by at least four journals, explaining the need for a young composer to make known his "essays in the dramatic genre."

The new schedule allowed for two rehearsals, though in fact there is evidence of only one. It was poor, not unlike, I suspect, nearly every young composer's first rehearsal. There was confusion, poor attendance, and bad behavior by unpaid musicians. Fétis reports the orchestra's bursting with laughter at one of the overtures, and both he and the *Mémoires* agree that the rehearsal simply petered out as the players slipped away.[53] The conductor Nathan Bloc, successor to Narcisse Girard at the Odéon and a close enough friend of Berlioz to have been called to duty on two other occasions, seems to have been more cooperative than accomplished.

The unplayable *Orphée* remained, except at the rehearsals, unplayed, as a result of the indisposition of Alexis Dupont and Bloc's inability to understand it. *Orphée* was replaced by the *Resurrexit*. Otherwise the concert came off essentially as planned, with the only known performance of two excerpts from *Les Francs-Juges*—an aria sung by the young Gilbert Duprez and the lovely *Mélodie pastorale* sung by Mme Lebrun, Duprez, and Dupont—and a *Marche religieuse des Mages,* probably the source for the later *Quartetto e coro dei maggi*.

Although the attendance was poor—the papers said the hall was nearly empty, and even Berlioz assessed it at but two-thirds full—and a good deal of money was lost, the concert was nevertheless a grand *succès d'estime*. The performers had come around, as performers do, and eventually cheered him. In the audience had been Auber, Hérold, Le Sueur, Reicha, and Nourrit. Fétis wrote admiringly of his "great natural talent" and "virile and energetic" style, and several other papers echoed those sentiments.[54]

It was not this concert, however, but the confluence of Beethoven and Shakespeare that had the greatest significance for Berlioz in 1828; it was this conjunction that turned his thoughts toward composing descriptive orchestral music. Circumstantial evidence suggests that *Roméo et Juliette* began to take shape in 1828: the librettist Emile Deschamps implies that the basic ideas came to them on the heels of the Odéon performances,[55] and two works of the period, *Cléopâtre* and the *Ballet des ombres*, have conceptual ties to the Romeo and Juliet story. He was soon to give birth to his first settings of *Faust* and "a colossal symphony," where his "infernal passion" might be described. It is significant that these kinds of ideas now took priority over the theater projects—an Italianized version of the English *Virginius,* several comic operas, and a grand opera were forgotten as quickly as they were conceived. In fact, Berlioz's radical turn away from the Le Sueurian repertoire of sacred music and opera to dramatic instrumental music should be reckoned the major artistic event of 1828.

*D*r. Berlioz, now owed a good deal of money by his son, refused to put up the cost of room and board for the 1828 prize competition, and it was left to Le Sueur to arrange the details. The cantata text, titled simply *Herminie,* described a scene in Tasso's *Gerusalemme liberata* where the Christian Tancred engages in mortal combat with the Saracen Erminia. Berlioz's cantata earned the second prize, which amounted to a year's free admission to the Opéra. On the basis of his prize, he applied to the government for an annual stipend, pleading the large size of his family and his father's exhausted finances. This initiative, not surprisingly, was denied.

Herminie would be of no particular interest were it not for the introduction on the first page of the theme that comes to be the *idée fixe* of the *Symphonie fantastique.* Berlioz may have gone into the contest with that page in mind—it is likely that he planned passages for adoption in the cantatas well in advance. The painters practiced assiduously, and of the composers Bizet is known to have tried his hand at a number of the texts given for earlier prize cantatas.

At the end of August, Berlioz left Paris for the first time in three years to visit La Côte-St.-André. He found his sisters approaching adulthood, titillated by balls and handsome young men. He paid the usual visits to the relatives in Grenoble and its outlying villages; Ferrand came to visit. The family sent him back to Paris with a pocketful of commissions: jewelry, a copy of the *1001 Nights,* and for Nanci the latest *romances* and guitar music.

Music for Goethe's *Faust* began to take shape in his mind that summer. Gérard de Nerval's translation of *Faust* had appeared at the end of 1827, and Berlioz's relish for it approached in intensity his involvement with Thomas Moore and even Shakespeare. While riding in a carriage somewhere near La Côte-St.-André, he set *Le Roi de Thulé* for voice and piano, experimenting with flattened melodic inflections and suggestions of the Swiss *ranz des vaches,* an idiom, purportedly based on the sounds of Alpine horn-calls, in which he had been interested for some time. Returning to Paris, he started work on a much expanded version of *Faust.* Its chronology is unclear, as are the circumstances surrounding its subsequent merger with the *Symphonie fantastique.* Berlioz apparently thought he had a good chance to be appointed composer of a *Faust* ballet written by Victor Bohain and already adopted by the Opéra. He summoned his well-placed connections in support of his candidacy, once again approaching, for example, La Rochefoucauld. Meanwhile a dramatic *Faust*—"an unworthy melodrama"[56]—had opened at the Théâtre de la Porte-St.-Martin, and the Opéra accordingly dropped the idea for its ballet. (It is worth noting here that Berlioz never knew Nerval well and did not look to him when, in 1846, he expanded the *Faust* music of 1828.)

By the time plans for the ballet had evaporated, he had already composed music for much of the rhymed poetry in Nerval's translation. These pieces he elected to have published by Maurice Schlesinger at his own expense. *Huit Scènes de Faust* is the first substantial expression of Berlioz's Shakespearean fever, and testimony, too, to an increasingly Faustian self-perception. The eight movements, each headed by a quotation from Shakespeare, constitute a bold announcement of his maturing style, especially in the radical and unheralded sprung rhythms of the songs of Brander and Méphistophélès. Equally radical is the absence of a common performing force and any linkage between the vignettes: *Huit Scènes de Faust* is the first of Berlioz's many collections to presuppose that the listeners will supply the appropriate dramatic contexts for themselves. In its kaleidoscope of musical images it is a direct precursor of such works as *Harold en Italie, Roméo et Juliette,* and *L'Enfance du Christ,* and as pronounced a departure from the overtures and *Scène héroïque* as the *Eroica* is from Beethoven's First and Second Symphonies.

Huit Scènes de Faust, dedicated to La Rochefoucauld, was published in the spring of 1829, at enough of a cost that Berlioz had to borrow money again, this time from a student. On 10 April 1829 he sent two copies of the work to Goethe, accompanied by an effusive note. Goethe was attracted by the forceful style of Berlioz's letter—"For some years now, *Faust* having been my ordinary reading matter, . . . "—and passed the score to Carl-Friedrich Zelter for evaluation. Zelter could see only "sneezing, croaking, vomiting. The work is an excrescence," he wrote, "the remains of a miscarriage from a hideous incest."[57] (Zelter showed the work to his pupil Mendelssohn, who was quick to agree with his teacher's negative impression.) Goethe, understandably, never wrote back.

The *Huit Scènes* had their admirers, however. Among them were the composer Georges Onslow and the German critic A. B. Marx, who vowed he had never seen anything so original. It apparently sold well. Meyerbeer, a resident of Paris for several months each year and on the verge of his greatest successes, asked for a copy and sent warm congratulations.

Berlioz's enterprises were now widespread and time consuming. A post as musical factotum for the Gymnase-Lyrique was offered him; he began to take English lessons three times a week. Alexandre Choron commissioned a work for his singing school at St.-German-des-Près, and Berlioz seems to have fulfilled this commission with an *O Salutaris* now lost. He set a *Chanson des pirates* from Hugo's new *Orientales* (published in 1829) and composed and published, again with the firm of Maurice Schlesinger, a sprightly *Ballet des ombres* to a text Albert Du Boys had fashioned from Herder's poetry. This fanciful chorus draws on a melodic and contrapuntal tactic to be used twice more, most prominently in the Queen Mab scherzo (ex. 3.3).

By early 1829 at the latest, Harriet Smithson, who kept returning to Paris in the hope of repeating her greatest triumph, could no longer have been ignorant of the young composer afflicted with such a serious case of romantic agony. She had her maid turn away his love letters, at least one of them in fractured English, and was protected wherever she went by no less formidable a chaperone than her mother. Berlioz, now thinking of Harriet as his Ophelia, next tried approaching her through her impresario and interpreter, an Englishman named Turner. She was baffled by his torment and alarmed by its intensity; he was stricken to hear rumors of her imminent departure for Brussels and Amsterdam.

In a last effort to attract her sympathies, he insinuated his *Waverley* overture onto the program of a benefit at the Opéra-Comique where she had agreed to appear in two acts of *Romeo and Juliet*. Their paths crossed at a rehearsal; it was here that she told her colleagues to "beware the gentleman with the eyes that bode no good."[58] The performance took place as scheduled on Wednesday, 25 February. But Berlioz's overture was done before the theater had begun to fill, and, experiencing a nervous attack at the promise of her entry, he fled the theater, not to hear the sound of her voice that night.

He ran directly to her apartments at 1, rue Neuve-St.-Marc—just opposite his own lodgings in the rue de Richelieu—and begged the landlord, M. Tarte, to secure a response to his missives. Harriet's reaction, when Tarte broached the matter with her the next day, was terse:

> "I already told you when Monsieur Berlioz first approached me two [months] ago, that I had him informed I was totally unable to share his sentiments. I fail to understand his perseverance."
> "So it is completely impossible?"
> "O, sir, nothing is more impossible."[59]

The last sentence haunted Berlioz for the two fatal weeks before she left for Holland. Perhaps she was engaged or, worse, already married.

Ballet des ombres, mm. 71–77:

Queen Mab scherzo (*Roméo et Juliette,* movt. IV), mm. 655–61:

EXAMPLE 3.3 Falling-fifth motive in the *Ballet des ombres.*

One senses his mind erupting, in early 1829, with almost hallucinatory sensations of Harriet and Shakespeare and Beethoven. There was a good deal more Beethoven to be heard: his friend Ferdinand Hiller played him the Beethoven piano sonatas, the Société des Concerts offered the Seventh Symphony on 1 March, and on 24 March he heard Baillot's quartet play ops. 131 and 135. At last he felt his forces multiplying, his capacities ready for a major undertaking. An enormous new symphonic work began to take shape in his mind: at once Beethovenian, Faustian, Shakespearean, and autobiographical.

In more tranquil moments his thoughts turned again to Thomas Moore: "He is her countryman: Ireland, always Ireland."[60] He had Thomas Gounet set about adapting some of the *Irish Melodies* and *Sacred Songs* from the French translations of Louise Sw. Belloc. (I think it unlikely the *Elégie en prose* comes from as early as 1827, as is usually maintained—for example, in the New Berlioz Edition. The source for the assertion is a phrase in the *Mémoires* concerning the events of 1827, to be sure, but there he merely ascribes the song to a period of acute longing for Harriet.) The work was done by December, and publication, paid for jointly by Berlioz and Gounet, was almost immediate. The *Neuf Mélodies* show the bright side of the Harriet affair, just as the *Symphonie fantastique* shows its darker manifestations. Berlioz himself loved the songs, later orchestrating three of them for his concerts.

A complete revision of the *Francs-Juges* libretto, with the hero's name changed to Lenor because there was an Arnold in Rossini's *Guillaume Tell,* finally arrived from Ferrand. Berlioz began the necessary musical revisions, only to have the libretto rejected by the jury at the Opéra before he was finished. (They found it long and obscure, though they praised the Bohemians' scene.) This time *Les Francs-Juges* was set aside definitively, its bits and pieces to serve other, more modern compositions.

Ferrand also helped arrange Berlioz's appointment as music journalist for a paper called *Le Correspondant,* an organ of Catholic leanings that liked to describe its sentiments as "political, artistic, religious, philosophical, and literary." Almost simultaneously, A. B. Marx invited Berlioz to report on the musical life of Paris for the Berlin *Allgemeine musicalische Zeitung.* To Berlin he wrote of new stage works by Auber, Bouilly, and Boieldieu; his opening gambit for *Le Correspondant,* "Considérations sur la musique religieuse," was more along the lines of the polemics he had written for *Le Corsaire.* During the summer of 1829 he completed his first sustained literary piece, a three-part article synthesizing his reactions to Beethoven. (There would later be a much more sophisticated Beethoven series.) So as not to offend, and in the French tradition of the anonymous reviewer, he signed these articles with an initial or left them unattributed. "Calamity," he describes this development: "I become a critic."[61] But his letters show that he was ecstatic over the appointments, and the extra money was not to be sneered at.

Doctors attributed the nervous attack he sustained in June to "excessive emotions." They counseled baths, but Berlioz preferred to regather his strength, after a brief stay in bed, through long walks in the country. Within a few weeks he was again holding court at his café table in the rue de Richelieu and priming himself for the *prix de Rome* competition. In 1829 he was confident enough of winning to make advance arrangements with Mme Dabadie, soprano at the Opéra, to sing the cantata. He sought to discover whether Cherubini still harbored grudges; Auber's election to the Academy offered great solace, for Auber, he thought, could be trusted to support him.

But the cantata text that July, called *Cléopâtre,* portrayed the great queen after the battle of Actium. Terrified, she asks the spirits of the Pharoahs if her own spirit will be granted welcome in their vaults. It was so Shakespearean a topic as to distract him altogether from his resolve to curb his excesses. He let himself be carried away, introducing the pulsating rhythms of a failing heart, shocking harmonic progressions, even forbidden enharmonic notation. Rich in orchestral color, overwhelming in dramatic power, *Cléopâtre* is quite the best of his *prix de Rome* cantatas. It is a fitting summary of the tumultuous months since *Herminie,* but for its text the equal of the *Huit Scènes.*

This was too much for the jury, however, a group by their own admission too conservative to grasp even half the implications of Beethoven. They suspected their petulant charge of purposeful ridicule. They were afraid to encourage his walk down "false paths." With Le Sueur ill in bed, there was no one to defend his interests. Moreover, the jury heard the cantatas on 2

August, during the dress rehearsal for *Guillaume Tell,* so Mme Dabadie was forced after all to send her sister, a timid voice student from the Conservatoire who had had no rehearsals. No grand prize was awarded, though two were promised for the next year.

The composers on the jury seem genuinely to have regretted that they could not give Berlioz the prize. Boieldieu, then fifty-four years old, cornered Berlioz on the street and confessed that he could not judge music he was incapable of understanding. "You had the prize in hand," he said, "and you threw it away." He invited Berlioz to call, in order that he might "study" his young colleague. Auber made similar gestures. Both men called Berlioz "volcanic,"[62] sealing his identification with that Chateaubriandesque adjective and foreshadowing Rouget de Lisle's remarkable letter of a year later, where he writes of Berlioz as a volcano in perpetual eruption.

He would not, then, have the stipend on which he had counted and would require further support from La Côte. The stalemate at the Institute triggered another round of parental unrest. He was ready to go home and explain the situation when his father agreed to a monthly stipend of 50 francs, rendering unnecessary a trip that promised to be unpleasant for all concerned. Berlioz's reasons for wanting to stay in Paris for the summer were sound. He had begun to plan another concert of his own works, similar to the one of May 1828. He had a number of composition students from whom he earned 40 or 50 francs monthly, as well as a new job with the publisher Troupenas, proofreading the piano-vocal score of *Guillaume Tell.* In fact, he had quietly fallen into the routine which he was to follow for the rest of his life, assuring daily survival with income from journalism and other modest appointments, planning for concerts of his own music, and composing in what time he had left.

When he was done with *Guillaume Tell,* he began to proofread the Troupenas editions of Beethoven's symphonies, which Fétis had revised by correcting what he thought could only be errors in the transmission of the sources. Berlioz found the scores "littered with impertinent emendations affecting the very stuff of the composer's thought and with even more presumptuous remarks scribbled in the margin." This philistinism could not go unchallenged. An incident followed, during which Fétis felt obliged to defend himself in the pages of his *Revue musicale.*[63] Berlioz had made his first literary enemy.

For the moment, however, that was of no concern: the most pressing matter was copying the parts for his autumn concert. It was scheduled for All Saints' Day, Sunday, 1 November. The program featured excerpts from the *Faust* music, his overtures, and the first Paris performance of Beethoven's "Emperor" Concerto, with Ferdinand Hiller as soloist. Applying once again to La Rochefoucauld, Berlioz secured the Salle du Conservatoire and, for the first time, the services of Habeneck himself as conductor. The orchestra was drawn as usual from his professional acquaintances; whatever he paid them seems to have been borrowed from Ferrand and Gounet. The chorus, probably made up of volunteers, was disappointing in its small size. He could afford a single rehearsal, on 30 October. There it was decided—perhaps because the baritone soloist failed to show up—to cancel Conrad's aria from *Les Francs-Juges* and the songs of Brander and Méphistophélès from *Faust,* for which he had copied parts never put to use.

Berlioz's stature was now such that his concert had a certain public appeal. Dozens of notables came, including the composition faculty from the Conservatoire, Maurice Schlesinger, and the painter Ingres, who would later sketch his portrait (see fig. 4.1). Audience and orchestra greeted him with enthusiasm. The *Francs-Juges* overture, played just after the Beethoven concerto, not only did not suffer from the comparison but rather seemed all the more apt. Only the sextet from *Faust* failed to seize interest; the revised *Resurrexit* with its four pairs of timpani, now approaching the form in which it was adopted for the Requiem, was thought as successful as the overture. Press reviews, including one published by A. B. Marx in Berlin (the connection was through the Schlesinger family) and one in the *Figaro,* were warm. The excellence of the performance revealed new facets of the music to its composer: he was surprised to find the power of his work more gratifying that the applause itself.

The concert also proved financially successful. Accounts show that he took in 528 francs as against 147.55 francs for the room, candles, heating, and service. After paying the copyists and other personal expenses, Berlioz reckoned a profit of 150 francs, a hundred of which he paid directly to Gounet against previous debts. La Rochefoucauld saw that he was sent an honorarium of 100 francs, though it was a draft on the king's account not payable until the following year.[64]

The documents agree that the All Saints' concert thrust Berlioz definitively into the limelight. He became a welcome addition to *soirées* and salons: the celebrated Sunday afternoons of Baron Trémont, an *amateur de musique;* gatherings at Kalkbrenner's; and Maurice Schlesinger's Friday evenings of Beethoven quartets. The authors who approached him to set their work included a fifty-year-old librettist with a *Tancredi;* Nerval, who brought his translations of Schiller; and old Rouget de Lisle, at work on an *Othello.*

His repeated bouts of overexcitement, which he dismissed as "spleen," had to be met with long periods of rest; his tangled emotions contributed to an attack of angina and left him susceptible to periodic tonsillitis. (On one occasion he lanced a boil in his own throat.) His teeth, which were nearly gone by late middle age, had begun to deteriorate. The latest cure for toothaches, tried by Berlioz and described by Balzac, was Paraguay-Roux, whose inventors advertised that "a toothpick, doused with Paraguay-Roux and applied to a sore tooth, will cure even the most acute pain on the spot."[65] Writing to his father of his dental problems, he also asks after a cure for his *ardeur fiévreuse,* for which Dr. Berlioz recommended a bland diet and abstinence from such stimulants as tea. His father must have been more concerned by the vivid descriptions of mental states bordering on mania: an expansive force erupting inside him, the frightening intensity of feelings, the inability to distinguish between physical and spiritual pain. The fact that a friend of the family had just committed suicide made his parents' alarm all the greater.

When well, however, Berlioz was able to enjoy a relatively fashionable lifestyle. It centered around gathering places in the rue de Richelieu: the Café Cardinal and Restaurant Drouot at the corner of the boulevards, the Restaurant Lemardeley at no. 100, the Café de la Bourse. Here he spent long evenings sipping the forbidden tea with his friends and talking ceaselessly of his enthusiasms. Otherwise he indulged in few of the traditional vices, recoiling, for instance, when he learned that Ferrand's parents thought he gambled. His wardrobe, replenished by his mother at Christmas, consisted of suits of various hues and fabrics, high collars, and bright cravats. These along with the shock of flaming hair and long sideburns must have made his appearance striking indeed, even for dandified Paris. His reading now inclined toward the contemporary Romantics: he was impressed that season, for example, by Hoffmann's *Contes fantastiques* and saw in the title an adjective of significance.

FIGURE 3.10 The Boulevard du Temple. Note the man on the corner having his boots shined, said to be the first person photographed. Daguerreotype (1839) by Louis Daguerre (1789–1851).

Early in January 1830 the turbulence and ferment of the preceding months settled into an immense orchestral composition "conceived in a new genre," his first full-fledged symphony. For a time the correspondence talks of an *idée fixe* haunting his life, the skeleton of a work forming in his mind. Soon there developed the notion that it would represent an *épisode de la vie d'un artiste,* where his "infernal passion" might be treated. By 16 April, in a letter to Ferrand,[66] he has roughed out a program for a *Symphonie fantastique,* with mention of enough technical details to suggest that the work was at an advanced stage. The symphony was done in plenty of time for a performance scheduled for 20 May, Ascension Day, at the Nouveautés. The major work on the most remarkable symphonic composition since Beethoven's Ninth was accomplished in a little over three months.

Two significant performances took place that February as Berlioz was hard at work on the symphony. A pair of his Irish Melodies, *Le Coucher du soleil* and the *Chant sacré,* was offered at a concert of the Athénée Musicale. Though buried in the middle of a long Thursday concert of new music at the Hôtel de Ville, they attracted the hushed attention of the audience and the favor of the press. (The celebrated tenor Adolphe Nourrit, too, enjoyed singing the Irish Melodies for salon gatherings, and that summer the *Chant guerrier* achieved for a short time the status of a revolutionary hymn.) And shortly after the famous opening night, Berlioz went to see Hugo's *Hernani,* the event of the season. It is a mark, I think, of his still limited grasp of the theater that he was only partially moved by the "sublime thoughts" he found in Hugo and on the whole preferred *Trente ans, ou La Vie d'un joueur,* which had been the talk of the previous season.

Sometime between mid-March and early April 1830, Berlioz met the eighteen-year-old pianist Camille Moke, by all accounts a ravishing young woman in the prime of her beauty. A pupil of Herz and Kalkbrenner, she was at the time the "adored angel" of Ferdinand Hiller. (His admiration, it later became clear, was platonic.) She taught piano at the boarding and finishing school of Mme d'Aubré. Berlioz had begun to teach guitar there the preceding winter (and remained on the school's prospectus through the 1840s), so he could pursue in propinquitous circumstance this acquaintance first made through Hiller or possibly at Baron Trémont's. While Hiller regaled Camille with stories of Berlioz and Harriet, she teased Berlioz that someone at the school admired him. The *Mémoires,* letters, and Hiller's autobiographical *Künstlerleben* agree that Camille was a vixen, warmed by Berlioz's reputation for ardor and anxious to taste it for herself.

Late that spring she came to Berlioz's room and announced her attraction to him,[67] decorating her confession with deprecations (*infamies*) of Harriet so vile that Berlioz fled blindly from Paris. He was gone for two days, wandering in the countryside, crying uncontrollably. At nightfall he fainted and fell into a ditch, waking there the next morning. His friends assumed he was dead. I suspect Camille told him that Harriet had been carrying on with her leading men. That was not so: Harriet's career may have been hurt by her virtue, but, as we shall see, she retained it.

Berlioz returned to engage Camille in a frantic, headlong, and frankly physical affair. She, unlike the other object of his affection, was very obviously attainable. The relationship lasted for the rest of that melodramatic year. In a few weeks Berlioz summoned up the courage to approach Mme Moke and ask for her daughter's hand. On 5 June he wrote to his parents for their consent to marry. The next day the couple set off together; they stopped in Vincennes, where on the night of 6 June they became lovers.[68] The exactitude with which Berlioz recalls the day a year later suggests that this escapade marked his sexual debut. Thereafter, he terms Camille his *maîtresse* on more than one occasion.

Camille's portrait (fig. 3.11) reveals but a hint of her beauty. Berlioz describes her to Nanci in the following terms:

> She is nearly as tall as I, of slim and graceful figure. She has superb black hair and large blue eyes which sometimes sparkle like stars and other times, when she is possessed by the musical demon, become clouded over as in death. She has a playful nature, an occasionally caustic and biting wit, which contrasts sharply with her basic goodness . . . At the piano, she is a Corinne.

"Her smile is like the sun breaking through the fog," he writes, and "When she amuses herself at the piano, you can imagine an army of fairies dancing on the keys of that harmonious instrument."[69]

The lovers were more than surprised on the 15th and 16th of June by news that the family in La Côte-St.-André consented to their marriage. The reaction of Mme Moke, a self-made shopkeeper whom Berlioz admired for her good taste and aristocratic lifestyle despite her limited means, was mixed. On the one hand, she could not deny his promise and the ease with which he already moved in the most prestigious artistic circles, and he was heir to a valuable estate. On the other, she, along with many other Parisians, was not quite convinced of his sanity and was put off by his obvious inability to maintain a household. In contrast to his meager income, Camille was making 10,000 francs a year. Mme Moke was too shrewd to turn Berlioz down cold, but instead tentatively agreed to the marriage's taking place after a year—certainly, she said, after he had attained a success in the theater. "She has only worked two years [and] has put nothing aside. Wait until she has amassed something. During this time you will do the same; your condition will improve; you will have advanced enough to be able to marry."[70]

The course of his romantic life was not his only preoccupation. Ever since he had fixed a spring debut for his new symphony, Berlioz had worried that the time was not ripe after all. The attraction was the good theater orchestra of the Nouveautés and the devotion to Berlioz of its conductor, Nathan Bloc.

FIGURE 3.11 Camille Moke, c. 1830.

The parts for the *Symphonie fantastique* had been copied and corrected. There was to be no turning back; he went so far as to urge his parents to come to Paris for the concert.

Conflicting productions by both the Société des Concerts and the Théâtre-Allemand limited his choice of extra musicians and promised to attract the most influential public elsewhere. A miserable rehearsal got under way amidst total confusion over music racks, chairs, candles, and space. The hundred-piece orchestra managed to finish only two movements from the *Fantastique,* the *Scène aux champs* and the *Marche au supplice,* before the enterprise was abandoned. Yet these quite thrilled their composer, and by publishing the symphony's program he had piqued the public interest. The concert was postponed until the autumn—it was already late in the season— and Berlioz learned once and for all the need to supervise the technical preparations for his concerts himself.

He vacationed in late May at the country house of one of his composition students, relieving his nervous condition somewhat despite a preoccupation with ideas for theater pieces of the sort that would secure Mme Moke's blessing. He formed a plan of action: to win the *prix de Rome* and its five years of subvention, spend as little time as possible in Italy, and then go on to Germany to stage *Les Francs-Juges* with the tenor Haitzinger in Karlsruhe or possibly with Spohr conducting it in Dresden. His passion for Harriet, now worked out in the *Symphonie fantastique,* could be left to subside. He bade farewell to Camille and her mother and on the afternoon of 17 July entered the grounds of the Institute and started to work. Earlier that day the music subcommittee had met and approved a text by J.-F. Gail, *La Mort de Sardanapale.*

The scenario is drawn jointly from Byron and from Delacroix's extravagant but wonderful painting of 1828. At the climax, the dissolute Assyrian king Sardanapalus, his concubines, and his eunuchs are consumed in flame, atop an enormous funeral pyre as the Medes and Babylonians storm his gates. In light of his experience with *Cléopâtre,* Berlioz was determined to curb his imagination within conventional boundaries, though the final tableau offered all too tempting possibilities. He worked rapidly, finishing a draft in a week, then scoring, polishing, and revising the work. Berlioz alone set a third stanza of text, probably written on the spur of the moment. He was the first to be finished and was ready to leave the Institute on the afternoon of Thursday, 29 July.

Anxious to be done with the Conservatoire and craving Camille's embrace, he would have been quick in any case. That day, however, there was a more pressing reason to leave: cannon fire from batteries in the Louvre had reached the Institute doors just across the Seine, and Berlioz, like every other student in Paris, was curious to find out for himself what was happening in the streets.

What had transpired was nothing less than the fall of the monarchy. Elections in late June had resulted in round defeat of the incumbent ministers, but on 25 July, before the newly elected parliament could meet, the king had had his controversial prime minister Polignac dissolve the Assembly, alter the election laws again, and abolish such freedom of the press as had been achieved under the Restoration. The press was in full insurrection by Monday, 26 July. The next day the courts decreed that the royal order of 25 July was contrary to La Charte, Louis XVIII's charter of suffrage of 1814, and therefore nonbinding. By noon the royal troops and Swiss guards had encircled Paris to contain the unrest. With cries of "Vive la Charte! Vive la liberté! A bas les ministres! A bas Polignac!" the citizenry took to the streets. Shots were fired and blood was drawn, inciting the crowds beyond the mere chanting of slogans. Street barricades built from that most convenient of revolutionary tools, the Paris cobblestone, were thrown up in several hundred locations; gendarmes and cavalry were caught in narrow alleys and pelted with firewood, flowerpots, and furniture. By nightfall the confusion was complete, and news of it had reached the students in the Institute during their evening encounter with the outside world.

On Wednesday the Hôtel de Ville fell, was retaken, and fell again, the cavalry barracks in the rue de Babylone were captured, and the French troops began to fraternize with the revolutionaries. On Thursday the citi-

FIGURE 3.12 Fall of the Louvre, 29 July 1830. The dome of the Institute is visible in the background.

zenry reached the Louvre and Tuileries. By the end of the day, a provisional government had been formed at the Hôtel de Ville, and the tricolor flew above Paris once more.

Just after 5:00 P.M. Berlioz stepped across the wounded in the courtyard of the Institute and into the streets. He dashed to Mme Moke's, where he found Camille to be unharmed, and then for three hours searched for arms to join in the uprising. Finding his two hunting pistols but no ammunition, he reported for duty and was sent to the Hôtel de Ville. With one bullet and some powder begged from passersby, he arrived to find that the *trois glorieuses,* as the July Days came to be called, were already over. On Friday the 30th, he joined a crowd marching to arrest Charles X at St.-Cloud, but the citizens, discovering at the Etoile that the soldiers had dispersed, returned quietly to town.

Within the week the streets were being repaired, and life had returned to normal. The government functionaries by and large retained their positions. On the other hand, 500 people had been killed, and a government had been overthrown. When the Bourbon Louis-Philippe, a cousin of Charles from the Orléans issue and its present duke, was invited to accept the *lieutenance-générale du royaume,* it seemed purely a measure of temporary compromise and safekeeping. But Louis-Philippe was there to stay: as "citizen-king" (which he became on 9 August, exchanging, it was said, the Napoleonic eagle for galoshes and an umbrella), he embarked on a shrewd program of liberal reform and industrialization. This relatively enlightened monarchy was to rule for another eighteen years; by 1840, with Guizot at the helm of the ministries, it was one of the strongest governments in Europe.

On 19 August the jury awarded Berlioz the long-coveted *prix de Rome* by a vote of 6 to 2. Berton dissented, still unwilling to encourage a composer down false paths, and Cherubini joined him. The prize left from 1829 was awarded Alexandre Montfort. Two days later the full Academy approved the awards, and Berlioz was able to write to his mother on 23 August of his victory.

Le Sueur wrote with rapture to Dr. Berlioz, apparently without the laureate's knowledge. The letter emphasizes money: Handel, Gluck, Paisiello, Rossini, and Méhul, says Le Sueur, all became wealthy. "Your son will do the same . . . and he will render the name Berlioz illustrious." He cites the young man's genius, developed well and precisely; his great talent; the facility of his work; and his great industry in seeing his works produced. The music, he says, is well thought out, grandly conceived, always new, of good direction, and off the beaten path. He speaks of Berlioz's imagination, innate warmth, and absolute genius in the fine arts, of his beautiful and rare quality of character—all lost without the support of a father and mother whom he cherishes and who should rejoice in him.[71]

In the aftermath of the July days, Berlioz prepared a splendid arrangement of the *Marseillaise,* with a large orchestra including four horns, six trumpet parts, and three pairs of timpani, as well as two choruses. At the refrain he calls for "tout ce qui a une voix, un cœur et du sang dans les veines." Published by the end of the year, it earned him Rouget's deep gratitude. In fact, it had turned out to be Berlioz's only contribution to the *trois glorieuses*—except, perhaps, for a very similar composition in Berlioz's hand, uncovered in 1984 in the library of the Geneva Conservatoire. The *Chant du neuf Thermidor,* another of Rouget's revolutionary hymns, is for a rather smaller orchestra, a soloist, and a chorus. The sentiments are the same as in the *Marseillaise,* concluding with what the authors, at least, felt to be a rousing refrain:

Chantons la Liberté, couronnons sa statue.
Comme un nouveau Titan le crime est foudroyé.
Relève ta tête abattue,
O France! à tes destins Dieu lui-même a veillé.

(Let us sing to liberty, crown we her statue. Like a modern titan, the evil has been struck down. Raise again, O France, thy bowed head: for God himself has watched over thy destiny.)

This work, too, doubtless comes from September 1830 or so. Berlioz gave the manuscript to Nathan Bloc, who must have taken it with him when he

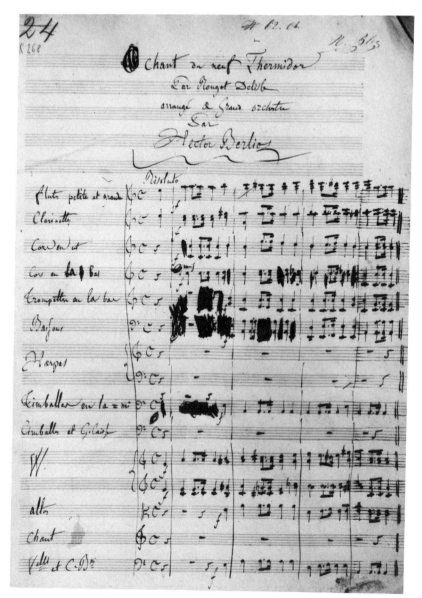

FIGURE 3.13 *Chant du neuf Thermidor,* title page of the autograph.

was called to Geneva in 1831 to lead a philharmonic society and later to direct the Conservatoire there.

Berlioz canceled his annual visit home to prepare for his travels and for the upcoming concerts: the prize ceremony, where *Sardanapale* would receive a full reading, and the performance of the *Symphonie fantastique,* which was set for 14 November, then postponed to 21 November, and finally to 5 December. He accepted an invitation from Narcisse Girard, now at the Théâtre-Italien, to compose a new overture. The work was to be a tribute to Camille, his Ariel, on *The Tempest* of Shakespeare. It would be "entirely new," summoning a chorus, glass harmonica, piano four-hands, and orchestra. He would show Camille that he could command his orchestra as well as she did her piano. Meanwhile they dined together, enjoying "devouring kisses, furious embraces," and poetic love. Harriet's return to Paris was noted only in passing, and Berlioz maintained his composure when he encountered her in person.

There were still monetary problems, for his stipend did not start until January 1831. Looking toward the expenses of his concert, he wrote away for a last round of loans, begging 500 francs from his friend Edouard Rocher and 200 francs more from his father.

He hoped for a time to be able to persuade the minister of the Interior to let him skip the sojourn in Italy. The Academicians were opposed to this course of action, attacking as it did the very foundation of their notion that Rome was a good place for a composer to mature. Rossini, on the other hand, sent word that "there's nothing to do there; he will be wasting his time." To Guizot, the new minister, he pleaded the pressing nature of his negotiations with the Opéra and other Paris theaters for what were in fact the vaguest of projects, suggested the greater value of going directly to Germany, and topped off his arguments with the notion that his nervous irritability would not be helped by the Italian sun. To this last extraordinary claim he appended certification from a doctor and endorsements from an illustrious quartet: Fétis, Spontini, Meyerbeer, and Le Sueur.[72] His editor at *Le Correspondant,* Carné, brought his own brand of pressure to bear. Nevertheless the word *impossible* was scrawled at the top of his petition by a functionary, and Guizot replied with that sentiment, couched in more exalted terms, on 14 December.

On Saturday, 30 October, after a general rehearsal on Friday before a full house, Berlioz was crowned with his laurel wreath. Spontini and Edouard Rocher came in his behalf, along with Mme Le Sueur and her daughters, but otherwise Berlioz was virtually bereft of support. Le Sueur was ill, Mme Moke and her daughter stayed away, and none of the family bothered to come. In a last, defiant gesture toward the Academy, Berlioz had added a conflagration scene at the end of his cantata, complete with an explosion for the percussion section. It fizzled in performance, however: the French horn player missed his entry, and the percussionists consequently had no cue. At this point, reported the *Journal du Commerce,* "we saw M. Berlioz jump to his feet, full of artistic rage, score in hand, seemingly overcome by a violent disturbance. Only with difficulty did they convince him to come and get the crown he had earned."[73]

Because of the aborted conflagration and the enthusiasm the cantata had induced in artistic circles, he scheduled it for performance on his December concert. But to Adolphe Adam he wrote that the cantata was a mediocre work not representative of the current state of his thought. He begged Adam to come instead to the Opéra to hear *La Tempête* given during a benefit at the Opéra for the musicians' pension fund; it was an entr'acte between act I of Rossini's *Le Siège de Corinthe* and a ballet. Ferdinand Hiller was to play the piano part that had been written for Camille. Again Berlioz sent the press a programmatic description, organizing the images of Ariel, Miranda, Caliban, Prospero, and of course the tempest itself into four sections, which he titles prologue, storm, action, and denouement. We know little of what went on at the concert of 7 November and nothing at all of a repeat performance announced for 26 November. Spontini, who now recognized the admiration of his disciple and his exceptional promise, went to all the rehearsals. According to Berlioz, at least, *La Tempête* was "an extraordinary success."[74]

The remaining weeks of the year were a time of frantic preparation for the December concert, the formal engagement to Camille, and the trip to Italy. To the new king, Louis-Philippe, he penned a fervent letter of invitation, which was only recently recovered:

> If Your Majesty deigned to honor this musical solemnity with his illustrious presence, it would be new proof of Your Majesty's solicitude for us liberators and would give me at the same time the most powerful of encouragements.[75]

The king's household responded with an encouragement of 300 francs. It was the first of many such gifts from the Orléans family, whose arrival on the scene was positively bracing to the artistic climate. The family members instructed their representatives in the professional bureaucracy to keep them informed of significant developments in the arts. They spent freely on these "gratifications" and "encouragements," enjoyed music in their various homes (Camille Moke, for example, played for the queen that September), and were often seen in the theater and concert hall. Moreover, both of Louis-Philippe's important prime ministers, Thiers and Guizot, were themselves gifted writers, inclined to recognize the fertility of their nation's art in ways that transcended anything offered by Charles X or, later, Napoleon III.

The concert of 5 December, with a large orchestra of by far the best players Berlioz had yet mustered, conducted by Habeneck, was easily his best to date. The *Symphonie fantastique* was received with ecstasy appropriate to the occasion, and this time *Sardanapale* went off without a hitch.

FIGURE 3.14 *Symphonie fantastique*, title page of the autograph. Note the citations from Hugo (upper left) and from Shakespeare's *King Lear* (toward bottom center).

FIGURE 3.15 Liszt in 1832.

Two Irish melodies, the overture to *Les Francs-Juges,* and a violin solo by Urhan completed the program. Fétis wrote, in 1835, that the audience was small, that there was scarcely anyone in the hall who was not either a friend or a guest. They thought they were having a nightmare during the whole performance, he says, but they did applaud the *Marche au supplice* for its novel effects.[76]

There can be no doubt that the *Fantastique* was admired by the progressives, however. Afterward Meyerbeer and Spontini led the applause, and Pixis came backstage to embrace the composer. An expensive score of *Olimpie* arrived the next day, signed "your affectionate Spontini." The most important of all the results of the December concert was that Liszt made his debut in Berlioz's life: he "forcibly led me off to dinner at his house and praised me with the most energetic enthusiasm."[77] They began at once to talk of a piano version of the symphony; Liszt promised to help with the arrangement, then borrowed the manuscript score.

What must have been a large monetary loss—the total cost had been well over 3,000 francs—went unnoticed. Berlioz had come of age; his apprenticeship was done.

A few hours after Berlioz's concert, Harriet Smithson appeared at the Opéra in the title role of Auber's *La Muette de Portici.* It was her benefit, aimed at the very public Berlioz had wooed that afternoon, but her performance is said to have been a failure. Though there is no mention of it in the documents of his life, Berlioz must have known about the benefit, as he knew about everything else going on in town. But he was dining with Liszt that night, and Harriet's appearance went unnoticed. It is significant testimony to their relative standings, however, that whereas the royal encouragement to Berlioz had been in the amount of 300 francs, Harriet was granted 1,000.

Even Mme Moke had been impressed by the *Fantastique,* having found the music "truly irresistible. Never in my life have I felt such musical emotion."[78] That week Berlioz and her daughter were engaged to be married on his return from Italy. They exchanged rings, tokens of the permanence of their love.

The last few days in Paris he spent largely in the company of Camille. Spontini came to bid him farewell and leave a letter of introduction to his brother, a priest in Rome. There was no time to respond to Rouget de Lisle's fine letter of 20 December, asking him to come discuss a libretto:

> We have never met; but it would give me great pleasure if we could. Your mind seems a veritable volcano in perpetual eruption. Mine never produced much more than a flash in the pan; the fire's going out, though there's still some smoke. But the richness of your volcano and the remains of my little fire combined might kindle something.[79]

Berlioz left his scores in care of Réty, the business manager at the Conservatoire. He stayed up well into the morning of 30 December 1830, penning Stéphen de La Madelaine a farewell letter at 2:00 A.M. At 8:00 A.M. he set out for La Côte-St.-André, welcoming the new year en route. Though bursting with new musical ideas, he saw his forced exile as a *fatal voyage* of separation. He left behind a growing circle of devotees and a few who were relieved to see him go.

Chapter Four

The Emergence of a Style
Francs-Juges and *Symphonie fantastique*

tanding before the Académie des Beaux-Arts to receive his laurel crown, Berlioz was no longer the "pale and disheveled" *habitué* of Odéon and Opéra, as he had once been described. His appearance must by that time have been more like the portrait made by Emile Signol at the end of the Italian sojourn, where he seems handsome, physically mature, petulant (fig. 5.5; Ingres's drawing, fig. 4.1, is closely related). Berlioz's peculiar brand of Romantic exuberance, at its peak from 1827 to early 1830, had begun to be tempered by his growing stature in the world of new music. His prodigious industry between his arrival in Paris in 1821 and the breathless events of 1830 had left him solidly footed in his trade, at the beginning of a promising career. He was now possessed of a certain degree of technical proficiency, a formidable mastery of the machinery and politics of music making, an easy command of the worlds of journalism and publishing, and above all a bright sincerity of purpose, proudly worn. He was, moreover, well on his way to becoming a cultivated man of letters, already swept into the current of literary goals and tactics that was Parisian Romanticism.

His artistic presence was in some respects defined by the way he had appeared, to all but a few insiders, to have burst onto the musical scene in 1828–29. His engraved scores and curious public concerts of that time seemed to be those of an original spirit proposing a radical new style, a perception Berlioz encouraged in his early autobiographical essays. Even those who found his work undisciplined were inclined to admire its stubbornly original elements. In fact neither Berlioz nor his musical language had arrived quite so abruptly: its more radical ideas had been brewing for more than a decade. It is not even true that the *Symphonie fantastique* announced in 1830 the arrival at maturity of a polished composer, for that is a distinction which must be reserved for works of the later 1830s, or perhaps even for *La Damnation de Faust*. What is astonishing is how each conceptual discovery of the 1820s, in literature and theater as well as in

FIGURE 4.1
Berlioz in 1832.
Pencil on paper;
attributed to Ingres.

music, threw open a new world of compositional ideas, and how each new world was embraced in support of a musical vision that is consistent from the *Fantastique* to *Les Troyens* and beyond.

Berlioz's understanding of musical meaning and his store of compositional devices were conceived in splendid isolation from the true issues of Viennese Classicism. He knew virtually nothing of the repertoire we often suppose to be the main forerunner of Romanticism—the instrumental music of Haydn and Mozart—and nothing at all of the masters of the High Baroque. Even after he had the wherewithal and inclination to learn older scores, his interest scarcely extended back before 1770, the year of Beethoven's birth. During the course of decades of important criticism, he mentions Lully and Handel only in passing. He was untouched—unlike his contemporaries in the German-speaking countries—by the long tradition of the courtly chapel-masters, those liveried servants who dutifully composed for a vast range of assured performances, from sacred service to dinner music and small-town theater. He knew little of the elegant architecture and the dynamic of harmonic departure and return that motivate and then propel the Viennese style. What

Berlioz did sense, instinctively, was the power of song to move the spirit, of the mighty alliance that might be concluded between music and a text already bursting with image and feeling. In that light it is anything but surprising that he found raw counterpoint, as it was taught him, cold, and the rules of the sonata, if indeed they were ever taught him in any systematic fashion, unattractive.

The middle and late 1820s, when Berlioz declared his material and spiritual independence, were years of synthesizing inherited and learned musical elements in service of his proposed compositional stance. The traits he later identified as the hallmarks of his style are "passionate expression, inward intensity, rhythmic impetus, and a quality of unexpectedness,"[1] and his musical grammar was developed on behalf of those goals. Briefly summarized, the elements of his musical syntax are a congenial melody, often constructed of irregular phrases; an altogether conventional repertoire of chords deployed in unconventional manner; a well-developed sense of the role of counterpoint in such musical design; and a flexible approach to genre and form. All this was revolutionary enough, at least for the 1820s and 1830s, to have cost Berlioz some tortuous working out. The percentage of genuine successes to be found in the works of the 1820s as measured by public and critical response, was relatively low. On the other hand, few such gifted composers have ever practiced so far from the central currents of compositional thought. Those who have, like Mussorgsky and perhaps Ives, are correspondingly fresh and direct.

The fact of the matter is that despite Berlioz's prodigious gifts and solid if somewhat eccentric grounding in technique, it took many years for him to work out the musical implications of the attitudes he assumed early on. It is reasonable to regard the 1820s as the decade of emergence of his style and the 1830s as the decade of its mastery.

Among the thorniest conceptual problems in understanding the Berlioz style is why the operatic stage in general, and the operas of Gluck and Spontini in particular, lured Berlioz so irresistibly, even after he had mastered a good deal of more modern music. Part of the answer lies in the stranglehold of theater over French music, indeed over French artistic circles in general. The Opéra was the uncontested proving ground for a composer of the time: it remained through most of Berlioz's career a sort of Panthéon of living music, the temple where the public came to sanctify what it took to be the nation's greatest art. Proof of this situation lies in the bizarre circumstance that when the Société des Concerts set about finding a new French symphony to perform, they could identify but one native composer, George Onslow, interested in providing it. Within this context the clear superiority of the Gluck and Spontini operas over anything else in the repertoire is a simple truism.

Much of the rest was vulgar and cheap, of passing musical value. In the mid-1820s, Berlioz's list of operas in this second category included *Le Rossignol, Les Prétendus, La Caravane du Caire,* and *Lasthénie*—that is, the work of such old-fashioned composers as Grétry and Hérold. Opera in Paris did have a knack for yielding a great masterpiece now and then, despite a prevailing climate of intrigue, scandal, and government intervention. The same milieu that produced Berlioz and the Société des Concerts brought forth the great Parisian works of Rossini, Auber, and Meyerbeer. But in the early 1820s that rejuvenation was still around the corner, and Berlioz, though eventually won over by all three composers, had a right to his biases and suspicions.

"The Jupiter of our Olympus," he said of his coterie, "was Gluck."[2] Gluck's was a noble solution to the issues of dramatic music, always simple, melodic, and appropriate to the drama. The two *Iphigénie* operas attracted the young Berlioz especially: they are, after all, Parisian works composed for the Opéra, to French texts, in that appealing genre called *tragédie-lyrique.* (*Armide* is a setting of Quinault's rather antiquated libretto first written for Lully. *Alceste* and *Orphée et Eurydice,* the other two Gluck operas in production at the time, are both Viennese works.) The heroine of the great *tragédies-lyriques* must have seemed especially appealing: Iphigenia, the daughter of Agamemnon and Clytemnestra, was sacrificed to the gods in

FIGURE 4.2
Gluck, c. 1775.
Terra-cotta
by Houdon.

order that her father's becalmed fleet might proceed to the siege of Troy; she is, therefore, a character in the epic struggle of Greeks and Trojans, just a few paces outside the boundaries of *Les Troyens*. It was as much the Frenchness of the tradition as the Greek antiquity of the subject matter, however, that drew Berlioz to Gluck. Gluck's work seemed the perfect accord of music with drama, a model for realizing his ideas, where before Berlioz had had only instincts.

In the dedication to *Alceste,* Gluck had written of his aims in what for Berlioz was telling fashion:

> I have felt that the overture ought to apprise the spectators of the nature of the action that is to be represented and to form, so to speak, its argument; that the concerted instruments should be introduced in proportion to the interest and the intensity of the words, and not leave sharp contrasts between aria and recitative in the dialogue, so as not to break a period unreasonably nor wantonly to disturb the force and heat of the action.
>
> Furthermore, I believed that my greatest labor should be devoted to seeking a beautiful simplicity, and I have avoided making displays of difficulty at the expense of clarity. Nor did I judge it desirable to discover novelties if they were not naturally suggested by the situation and the expression. There is no rule which I have not thought it right to set aside willingly for the sake of an intended effect.[3]

In late 1834 Berlioz wrote an analysis of *Iphigénie en Tauride* which suggests that the most memorable first impression of Gluck in performance was the richness of the orchestral sound. "To hear a full orchestra, to read a full score, all that had been until then but a dream I could only hope someday to realize."[4] He was especially intrigued by the delicate strokes of orchestration: the "chaste color" of flutes in the low register in the *marche religieuse* from *Alceste* and the dramatic appearance of trombones for the accompanied recitative of Orestes in act III of *Iphigénie en Tauride* ("Quoi! je ne vaincrai pas ta constance funeste?"). He detected and shared Gluck's passion for his dramatic situations, as expressed in such passages as the underworld scene in *Orphée* and the characterization of arch-villain Hidraot (Hydraotes, magician-king of Damascus) in *Armide*. Berlioz's memory of vivid details from Gluck is striking indeed, documented time and again in his correspondence and criticism. The intelligibility of Gluck's text, too, delighted him, and offered bold precedent for his own novel ideas on declamation.

As an example both of Gluck's effect on Berlioz and of Berlioz's careful scrutiny of how Gluck operates, here is a portion of the entry on violas from Berlioz's *Traité d'instrumentation*.

> One recalls the profound impression that [the viola] always makes in the passage from *Iphigénie en Tauride* where Orestes, panting, overcome with fatigue and remorse, falls asleep singing "Calm returns to my heart." The quietly agitated

orchestra, meanwhile, offers sobs, convulsive plaints, punctuated incessantly by the frightening obstinate groans of the violas. Not a single note of voice or instrument is without sublime intent in this matchless inspiration, but one must recognize that the fascination the passage has for its listeners, the sensation of horror that causes the eyes to open wide and fill with tears, is principally due to the viola part: to the timbre of its third string, to its syncopated rhythm, and to the strange effect of the unison made by its syncopated A, brusquely interrupted by another A from the basses, in a different rhythm.[5]

Gluck, then, is Berlioz's rooting in Classicism, a guiding presence in both *Les Troyens* and *L'Enfance du Christ*. Berlioz was right to boast, early on, of his expert knowledge of this increasingly neglected repertoire, and by the end of his career he was himself widely regarded as Gluck's most persuasive advocate. He often programmed the great scenes for his concerts, developed for Mme Viardot the version of *Orphée et Eurydice* still most frequently performed, participated in revivals of *Alceste* and *Armide,* and was the spirit behind the regal edition of Gluck's *tragédies-lyriques* published by Simon Richault and his successors beginning in 1873.

Spontini's operas attracted Berlioz, too, and for similar reasons. Their technical attributes are a generation closer to Berlioz; from a strictly musical point of view—putting aside for the moment the question of subject matter— "it is arguable that the major force in shaping Berlioz's musical style was not Beethoven or Weber or even Gluck but Gluck's successor and inheritor at the Paris Opéra, Spontini."[6] Again, Berlioz is drawn to the great Paris *tragédies-lyriques: La Vestale, Fernand Cortez,* and, to a somewhat lesser extent (because there was no full score available to him until Spontini gave him one in 1830), *Olimpie.* He writes of Spontini nearly as often and as extravagantly as of Gluck, citing his "inexpressible admiration" for work of such genius: "it is true, it is strong, it is beautiful, it is new, it is sublime."[7]

Berlioz was drawn most of all to Spontini's way of controlling the grand design of his operas, his lavish stage settings and abrupt turns of plot, his pacing of tableaux and brilliant juxtaposition of contrastive musical forces, as, for example, in the joint choruses of Spaniards and Mexicans in *Cortez.* "One might almost say," he wrote, "that the second act of *La Vestale* taken as a whole is just one gigantic crescendo, the *forte* of which does not come till the final scene with the veil."[8] We know Berlioz to have turned to the *Marche triomphale* in *Olimpie* (act III, sc. vi) for guidance with his own music for the appearance of the Trojan horse in *Les Troyens.*

Spontini's graceful and refined brilliance constituted, but for Berlioz's own *Les Troyens,* the last breath of lyric tragedy in France. The feverish public admiration for a naïve, apparently simplistic theater—based, thought Berlioz, on crass effects repeated many times over—snuffed out the flame of Spontini's genius once and for all. It would take Berlioz another three decades to bring himself to try his hand for the first time at an overall design following the model of Spontini's masterworks.

FIGURE 4.3 Spontini in 1830.

At the time his own style was emerging, it was more useful for him to imitate details: intricate accompanimental figurations, for instance, and the lyric sweep of Spontini's melodies. To illustrate the clever use of trombones for his *Traité d'instrumentation,* Berlioz chose a passage from *La Vestale,* the sort that obviously served as a point of departure for his own ideas (ex. 4.1a). Berlioz often used this kind of textural gesture to establish scenic identity, as in the pantings that begin *Herminie,* for example, or any one of the dozens of restless accompaniment figures that tint his broad tenor-range melodies (ex. 4.1b–c). The influence of Spontini's melodic style, especially in the arias of slower tempo, can be sensed in the growing sophistication of Berlioz's own melody, first manifest, I think, in the *prix de Rome* cantatas. Berlioz's fondness for the grand march and, perhaps, the ease with which he composed the sparkling ballet music for *Faust* and *Les Troyens* are part of Spontini's legacy, too. He was taken by the march in triple meter in act II of *Cortez* ("Le repos de la gloire"), and this metric trick alone has far-reaching general implications and at least one specific one, for the duet of the sentinels in act V of *Les Troyens* was first conceived as a march in $\frac{3}{4}$.

a. From Spontini's *La Vestale: Chœur et Marche funéraire* (act III, no. 17), as given in Berlioz's *Grand Traité d'instrumentation* (p. 222; example reduced and abbreviated):

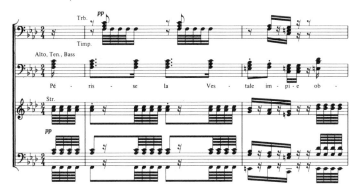

b. *Herminie*, mm. 1–4:

c. *Symphonie fantastique*, movt. III, mm. 67–70:

EXAMPLE 4.1 Decorative figuration in Spontini and Berlioz.

Berlioz, then, picked and chose from the existing repertoires for his tutelage, and he found ample material there to attract his sympathies. He was not immune to the novel ideas of composers who pleased him less than Gluck and Spontini; this is especially true of the large body of Revolutionary and Napoleonic ceremonial music, notably of Gossec (with his revolutionary marches for wind band and, in his nativity oratorio, an offstage chorus of angels) and Méhul (in, for example, his *Chant national du 14 juillet 1800,* which calls for two choruses and two orchestras, embodies a number of spatial effects, and was first given in the church of the Invalides). The first manifestation of this particular genre, if it was not already alluded to in the Mass of 1824, is the 1830 setting of the *Marseillaise,* with its giant orchestra and bold strokes of harmonic color.

Berlioz also enjoyed the music of Salieri and Sacchini, the Parisian operas of Rossini, and such little Mozart as he knew. (He could not help being put off, at first, by the public's adulation of Rossini, but studied *Guillaume Tell* [1829] closely and with growing affection.) Of Meyerbeer, whose star was just beginning to rise, Berlioz was a staunch admirer, ultimately gleaning more from him, I think, than he ever said. Meyerbeer's inexhaustible fertility and mastery of the politics of the Parisian stage must have been powerful lessons for his younger colleague.

But it was Le Sueur's pedagogical skill that united these varied impressions, gathered from so many disparate sources, into a disciplined grammar. Le Sueur's principal triumph was to foster in his pupil a sense of daring: Berlioz cannot have failed to grasp the precedent of his teacher's own iconoclastic behavior in years long past. And it was Le Sueur who, though he saw little use for music of abstraction, had himself been happy enough to blur the distinctions between the two conventional genres of French music of his time, opera and Latin motet. The effect of Le Sueur's view of amalgamating styles is apparent in Berlioz's earliest efforts at composing sacred music and, later, in his purposeful merger of the symphonic and operatic genres as well. Le Sueur's biographer Jean Mongrédien argues that his subject constitutes the true link in French music between Gluck and Berlioz, an association he finds expressed in Berlioz's notions of musical space, narrative description, timbre, and acoustics.[9] Yet Saint-Saëns, whose criticism always seems apt, saw Le Sueur's influence as prevailingly negative: Berlioz's excellences, he said, were inimitable, and it is his faults and insecurities that show the influence of Le Sueur.

The rest of Berlioz's musical education can only be reckoned as haphazard. Catel's little treatise offered proper grounding in chord structure and harmonic linkage by good counterpoint; it even included some figured bass. But Catel offers few admonitions concerning what *not* to do. His examples of modulation and acceptance of enharmony and diminished-seventh sonorities as ways to move about are more than a little progressive compared with the ideas of Cherubini and Berton (both of whom wrote treatises not mentioned, and apparently not studied, by Berlioz); it may be that Catel's role in Berlioz's orientation to harmony was great indeed.

The only other formal tutelage offered Berlioz was Reicha's. No matter how unappealing Berlioz found the subject matter, the counterpoint class was clearly of great significance to his professional orientation. Berlioz's descriptions of Reicha are appreciative, and there are many accounts by other pupils of his excellence as a didact. Reicha was an eccentric composer, much taken with free, "modern" styles. His irreverent fugues composed "in the modern style" (see, for example, ex. 4.2) obviously intrigued Berlioz. Set beside Reicha's flights of fancy, Berlioz's many fugal movements seem positively traditional. One should not be misled by Berlioz's intemperate remarks about counterpoint or by the drunken "Amen" in *La Damnation de Faust.* The sure command of the opening of *Harold en Italie,* the fugal marches in the Requiem and *Roméo et Juliette,* and the Witches' Round Dance all offer convincing evidence that he mastered Reicha's subject matter well.

Berlioz was for all intents and purposes on his own by the start of that electrifying season of 1827–28. The music that followed—*Huit Scènes de Faust, Neuf Mélodies,* and the *Symphonie fantastique*—is anything but derivative. It is easy to contend that the paucity of Berlioz's formal instruction resulted in an unbridled maverick's being loosed on the world of composition, but I doubt he would have profited much from further instruction. What he did not learn from a teacher of the rudiments of harmony and form he would work out for himself, just as he worked out for himself the grammar of conducting. Fétis's advice, to tell "the young calumniator of counterpoint and fugue to give up subjects that he valued so little and to put himself at the free disposal of his genius,"[10] was better than he knew.

EXAMPLE 4.2 Exposition of Fugue no. 31 from Anton Reicha's 36 *Fugues* (Vienna, 1803).

Early in his career—after the second performance of the Mass (November 1827), according to the *Mémoires*—Berlioz gathered up and burned much of his major work: the Mass (except for the *Resurrexit*), *Beverley, Estelle et Némorin,* and the oratorio on the crossing of the Red Sea. A "coldly impartial glance" had shown him how little they were worth. At some point in midcareer, he destroyed the sources for much of what was left from that period: the *Resurrexit,* the *Scène héroïque,* much of *Les Francs-Juges,* much of *Sardanapale, La Mort d'Orphée, Huit Scènes de Faust,* and *Rob-Roy.* This second episode can be placed with some certainty, I think, between the completion of *Faust* in 1846, when the *Huit Scènes* was drawn whole into the larger composition, and the first stage of serious work on the *Mémoires* in 1848, when Berlioz writes of the bonfires. (His revisionist attitude was clear as early as 1839, however, when Berlioz and his publisher reassigned the opus number 1 from the *Huit Scènes* to the score and parts for the altogether less striking *Waverley* overture.)

Only in the cases of *Les Francs-Juges* and *Sardanapale,* however, was he successful in destroying much of the music, for each of the other works was preserved in sources Berlioz could not reach: the *Resurrexit, Scène héroïque,* and *Orphée* in presentation copies; *Rob-Roy* in an *envoi* sent to the Académie des Beaux-Arts from Rome; and the *Huit Scènes* in multiple printed copies, several of which had by that time already left France. (The print run for that publication cannot have been much greater than several dozen copies, and more than a dozen still exist.) All of these works provided Berlioz with substantial passages for his masterpieces of the 1830s and 1840s. What he saved of *Sardanapale, Les Francs-Juges,* and the unfinished opera *La Nonne sanglante* (1841–47) were precisely those movements which might still serve his purposes. He was to keep that material in his workroom in case it were to come in handy later on: "à consulter," he marked one fragment, "à brûler après ma mort."[11] Even the short fragment of *Sardanapale* left to posterity shows melodies adopted for *Roméo et Juliette* and *Les Troyens.*

There is nothing unscrupulous about the practice of self-borrowing, and Berlioz freely attests to it in his writings: "I have used here and there," he writes, for instance, of *Les Francs-Juges,* "the best ideas from this opera, developing them for later works. What is left will probably go through the same process or else be thrown away."[12] Berlioz's self-borrowings amount to a good case of musical thrift. The surprise comes in the ease with which he recasts the same music into sharply different settings: consider, for example, how "Et iterum venturus est" from the *Resurrexit* becomes "Assassiner un Capucin" in *Cellini* (see ex. 3.1). Two of the more interesting smaller-scale borrowings appear in example 4.3.

It was because of self-borrowing, we may reasonably conclude, that Berlioz came to rip out two of the movements of *Les Francs-Juges,* leaving just enough notation in the margins for us to identify some of the music. He

a. From *Cléopâtre* in *La Tempête:*

Cléopâtre, movt. III (*Méditation*), mm. 77–84:

Ouverture de La Tempête, mm. 230–37:

b. From *Sardanapale* in *Les Troyens:*

Sardanapale fragment, mm. 28–36:

Les Troyens, no. 10 (Cassandre's aria), mm. 53–60:

EXAMPLE 4.3 Self-borrowings.

destroyed six other movements altogether. Of *Les Francs-Juges,* only the overture, five of the original movements, and the revised libretto of 1829 remain. As the revised libretto refers to movements already completed, a fairly good idea of the total content can be deduced.

Though ill-fated from the start and left to us in the most fragmentary of states, *Les Francs-Juges* is nevertheless the most detailed primary evidence of Berlioz's style before he discovered Beethoven and is the major product of his Le Sueurian period. If the opera shows artistic dependence, it is on the world of *Der Freischütz,* where similarly dark characters lurk in the forest and similarly naive peasants cavort about. Berlioz is at his best in such contrasts of bright and lugubrious, in the juxtaposition of pastoral and diabolical. In that sense the step in dramatic conceit from *Les Francs-Juges* to the world of the *Symphonie fantastique* is small indeed.

The story concerns the usurped throne of Breisgau and the tyranny of a band of vigilantes (*Francs-Juges:* roughly, "self-appointed judges," the

Vehmic tribunals of medieval German history) over a simple folk, the *bohé-miens et bohémiennes, bergers et bergères*. The pretender Olmerik (bass) has seized power by murdering his brother the king, yet can perpetuate his authority only by eliminating the true heir, his nephew Lenor (tenor). (In 1826, as we have noted, this character was named Arnold.) Lenor loves the princess Amélie, betrothed to Olmerik; she returns the sentiments. The first two acts set forth the problem, the love interest, Lenor's role as hero, and the villainy of Olmerik's horde; in the third act Lenor is led to the cave where the black-hooded judges, in mystic ceremony, prepare to decide his fate.

"Where are your enemies?" asks Olmerik of Lenor, in a passage symptomatic of the libretto as a whole. "Within your ranks." "Your accomplices?" "The heavens!" "Your arms?" "Hope, the people's misfortune, and the horror of tyrants." In the nick of time, the citizens raid the castle. Olmerik, refusing to be taken alive, leaps into the arms of a colossal bronze statue and is engulfed in flames.

The principal setting is a town square dominated by an ancient fortified castle and encircled by a dense wood; among the parapets is a bell tower of great significance. The cavern of the Francs-Juges might well be found in the Wolf's Glen: it is sinister, lit by reflections of a distant moon, and furnished with a circle of twelve stone chairs and an immense table covered in black fabric. The blackness is in studied contrast to the colorful song and dance of the rustics elsewhere in the opera.

Each detail of the setting and plot was clearly conceived by Berlioz for its promise of musical expression, down to the chiming of the clock tower at the most critical moments in the story. One has the strong sensation that Berlioz played a predominant role in forging the libretto, and that Ferrand's work was limited to the hacking out of rhymes. In the 1829 libretto appear such indications as, for the opening of act III, "The orchestra expresses the sorrow of nature and the sad disquiet that foreshadows extraordinary events." The best numbers seem to have been the successive peasant scenes at the close of act I (sc. viii: "Mêlons à la voix des trompettes") and at the opening curtain of act II ("L'ombre descend dans la vallée"); an aria by Lenor's liegeman Conrad, of which Berlioz thought highly enough to include in a public concert ("Noble amitié"); an orchestral interlude representing Lenor's troubled slumber; and the hymn of the Francs-Juges ("Des célestes décrets").

The preserved music is competently set out and, like the libretto, displays a sensitivity to good theatrics and a fertility of novel ideas. The orchestral writing is in the mold of Spontini from the very first (ex. 4.4a). Pastoral elements dominate the texture of the first two acts, and Berlioz flirts willingly with sounds of herdsmen's pipes and their echoes, what was called the *ranz des vaches* (ex. 4.4b). Berlioz thought the charming though primitive *Mélodie*

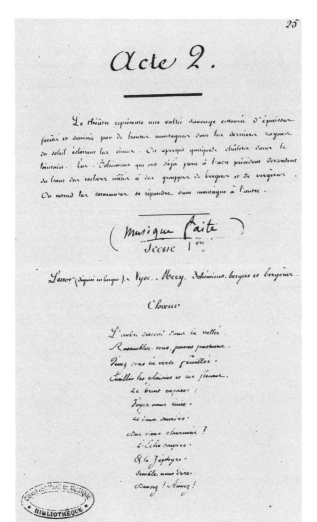

FIGURE 4.4
Les Francs-Juges, libretto.
The opening tableau of act II.
Berlioz has written *musique
faite* near the middle of the
page.

pastorale worthy of programming on his concert of 26 May 1828. He prepared a piano reduction, probably for rehearsal use; consequently a late version of the movement has been preserved (ex. 4.4c).

What little has been preserved of the hymn of the Francs-Juges suggests a lugubrious slow march (ex. 4.4d). This important scene, incidentally, includes a melody later found greatly augmented in speed at the beginning of (and elsewhere in) the Roman carnival in *Benvenuto Cellini* (see ex. 7.19a). But the most intriguing movement is one of those for which the music has been nearly destroyed: the first scene of act III. Lenor appears by dark of night to keep his fatal rendezvous with the Francs-Juges; after a brief invocation

a. *Chœur du peuple* (no. 1), mm. 1–14:

b. *Chœur de bergers* (no. 6), mm. 1–21:

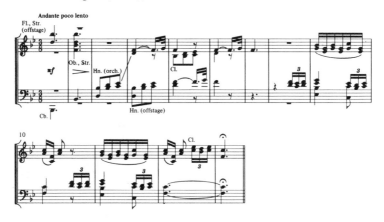

EXAMPLE 4.4 *Les Francs-Juges.*

c. *Mélodie pastorale* (no. 7) in a piano reduction by the composer, mm. 1–10:

d. *Hymne des Francs-Juges* (no. 12), mm. 7–11:

EXAMPLE 4.4 (*continued*).

to the heavens, he stretches out on a bank and falls asleep. Here the libretto reads as follows:

> His sleep is agitated and painful. The melodies and images of the preceding acts appear to him in a confused dream and mingle in his imagination. The orchestra recalls one-by-one and in quick succession the motives of the pastoral scenes, the march of Olmerik's guards, the end of the finale of the first act, the "anathema of the Franc-Juge."

Among these reminiscences are a tune used for the trombone solo in the *Symphonie funèbre et triomphale* and four notes from the descending scale used at the start of the *Marche au supplice*—a tiny but convincing detail that supports the contention that the *Marches des gardes* and the *Marche au supplice* from the *Fantastique* are at least related. Most interesting of all is the suggestion that in *Les Francs-Juges* Berlioz dabbled for the first time—demonstrably, at least—in two of his stocks-in-trade: the musical reminiscence and the march. It was with his marches that Berlioz routinely found his greatest degree of popular success.

The overture was doubtless the last movement of the opera to be composed; indeed the opening Adagio may have been revised with Beethovenian harmonic strategies in mind. In formal procedure it heralds Berlioz's habitual first-movement technique: a slow introduction, two contrastive sections but a single main theme (in this case, as in many others, the one in the second position), an intervening section related to but by no means the same as a sonata development, the return of the major sections in a new context, and a drive to peroration, followed by a grand coda. It begins in F minor with a sinister, interrupted figure, which grows into the solemn brass theme in D♭ we know to be associated with Olmerik (ex. 4.5a).[13] The cadence is in the flamboyant brassy style of which Berlioz was so fond, with strong reliance on ♭VI–V–I in the bass prolonged by unison scales and arpeggiation of the dominant triad in the winds—the whole similar in structure to the climaxes of the Requiem (ex. 4.5b). This point of arrival in D♭ (note the *Freischütz*-like exclamation of the piccolo, which occurs again in *Faust*) is immediately deflected by chromatic meandering to C as dominant of F minor, building to climax through insistent, Gluckian throbs of trombones and bassoons whose dotted figures are filled in by a mirror image in the timpani.

The Allegro opens with a busy, scalar figure in eighths (see ex. 4.6b)—one could not call it a theme, for it never achieves much by way of identity—in first violins. These are joined, after much to-do with D♭– or D♮–C over B♮–C, by canonic entries from the other string sections. The figure, augmented into quarter notes in the bass instruments, dissolves into a passage-work transition over descending whole-note chromatics in the brass; the brass make it clear that the descending chromatic to ♭VI–V–I is the governing harmonic feature of the work. The Savoyard second theme, taken (according to the *Mémoires*) from the quintet composed in La Côte-St.-André, is un-

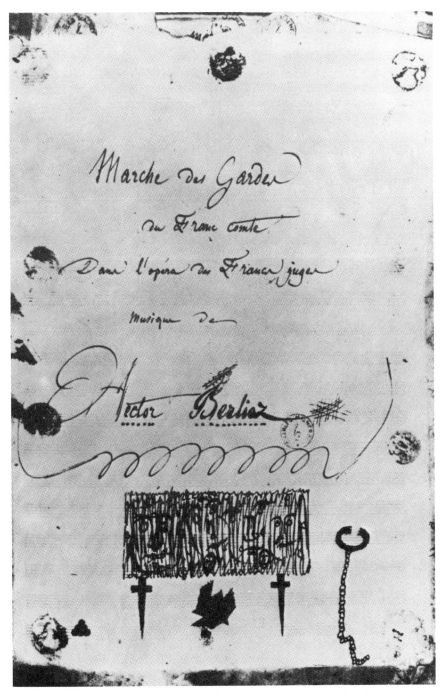

FIGURE 4.5 *Symphonie fantastique,* the original title page of the *Marche au supplice.*

a. Olmerik's theme, mm. 20–23:

b. Mm. 40–45:

EXAMPLE 4.5 *Grande Ouverture des Francs-Juges,* Adagio.

derscored by a bright, syncopated accompaniment in the Mediterranean fashion. Its clear-cut symmetricality at the beginning strikes the ear as naive in squareness, but Berlioz deflects (at mm. 131–34 and again at 140–42) opportunities for closure, extending the melody to thirty-one bars (ex. 4.6a). This setting-forth is repeated in the winds, with a counterpoint in the strings constructed of the opening figure, foreshadowing a tactic of which we see a great deal more in later works (ex. 4.6b). The following passage of nearly 150 bars, which takes the place of a customary development, prolongs C minor beneath a long, sustained melody in a rather successful setting for paired flutes and clarinets. This melody is an augmentation in whole notes of Lenor's invocation ("Descends et viens rendre à mes songes / Le calme qui fuit mes douleurs"; ex. 4.6c).[14] I think we must concede, however, that this rather clever idea ultimately fails, for the ear loses track of the tune.

Berlioz's figuration of the long pedal point in the development (mm. 282–329) is representative of his quite primitive notion, in the mid-1820s, of fleshing out a texture. With the bass drum solo in the distance—Berlioz added it to have something to play for himself—and a timpani solo in juxtaposed $\frac{3}{4}$, the passage begins to grow toward resolution; at the point of arrival, though, it is harshly thrust into E♭ for a full, though false, recapitulation of the second theme. (Note the charming embellishment in m. 355, and note, too, how that promising stroke is left behind to die, forgotten.) The theme restated, Berlioz settles on another dominant pedal, with melodic allusions to the opening figure. When the "true" recapitulation occurs, it is scarcely perceived, being hidden *pianissimo* under a new decoration in the upper winds. The recapitulation of the second theme is in F major, where the overture stays to the end. What actually transpires, though, is more than anything else an operatic crescendo. The melody creeps in after a full strophe

a. Mm. 120–50:

b. Mm. 151–58:

c. Mm. 194–203, 208–19 (Lenor's theme):

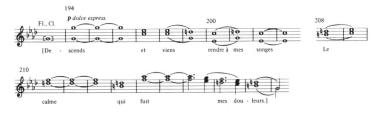

EXAMPLE 4.6 *Grande Ouverture des Francs-Juges*, Allegro.

of accompaniment alone, then rolls headlong into triplet fanfares, a stretto, Olmerik's D♭ theme, a grand chromatic wedge, and a rather traditional charge to final cadence.

Although an adolescent quality and hint of structural incoherence cannot be denied, there is much in the overture, as elsewhere in *Les Francs-Juges*, to suggest movement toward the mature style. The heavy reliance on modal mixture (here, between F minor and F major), the affinity for ♭VI–V–I as a cadential pattern to hint at unrest or mystery, the electrifying *tutti* cadences—all these were soon to be used less self-consciously. The weaknesses of the overture have to do with its somewhat miscellaneous feel: the melodic materials lack unity, and the elision of sections is tentative at best. Berlioz is still uneasy with his large performing force, relying too much on massive doubling and tedious passage-work and accompanimental device. The most engaging attribute is the full nineteenth-century orchestra itself, with its contrabassoon, four horns, two natural trumpets and a piston trumpet—note the almost anachronistic sound, for 1826, of the diatonic passage for trumpet in mm. 40–45—and two ophicleides. The second one, in low B♭, is put there to reach the lower octave toward the end; this and the contra-bassoon part appear to have been added after 1826. Berlioz had begun to pepper his scores with instructions to the performers, particularly the per-cussionists ("une Cymbale suspendue, baguette d'éponge"; "même mouve-ment que le reste de l'orchestre"); the forlorn flute obbligato above the reprise of the theme is marked "expression mélancolique." By and large, the writing for brass and percussion is much superior to that for the woodwinds and strings, a problem that would take Berlioz some time to remedy.

It is a dubious undertaking to judge the overture without knowing just how it relates to the opera that followed. As a free-standing concert work, which in fact it amounted to by the time of publication, it can be considered a success only in its promise and intensity. The seeming allusions to the concert overtures of Beethoven, Schubert's Great C-major, and the early Mendelssohn, though tempting to infer, are false. Berlioz discovered these effects quite independently of a repertoire with which he so far had virtually no experience.[15]

Simultaneous with his discovery of Shakespeare, Berlioz began to ex-periment with the texts of true Romanticism and—perhaps as a result of seeing himself as an archetypal tragic hero—to weave personal references into his music. It probably was the discovery of Shakespeare, shared with the other young artist-heroes of nineteenth-century France, that drew him so forcefully into the brotherhood of Romanticism; in any event Shake-spearean tragedy and the Faustian mystique were of a type in his mind. Berlioz was seized by Shakespeare's almost mystical gift for getting to the heart of a dramatic conflict, for penetrating the secrets of intense love—secrets Berlioz suggests, in the text of *Roméo et Juliette,* he carried with him to Heaven. Again and again, as the years passed, he would take up the images of a favorite play and distill them in musical terms. The idea for *Roméo et Juliette* may well have been the first; then came the settings to evoke *The Tempest* and *King Lear,* and later a funeral march for the last scene of *Hamlet,* the love scene in *Les Troyens*—for the situation comes from *The Merchant of Venice*—and of course *Béatrice et Bénédict.* Not a few works from the late 1820s are headed with epigraphs from the tragedies. Of these the most moving is surely the half-line at the head of the autograph of Cleopatra's meditation: "What if, when I am laid into the tomb . . ." This is a reference to Juliet's act IV soliloquy, of which it is said that Harriet Smithson's delivery, with gesture and pause after the word "tomb," sent a shudder through her audience.

Berlioz cannot have understood the English well in 1827, but what he knew he apparently memorized from the inexpensive, pocket-sized editions in French and English published for patrons of the Shakespeare season. (In 1835 an admirer gave him a complete set of Shakespeare in Le Tourneur's translation, as modernized by Guizot [1821].) Shakespearean tragedy became his new obsession. He read it—often aloud, to anyone who would listen— and quoted from it for the rest of his life. In his declining years he took solace in it and wept at its beauty. From 1827 on he associated just about any upheaval in his own life with its Shakespearean counterpart. Of an English troupe arriving in Paris in 1844 he writes: "Oh, I cried this morning—cried while running errands—thinking of Hamlet, of Ophelia, of all that is no more, of all that has ended up like poor Yorick."[16] A skull he found in an Italian cemetery sat in his study until his death, a constant reminder of the graveyard scene in *Hamlet.* And of course Shakespeare was inextricably linked with Harriet, so much so that Berlioz was never comfortable with anything but the myth of Harriet as the embodiment of her characters.

In Beethoven Berlioz saw a path to this new dramatic manner. "Now that I have heard the terrifying giant Beethoven, I know exactly where musical art stands; the question is to take it from there and push it further."[17] His 1838 series of articles on the Beethoven symphonies is the culmination of years of study during which he mastered most of the orchestral repertoire. His long treatment of the Beethoven scherzo (wherein he translates the term for his readers as "charmant badinage"[18]) bespeaks his particular admiration for that kind of movement. His remarks on the first movement of the *Eroica* are masterly: he draws attention to the foreboding start, the delayed *tutti,* the power of the metric hemiola. ("The rhythm is exceptionally remarkable in the frequency of syncopation and in the superposition of duple meter thrown, by accentuating the weak beats, on top of the triple."[19]) Of the celebrated arrival at recapitulation, he writes at considerable length—though somewhat stodgily, as if trying to cope with the inadequacy of language to convey his excitement:

> We shall content ourselves with describing one especially curious [treatment of the theme]: the subject of many discussions, a reading which the publisher corrected in the score, thinking it a typographical error, but which has been

reestablished following a more amply informed authority. The first and second violins alone are sustaining, in tremolo, a major second (B♭–A♭)—a portion of the dominant seventh chord of E♭—when a horn, as though mistaking itself and entering four measures too early, timidly sounds the beginning of the principal theme, which deals exclusively with the notes E♭–G–E♭–B♭. You can see what a strange effect this melody of the three notes of the tonic chord must have against the dominant chord, the disparate character of the components greatly weakening the juncture. But at the moment when the ear is on the verge of revolting against such an anomaly, a vigorous dominant *tutti* overtakes the horn and, ending *piano,* leaves the cellos to return with the theme over the appropriate harmony.[20]

Berlioz is similarly impressed by the dissolution of the funeral march, with all its implications for a music of space and time, and again sees the effect in expressive terms: "the shreds of the lugubrious melody, alone, naked, broken, crushed" and the wind instruments "shouting a cry, a last farewell of the warriors to their companion at arms."[21] (He will use the same idea for himself, to considerable advantage, in the funeral marches for *Roméo et Juliette* and *Hamlet.*) The most interesting description from the essay on the Fifth Symphony concerns the transition to the finale: "The notes of the timpani are Cs; the key of the movement is C minor; but the chord is A♭, long sustained by the other instruments; beside it the distant hammer of the timpani on the C tends to suggest the prior key. The ear hesitates . . . One doesn't know how this harmonic mystery will end."[22]

This sort of analysis is a good deal more technical than the essays usually found in the periodical literature of the time, suggesting that Berlioz was determined to lead his readers through mysterious territory for the first time. Alongside the "hard" analysis, though, invariably comes a characterization of the poetry of Beethoven. The celebrated Allegretto of the Seventh Symphony—easily the most beloved movement, to nineteenth-century audiences, of the symphonic repertoire—he terms a "rainbow of melody"; the bass ostinato beneath the second A-major trio calls forth a citation from Thomas Moore, the same one used as the epigraph on the title page of *Huit Scènes de Faust:*

> One fatal remembrance, one sorrow that throws
> Its black shade alike o'er our joys and our woes.

And of the "profound sigh" ending the movement he says, "The rest is silence."[23]

But for Berlioz the most sensational Beethoven was the Sixth Symphony, with its descriptive subtitles and especially its storm, "a magnificent horror" causing the most profound vertigo.[24] It is telling that Berlioz limits his remarks on the Sixth to the manner in which the program is deployed. The birdcalls invite his particular scrutiny; he finds that the nightingale fails by comparison with the quail and cuckoo, whose songs, consisting of two precise pitches, can be reproduced exactly. (He had himself written birdcalls at the start of *La Mort d'Orphée,* one of them marked "turtledove.") He is much taken with the "imperturbable naivety of the old bassoon" in the peasant dance, the effect of whose lazy sliding out of kilter is ordinarily lost on the public. Of the storm he says, "I despair of giving any idea of this prodigious movement: one must hear it to understand the degree of truth and sublimity which pictoral music can attain in the hands of a man like Beethoven."[25]

What he does *not* see in Beethoven is Classicism, nor does he seem to have much sense of Beethoven's strides in motive and development. Rather he sees the symphonies as pillars of expressionism, the stuff of Romantic struggle, and quite naturally to be identified with. "It is no longer just music: it is a new art." Berlioz associated the music with Beethoven's tragic life: "those somber tableaux of the sentiments of the human heart, those sad meditations wherein the author seems to breathe the regret of lost happiness, those painful tremblings mixed with cries of rage."[26]

Berlioz's ability to grasp the essence of Shakespeare and Beethoven, without flinching as his contemporaries did, is a mark of his genius. Now the path to the future was clear. He turned from operatic genres to symphonic ones and gave free rein, as Fétis suggested, to his gifted ear. His curiosity expressed itself in daring experiments: with rhythm and meter, with the acoustical qualities of individual halls. Considerations of space, panorama, and vignette began to dominate his musical style. His fondness for musical instruments grew into genuine love of the orchestra as a medium, and he willingly incorporated into his orchestra each new refinement of the instrumental force: the modern English horn, valved brass instruments, pedal harps, the new instruments of Adolphe Sax.

*T*he marked sophistication of the last works of the decade has its roots in the *prix de Rome* cantatas. In one sense the annual competition was the most ephemeral of musical events; it nevertheless required advance planning by contestants, and Berlioz, like the others, surely entered the Institute with good musical ideas already in mind. Each of the cantatas has its moments of vision: the *tableau musical* in *Orphée,* where the wind vibrates strings of the half-destroyed harp, for example, and the dramatic decrescendo to closure in *Herminie.* The only cantata topic to excite him much, however, was *Cléopâtre,* and with that scene he almost succeeded in making of the stifling genre something of note. (The cantata texts he invented for the *Mémoires* are amusing; in fact the opening recitatives were just as excruciating as he suggests, including the anticlimactic first line of *Cléopâtre,* "C'en est donc fait.") By the time he reached the passage of Cleopatra's invocation to her ancestors, he was in a white heat of Shakespearean excitement, the standards of the jury long forgotten: the conceit might as well have been from *Romeo and Juliet*. As though the enharmonic transition to F minor at the start of the scene were not daring enough, what follows is extraordinary harmonic progress by any measure (ex. 4.7). This seeming comfort in technical manipulations of harmonic vocabulary is a far cry from the tentative tactics of the *Francs-Juges* overture. Berlioz seems at ease, too, in his startling conception of the *Huit Scènes de Faust*. He is assured in deploying his forces; the sextet—the *Concert des sylphes*—is a shimmering exercise in delicacy of orchestral color. When he writes for the solo voice it is with a flawless sense of linear accent freed of unwarranted downbeats, a discovery that leads to the rhetoric of his most ambitious songs, such as *Le Spectre de la rose*.

a. Analysis of voice-leading:

b. Reduction:

EXAMPLE 4.7 *Cléopâtre*, movt. III (*Méditation*), mm. 12–49.

In the areas of rhythm and melody, Berlioz's growth is clearest of all. The solos of Méphistophélès, along with Brander's drunken revelry, deal in scherzo-like phrase groupings and displaced accent—a sort of sprung meter of such rhythmic intricacy that all three arias have become standard preliminaries for singing competitions (ex. 4.8a,b,e). Given their forerunners, Marguerite's two songs are astonishingly refined in melodic lyricism, a function of both their phrase structure and their chromatic inflection. The gothic quality of the *ballade, Le Roi de Thulé,* results from what Berlioz hoped would be a modality, imparted by the ♯4 and ♭6 (ex. 4.8c). (He discusses ♯4 as a way of imbuing a melody with local color in a letter of November 1828, which has to do with a Swiss waltz and the acoustical properties of alphorns.[27]) *Le Roi de Thulé* is a prototypical Willow Song. The singer is not to try to express the text, writes Berlioz: "It is clear that nothing occupies Marguerite less at the moment than the problems of the King of Thule; that is an old story from her childhood, which she is but distractedly humming."

Marguerite's *romance*—which should be considered alongside Schubert's setting of the same scene in *Gretchen am Spinnrade,* with all that that comparison says of tradition and heritage, of the power of imagination, and of the sound of a language—is more exceptional still. Its languid meanderings make the much-discussed wending of the *Fantastique*'s *idée fixe* seem tame indeed. Here, perhaps, is the archetypical Berliozian melody: a ten-bar phrase, elegant chromatic inflections, double appoggiatura and fall to the dominant pitch (mm. 17–19), all beautifully declaimed and sympathetic to the low soprano voice (ex. 4.8d). The throbbing of a troubled heart, paramount in the accompanying figuration, is shared by the singer in her departures from the refrain. Note how Berlioz, in some respects like Schubert, implies the refrain after the climactic last line of the poem: "to see my soul expire in his kisses." Schubert returns to the text of the refrain ("Meine ruh' ist hin") and lets it subside; Berlioz leaves the thought to the English horn and lets it merge into the soldiers' chorus. Lest there be any doubt that Berlioz's idea of dealing with texts had greatly improved since the miserable libretto of *Les Francs-Juges,* note that the text of this *romance* is largely rewritten and reordered from Nerval's verses, surely by the composer himself.

Berlioz was right in viewing *Huit Scènes de Faust* as the best of his works to date and in assigning to it his opus number 1. It was to serve him well as the framework for the larger dramatic legend of 1846. When he became affiliated with the periodical *La Romance* in 1834, he tried to have excerpts from the *Huit Scènes* published there; in 1860, however, he wrote to Fétis that the work had been badly composed.

The simpler, more transparent texture of the Irish Melodies is enchanting, too, and it is unfortunate that, like the scenes from *Faust,* the collection has a diversity that tends to preclude performance—a problem exacerbated by Malherbe and Weingartner, editors of the first complete edition, who divided up the group according to performing force. (The nine songs appear in order,

a. *Ecot de joyeux compagnons (Histoire d'un rat)*, no. 4, mm. 7–29:

b. *Chanson de Méphistophélès (Histoire d'une puce)*, no. 5, mm. 9–24:

c. *Le Roi de Thulé: Chanson gothique*, no. 6, mm. 7–10:

d. *Romance de Marguerite*, no. 7, mm. 12–21:

e. *Sérénade de Méphistophélès*, no. 8, mm. 3–17:

EXAMPLE 4.8 From *Huit Scènes de Faust.*

following the *Nuits d'été,* near the beginning of the late collection of 32 *Mélodies.*) The *Neuf Mélodies* aim to achieve Irish rusticity by strong reliance on octaves, open fifths, and other simple structures in the left hand of the piano part and arpeggiated figures in the right, these to suggest, I suppose, the Irish harp. Berlioz's favorite, because it alluded to his passion for Harriet, was the *Elégie en prose.* The more interesting are the songs of fair Celtic women: *Hélène* and *La Belle Voyageuse,* both of which were later recast for orchestra, and the bilingual *Adieu, Bessy / Farewell, Bessy.* These are declaimed in the new manner, freely and unconstrained by convention (ex. 4.9).

*B*erlioz composed the *Symphonie fantastique*—"furiously," his mind "boiling over"—with a clear intent of unifying the elements of his musical understanding thus far in a work of substantial proportion, to give full vent to his urges for freedom, naturalism, and intensity. There were to be "fire and tears within."[28] One of the striking characteristics of the *Fantastique* is the interplay of the elements that constitute its "programmatic" background, for the work seethes with both literary and biographical allusions. It was not just a matter of working through the two notions that motivated Berlioz to begin with: a descriptive symphony on *Faust* and the *idée fixe* he could not banish from his mind. ("Une idée fixe me tue," he had written.[29]) As it concerns the troubled heart of an artist-hero, the sym-

a. *Hélène,* mm. 14–21:

b. *La Belle Voyageuse,* mm. 5–12:

c. *Adieu, Bessy,* mm. 17–22:

EXAMPLE 4.9 From *Neuf Mélodies.*

EXAMPLE 4.10 Theme of the opening Largo from the *Symphonie fantastique*, with text of Florian's *Je vais donc quitter pour jamais* underlain; after reconstructions by Julien Tiersot and Nicholas Temperley.

phony is related to Chateaubriand's *René* and to that great writer's concept, amplified elsewhere, of a *vague des passions,* a Romantic welling-up of emotion that could easily be confused with an attack of spleen.[30] The countrified lyricism of the first and third movements is clearly Savoyard in origin, and we know the melody of the opening Largo to have been a song composed during his teenage years to the words of a *romance* in Florian's *Estelle* (ex. 4.10). The Witches' Sabbath is as much related to the Wolf's Glen and to Hugo's *Ronde du sabbat* as it is to *Faust,* and the concept of the opium dream seems to have originated with Berlioz's reading of Thomas de Quincey's *Confessions of an English Opium Eater* in the very free translation of Alfred de Musset (Paris, 1828). (There is little other evidence, incidentally, to suggest that Berlioz experimented with hallucinogens. He was mildly addicted to coffee and cigars and enjoyed an occasional cognac or glass of champagne. A progressive dependence on opiates in his later years was related to the onset of an intestinal disorder to which he eventually succumbed; the only other hint of drugs surrounds his lame attempts at suicide in 1831 and 1833.)

The title page of the autograph score of the *Symphonie fantastique* makes two further literary allusions, with an epigraph from the French edition of *King Lear,*

As flies to wanton boys, are we to the gods;
They kill us for their sport.[31]

and a long citation from Hugo's *Feuilles d'automne* on the trials of youthful passion. Both were added to the original title page during the great revisions of the work in 1831–32, the period during which he came to see his life as a Romantic novel.

To explain the context of the drama represented in his work, Berlioz published the notes that had served to organize his thoughts. These appeared in the newspapers and as a leaf to be read by concertgoers before the symphony got under way. It seems a natural step for a composer anxious to declare membership in the confraternity of Romantic writers, an altogether logical extension of the movement subtitles in the Pastoral Symphony. The program of the *Fantastique,* like the music, was subject to modifications and changes over the years of its refinement. Ultimately—and well after the program had appeared in the published score—Berlioz elected not to publish the story in the printed concert programs, though so far as I know only in France and only because the auditors could be assumed to know it already. The aesthetic rightness or wrongness of the program, which has occasioned much fuzzy-headed writing, seems less important than its existence and its undeniable impact on other composers and other works. To deny that Berlioz meant the program to be followed—or assert that he thought better of it— is foolish; to see it as the first chapter of a lifelong struggle to reduce the narrative requirements of evocative music while at the same time setting the appropriate stage is, I think, critical. The program is Berlioz's most seminal homage to Beethoven and arguably his most important legacy to other composers.

The *Symphonie fantastique* is thus the first major composition to test Berlioz's notions of imitative dramatic music on a large scale, the first of four primarily orchestral works—the others being *Harold en Italie, Roméo et Juliette,* and *La Damnation de Faust*—to address the question. His rhetoric, to be viable, required that instrumental music deal directly with human situations—the love, for example, that develops between two strangers as if by fate. Once having made such a connection, he summoned all of his materials to support it, freely drawing on any genre or medium that struck his fancy. Here, and for the rest of his career, he wrote a music of tableau and vignette, relying on his listeners to supply for themselves whatever narrative would make the evocations satisfying and complete. This orientation to a story relieves the composer of responsibility to relate its every detail.

Berlioz did not shrink from direct imitation. It is obvious, in the *Scène aux champs* of the *Fantastique,* that the play of English horn and offstage oboe is to represent "two shepherds piping a *ranz des vaches* in dialogue," and that the timpani are "distant sounds of thunder." It is but a small step to hear, at the end of the *Marche au supplice,* the slam of the guillotine, the thump of head falling into basket, and the *hourrahs* of the crowd. We need not be embarrassed by these discoveries, for the effects are there to be discovered—conspiratorial winks of composer to listener. To ignore these depictive touches or to dismiss them as unworthy of a lofty composer is to miss some of the most elegant moments in, for example, the *scène d'amour* and the tomb scene of *Roméo et Juliette* or the *Chasse royale* from *Les Troyens.*

It is not enough, in short, to hear these works as Romantic, free-wheeling versions of the tried-and-true procedures. The committed listener, who has learned to participate in the purely structural drama of, say, the instrumental works of Bach and Mozart and who knows sonata form, rounded binary, and the rest, must alter his or her expectations. The rules are different.

The novel organizing device of the *Fantastique* is its use of the *idée fixe,* the graceful theme of the Beloved that is transformed into appropriate guises for each of the succeeding movements. (It is complete only in the first.) Here again Berlioz broaches the issue of that most Romantic of ideas, nostalgic recollection, but on a much larger scale than in his previous works. The manner in which the *idée fixe* is deployed is another idea gleaned from Beethoven, in this case from the Fifth Symphony. (The movement-by-movement recollection at the end of *Harold en Italie* is, by contrast, a direct reference to the kind of recall practiced in the Ninth.) Berlioz's aggressive rewriting of the *idée fixe* as the symphony takes its course, especially the "mockery of the Beloved" at the Witches' Sabbath, carries the notion of cyclicism well past Beethovenian practice, however, and provides the point of departure for a formidable chunk of his midcentury repertoire.

Berlioz imparts his fantastic vision in an extravagant display of orchestral writing. Unlike Schumann and Chopin, he has little difficulty manipulating the textures and sonorities of the new Romantic orchestra. Indeed, harnessing the orchestra in support of a dramatic vision constitutes his fundamental orientation to symphonic music. His previous experiments with orchestral possibilities—the passages with clarinet bells in silk sacks, *divisi* strings, *col legno,* and the many other such effects encountered in the early works— have begun to pay dividends. (The clarinet-in-the-bag, which made its debut in *Orphée,* was a favorite effect; he later described it in the *Traité,* refined the idea in various ways, and talked of it in his *Mémoires.*) The *Fantastique* introduces to the symphony orchestra a clutch of instruments from the opera house and military band that rapidly become permanent members: English horn, for example, E♭ clarinet, harps, bells, and novel percussion. Later Berlioz would use these with more subtlety and tact; in the *Fantastique* each is associated with a particular expressive effect. To my mind the two passages that stand out most startlingly in terms of orchestration are the opening of the ball scene, where *two* harps, as though tuning and warming up, establish the smoky ambience appropriate to the salon music that follows, and the ghostly beginning of the last movement, with the eight-part *divisi* strings articulating a dramatic sonority, the whole concept as splendid as the curtain rising on an eerie stage lit in green and purple.

Berlioz thought of the orchestra as his own particular instrument. Though he owned a piano from the 1820s on, it was for the purpose of learning how to accompany singers. (A guitar was always to be found in his study, too, but it was a souvenir, not an instrument for composition.) He likened composition to commanding an army of instruments, with the different ranks deployed on a battlefield of harmonies left virgin by the conservatives: soldiers at last free of their routine drills to do true battle.[32]

Berlioz disliked the notion that his was an Italianate style, because that suggested the style of Rossini, with its banal rigidities and routines. To the extent that "Italianate" suggests an approach to composition governed by melody, however, the terminology is apt; one of Berlioz's fondest beliefs, in fact, was that he was an inspired melodist. The *Fantastique* is predominantly a work of song, of melodies that themselves generate the bass lines, accompanying figurations, and even formal structures. It is partly this attitude toward musical content that led Berlioz to such discoveries as the *réunion des thèmes,* that juxtaposition of apparently unrelated melodies used to such magnificent effect in the fifth movement. In the *Symphonie fantastique* the melodic freshness is primarily a matter of phrase length, as in the extension of the *idée fixe,* with its spun-out, overweight consequent. Likewise the primacy of melody is what ultimately makes strophic forms the most congenial forum for his musical ideas.

At first the matter of form was troublesome for Berlioz; we saw earlier the uneasy fashion with which the sections of the *Francs-Juges* overture are glued together. He grasped, intuitively enough, the notion of main theme and contrastive section, but had little feel for dramatic arrival in harmonic dominance, or for developmental practice as a process of unifying disparate musical elements. Even when he tried his hand at ordinary first-movement practice, as in the *Fantastique,* he had difficulty sustaining the drama with much interplay of the stated material, routinely veering off into textural manipulation and harmonic surprise. In this particular development, he is in a certain dilemma after twenty-one measures and simply alights on a dominant fanfare to his brief recall of the second theme (see movt. I, mm. 187–91). The first movement, indeed, is scarcely a sonata at all, but rather a simpler arch, with the "false" dominant return at mm. 238–39 as its keystone. And in the *Marche au supplice,* the only thing that suggests sonata practice is the pair of repeat signs.[33]

It is for such reasons as these that Berlioz's architecture takes some getting used to, for the music is propelled by other than the expectation of particular events. His formal procedures fall more usually into such arrangements as A–B–excursion–culmination (for example, *Les Francs-Juges*), or A–B–superposition of A and B–coda (for example, *Fantastique,* movt. V; *Fête chez Capulet*), or A–B–A–C–A–coda, but with little sense of "rondo" (for example, Marguerite's *romance; Fantastique,* movt. II). The weight of the movement is nearly always thrown to the end, best viewed as the peroration. But it is within these contexts of free sectionality that he achieves his most ravishing effects: the Offertoire in the Requiem, for example, and the closely related idiom of Juliet's funeral procession, or the free strophes of Iopas's aria in *Les Troyens,* act IV.

By the same token it is true that the function of Berlioz's chord progressions is determined more by the need to express the dramatic context than by conventional harmonic practice. The vocabulary of chords is actually quite small, but Berlioz is prone to draw on "foreign" sonorities for surprise value or expressive effect: recall the exquisite moment in Cleopatra's invocation where he lands on an E-major triad while in the key of F minor, and the bold juxtaposition of tritone-related chords in the *Marche au supplice* (ex. 4.11). Sometimes such harmonic effects are less successful, as in the first-inversion chromatics in movement I (mm. 198–222), seemingly unmotivated by anything that has come before. But in general terms Berlioz appears supremely confident in the ability of his harmonic language to create the effects he desires.

Edward T. Cone, who translated Robert Schumann's analysis of the *Symphonie fantastique* and then amplified it,[34] offering in sum a much more detailed view than I shall attempt, shows how Berlioz goes about unifying the *Fantastique* particularly in terms of overall tonal cogency, often by structural revisions on a very large scale. As the work now stands, the key relationships form a clear if somewhat uncommon progress in C: C major–A major–F major–G minor–C major: I–VI–IV–v–I. Berlioz's mixing of major and minor modes, by then habitual, was nevertheless in 1830 (and even five to ten years later, when the *Fantastique* was starting to draw international attention) exceptionally novel. It is this interplay of the major and minor scale degrees, moreover, that brings the symphony's predominant motivic relationship to the fore: A♭–G, the flatted sixth scale degree descending to the dominant pitch. We sense this relationship from the moment of the prolonged A♭ pedal at the cadence of the introduction, *Rêveries* (and remember Berlioz's remarks on the transition to the last movement of Beethoven's Fifth, where the procedure is similar). It is reconfirmed in the *idée fixe* itself, where A♭–G and its alternation with A♮–G emerge as a point of structural identity. Indeed, this flirtation of major and minor sixth as embellishment of the dominant pitch is a hallmark of Berlioz's melody (ex. 4.12).

Other structural coherence is achieved through Berlioz's strong sense of framing, which extends from the use of the long introduction and religious coda as a frame for the first movement to its balance with a very similar structure in the fifth. It seems no accident that the unusual A major of the second movement is softened by an introduction in A minor, bridging the gap left by the C-major conclusion of the previous movement, or that the G-major *hourrahs* at the end of the G-minor march form an appropriate transition to the finale, making of the march a movement-long upbeat to the Witches' Sabbath.[35]

Berlioz's mastery of rhythm and meter continues to develop in the *Fantastique*. He has not yet reached the level of experiment with metric juxtaposition that he will find with *Harold*, but at one point in the fifth movement of the *Fantastique* he certainly adumbrates that practice (ex. 4.13). Note, in bar 399, that the vicious overlapping hemiolas commence with a splendid

EXAMPLE 4.11 *Marche au supplice*, mm. 154–56.

Symphonie fantastique, movt. I, mm. 87–94:

Requiem, movt. I, mm. 83–86:

Love scene from *Roméo et Juliette* (movt. III), mm. 153–55:

La Damnation de Faust, movt. I, mm. 1–8:

EXAMPLE 4.12 Alternation of major and minor sixth in Berlioz's melody; after a table by Edward T. Cone (Cone: *SF*, p. 277).

clash of B♮ and C. Consider, too, the sheer variety of note values in the orchestral hiccups in the third movement (mm. 87–102), which are without precedent in the orchestral repertoire, so far as I know, and the ambiguities of implied meter ($\frac{3}{2}$? $\frac{6}{8}$? $\frac{12}{8}$?) at the opening of the fifth movement.

Berlioz seldom left major works like the *Symphonie fantastique* to stand as first written; they were always subject to his efforts to polish imperfections. This long process of maturation and revision—of retroactive composition, as it were—was prompted mostly by his experience of his music in live performance; it is one of the best testimonies to the power of his self-

EXAMPLE 4.13 *Symphonie fantastique*, movt. V, mm. 395–403.

criticism. The *Fantastique* grew in a variety of ways from what it was in
April 1830, mutating for nearly fifteen years both in overall form and in
minor detail. Berlioz repositioned the *Scène aux champs;* once the second
movement, by mid May 1830 it had become the third. The original movement-by-movement parallel to Beethoven's Sixth was thus sacrificed, but the
net effect—with the march as anacrusis to the finale, as the Storm is in
Beethoven—is much the same. Another radical change was the superposition
of the oboe plaint toward the end of the first movement (m. 358ff.) over
preexisting material in strings. (This is but one of several lyric melodies that,
but for the documentary evidence, the ear would not have detected as having
been added on top of what was already there.) We cannot be certain exactly
when each of the changes to the *Fantastique* was effected, though the majority of them must have been related to the wholesale recomposition done
in Italy in 1831–32.

Among the editings that resulted in a stronger overall design were the
addition of the passage concerning the artist's "religious consolations" at
the end of the first movement and a significant change in the ending of the
ball scene. In the ball scene Berlioz added a coda and introduced two horn
parts to the original pair, along with a new clarinet part. The cornet obbligato
for the second movement was presumably composed for J.-J.-B. Arban, the
trumpet virtuoso known to all modern trumpet students for his method
book.[36] In my view the cornet part is a stroke of genius that should be
retained, redolent as it is with the sounds of pleasure palace and Musard
quadrille.

Berlioz was, in short, the most scrupulous of revisers. Tinkerings such as
these went on, for most compositions, until the work was engraved and
offered for sale to the public. In writing of the many dramatic changes in
Roméo et Juliette, he summarized this attitude toward the composer's art:

If there are other blemishes that I have missed, at least I have tried sincerely and with what judgment I possess to detect them. After which, what can a composer do but admit candidly that he has done his best, and resign himself to the work's imperfections?[37]

The fifth movement, *Songe d'une nuit de sabbat* (Dream of a Witches' Sabbath) is in many ways the focal point of the *Fantastique*. It is in a sectional, semi-sonata form (ex. 4.14a). Built into it are numerous details that relate it to the other movements. The progression of key areas in the introduction, for example, closely parallels the opening of the first movement, notably in its emphasis of, in C minor, III (E♭) and the prolongation of the VI–V–I cadence. The outer movements embrace other similarities of overall architecture as well. And the free interchange of parallel major and minor that has characterized much of the *Fantastique* is retained through the emphasis of ♭3 and ♭6 scale degrees in C major.

The scene opens in evocation of some dark meadow where the supernatural is commonplace and goings-on by dark of night are to be expected: diminished-seventh chords in the string parts *divisi, con sordini,* and *a punto d'arco* set the musical stage. Sounds of grotesque masculine laughter are heard in the brass, then shrill feminine giggles and their distant echoes (ex. 4.14b).

From a distance is heard the *idée fixe,* played by C clarinet in a cocky $\frac{6}{8}$ march: "It is she, coming to join the sabbath." With a great *tutti* entry—the brass with bells in the air—there is much scattering about in E♭ moving to the dominant: "a roar of joy at her arrival." Now the grotesque setting of the *idée fixe* is heard full force, played by the E♭ clarinet joined by piccolo: "She takes part in the devilish orgy." The percolating bassoon figurations at one point filled every bar, then were reduced to the present reading because they were found to be too difficult;[38] these are joined by arpeggios in the lower strings and a cadence figure in all upper instruments in unison. A string of chromatics in thirds (mm. 72–75) heralds the tumble of syncopations that manages to wrench the meter, for a bar, into ¢ (mm. 78–81). Foreshadowings of the witches' Round Dance are asserted but quickly silenced.

The toll of bells in C and G—instruments borrowed from the Opéra, where they were used for many a stage piece—sounds "the very witching hour of night," extending into a funeral knell. Bassoons and ophicleides play the Gregorian *Dies irae,* imitated in successive levels of diminution by the rest of the orchestra. The bells clang on at incessant but irregular intervals. The last low G of the bells is prolonged by reiterations in the brass and the bass drum roll played by two players. A strong dominant is achieved, and the Round Dance begins.

Here the ambiguity of Berlioz's formal practice is clear. The *Ronde du sabbat* is actually the second major section of the Allegro (the *Dies irae*

a. Outline of formal structure:

Introduction		Exposition			Development			Recapitulation			
		Int.	I	II	(folding-up)	drive to:		I *Dies irae*		drive to:	Peroration
Night / *idée* / Roar / *idée*		Knell	*Dies irae*	Round Dance				II Round Dance			
1	21	29	40	102	127	241	305	363	408	414	485	496
dim7	C	E♭		C min		C–G	E♭		C			
I	♭III		i		I–V	♭III		V	I		iv–V–	I

		Introduction		
Night, Laughter	Grotesque *idée fixe*	Roar of Joy	*idée fixe* & devilish orgy	
1	21	29	40 61 69 82	
a♯dim7–C– f♯dim7–C– b dim7–	C – G	E♭–B♭	E♭ Cm A♭ G	
vii7ish	I V	♭III – V	♭III i ♭VI V	

b. Introduction:

c. Movt. V, mm. 241–47, fugue subject and countersubjects:

EXAMPLE 4.14 *Songe d'une nuit de sabbat*, movt. V of the *Symphonie fantastique*.

having been the first), but this is the first true arrival in C major, and (to follow Cone's reasoning) all of what comes before now seems to have been preparatory. The Round Dance is a genuine nineteenth-century fugue, with a countersubject split between two voices (ex. 4.14c). The formal exposition yields to an episode taking up ♭III and ♭VI. An incomplete counterexposition (subject in V, then I) dissolves into a development, as though the energy of the dance were slacking off, fragmenting away in Beethovenian fashion to be replaced by reminiscences of the *Dies irae*. With a pronounced A♭–G the basses prepare the dominant, though the effect is somewhat muted by the persistence of E♭ in the bassoons. Indeed, this dualism continues for a time, with the dance tune heard (this once) in thirds. The drive to peroration begins with a timpani roll and cellos alone, then adds instrument after instrument in an inexorable crescendo that puts Rossini's formula to shame. The movement regains its momentum.

A unison recapitulation of the dance in C major has just begun when, in the first of those dual recollections we like to call *grandes réunions des thèmes*, it is joined by the *Dies irae* in winds. A smallish redevelopment—a musical stepping back—features the bone rattling of the upper strings, *col legno*, and material from the Round Dance stated in the same generally mocking terms as the *idée fixe* at the beginning. Berlioz drives to his final cadence with the ♭6–♮6 allusion to the *idée fixe* (mm. 496–507) and a thrilling surge of his orchestral force (mm. 512–24), with trombones and piccolos coming to the fore *à la* Weber.

*W*hat did the auditor of the 1830s make of this shocking First Symphony? The world of the *Fantastique* must have seemed every bit as disruptive, even to intellectuals, as Victor Hugo's *Hernani* had been. The parallel octaves of leading tone to tonic in the first bar of the symphony seem just as purposeful an announcement of iconoclasm, though Berlioz would have denied it, as was Hugo's celebrated *enjambement* at the start of *Hernani*. So modern a composer as Schumann could not believe the opening and assumed the bassoon's B♮ to be a misprint.

Parisian liberals welcomed the breath of excitement. This was especially (and progressively) true of the *littérateurs* who had shared in the Shakespeare fever—secondary writers such as the brothers Emile and Antony Deschamps and eventually figures such as Vigny, Balzac, and even Hugo. Traditionalists disliked the bombast, about which they were to make a myth during Berlioz's lifetime. Rossini coined, it is said, the best of his *mauvais mots:* "What a good thing it isn't music."[39] The conservative faction at the Conservatoire was quick to voice its reservations.

But the press, preoccupied with political matters, paid little attention to the first performance. Two of the three known reviews reported a success, however, and in relatively enthusiastic terms. Fétis devoted a page of his

Revue musicale to the work, at once enthusiastic and reserved: the music, he said, "excites more astonishment than pleasure."[40]

In Germany, the ever-curious Schumann eventually learned of the *Symphonie fantastique* through Liszt's piano transcription (1834), and it was the combination of Liszt's transcription and Schumann's analysis that finally focused the attention of the European musical elite on Berlioz. Schumann was quick to note the futility of trying such music at the piano, finding the orchestral effects the most notable aspect of the style. The novelty of the *Fantastique* was offset by a brazen grammar that offended German ears: Schumann labeled Berlioz "an adventurer." But of his admiration there can be no doubt, for he also dubbed Berlioz "the terror of the Philistines."[41]

Chapter Five

A Sojourn—A Courtship—A Birth
(1831–34)

The new year, 1831, found Berlioz on the first stage of his *prix de Rome* journey. Still uncertain of his ultimate plans, he had decided to start out to Italy alone, leaving the other laureates to their slow coach across the Alps. He arrived in La Côte on about 3 January. The family accorded him a warm welcome—the first in years—and he began to relax and enjoy a period of unaccustomed leisure, taking care, however, to assure the director of the French Academy in Rome, Horace Vernet, of his impending arrival. In fact it was several months before he resolved to complete the residency in Rome, if residency it can even be called. During the first third of 1831, his recurrent notion of abandoning the prize and returning to Paris was counterbalanced only by the long-term monetary advantage of seeing the venture through.

In the third week of January Berlioz and the ladies of the family went to visit their Grenoble relatives. For once he was vivacious and witty in company by then accustomed to his boorish moods. His female cousins were pleased to chatter about his engagement ring.

Already he was begging friends in Paris for news, alarmed to have received but a single letter from Camille and her mother. Ferdinand Hiller, moreover, had written hinting that she might be involved with someone else. Camille's studiedly formal response to a sweet letter from Nanci—"That you will call me sister is my dearest hope," Nanci had written[1]—suggests that Hiller may have been right. (Fifty years later Hiller recalled having been convinced that she had already decided to betray Berlioz before he ever left Paris. "All I did," Hiller wrote to Hippeau in 1882, "was to tell him what everybody knew . . . Our poor Berlioz was never happy in his relationships with the fair sex, but it was, after all, his own fault."[2]) One has the strong sense that the periods of dalliance during these months had to do with exchange of post to and from Paris, and that the urgency was mainly a question of getting to the next *poste restante.*

On 8 February, a month behind the schedule expected of *prix de Rome* winners, he traveled from La Côte to Lyon and thence to Marseille, where he arrived late in the afternoon of 12 February. After arranging to take a Sardinian ship to Livorno whenever the captain came to the conclusion that the weather was right, Berlioz was free to revel in his first exposure to the sea. He took a boat tour of the harbor, climbed among the rocks, sought out acquaintances from the Paris Conservatoire, and that evening went to the theater. (A trip to the local opera house, in each of the many dozen cities he would eventually visit, is perhaps the most consistent of his habits.) He retained fond memories of Marseille, to which he would return with pleasure for a pair of concerts in 1845.

The voyage of the small brig was troubled first by becalmed seas and then by a storm that threatened it and all aboard, though more because of the captain's ineptitude than for any other reason. This was Berlioz's first brush with death: to avoid the agony of a prolonged drowning, he wrapped himself tightly in his heaviest coat, reasoning that the weight of the sodden garment would take him directly to the ocean floor. There was a certain tranquility to his contemplation of a watery grave: he was later to reflect of the incident that "death is more unpleasant from afar than from near."[3] He never again embarked on a sea voyage, however, confining his later nautical experience to routine crossings of the English Channel and a day or two on the Danube. The ship arrived safely in Livorno on about 25 February, the four-day trip having lasted nearly two weeks.

Revolutionary activity in the Papal States meant that all travelers, especially long-haired young Parisians, were to one degree or another suspect. So it was that the papal nuncio in Florence refused to validate Berlioz's passport, and he had his first taste of the police harassment that was all too frequently brought to bear that year on young artists abroad. ("What is there to fear from men," wrote George Sand, "when one has a valid passport in one's pocket?"[4]) He spent nearly two more weeks, in late February and early March, waiting in Florence for Horace Vernet to clear his safe conduct on to Rome.

He made of the forced hiatus an opportunity to discover native Italian opera, attending Bellini's *I Capuleti e i Montecchi* and Giovanni Pacini's *La Vestale*. The experience was not to his taste. Bellini's treatment of the Romeo and Juliet story, in particular, so shocked him that he outlined his objections in notes that became the source for an important essay of 1832 and, indirectly, a plan for his own Romeo and Juliet symphony. By the time he was allowed to proceed to Rome, he was already thoroughly disappointed with Italian stage music and appalled by what he had so far discovered of Italy in general.

He arrived in Rome one evening in early March—perhaps the 10th—at dinner time. The other prize winners, representing the five fine arts, were found to be in boisterous good humor, and for a few days Berlioz joined in the general merriment, clowning with the composer Montfort; the painters Signol and Gibert and Bézard; the architects Duc, Lefebvre, Garrez, and Dellanoie; and the sculptor Antoine-Laurent Dantan, older brother of the soon-to-be celebrated caricaturist Dantan, *jeune*. There were others, too: expatriates, hangers-on of all sorts, and such particular friends as the womanizer Isidore Flacheron and the brilliant twenty-two-year-old sculptor Antoine Etex, who in a few years' time would be found chiseling the monumental statues on the Arc de Triomphe. With Bézard, Gibert, and Delannoie, Berlioz formed that year a Gang of Four, devoted to "absolute indifference in all that pertains to matter."[5] Like nearly everyone else, he was charmed by the affable director Horace Vernet, a painter of landscapes who at the age of forty-two looked like a teenager, and by Vernet's wife, their daughter Louise, and the grandfather Carl Vernet, a devotee of music who took delight in Berlioz's unpredictable company, especially the monologues on Gluck.

The Villa Medici, perched on the Pincian Hill atop the Spanish steps, commanded a stunning view of the city, with St. Peter's in the distance. The view was regal: "one of the most splendid in the world."[6] Nearby, in the Borghese gardens, stood the country house of Raphael. The romance of it all, and the promise of visits to Naples, Calabria, and Sicily, briefly masked Berlioz's growing anxiety.

Ultimately, however, still angry at having had to leave Paris during the height of his success, suspicious of the worth of studying Italian music at

FIGURE 5.2 Rome: the Bridge and the Castle of St. Angelo with the Cupola of St. Peter's. Oil on canvas; Corot.

all, and separated from his fiancée, Berlioz enjoyed but fleeting moments of happiness. Rome was an excellent place for painters and architects to learn their trade, he imagined, but it was not a healthy place for musicians. The oppressive atmosphere—the *aria cattiva*—bothered his lungs, and it threatened to grow intolerably hot. He was unamused by the Italians as a people—finding them dirty, lazy, unfriendly, nearly always asleep, and if awake, behaving like eight-year-old children—and was clearly frightened of the anti-French sentiment, with its constant threat of physical violence, that could be felt in various quarters of Rome.

His loneliness was augmented by the alarming absence of mail. Although he had spent more than a month in transit, there were no letters waiting for him in Rome, nothing to allay his concern over Camille. He wrote frantically to Gounet, asking him to check on the situation *chez* Moke in the Faubourg Montmartre; soon he was threatening to return to Paris. In early April, probably on the 4th, he did exactly that. Leaving word with a fellow pensioner to forward his mail, he simply fled the Academy. So far without any particular plan of action, he took the route north, homeward.

In Florence he was detained by another attack of tonsillitis and spent a week in bed, revising the *Symphonie fantastique* during his more lucid moments. Once recovered, he interspersed vain stops at the post office with afternoons reading *King Lear* by the river Arno and sightseeing at the Pitti Palace and the cathedral. A funeral was in progress at the cathedral; a young woman had died in childbirth. Berlioz joined the procession to the morgue, bribed the porter, and when the mourners had gone entered and kissed the hand of the dead *bella sposina*. The next day, still in funereal temper, he witnessed at the Church of the Santo-Spirito a somewhat more exalted burial. This time it was a Bonaparte: Napoleon's nephew, Napoleon-Louis.

When the long-awaited letter from Paris arrived, it was not from Camille at all, but from her mother, and it announced the marriage of her daughter Camille to Camille Pleyel, piano manufacturer and son of the famous publisher. (It did not last: the female Camille earned a reputation for her scandalous behavior with men, and Pleyel left her four years later, in 1835.) Berlioz's first reaction was blind fury at a hideous crime, "un abus de confiance."[7] He would go to Paris, murder the newlyweds and the perfidious mother, and then, for good measure, shoot himself. He would be a modern incarnation of Cellini's *Perseus,* which he had just admired in the piazza della Signoria.

The revisions for the *Symphonie fantastique* were not done, with the *Scène aux champs* still to be revised and the new scoring and coda for the second movement not yet final. As a last testament, he left a note in the manuscript score begging Habeneck to complete his rescoring and then perform the revised symphony. This account from the *Mémoires* is substantially confirmed by the autograph score, wherein an annotation, later covered by cross-hatching, reads:

> I don't have time to finish it myself; let somebody finish it, then, as in my other copy. All the parts will need recopying.[8]

He had equipped himself, from the store of weapons used by the pensioners to ward off intruders, with two double-barreled pistols—enough for the four planned shots—some laudanum and strychnine for the journey, and the

FIGURE 5.3
Caricature of Berlioz,
c. 1831.

disguise of a lady's maid, in which extraordinary garb he proposed to get within range of his victims. He left for France in the postal coach. In Genoa, according to a possibly fanciful explanation concocted for Horace Vernet, he threw himself into the sea, was pulled out by some fishermen, and vomited salt water for an hour. By 18 April he was still short of Nice, in the village of Diano Marina, but his anger was spent. The women in Paris no longer seemed worth murdering.

It remained only to find out from Vernet if his pension had been canceled. Berlioz went on to Nice, hoping that because he had never technically arrived in France—Nice was then held by the House of Savoy—his position with the Academy would not have been jeopardized. He took lodgings with a widow in the marina village of Ponchettes and proceeded to spend a month recovering from his ordeal. Vernet approved of the plan, saying in paternal fashion that his name had not yet been crossed off the register of pensioners and that news of his rash behavior was unlikely to reach officials in Paris. Berlioz regained his composure in part by describing the sensational events in long letters to his family and friends. His immense communique to intimates in Paris—Gounet, Narcisse Girard, Hiller, Desmarest, a *littérateur* named Richard, and a friend from the Faculty of Medicine named Jules Sichel—foreshadows the travelogues that constitute the bulk of his *Voyage musical* (1844) and *Mémoires*. His powers of description had been reawakened, and they soon found further expression in the text of *Le Retour à la vie*.

That charming city, "my laughing Nice," awakened, too, a rapture with the sea. So far he had met the Mediterranean only in unfavorable circumstances, and by winter. Now it was spring, and the immensity, truth, and finality of the sea overwhelmed him. He found a degree of female companionship and, ending nearly a year-long abstinence, made love to a young woman on a beach, the sea washing up against their legs.[9]

The remaining three weeks he remembered as the happiest of his life. He returned spontaneously to composition, completing sketches for his next major work, an overture after Shakespeare called *Le Roi Lear*. Then he began to rough out a second overture, this one taking Walter Scott's *Rob-Roy* as a title, and ruminated on further refinements of the "new" *Symphonie fantastique*—though he had left the score in Florence—and an autobiographical sequel. Wandering along the beach with sketchbook in hand may have seemed glamorous to a young man rejoicing in springtide romance, but to the local police it appeared to be suspicious behavior. Berlioz was summoned to the police station, cross-examined about the dubious practice of sketching music without a piano, and told to leave town.

Lear (and not the overture *La Tour de Nice*, which was written during another visit to Nice, in 1844) was finished on about 10 May, and on the 19th Berlioz left to return to Rome, traveling, as he had come, over the spectacular Corniche route—the ancient Via Aurelia—to Genoa (21 May), then Lucca (22 or 23 May) and Pisa (24 May), where he visited the Leaning Tower. In the cemetery at Radicoffani he picked up a skull, and he carried it in his bag through the remainder of his Italian sojourn to use for a lap desk. (In Paris the skull sat on a table in his workroom, filled with writing sand; at the time of his death, it was rumored to be Harriet's.) He stopped in Florence to acquire another visa and collect the belongings he had left behind, then spent the last three days of the month on the road to Rome in the company of monks bound there for Corpus Christi.

At the town of San Lorenzo Nuovo, on the banks of the Lago di Bolsena, he left his companions in the coach and spent the day walking southward fifteen leagues (probably some 35 or 40 miles) alongside the lake. During that promenade he conceived and wrote the text of his *Mélologue: Le Retour à la vie*, the sequel to the *Symphonie fantastique*—an autobiographical essay, wherein love of art replaces lust for woman and is seen as the only successful philosophy of life. He soon sent to Paris for the music he intended to reuse for the work.

Berlioz and the monks arrived in Rome in time for the Corpus Christi procession (Thursday, 2 June), an event that in La Côte-St.-André always aroused the public to a fevered pitch of spiritualism. In Rome, he imagined, that display would be augmented manyfold, surely including performances of the great ceremonial and religious music of the Vatican and ending with an appearance of the pope himself. Instead he found deteriorating cardinals, execrable counterpoint, and a procession devoid of dignity: "There it is," he wrote, "the capital of the Christian world, the place we are sent to admire musical masterpieces."[10]

Recovered for the most part from his mangled engagement and flirtation with murder and suicide, he set about assembling and revising the music for the *Mélologue*—all of it borrowed from works of the late 1820s.[11] The completed "monodrama" consists of six monologues and six excerpts of music, the last of which is the full *Tempest* fantasy. It was to be a vehicle for the great tenor Adolphe Nourrit at the first concert Berlioz could arrange on returning home. Among its features was a splendid attack on Fétis, intended to "clip his wings" for correcting Beethoven; Berlioz hints of this passage in a letter to Hiller, but urges him to keep the matter in confidence. There was, too, a chorus of spirits, its music borrowed from *Cléopâtre* but its text in an "ancient Northern dialect," "a strange language, like a great voice emanating from some unknown world, incomprehensible to us":

O sonder foul, sonder foul leimi,
Sonder rak simoun irridor!
Muk lo meror, muk lunda merinunda
Farerein lira moretissò.

The papal censors, according to an account Berlioz probably trumped up, gave him difficulty over its publication.[12]

June 1831 was the first full month he actually spent in Rome. In part, that was the result of necessity: the Nice adventure had cost him 1,050 francs, nearly half his first year's pension. He had no choice but to settle into the routine of the Academy and such diversions as hunting in the Roman countryside, Vernet's Thursday balls, and the Sunday cotillions of the French ambassador. (Berlioz seldom danced, he wrote his impressionable younger sister; the opportunity to gaze at the young women present at these parties was their chief attraction.) Many evenings ended at the Café Greco, a mail drop and haven for foreign artists. "Dark, dirty, and ill-lit," it was the "most odious place imaginable."[13] Berlioz nonetheless encountered there a number of artists who became important figures in his life: Glinka, Heine, Auguste Barbier, Brizeux, and possibly Stendhal, to name but a few. It may have been at the Café Greco that Berlioz met Mendelssohn, who had been in Rome since late 1830.

The greater attraction was the out-of-doors, where country promenades were soon a regular activity. Two weeks after returning to Rome, Berlioz and a friend set out by foot one Saturday afternoon on an excursion to Tivoli, with its "ravishing and original" cascades at the Villa d'Este and Hadrian's villa nearby. It was too hurried a trip, and almost immediately Berlioz began to plan a longer visit. He had found it easy to be pleasant with the natives, the first Italians he had enjoyed, and their Byronesque brigandry attracted him more than anything he had encountered elsewhere in Italy.

Rome, by contrast, meant the boring life of a bachelors' barracks. The quarters were small and cramped; by night the residents had to arm themselves against insurgents. His cohorts he found to be vulgar, short of artistic soul: of the great living composers, for instance, they preferred Bellini, thinking Rossini "too grave." There was, Berlioz alleged, nothing to read, no music, no theater, and little by way of spiritual excitement. (The part about the books is not true: Berlioz himself refers to the arrival of reading matter from Paris on more than one occasion. What is true is that many of the books he wanted to read were on the papal index.) The first allures of Rome had faded entirely: the civilization, he concluded, was two centuries behind, and the city was "the stupidest, the most prosaic that I know."[14]

His colleagues at the Villa Medici, according to Ernest Legouvé, who first heard of Berlioz there, admired him for his talent and exceptional intelligence, but they suspected him for the eccentricities they had begun to see as studied affectation. Berlioz was more of a success with the few women about the Academy. Ladies are quicker than men, Legouvé explained, to perceive superiority in those around them.

Berlioz was less successful still at impressing Mendelssohn, whom he had encountered briefly before he left for Nice and with whom he now tried to build a friendship.[15] He was clearly attracted to Mendelssohn, describing him in long strings of adjectives: grave, delicate, gracious, sensitive. Mendelssohn's talent seemed enormous, superb, and prodigious. In character he was virginal, still preserving some fundamental beliefs, and a little cold, but Berlioz liked him nonetheless—and despite his poor French, which Berlioz enjoyed ridiculing. They visited Tasso's tomb together and went riding in the countryside, talking of Shakespeare, scherzos, Queen Mab, and their shared dislike for Italian standards of musical performance.

Mendelssohn found Berlioz on the whole distasteful—attributing part of the problem to his inelegant ramblings about women—and wrote home of his new acquaintance in the following terms:

> *** distorts himself, without a spark of talent; groping around in the dark, he deems himself the creator of a new world—then he writes the most hideous things, and dreams and thinks of nothing but Beethoven, Schiller and Goethe; at the same time full of unbounded vanity, and looking condescendingly down upon Mozart and Haydn, so that all his enthusiasm is very questionable to me . . . Me, who would like to bite *** to death [actually, "strangle him"], until suddenly he raves again about Gluck, when I am forced to acquiesce—yet I like to go to walk with them both [that is, Berlioz and Montfort], because they are the only musicians here, and very pleasant, amiable people—all that makes the most comical contrast. You say, dear mother, that after all *** must attempt something in Art; there I am not at all of your opinion; I believe he wants to marry, and is really worse than the rest, because he is more affected. Once for all I cannot endure this inside-out enthusiasm, this despair presented to the ladies, this genius in black letters, black on white; and if he were not a Frenchman (with them one always can live agreeably, and they always know how to say something and to interest you), it would be intolerable.[16]

Berlioz recognized himself in the asterisks when the letter was published in the early 1860s, but by then he could attribute its negative tone to Mendelssohn's youth and lack of familiarity, at the time, with his music.[17] Berlioz and Mendelssohn shared precious little but their profession and their gentility. On this both men agreed.

In 1831 Berlioz gave Mendelssohn the last remaining copy of his *Neuf Mélodies* and showed him the new *Le Roi Lear* and even *Rob-Roy*, before it was beginning to approach completion. Only later did they become familiar with more than the rudiments of each other's music. Mendelssohn had probably met Berlioz with preconceived negative impressions based on the *Huit Scènes de Faust*, which Zelter had shown him. Soon after Mendelssohn left Rome for Paris, Berlioz was able to learn the First Symphony, but only from a reduction for salon musicians. Later he discovered the "ravishing" *Midsummer Night's Dream* music—could the scherzo therein have been born, in fact, of their conversations?—and became noted for his conducting of Mendelssohn's works.

The overtures and *Mélologue* were not the only products of his imagination during the spring and summer of 1831. He had drafted a plan and some of the words for a "colossal oratorio" on *Le Dernier Jour du monde* (The last day of the world) in Florence that April, a time when we know him to have been occupied with thoughts of death and judgment. It was doubtless preconceived as a vehicle for reusing the *Resurrexit* from the early Mass. In late June, Berlioz worked out a detailed scenario for this extravaganza, to be produced in festive surroundings—at the Opéra, or at the Panthéon, or in the *cour carrée* of the Louvre—then wrote to Ferrand inviting him to do the poem, to "put muscles on the carcass."[18] Soloists, chorus, an orchestra of sixty, and another of two or three hundred would be sufficient to tell the story:

> The people, having arrived at the last stage of corruption, indulge in every sin; a sort of Antichrist governs them despotically. A few worthies, led by a prophet, cut off in the midst of this general depravity. The despot torments them, kidnaps their virgins, insults their beliefs, and has their holy books destroyed during an orgy. The prophet comes to reproach him for his crimes and announces the end of the world and the Last Judgment. The enraged despot has him thrown into prison and while indulging again in impious sensual pleasure is surprised in the middle of a feast by the terrible trumpets of the Resurrection. The dead leaping from the tomb, the damned crying frightfully, the shattering world, the thunder of heavenly hosts make up the *finale* of this musical drama.[19]

Either the letter was lost or, more likely, the idea failed to arouse Ferrand. Berlioz wrote him of the project once more in January 1832, starting over again, and by this time the oratorio had evolved into an opera.[20]

On 8 July Berlioz left, by himself, for a two-week visit to Subiaco, a small village 35 miles east of Rome in the Abruzzi mountains.[21] In geographical setting and coziness of ambience, it was not unlike La Côte-St.-André. He was pleased by the simple lifestyle and the remote, isolated quality of the place: "Oh! how well I could breathe; how much I could see; how handsomely I lived!"[22] Armed with his rifle, an old guitar, and his sketchbook, he wandered aimlessly in the mountains, enjoying chance encounters with the peasantry, bathing in the streams, tramping over the rocks, passing an evening or two in the inn of nearby Civitella. He imagined himself a chamois hunter and recalled a hunter's song to sing: *Sur les Alpes, quel délice.* (He had jotted down the tune in a letter of 2 July to Mme Le Sueur, referred to it again in correspondence from Subiaco, then later harmonized it and presented the work in a concert.) He drank too much of the local *eau-de-*

FIGURE 5.4
Berlioz playing the guitar,
c. 1832.

vie—the only time in his life he mentions overindulgence—and smoked many cigars. He met what he imagined to be an authentic brigand, one Crispino, who serenaded his *ragazza* with a song and accompanied himself one-man-band fashion on the musette, mandolin, guitar, and triangle. Berlioz played the guitar for Crispino and his friends and sang them Gluck, arias from *Guillaume Tell,* and songs of his own composition. Everything he missed in Rome he found in the Abruzzi.

This first trip to Subiaco was a well of inspiration in a year that had already been profitable in that regard. He saw peasant children with tambourines dancing the saltarello and heard for himself the uncouth sound of bagpipes, the mandolin, and the strolling *piferrari.* He found in the music of the peasants ethnic elements for which he had a natural affection, and just as inexorably as if he had gone to the Abruzzi specifically to study rustic music, its ideals manifest themselves again and again in his later works. The peasants' devotion to the madonna is evoked in the pilgrims' march in *Harold* and in processions in both *Benvenuto Cellini* and *La Damnation de Faust.* A version of Crispino's serenade can be heard in the third movement of *Harold en Italie;* the more authentic version, with its fifth-dominated Italianate melody of a sort that begins to pervade Berlioz's idiom, appears in *Benvenuto Cellini* (ex. 5.1).

*B*erlioz's flirtation with St.-Simonism, that eccentric religio-socialist cult which numbered among its admirers Vigny, Liszt, Nourrit, Balzac, and Sand and among its disciples the composer Félicien David, reached its peak with a letter of 28 July to one of the most important lieutenants of the movement, the lawyer Charles Duveyrier, the St.-Simonian "Poet of God." Berlioz was doubtless introduced to the movement by the cellist Tajan-Rogé in 1830, just before he left Paris for Rome; he probably attended some proselytizing lectures in the Salle Taitbout or one of the *soirées* at the St.-Simonian lair in the rue Monsigny—dance-and-conversation parties that attracted a number of other prominent musicians in those months. "Several artists—Liszt, Berlioz, Nourrit—are approaching us," wrote the *père suprême*, Barthélémy-Prosper Enfantin, in October 1830.[23]

To Duveyrier, whom he addresses as "father," Berlioz writes that he has discovered that Cendrier, a French architect living in Rome, is "one of us." They have talked of the movement, and Berlioz has read a bundle of back issues of *Le Globe*, the St.-Simonian newspaper. Whatever doubts he had had in Paris have largely been overcome.

EXAMPLE 5.1 Goldsmiths' refrain in no. 10 of *Benvenuto Cellini*; compare with Crispino's song as given in the *Mémoires*, chap. 38.

Concerning everything having to do with *the political reorganization of society,* I am now convinced that St.-Simon's plan is the only true and complete one. But I must tell you that my ideas haven't changed at all on the issues pertaining to the supernatural, to God, to the soul, and to another life. I imagine that this will not be an obstacle to my uniting my wishes and my efforts with yours on behalf of the largest and poorest classes . . . Write to me about this matter, and I will respond quickly, outlining my ideas on the manner of my musical contribution to the Great Work when I return to Paris.[24]

Berlioz, in short, admired the St.-Simonians' concern for the poor and belief in social equality and was willing enough to engage his own talents in support of the *famille.* But it was only the egalitarianism that attracted and not, for example, the *Globe*'s meandering views on art or Enfantin's half-crazed sermons. Berlioz was repulsed by politics in general, and his philosophy of government was confused at best. We know nothing more of any affiliation with the group, though several of his later works praising industry seem in one way or another descendents of the St.-Simonian tenets. St.-Simonism was in the air, however, and every French artist of the time knew something about it.

Ralph Locke, in his book on how the movement affected music and musicians,[25] suggests that *Le Dernier Jour du monde* may have been the work intended for the St.-Simonians. Later, Dido's peaceable, laboring kingdom bespeaks St.-Simonian ideals, and Tajan-Rogé reappears in Berlioz's life, still upholding the ideals of the movement, during the 1847 sojourn in Russia. Berlioz developed a utopian dream of his own: he was to call it Euphonia, a mythical civilization where everyone is a musician. But in *Euphonia,* Berlioz dismisses the pomposity of St.-Simonism as a *grotesquerie:* "The St.-Simonians claimed to know how to make work attractive. They kept the secret well."[26]

His letter to Duveyrier of 28 July 1831, bearing the address of the notorious newspaper *Le Globe,* never reached Paris, having been intercepted by the Austrian censor. Metternich himself warned the Austrian ambassador in Rome of the radical in their midst.[27]

August and September constituted one of the few periods of more than six weeks that Berlioz spent in Rome. Even then there were day trips for hunting, on one of which he shot sixteen quail, seven waterbirds, a snake, and a porcupine. In August,[28] suffering from spleen, he set another poem of Thomas Moore, a "psalmody for those who have greatly suffered and whose souls are sad unto death," a *Méditation religieuse* for chorus and seven wind instruments. He responded positively to an invitation to write of his Italian adventures for the *Revue européenne,* successor to *Le Correspondant.* The resulting "Lettre d'un enthousiaste," along with a chapter he wrote for a travel book called *Italie pittoresque,* published in 1836, are a major source of our knowledge of his Italian travels. Together they became the Italian portion of the *Voyage musical en Allemagne et en Italie*, published in 1844, and in turn the source of chapters 31–43 of the *Mémoires*.

In late September, Berlioz left Rome in the company of two colleagues from the Academy, traveling prosaically by coach, for a tour of Naples and its surroundings. (On the way, he wrote an otherwise unidentified chorus—"improvised, as one does improvise, while waiting for the sun to come out.") There were stops en route at the Benedictine abbey of Montecassino,[29] the ruins of ancient Capua—Hannibal's capital, where the victorious Carthaginians were said to have abandoned themselves to licentiousness and ultimate defeat—and the palace, gardens, and cascades of the King of Naples. On 1 October they arrived in Naples, where Berlioz's first duty was to visit Virgil's tomb on the cape of Posillipo. There was a breathtaking sunset into the sea, and it loosed a flood of Virgilian memories from his childhood.

Berlioz walked up Mount Vesuvius and into the crater, though his friends hired donkeys. The volcano's lava fulminating inside a cool crater seemed to him an apt symbol of his own creative urges, all the more so as news of a volcanic eruption in Sicily, with the sea welling up to extinguish it, had just reached the travelers. Naples was cleaner and more appealing than Rome, the local peasants to be admired for "their profound instinct for stealing, their wit, and their moments of sheer spontaneous goodness." The ruins of a bygone civilization, alongside the timeless bay and the volcano, evoked at last the sensations of antiquity he had so long anticipated of Italy.

On this journey the evenings of opera at the historic theaters—the Teatro San Carlo and the Teatro del Fondo—were of secondary interest to the wanderings by day, though there Berlioz was impressed for the first time with Italian performances. He may have gone to Capri. From Baia, the locus of episodes in the lives of both Aeneas and Nero, Berlioz embarked for the Isle of Nisida, there to spend the day among the fruit trees, inviting his guides to share his lunch of pasta. Last of all came Herculaneum and Pompeii, where he found in the museum a display of musical instruments recovered from the ashes. "I tried two pairs of tiny cymbals."[30]

Berlioz had gotten as far south as Castellammare, intending to continue all the way to Calabria and Sicily, when his money ran out and he was obliged to turn back. He missed Sorrento, Amalfi, and Paestum, all of which he had hoped to visit, and passed up a boat trip to Ischia. For economy's sake, he elected to travel homeward by foot, sending his belongings ahead with a porter and joining forces with a pair of Swedish army officers. They wended their way back toward Rome via San Germano and the waterfalls of the Isola di Sora, three vagabonds dining on stolen fruit, some eggs, and an occasional loaf of bread. In Alatri, he fell sick with a fever caused, he thought, by the fleas in his bed.

After seven days on the road—on through Capua, Arcino, and Anticoli—Berlioz arrived, with blistered feet, in the familiar surroundings of Subiaco, where he stayed for three days. After another day and night in Tivoli, he made his way back to Rome and the Villa Medici. "Never," he wrote, "has a trip interested me so much."[31]

By early November he had reestablished himself at the Academy and begun to collect the news from Paris and La Côte-St.-André. Except for the good tidings of Nanci's engagement to the lawyer Camille Pal, there was little but bad news. The cholera epidemic that had terrorized southern Europe was now threatening the Villa Medici, leaving hundreds of dead each day; corpses were being dragged in an unbroken procession of carts through the streets of Rome. The cholera was certain to reach Paris. There were riots in Lyon, where Ferrand and his relatives might be endangered.

The news from Paris dealt largely with the "matrimoniomania"—a term that crops up again in *Béatrice et Bénédict*—spreading among his intimate friends. To the news of Nanci's forthcoming marriage and that of Ferrand was added the discovery that his friends Albert Du Boys, Auguste Berlioz, Edouard Rocher, and the count Carné—among others—were all married or about to be. These developments coincided in unwelcome fashion with his efforts to extricate himself from the hostile memories of his own flirtations with matrimony. He tried to make amends to Ferdinand Hiller, from whom he had essentially stolen Camille, and to erase the whole incident by sending back "to our Holy Virgin" her letters and trinkets, in the baggage of the homeward-bound architect Duc. Thoughts of Paris led to disappointment at missing performances of Beethoven's Ninth and Meyerbeer's *Robert le diable* and the recitals of Paganini. All this turned into the case of spleen—best defined, I suppose, as tragic boredom—he mentions repeatedly in his writings from those months. "My life so far," he concludes, "has been a bizarre and romanesque web of adventures and painful emotions."[32]

Sophomoric dormitory life brought him out of his misery: the naughty couplings of the young men with each other's mistresses and other people's wives. One of Berlioz's better tales of Italy is his sad story of Vincenza, Gibert's mistress, who meets a tragic end in the Tiber.[33] ("As for the indolent Creole, Gibert, . . . he is still in Rome, where he spends a third of his life dozing, a third sleeping, and a third doing nothing.")

Among the serious requirements of the *prix de Rome* composers was to send an annual *envoi* to the Académie des Beaux-Arts, demonstrating what they had accomplished so far. Berlioz had not actually finished much of anything and was hardly disposed to send his one promising work, *Le Roi Lear,* for examination by the Institute. For his 1831 *envoi*, he hired a scribe, paid with 4.50 piasters from his Villa Medici account, to recopy the *Resurrexit* from his 1824 Mass (probably following the manuscript used for the November 1829 performance). The receipt is dated 15 April 1831—when Berlioz was in Nice, just a few weeks after he had first arrived in Italy—but the *envoi* does not seem to have been sent until the end of the year.

Winter was approaching; but for a brief visit to Tivoli and Subiaco in mid-November, he was confined to Rome by the weather. There was time for reading—the recent work of Hugo, among others, including *Notre Dame de Paris*—copying of parts for the *Symphonie fantastique* and its sequel, and some light composition. For the Christmas amusement of the French exiles, he penned a brief angels' chorus, now lost, and a *Quartetto e coro dei maggi*.

But the major business of the holiday season and early January was to polish his article on "L'Etat présent de la musique en Italie" for the *Revue européenne*, ultimately retitled "Lettre d'un enthousiaste." The long essay, developed from impressions he was now systematically recording in his pocket albums, is the first of the splendid reports that became a stock product of his travels. Berlioz proved himself a natural autobiographer, possessed already of a fetching combination of insight and wit. His correspondence, too, is convincing proof of his growing expertise as a travel writer; indeed, the common sentiments, turns of phrase, and even entire passages repeated in clots of letters and in his later essays suggest that he was often relying on some manner of journal, now lost.

Dr. Berlioz sent the money his son had begged, but not without provoking a squabble. Berlioz seems to have reckoned that the annual pension of 1,000 francs promised by his family on the occasion of his engagement still applied if he remained single—"en restant garçon," as he put it. Dr. Berlioz, quite naturally, imagined otherwise. Moreover Berlioz had found other antagonizing passages in his latest letter from home—perhaps suggestions of possible mates—and had recoiled with a manifesto of independence. "Any forced conditions, any obvious brakes, anything which hinders my liberty in the least," he replied, "is absolutely insupportable to me." He would rather do without assistance altogether than have strings attached. As for the matter of marriage, he says he has a few ideas, but refuses to be drawn into anything conventional. "I know too well that an ordinary marriage, that which is called a proper marriage, a tranquil and moderate marriage, would be death."[34]

A fourth and last trip to Subiaco in early February 1832—where he heard the crack of ice for the first time since arriving in Italy—resulted in the best of the Italian compositions, *La Captive*, set to a poem from Hugo's *Orientales*. Berlioz jotted down the melody and bass in the corner of a tavern, sitting by the fire; in Rome he fashioned a piano accompaniment, which he tried with Louise Vernet, who may have become an object of his fancy.[35] (He was, surprisingly enough, at the piano; Mlle Vernet was the singer.) *La Captive* became a *succès de salon;* the other women were envious and begged for a similar memento. Copies were made and spread about, and the servants sang *La Captive* while at their work—to the point where Horace Vernet begged him not to compose any other music of such charm.

The highlight of the winter season was the French ambassador's costume ball at the end of February, to which Berlioz went dressed as a soldier of fortune, Walter Scott's Allan, in Scottish kilts and tartans. Now a killing influenza epidemic swept Rome, and for much of the month of March Berlioz was ill with another throat infection. The political relations between France and the Holy See—France had occupied the port of Ancona—had become so strained that the pope forbade circulation of the French papers. The confluence of the epidemic and the military troubles dampened the Carnival celebrations on Mardi Gras, 6 March. Thus, as he had not arrived in Rome in time for the carnival the preceding year, Berlioz never saw for himself the full-fledged Roman Mardi Gras that he depicts with such brilliance in *Benvenuto Cellini.*

There was little left to do but count the days until he could leave for home, his departure having been set for 2 May. Vernet, understanding the difference between the needs of composers and those of the painters and architects who counted for the majority of his charges, agreed to allow him to go on to Germany, after the briefest of sojourns in Paris, voiding the customary second year in Italy. Berlioz would in fact have left in March but for the necessity of sitting for a portrait to hang in the refectory. The remaining weeks were devoted to getting his business affairs in order. Hiller, on the verge of leaving Paris, had written for repayment of a loan. Berlioz authorized him to open the package of belongings returned by Camille Moke, remove the *prix de Rome* medal, and pawn it in the passage des Panoramas— a common practice of the time. Hiller did so, leaving the rest of Berlioz's package in the care of Thomas Gounet.

FIGURE 5.5 Medal of Berlioz, Rome, 1831.

In late March Berlioz made a last sightseeing trip, this time to Albano and the lake there, Frascati, and Castel-Gandolfo.

*T*he Italian soujourn made of Berlioz a vagabond. The lack of anyone to share his particular enthusiasms and the difficulty of the language led him to seek out new freedom, greater still than the independence he had found in Paris. His aimless wandering invariably ended with his having discovered serenity and renewed purpose. Decked out with his cane or rifle, purse, and portfolio, he had wandered alone in the corridors of ancient Latium, his imagination swimming in visions of Virgil and Tasso, Hannibal and Nero, Aeneas and the others. A wealth of images and thoughts collected in his mind, to be filed away and later to yield great dividends. Berlioz's discovery of Antiquity and The Folk and especially Nature ranks with the revelations of Beethoven and Shakespeare among his most important formative influences. His thoughts were full of the *rochers* and *torrents* mentioned in a dozen or more letters from Italy; of the word *agreste* ("rustic"), which had crept into his working vocabulary; of brigands and vagabonds and their "orgies"; of columns and moonlit arcades; of antique cymbals; of strolling *pifferari* and their oboe-like *pifferi*; of the saltarello; of the tambourine; of smoky taverns; and even of the wines of Orvieto, Lambruschino, and Lacryma Christi. Most significant of all, perhaps, is his embrace of Italianate movement, the bustling rhythmic frenzy that marks the next great step forward in his style. He thought himself isolated, in exile, deprived of the excitements of art, trapped in a rarified atmosphere, but in truth the "savage life" had also revealed to him "all the charm of absolute physical freedom."[36]

In his last two weeks, Berlioz had a copyist prepare his second *envoi* from Rome: the *Quartetto e coro dei maggi,* almost surely a reworking with Italian words of the 1828 *Marche religieuse des mages,* and his overture *Rob-Roy.* (Berlioz himself used the same regal-sized manuscript paper for a fair copy of the *Mélologue* and the revised second movement of the *Symphonie fantastique.*) The cost of the *envoi* was 9 piasters and 15 baiocchi, the receipt dated 31 May—a month after he left Rome. He also postdated receipts for the last payments of his pension and board.

On Wednesday, 2 May, after an affectionate farewell from the Vernets, Berlioz climbed into a battered old wagon and began his journey northward, never to return to a land he had grown to love more than he yet knew. Just before leaving he had purchased a pocket album and sketched in it a setting of *Dans l'alcôve sombre* from Hugo's *Les Feuilles d'automne* (1831). This album now became a travel diary, in which he entered each expense of the trip, some narrative impressions of the journey, and here and there a musical sketch. The sketchbook allows us to reconstruct a relatively firm chronology of the trip homeward from Italy.[37] It appears that Berlioz covered between 30 and 50 miles each day.

His first notion was to spend several days sightseeing in Terni, noted for its lake and spectacular waterfalls; he arrived there after two nights on the road (2 May in Civita Castellana; 3 May in Vigne or Narni, a "delicious countryside like those painted by Poussin").[38] He spent three days in Terni (4–6 May), then continued in the direction of Florence, through Spoleto (7 May) and Perugia (8 May). After an overnight stop and some sightseeing by the Lago di Trasimeno (9 May), he passed through Castiglion (10 May) and Incisa (11 May). It is surprising to find that after a visit to the lovely basilica of Santa Maria degli Angeli he failed to climb the hill to Assisi, only a few miles away. In general his interest during these last days in Italy was primarily in landscapes and people: he was quick to report to the local theaters to see operas he invariably disliked, but scarcely remarked the exceptional art and architecture he encountered along the way home.

He arrived in Florence on 12 May and stayed for two days, probably until the morning of the 15th. There he sought out the tenor Gilbert Duprez, whose career was blossoming in Italy and whom Berlioz hoped soon to use in a Paris concert, and accompanied him to a performance of *La Sonnambula* at the Teatro della Pergola. (Duprez's Florence address appears in the sketchbook.) He obtained his Austrian passport for travel in Lombardy-Venetia, went shopping for Florentine straw hats for his sisters (of which souvenirs there is much talk in the correspondence with his family) and a walking stick for himself, mailed a letter, and had his boots refurbished. Quarantines occasioned by the cholera epidemic forced him to abandon a plan for Napoleonic side trips to Elba and Corsica.

FIGURE 5.6 Sketchbook of 1832–36. The journey homeward from Rome: Florence, Bologna, Modena, Parma. Note the customs duties paid for the straw hats bought in Florence for his sisters.

The long march across the Apennines to Bologna was cruel—"quite cold, with a wind that could blow you away"[39]—though apparently accomplished in a day. Berlioz paid stiff customs duties for the hats and his other purchases, taxes totaling several times their original cost, at the many economic borders he now encountered: Bologna, the duchies of Modena and Parma, Lombardy–Venetia, Piedmont, and France. From Bologna (15 May) he passed through Modena (16 May), Parma (17 May), Fidenza and Piacenza (18 May), and Lodi (19 May). Just twenty miles short of Milan, he paused in Lodi to visit the bridge where in May 1796 Napoleon had led his dramatic charge against the rear guard of the Austrian army.

The stopover in Milan included a trip (probably 21 May) to the Teatro della Cannobiana to hear *L'Elisir d'amore,* which had opened there on the 12th. He recorded expenditures for dinner, ice cream, a shave, and new gaiter straps before departing on the morning of the 23rd for Piedmont. He was in Turin by the 25th, a Friday, where he stayed for three days to enjoy the unexpected attractions of the city and its theater. On Monday the 28th, he was on the road to France.

Berlioz had spent nearly a fortnight in territory redolent with evocations of Napoleon's first Italian campaign, that dramatic time wherein much of the seed of the Napoleonic legend was sown, as the Little Corporal repeatedly trounced the Austrians, to the glory of France. Overwhelmed with excitement, Berlioz was now in sight of the Alps, and France was but a few leagues distant; his emotional state, confused by the conflicting sensations of farewell and triumphant return, welled up in an outburst of letter writing and composition. He paused to scribble out the first of many ideas for a Napoleonic military symphony: penciled prose sketches followed by a musical passage reminiscent of the finale to Beethoven's Fifth (ex. 5.2). The work would consist of two movements, "Farewell, from the summit of the Alps, to the brave fallen in the battlefields of Italy" and "Triumphal entry into Paris of the conquerors."[40] In 1846 this idea is briefly reasserted, in response to an invitation from the Duc de Montpensier, in the form of a planned military symphony—"a subject of which I once spoke"[41]—with a chorus of 3,000 men. A description written at the time of the Te Deum, in 1855, may also hark back to the spirit of the 1832 sketches: "At the moment General Bonaparte passes underneath the arches of the cathedral, the Te Deum bursts forth from all directions, standards are lowered, drums beat, guns sound, and bells ring out in great peals."[42] The Napoleonic symphony went unfinished, but its underlying idea occupied him for two more decades.

Berlioz had taken care to ready himself—with a certain gusto, in fact—for his own triumphal entry into France: his hair and beard were freshly trimmed, his clothes and boots had been spruced up, and he was doubtless carrying his new stick. He rode with mounting excitement from Turin to Grenoble via Susa (27 May), the Mont-Cenis pass (28 May), and St. Jean-de-Maurienne (29 May) and Chapereillan (30 May), arriving in Grenoble on the evening of 31 May. He went to considerable lengths to surprise his sister, returning three times to her house in the company of Casimir Faure, at last finding her at home. Faure went in and announced, "Madame, I have brought a gentleman who has news of your brother"—and in walked, as Nanci put it, "you-know-who."

But she was not entirely amused. Her new husband was having his evening nap, and it had not been her intention to show him off with "the stupefied look of a man just waking up and rubbing his eyes."[43] Berlioz stayed less than a day, then went on to La Côte-St.-André, where he must have arranged a similarly grand entry. It was late spring, one of the loveliest times of the year in the Isère, and the freshness of his native land compared favorably even with that of Naples.

O f the two years he was to have spent in Italy, Berlioz actually stayed fourteen months, less than half of those at the Villa Medici. For all his violation of the terms of the award, he had done very nearly what the laureates were expected to do, having absorbed deep inspiration from the surroundings and the people. The value of the friendships he made—with figures from Duc and Vernet to Mendelssohn and Heine—is immense. Ideas gleaned from Italy and souvenirs of the trip would dominate his compositional thought for a decade and continue to crop up in his music for the rest of his life. Moreover during this period Berlioz grew measurably in sophistication and maturity of self-perception. His most violent impulses were nearly spent—there would be few other eccentricities on the scale of the Nice incident, the *bella sposina,* and the strange text of the *Mélologue*—and but for the reawakening of his passion for Harriet Smithson, his life from here on would be decidedly tamer.

He planned to spend several months with his parents in La Côte-St.-André, for he had promised not to show himself in Paris before November.

EXAMPLE 5.2 Sketch for the *Symphonie militaire*, sketchbook, fol. 10ʳ.

He would assiduously compose and copy orchestral parts, return to Paris late in the year to give two or three concerts of his *Symphonie fantastique* and *Mélologue,* and then, following the rules of the *prix de Rome,* go on to Berlin with a cargo of works ready for presentation to the German-speaking world. The advantage of staying in La Côte was strictly fiscal: if there were any difficulty collecting his pension, he could go from time to time to nearby Chambéry, then in the Kingdom of Sardinia, to sign the receipts.

Life in La Côte was, on the whole, as Berlioz imagined it would be. Tensions in the family had eased somewhat as the result of the *prix de Rome* and Nanci's good marriage. Their father had aged, saddened by the departure of his elder daughter and troubled by the academic difficulties of his younger son Prosper. Prosper, now twelve years old, had tantrums, refused to study Latin, and, when it suited his purposes, forgot how to dress himself. Berlioz was sympathetic to his problems, which he attributed to provincial education, and suggested that his brother come to school in Paris. With Adèle he nurtured the relationship proper to adult siblings; they went together on long, silent walks over the plain, shielded from the summer rain by a shared umbrella.

In July, Berlioz returned to Grenoble to stay with his sister and brother-in-law, but this visit did not go well. Never one to hide his boredom with prosaic topics of conversation, he was unpopular with his new in-laws. He was uncomfortable in a world of magistrates and doctors, and Nanci's husband Camille insisted on discussing artistic matters with him, championing, Berlioz thought, the *passé* in art. "It is in these situations that I am dangerous."[44] Nanci could not help being peeved: "Not once did he come to my house without a somber and ferocious look; if his visit to Grenoble cost him such effort, I can't imagine why he stayed so long . . . His glacial silence often broke my heart."[45]

His glacial silence may have had something to do with their concern over his unseemly bachelorhood. His father suggested a certain Louise Veyron as a possible mate; two former possibilities, his cousin Odile Berlioz and Estelle Dubœuf, had since been married. Berlioz's own thoughts, it is certain, were turning once again to Miss Smithson. But marriage was a lesser concern: "I need liberty, love, and money,"[46] he wrote at the time, pointedly omitting the matter of a wife.

With the forthcoming season in mind, he spent the summer copying parts; those for the *Mélologue* have recently been recovered. The Hugo song, *Dans l'alcôve sombre,* was abandoned, possibly as his interest in Louise Vernet subsided. To Mme Vernet he wrote:

> I had very much hoped to send to Mlle Louise a small composition similar to those she likes; but what I had written did not seem to be worthy of summoning a smile of approbation from the gracious Ariel, and so I followed the advice of my *amour-propre* and burned it.[47]

Whatever pleasure he may have derived from *boules* with the townsmen or hunting with his younger brother was soon overcome by renewed longing for Paris. The time appointed for his return was nearing, and there were countless tasks to be accomplished before the concert season began. On 28 October, after twenty-one weeks in the bosom of his family, he took out a passport and made ready to assault the metropolis. This stay in La Côte had been the longest of his adult life; he would return there but twice more, and he was never to see his mother again.

He paused in Lyon on 2 and 3 November with the thought, once again abandoned, of seeing Ferrand. At the municipal theater there he heard a movement from Beethoven's Sixth; though merely the accompaniment for a ballet, it was nevertheless the first serious music he had heard in half a year. He reached Paris on Wednesday morning, 7 November, and dined that evening with the Le Sueurs. There he learned that two weeks before, his first *envoi* from Rome—the recycled *Resurrexit* and *Et iterum*—had been favorably reviewed by the Academy. After dinner he met Gounet for tea at the Café Feydeau.

Discovering that his former rooms in the rue de Richelieu were occupied, he established himself across the street in a vacant apartment at 1, rue Neuve-St.-Marc, by strange coincidence the very lodgings Harriet Smithson had left the previous week for a hotel in the rue de Rivoli.

*M*iss Smithson was on the verge of opening her own English theater company at the Théâtre-Italien. She had parted with William Abbott and the remains of the original troupe after an incident in Bordeaux in 1828. It concerned the matter of her salary:

> She told Mr. Abbot [*sic*] that she was the great feature and sole attraction and demanded an increase of remuneration equal to the combined salaries of the whole company! Mr. Abbot very properly told the lady that her demand was preposterous, and that he could not, and would not, even if he could, comply with it. The manager was firm, and the lady obstinate; accordingly the company was disbanded, and had to retrace their steps.[48]

Since then her career had taken her to London, without much success, on a tour of the English provinces, back—as we have seen—to Paris (1829–30, at the time of her benefit), to England for eighteen months, and now again to Paris. She was determined to establish her own company there rather than attempt a tour of America.

Though Harriet herself enjoyed an unqualified triumph in the title role of *Jane Shore,* with which her troupe opened on 21 November, they were successful neither with the critics nor at the box office. The repertoire was nearly the same as in 1827, but its magic had vanished. Harriet was not a gifted impresario—the incident in Bordeaux foreshadowed that, and her letters reconfirm it—nor did she have Berlioz's knack for dealing with French bureaucrats. She had grown plump. Berlioz, however, found in her decline some encouraging signs: "She has so changed in every respect that she will no longer play tricks on me."[49]

Preparations for his December concert, billed for the 9th, went more smoothly than he had expected. The technical arrangements were made easier both by the new government and by his celebrity: the hall was secured forthwith; the musicians, over 100 of them, were eager to offer their services. Habeneck would be honored to conduct, and even Cherubini found the wherewithal to appear "enchanted to see him again." The posters announcing a new chapter in the "Episode from an Artist's Life" piqued the public curiosity.

But there were inevitable dilemmas. Recruiting a chorus was difficult, and the ensemble proved disappointingly small. A graver matter was that Louis Véron, the new director of the Opéra, refused to authorize an appearance by his leading tenor, Adolphe Nourrit, for whom the text and tenor solos of the *Mélologue* had been intended. Berlioz turned to Alexis Dupont, Nourrit's heir apparent and a future Benvenuto Cellini, for the tenor solos; the tragedian Bocage, just embarking on what was to be an impressive Paris career, would narrate.

On 9 December the *Symphonie fantastique*, handsomely rewritten, was given a reading that far surpassed the 1830 performance; the *Mélologue* was greeted favorably by a public becoming accustomed to the latest tenets of Romanticism. In the audience were such old friends as Pixis, Nourrit, and the formidable Alexandre Dumas, rumored to be preparing a libretto for Berlioz, and such newer acquaintances as the wealthy Ernest Legouvé, the novelist Eugène Süe, and the great Paganini, "with flowing hair and piercing eyes and a strange, ravaged countenance, a creature haunted by genius, a Titan among giants"[50]—all there to learn of Berlioz's art firsthand, many for the first time. And in one of the boxes, alongside Liszt and Hugo, sat Miss Smithson, brought there by a correspondent for the English newspaper *Galignani's Messenger*. She was studying the printed libretto of the *Fantastique* and its sequel and seemed to be intrigued. (This publication was one of the season's more attractive souvenirs: any number of copies ended up in distant places.)

Indeed, *Le Retour à la vie*, being a timely work, almost a roman a clef, was more appealing in December 1832 than it would ever be again. The butt of the tirade against "profaners who dare take their hand to original works and submit them to horrible mutilations which they call *corrections* and *improvements*" was made clear to all when Bocage mimicked Fétis's high-pitched voice. (The passage goes on to draw the analogy with birds who sully statues in a public park, then preen themselves and strut about as though they had laid a golden egg.) Both that outburst and the end of the same monologue, where the narrator dons a holster, pistols, and a saber,

FIGURE 5.7
Pierre Bocage,
the artist in
Le Retour à la vie.

were interrupted with applause. The audience greeted the lines on Shake-spearean love—

Oh, that I might find that Juliet, that Ophelia, my heart longs for. Oh, that I might intoxicate myself with that joy mingled with sadness which is true love and, one autumn evening, rocked with her by the north wind on some savage heath, sleep at last in her arms—sleep that last, melancholy sleep.

—with knowing glances at the principals.

Afterward Bocage, overcome with emotion, embraced Berlioz in the cor-ridor. Paganini, too, was moved: "Monsieur," he said, "you are beginning where the others [that is, Beethoven and Weber] ended."[51] Gentlemen in the streets tipped their hats to Berlioz for days afterward; two dozen newspapers, by his estimate, carried reviews. Some money had been made. Everything had been successful enough that a second concert—"généralement rede-mandé"—was announced for 23 December. A conflicting dress rehearsal at the Opéra, and Habeneck's resulting inability to appear, forced a postpone-ment until 30 December.

Within a day or so word reached Berlioz that Harriet Smithson had at last been won over by his art: she had recognized their portraits and had wept. He begged—"in the name of pity; I dare not say of love"—to see her. Mutual friends arranged a formal introduction, which probably occurred on 15 December. Three days later a more touching scene was played: she relayed

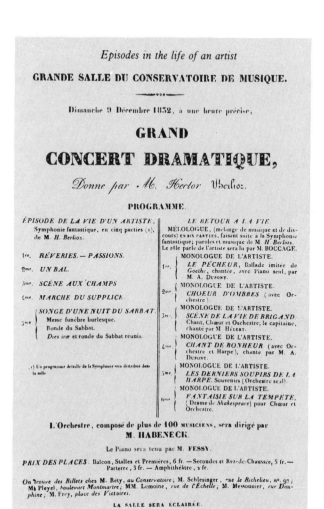

FIGURE 5.8
Program for the first
performance of
Le Retour à la vie,
9 December 1832.

her sentiment of affection—"Eh bien, Berlioz, je vous aime"—and he, like
Othello in act I, scene 3, recounted his life since last they had met, Camille
and all. She wept again and kissed him; they walked slowly about her parlor,
dreaming of their future together. "A constant love of five years [had] resisted
all, even an episodic passion."[52]

Drunk with passion, blind with joy, Berlioz rushed headlong into this new
romance. His courtship became the main object of a ten-month period during
which he accomplished virtually nothing else. By early January 1833, there
was talk of marriage, an idea that could have pleased neither Harriet's invalid
sister nor her aged mother. Liszt, now Berlioz's closest confidant, did his
best to counsel against what he, too, considered a foolish step. To Marie

d'Agoult he wrote poignantly of the affair: "Poor Berlioz: how often I see myself in him. Here he is beside me, and just a moment ago he cried, sobbing in my arms."[53]

Berlioz begged Liszt to conceal his misgivings from their friends, for this was the unique, poetic love of which he had dreamed and written. "One must respect love and enthusiasm when they are as profound and as intimate as those which I feel," he cautioned,[54] and for one of the first of many times drew the analogy between his biography and fictional narrative: "What an unlikely novel is my life."[55] The remark is astonishingly apt, a *de facto*, if subconscious, admission of his quest for a relationship found, in truth, only in books.

*T*he second of his 1832 concerts, on 30 December, was as successful as the first. The *Francs-Juges* overture was added before the "Episode from an Artist's Life," and the French were introduced for the first time to *La Captive*, sung by Mme Boulanger with piano accompaniment and a newly composed cello obbligato, played by Desmarest. Maurice Schlesinger, impressed with both concerts, bought and soon published the four works amenable to the salon: *La Captive* (with a dedication to Louise Vernet), *Le Pêcheur*, the *Chant de bonheur* (with a dedication to Miss Smithson), and the *Chant des brigands*.

The final accounts for the two concerts showed enough of a profit to have allowed Berlioz to repay some of his debts. His overall financial picture was more positive still, for despite the fact that he was not yet close to leaving for Germany, he had requested, and been granted, his 1833 pension.

Between the two concerts, in the *Revue de Paris* of 23 December, appeared the first biography of Berlioz, an eighteen-page article signed by the critic Joseph d'Ortigue. Berlioz had drafted an autobiographical sketch for d'Ortigue to follow, but got only as far as the incident of the *bella sposina* in Florence; d'Ortigue then covered the back page of Berlioz's manuscript with notes on more recent developments: "Paganini," "écrivain," and references to Hugo and the quartets of Beethoven.[56] The beginning and end of the finished piece are d'Ortigue's; most of the rest is by Berlioz.

"The name Berlioz is on every tongue: it rebounds in the salons, the theater foyers, and even in the streets," he writes. Toward the end is one of the best contemporaneous descriptions of the composer's appearance:

Berlioz is of average height and well-proportioned; yet seeing him seated you would suppose him much taller because of the vigor of his face. He has fine, individual features; an aquiline nose, delicate thin-lipped mouth, prominent chin, deep-set, penetrating eyes, sometimes dulled and clouded over with an expression of melancholy. His forehead, already furrowed with wrinkles, is partly covered by a mane of fair, wavy hair.[57]

The 1832 biography/autobiography is an important document for other reasons as well. It contributed to the worsening of the rapport between Berlioz and his family, for it dwells heavily (as do the *Mémoires*) on Dr. Berlioz's use of the allowance as leverage to discourage his son from becoming a composer. Moreover, it divulged for the first time the story of Berlioz's work as a chorister for the Nouveautés—a secret he had so far kept from nearly everyone, even his housemate at the time, Antoine Charbonnel. This new development, coinciding as it did with the climax of the Harriet affair, bent the fragile truce with La Côte-St.-André to its breaking point.

D'Ortigue was the first to draw the parallel between Harriet's awakening love and and the subject matter of George Sand's novella *La Marquise*, recently published in the *Revue de Paris*, a romance in which the hero is a comedian named Lélio. D'Ortigue couched his observation in the following manner:

> An unknown English actress played the role of Ophelia in *Hamlet* and was justifiably admired for it. Berlioz saw her, and from this moment a sudden love, its cause and effect inexplicable, frightening in its violence and tenacity, seized his heart. Such a sentiment can only be compared with that singular passion of the marquise de R*** for the actor Lélio, which a gifted writer has described with so much skill in the *Revue de Paris*.[58]

Berlioz was not formally to adopt the title *Lélio* for his *Mélologue* until after the Weimar performance of 1855, when the score was published; it seems clear, however, that the idea was d'Ortigue's.

Finally, there is the matter of the citation from "Ce siècle avait deux ans," the first of Hugo's *Feuilles d'automne*, with which the biography concludes:

> Certes, plus d'un vieillard sans flamme et sans cheveux,
> Tombé de lassitude au bout de tous ses vœux,
> Pâlirait s'il voyait, comme un gouffre dans l'onde,
> Mon âme où ma pensée habite comme un monde;
> Tout ce que j'ai souffert, tout ce que j'ai tenté,
> Tout ce qui m'a menti comme un fruit avorté,
> Les amours, les travaux, les deuils de ma jeunesse;
> Mon plus beau temps passé sans espoir qu'il renaisse;
> Et, quoique'à l'âge encor où l'avenir sourit,
> Le livre de mon cœur à toute page écrit.[59]

> (More than one ardor-less, hairless old man,
> Overcome with weariness at the end of his desires,
> Would pale were he to see, as at the bottom of some whirlpool,
> My soul, where my spirit mundanely dwells:
> All that I have suffered, all I have tried,
> All who have lied to me—like shrivelled fruit,

The loves, the work, the sorrows of my youth;
The best years of my life gone by with no hope of recovery;
And though yet at the age when the future still smiles,
My heart's book of hours is already full.)

These same lines appear in the printed libretto for the 1832 concerts and on the title page of the *Symphonie fantastique* autograph, to which they had been added in 1831 or 1832. The image of one's life as an open book veritably dominates Berlioz's self-perception. It comes to intrigue, then haunt, him more than any other conceit.

*H*arriet invited Berlioz to see *Romeo and Juliet* but barred him from the rest of her new season because, she told him, she feared for her emotions. In fact she must have been embarrassed by the cramped, second-rate theater in the rue Chantereine to which her troupe moved in January. Brushing aside his obligation to go on to Germany, Berlioz and his prospective spouse now thought to alternate half years in Paris and London. Harriet was apparently unconcerned with his lack of money—"At least you cannot suspect that it is not for yourself alone that I love you"[60]—and Berlioz seems to have been altogether oblivious to her perilous artistic position. The question of living expenses for a celebrated lady who would surely require servants and a modish wardrobe seems not to have given them pause: they would establish their nest egg with a joint benefit, then, comfortably heeled, inform the parents of their intent to marry. How they managed to work through the details of even this naive plan is difficult to imagine, as neither had mastered the other's tongue: their discussions could only have been macaronic, with a good deal of misunderstanding in both directions.

Berlioz had already written Nanci of the romance and now hinted of it to Adèle, confessing that Harriet feared his love might be nothing more than the effect of an overly active imagination. He also made the mistake of writing to the Ministry to request reimbursement of 500 francs in expenses incurred for his December concerts. The Ministry responded of the impossibility of so doing and reminded him that he was to have been in Germany on 1 January, engaging him "to get there without delay."[61]

On 3 February, feeling "the dénouement approaching,"[62] he wrote to his father for permission to marry. He knew already that the reaction would be negative: she was older than he, an actress, and a Protestant. The response from his family was to enlist uncle Félix Marmion to undertake a fact-finding mission on their behalf. Marmion was already annoyed with his nephew for having failed to send him a single letter from Italy and for waiting two weeks after his regiment had been garrisoned in Paris to call. (In fact Berlioz had watched and enjoyed the grand progress into Paris of Uncle Félix and his troops.) Marmion set about his task by visiting Alphonse Robert, who told him flatly that Harriet was ruined. On 9 February, he went to the Théâtre Chantereine to see for himself. Appalled by the modesty of the hall, he was nevertheless taken by her "remarkable traits and her exquisite sensitivity of voice and nobility of gesture." And, he reported frankly, he had little hope of dissuading his self-centered nephew. "It would be folly to expect that Hector might make the least sacrifice to the will and scruples of his family."[63] He would attempt to see Miss Smithson, though, if he could find a good interpreter.

On 14 February, having had the expected veto from his family, Berlioz went to a lawyer named Guyot and signed the papers necessary to instruct a La Côte counterpart, Just Pion, to deliver the first of three legal documents needed to marry without the consent of one's parents: the *sommations respectueuses,* or formal requests not to be disinherited. Pion refused to figure in shaming the Berlioz family, however, so Berlioz was forced to beg Edouard Rocher (who had returned to live in La Côte) to take care of the matter. The law required the signed documents to be hand-carried to the notary and thence to the parents; mail was out of the question. Rocher, after no little vacillation, delivered himself to the notary Simian with the first *sommation*; he and his family had concluded that the best method of opposing Berlioz was legally, without underhanded dealings.

O f all the periods of strain between Berlioz and his family, the next eight months are surely the saddest: 1833, indeed, is a year of little artistic progress and enormous domestic unrest. It is tempting to sympathize with his view that the love awakened five years before, rekindled in Rome (encouraged, it seems, by Mme Vernet, when she allowed Harriet's name to slip into a discussion of Shakespeare, and Berlioz was promptly seized by an attack of nerves),[64] and now finally shared by the Irish actress was the stuff of an ideal artists' marriage. His family and intimates—Liszt, especially—might more honorably have tried to be supportive, or at least less hostile. Yet for the most part their actions seem honorable enough, and a host of their reservations proved, in the end, well founded.

There was abundant evidence to support the view that the world of the vagabond actor was exactly what his friends and relations imagined it to be: "sordid business," a half step removed from the circus. In Bristol, for example, Harriet had played in repertoire with Mme Saqui, who danced "her much-admired Pas-Seul, on the Single Rope" and went on to thrill Parisian audiences with similar feats at the age of seventy-five.[65]

Harriet was for all intents and purposes, as Alphonse Robert and Uncle Félix had reported, ruined. At one point Dr. Berlioz offered the bizarre prophecy that his son would end up a gambler, which did not happen, then

FIGURE 5.9 Nanci Berlioz.

suggested he would finish by leaving Miss Smithson for another, which did. The most poignant and in some respects convincing argument against the pairing came in April, when Rocher presented his "cher Hector" with the reasons why he would deliver no further *sommations:*

> You are called to an illustrious career in an art which it seems must develop greatly under the influence of your genius. And you sacrifice this entire future to a deadly love which halts you in your course, strikes you with indifference, turns you from your true destiny, and makes you the unhappiest of men.[66]

Berlioz would brook none of it. He threatened not to open any further mail from La Côte and sharply rebuked Rocher: "You alone have done me more harm than a host of others."[67] There would not be another letter to Rocher for more than two years. The break in the correspondence with Nanci lasts from 5 February 1833 to 21 February 1836, except for a brief, self-satisfied note in October describing Harriet's virginal condition; with his father, the interruption is from 23 February 1833 to 6 May 1835, except for a note announcing the birth of Louis. Even Uncle Félix is cast aside, and he leaves Paris without once visiting the newlyweds. What is certain is that Berlioz's unpredictable behavior compounded the agony for all concerned.

This state of affairs came to a head on the afternoon of 1 March, when Harriet broke her leg while descending from her cabriolet. Not waiting for the assistance of her chambermaid, she caught her skirt, turned her foot on the step, and broke both bones of her leg. Her cries of agony lasted for two days, and it was feared that she might be permanently lame. Marmion and Alphonse Robert, whose dinner invitations had so far been ignored, decided to call on Berlioz and persuade him to share his grief with them. But Berlioz held back: "You would engage me in a conversation that I don't want to hear."[68]

In fact the accident was causing Berlioz his share of second thoughts. He wrote Rocher to discontinue the *sommations:* "I no longer need to be married. If Harriet absolutely wants it later . . . "[69] Within two weeks he had changed his mind again, but by then he had learned of Rocher's disinclination to be further involved in the affair; he would need to find another way to present the remaining documents. By mid-April it was clear that the second *sommation* had never been delivered. He booked passage on a mail coach to carry it home himself, then reconsidered that, too. The effect of such a visit on a respectable family of La Côte-St.-André, where "the houses are made of glass and daily life is open to view,"[70] would have been more shattering even than the arrival of the *sommations*. Dr. Berlioz had already written directly to Miss Smithson not to count on an inheritance: he would rather sell his property, he said, than leave his eldest son an estate where she might live. Nanci filled mailbags with pompous and unflattering analyses of the situation; only nineteen-year-old Adèle, a "good and dignified child,"[71] seems to have wanted to understand and serve as confidante. At length the Justice of the Peace in La Tour du Pin, M. Charavel, agreed to deliver the remaining documents. The third and last arrived on 5 June; if there were no further legal response, the couple could be married at the beginning of September.

The agony was compounded by the shortage of money. Going with Harriet to England would cost Berlioz his only assured livelihood, the annual 3,000 francs from the *prix de Rome*. Suicide seemed more than once the only satisfactory resolution to his trials, but, as on previous occasions, the need to live for his art reasserted itself in due course. His ambition had not gone unchallenged by the brilliant success of Meyerbeer's *Robert le diable:* the issues of the new style were clear, and perhaps he, too, might secure a libretto from Scribe and outdo Meyerbeer. Another Shakespearean play was tempting him in any case, the comedy *Much Ado About Nothing*. In early 1833 he prepared a scenario for a Beatrice-and-Benedict opera, an idea resurrected in different guise in 1852 and again in the early 1860s.[72]

Despite the hiatus in his composition, he and Liszt were for the moment the most fashionable artists about town, the "curiosities of the musical season."[73] D'Ortigue describes a *séance* in a piano showroom where Liszt erupted at the keyboard, gazing the while at Berlioz, "his echo"; afterward they embraced, and Berlioz cried "O mon cher sublime, how I love you." (Legouvé recounts a rather similar scene.) Liszt's Vauxhall concert of 12 March, to benefit the poor of the second *arrondissement,* included the *Francs-Juges* overture, conducted by Girard and played by the Opéra orchestra. It was the first of their joint appearances, the beginning of the public's asso-

FIGURE 5.10 Adèle Berlioz.

ciation of the two lion-maned young visionaries—the confluence of what many came to believe were the brains behind The Artwork of the Future.

Harriet Smithson had been in rehearsal for a benefit performance at the time of her accident, and it now fell to Berlioz to see the project through: her astronomical medical expenses gave the project added urgency. He did much of the correspondence in her behalf (letters survive in his hand with her signature), and he engineered an honorarium from the royal household of 200 francs, though this was far less than Harriet had once been accustomed to receive. He was less successful still at helping her secure a permanent charter for her troupe.

The performance to benefit Miss Smithson was announced for 2 April at the Salle Favart, where her ill-fated company, now in shambles, had begun its season. The best actors and musicians in Paris agreed to perform, with musical selections set between the acts of Racine's *Athalie* and a vaudeville called *Les Cabinets particuliers*. Liszt and Chopin offered a piano duo, Urhan a work for viola *d'amore*, and Huerta a guitar solo. Only Paganini declined to play, and the press noted his absence, grumbling, "It seems that M. Paganini has undertaken the immutable resolve never to break *his* leg."[74] (On the occasion of Paganini's recital at the Opéra, 14 April, Berlioz responded in kind; he skipped the program, pleading a "violent indisposition.") The receipts of the Smithson benefit, in excess of 6,000 francs, were put against Harriet's most pressing debts.

Berlioz suffered a setback of his own shortly afterward. Habeneck and the Société des Concerts had agreed to play his *envoi* from Rome, the *Intrata di Rob-Roy MacGregor*, and at the concert on 14 April it failed roundly. Why that should have been so is not clear. It is true that the work is formally diffuse, but certainly no more so than the *Francs-Juges* overture, which enjoyed its fair share of popularity. *Rob-Roy* is a bright work, brimming with rhythmic and melodic invention, the first of his compositions to adumbrate the lively Italianate style that reaches its zenith with the Roman carnival scene from *Benvenuto Cellini*. There are other remarkable effects that foreshadow later practice: juxtaposed against the $\frac{6}{8}$ toward the end of the overture, for example, is figuration in $\mathbb{C}$. The Scottishness of the subject matter is expressed in the first theme, where the tune is based on Robert Burns's *Scots wha' hae wi' Wallace bled* (ex. 5.3a).[75] (Note the prominent "Scotch snaps" in Berlioz's version.) Two of the melodic gambits, indeed, would soon be borrowed for the first movement of *Harold en Italie*. Both are first stated by English horn in *Rob-Roy*, by the solo viola in *Harold* (exs. 5.3b–c). More important yet is the extravagant orchestration of the melody's second appearance, which, with only light refinement (including the addition of the canonic echoes), constitutes one of the most exceptional passages in *Harold* (ex. 5.3d).

"Long and diffuse," writes Berlioz in the one line devoted to *Rob-Roy* in his *Mémoires*, "performed . . . in Paris and very badly received, I destroyed it immediately after the concert."[76] That is not quite true, for he reused its best material, in the same key and with many of the same details, several months later when he began *Harold en Italie*. *Rob-Roy* developed into the first movement of *Harold* not so differently from the way any other work improved as it evolved. His dismissal of the overture as worthless is off the mark.

There was a certain improvement in Berlioz's financial standing in the spring of 1833. He had been able to convince the Ministry of Commerce and Public Works, responsible for the Department of Fine Arts, to continue his pension on the assurance that his trip to Germany would be made in 1834. Liszt was arranging the *Symphonie fantastique* for piano solo, and sales of the published edition promised to be excellent. In April or May Berlioz was engaged by an ambitious new literary journal, *L'Europe littéraire*, published by Victor Bohain and Alphonse Royer. The pay of 50 centimes per published line of text was good, especially as most of what Berlioz eventually published there had already been written. Moreover, the paper counted among its correspondents many of the best Parisian writers— Nodier, Dumas, Musset, Heine, Balzac, Janin, not to mention the music critics Castil-Blaze and Henri Blanchard—and among its backers some of the most important figures in French commerce and banking. The affiliation offered innumerable opportunities to meet and discuss issues of Romantic art with the writers on the staff and turned out to be one of his most extended associations with "capitalists."[77]

His main duty for the short time the journal remained solvent was to produce that spring a series of musical *soirées* sponsored by the paper and given in their building in the Chaussée d'Antin. This series was conceived

a. *Scots wha' hae wi' Wallace bled:*

Rob-Roy, mm. 10–19:

b. *Rob-Roy*, mm. 170–73:

Harold en Italie, movt. I, mm. 173–76:

c. *Rob-Roy*, mm. 260–63:

Harold en Italie, movt. I, mm. 38–41:

EXAMPLE 5.3 *Intrata di Rob-Roy MacGregor.*

d. *Rob-Roy*, mm. 301–04:

EXAMPLE 5.3 (*continued*).

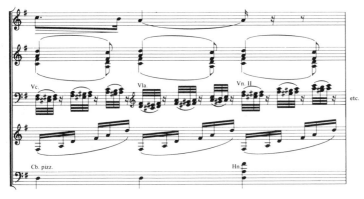

Harold en Italie, movt. I, mm. 73–76:

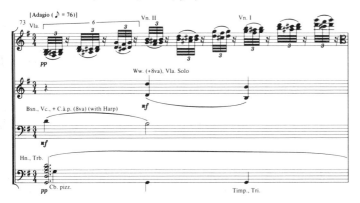

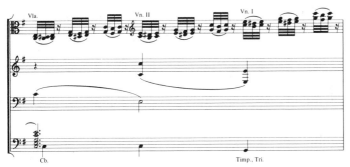

EXAMPLE 5.3 *(continued).*

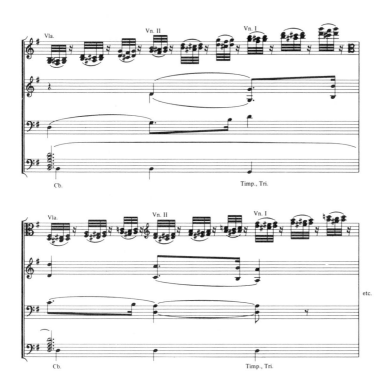

EXAMPLE 5.3 (*continued*).

along the lines of Fétis's *concerts historiques,* which had been sponsored by his *Revue musicale.* At least two of the four concerts given in the series were primarily Berliozian events, featuring his friends as performers, his own compositions, and arrangements he prepared especially for the occasion. (He was probably in charge of the other two, as well, though information on them is more scarce.) The first, on 2 May, was a lavish *soirée:* on the program were the three middle movements of the *Fantastique,* both early overtures, the song *Le Pêcheur* from the *Mélologue,* a guitar solo by Trinitario Huerta (just then setting the capital ablaze with his own brand of virtuosity), and a brass quintet apparently by Jacques Struntz. The concerts rapidly evolved—*faute d'argent,* I should think—into more intimate events; the most interesting was the last, on Thursday, 6 June. Here the program included the two recent songs *La Captive* and *Le Pêcheur,* sung by Boulanger; "six airs"—almost surely the Irish Melodies—sung by Stéphen de La Madelaine; another guitar solo, this time by Sor; a sextet played by Narcisse Girard and his friends; and two hunting songs arranged by Berlioz for ten male singers and, possibly, the players from the sextet. These lush choruses of vagabondage were *Le Chasseur de chamois* ("Sur les Alpes, quel délice"), of which he had written to Mme Le Sueur from Rome, and the first of two performances of Weber's *Lützow's wilde Jagd,* op. 42, no. 2, called in French the *Chanson des Hussards de la mort.* Two fragments of the Alpine song have been preserved in the autograph score of the *Symphonie fantastique;* Liszt uses the same melody in one of his *Fleurs mélodiques des Alpes.* Schlesinger's publications of *La Captive* and the excerpts from *Le Retour à la vie* seem to have been timed to profit from the *Europe littéraire* concerts.

Berlioz's talents as an entrepreneur did not go unappreciated in the competitive world of music publishing, where journals regularly tried to outdo one another in premiums offered to subscribers. Later he would be involved with concerts sponsored by other journals, including *Le Ménestrel* (1834), the *Revue et Gazette musicale* (1840), and *La France musicale* (1840). But he published only two articles in *L'Europe littéraire:* a redaction of his "Lettre d'un enthousiaste" and a two-part article on the Rome-prize competition, later adopted for chapters 22 and 23 of the *Mémoires.* The journal limped on through February 1834, but without Berlioz, who by December of 1833 had become music critic for the much healthier journal *Le Rénovateur.* It is this latter appointment that should be reckoned his first full-scale post as music critic.

His compositional, or pre-compositional, activity of 1833 was expended on the planning of any number of dramatic projects, none of which came to fruition. Ferrand had never delivered the libretto for *Le Dernier Jour du monde,* so Berlioz managed in June to persuade Emile Deschamps and Jules de St.-Félix to fashion one, providing them with an autograph scenario:[78]

> A prophet, a sinner, choruses of religious men, choruses of sinners, choruses of angels announcing the arrival of the supreme judge, choruses of the dead risen from their tombs ... First the prophet announcing to the believers that his predictions are about to come true ... Grave prayer of the believers, begging the supreme judge not to confound them with the pious. Solo of the sinners, voluptuous and orgiastic scene interrupted by the call of the celestial trumpet and the voice of the archangels summoning the dead. Final universal chorus.

But this idea, too, was refused, that August, by the Opéra. It may not have helped his chances much that Berlioz had behaved boisterously at the premiere of Cherubini's *Ali-Baba* on 22 July.

In honor of the *trois glorieuses*—annual celebration of the July 1830 revolution having become, while Berlioz was gone, a national holiday—the government was planning to reconstruct a statue of Napoleon at the top of the column in the Place Vendôme. The festivities included an outdoor concert conducted by Habeneck, for which Berlioz rearranged the last two movements of his *Scène héroïque* for two choruses and a wind band of 250. The "new" work was rehearsed in the studio of the painter Ciceri (on the grounds of the Conservatoire) on 22 July and twice thereafter. At the performance on the 28th, however, the candles ran out before it could be played, and instead the concert closed with patriotic hymns everybody knew by heart:

the *Marseillaise* and *La Parisienne*. (Plans to repeat the concert at the Opéra were short-lived.) Indoors, Berlioz had found Habeneck's program moving, especially the patriotic chorus that closes act II of *Guillaume Tell*. Out-of-doors, it was less successful: "Music is decidedly not made for the streets"[79]—a sentiment he was to repeat on hearing Tilmant's outdoor performance of his own *Symphonie funèbre* in 1846.

It may have been in conjunction with this festivity—or perhaps when he was working on the *Fête musicale funèbre* in 1834—that Berlioz penned into his sketchbook a surprisingly good poem on the death of Napoleon, which begins as follows:

> Inclinez-vous, brillants faisceaux,
> Drapeaux, voilez vos couleurs éclatantes
> Soldats, baissez vos armes triomphantes
>> O France, mère des héros,
>>> Pleure
>>> Pleure
>> Napoléon n'est plus!

> (Bow, brilliant torches,
> Flags, furl your bright colors,
> Soldiers, lower your triumphant armaments:
> O France, Mother of Heroes, weep:
> Napoleon is no more.)

So far as we know, he never composed the music, but the sketch is one of our first examples of Berlioz's fashioning his own texts.

He visited Harriet each evening in her rooms in the Hôtel du Congrès on the rue de Rivoli. She was convalescing slowly, nursed by her "damned hunchback" sister, who wished she were strong enough to throw Berlioz out the window. After four months as an invalid, Harriet was just beginning to walk again. She had wanted to go back to London to recover, but had fallen into "absolute destitution," as she wrote to the royal family in a plea for cash. Berlioz, meanwhile, sensing things coming to an uncertain head, at one point arranged for Hiller to be executor of his manuscripts in the event of some *malheur définitif*. Early in August a violent incident in Harriet's rooms led to almost precisely that conclusion.

The marriage license, it transpired, had to be secured thirty days before the wedding, now planned for the first week of September. The couple had returned triumphantly home with the document, only to see Harriet's sister snatch and destroy it. Harriet concluded, for her part, that perhaps they should indeed wait a few more months. At this point Berlioz swallowed a bottle of opiates, then had second thoughts of his own. A dose of ipecac induced him to vomit for two hours, and the whole experience left him "near death," he imagined, for three days. Harriet was confused more than ever by the incident and in any case frantic with worry, but still declined to accompany him to the *mairie* for a new license.

And so Berlioz decided to leave after all for Berlin—in the company of a "poor young girl of eighteen years,"[80] trained in music, escaped "by happenstance" into his arms from the clutches of a villain who had kept her enslaved since childhood. By 30 August Berlioz had his passport in hand and was ready to leave. The girl, he imagined, could sing in his choruses.

It is difficult to know what to make of this silly turn of events. I think the lovers had fallen prey to outward declarations of their subconscious fears; surely much of it was staged, or imagined. But it was by no means the last showdown between the proud actress and the passionate composer.

This particular crisis was resolved on 3 September, when Harriet came to his lodgings to fetch and accompany him to city hall. Bans were published for a wedding in thirty days. (The young girl was left to the care of the critic Jules Janin, who may have arranged the whole affair thinking that the diversion would do his colleague some good.) Berlioz and Harriet spent the next four weeks trying to establish a semblance of financial footing, soliciting the aid of, among others, Vigny and his mistress, Marie Dorval; Dorval quite graciously arranged to help with another benefit concert to pay off Harriet's debts.

*H*arriet Constance Smithson was married to Louis-Hector Berlioz on Thursday, 3 October, at the British embassy, before a chaplain named Luscombe. The ceremony followed both the English and the French customs. Liszt, Robert Cooper, and the composer Jacques Strunz served as witnesses, as Hiller and Heine stood by. Berlioz appeared to be calm; Harriet cried tenderly. Hiller later recalled the ceremony as having been subdued and rather sad.[81]

For their wedding trip they went to a small house in Vincennes rented for the month with money lent by Thomas Gounet. (Harriet had installed herself there a few days before the wedding.) Harriet's sister finally left them to themselves—she disappeared from their lives altogether, probably to England, where she died in 1836—and there were no servants to interrupt them; this was almost certainly the first time they were ever alone together for a period of more than a few minutes. As neither of them knew how to cook, they brought a wedding dinner to the house from a local restaurant. He found her pure—"Vierge, tout ce qu'il y a de plus vierge"[82]—and was quick to tell his intimates, Liszt in particular, of this unexpected development. The effort of the wedding-night responsibilities, he coyly wrote, left him exhausted.

Berlioz's father assumed the marriage had taken place three months before, just after the last *sommation*. In his *Livre de raison* he noted: "married, despite his parents, to Harriet Smithson in July 1833." Only Adèle shared her brother's delight; he responded by sending her a lithograph of Harriet's portrait, but instructed the postmistress to deliver it only to his sister and told Adèle to keep it hidden.

FIGURE 5.11 Certificate of marriage.

They dwelt in Vincennes for two weeks, sustained by Gounet's 300 francs. After the first weekend, Berlioz returned to Paris on daily errands, among the first of these a trip on 6 October to hear Hugo read his new play, *Marie Tudor*. They enjoyed their rustic idyll, walking every day in the lovely gardens of Vincennes and enjoying the excellent autumn weather.

On 16 October, they returned to the apartment in the rue Neuve-St.-Marc, their home for six more months. Among the early well-wishers were such friends as Gounet, d'Ortigue, and Alphonse Robert and their spouses, who came for tea and sometimes dinner. The newlyweds made their own calls from time to time, when Harriet enjoyed signing guestbooks as Mme Berlioz-Smithson; occasionally they went together to the Opéra. Harriet and, especially, her husband drew closer to Vigny, both for the poet's useful relationship with Marie Dorval and for the promise of future collaboration: after he finished *Chatterton*, Vigny indicated, he might well be induced to write something for Harriet, or possibly even to collaborate on an opera. The closeness of the relationship came to cause them all some discomfort when public reaction to *Chatterton* was at issue.

Their future plans varied: one day they would imagine going to Germany by winter; then they would dream of giving joint drama-and-music events in Paris. In December, Berlioz went so far as to try to enlist Spontini's aid in helping his wife secure an appointment in Berlin. There is a certain bittersweet quality to their bliss, apparent in the correspondence of the period. Harriet was reticent, perhaps frightened, about things in general: Berlioz often uses words like "timid" and "dignified" to describe her. There is frequent reference to weeping together.

The presentation ceremony for the *prix de Rome* that 12 October included, as usual, an evaluation of the works submitted from Rome the previous year. Of Berlioz's *Quartetto e coro* the committee complained that it "is not, properly speaking, a complete work; it seems to be no more than a preparation. In this sort of prelude, we find to our regret little melody, few firm ideas, a pretentious format, a total absence of that sentiment of unification" . . . and so on. Concerning *Rob-Roy* and its failure with the Société des Concerts they observed merely that "the author having been judged by the public, it is not up to us to comment."[83] The newspapers spoke of these "severe remonstrances," but there is no evidence that Berlioz attended the ceremony or that he much cared.

The Berlioz-Smithson benefit planned with the assistance of Vigny and Mme Dorval was set, after a failed attempt to secure the Odéon, for 17 November at the Théâtre-Italien (playing in the Salle Favart). Like the performance of the preceding April, it would be an unwieldy combination of spoken drama—in two languages—and concert. The program as announced consisted of the first act of Dumas's *Antony* with Mme Dorval, the fourth act of *Hamlet* with Harriet, and a complete concert: Weber's *Konzertstück* with Liszt as soloist, the entire *Fantastique,* the *Sardanapale* cantata with added explosion, the *Francs-Juges* overture, and the Weber hunting chorus heard earlier in the year at one of the *soirées* of *L'Europe littéraire.*

Put simply, this benefit was a disaster, one of the debacles of Berlioz's career. Too much had been scheduled, for one thing, and the bits and pieces had not been properly timed. Dumas and Marie Dorval had arranged a claque for *Antony;* the English community was disinclined to come to the theater on a Sunday evening to cheer the rival heroine. The performance was an hour late getting under way, as one of the actresses waited for her dress to dry. Harriet was still stiff and uncomfortable, her celebrated mime and graceful carriage overshadowed by the undeniable vestiges of a limp. The house musicians were resentful of the extra duty; in any event they were contracted only until midnight, and the concert did not even begin until 11:45. And Berlioz tried to conduct, with the result that the *incendie* in *Sardanapale* fell apart once more.

Eugène Sauzay was sitting in the front desk of violins—he erroneously recalled the evening as the occasion of the first performance of the *Fantastique*—and observed the misadventure firsthand. Berlioz maintained his composure well, he said, though the public had become restless and noisy, and members of the orchestra were shouting "enough." By the beginning of the symphony, only the paid extras were left, a few strings and one trombone player. Meanwhile the house musicians, who had slipped out during the Weber chorus, discovered the basement exit blocked by a harpist and her harp. There was general commotion both above and below stairs, with Berlioz crying "Ayez pitié de moi!" and promising to repeat the concert in a week. Those left in the audience were his partisans, who roared back, "Au Conservatoire: une autre fois."[84]

For all that, the benefit cleared some profit, something on the order of 2,500 badly needed francs, and the government sent its customary gratuity of 200 francs. It is not clear just how far in debt Harriet Smithson actually was, but the amount of money applied to its retirement in 1833 was now approaching 10,000 francs—an enormous sum by any measure—and yet she was still unable to pay her dressmaker's note.[85]

Berlioz was as good as his word; though it took some doing, he engaged the Salle du Conservatoire, an excellent orchestra, and the services of Narcisse Girard for a concert on 22 December. This time the *Symphonie fantastique* was well played. The public, however, was beginning to tire of it, and d'Ortigue for one admonished that "he forget for a time his *Symphonie fantastique*; posterity will return to it. May he yield himself to other inspirations."[86] More interesting were the first performances of the overture written in Nice, *Le Roi Lear,* and two new songs, *Le Paysan breton* ("The peasant from Brittany," probably with piano accompaniment) and the *Romance de Marie Tudor,* a setting of the lullaby from Hugo's play. Liszt—who, perhaps not coincidentally, also wrote a work to the same Hugo text—appeared again at the piano, this time in less trying circumstances.

By the new year, Harriet suspected she was with child.

*B*erlioz's return to composition began slowly with the *Marie Tudor* song, now lost (perhaps buried somewhere in *Benvenuto Cellini*), and *Le Jeune Pâtre breton,* a miniature that rivals *La Captive* in its grace. Even discounting the time that must have been consumed with his pursuit of Harriet, he had wasted a good deal of effort on dramatic scenarios that did not pan out. Two others were afoot at the turn of the year: a rewriting of portions of *Les Francs-Juges* called *Le Cri de guerre du Brisgaw* (The war cry of the Breisgau), with new words by Gounet and incorporating the new song of the Brittany woodman, and a dramatic setting called *Les Brigands* to a text after Schiller's *Die Räuber* (as was Verdi's *I Masnadieri*). His domestic responsibilities, notably including the child on the way, offered strong inducement to get down to serious work. His long-dormant career blossomed now in extraordinary fashion, with diligent labor and a clear understanding of his priorities leading to almost invariably successful works. The remainder of the decade would see his most sustained period of accomplishment, beginning with the viola concerto that became *Harold en Italie* and the selection of the life of Benvenuto Cellini as the subject for his next opera.

Although the long saga of disagreement with his family was drawing to an end, Berlioz had little hope of financial support from La Côte—except, of course, for the inheritance he would someday receive. He could count on two more years of his annual pension of 3,000 francs, if he could convince the authorities of his firm intention to go to Germany. (He had already collected his first payment for 1834, assuring the bureaucrats that he was on the verge of departure.) But his financial solvency was threatened now by the need to find a suitable family residence.

Late in January Paganini, perhaps embarrassed by his failure to appear at the Smithson benefit, came to ask Berlioz for a new concerto for viola, with a view toward performing it during his upcoming London season. They agreed on a work for chorus, orchestra, and solo viola, tentatively to be called *Les Derniers Instants de Marie Stuart*. Berlioz rushed to place announcements of the commission in the press[87]—too quickly, as it turned out, because the work emerged in radically different guise. It became his principal concern of the new year, taking flight from the wreckage of *Rob-Roy*.

In early April, on the 8th or 9th, the couple moved to a four-room furnished cottage in Montmartre at 10, rue St.-Denis,[88] a half hour from central Paris. There was a garden with a ravishing view of the plain of St.-Denis, and the cost, at 70 francs per month, was low. It was, in short, a hermitage, far enough from the rigors of the city to allow Berlioz the quiet to compose, an appropriate retreat from the social calls of which they had begun to weary. Harriet, who imagined herself to be in temporary semi-retirement, was delighted to be alone with her husband and to accompany him on long walks in the country. Berlioz found the new life pleasant indeed; its only drawback, he noted, was the constant prattle of the nightingales. The work for Paganini evolved easily from a two-part concerto into the four-movement dramatic symphony *Harold en Italie*, a work conceived in domestic bliss and completed in the tranquility of their new home. So, too, were a host of other projects brought toward completion in the spring and summer of 1834. It was a time of conspicuous achievement, as Harriet approached her confinement.

His best hope of assured income seemed to lie, however, in his work for all manner of periodical publications. By 1834 he was writing regular weekly articles for *Le Rénovateur*: novelettes, reviews of the new season of the Société des Concerts, a study of the Müller Quartet from Brunswick and its performances of the Beethoven repertoire, an extensive article on the production of Mozart's *Don Giovanni* that had opened in March (as *Don Juan*, with French text by Emile Deschamps and Castil-Blaze). He also wrote a life of Gluck. This was first intended for a journal called *Le Publiciste*,[89] but was instead sold to Maurice Schlesinger's *Gazette musicale*, with the result that by the end of April, Berlioz was writing regular reviews there. The *Gazette musicale* was in the process of succeeding Fétis's *Revue musicale* as the most influential of the Paris music journals; the *Revue musicale* declined quickly after Fétis moved to Brussels in 1833, and eventually his magazine was absorbed into Schlesinger's paper, which by 1836 bore the name *Revue et Gazette musicale*.

But only a portion of the work for which Berlioz had been commissioned appeared in those papers. He had agreed, for instance, to do biographies for an *Encyclopédie du XIXe siècle,* which appears never to have been published. Then progress on *Harold* was interrupted by an urgent request in April to summarize his recollections of the Italian adventure in *Italie pittoresque,* one of those lavish illustrated publications of the time delivered to subscribers in installments; this finally appeared in 1836, though Berlioz's work had been submitted long before. He also sold short *romances*—*Les Champs* and *Je crois en vous*—to fashion magazines, and these were sufficiently successful that he was asked to do more of the same. There is no question that Berlioz was recognized now for the fluidity of his pen, or that his opinions were widely deemed a marketable commodity. The pay raised his monthly income to a decent level for an artist of merit, something on the order of 400–500 francs each month.

Otherwise his creative work went on without much bother from the outside world. He and Harriet were essentially untouched, for example, by the Paris repercussions of the Lyon uprisings that April. There were impromptu dinners for those who could make the trip to Montmartre; among these was a fine picnic with Vigny, Antoni Deschamps, Hiller, Liszt, and "Chopinetto mio," who had been summoned with light-hearted invitations in fractured Italian.

Berlioz also continued to negotiate on Harriet's behalf with various enterprises and fledgling theatrical concerns. The most promising was a new venture by Narcisse Girard and his acquaintances, who had secured a nine-year privilege on the Théâtre Ventadour. They would open a Théâtre-Nautique, so called because it was to have a large basin where naval maneuvers could be simulated, to give "nautical and other sorts of pantomime, mixed with dancing."[90] Berlioz briefly envisaged composing a work for the opening, a vehicle for Harriet; she was engaged by the company in June and expected to make her debut in October.

During those months he also attracted the attention of the powerful Bertin family, publishers of the *Journal des Débats*—one of the two or three most important daily papers in France. It was a significant development in his career when Edouard Bertin, who was on the governing committee of the Opéra,[91] offered to intercede on his behalf with Véron. In May the talk was of a five-act *Hamlet;* then the discussions turned to using Hugo's *Notre Dame de Paris* for a grand opera—though it was known that Hugo loathed musical settings of his works. (This project was left to the elder Bertin's daughter, Louise, and would involve Berlioz intimately before it was done.) Within the year, Berlioz had found with their paper the best appointment he would ever have, and the Bertins did indeed clear the way for an assault on the Opéra.

It was in this context that Berlioz settled on the autobiography of the sixteenth-century Florentine sculptor Benvenuto Cellini as the source of a comic libretto. He seems to have been introduced to the idea, and possibly the autobiography, by Alfred de Vigny; in Florence he had admired the famous statue of Perseus. Berlioz drafted his own scenario and probably a portion of the text, as was his habit, and submitted it to the Opéra-Comique, then asked Vigny to do the words. But Vigny was preoccupied with *Chatterton* and thus passed the work on to a writer named Léon de Wailly; Wailly subsequently asked Auguste Barbier, one of Berlioz's friends from the Roman days, to assist. The team was at work by summer. The Opéra-Comique declined their effort—fearing the composer's personal eccentricities, it appears, more than the music he might write—but Berlioz by that time had already composed the central tavern scene with the goldsmith's chorus: "the first scene, the *chant des ciseleurs de Florence,* in which they are carried away with themselves to the last degree."[92] He was also well embarked on another scene, Teresa's first aria, later removed from the score but reused in the *Rêverie et Caprice* for solo violin.

The entire summer was devoted to frantic preparation for the autumn concerts. (The Société des Concerts had declined his offer of *La Tempête* for their forthcoming season.) In addition to *Harold en Italie,* which was finished and dated on 22 June and dedicated to Humbert Ferrand, he orchestrated three of his earlier songs—*La Captive, Le Jeune Pâtre breton,* and (from the *Mélodies irlandaises*) *La Belle Voyageuse*—and composed a fourth—*Sara la baigneuse.* These would constitute the *partie vocale* of his concerts.

Harriet's pregnancy was difficult from the first; the severity of her morning sickness had caused them both alarm. At thirty-four she was old to be having a first child. She was, moreover, too heavy and found herself altogether unprepared for the repeated episodes of aches and pains to which she was prone. Neither she nor her husband had acquired any expertise in running a household and supervising servants; now, because she would be returning to work soon after the birth, they needed a nurse. The issue of the nurse terrified her: she could not bear the thought of having her child nourished outside the home and did not know where or how to look for a resident wet nurse. The English neighbors and Alphonse Robert and his wife succeeded in allaying only some of her fears.

The labor and delivery were difficult, too, lasting some forty hours. But all was for the best: a handsome boy was born on 14 August. The proud godfather Thomas Gounet looked on as the baby was baptized later in the month, "not Hercule, Jean-Baptiste, César, Alexandre, or Magloire—but a simple Louis."[93]

Chapter Six

Affairs of State
(1834–40)

he baby pleased his parents a good deal more than either of them had expected. Within a few weeks they were immersed in the start of the new season of concerts and theater, but for the moment they took keen pleasure in the delights of parenthood, their thoughts well removed from the annual, relentless quickening of pace just beginning to be felt downtown. Berlioz was proud to identify some family resemblances: Louis had reddish hair, an aquiline nose, and "pointed cartilage on his ears, like mine."[1] He was a well-formed lad and strong, prone to nocturnal lustiness. The late summer and early fall were blissful, the family as close as it would ever be. A spirit of geniality, in turn, pervades the first sketches for *Benvenuto Cellini* and the excellent additions to Berlioz's growing corpus of songs.

There were gifts for the infant from La Côte-St.-André. Adèle, who had been charmed from the beginning by the idea of Harriet, took seriously her responsibilities as Louis's godmother. The family was now for all intents and purposes reconciled with its Parisian branch, and its members grew still closer as the adult children built stable lives for themselves and began, in their turn, to inherit responsibility for the care of their aging parents. But only Adèle was ever to know Harriet and Louis intimately; Berlioz's mother never saw either of them, and the good doctor met Louis a single time, when he was nearly grown.

Harriet and the nurse, Marie, enjoyed showing Louis off, particularly to the English populace, during their promenades through the shaded walkways of Montmartre. They liked to accompany Berlioz halfway down the hill each morning, then be waiting there on the rocks when he returned in late afternoon. It was an idyllic existence that could be of only fleeting duration and had vanished altogether before Louis was three months old. Journalistic duties called his father to town several evenings each week; it was expected that Harriet would soon be appearing at the Théâtre-Nautique. An already delicate balancing of the two careers was complicated by the need for both

FIGURE 6.1 Berlioz's house in Montmartre.

parents to wend their ways up Montmartre every night, a journey exhausting by foot and expensive by cabriolet. After six months in Montmartre, the family and servants settled that October into a modest, unfurnished flat at number 34, rue de Londres.

The rue de Londres is north of the rue St.-Lazare in what was then the new *quartier* of St.-George. Above the center of town and west of the theaters, it was at the time a proper and refined area of apartment buildings, acceptable for a composer of stature, though a far cry from the regal conditions under which Rossini lived in Passy and the great townhouses where the stars of the Opéra liked to dwell. In many ways the establishment of the household in the rue de Londres is indicative of Berlioz's good, if not quite glamorous, standing in the field. So, too, had his other residences been appropriate to his lifestyle: he had spent his first Paris years with the rest of the student population on the Left Bank and in the Cité; later he had lived near the boulevards as a fashionable dandy. The countrified life of Montmartre had been good for his composition, but in the end it was inappropriate to his growing responsibilities and enterprises.

But for a brief return to Montmartre in 1835, Berlioz spent the rest of his career within a few blocks of the rue de Londres. The rue de Provence, where he lived with Marie Recio, is a few streets south; the rue Blanche, where Harriet spent her declining years, lies just behind the church of the Trinité. Berlioz lived his last thirteen years a bit farther north, first in the rue Vintimille, then at 4, rue de Calais; these streets intersect at what is now known as the square Berlioz.

Acquiring furniture befitting a professional couple and, more urgently, their important guests became a matter that concerned them for several more years. Their monthly rent did not include firewood, and the need to keep apartment and family warm during the winter—one of the many aspects of household management with which neither of them had prior experience—further tried an already marginal budget. They struggled, amateurishly, to keep domestic accounts.

Berlioz's annual cycle of professional activity now became remarkably routine, as assiduous effort every spring and summer yielded new compositions to be presented in November and December. He devoted his autumns to the administrative and technical preparations for his concerts. Negotiating with publishers, on the other hand, went on the year round. Berlioz was dealing in the mid-1830s with three major Paris publishers—Maurice Schlesinger, Simon Richault, and Adolphe Catelin—and although he did not intend to countenance publication of his symphonies until after he had conducted them in Germany, most of the rest of his works were published in relatively short order.

The journalism, too, was a year-round affair with little interruption, a particularly taxing obligation during the period when he worked for three papers at once. Berlioz wrote an average of one major article each week during these years and was surely responsible for hundreds of the unsigned bits of news and gossip that appeared beneath such headings as "Nouvelles" or "Chronique Musicale." On top of all this came the more substantive pieces: the novellas, the autobiographical essays, and protracted analyses of Mozart, Beethoven, Gluck, and such individual masterpieces as Rossini's *Guillaume Tell* and Meyerbeer's *Les Huguenots*. There were more than a few invitations from less august sorts of journals, those that published bagatelles for the salons of elegant women and the delectation of well-to-do teenage girls. He had composed *Les Champs,* the previous April, to one such commission; in September the *romance Je crois en vous* appeared in a fashion magazine called *Le Protée*. Soon this charming little song was reused for *Benvenuto Cellini,* where it serves as the *Ariette d'Arlequin* in the carnival scene.

Harriet began her rehearsals at the Théâtre-Nautique in October. Their season of mediocre ballet-pantomimes had opened 10 June with bastardized mockings-up of *Guillaume Tell* and E. T. A. Hoffmann's *Les Ondines*. It continued with *Le Nouveau Robinson* and a *chinoiserie* called *Chao-Kang,* none of which curried much but scorn from the critics. (Berlioz did his best to be supportive by writing frequently, and passively, of the new venture.) Harriet opened on 22 November, cast as the wife of the condemned man in a dark pantomime called *La Dernière Heure d'un condamné* and playing opposite the perpetrator of the work, a choreographer named Louis Henry. The press allowed that she was the "perfect *artiste*" and a "gifted actress" and mentioned the "fidelity and painful truth" of her interpretation;[2] there is the strong implication that she was the only attribute of the piece. Both Harriet and her husband, though for different reasons, attached immense importance to what they hoped would be her triumphant return to the stage. In fact *La Dernière Heure d'un condamné* finished the poor company off. The actors were dismissed soon afterward, and the management announced its bankruptcy before anyone was paid. The government received the remaining assets of the company in February 1835. Not a word of the failure appears in Berlioz's correspondence.

The goal of his own continuing calendar of public concerts was to program his major works often enough that they might become familiar, instead of merely shocking. Yet there was the ever-present danger of the public and critics' growing bored with it all: the *Symphonie fantastique* was by now widely known and could no longer serve as the focus of a concert, yet he had so far completed only one other sizeable work, *Harold en Italie*. It is perhaps for this reason that the repertoire for the concerts of November and December 1834 changed with each published announcement. The *Mélodie pastorale* from *Les Francs-Juges* was programmed, then canceled, as was the *Chœur des Ciseleurs de Florence*—the opening tableau from the first version of *Cellini*. (The correspondence suggests that no bass could be found, but I suspect that the scene from *Cellini* had not been finished.) Perhaps, for once, *Sardanapale* could be made to explode on cue.

Liszt's participation was so far uncertain as well, and the news that Heinrich Ernst, the prodigiously gifted twenty-year-old German violinist, would appear in one of the concerts proved to be false. Things had not gone as planned with Paganini and *Harold* either. According to the *Mémoires*, Paganini had taken a look at the manuscript of the first movement and found the solo part to lack sufficient opportunity for virtuoso display—an eventuality Berlioz had feared even as he composed it. But that is not the only reason for Paganini's disappearance from Paris: he had refused to play in a benefit concert for the victims of the Rhine floods and cholera epidemic, and Janin, a native of the Rhineland, had published in the *Débats* a vitriolic attack on his parsimony.[3] Paganini was mightily offended, for in fact the problem was that his health was ruined. By September 1834 he had gone home to Italy.

Berlioz never heard Paganini play in concert. The "Titan among giants" had come to Paris in 1831 and then again "with the cholera" in 1832, while Berlioz was in Italy; Berlioz had missed Paganini's recital in April 1833. They nevertheless managed to develop a certain friendship, conversing, once Paganini had lost his voice, in reverse Beethoven-style, with Paganini's half of the conversation scribbled into Berlioz's pocket albums.

He had booked the Salle du Conservatoire for a series of four biweekly concerts on Sunday afternoons in November and December; the major attraction was to be the first performance of *Harold en Italie*. The solo part had been placed in the care of Chrétien Urhan, a musician of such piety that

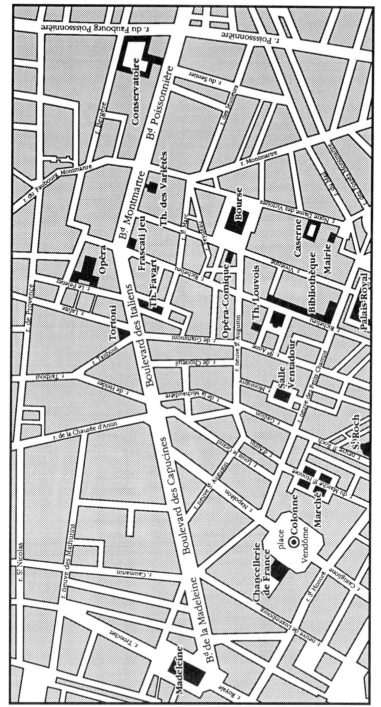

FIGURE 6.2 Berlioz's Paris (1830s).

FIGURE 6.3 Paganini in Paris.

his contract at the Opéra provided he might always have his back to the stage, the better to preclude some unwitting assault on his sensibilities. *Le Roi Lear* was announced for a second performance, with older works, solos *di bravura*, and the results of Berlioz's summer labors to fill out the programs. The most interesting of the new settings was another *Orientale* of Hugo, *Sara la baigneuse*, for male quartet and orchestra; for the same performing force, Berlioz rearranged his Irish melody *La Belle Voyageuse*. (The singers were Puig, Boulanger, Henze, and a baritone identified as "***," who I suspect was Berlioz himself.) The young soprano Cornélie Falcon—Alice in Meyerbeer's *Robert le diable*, and soon to be Rachel in Halévy's *La Juive* and Valentine in *Les Huguenots*—was engaged to sing the new orchestrations of *La Captive* and *Le Jeune Pâtre breton*. She was successful enough to be allowed a Bellini encore at the concert of 23 November. Berlioz could not afford a chorus for the series—which probably explains the unusual settings for male quartet—but the orchestra numbered nearly 100. Narcisse Girard agreed to conduct.

Berlioz opened his winter season on 9 November, not with *Harold* but with the *Symphonie fantastique*, *Le Roi Lear*, and the two new works for quartet and orchestra. On 23 November, the day after Harriet's debut at the Nautique, *Harold en Italie* and the new orchestrations of *La Captive* and *Le Jeune Pâtre breton* were presented for the first time before a sympathetic audience that numbered among its members Chopin, Liszt, and Hugo. For the first time, too, a member of the royal family was present, the Duc d'Orléans, crown prince of the kingdom. Presumably he had come to see for himself the author of the several bizarre letters Berlioz had addressed to him, the most recent of which had ended with the remark

> Perhaps, after having heard my music performed by 130 young people, all of whom are more or less touched by the same disequilibrium for which I am criticized, Your Highness will decide for himself, as my friends have done, that a room at [the insane-asylum in] Charenton is not what I most urgently need.[4]

It was not *Harold* but rather *La Captive* that captivated the public. The press called it "a masterpiece of melodic skill and orchestration."[5]

At the third concert, postponed from 7 December to 14 December, *Harold* was offered again, with more assurance. But this time it was the appearance of Chopin, playing the *Romance* from his E-Minor Concerto, that attracted the rapt attention of the audience, for this was one of only a handful of occasions on which he appeared before the Paris public. After the third concert, Berlioz considered his options and concluded that, as the musicians had volunteered their services, he could manage a fourth concert on 28 December. Liszt played two movements of his arrangement of the *Fantastique*, and *Harold* was heard for the third time.

Though we know little about what the composer thought of the artistic results of this ambitious series, it is clear that his concerts were, at the very least, a triumph of organization and production. He may not have been in much of a position to judge musical merit: he played the cymbals in at least two of the concerts and may have sung in them, too. All the other indications are of a stunning artistic victory. *Harold* seems to have fared poorly at the hands of the mediocre Girard, but the *Marche des pèlerins* was encored at every playing and soon was popularly regarded as the best thing Berlioz had yet composed. Urhan, who played the work time and time again, must have been superb: "Ever faithful, ever attentive and careful, he always gave to that difficult part such melancholy poesy, such sweet color, such religious revery."[6] *Le Roi Lear* met with acclaim as well; Antoni Deschamps published dithyrambic verses "To Hector Berlioz, after having heard his overture on King Lear" in the *Revue de Paris*.[7]

The financial results were better than marginal: there was a clear profit of perhaps 2,000 francs. The Berlioz household had been counting on income from Harriet's performances to meet the cost of Louis's nurse. What little Harriet earned, however, she was never paid, and so their domestic budget was thrown into disarray. Berlioz begged d'Ortigue not to mention his monetary embarrassment in the press, but at the same time quietly began to investigate other possibilities for raising some capital. They filed suit, for example, to recover Harriet's fee. Eventually this undertaking was settled in their favor, but not before the director of the company was in debtors' prison, with the lawyers' fees and court costs nevertheless to be paid. The suit was ultimately a money-losing proposition all around. The financial crisis of 1835 was perhaps the most severe of Berlioz's adult life.

Harriet bore all this well. Berlioz regarded her willingness to stake the family capital, time and time again, on his musical productions to be the greatest proof of her artistry. It must also be understood that measures of poverty varied considerably according to one's position in society: the Berlioz household never went without servants, adequate lodging, good food and drink, and decent clothes. There were always good schools for Louis. Those who bore the burden of his fiscal ailments were his more prosperous friends and patrons, who advanced him needed money, and the shopkeepers and other merchants, who were simply expected to take promissory notes.

Rescue came, as was usually the case in Berlioz's career, from his talents as a writer. In October 1834, the *Gazette musicale* printed Berlioz's novelette *Rubini à Calais*.[8] Five days later the *Journal des Débats* reprinted it, complimenting the author on his "verve" and "spirit," and within a few weeks the Bertins had discussed with Berlioz the possibility that he might replace Castil-Blaze as the music critic for their paper—an irony Berlioz was careful never to mention. It was agreed that he would cover the Conservatoire concerts and *variétés musicales;* Jules Janin would continue, for a time, to review the Opéra and Opéra-Comique; and Delécluse would deal with other lyric theater. Berlioz began serious criticism for the *Débats* in January 1835, but did not regularly sign his articles until January 1837, largely because he simultaneously published a good deal of the same material in the *Revue et Gazette musicale* and *Le Rénovateur*. For the time being, he was content to sign himself merely H***. It was no secret in professional circles who the author was.

His association with the *Débats* made Berlioz, at one stroke, a powerful critic. Through all the political thicks and thins of the next three decades, and with remarkably few interruptions, the *Débats* remained an influential and most often respected publication, among the most significant of the several dozen Paris periodicals that sent reviewers to concerts. Berlioz stayed on consistently good terms with the Bertins (Louis-François, the father and founder, his sons Armand and François-Edouard; and his daughter Louise-Angélique, a composer), and they along with the formidable Janin were of immediate and continuing support to his career. The Bertins moved in aristocratic circles where Berlioz so far lacked many contacts. This new access to wealth and power was critical to his plans for taking on the Opéra, where his disinclination to wheedle and deal otherwise put him at a disadvantage.

FIGURE 6.4 Study for the portrait of Louis-François Bertin; Ingres.

Berlioz was hired by Louis-François Bertin and eventually submitted his resignation to Edouard Bertin, but it was with his contemporary Armand Bertin that the friendship was intimate.

The Opéra's first masked ball of the new year, on 10 January, featured a parody of the *Fantastique* called "Episode in the Life of a Gambler," pasted together by Adolphe Adam. The comedian Arnal played the artist—"I shall depict my personage from head to foot: in the repeat of the first Allegro I shall show you how he ties his cravat"[9]—declaiming his part from beneath a grotesque red wig. Berlioz was there, I think, and probably took care to appear amused. But he cannot have thought much of this new mark of notoriety.

Fertilized by the tenets of the 1830 Revolution, the flower of musical Romanticism reached full bloom in early 1835. Chopin was at the height of his celebrity, Auber, Halévy, and above all Meyerbeer were dominating the stage with their style of grand opera that put the efforts of Spontini, Berton, and Le Sueur permanently to rest. Liszt's public and private affairs were the source of citywide amazement, as fine a topic of gossip as the tight fist of

Paganini had been a few months earlier. Bellini's *I Puritani* opened on 24 January, Halévy's *La Juive* on 23 February. Berlioz, who had begun to move freely in this cosmopolitan circle, also counted as friends the formidable writers then in the throes of creating the masterpieces of Romantic literature: Hugo, Alfred de Musset, George Sand, and Balzac. With the painter Delacroix, who was also reaching his peak, he had at least passing acquaintance. But he was never a true *habitué* of the literary salons, preferring evenings at his work table to the chatter of poets and their ladies.

Berlioz went alone to the most anticipated literary event of the year, the opening night of Vigny's *Chatterton* on 12 February. Harriet, fearing she would find the inevitable memories of her lost career too much to bear, stayed home. That was a wise decision, for Marie Dorval as Kitty Bell scored a triumph. The contrast with her own fate would have been crushing.

Liszt and Berlioz, hoping to capitalize on the excitement in the air, announced a joint concert for 9 April, a Thursday night. It was a daring choice of dates, for it put the concert squarely in the middle of Lent, the peak of the season for the Société des Concerts. (Liszt made his debut with that orchestra on Good Friday, 17 April, and Chopin appeared with them on 26 April, the Sunday after Easter.) Neither the Salle du Conservatoire nor the best professional musicians would be at liberty, so the affair was kept simple, billed as a benefit "for the profit of a poor family." An adequate venue was found in the Salle St.-Jean of the Hôtel de Ville. Boulanger opened the program with *Le Pêcheur,* accompanied by Liszt; this was followed by the first performance, postponed since the previous November, of Liszt's symphonic fantasia for piano and orchestra on two passages from *Le Retour à la vie: Le Pêcheur* and the *Chanson des brigands.* The orchestral works were the *Fantastique* and a movement from *Harold,* conducted by Girard.

The results were satisfying enough that a second concert along the same lines seemed appropriate, though it was feared that the inviting spring weather would compromise the attendance. The mighty pair took the Salle du Conservatoire on Sunday, 3 May, for a program featuring the *Fantastique* and its epilogue, separated by a Moscheles *solo di bravura* for Liszt alone. A large public came, partly because it was announced that the king and queen would appear. (They did not in fact attend, though the royal household sent its customary tip.) Berlioz, however, thought the afternoon a failure: the orchestra, which consisted largely of students from the Conservatoire and had had but a single rehearsal, was not equal to the demands of the music. The Berlioz-Liszt concerts marked a fitting end to Liszt's twelve-year residency in Paris. Shortly afterward he went to Geneva, soon to be joined there by Marie d'Agoult to await the birth of their child.

Two more Berlioz concerts took place before the summer hiatus. On 4 and 25 June, the small orchestra of the Gymnase-Musical, conducted by Théophile Tilmant, *aîné,* played *Harold,* the overtures, and *Le Jeune Pâtre breton.* What motivated these unusually late concerts is uncertain: perhaps they were the first salvo in a campaign to secure Berlioz the privilege of musical direction at the Gymnase, though that episode is associated for the most part with 1836. Berlioz incurred little or no financial risk, and no profit, from the two events.

$\mathcal{P}$aris was shocked, and Berlioz's life—it later turned out—immeasurably changed, by a thunderstroke that shook the foundations of the French government one stormy afternoon that summer. On 28 July 1835, the Corsican Giuseppe-Maria Fieschi and his accomplices attempted to assassinate King Louis-Philippe during his royal progress commemorating the first of the national holidays. With an "infernal machine"—several large guns rigged to fire simultaneously—Fieschi and his co-conspirators fired into the convoy from their rooms in the boulevard du Temple. The salvo felled eighteen people, including a military hero, the Maréchal de France Edouard-Adolphe Mortier, duke of Treviso, the king's commander-in-chief. (Louis-Philippe, grazed on the face by shrapnel and astride a wounded horse, collected himself and commanded, "Messieurs, continuons.") After the inevitable period of official mourning and the equally inevitable guillotining of the assassins, the government began to ruminate on a suitable memorial for the following year. Soon its representatives approached Berlioz to commission a Requiem mass.

It happened that, though abed with a tonsillitis attack as serious as the one in Florence, he was already at work on a ceremonial composition along those very lines. This was, in fact, his major enterprise of 1835, a *Fête musicale funèbre* "in memory of the illustrious men of France," combining his inclinations toward a military symphony of some sort with his growing interest in staging a colossal *fête musicale* on the order of the German festivals of which he had read acccounts. His recurrent urge to compose something monumental, something Napoleonic, was taking shape as a third symphony, in seven movements, intended for first performance in November. It seems clear from a manuscript plan listing the proposed orchestral force (see fig. 6.5)[10] both that the work was an outgrowth of the symphony conceived in the Alps in 1832 and that the ultimate fruit of the idea was the Requiem of 1837 and the *Symphonie funèbre et triomphale* of 1840.

Berlioz labored diligently at this project through early autumn. As the concert season drew closer, however, it was obvious that the *Fête musicale* could not be finished in time to allow a proper production. Berlioz took one of the two completed movements—the other is almost surely equivalent to the *Marche funèbre* in the *Symphonie funèbre et triomphale*—and refashioned it as the Napoleonic cantata *Le Cinq Mai*, commemorating the emperor's death on St. Helena in 1821. The sentimental poetry of P.-J. de Béranger was from a bygone time, but its "grand and sad" leanings excited Berlioz, especially the refrain:

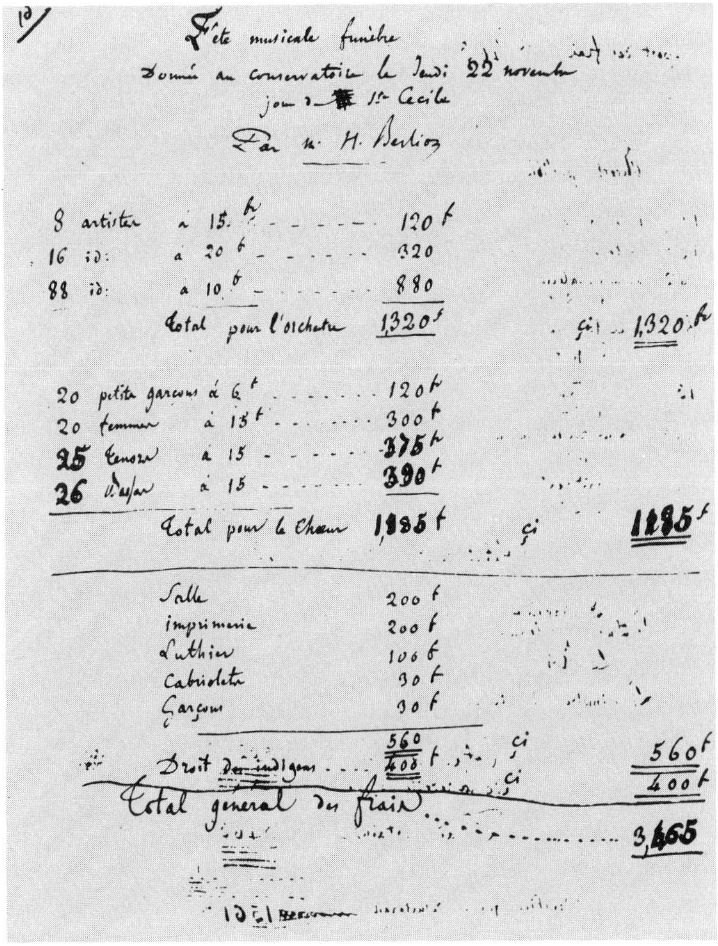

Fête musicale funèbre
Donnée au conservatoire le Jeudi 22 novembre
jour de Ste Cécile
Par M. H. Berlioz

8 artistes	à 15 f	120 f		
16 id:	à 20 f	320		
88 id:	à 10 f	880		
Total pour l'orchestre		1,320 f	ci	1,320 f
20 petits garçons	à 6 f	120 f		
20 femmes	à 15 f	300 f		
25 ténors	à 15	375 f		
26 basses	à 15	390 f		
Total pour le Chœur		1,185 f	ci	1,185 f
Salle		200 f		
imprimerie		200 f		
Luthier		100 f		
Cabriolets		30 f		
Garçons		30 f		
		560	ci	560 f
Droit des indigens		400 f	ci	400 f
Total général des frais				3,465

FIGURE 6.5 Plans for a *Fête musicale funèbre* envisaged for 22 November 1835. (First of four pages.)

> Pauvre soldat, je reverrai la France:
> La main d'un fils me fermera les yeux.
>
> (I shall see France again, poor soldier,
> The hand of a son will close my eyes.)

This is apparently an allusion to Napoleon's dying words: "*Mon dieu* . . . the French nation . . . my son . . . head of the army." Berlioz implies in the *Mémoires* that the poem had been on his mind as early as the 1820s and again in Rome in 1831, at the time of the tenth anniversary of Napoleon's death: "after two years," he says, he came on the music for the refrain as he fell into the Tiber.[11]

Le Cinq Mai is generally held to be one of Berlioz's failures. There is a strong sensation of routine, almost mechanical setting of a mawkish text. Yet to its composer it was a favorite work: aside from the first two symphonies and the more popular overtures, it was among the works he most frequently programmed during his European travels, played a dozen times after 1835. Berlioz added *Le Cinq Mai,* as though he had forgotten something important, to the 32 *Mélodies* of 1863 (thus 33 *Mélodies,* 1864). He performed it through the 1840s and as late as 1857 can be found attempting to secure a German publisher for it.

The last payment of the *prix de Rome* pension, his only assured income, came in late June 1835, after the functionaries had given up on the issue of the trip to Germany. It thus became more urgent than ever to find some permanent position with a stipend attached, the sort of administrative or teaching post that everyone from Le Sueur and Cherubini to the riff-raff composers seemed to enjoy. It had to be something that would occupy only a portion of his time, leaving him uninterrupted periods to compose; it should begin with several months of leave to finish *Cellini.* In truth Berlioz already had such a position with the *Débats.* Journalism did, after all, take only part of his time, and it kept him in the thick of Parisian musical life. But he dreamed of freedom from it, knowing he had committed himself to too much piecework for the press. He was writing more than ever: for the *Débats,* the *Gazette musicale, Le Monde dramatique,* and, still, the poorly paying *Rénovateur.* His affiliation with this last journal ended with its absorption by *La Quotidienne;* his last essay appeared at the end of 1835.

The concerts usually produced some income, but there was always risk of a major loss. Harriet still had unpaid medical bills and obligations to her associates, Berlioz still owed money to Edouard Rocher, and there was talk in La Côte of unpaid expenses relative to the *sommations respectueuses.* Their apartment was poorly furnished. He could no longer live a student or bohemian existence, but rather had to arrive at the theaters and concert rooms of Paris by carriage, attired in stylish evening dress. Dr. Berlioz appeared willing to send money from time to time, but since his retirement had little new income of his own; his son would only have accepted it in situations of dire emergency anyway. Even discounting the debts to be repaid, the household required 6,000 francs annually, or 500 francs a month, to make ends meet. Without the prize stipend, he would fall at least 100 francs short of that every month.

The situation was desperate enough that Berlioz arranged to have mail concerning financial matters delivered to Maurice Schlesinger's shop, the better to spare Harriet undue alarm. Plans for an American tour, which might lose money, were laid aside. In October the household moved once again to Montmartre, to economize and probably also to get Harriet away from the theater district, now that her career was over.

Almost immediately there were encouraging signs, for in mid-October an *opéra semi-séria* to be called *Benvenuto Cellini* was received, at least in principle, by the Opéra. This development was reported to the papers, doubtless by Berlioz himself.

Three concerts had been set by Berlioz and Narcisse Girard for the winter of 1835, originally for 15 and 22 November and 6 December, all Sunday afternoons. The first, delayed until the 22nd, offered 130 performers in a strange program that began with Girard's overture to *Antigone* and concluded with his arrangement for orchestra of Beethoven's "Moonlight" Sonata. *Harold en Italie* was the centerpiece, receiving at last a fine performance from all the forces but Girard and assuming from there on a place in the canon of Berlioz's masterpieces. Mlle Falcon sang an aria from Meyerbeer's *Il Crociato* and *Le Jeune Pâtre breton;* a note in the program reminded members of the audience that *Le Jeune Pâtre breton* was offered for sale by Schlesinger. *Le Cinq Mai* had its first performance, with the solo part sung by twenty basses. The *Revue et Gazette musicale* commented:

> We have learned that this work was a part of a vast composition of varied character to have been performed at the Panthéon. Because of the immensity of the nave [there] and the mass of air to be set in motion, the author thought it necessary to assign the solo bass role to twenty voices.[12]

What happened afterward to cause the rupture between Berlioz and Girard, his long-time friend and conductor, is in fact rather more complicated than the composer recounts, for no single incident precipitated it. Berlioz's growing antipathy toward Girard's abilities—he had conducted the *Francs-Juges* overture badly, in 1833, and could never get the hang of the metric ploy in the third movement of *Harold*—was now complete, and he resented, under those circumstances, that Girard took half the profits from their joint ventures.[13] They quarreled and postponed the next concert; by 13 December, Girard's name had disappeared from handbills and programs.

The direct result of his not wanting to split the earnings was that Berlioz took the vastly more significant step of becoming, once and for all, his own conductor. He gave *Le Roi Lear* and *Le Cinq Mai* and the two symphonies; Mlle Falcon sang songs including a "Keepsake-lyrique" by Meyerbeer. Meyerbeer was there, seated with George Sand, who later recalled their encounter:

> Do you remember, *maître*, the evening I was honored to run into you at a concert of Berlioz? Our seats were quite poor, for Berlioz was extravagant in sending out complimentary tickets; but it was a true stroke of luck that the crowd and chance swept me there. They played the *Marche au supplice*. I shall never forget your sympathetic handshake or the effusion of feeling with which your celebrated hands, so often filled with crowns, applauded the great mis-

FIGURE 6.6 Narcisse Girard.

understood artist, who was struggling heroically against his ungrateful public and harsh destiny. You wanted to share your trophies with him, and I went away with tear-filled eyes.[14]

Suddenly there opened up in Paris an ideal permanent post. The Théâtre du Gymnase in the boulevard Bonne-Nouvelle, about three blocks from the Conservatoire, was so called because it was across the avenue from the Gymnase-Dramatique. It was let in the summer of 1835 to entrepreneurs eager to create a much expanded Gymnase-Musical in order "to render great service to musical art: popularizing the masterpieces of the great composers, offering to talented instrumentalists the opportunity to be heard in concert, and lending to young composers the precious resources of an orchestra both accomplished and sagely conducted."[15] The concerts, during the season, were to be on Sundays, Mondays, Wednesdays, and Fridays, at 8:00 P.M. All was in keeping with the traditions of the friendly house, which was first envisaged as a place where "the students of the Conservatoire might exercise themselves without pretention and for an indulgent public, before appearing in a major theater."[16]

Sometime in middle or late 1835, the Bertins secured Berlioz the post of musical director for the new Gymnase-Musical. Or at least they thought they did, and Berlioz himself believed the contracts to have been signed and sealed. There was the promise of nearly 12,000 francs of annual income, almost exactly the amount he needed for a comfortable way of life: 6,000 francs of direct salary, proceeds of benefits for the conductor with an estimated value of 4,000 francs, and the performance fees, or *droits d'auteur,* for each of his own works presented there, valued at perhaps another 2,000 francs. It was a perfect position for him, near the top of established musical enterprise. He would stage operas, theater pieces, and concerts and perhaps create there a singing school like Choron's.

As quickly as this opportunity had materialized, however, it vanished. The minister of the Interior, Thiers, forbade singing in the hall—not wishing, presumably, to encourage competition with the Opéra and Opéra-Comique—and it was beyond Berlioz to imagine any serious musical enterprise without at least the possibility of a chorus. Anything else was merely an excuse for another ballroom, like Musard's, for quadrilles and the latest novelties. Tilmant became permanent conductor.

*T*he cheerless winter was made all the more trying for the Berlioz household by the difficulty of heating their new apartment. Louis had been ill for a month in October and was not yet fully recovered; Berlioz found that tending to him in the night, padding over the cold floors in bare feet, aggravated his own tonsillitis. Harriet did not go out much, partly because of the expense and partly because of her distrust of the servants. Both parents complained of their insolence and greed—"you have to give them *coffee*"[17]—and imagined in bourgeois fashion that things were worse since the July Revolution than before. Louis had so far uttered nothing intelligible, a common problem of bilingual households, but one that worried his parents nonetheless. Harriet fretted over the collapse of serious theater in England, the lack of news from her family, and her inability to go shopping for herself.

Yet there is evidence that she and Berlioz found strong consolation in each other, and that their affection for one another continued to grow. They had gradually restored the relationship with the rest of his family: Berlioz's brother Prosper sent Louis *joujoux,* and the family would have been happy enough to send a maid from the Isère, if only one could be found. Adèle, who liked to send bonnets and other apparel for Louis, was still the most popular of the relations, especially with Harriet. Dr. Berlioz urged his son to take the lead in thawing the icy relations with his elder sister. Berlioz objected: it was Nanci who had broken off the correspondence to begin with; he was the older of the two; it was *his* marriage that she had objected to. "Nanci is afflicted, like so many people, with presumption disguising itself as apparent reserve, which often leads her to judge things she cannot understand."[18]

So Nanci wrote first, and on 21 February, Berlioz responded that all was forgiven and extended his hand in friendship:

Here is my life in four words: I am very happy—to have the best and most-loved wife in the world. But I suffer greatly from all the privations I see her enduring without complaint; by her isolation, and above all, by the loss of her immense talent. Her forced inaction is killing her.[19]

There seems to have been a certain lack of resolve on Berlioz's part, in these early months of 1836, as to what to undertake next. The only serious work he completed was an arrangement for piano, four-hands, of the *Francs-Juges* overture, with which Chopin and nearly every other pianist of his acquaintance provided assistance. This publication was intended to complement the full score; both were to appear under the imprint of the publisher Simon Richault. Ideas for the new *Benvenuto Cellini* dominated his imagination, but he was reluctant to begin the work with neither a written contract from the producers nor, apparently, the complete libretto. Berlioz had hoped that Auguste Barbier, one of *Cellini*'s librettists, would be named to succeed Véron as director of the Opéra—that would make his own production quick and easy—but a devious impresario named Edmond Duponchel was appointed. At least Duponchel was subject to the influence of the Bertins.

The cantankerous minister Thiers, who had denied Berlioz the privilege of the Gymnase-Musical, now forbade a written contract for *Cellini*. The Opéra wanted a simple, light work, unlike the epic *Cellini* of Berlioz's dreams, and yet seemed unable to specify the details of what would be deemed acceptable. Meyerbeer and the Bertins, nevertheless, urged Berlioz to carry on, all but assuring him that sufficient pressure could be brought to bear once the opera was done. He was fully swept up in the composition by late spring.

Berlioz and Harriet went together to the premiere of *Les Huguenots* on 29 February, the first time she had accompanied him out since the Christmas holiday. He had done his homework with regard to the new opera, having attended the rehearsals and studied the manuscripts of that "musical encyclopedia" on whose success hinged, he thought, the promise of serious art in France. He was delighted with Meyerbeer's accomplishment—"c'est superbe"—and with its popular reception, measured both at the box office and in the sale of vocal scores, excerpts, and the usual parlor arrangements. He devoted three of his articles in the *Revue et Gazette musicale* that March to an act-by-act analysis of the opera, then reexamined the work for the *Journal des Débats* when the published score appeared later in the year. He admired the orchestration, especially Meyerbeer's skilled deployment of the eight harps at the end, and the use of the Protestant chorale *Ein feste' Burg*. *Les Huguenots* showed taste and reason, the control of ordered thought. It was superior to *Robert le diable*, he declared, and would prove to be Meyerbeer's masterpiece. He looked forward to shaking the hand of the man who had written it.

Harriet Berlioz-Smithson may have had little commercial viability in a land where her repertoire was limited to mute parts, three great Shakespeare roles, and Jane Shore, but she still had a certain social draw—the whiff of legend remained about her—and could offer moving revivals of her handful of significant scenes. She retained her *entrée* into an elevated level of society. It was thus that she became attached to the household of a certain Castellane,

FIGURE 6.7 Meyerbeer, c. 1835.

presumably the Comte de Castellane, a French military hero. There she recreated her triumphs before two or three hundred invited guests. The journal *La Quotidienne* gushed over her appearance during the week of 20 March as Ophelia, complimenting her noble inspiration and poetic sensibility in the mad scene and summarizing the reaction of the audience in the words, more or less, of Laertes: "Thought and affliction, passion, hell itself, she turns to favor and to prettiness" (*Hamlet* IV, 1, lines 187–88).[20] (The tone of these remarks has an acutely Berliozian ring, as though his influence, and possibly his pen, were involved.) She offered similar evenings *chez* Castellane through 1837, thus extending her career well past the date usually given for her last public appearance.

Sigismond Thalberg, a twenty-four-year-old virtuoso pianist of uncertain parentage, made his appearance that season in Paris, determined to claim for himself the kind of adulation so recently garnered there by Paganini and Liszt. Berlioz was quick to enlist his services for a concert to follow the season of the Société des Concerts, during which Thalberg had appeared with great success. The date was tentatively and somewhat curiously fixed for 28 April, a Thursday afternoon just four days after the last Société concert, then abandoned. Berlioz's relationship with Thalberg was stormy

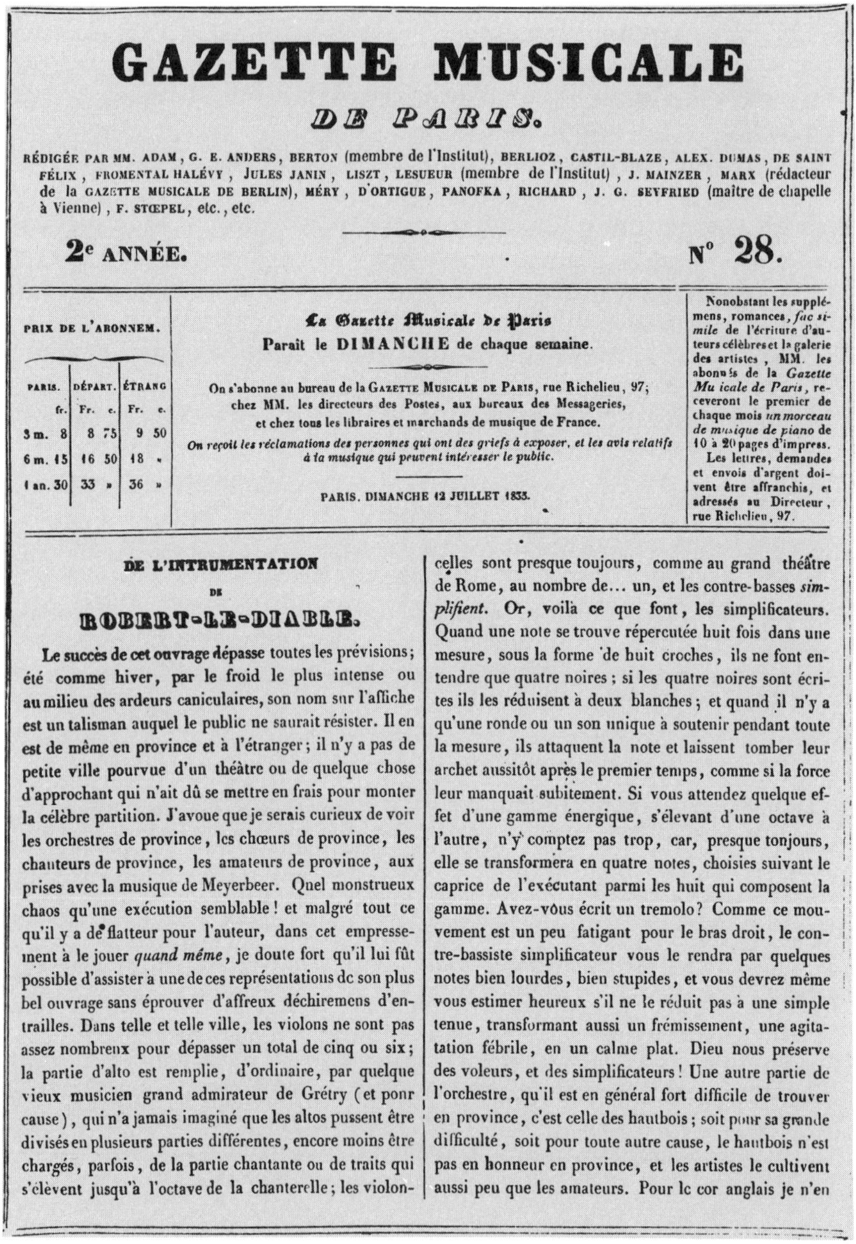

GAZETTE MUSICALE
DE PARIS.

RÉDIGÉE PAR MM. ADAM, G. E. ANDERS, BERTON (membre de l'Institut), BERLIOZ, CASTIL-BLAZE, ALEX. DUMAS, DE SAINT FÉLIX, FROMENTAL HALÉVY, JULES JANIN, LISZT, LESUEUR (membre de l'Institut), J. MAINZER, MARX (rédacteur de la GAZETTE MUSICALE DE BERLIN), MÉRY, D'ORTIGUE, PANOFKA, RICHARD, J. G. SEYFRIED (maître de chapelle à Vienne), F. STŒPEL, etc., etc.

2e ANNÉE.　　　　　　　　　　　　　　　　　**N° 28.**

| PRIX DE L'ABONNEM. | | | | La Gazette Musicale de Paris | Nonobstant les supplémens, romances, fac simile de l'écriture d'auteurs célèbres et la galerie des artistes, MM. les abonnés de la Gazette Mu icale de Paris, receveront le premier de chaque mois un morceau de musique de piano de 10 à 20 pages d'impres. Les lettres, demandes et envois d'argent doivent être affranchis, et adressés au Directeur, rue Richelieu, 97. |

Parait le DIMANCHE de chaque semaine.

PARIS.	DÉPART.	ÉTRANG	
	fr.	Fr. c.	Fr. c.
3 m. 8	8 75	9 50
6 m. 15	16 50	18 »
1 an. 30	33 »	36 »

On s'abonne au bureau de la GAZETTE MUSICALE DE PARIS, rue Richelieu, 97; chez MM. les directeurs des Postes, aux bureaux des Messageries, et chez tous les libraires et marchands de musique de France.

On reçoit les réclamations des personnes qui ont des griefs à exposer, et les avis relatifs à la musique qui peuvent intéresser le public.

PARIS. DIMANCHE 12 JUILLET 1835.

DE L'INTRUMENTATION
DE
ROBERT-LE-DIABLE.

Le succès de cet ouvrage dépasse toutes les prévisions; été comme hiver, par le froid le plus intense ou au milieu des ardeurs caniculaires, son nom sur l'affiche est un talisman auquel le public ne saurait résister. Il en est de même en province et à l'étranger; il n'y a pas de petite ville pourvue d'un théâtre ou de quelque chose d'approchant qui n'ait dû se mettre en frais pour monter la célèbre partition. J'avoue que je serais curieux de voir les orchestres de province, les chœurs de province, les chanteurs de province, les amateurs de province, aux prises avec la musique de Meyerbeer. Quel monstrueux chaos qu'une exécution semblable! et malgré tout ce qu'il y a de flatteur pour l'auteur, dans cet empressement à le jouer *quand même*, je doute fort qu'il lui fût possible d'assister à une de ces représentations de son plus bel ouvrage sans éprouver d'affreux déchiremens d'entrailles. Dans telle et telle ville, les violons ne sont pas assez nombreux pour dépasser un total de cinq ou six; la partie d'alto est remplie, d'ordinaire, par quelque vieux musicien grand admirateur de Grétry (et pour cause), qui n'a jamais imaginé que les altos pussent être divisés en plusieurs parties différentes, encore moins être chargés, parfois, de la partie chantante ou de traits qui s'élèvent jusqu'à l'octave de la chanterelle; les violon-

celles sont presque toujours, comme au grand théâtre de Rome, au nombre de... un, et les contre-basses *simplifient*. Or, voila ce que font, les simplificateurs. Quand une note se trouve répercutée huit fois dans une mesure, sous la forme de huit croches, ils ne font entendre que quatre noires; si les quatre noires sont écrites ils les réduisent à deux blanches; et quand il n'y a qu'une ronde ou un son unique à soutenir pendant toute la mesure, ils attaquent la note et laissent tomber leur archet aussitôt après le premier temps, comme si la force leur manquait subitement. Si vous attendez quelque effet d'une gamme énergique, s'élevant d'une octave à l'autre, n'y comptez pas trop, car, presque tonjours, elle se transformera en quatre notes, choisies suivant le caprice de l'exécutant parmi les huit qui composent la gamme. Avez-vous écrit un tremolo? Comme ce mouvement est un peu fatigant pour le bras droit, le contre-bassiste simplificateur vous le rendra par quelques notes bien lourdes, bien stupides, et vous devrez même vous estimer heureux s'il ne le réduit pas à une simple tenue, transformant aussi un frémissement, une agitation fébrile, en un calme plat. Dieu nous préserve des voleurs, et des simplificateurs! Une autre partie de l'orchestre, qu'il est en général fort difficile de trouver en province, c'est celle des hautbois; soit pour sa grande difficulté, soit pour toute autre cause, le hautbois n'est pas en honneur en province, et les artistes le cultivent aussi peu que les amateurs. Pour le cor anglais je n'en

FIGURE 6.8 Berlioz's article on Meyerbeer's *Robert le diable*, in *Gazette musicale*, 12 July 1835.

at first, for by the beginning of the 1836–37 season the rivalry with Liszt was heated and Berlioz was of course a partisan of the Liszt camp. (Whatever personal animosity there may have been between the two pianists reached a relatively amicable resolution in the course of the memorable concert of March 1837, at the home of the Princess de Belgiojoso—the so-called pianistic duel.) Thalberg eventually became a good friend and was the composer of a fantasia, op. 58, on the *Apothéose* from the *Symphonie funèbre et triomphale.*

In April, just after Berlioz had finished his own four-hand version of the *Francs-Juges* overture but before it appeared in print, he stumbled onto a hackneyed four-hand arrangement published by Friedrich Hofmeister of Leipzig in 1833. Though based on the published orchestral parts, it was arranged in the fashion perfected by Castil-Blaze, such that a composer might not recognize his work: the piano figuration was simplified, and the arranger missed the point of the long C-minor augmentation of Lenor's theme. This was all the more annoying in view of Berlioz's by now well-established position on the arrangers of Beethoven and Weber. He spewed forth on the matter in a letter to Liszt of 28 April, then published a lengthier attack in the *Revue et Gazette musicale* of 8 May, in the form of an open letter "To Monsieur Hofmeister, Music Publisher of Leipzig."

> It is NOT MINE, and I can hardly recognize my work in what is left of the overture. Your arranger has butchered my score, clipped its wings, rearranged its parts, and sewn it back up again such that I find a ridiculous monster in its place; I beg him to retain the honor for himself alone.[21]

The only scores he will recognize are his own, published by Richault in Paris and Adolf Martin Schlesinger in Berlin, although even at that—he notes—the Berlin score does not contain the "light emendations" suggested to him by Chopin, Georges Osborne, Ludwig Schunke, Wojciech (called Albert) Sowinski, Julius Benedict, and Carl Eberwein. The incident rankled as late as 1852, when Berlioz took care to note on a list of his published works that "this arrangement, done by the author with the assistance of the three capable pianists Chopin, Benedict, and Eberwein, is the only faithful one, and conforms to the score."[22]

And well it might have rankled. Schumann had tried to learn the work for an essay that spring in the *Neue Zeitschrift für Musik* and complained that the Leipzig edition he had used must be "a miserable skeleton, one for which the composer would have the right to sue the arranger." Schumann later reprimanded a correspondent for criticizing the overture without hearing it: "You have no idea of the way he deploys an orchestra."[23]

Les Francs-Juges was nevertheless the only orchestral work of Berlioz available for purchase, and more than one orchestra wished to investigate this accomplishment of the brilliant new star on the horizon. Moscheles had tried to lead the Philharmonic Society of London through the overture in early 1834, but had been forced to abandon the "nonsensical *charivari* of dance music and pathos *with bass drum,* with a noise loud enough to deafen, and so extravagant that the audience and the orchestra burst into laughter."[24] A reading in Marseille had met with a similar fate. The work was performed more successfully in Leipzig, by which time there was a published score; it was this concert that Schumann attended. Within a few months *Les Francs-Juges* had been heard as well in Aix-la-Chapelle, Cologne, Berlin, Bremen, Weimar, and Vienna. In France, by the end of 1835, it had been played in Dijon, Douai, and Lille. Of the Dijon performance, a correspondent wrote to the *Gazette musicale* in charming terms:

> We dared attack Berlioz's overture to *Les Francs-Juges,* and we had to battle with all the provincial limitations. But the more difficult the task, the more we put our zeal to work. Eventually we emerged from the struggle with the honors of battle, that is to say, to the noise of applause.[25]

This was Berlioz's first experience with performances beyond the scope of his own direct control. They seemed to him new proof of the danger of circulating his works, at least until he had toured Germany himself. Weber had allowed copies of his operas to be made, and that was enough for him to lose control of them forever. The fear of being translated into nonsense by an unfaithful or incomplete performance, he wrote in a moving letter to Schumann, was more than he could bear. His symphonies were too young to travel without him.[26] He was firm in his resolve to publish neither scores nor parts to the symphonies until after he had personally introduced them to the great concert halls of Europe, and he kept that resolution steadfastly and adamantly, never minding the resultant delay in achieving the international stature he warranted. "[I am] absolutely determined not to allow anything to be published until I have visited Germany."[27]

The Bertin family had already accomplished a great deal for Berlioz and his career, and the infrequent favors they asked of him could under no circumstance be declined. Serving Louise Bertin as musical factotum for her opera, *Esmeralda,* must nevertheless have been a distasteful task, in view of the fact that every day spent with it delayed *Benvenuto Cellini*—both the composition and its production—that much longer. That he did it with such grace is testimony to his affection for the family and for Hugo; Hugo's having this once fashioned a libretto was in turn a mark of his own affection for the Bertins. Berlioz reviewed and corrected the score and suggested revisions, a task for which he was well paid by Louise Bertin's father. He denies having written any of the music himself, though everyone from the chorus members to the salon-goers gossiped that he had; his main suggestion, he wrote, was for an improved ending to Quasimodo's Bell Song in act IV.

More significant than whatever details he added to the score was his work on the production. Mlle Bertin, partially paralyzed, was not mobile enough to supervise things herself. For the better part of the year, Berlioz watched over copyists, coached soloists, and rehearsed the chorus. Tradition dictated that only Habeneck could conduct the performances, but it was Berlioz who put the singers through their paces, confronting and overcoming their limitations in intelligence, gesture, and pitch. It was good practice for *Benvenuto Cellini,* especially the strong dose of politics: the reputation of the *Journal des Débats* was popularly supposed to be at stake. By the end of the summer, he was expecting a good production, although he could not escape the conviction that the solo roles were weak and the orchestration heavy-handed. The choruses, on the other hand, he found most attractive. They were scheduled to open in early fall.

Esmeralda's labor and delivery came just as Berlioz's own opera was beginning to take definitive shape. Envious of the reception accorded *La Juive* and *Les Huguenots,* he grew hungry for a victory of his own. He had abandoned himself to the composition, and *Cellini* was at last going smoothly.

The libretto for the new version was in two acts of two tableaux each. Barbier, who had found the original scenario disjunct and tedious, persuaded Berlioz to move the action from Florence to Rome, the better to permit the Roman carnival and a convincing appearance of the pope. The Opéra had made it clear that they expected something in the "moderate genre, more gay than tragic." The story became a simple tale of Cellini's struggle with power, and the superfluous incidents, like the siege of Rome and Cellini's role in the death of a Bourbon constable, were deleted from the draft. The necessary spectacle would be provided by the two Mardi Gras tableaux: the one in the tavern with Cellini and his goldsmiths, which Berlioz had written in 1834, and the "follies and joyous tumult" of the Roman carnival. Barbier noted the many parallels between Cellini's personality and Berlioz's and rather enjoyed fashioning a life of Cellini centering pointedly on love of art and combat against those who would cheapen it.

It appears that the great majority of the composition, beyond the scenes roughed out in 1834, was done in the summer of 1836, with the most intense activity occurring during the July holiday from *Esmeralda*. Berlioz wrote with vigor, from time to time fleshing out his opera with bits and pieces of earlier compositions. Composing *Cellini* seemed playful by comparison with his exercises in the symphonic genres, except that there was three times as much music to write. He was all but done by the end of the year, and the work could have been produced in the spring of 1837. In fact it waited in reserve for nearly two years.

Harriet's sister, the invalid for whom she had cared until her marriage, died in June. Louis had begun to speak something like a language—Polish, Berlioz imagined—but was becoming a difficult child, violent in a manner his parents characterized as "just barely wise." He enjoyed perching in the open window over the street for the commotion that would always ensue. There were continuing problems with the maids: one of them took Louis into town, where he pinched his finger in a café door and subsequently lost a fingernail; a successor taught him, Harriet imagined, to dislike her. Meanwhile Berlioz was engaged by his father to inquire into academies for his brother Prosper, who was coming to Paris to finish preparatory school before matriculating at the Ecole Polytechnique.

During Schlesinger's summer holiday, Berlioz was acting editor of the *Revue et Gazette musicale*. He had once again taken on too much literary work—essays for an *Encyclopédie catholique* and lives of composers for a *Biographie des hommes illustres d'Italie*—and thus there was little time, that summer and fall, even to correspond. The family moved back to the rue de Londres in late September, to an apartment at number 35, reluctantly abandoning the Montmartre garden they had loved. The pace of rehearsals for *Esmeralda* doubled, first to daily, then to twice daily.

Harriet went with her husband on 14 November to the opening of *Esmeralda*. It fell flat, with only the Bell Song reckoned to have been a success. Cries of "A bas les Bertin! à bas le *Journal des Débats*" rang from the parterre. It was widely rumored that Berlioz had written the Bell Song, and Dumas, who did not like the Bertins, lent his considerable weight to the myth by shouting "C'est de Berlioz; c'est de Berlioz." Berlioz went alone to the remaining performances, most of which were limited to the first act, with a ballet after the interval, a tired formula that he would come to know all too well.

Liszt returned to Paris for the new concert season, and Berlioz naturally engaged him for his Sunday concerts that December. On the 4th, the *Fantastique* and *Harold* were juxtaposed for the first time in two years, separated by the Bell Song from *Esmeralda* and other solos; on the 18th, Liszt offered his fantasia for piano and orchestra on themes from the *Mélologue* and two movements of his transcription of the *Fantastique*, with two movements from *Harold* at the end of the program. At both performances the *Marche des pèlerins* was interrupted by applause, led, according to one observer, by Cherubini and Meyerbeer. Heine found the Berlioz-Liszt concerts the zenith of an already memorable season.[28] The 1836 concerts were financially successful, with a before-tax profit of 1,760 francs, and admired by the critics as well: one of the reviews looked forward to the timely production of "his operas."

Through the intercession of Dumas, Harriet's mad scene from *Hamlet* was placed on a benefit for the great actor Frédérick Lemaître at the Théâtre des Variétés. On 15 December she was seen by the paying public for the last time. Jules Janin wrote lyrically of her mystique: "She is noble, she is beautiful, she is intelligent. We owe to her that she was the first actress to have understood Shakespeare."[29]

Louis was the center of attention for the holiday season, proud recipient of a drum from his godfather Thomas Gounet and a silver place setting from Nanci. Harriet was at last comfortable leaving him at home and willing to join her husband from time to time at the theater. They were occasionally accompanied on these outings by Félix Marmion, now colonel and commander of the Second Regiment of Dragoons, stationed in Paris; they went together on 17 April, for example, to *Guillaume Tell*, where the tenor Duprez made his debut, replacing the legendary Adolphe Nourrit. The influenza that swept Paris that winter, leaving over 1,500 dead, seems to have missed Berlioz and his household, though he was bedridden for a time with some other ailment. Grandfather Marmion died in Meylan that March, attended by Berlioz's mother and his two sisters. Meanwhile, Berlioz fulfilled what appears to have been an obligation incumbent on all male citizens by joining the National Guard. His father paid for the uniform.

*B*ut for the orchestration, *Benvenuto Cellini* was complete by early spring 1837. It stood third, after Niedermeyer's *Stradella* and Halévy's *Guido et Ginévra*, on the list of works awaiting production at the Opéra—fourth, if Auber finished his *Le Lac des fées*. Auber was, after all, a professor at the Conservatoire and a member of the Institute; his work would automatically be granted priority. The Opéra was capable of mounting one or two new works a year, not counting ballets, but productions invariably lagged behind schedule, and the wait stretched on for another two years. *Stradella* opened on 3 March 1837 and *Guido* a year later, on 5 March 1838. Auber's opera opened on 1 April 1839.

In early 1837 Janin ceded to Berlioz the responsibility of covering the lyric theater for the *Journal des Débats,* just as Berlioz's stints as acting editor of the *Revue et Gazette musicale* were growing more and more frequent. (Maurice Schlesinger ran a major publishing house as well as the *Gazette* and was often away in Berlin to consult with the other half of the enterprise, run by his father Adolf Martin.) Berlioz had begun to sense his power as a journalist: he saw that the criticism had become his ram for breaking down the door of the Opéra and grew confident that *Cellini* would be mounted one way or another. Meanwhile, it was necessary to treat *Stradella* kindly, though to his intimates he confessed that the opera was "dead, without remission."[30] *Esmeralda* had been a hundred times more interesting.

The minister of the Interior for the cabinet of September 1836 was Count Adrien de Gasparin, whose well-meaning if rather conservative vision was to restore French ceremonial music to the primacy it had enjoyed before the dissolution of the Chapel Royal in 1830. He intended to appropriate several thousand francs annually to commission grand sacred works in the patriotic style, and he meant to start with a composition by Berlioz. While Berlioz was petitioning him on another matter, probably a request for the Salle du Conservatoire, Gasparin turned the conversation to a work commemorating Maréchal Mortier and the other citizens killed by Fieschi and his accomplices in July 1835.[31] It should be suitable, too, for the *trois glorieuses* and would probably be given at the Invalides. The timing was perfect: Berlioz had, of course, been aching to set such a text. He had a good deal of appropriate music already at hand, and with *Benvenuto Cellini* essentially finished in March or early April, he had several months free to do the work. He calmly demanded 500 performers of the minister, expecting 400 in the end, then went home in a frenzy to start work. The official commission was tendered by decree of 22 March and announced by the papers in early April. As it happened, this was just as Gasparin left office, but the negotiations appeared to be well past the point of turning back.

From the start, however, there were complications. Cherubini had finished a second Requiem, in D minor, and naturally assumed the government would look first to him for the music commemorating Mortier. This was enough to cause sharp discomfort at higher levels, such that the director of Fine Arts, Cavé, was led to announce his flat opposition to the Berlioz work. (Berlioz's relations with the new minister, Montalivet, remained nonetheless cordial.) Halévy took the astonishing step of coming to the *Débats* to plead Cherubini's case with Bertin. Some read Berlioz's letter to Cherubini of 24 March—after Berlioz had his commission in hand—as high sarcasm; I lean toward interpreting his remarks as those of genuine gratitude. "I am deeply touched by the notable self-effacement," he wrote, "which has led you to withdraw your admirable Requiem from the ceremony at the Invalides."[32] Cherubini certainly had the power to get his way, were he determined enough.

After a period of intellectual upheaval over the work, during which he experienced accesses of intoxicating dizziness—"My brain felt as though it would explode with the pressure of ideas"—Berlioz dominated his subject matter.[33] The eruptions stopped, the lava cooled. Having taken the time to master text and concept, he composed the Requiem methodically and quickly, movement by movement, beginning with the *Prose des morts* (the *Dies irae* through the *Lacrymosa*). The ideas came to him faster than he could notate them; he adopted a style of musical shorthand in which he sketched out his ideas in pencil on large score paper, then prepared the finished autograph full score by covering the same pages in ink. He used the traditional Requiem text freely, not hesitating to rearrange this poetry "of gigantic sublimity" to suit his purposes. His musical vision of the Last Judgment, like Dante's literary one, was as a step in the progress from Purgatory to Paradise.[34]

By late May he was to the point of mapping out the work remaining, day by day:

To orchestrate:

Dies irae and Tuba mirum	3 days
Rex tremendae	3
Sanctus	4
Lacrymosa	4
Agnus	4
Offertoire	3

The Requiem and Introit, along with the Quid sum miser and the Quaerens me, will take   8 days

    Total for all this: one month (June)[35]

The work was indeed finished, except for minor details, on 29 June 1837, well in time for the July celebrations.

The promised fee was in the amount of 4,000 francs, above and beyond the expenses of the production. This would be enough for Berlioz to pay most of the last debts of courtship and marriage. He wrote to Edouard Rocher asking him to pay the fees owed to Simian, the notary, and promised quick repayment of his remaining obligations. Harriet was still appearing in Castellane's galas before such figures as Hugo and his wife Adèle; her portrayal in act V of *Jane Shore* on 7 May was thought especially moving. There was hope that through the influence of Mme d'Agoult, George Sand might be induced to create a role for Harriet in one of her plays, a part, perhaps, for an English woman who speaks French with difficulty and a pronounced accent. Berlioz contributed the idea that such a plot could revolve around a misunderstood word. Nothing came of his idea.

Technical preparations for the Requiem were more complex than those for any other work he had yet composed. Carpenters had to be engaged to build the necessary scaffolding at the Invalides. (Napoleon's tomb was not yet there.) Dozens of chorus parts were prepared directly from the manuscripts of Berlioz and his copyist by the firm of Mme Bobœuf, using the novel process of lithography. Extra trumpet and trombone players had to be found among the students at the Conservatoire and elsewhere. Rehearsals commenced in late June with three meetings of the chorus, and there seemed no reason to imagine that the production would not be well prepared by 28 July.

Then, with the work finished and the rehearsals under way, Berlioz learned—indirectly—that the celebration of the *trois glorieuses* was to be reduced to a bare minimum and that the solemnity in honor of Fieschi's victims had been canceled. The governments of Austria and Russia had complained of the ostentatious celebration of revolutionary sentiment; the press muttered that "many people commemorate the July Revolution only out of great desire to continue it or to have another."[36] The treasury for such national celebrations was in any event depleted by the marriage of Louis-Philippe's oldest son and heir, the Duc d'Orléans, to Hélène of Mecklenburg-Schwerin. Money from the national coffers had flowed lavishly for the royal wedding of 30 May. There was a grand entry of the bride to the chateau at Fontainebleau, a procession of the newlyweds through the Arc de Triomphe on 4 June, and festivities at the Champ de Mars on the 14th. The city of Paris offered a banquet on the 19th, and finally there was a grand ball at the Opéra on the 22nd. Soon afterward, Harriet was presented an honorarium by a lady-in-waiting to the Princess Hélène; perhaps she was in some way involved with the wedding festivities. And it was already known that there would be another royal wedding later in the year, with corresponding expenses.

Canceling the Requiem was not, as Berlioz naturally imagined, a personal attack by the ministry, or a slap in the face of serious music. Not until 1840 was France again to celebrate the July revolution with great ceremony, and then the government did indeed turn first to Berlioz. Nevertheless the decision seemed at the time a setback of stunning proportion. He had neither recourse nor resource to present a work he knew was brilliant; like Robinson Crusoe, he had built a canoe too large to launch by himself.[37] The Requiem needed its association with a ceremonial event; it needed a church and several hundred performers; the financial risk was far too great to bear alone. For a time, he thought that he would not be able to go on breathing, but at length he regained his composure: the work existed, after all, and he had a hard head.[38] One way or another, he would see to a performance.

Uncle Félix reported to La Côte that his nephew was right to be vexed by the vagaries of government. He needed to be heard by powerful people, by officials who were not, for the most part, connoisseurs. Marmion took it upon himself to remind the minister of his responsibility to deal honorably with the work and of the government's obligation to pay the legitimate expenses of the enterprise. So, too, did Bertin. But the net result was to reconfirm Berlioz's distaste for politics and government: the excuse "par raison politique" for avoiding contracted obligations was symbolic of the vagaries of public will, especially where art and artists were concerned.

Berlioz owed his copyist and the lithographer 3,800 francs for the parts alone, and the expense of the three rehearsals was so far unreimbursed. Then there was the matter of the 4,000-franc fee for the composition itself. The months of September and October were wasted on negotiations; in the end, when a lawsuit threatened, the expenses at least were paid.

The Berlioz household moved again in October to 31, rue de Londres, their last home together.[39] Le Sueur died on 6 October, mostly of old age. With heavy heart, Berlioz joined three members of the Institute in carrying the funeral awning; his obituaries of Le Sueur appeared on 15 October in both his papers. While guest editor of the *Revue et Gazette musicale* for two months, he took the opportunity to publish a novelette he called *Le Premier Opéra*, a thinly disguised essay on the unpaid commission.[40] For the dilemma of the Requiem mass was far from resolution. The inspectors-general had paid the most pressing of their obligations but seemed disinclined to see the work presented. The Ministry of the Interior continued to excuse itself on the grounds that all the money allocated for events of pomp and circumstance had been spent.

Just as it seemed that drastic measures might be necessary, an appropriate occasion for the Requiem suddenly presented itself. The governor-general of the French colonies in North Africa, Charles, comte de Damrémont, had ordered a siege against the city of Constantine in Algeria. Where a similar attack against the Ottoman dey Ahmed in 1836 had failed, this one was victorious, though at considerable mortal cost. Damrémont was wounded on 11 October and died the next day; the city fell to his armies on the 13th. The return of the general's body was to be recognized with a national commemoration both more timely and more stately than the occasion for which the Requiem had originally been commissioned, and it would be paid for by the much richer Ministry of War.

Berlioz's Requiem was the obvious choice for the funeral, but still he felt it necessary to fire off a fusillade of letters aimed at assuring the performance and reminding the authorities of its physical requirements. An agreement was reached between the ministers of War and the Interior by which 10,000 francs were allocated by the War Ministry for the event and the Interior would satisfy the remaining expenses from the previous July—that is, the composer's fee. The amount of the allocation meant that the work would be presented with rather smaller forces than Berlioz had first imagined— some 300 performers, in total—but the promise, this time, was definite. The arrangements were announced on 19 November. Habeneck was to conduct, by traditional protocol of his office as the king's chapel-master. Berlioz would serve as assisting conductor, occupying himself with the timpani players.

Rehearsals were begun anew, and the progress of the general's coffin, reported by signal fires and dispatches, was monitored in order to establish a firm date for the solemnity. After an open general rehearsal on 4 December, the work was presented the next day before a large audience which included one of the most influential groups of government dignitaries, including the Duc d'Orléans, ever to attend a concert by Berlioz. Also there were his devoted colleagues and friends, among them Adèle Hugo, Legouvé, Louise Vernet and her mother, and Harriet and Louis (who was enchanted by "his father's trumpets"). During the brass and percussion of the Last Judgment, a member of the chorus was seized with a nervous attack; the curate burst into tears at the altar and had to be led to the sacristy to regain his composure.[41] Duprez, as tenor soloist, acquitted himself admirably. It was a near-perfect performance, the delight of the public, and the talk of Paris. The composer's friends were in high exultation: it was agreed that he had surpassed himself, and that it would be impossible to do better or to produce music of greater effect. Many declared that they had never been so moved by a musical work. "Hé bien," wrote Legouvé, "êtes-vous content?"[42]

Indeed he was happy, but for an accident which befell the beginning of the *Tuba mirum:* here, the *Mémoires* have it, Habeneck indulged in a favored habit by pausing to take a pinch of snuff at the critical moment of transition. However unlikely the pinch of snuff incident seems in the retelling, it appears an established fact that something went wrong there, and that Habeneck caused it. In view of the evidence of how Habeneck conducted, the inference is clear that he let his guard, and probably his bow, fall as the lugubrious *Dies irae* played itself; perhaps, as was sometimes his habit, he did not move

FIGURE 6.9
Habeneck and
his snuffbox.

at all. (Mendelssohn, too, is known to have ceased conducting during longer movements, "when he knew they were safe, with a little nod, as much as to say 'This will go very well without me'."[43]) The brass fanfare preceding the *Tuba mirum* caught him unaware.

It was a simple mistake, no worse than countless others caused in that era by the prevailing style of conducting. Berlioz rescued the passage, he says in the *Mémoires*, by marking the new tempo himself. Where Berlioz and Habeneck did part artistic company was over *Benvenuto Cellini* the following year: Berlioz viewed Habeneck as unnecessarily ill-humored over having to conduct the difficult opera, which he would have liked to lead himself, and Habeneck found the young composer's repeated insistence on faster and faster tempi to constitute an unseemly and arrogant tampering with his prerogatives.[44]

How much the listeners could have grasped of the Requiem is not clear, for it could not have been heard in circumstances less conducive to understanding it. Those who came to hear the music were seated at great distance from the catafalque, the performers, and the many general officers of the military who had come to pay their last respects. The bereaved wept loudly. The priests chanted the Gregorian funeral service throughout, with no regard to the music being performed. Berlioz's music did not recede into nothingness, as he had meant the ceremony to end, for the clerics insisted on a polyphonic Te Deum in *fauxbourdon* at the conclusion of the funeral.

Yet only three reviewers of the several dozen who wrote of the event offered negative impressions—and none of those had been seen there. Jules Janin raved in the *Débats* ("The effect of this Requiem was all powerful"),[45] as did Auguste Bottée de Toulmon in the pages of the *Revue et Gazette musicale*. Montalivet sent the composer an unexpected honorarium of 1,000 francs to recognize the exceptional accomplishment, thus resolving Berlioz's most pressing debts for the year. Arrangements were made with Schlesinger for immediate engraving of the score, and a subscription drive was opened: the list price was 90 francs, with advance subscribers paying only 30.

Of the many ecstatic notes he received, the most satisfying must have been the one from the minister of War:[46]

> Sir, I hasten to express to you all the satisfaction I sensed in hearing the performance of the Requiem Mass of which you are the author, and which has just been sung at the funeral service for General Damrémont.
>
> The success obtained by this beautiful and severe composition complimented with dignity the solemnity of the occasion. And I am pleased with myself for having been able to furnish you with this new occasion to tap the talent which puts you in the first rank of our composers of sacred music.
>
> Accept, Sir, the certainty of my most distinguished regards.
>
> Le Pair de France,
> Minister-Secretary of State for War,
>
> Bernard

His luck had finally turned.

---

*W*hen Schlesinger asked Berlioz for a notice on the sumptuous New Year's albums that were gracing Parisian parlors, Berlioz was so exhausted and exasperated that instead of a review he published an open letter begging to be left alone to finish the overture to his opera. Another explanation for this retreat from journalism is that he wished to maintain a low profile before the opening night of *Cellini,* not daring to anger the musical establishment. He held firm in his partial retirement. Although he continued to write weekly for the *Revue et Gazette musicale,* columns for the *Journal des Débats* appeared only sporadically for the rest of the year, something on the order of once a month, not to resume until the spring of 1839.

Early in the morning of 17 January, after a performance of *Don Giovanni,* the Salle Favart and all the properties of its resident company, the Théâtre-Italien, burned to the ground. A faulty gas jet in the heating system of the scenery warehouse had started the fire; there was not enough water in the neighboring Chinese baths to put it out, and the efforts of the bucket line had thus been for naught. Severini, the director of the Théâtre-Italien, leapt from a window and was killed. Now there were only two serious music theaters left in Paris: the Opéra and the Opéra-Comique, the latter playing at the time in the Salle de la Bourse.

This was just the sort of unexpected turn of events that might afford Berlioz his permanent job. Hardly had the smoke dissipated than he was writing to the Ministry to secure the privilege of reorganizing the theater.[47] His proposal was to reopen the Théâtre-Italien in the Salle Ventadour—the very building that had housed the ill-fated Théâtre-Nautique. He would produce the latest works from Italy or by the Italian masters of Paris; and in the summer months he would offer other opera and, to be sure, English tragedy. He would establish a formidable company, made up of the best singers available.

His petition was complicated somewhat by the fact that the matter of payment for his Requiem was still unresolved. The Minister of War had kept his end of the bargain, but there was still discussion of the fee owed to the composer. When they told him at the Ministry of the Interior that they had disposed of the 4,000 francs (or, as Berlioz put it, "to speak French—they had stolen them"),[48] he became blue with anger, made a scene in front of the minister's secretary, and threatened to compile a detailed account of the whole sordid mess for the *Journal des Débats*. The order for payment was issued directly, on 23 January 1838, and Berlioz collected his money the next week, but the display could not have improved greatly his chances of securing the privilege of the Théâtre-Italien.

His mother died on 8 March. She and her family had never made the long-promised trip to Paris to meet her grandchild and daughter-in-law, nor had she ever heard her son's mature work. Dr. Berlioz informed his four children as to the provisions of her estate; Berlioz's annual pension from his mother's holdings would be some 1,200 francs. Dr. Berlioz, looking to the future, promised to divide his own estate into equal parts. If Berlioz wished to finish his days "beneath the paternal roof," his father would leave him a home, presumably the house in La Côte;[49] otherwise he would have the property sold for cash. Nanci's husband Camille Pal took over the supervision of the family properties; Berlioz begged his father not to think of such dark matters and urged him, again, to come to Paris.

Later in March, *Benvenuto Cellini* finally entered rehearsals, slowly at first, with the coaching of soloists, then with growing frequency through the summer.

The Théâtre-Italien initiative was but one of several efforts Berlioz undertook during those months to secure for himself a salaried post in teaching or artistic administration. The death of Louis-Victor Rifaut—the pianist who had not been able to play *Orphée* in 1827—left a vacancy in harmony instruction at the Conservatoire, for which Berlioz proposed himself. Cherubini convinced him that one needed to be able to play the piano to teach such courses and forced him to withdraw. "Come, embrace me," said Cherubini when the interview was done. "You know how fond I am of you."[50] (Ultimately an equally suspect pianist, Paul-Emile Bienaimé, was named to the post.) There was also talk that Berlioz was on the list for the Legion of Honor, to be conferred on the king's official birthday in May, and that honor carried with its cross a small annual pension; a few months later his candidacy as master of the royal chapel was briefly at issue. But the Legion of Honor was delayed for nearly a year, as was any other appointment.

For much of the spring it seemed that the proposal for the Théâtre-Italien was on the verge of ministerial approval. On 12 June Berlioz and his consortium were asked to deposit 10,000 francs, 5 percent of the capital necessary to underwrite the venture. There was opposition to the plan, however, led by the deputy from the Isère, and the project came to its end on 19 June when the Chamber of Deputies defeated the proposed legislation. By this time, however, Berlioz had had his fill of capitalism and of plans for reconstructing halls: he was an artist, ill equipped for such tedious and ultimately trivial pursuits. He was notified on 21 June to reclaim the deposit and was happy to do so. The end of this story is ironic, for the Théâtre-Italien was indeed reorganized, some years later, along precisely the lines Berlioz proposed in 1838.

Habeneck sent news from Lille of a brilliant performance of the Lacrymosa from the Requiem. There had been five to six hundred performers at the Féstival du Nord on 25 June, and several thousand people in the audience. The excitement was repeated the next day. Berlioz reckoned that all must have gone well indeed for the old wolf to have bothered to write. He was careful to place this news in the *Revue et Gazette musicale,* quoting Habeneck's letter in full and reminding readers of their opportunity to subscribe to the published edition.

The time he had taken off from criticism, along with the failure of the Théâtre-Italien venture, caused substantial monetary embarrassment just as *Cellini* was reaching fruition. It was the proper moment for a dramatic step: to claim the 1,200 francs from his mother's estate, for example, and to extend his financial obligation to Legouvé by perhaps another 1,000 francs. Whatever the precise total of his loan, Legouvé had become *Cellini*'s guardian angel. He had given "the metal to cast Perseus, and thus Benvenuto owes you his work, however it is":[51] he had earned its dedication.

The pace of the orchestral and choral rehearsals quickened as the summer went by. In addition to supervising the formal rehearsals, Berlioz coached the soloists at their homes, often spending six hours a day preparing *Cellini.* The score surpassed in difficulty anything he had written—or indeed would ever write. The libretto, too, was unusual, and the sum of the parts seemed daunting by comparison with the modernisms of Meyerbeer, Halévy, or Rossini. The chorus grumbled at first and declared the music *inexécutable,* but little by little came to enjoy their rambunctious parts, now and then bursting into spontaneous applause. Mme Dorus-Gras, his Teresa, proved a delight: diligent and sympathetic, she willingly delayed her summer holiday to prepare her part. Nevertheless, Berlioz grew fearful of opening night, especially of the retribution from critics he had had the temerity to offend in his own columns. And he could not control his own production from the orchestra pit, forbidden the baton by ironclad traditions of the house.

By July there were two rehearsals each day, one in the morning and one in the early evening. The final text went to the censor, who required the authors to remove Pope Clement VIII; Berlioz and his associates scrambled to make the necessary corrections to libretto and music, replacing the pope with a cardinal named Salviati. The censor also complained of the litany in the second act—"Vas spirituale Maria sancta mater ora pro nobis," etc.—but left this matter open pending the experience of the first performances. Berlioz, already overworked, fell violently ill in late July with a nervous attack brought on by the orchestral rehearsals. The crotchety old men played hundreds of wrong notes, he wrote, were manifestly unable to sense the metric tricks, and indulged in the foolishness typical of unwilling players. Habeneck was civil, but just barely.

The premiere was postponed by one week, then by another. Yet by opening night the composer sensed that confidence which can only come from there being no other choice, and he thanked his artists in a profuse note:

To Messieurs, the Artists of the Opéra
Messieurs
   Now that my work is about to be presented, I feel the need to thank all the artists participating in its performance for the zeal and the patience they have brought to the difficult work of the rehearsals.
   Whatever befalls my score, I shall always keep the memory of the indications of interest and devotion which I have had from MM. the artists of the Opéra, and I beg them to accept my expressions of gratitude.[52]

Benvenuto Cellini at last opened to the public on Monday night, 10 September. Habeneck conducted a distinguished cast made up of the highest-ranking singers at the Opéra, the best singers, indeed, of the nation: the tenor Gilbert Duprez as Cellini; Mme Dorus-Gras as Teresa; Rosina Stoltz as Ascanio, the role in which she began her spectacular and controversial rise to the pinnacle of her profession; Prosper Dérivis as Balducci; and J.-E.-A. Massol as Fieramosca. *Cellini* was surely a *succès d'estime*. The thinking public discovered in the opera, especially the first act, the same vividness and color the composer himself treasured in it for the rest of his life. But except for the overture, the work failed to impress the general audience. It was unfortunate that the merit of *Cellini* rested so heavily on its first act, for certain influential segments of the public made it a point of honor not to arrive before the second curtain. Berlioz's opera had only two acts, with the four most successful movements—Teresa's cavatina, Cellini's aria "La gloire était ma seule idole," and the tavern and carnival scenes—all before intermission.

Opening night was not the abysmal failure many writers have made it out to be, but it was far from a rousing success. Berlioz knew from the beginning that his work would have to prove itself over many rehearings, and thus it was not a little encouraging that the second and third performances, on 12 and 14 September, fared better with both the artists and the audience. But after first nights it is open season on passages that displease singers, man-

FIGURE 6.10 Poster announcing the first performance of *Benvenuto Cellini*.

agement, and especially the public. Berlioz was constrained to eliminate passage after passage, including much of the sextet in act II. It was all done in a rush, with the result that no one performance was quite the same as any of the others. The difficulties with the text of the denouement and the corresponding musical problems of the second act—nothing in the rest of the work has close to the élan of the tavern scene and the Roman carnival— were insurmountable, at least for the moment. Painstaking corrections of detail and an overall rethinking of the structural flaws would have to come later.

Cellini might have fared markedly better with only a half-dozen more performances. But Mme Dorus-Gras had a right to her vacation, and further performances were postponed until her return. Meanwhile, Duprez could not hide his unhappiness with the title role, his second creation (after the male title role in *Guido et Ginevra*) at the Opéra. The women soloists garnered the bulk of the critical attention—and rightly so, according to the composer. Duprez disliked Berlioz's idiosyncratic tunes, having found his music overly demanding in stamina and tessitura. ("Le talent de Berlioz," he wrote in his 1880 recollections, "n'était pas précisément mélodique."[53]) His wife was in labor when he left her to sing the third performance; during the last act, he spotted the doctor in the wings, got befuddled, and never regained his place. (The news was good: Madame had been delivered of a boy, their first son.) Duprez, too, took a holiday, and he resigned the role

FIGURE 6.11 Costume renderings for Cellini and Teresa in *Benvenuto Cellini*.

before he left town. It seemed to Berlioz the most acute sort of betrayal, particularly as he had praised Duprez's debuts in *Guillaume Tell* and *Les Huguenots* a few months before. But in such situations as these, a composer has little recourse. *Cellini* was advertised in November and December, but not given.

Alexis Dupont came forward to learn the tenor part and, though he found it more difficult than he had expected, had mastered it by January. By that time, however, *Benvenuto Cellini* was essentially dead, and Dupont had but a single opportunity to sing both acts. Liszt, who was to become the great champion of *Cellini,* shrugged his shoulders on hearing the bad news: "Nevertheless, Berlioz remains the most vigorous musical mind in France."[54]

The opera did occasion a typically Parisian war of pamphleteers. The *Débats* had done its best to prepare the way for *Cellini;* yet Joseph Mainzer launched an attack in a leaflet he called *De M. Berlioz, de ses compositions et de ses critiques musicales,* and Blaze du Bury followed suit in the *Revue des deux mondes.* A cartoonist dubbed it *Malvenuto Cellini* ("with literary pasquarelloisms and musical harlequinisms; at the end of the parade a big statue will be cast [in bronze], and the composer, too"; fig. 6.12). The London *Musical World* ran a long article on the opera, the first major study of Berlioz in the English press. Noted musicians wrote letters to editors about *Cellini* and occasioned lively responses. D'Ortigue entered the fray in 1839 with a 350-page book in favor of Berlioz's work, surely polished by the composer, called *De l'école musicale italienne et de l'administration de l'Académie Royale de Musique à l'occasion de l'opéra de M. H. Berlioz.*

Berlioz himself attributed the failure, with some justification, to the libretto. Auguste Barbier, on the other hand, argued that the libretto was constrained by the givens from the composer and (he was, after all, the librettist) that it was fundamentally a good text. The failure had to do with the composer's politics:

> Before presenting himself on the lyric stage, M. Berlioz had mixed criticism with composition. A fine writer and able polemicist, a lively and mordant satirist, he

FIGURE 6.12 "L'Homme-orchestre: *Malvenuto Cellini.*"

proclaimed his opinions incisively and even excessively with regard to some of the most renowned of his colleagues. They forgot nothing of these opinions, and when he presented himself as a dramatic composer, he was judged with severity by all those who neither shared his opinions nor admired his talent.[55]

Barbier also detected an excess of exuberance in the harmonic language and lack of experience in writing for the operatic voice. Like many others, however, he was well taken with the beauty of the music.

The composer was the model of sanguine resignation. He knew of the enemies his *feuilletons* had caused, and that his opera might perplex even his admirers. He suspected he and his librettists had been wrong to imagine that a book concerning art and artists could have interested a public more content to see (and not hear) operas about political events. *Cellini* was, in fact, a burst of old-style Romanticism, with hearty and purposeful mixing of styles—partly as a result of its complex history, partly out of artistic principle—that confused its audience; Berlioz had been as experimental and as unorthodox as Hugo or Vigny, and their work had been similarly received. At some later time, he was confident, the opera would prove itself. And that prophecy was in some sense fulfilled, but not in Paris. After four full performances of *Cellini* in 1838 and three offerings of act I in 1839, his dramatic music would not be heard at the Opéra again until well after his death, and to this day not one of his operas has a significant place in its repertoire. By contrast, Gounod's *Faust* had 424 performances before 1876, and even the strange *Freischütz* with which Berlioz was to be affiliated in the 1840s had over 60 performances in five years.

Berlioz had sold the rights to *Cellini* to Adolphe Catelin, the publisher of *Le Jeune Pâtre breton* and the *Chant des bretons,* for a modest price. He then had second thoughts and arranged, under somewhat false pretenses, to have them transferred to Schlesinger. Schlesinger published nearly everything from the opera that lent itself to home performance—nine excerpts in all, two of them from plates Catelin had already produced; shortly thereafter he offered the overture in score and parts. Otherwise *Benvenuto Cellini* remained unpublished and therefore unavailable for study.

The Requiem, on the other hand, appeared in October 1838, Maurice Schlesinger's handsome score constituting Berlioz's first luxuriant publication. The dedication was to Gasparin, who had commissioned it. This score was followed by those of the *Waverley* and *Benvenuto Cellini* overtures and, after some delay, the parts and later the score of *Le Roi Lear.* Liszt began a piano transcription of *Le Roi Lear* in 1837, but never finished it.

Prosper Berlioz, eighteen years old, arrived in Paris during the last week of October to enroll at a preparatory academy. Berlioz, Harriet, and particularly the four-year-old Louis had looked forward to his arrival: Harriet planned a large welcoming party, and Louis hoped to go on hunting trips with his uncle. Berlioz was delighted to have Prosper close by and took every

FIGURE 6.13 [9 *Morceaux détachés de*] *Benvenuto Cellini*, title page (Paris: M. Schlesinger, [1839]).

opportunity he could to be with him. After a brief stay in the rue de Londres, the boy took lodging at the pension Babil and began his studies. He was not happy in the school, an institution intended primarily for younger children. His advanced age for primary study, the history of his difficulties at home, and the tone of Berlioz's remarks to his father—"He is slow spirited, but sooner or later will develop in a most remarkable manner"[56]—all suggest that Prosper had some sort of learning disability or perhaps was retarded. He had always been frail.

The nervous attack Berlioz sustained in late summer had turned by autumn into a severe bronchitis that plagued him for the rest of the year. Ill health combined with the uncertainty surrounding the fate of his opera caused him to let the dates proposed for his end-of-year concerts come and go; at length the concert dates were fixed for 25 November and 16 December, Sundays three weeks apart. Berlioz, too ill to go out, attended to most of the organizational work for the concerts by mail and messenger; the correspondence of November and December thus provides unusually precise documentation of his style of concert management. By late November it was clear that he was too ill to appear, and Habeneck agreed to conduct the first concert in his stead.

The concerts featured the symphonies and overtures, and Mmes Stoltz and Dorus-Gras sang their arias from *Cellini*. The programs also included an aria from Gluck's *Alceste,* sung by Mme Stoltz, and a "madrigal" of Clari, *Cantando un dì,* actually one of his duo cantatas with continuo, known to Berlioz from the Paris print of 1823. (He may have learned of Clari while writing his biographies of Italian musicians some months before.) He was well enough to conduct the concert of 16 December. Cognizant of how little new work there was to offer, he programmed both the *Fantastique* and *Harold* to improve receipts. The 1838 concerts, like most of the performances from the second half of the decade, were warmly received. The revival of Gluck was especially appreciated; indeed, the violinist Seghers, *aîné* had to leave the stage after the selection to regain his composure.

It is worth emphasizing once more how routinely successful the concerts from 1836 on had become. No one else was producing anything remotely so audacious. The Berlioz seasons were followed attentively by the press and anticipated with pleasure by the intellectuals. The artists valued their participation in the Berlioz concerts and came to recognize the concerts as fixtures of Parisian life.

Paganini had returned to Paris to appear at the Casino Paganini, his barely legal pleasure dome for music, dance, conversation, and most especially gambling. His backing of the casino was an ill-advised venture that only exacerbated the tarnish of his public image and led eventually to a national prohibition of such lairs. He was, however, induced to come to the concert of 16 December, where for the first time he heard the masterpiece he had commissioned. At the conclusion he led the exhausted and trembling composer back to the stage, to the surprise of the musicians packing to leave, and tried to make a speech. With his beloved son Achille struggling to make sense of his croaking noises, he fell to his knees before the startled orchestra, kissed Berlioz's hand, and declared him, again, to be the successor to Beethoven. Then he disappeared.[57] It was a fully public meeting of two of the most carefully watched figures in music, the meteoric encountering the volcanic.

Berlioz, still afflicted with bronchitis, could only take to his bed. On Tuesday morning 18 December, Achille Paganini entered his bedroom with "a letter that requires no response"[58] and hastily backed away. In the envelope was a draft on the Rothschild bank for 20,000 francs as a token of Paganini's homage, along with a rapturous note in Italian which began,

Beethoven having left us, only Berlioz can make him come alive again.[59]

Not for two more days was Berlioz able to leave his bed; his first duty then, of course, was to visit Paganini at the Néothermes, in the rue de la Victoire. The violinist wept to see him; they embraced, then conversed after their fashion. Paganini did not need to be thanked, he said, for the gift had given him the greatest satisfaction of his life. "You have introduced me to emotions I never suspected."[60] He stayed in Paris long enough to see the fourth performance of *Cellini*, on 11 January 1839, and grant an interview to Morel ("I did it for Berlioz, and for myself," he said),[61] then left for Genoa and Nice. The press was riveted by the news. Schlesinger went so far as to publish facsimiles of Paganini's note and Berlioz's response in the *Revue et Gazette musicale*. Inevitably there was negative reaction, too: someone wrote to Berlioz begging him to blow his brains out, and he imagined that if he were Spanish or Italian, he would have been assassinated twenty times over.

Neither king nor minister, said Janin in one of his typically apt essays, could have offered an artist such tribute. Paganini's gift surely ranks with the patronage of King Ludwig of Bavaria and Mme von Meck, and nothing can match the circumstances of its delivery. Berlioz took the money—nearly twice what he lived on annually—and, at long last, paid his remaining debts to Legouvé and Edouard Rocher and began to think of a major new composition. It may have been at this point that he abandoned a strange cantata on Ballanche's *Erigone,* of which a few fragments have been preserved, for more significant pursuits.

On the heels of the excitement came news that Gasparin, once again the minister of the Interior, had appointed him assistant librarian (*sous-biblio-thécaire*) of the Conservatoire, a lifetime sinecure with an annual stipend of some 1,500 francs. This salary of 125 francs a month—minus 7 francs of tax; Berlioz always speaks of it as 118 francs—was actually that of the head librarian, Berlioz's close friend Auguste Bottée de Toulmon, who served without pay. There were only a few duties attached, mostly the acknowledging of gifts to the collection. The position was, moreover, appropriate to his reputation as a savant: it gave him the opportunity to pursue his curiosities at leisure and in an office of his own. It was both a fitting appointment and an ironic one: fitting because he had garnered much of his initial excitement over composition in that very library; ironic because Cherubini had thrown him out of it, yet now professed to be happy to see him on the staff. Berlioz had just turned thirty-five years of age.

The unexpectedness of the Paganini incident overshadows two other important results of the 1838 concerts. The president of the London Philharmonic Society, Lord Burghersh, approached Berlioz to inquire about the possibility of his conducting a two-month series of concerts in London. And Stephen Heller, who enthusiastically reviewed one of the concerts for the *Revue et Gazette musicale*,[62] became Berlioz's most important new acquaintance of the year. Heller moved to Paris in 1838 from Augsburg and must have met Berlioz at Schlesinger's establishment shortly thereafter. They became good friends and in due time grew old together. Berlioz admired Heller's sense of humor and erudition, and they shared literary affinities. Compositionally they were very different, for Berlioz wrote bold symphonic music, whereas Heller composed salon pieces for the piano, works Berlioz found melancholy and almost religious in their ardor. In short they were brothers in "the small family of humble musicians who love and respect their art."[63] It was through Heller that Berlioz met and befriended other members of that small family, such as the German pianist and conductor Charles Hallé, who had arrived in Paris in 1836.

The fourth performance of *Benvenuto Cellini*, having been announced for and then postponed from both 21 November and 2 December, "owing to the illnesses of the singers," was finally given on 11 January, with Dupont in the leading role. Dupont lacked force and seemed apathetic to some, but he did his best in difficult circumstances. After that, only the first act of *Cellini* was offered, on double bills with a ballet—the standard formula for squeezing the last *sou* out of a failed work—once in February and twice in March. Berlioz wrote Duponchel a terse note withdrawing the work on 17 March 1839.

It had taken Paganini's magnanimous gesture to get him working again on a major composition, this one a symphony with Romeo and Juliet represented not by singers but by the infinitely richer voices of the orchestra. The questions surrounding Paganini's gift—whether he was attempting to buy posthumous glory and whether the backing actually came from some powerful figure like Bertin[64]—are irrelevant. Paganini's gift offered incentive and at least in theory some time free from journalism. (In fact 1839 shows thirty-three newspaper articles, including regular reports for both the *Revue et Gazette musicale* and the *Journal des Débats,* though there were a few long breaks.) What Berlioz no longer had to do was concern himself with old debts. Within two weeks, he was hard at work on *Roméo et Juliette.* He sent a scenario to Emile Deschamps, whose "most musical facility" he admired, then wrote to Liszt and Ferrand that he had begun his new symphony, and dated a draft of the *Fête chez Capulet* "commencé le 24"—24 January, that is, 1839.

The new symphony was the main work of the winter, spring, and summer. Berlioz reports feverish activity and sleep lost over the work in his letters from early spring; by May he writes, in much the same manner he had spoken of the Requiem, that the euphoria had passed and he was working in cold blood.

Prosper Berlioz, whose health was never especially good, died at his pension on 15 January, presumably of a respiratory infection. He had just been to *Cellini*, where he had enjoyed himself.

Berlioz planned and then retreated from a concert on 1 March: a *fête musicale* at the Théâtre de la Renaissance or one of the large rooms in the Hôtel de Ville, to feature the big movements of the Requiem and *Le Cinq Mai*.[65] He had heard·in late February of Adèle's engagement to Marc Suat, a notary; they were married on 1 April. There was much to distract him from his work in May as well. Ferdinando Paër, one of the professors of composition at the Conservatoire, died on 3 May, and Berlioz proclaimed himself a candidate for the vacant chair, as did Halévy, Elwart, Niedermeyer, and others; Berlioz's nemesis, the patrician Carafa, who had already succeeded to Le Sueur's seat in the Academy, was elected to the professorship. Berlioz was never seriously considered for Paër's duties at court either, despite his optimism in that regard. Also May saw the arrival in Paris of the body of the tenor Nourrit, who had killed himself that March by leaping from his hotel window in Naples. Nourrit had been an ardent supporter of Berlioz since the late 1820s, and the grateful composer thus felt obliged to attend the burial. He was the only significant composer present.

The day before the burial, he was decorated with his ribbon and medal of the Legion of Honor—to which he had been elected two months earlier—along with Duponchel, director of the Opéra, and Bordogni, the singing teacher. In the *Mémoires* he remarks that he would not have given thirty *sous* for the honor, but in fact he was proud of it. Meyerbeer stood as his sponsor. Spontini, whose feelings were hurt by that choice, had his measure of reward soon enough: he was elected to the Institute in June.

Adèle and her new husband Marc Suat arrived in Paris in late May on their wedding trip. There were at least tentative plans for them to take Louis back to La Côte-St.-André to meet his grandfather, though this idea was at some point abandoned. The family seem to have regarded Suat as a poor match for Adèle, perhaps because of his modest social circumstance or the distance he lived from La Côte, but Berlioz liked him from their first meeting and was always more intimate with Suat than with Nanci's husband, Camille Pal. They toured Paris together that May, Adèle's portrait was made, and Berlioz took them to have tea with Alfred de Vigny. They agreed to urge their father, who since the death of Prosper and the marriage of Adèle was alone in La Côte-St.-André, to come to Paris, perhaps bringing Nanci and her husband with him.

Roméo et Juliette was on schedule and would be ready to present at the concerts of November and December. To Carolyne Sayn-Wittgenstein, Berlioz wrote in 1856 that the *Scène d'amour* and the *Serment de réconciliation* were the most difficult to compose, yet the tomb scene was in fact the last to be completed. Berlioz signed and dated his autograph on 8 September

1839. Among the first to see the new manuscript was Moscheles, who had come to make Berlioz's acquaintance during his visit to Paris. Moscheles admired the excellent penmanship, but professed that the music was too much for him to grasp.

On 17 September another sojourner quietly arrived in Paris: Richard Wagner. He and Berlioz almost surely met—or at least learned of each other—soon afterward, for Wagner's name is entered in Berlioz's hand on a seating list for one of the first performances of *Roméo et Juliette*. Their initial encounter was probably in the offices of the *Revue et Gazette musicale*, for which Wagner wrote some criticism. But Wagner was living poorly, eking out a subsistence with the journal and extracting from the operas in vogue suites for chamber ensemble, and Berlioz could have paid him little heed at the time. He did not, for example, cover the 1841 *Revue et Gazette musicale* concert where Wagner's *Columbus* overture was given.

From the completion of *Roméo et Juliette* in early September until the first performance in November, Berlioz was occupied with arrangements for the premiere: parts to be copied, chorus parts to be lithographed, and rehearsals to be got under way. Such matters as the different-colored dresses for the Montagus and the Capulets had to be negotiated with the affected parties and resolved. The soloists and the prologue chorus, all of whom came from the Opéra, were rehearsed during the intermissions of performances there; the bass had been receiving private coaching since mid-October. The orchestra was drilled through a novel system developed by the composer and later adopted everywhere: sectional rehearsals. One full rehearsal, on 14 November, preceded the sectionals, and the public dress rehearsal was called for the 23rd. Hearing *Roméo et Juliette* in its entirety for the first time so positively affected the performers that the success of the work seemed assured.

Roméo et Juliette is, if not Berlioz's most ambitious work of the 1830s, surely his best one. It was presented to the Parisian public in three successive concerts under his own direction on 24 November, 1 December, and 15 December 1839, all Sundays, at 2:00 P.M. in the Salle du Conservatoire. Louis Alizard, whose "grave and unctuous" bass voice Berlioz admired,[66] was Père Laurence. Alexis Dupont, who had replaced Duprez as Cellini the year before and who was the tenor soloist at the first performance of *Le Retour à la vie*, sang the tenor scherzetto, *Mab la messagère*. Mme Stoltz had been announced as the female soloist and apparently had expected to sing the part all along, but she did not appear, perhaps having found the *Strophes* too low. It was Emily Widemann, a contralto, who actually sang the aria. (Mme Stoltz did go to the concert and sent Berlioz a congratulatory note on his triumph.) To the program of the third performance, Berlioz added movements I and II of *Harold en Italie* and Teresa's *Cavatine* from *Benvenuto Cellini,* sung by Mme Dorus-Gras; he may have cut portions of the prologue and the entire tomb scene to allow for the other works.

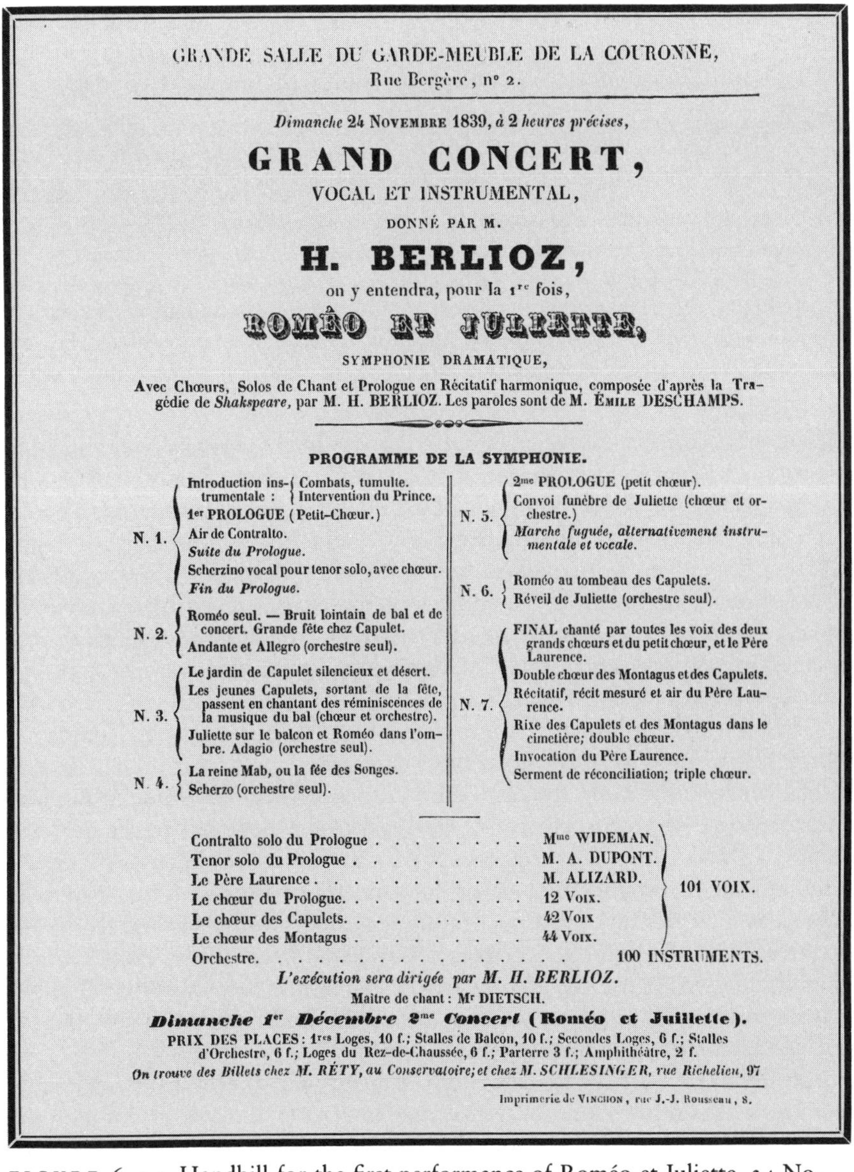

GRANDE SALLE DU GARDE-MEUBLE DE LA COURONNE,
Rue Bergère, n° 2.

Dimanche 24 Novembre 1839, à 2 heures précises,

GRAND CONCERT,
VOCAL ET INSTRUMENTAL,

DONNÉ PAR M.

H. BERLIOZ,

on y entendra, pour la 1re fois,

ROMÉO ET JULIETTE,

SYMPHONIE DRAMATIQUE,

Avec Chœurs, Solos de Chant et Prologue en Récitatif harmonique, composée d'après la Tragédie de *Shakspeare*, par M. H. BERLIOZ. Les paroles sont de M. ÉMILE DESCHAMPS.

PROGRAMME DE LA SYMPHONIE.

N. 1.
- Introduction instrumentale : { Combats, tumulte. Intervention du Prince.
- 1er PROLOGUE (Petit–Chœur.)
- Air de Contralto.
- *Suite du Prologue.*
- Scherzino vocal pour tenor solo, avec chœur.
- *Fin du Prologue.*

N. 2.
- Roméo seul. — Bruit lointain de bal et de concert. Grande fête chez Capulet.
- Andante et Allegro (orchestre seul).

N. 3.
- Le jardin de Capulet silencieux et désert.
- Les jeunes Capulets, sortant de la fête, passent en chantant des réminiscences de la musique du bal (chœur et orchestre).
- Juliette sur le balcon et Roméo dans l'ombre. Adagio (orchestre seul).

N. 4.
- La reine Mab, ou la fée des Songes.
- Scherzo (orchestre seul).

N. 5.
- 2me PROLOGUE (petit chœur).
- Convoi funèbre de Juliette (chœur et orchestre.)
- *Marche fuguée, alternativement instrumentale et vocale.*

N. 6.
- Roméo au tombeau des Capulets.
- Réveil de Juliette (orchestre seul).

N. 7.
- FINAL chanté par toutes les voix des deux grands chœurs et du petit chœur, et le Père Laurence.
- Double chœur des Montagus et des Capulets.
- Récitatif, récit mesuré et air du Père Laurence.
- Rixe des Capulets et des Montagus dans le cimetière; double chœur.
- Invocation du Père Laurence.
- Serment de réconciliation; triple chœur.

Contralto solo du Prologue	Mme WIDEMAN.	
Tenor solo du Prologue	M. A. DUPONT.	
Le Père Laurence	M. ALIZARD.	101 VOIX.
Le chœur du Prologue	12 Voix.	
Le chœur des Capulets	42 Voix	
Le chœur des Montagus	44 Voix.	
Orchestre.		100 INSTRUMENTS.

L'exécution sera dirigée par M. H. BERLIOZ.
Maitre de chant : Mr DIETSCH.

Dimanche 1er Décembre 2me Concert (Roméo et Juillette).

PRIX DES PLACES : 1res Loges, 10 f.; Stalles de Balcon, 10 f.; Secondes Loges, 6 f.; Stalles d'Orchestre, 6 f.; Loges du Rez-de-Chaussée, 6 f.; Parterre 3 f.; Amphithéâtre, 2 f.

On trouve des Billets chez M. RÉTY, au Conservatoire; et chez M. SCHLESINGER, rue Richelieu, 97

Imprimerie de VINCHON, rue J.-J. Rousseau, 8.

FIGURE 6.14 Handbill for the first performance of Roméo et Juliette, 24 November 1839.

There were just over two hundred performers: a hundred instrumentalists, more than forty singers in each of the two choruses, twelve singers in the prologue chorus, and the three soloists. The creative rehearsal scheme and efficient use of time led to an exceptionally polished performance. Players and singers acquitted themselves with glory; Berlioz was delighted with Alizard. The composer himself conducted with such dignity and power that, with these performances, he entered the ranks of the great conductors of Europe.

The triumph of the first performance was repeated twice more. Berlioz describes the concert of 1 December to his father as follows:

> The second performance of *Roméo et Juliette* was a total success. They showered me with applause, shouts, tears, and all the rest.
>
> At the end of the concert, [after] the reconciliation of the Capulets and Montagus, the orchestra and choruses stood and filled the hall with cheers, while the public offered shattering applause from parterre and gallery. For a moment I was afraid of losing my *sang-froid,* the thing I fear most, but I kept calm.[67]

Of the third concert, he wrote Adèle: "The performance was overwhelming. Nobody had ever dared give the same work three times in a row."[68]

The reaction of the public—which included the queen and at least two of her sons, Berlioz's uncle Auguste Berlioz and his family, Balzac, Vigny, Gautier, Beethoven's amanuensis Schindler, and Wagner—was ecstatic. The press, though guarded on the subject of the choral recitatives, concurred. Janin's notice in the *Journal des Débats* concluded: "The success was as great as it ought to have been. The terrifying gamble that Berlioz made was won, completely won." An Englishman "bought" the composer's baton from a servant for 120 francs. Catelin published the *Strophes* on Tuesday, 3 December, in time to profit from the excitement.

The concerts did well, too, at the box office. For the first time in Berlioz's career, people were turned away. He reckoned a personal profit of 1,200 francs, 13,200 francs of receipts less 12,000 francs of expenses. This was only half the income from some of the concerts of 1835–36, but it must be viewed as a large sum, given the cost of performers and parts and the luxury of three full performances. The total budget had been on the same order of magnitude as that for the Requiem; the difference here was that Berlioz's private purse was at stake, whereas before he had enjoyed the backing of one of the richest governments in the world.

Yet just after the first concert, Berlioz mentioned "several little changes I want to make in my score,"[69] and revisions of both a major and minor sort would continue for another six years. Paganini never saw or heard the work he had fostered with his gift and of which he was the dedicatee.

Berlioz spent January marking time and remarshaling his forces after the letdown that always follows great undertakings. The cycles of exhilaration and exhaustion during the months just past were succeeded by a period of depression. His family did not help by harping on the reference in Janin's review to Berlioz's continuing financial embarrassment. Paganini wrote from Nice imploring Berlioz to help him with the paperwork necessary to resolve the 50,000-franc assessment on his casino. Having left France definitively, Paganini had thought he was safe from the fine; in Nice, he had received a French vice-consul and a representative of the casino, who seized his musical instruments to hold for ransom.[70]

Habeneck was ill, perhaps terminally, and there was some thought that Berlioz might eventually succeed him as principal conductor at the Opéra. There were negotiations with Scribe for a three-act grand opera. Berlioz was offered a libretto—not long before he would have deemed that a great victory—but he could not yet face the physical and emotional strain of producing another opera and so returned it unread. He ventured out to conduct the seventh *Gazette musicale* concert on 6 February, where the brilliant reception accorded the *Benvenuto Cellini* overture gave a critic or two second thoughts about the worth of the opera. But he was suffering from spleen: his youth was fleeing—"I feel 110 years old"[71]—and he had no notion of what to do next. By February this mood had turned into a full-fledged attack of the nervous system, and he took to his bed with uncontrolled trembling. Harriet was suffering from tonsillitis, and Louis had the measles.

The long-delayed score of *Le Roi Lear* finally appeared, three months after the orchestral parts had come on the market. Berlioz sent the autograph manuscript,[72] for which there was no more use, and a copy of the printed score to his friend and patron Armand Bertin, its dedicatee, along with the most poignant of his letters of dedication:

> I am sending you our *Roi Lear* overture, which is finally published, along with the manuscript which I beg you to keep.
> The dedication of a piece of music is banal homage, which has no worth except for the merit of the work, but I hope you will accept this one as the testimony of the grateful friendship which I have held toward you for a long time.
>
> H. Berlioz
12 February 1840

Soon after *Lear* became available in score and parts, it was programmed by the more adventurous orchestras in Germany: Frankfurt, Brunswick, and Bremen. It enjoyed a good reception, similar to that which had been accorded *Waverley* in London the year before. Moreover Lecourt, a lawyer and dilettante musician of Berlioz's acquaintance, wrote from Marseille about a successful performance of *Le Roi Lear* there. Berlioz wrote to thank the musicians, advocating for further ventures the system of sectional rehearsals he had used in *Roméo et Juliette*. Later he heard of a Mainz performance of *Les Francs-Juges* overture, conducted by Lachner on 24 June, to celebrate the dawn of a fifth century of printing from movable type.

Early in 1840 he began to investigate the possibility of organizing a performance of his works, apparently to include fragments of his Requiem, by massed choruses and instrumental forces at the Panthéon; this idea was summarily rejected by Jean Vatout, the director of Monuments, who had had to deal with the practical arrangments for the Requiem. Berlioz was consoled by the discovery that the Musical Society of the Upper Palatinate in Munich had programmed a festival performance of the Requiem. For a time it seemed that a German tour might be arranged to coincide with the performance, but this undertaking, too, came to nothing.

In April or May, meanwhile, he learned of a more intriguing festival: the tenth anniversary celebration of the July revolution was to include the removal of the victims' mortal remains to a new resting place in the Place de la Bastille. They would be buried beneath a new column, designed by his *prix de Rome* colleague Joseph-Louis Duc. A new wave of Napoleonic fever was in the air as well. On 5 May, the anniversary of the emperor's death, Berlioz had been to the commemorative ceremony in the Place Vendôme and had reread Hugo's *Le Retour de l'empereur* and *Ode à la colonne* with rapture. His first thought was to profit from the occasion by publishing *Le Cinq Mai,* but the king declined to offer his patronage and the forward momentum was lost. Nevertheless Berlioz found himself swimming, once more, in Napoleonic ideas.

FIGURE 6.15 Duc's column in the Place de la Bastille.

It was fitting and appropriate for Berlioz to receive an official order from yet another minister of the Interior, Charles de Rémusat, to provide music for the *fêtes de juillet*. The *Revue et Gazette musicale* reported in early June that Berlioz was to receive 10,000 francs for a funeral march and solemn music to be played as the bodies were lowered into the ground. Berlioz added an Apotheosis, which he imagined would conclude the ceremony after the sealing of the graves, at the time when the attention of the crowd was certain to be drawn to the new column. The march would be "bleak, but awe-inspiring."[73]

The lateness of the formal commission obliged him to compose his new work at breakneck speed. The *Grande Symphonie funèbre et triomphale* was written, by his account, in forty hours; he pronounced it complete on 19 July, just over a week before the ceremonies. The scoring was for a large military band, with trumpets and drums, six horn parts, two ophicleide parts, and military woodwinds with piccolo.

The speed of composition is attributable in part to self-borrowing: the center movement, his *Hymne d'adieu,* was in large measure borrowed from Lenor's *Invocation* in *Les Francs-Juges*; one idea came from the *Scène héroïque,* and the two outer movements may have been sketched as early as 1835 for the *Fête musicale funèbre.* The complete work was first called, simply, *Symphonie militaire,* one of the subtitles proposed in 1832 for *Le Retour de l'armée d'Italie.*

He was to hire and pay the musicians himself, out of his expense account of 10,000 francs. They would all have to be in the uniform of the National Guard. The work was rehearsed in the Salle Vivienne at 11:30 A.M. on Sunday, 26 July. The general impression was of another splendid work, entirely new in conception. The manager of the Salle Vivienne contracted, on the spot, for four performances at a later time.

The events of 28 July began with a memorial service in the church of St.-Germain l'Auxerrois, facing the east front of the Louvre, where the coffins were on display. The cortege left the church in the direction of the Place de la Concorde, turned right past the Madeleine, and proceeded down the boulevards to the Place de la Bastille, a distance of nearly nine miles. Berlioz marched at the head of some two hundred instrumentalists drawn from the excellent military bands of the region. Both the funeral march and the Apotheosis were played several times in searing heat. The separation of the trumpets and drums made coordination difficult; for the most part, the music disappeared in the street, and any one person along the route could have heard only a few bars. At the Bastille, the slow, introspective second movement, a funeral "oration" written for the trombonist Dieppo, was played while the ceremony was going on. When the time came for the Apotheosis, the first time the officials might have grasped something of the magnitude of the work, the military units re-formed and departed to a cadence of side-drums, obscuring the great finale.

Thus the wild enthusiasm of the crowd, partisans and detractors of Berlioz alike, came as an unexpected pleasure. Cavé offered a "pompous appreciation" on behalf of the minister. Adolphe Adam, who liked "neither the man nor his style," approved of the peroration in the *Apothéose* which "was considerably superior to all he has done so far." Habeneck concluded that "the bastard has some damned fine ideas." "This symphony," Wagner later wrote to the Dresden *Abendzeitung,* "will exalt the hearts of men so long as there is a nation called France." The officials were delighted. Paris itself had been his backdrop; one could not ask for a better setting for a fourth symphony.[74]

The expenses of the production came to 6,901 francs. Berlioz persuaded Rémusat to give him all 10,000 francs of the governmental allocation, and when the accounts were clear, his profit came to something on the order of 2,800 francs. Making the events of July especially satisfying was that by this time Berlioz knew that Napoleon's remains were to arrive in Paris during the fall and be set in a fantastic tomb in the rotunda of the Invalides. He imagined that they would ask him for a heroic song for the entry into Paris—doubtless at the last minute.

The minister regretted the conditions under which the *Symphonie funèbre* had been heard and encouraged Berlioz to offer the work again. To that end it was repeated on 7 and 14 August in the Salle Vivienne, and here the public had the opportunity to absorb the much-heralded work. Queen Marie-Amélie took tickets. Again it was well received: indeed, it had become almost popular.

Finally, in late summer, there was the leisure for a visit to La Côte-St.-André. Sometime in the third week of August, he set out for the Isère by coach. He left Harriet and Louis in Paris.

Chapter Seven

Portrait in 1839–40
Works of the Golden Decade

The Legion of Honor and the sinecure at the library of the Conservatoire seem modest enough rewards for the splendid work of the decade since the *Symphonie fantastique*. But these, along with the commissions for the Requiem and the *Symphonie funèbre,* should be reckoned conspicuous indications that Berlioz was widely recognized as the nation's most interesting composer. His standing in Paris can likewise be measured by the unflagging audience interest in his concerts and by the exceptional group of artists he could number as his intimates. Internationally, Berlioz's music had so far been perceived as a curious phenomenon, an unlikely product of a land otherwise appreciated mostly for its comic opera. The speed with which the published scores of the *Francs-Juges* and *Waverley* overtures were translated into public performances in the German-speaking countries and England, however, and the critical attention focused on Liszt's transcription of the *Fantastique* are telling signs of nascent international interest. There would always be hostility, and so unusual a composer naturally attracted the irreverent attention of cartoon-mongers and other *charivarists*. It was surprising, as Saint-Saëns pointed out, that Berlioz encountered anything but hostility in a city where one still heard Beethoven described in some quarters as scandalous and where the symphonies of Haydn were still said to be noisy.

The lithograph of Berlioz from the time of the Legion of Honor and *Roméo et Juliette* (fig. 7.2) shows a still-youthful man of apparent enthusiasm, so far without a hint of the resignation obvious in the likenesses from later years, though d'Ortigue's description of 1832 talks of melancholy eyes and a prematurely wrinkled forehead. By 1840 Berlioz had achieved, moreover, a new poise and reserve—at least before the public, most of the time. Even the fanciful plaster bust by Dantan *jeune* (see fig. 7.1) is, in its own way, heroic.

Ernest Legouvé emerged in the 1830s as the composer's great patron and confidant. It was he who cheerfully relieved Berlioz's most pressing monetary woes of the 1830s by judicious loans of 1,000 francs here and there, and who earned for his generosity the dedication of the published *Benvenuto Cellini* overture. (Had a complete score of the 1838 version been published, that, too, would have been dedicated to him.) Legouvé first heard of Berlioz at the Villa Medici in 1832, just after the composer had departed for Paris. When Louise Vernet sang *La Captive* at one of what must have been multiple presentations for passers-through, he developed a sympathy for its composer and left Rome armed with a letter of introduction. He sought Berlioz out in November at the establishment of the Italian hairdresser Decandia, and the two went off to the opera together, well coiffed, happy to discover their shared affinities for Shakespeare, *Don Giovanni,* and Romantic poetry. Berlioz was taken at once by the ease with which Legouvé carried his obvious wealth and by his willingness to use it to altruistic purpose.

Legouvé entered Berlioz's life just as the courtship of Harriet was reaching its climax and was thus drawn directly, perhaps inexorably, into that adventure. In 1833, he was summoned to bear witness to one of Berlioz's paroxysms of despair; later, he wrote the text of *La Mort d'Ophélie,* a song strongly evocative of Harriet. Legouvé also advised Berlioz on the libretto of *Les Troyens.* They were thus intimates for more than three decades, and

Legouvé's *Soixante Ans de souvenirs* of 1886 includes one of the most entertaining and sympathetic—though far from error-free—recollections of the composer that we have.[1]

In the 1830s he and Berlioz moved, says Legouvé, in a circle of friends that included Eugène Süe and Victor Schœlcher and above all Liszt; he recounts one of the several recorded incidents of Berlioz's weeping in the dark as Liszt played Beethoven. "Look at him," said Liszt afterward: "the heir apparent." (Liszt, incidentally, is one of the handful of acquaintances Berlioz brought himself to address with the familiar *tu* form; the only other of his intimates so honored were d'Ortigue, Edouard Rocher, the architect Duc, and, later, the English critic Davison.) Legouvé's most striking recollection, perhaps, is of the hypnotic power of his friend's exegeses of Beethoven. These were better even than his written criticism, Berlioz's obvious expertise enhanced by "his expression, his gestures, tone of voice, tears, exclamations of enthusiasm, and those sudden flashes of inspired imagery ... An hour spent like this taught me more about instrumental music than a whole concert at the Conservatoire."[2] It was this sort of rabid intelligence

FIGURE 7.2
Berlioz, c. 1839.
Note the Legion of Honor
in his lapel.

that made such a profound impact, at Legouvé's, on the powerful minister Guizot.

The years between Berlioz's marriage in 1833 and the end of the decade constitute the brief period of familial happiness that was to be his. Both Berlioz and Harriet enjoyed their child, and despite the failure of her career, Harriet was for a time a constructive member of the household. For both of them family life and domestic management were uncharted territories, and they had to feel their way through the ordinary concerns of daily life: childrearing, servants, firewood, and furniture—even the grave matter of how to stock a wine cellar. (The wine had come from La Côte, as had a table and bed linens.) Louis's behavior, which was problematic from the first, was affected by the tensions of his bicultural parentage and the language barriers at home. Neither of the parents seems to have had an inkling of how to deal with it. On the other hand, supporting a wife and child made Berlioz more responsible than before and resulted in a general strengthening of his forces: with a few exceptions—the usual winter infections and occasional bouts of nervous exhaustion—he was in good health. The middle and late 1830s were thus constructive years, during which he managed to carve out time to produce a substantial work each year, a record unmatched elsewhere in his career.

By the end of 1840, on the other hand, Berlioz must have begun to sense the decline in Harriet's physical and mental health. It is difficult to know quite what to make of her, even with—or perhaps because of—all we now know about her. The alcoholism to which she would fall victim in the 1840s cannot explain the many eccentricities of her behavior in the 1830s. Why did she never learn French? Why are her surviving letters so breathless and scatterbrained? Why did she flatly refuse to travel—to England, Germany, or even La Côte-St.-André? Why did she, once a lovely woman with an enviable career, grow so large so quickly? (The painting of Harriet now owned by Hugh Macdonald shows a lovely woman of vivacity, poise, and charm; in a lithograph of 1828 "designed after Nature," there is already the hint of portliness.)[3] Harriet, I suspect, was neither greatly intelligent nor, outside the theater, especially imaginative.

We know precious little of Berlioz's private life with her. At first, they could scarcely have communicated except through gestures and phrase-book formulas; they slept in separate bedrooms from the beginning. It is clear that she subconsciously blamed Berlioz for the loss of her career, but it is equally certain she made little effective effort to reclaim it for herself. Despite Berlioz's appreciation of her willingness to endure hardships so that he might produce his concerts, the fact is that there is little other indication of much support for his artistic needs or of enthusiasm for his music. She manifestly failed to bring a *sou* into the household budget; Berlioz's job of repaying her many debts, by contrast, was monumental. It is easy to see the fore-

FIGURE 7.3 Berlioz, c. 1839.

shadowings of a marital crisis. But during the mid-1830s the truth had dawned on neither of them; on the contrary, it was a time of unusual tranquility in domestic affairs, and as a result we have been left great music of exceptionally even keel.

The artistic goals that preoccupied Berlioz in the 1830s are clear: to give vent to his longing to set a Napoleonic work, to deal with his vision of apocalypse, to continue his experiments with the dramatic symphony, and to compose a grand opera to rival those of Meyerbeer and Halévy. The first two goals were achieved with the Requiem and the *Symphonie funèbre,* though Berlioz would twice more return to the "imperial" style. *Harold en Italie* and *Roméo et Juliette* are in some sense experimental efforts on the path toward *Faust.* The assault on the Opéra failed, of course, but *Cellini*'s failure had at least one positive result, and that was to deflect the composer's interests toward other genres at a time when further operas could only have met with similar failure.

His lifestyle was largely governed by the necessity of attending to business other than the composition of new music: journalism, rehearsals, dealing with his publishers, proofreading, arranging for and conducting his concerts. During these periods he would rise with the rest of the household to attend to his immense correspondence, usually penning three or four notes and a long letter or two at the beginning of every day. He would satisfy the demands of his newspaper work as best he could, then set out for town on daily errands, stopping perhaps at Schlesinger's to deal with the *Revue et Gazette musicale* or check on the progress of his published music, then at the Conservatoire to consult the business manager about contracts and ticket sales, then at the apartments of various journalists to bring them up to date on his enterprises. (It was customary to call on members of the press corps to introduce them to new works, a custom Spohr termed barbarian. Meyerbeer had press conferences with food and drink, but Berlioz would not have been able to afford that sort of thing.) There might be rehearsals for *Esmeralda* or *Cellini* at the Opéra, then something to attend at night. He traveled by foot during the day, but in the evenings took care to arrive at the Opéra in a cabriolet. He never, if it could be avoided, wore an overcoat.

The sketchbook of 1832–36 gives an idea of one day's work,[4] no more intense than many another, just before the concerts of December 1836:

Today Monday 28 [November 1836]:
Go to Liszt's. [He was to play at one of the December concerts.]
Go to Schlesinger's to get money.
Attention: To Mantoue's for the poor tax.

Carry or send [announcements of the concerts to] the rest of the papers.
Go to the *Débats.*
Rue de Rohan for the business with Urhan.
Write to [the young Ambroise] Thomas [to invite him to the concerts].
Go to Pape's [the piano maker, from whom Berlioz rented the piano for the concert].
Carry [tickets for] the boxes to Pacini.
Go see Mlle Bertin [since the concert was to include the Bell Song from *Esmeralda*].
Send tickets to Ch[arles] Maurice [a critic].

Send [tickets for] the box to the rue de Rohan.
Have the large programs of the Symph[onie fantastique] printed.
Send Barbier [an announcement of the concert, or perhaps some tickets].

On such days of errands and business in town, he would not find the leisure to compose music until the late evening, when he could relax in an armchair by the fire and ponder compositional issues at whatever length they demanded. For some of *Cellini* and all of the Requiem and *Roméo et Juliette,* however, he enjoyed the luxury of long blocks of uninterrupted time; once his imagination was loosed and the way was clear, he could work with formidable speed and agility. He completed *Harold* in a few months, much of *Cellini* in the summer of 1836, and the whole of *Roméo et Juliette* in the nine months between January and September 1839. The summer was usually the most profitable season for composition, because theater closings made it a slack time for reviewers. Productions at the Opéra, however, continued through much of the summer, and these were often in the most interesting stages of rehearsal in July and August, as the fall premieres began to come together.

*B*erlioz's work habits have much to say of his musical purpose. Because virtually all of his music is related to subject matter of one kind or another, there is for most of the major works a period of what he calls "dominating his subject," a time of intellectual ferment during which the subjective elements settle themselves into pleasing focus. It is the occasion for perusing musical possibility, and those ideas that fail to progress are pushed aside to await some more appropriate climate. (In 1833, for example, he considered a "very gay Italian opera" on *Much Ado About Nothing,* then abandoned the idea; he returned to it unsuccessfully in 1852 and successfully in the 1860s.) One can sense from the various documents of his life the beginnings of the unrest, the percolation of spirit, that precedes the white heat of notation—most of all, perhaps, in the repeated references to colossalism and a haunting *idée fixe* just before the *Fantastique.*

Whereas the great symphonies of Classicism often take flight from a central thematic or harmonic event, Berlioz's masterworks nearly always start from a perceived association of music and image. For the Requiem, it was the trumpet calls heralding the Day of Judgment; for *Roméo et Juliette,* the first idea (or, at least, the place he started the full score) was Romeo's love song heard through the dazzling tumult of the *Fête chez Capulet;* for *Cellini,* it was the scene in the tavern, where the smiths sing an apostrophe to their noble art. Works would inevitably expand in size as he thought about them: *Harold,* for example, began with an idea for a one-movement work that then expanded itself to four. Nearly all his great compositional statements reflect some intensely personal experience as well, some intimate identification with the matter at hand. *Roméo* and *Harold* and *Cellini* and the rest were thus intended, from the first, to evoke a phantasmagoria of images and musical relationships, a Chagall-like canvas of scenes entrenched as firmly in the composer's memory as in his imagination.

Compositional decision-making would at some point progress from these visionary but general issues to the detail of musical design. The first melodic ideas usually occurred to him spontaneously, as the "right" music for some dramatic issue at hand. Berlioz tells several anecdotes of abrupt inspiration: the story of the *Elégie en prose,* where the poetry book fell open to just the right place; the accidental swim in the Tiber that led to the refrain ("pauvre soldat") in *Le Cinq Mai;* the military symphony conceived in the shadow of the Alps. While composing *La Damnation de Faust,* Berlioz tells us, he became so immersed in his thoughts that he was swept by a crowd onto an excursion train and ended up in the suburban village of Enghien before he noticed what was happening.

On these occasions he was in the habit of using a pencil to jot down his thoughts—fragments of melodies, hints of the text—on whatever paper was handy: one of the pocket albums, perhaps, or the empty back cover of a manuscript orchestra part in his lap. Example 7.1 shows, for instance, the early sketches for Hugo's *Dans l'Alcôve sombre.*

Cases of spontaneous inspiration followed by immediate, finished composition are few and far between. Among these impromptus are such songs as the *Elégie en prose* and *La Captive,* along with certain pregnant ideas forced into early delivery by firm concert dates, such as the Hungarian March and much of the *Symphonie funèbre.* But in each of these cases a later, "definitive" version comes to succeed the hurried one.

Berlioz labored as diligently and systematically as anybody else to work out the implications of germinal ideas. After refining and extending the melody, he would build the bass line, the inner voices, and, last of all, the accompanimental figurations and textures. By this time, he was working in more or less full score: any number of unfinished passages show complete melodies, a line or two of counterpoint, then uncertain dabbling with the other voices, often in pencil. There is little evidence that he had rigid structures in mind while first composing; he was generally cognizant of principles of working out and structural return, but true formal constraint was generated anew for each movement, as though it, too, were a conclusion drawn from the argument.

At home, he worked at a table before gathered sheaves of score paper, surrounded by his albums and miscellaneous bits and pieces of paper, his pencils, quills, ink, rulers, and writing sand. He was proud that composition, for him, did not often involve a keyboard: "I compose without instrument," he wrote to Rellstab in 1838, "for I do not play piano at all."[5]

EXAMPLE 7.1 Sketch for the first stanza of Hugo's *Dans L'Alcôve sombre,* sketchbook, fol. 2[r].

A rather shocked description of his workroom in the rue de Londres was left by the composer Léon Gastinel.[6] Berlioz had taken over an attic room, just beneath the mansard, equipped with only a table, a chair, and his guitar—a souvenir, not an instrument for composition, played most often when Louis wandered in. Other accounts note his pistols hanging on a wall (the ones he was going to use to dispatch Mlle Moke and her accomplices?) and the skull on the table. Later there was a large, glass-front cabinet in the workroom, filled with his manuscripts. Berlioz did in fact like to have a piano nearby, at least, and owned one as early as 1826. From time to time other instruments, usually the new and curious, lay about the room awaiting his scrutiny; in the *Mémoires* he says that he should like always to be surrounded by the orchestral instruments while he worked.

By the mid-1830s Berlioz sometimes found musical ideas coming to him faster than he could write them down. It is at this point that references to "a kind of musical shorthand" begin to appear in his writings. Peter Cornelius mentions the shorthand, too, though in association with the story of *La Captive,* which took place earlier, in Subiaco. Although no primary evidence of this sort of shorthand has been identified, what we do often see—and what Berlioz and Cornelius may have been describing—are layers of light pencil in the autographs, most of them now virtually illegible by virtue of having been covered with the notation in ink. Berlioz also used figured-bass symbols, usually to remind himself of proposed chord structures.

I cannot say for certain just how extensive other preliminary sketching may have been. Ten years ago, we knew of only the large body of sketches for *Les Troyens* and two pages of work on the *Invocation à la nature* from *Faust;* to those we can now add two fine pages of work on the *Marche pour la présentation des drapeaux* from the Te Deum (see ex. 7.4) and the material in the sketchbook of 1832, notably some extended sketches for *Cellini* and *Je crois en vous.* In most of these cases it appears that notated composition can be traced, without substantive gaps, from first attempt to full score. Put another way, it seems as though Berlioz exhausted the possibilities of one- or two-lined sketching in short order and proceeded as quickly as possible to open score. My hunch is that several reams—but not several hundred reams—of sketches and drafts have been lost to posterity; that is the implication of the fact that whenever preliminary sketches exist at all, they are very dense and relatively short. But one cannot discount the possibility that Berlioz was so fluent that in many cases he required no sketching at all. Either way, a parallel is better drawn with Mozart (or, though Berlioz would have hated it, Rossini) than with Beethoven.

The preserved sketches from this stage of composition, what might be thought of as the advance toward full score, are surprisingly alike over the long span from 1834 to the late 1850s, suggesting that Berlioz's routine had by the time of the Requiem and *Benvenuto Cellini* become essentially fixed. He works in single staves, or pairs of them, setting the text and experimenting with the outlines of his melodies, then trying out various harmonic progressions, often notated in the same staff as the melody. He usually begins on the right-hand side of an opening, reserving the left-hand pages for continuation or intensive work on difficult passages; the segments are connected by letter references and, occasionally, such instructions as "allez à B; non, allez encore en Sol♭ à A."[7]

Take, for example, what is obviously an early sketch for the beginning of the tavern scene in *Cellini*, found in the pocket sketchbook and probably prepared in 1834 (ex. 7.2a–b).[8] The two openings devoted to the passage suggest the work of a couple of hours; at their conclusion, Berlioz is ready to rough out the first sixty bars of the full score. He begins by copying out the text; the phrase "pas de chansons à boire" seems to be an afterthought, to rhyme with "soient un hymne à la gloire":

CHŒUR:	A boire, [à boire, à boire]
BERNARDINO:	Chantons!
CELLINI:	Soit, mais pour Dieu! pas de chansons à boire,
	Pas d'ignoble refrain
	Sentant la cuisine et le vin,
	Chantons: mais que nos chants soient un hymne à la gloire
	Des Ciseleurs et de notre art divin.

(Note the textual variant: *cuisine* for the later *taverne*.) To the left, he sketches an orchestral ritornello in $\frac{6}{8}$, in G minor. By the next page, the key of the scene is G major, though with considerable reliance on the flattened sixth degree, E♭, and on the relative minor. At first glance there seems little relation with what was finally adopted for the orchestral introduction, but I think the gestural similarity of certain figures cannot be denied (ex. 7.2c). On the right-hand side of the next opening, Berlioz sketches the call to drink, "à boire," essentially as it appears in the finished version, changing his mind only about the scalar rise to cadence, where apparently a diatonic figure was substituted for a chromatic one, reducing the overall length to a more manageable four-bar subphrase (ex. 7.2d).

Bernardino offers his modest suggestion, "Chantons!", and this is answered by Cellini as far as "chansons à boire," with the rhythm of the declamation clear, though the precise pitches are rather less so. (In one scrambled spot, Berlioz resorts to writing out the pitch names, *ut–ut–ut–re*.) At this point, the composer has a better idea: Bernardino will begin with a brief tra-la, the effect of which is to give some musical substance to his one-word exhortation; tra-la-ing goes on to become a motive in the opera, identified with the carefree spirit of Cellini's apprentices. Berlioz connects the progression of ideas with the letters A and B (ex. 7.2e). (This is all sketched in G; the abrupt shift to the mediant B major at Bernardino's entry is a later embellishment.) Cellini's recitative then works itself out more or less effortlessly, the major issue being the shape of its midsections. Note,

a. First sketch, sketchbook, fol. 17ᵛ–18ʳ:

b. Second sketch, sketchbook, fol. 18ᵛ–19ʳ:

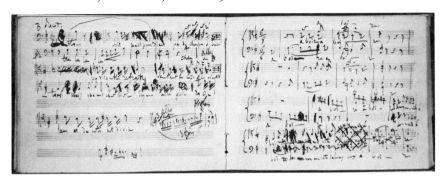

c. Sketch, mm. 1–2:

Final reading, mm. 1–2:

Sketch, mm. 14–16:

Final reading, mm. 14–20:

EXAMPLE 7.2 Sketches for the tavern scene in *Benvenuto Cellini*.

d. Sketch, m. 10ff.:

à   boi - re ser-vez nous vite à   boi - re ser-vez .nous vite servez   nous   à boi -

boi - re ser - vez nous vite à   boi -

e. Sketch progress, fol. 18ᵛ:

tra - la - la la   Chan

- tons   Soit mais pour dieu pas de chansons à boire

pas d'ignoble re - frain sen - tant la cui-sine et le vin   ·   etc.

f. Transition to hymn:
Sketch:

Final reading:

EXAMPLE 7.2 (*continued*).

too, the hints, at the transition point, that the hymn tune and its introduction
are already well thought out (ex. 7.2f).

Consider, further, the afternoon's work in which the ravishing song *Je
crois en vous* takes shape—doubtless in a rush to meet the publisher's
deadline (ex. 7.3). The pencil sketch[9] bears little similarity to the completed
score but for the leap of a sixth at the point of refrain; the first ink sketch
is scarcely closer, though the melodic shape is beginning to emerge, and
Berlioz has conceived a firm idea for the last line of the poem, "Je crois en
vous." But by the third try, the second in ink, he has come close to a final
pass. The languidly falling fifths, interlocked by thirds—an old trick, in

fact—are isolated as the principal thrust of the accompaniment and given considerable attention to the left of the principal sketches. The work was published in D♭ and is cast in D in *Cellini*.

Je crois en vous, incidentally, is meant to be printed as a single stanza of music. Malherbe and Weingartner's edition subtly violates its integrity—and that of several other such songs—by writing out the music anew for each strophe.

A similarly rapid genesis can be seen, two decades later, in the sketches for what came to be called the *Marche pour la présentation des drapeaux*, in the Te Deum. These two pages (ex. 7.4) are found at the close of a manuscript vocal score[10] for an early, unperformed version of the work, proving beyond doubt—among other things—that the *Marche* was a late addition. They are in the key of B major, not B♭, suggesting association with the second movement, *Tibi omnes*, which is in that key. It can be shown, I think, that this march originally had something to do with the coronation of Napoleon III in 1852 and the jubilant Te Deum intended for that ceremony; in 1855 the occasion was different, as was the placement of the march and, therefore, its key.

The page marked *adopté* is clearly the latter: the metric placement of the first strain is as in the final version, and the completed movement follows the sketch measure by measure, except for matters of detail. The nine-bar introduction with drum rolls, however, appears in neither sketch. Berlioz begins sketching with a good notion of the march theme and of a second subject based, apparently, on the Judex crederis at the end of the Te Deum. The melody is complete, with some of the supporting harmony sketched in and ideas for the bass progression notated in ledger lines beneath the staves. (There is sparse reference, in the finished march, to the half-note figure that in the sketch effects the retransition.) Berlioz seems to have concluded his initial effort at the end of the sixth staff. So far, there is little indication of the two references to the first movement that will constitute the middle section of the march: a fugal treatment accorded the main subject of that movement, and the descending *cantus firmus* for organ—what Berlioz calls the *point d'orgue* (see mm. 52–72 of the full score).[11]

At this point, relatively content with the formal structure and overall scope of his march, Berlioz goes on to attempt a continuous draft on one line. The second page of sketches finishes by outlining every measure of the work, including the passage of thirty-seven bars later found deleted from the autograph score and manuscript parts. It is *during* this sketch that he conceives, for the first time, of the first-movement citations, and he returns to the empty staves at the bottom of the previous page to work them out. From this juncture he uses both pages at once, working out the treatment in whatever empty space he could find. He soon solves his difficulties with the imitation, finds himself content with the plan, and marks the second sketch *adopté*. The next step was to move to the full score.

a. Sketchbook, fol. 31ᵛ–32ʳ:

b. Sketchbook, fol. 30ᵛ–31ʳ:

EXAMPLE 7.3 *Je crois en vous.*

His attention to detail is scrupulous: we find passages shifted to the left and right by half-measures, careful smoothing-out of seams, new melodic ornamentation, and determined attention to every turn of phrase that on second thought seemed mundane. The sketches, in short, do not limit their attention to any one issue of composition to the exclusion of others; rather Berlioz can be seen assaulting the entire citadel at once.

I said, at the beginning of this digression, that I was unwilling to deduce the existence of lost sketches along these lines for all the major works. This is at least in part because the preserved sketches are mostly for daring movements. Or is it that sketching becomes necessary when things start out being too ordinary and become daring along the way? Ultimately, in either case, that is what is exciting about them: to watch, for example, the rushing

a. First sketch (found in a manuscript vocal score of the Te Deum, F-Pc ms
17998):

EXAMPLE 7.4 Sketches for *Marche pour la présentation des drapeaux*.

b. Second sketch:

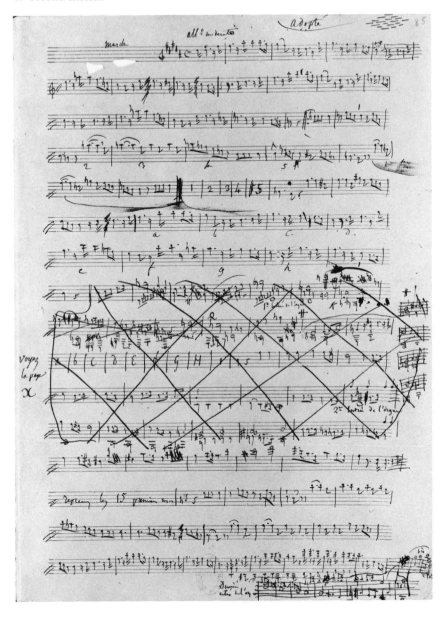

EXAMPLE 7.4 (continued).

waters in the *Invocation à la nature* from *Faust* develop their identity is to witness the mundane becoming sublime (ex. 7.5).[12] Some of the most elegant ideas of the great fourth act of *Les Troyens,* particularly the stunning verse structure and harmonic surprise of the song of Iopas, first emerge during the process of sketching.

After having established the general structure of a movement in his mind, Berlioz would transfer his attention to the full score and begin again, working out details, interludes, orchestral interjections, and decorations of all sorts. Beginning with this stage of the composition, the sketches are less obviously connected, for by then he was in the habit of using whatever scrap of paper was handy to resolve problems too complex for working out, in faint pencil, in a manuscript he did not intend to recopy. Points of transition gave him the most trouble: in one of the *Cellini* sketches, he tries a half-dozen alternative solutions to the same eight-bar junction.

The evidence for this kind of sketching is found on many dozens of scraps of paper. There must have been many more, most of which were simply thrown out. But from time to time Berlioz would turn over a piece of sketch paper, use its blank side to copy out some revised reading, cut that out, and paste the revision into the main manuscript. Often, then, the correction slips (called *collettes* in French) pasted into the score have sketches on their verso surfaces; the collettes tend to cover blocks of manuscript that have become too messy, during the compositional process, for presentation. Most often the original surface shows some routine technical problem encountered, solved, and then covered over. Example 7.6 shows a transposition table for the natural horns in the finale of *Roméo et Juliette.* Example 7.7 shows work on a passage for saxhorns from the Te Deum—in fact, for the *Marche pour la présentation des drapeaux* I have just treated; it is found on the verso surface of a collette in the autograph of *Benvenuto Cellini.*

The foreshadowings of later movements that can be heard in the recitatives near the beginning of *Roméo et Juliette* were the product of a revision effected in Vienna and Prague at the end of 1845 and beginning of 1846; a sketch for the interlude based on the *Fête chez Capulet* has been preserved as a collette-verso (ex. 7.8). With that observation, I have confused sketching for first composition with sketching for later revision, and purposefully so. Berlioz (like most composers) sketched whenever he needed to and went on "composing" long after a work was "finished."

Indeed, the most unusual characteristic of his creative process, in view of his obvious delight in the orchestra and its possibilities, is that he is quick to declare a work done before he has gotten around to the final orchestration. "I have finished," he would write of a piece; "now I have only the orchestration left to do." He would have told his pupils, had he had any, that orchestration was something you do to a finished work. Nevertheless, as I have noted, orchestral effect is for Berlioz part and parcel of the very

a. As sketched (found in the *Harold en Italie* autograph, p. 156 collette verso):

b. As completed:

EXAMPLE 7.5 The *torrents* motive in the *Invocation à la nature*.

EXAMPLE 7.6 Transposition table for brass in movt. VII, mm. 6–8, of *Roméo et Juliette* (found on the verso surface of a collette, p. 396 of the autograph).

inspiration for much of his best music: the orchestration comes at both the beginning and the end of the process.

He seldom showed his unfinished work to other musicians, not because he feared adverse reactions, but "because I wish to follow caprice's path straightway"[13] and not be turned from that course by the impressions of well-meaning and trusted friends. When he did show friends an unfinished work, he invariably regretted that they had seen the piece before the refinements were done. (He retreated slightly from this position toward the end: *Les Troyens* incorporates the suggestions of many friends, several of whom examined the score while it was in progress.)

It should be apparent that what is ultimately more interesting than the way they are assembled the first time is the manner in which the great works develop once they are done and first performed. Berlioz is facile in the first stages of composition, meticulous in the succeeding steps, and positively Beethovenian in his dissatisfaction when it comes to the finished work. He

EXAMPLE 7.7 Transposition sketch for a passage for saxhorns and cornets in the *Marche pour la présentation des drapeaux* from the Te Deum, later deleted (see NBE, X, 189–90) (found on the verso surface of a collette over p. 128 of the first volume of the *Bevenuto Cellini* autograph).

EXAMPLE 7.8 Sketch for the orchestral interlude in the prologue to *Roméo et Juliette*, movt. I, mm. 37–62 (found on the verso surface of a collette over p. 63 of the autograph).

is almost neurotically subject to the uneasy feeling that he has not yet done his best. This is partly because each of the major works embodies a fresh view of musical form and texture: he would discover as he composed, and it was often toward the end of the experience that he found the true implications of his labor. It was only natural to want to go back again to spruce up, refine, polish, and balance his work, particularly as he came to know its specific problems through multiple performances. No composer more scrupulously attends to the weaknesses and flaws he perceives in his work or pays more attention to the advice of thoughtful listeners, once he is ready for it.

Examples of this care extend down to the most minute of details, as for example a routine figure from the *Fête chez Capulet,* rendered, at a late moment, into something more stylish (ex. 7.9). So significant a change as the unification of *Harold en Italie* through the use of a recurrent theme seems to have been a late idea, though in this case certainly from before the first performances.

He lavishes particular attention on the musical imagery. This is nowhere clearer than in the autograph and related sketches for the Pilgrims' March in *Harold.* Here the image is of an Italian landscape, viewed by the hero from some lofty perch, and of a procession of monks intoning their evening prayer. At the end of each phrase of the march, Berlioz suggests the chanting and the toll of a distant monastery bell, using for the bell a "dissonant" C against tonic and dominant triads of B major. It was a magnificent idea, though overdone at first, and correspondingly shocking to the public; the autograph materials show systematic reduction in the length of dissonance, to the point where the last version is dissonant only from the most conservative of viewpoints (ex. 7.10). Similar concerns inform the in-progress changes to the tomb scene from *Roméo et Juliette,* where Berlioz is anxious for the accompaniment of Romeo's invocation to suggest his inner torment, but not to the point of overwhelming the lyrical melody (ex. 7.11). Changes of various degrees of magnitude go on and on, from the addition of the waltz motives to the appearance of the *idée fixe* in the second movement of the *Symphonie fantastique,* done a full fifteen years after the first performance, between the second proof and publication of the score (ex. 7.12), to the removal of full stanzas from strophic compositions, to the reframing of *Lélio* for Weimar, to the wholesale reworking of *Roméo et Juliette* in Vienna and Prague. A French composer would call this process of putting things just right the *mise au point,* or *mise au net.*

The compositional concern that governs these retroactive changes is the endless quest for perfection of balance, symmetry, reason, and frame. The late revisions lend enormous structural enhancement to such works as the *Fantastique* and *Roméo et Juliette,* both of which were heavily revised, and even to the Requiem, which was simply touched up from time to time. A radically different sort of growth toward perfection is seen in the genesis of *L'Enfance du Christ,* a process I shall have cause to examine in some detail. Once one has a feeling for the power and the profound vision of these changes, the central tragedy of Berlioz's music becomes clear. For neither of his longest two masterpieces, *Benvenuto Cellini* and *Les Troyens,* ever received its "final" touchings-up—efforts that might have restored *Cellini* to a well-paced adventure based on the original Paris version, but incorporating the lessons of Weimar and perhaps London; efforts that might have led to discovery of a better ending for *Les Troyens.*

a. Original:

b. Revision:

EXAMPLE 7.9 Details from the original reading of the *Fête chez Capulet* in *Roméo et Juliette* and its revision, made sometime after the Vienna and Prague performances of 1846.

a. First version:

b. Second version:

c. Third version:

EXAMPLE 7.10 Revisions to the "dissonant convent bell" effect in *Harold en Italie*, movt. II, mm. 278ff., as seen in the autograph, pp. 137 and 139.

The layers of revision came to an end, usually, with a work's publication. The published score and parts then became definitive sources—for performance, the composer's own use, and posterity. At this point, Berlioz could only accept the infelicities of his work; I cited earlier his touching remark about resigning himself to unavoidable blemishes and imperfections.[14] Or, as he put it in the outburst to Hofmeister over the *Francs-Juges* overture, if a work is good, one must "respect the form, the thought, and the details, including the mistakes."[15]

After publication of a work, Berlioz was even prepared to give away the autograph score. He presented the *Fantastique* and the *Symphonie funèbre* to d'Ortigue, *Harold* to Morel, *Le Roi Lear* to Armand Bertin, and the elegant autograph of *Roméo et Juliette* to Georges Kastner. On the cover of this last is the following inscription:

> You will pardon me, my dear Kastner, for giving you such a manuscript: its German and Russian campaigns have covered it with wounds. It is like those flags "that return from battle," says Hugo, "more beautiful because they are torn."
>
> Paris, 17 September 1858
> H. Berlioz[16]

a. As sketched in pencil and covered in ink, autograph p. 310, original surface:

b. As begun in ink draft, autograph p. 309, original surface:

c. As resketched and simplified, autograph p. 309, original surface:

d. As adopted:

EXAMPLE 7.11 Romeo's invocation in movt. VI of *Roméo et Juliette*, mm. 48ff.

a. Reading in autograph:

b. Reading in published score of 1845:

EXAMPLE 7.12 *Symphonie fantastique*, movt. II, mm. 129–34.

Berlioz's calligraphy is elegant from the beginning of his career to the end. Most of the autographs are so clear as to have served the engraver of the published edition directly, without an intermediate fair scribal copy. Berlioz enjoyed a friendly rivalry with his head copyist over the matter of who could produce the handsomer work; for important projects like the lithographed masters for the Te Deum chorus parts, he divided the work equally with his copyist, and his half is, to be sure, just as good or better. The autograph full score of a major work also served its composer as conducting score, at least until the published edition appeared, and thus amounts to a sort of diary of its development in concert.

*S*eeing even a short composition through performance and subsequent publication was always a monetary gamble. Berlioz published many of his works at his own expense, and that usually amounted to a flat loss. In some respects, however, issuing multiple copies became easier and decidedly cheaper as the decades went by: engraving and, more significantly, lithographic processes had by midcentury replaced individual scribal copies as the most efficient manner of circulating scores and parts. An 1837 "Guide des Prix" in a Paris almanac gives an idea of the prices for such work: 25 centimes per copied page of twelve staves, including paper; twice that for the more complex notation needed for piano, harp, and guitar parts. Engraving was 1.75 to 2.25 francs per page; the plates were another 1.40 francs for each pound of copper; the ornamental title page was 2.25 francs, exclusive of any illustrators' fees. The printing itself was 1.50 francs for ten pages. Hence fifty copies—an average or slightly above-average print run for the era—of the modest *romance Le Jeune Pâtre breton,* which he first published at his own expense, cost Berlioz something on the order of 65 francs.

One can calculate the cost of the thousands of pages of copy for the orchestral parts of the Requiem, and of the three hundred lithographed chorus parts, which even today fill twenty-six boxes. To that was ultimately added the cost of the engraved score of over 150 plates—the edition paid for in this case by subscription; of corrections to the manuscript and published performance material on the occasion of revisions to the score; of the preparation and engraving of the two further editions of the score, and so on. Even so, neither vocal scores nor orchestral parts for the Requiem were published during Berlioz's lifetime.

When a publisher was interested in buying the property of some musical work—that is, when there was hope of clearing a profit—the composer garnered a few hundred francs in fee, some copies of the score, and the assurance that the other expenses would be borne by the publishing house. Berlioz's publisher paid him 100 francs for the *Chant des chemins de fer* in 1849, and the same for his arrangement of Bortniansky's *Chant des chérubins* and *Pater noster* in 1850; Richault offered Berlioz 700 francs, ten copies of the full score, and a complete set of parts, including multiple strings, for *La Damnation de Faust.*

A composer sold his property "pour tous pays," though Berlioz sometimes managed to reserve rights to republish a composition in Germany or England and occasionally indulged in shady dealings when a foreign publisher indicated interest in one of his works. Only for the rights of *Les Troyens* did he reap a substantial amount of money, but that sale went sourest of all. His relationship with his publishers was, on the whole, quite good, though that did not prevent him from behaving disagreeably when corrections or revisions had to be made at the last minute or when parts promised in time for a concert failed to arrive or arrived too flawed for use.

Except for some excerpts requested by kings and princes for their palace libraries, virtually no scribal copies of the orchestral scores were prepared. For the larger works with chorus, on the other hand, manuscript piano-vocal scores were made for the chorus master and his accompanist. Berlioz prepared the piano reductions for these manuscripts himself, and with increasing fluency. For the published piano-vocal scores, however, he usually engaged the services of a professional pianist—Hans von Bülow for the *Cellini* overture, Saint-Saëns for *Lélio,* a young pianist named Théodore Ritter for *Roméo et Juliette,* and Ritter and Amédée Méreaux for *L'Enfance du Christ.* The piano arrangements inevitably caused misunderstandings, hard feelings, and lengthy delays: Berlioz thus did his own reductions of *Benvenuto Cellini, Les Troyens,* and *Béatrice et Bénédict,* all toward the end of his career. Pauline Viardot helped him with the piano score of *Les Troyens*—they were inordinately, perhaps inappropriately, fond of their sessions together—but the legend that she corrected the full score and rewrote the bass lines is the invention of her son.

The stage was set for Berlioz and his concerts by the Société des Concerts du Conservatoire, an organization that had radically improved the climate for symphonic music in France since its establishment in 1828. With its virtuoso players and competent conductor, a growing library of orchestral parts, and—significantly, as this was a luxury the German court orchestras did not share—an intimate concert room designed expressly for orchestral and choral performance, the Société began its life with considerable advantages. Because it had little by way of ancestry and little to do with either the opera house or the princely chapel, it was receptive to new ways of doing things and thus became an admired and imitated setter of precedents. From the beginning the Société des Concerts was an immense success with the public and professional musicians alike, and from the beginning it served Berlioz as a model for his own concerts. The relationship between Berlioz and the Société des Concerts was always reserved and often outwardly hostile—a state of affairs for which the orchestra's governing committee was in large measure responsible—but their paths often intersected: Berlioz lent the Société his talents as percussionist from time to time, and for three decades he was the most influential journalist to write about their concerts.

Berlioz organized, produced, and after 1835 conducted between two and four concerts a season, feeling his way at first, learning from his mistakes, and over the years quite perfecting the system. He came to look forward to these public presentations as the culmination of each year's tedious and intensely private business of composition. His mastery of concert production became so complete that others turned to him, time and time again, for help in offering concerts of their own. More than a dozen letters of Berlioz painstakingly set out the necessary preparations and expenses for some neophyte to the Paris scene; giving this kind of advice later became his way of returning some of the favors bestowed on him in Germany.

He contracted, if he could, the best Parisian instrumentalists and singers for his works. Working repeatedly with good professional musicians, learning their strengths and their foibles, gave him a new assurance in dealing

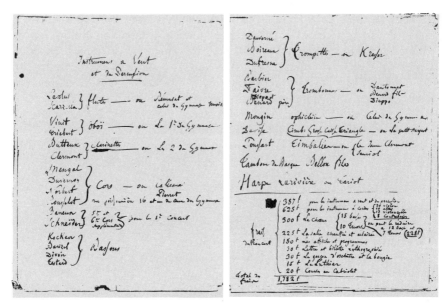

FIGURE 7.4 List of players for Berlioz's concerts of November and December, 1835.

with the orchestral force as composer. Yet as a free agent, unlike the rule-bound Société, he could engage whomever he wanted at whatever terms he could negotiate: he might hire 100 or 150 musicians, professionals both good and less accomplished, students, and even amateurs, as matter-of-factly as he hired the thirty or forty first-class players who dominated the market. The students at the Conservatoire and the other pit musicians in town were a veritable treasure trove for the festival concerts, which brought together forces in numbers only to be found in the largest cities of Europe. (When Berlioz conducted festival concerts in Baden, Strasbourg, and north Germany, the extra musicians were brought from neighboring municipal orchestras by rail, at the producer's expense.)

Invaluable assistance in producing these events was provided by Berlioz's librarian and head copyist, Rocquemont, whom he describes as "a man of uncommon intelligence and a tireless worker who out of regard for me—as sincere as mine for him—has rendered me unforgettable services on many occasions."[17] Rocquemont lived in the rue des Martyrs, Montmartre, convenient to Berlioz's dwellings; gradually he became a factotum, carrying instruments and performance material from place to place, conducting an occasional rehearsal, standing guard duty when sabotage was expected, and caring for Berlioz's library during the composer's frequent absences from Paris. Rocquemont seems also to have sung tenor, from time to time, in

Berlioz's choruses, for his signature appears at the head of a tenor part or two.

Rocquemont engaged and supervised subcontractors for the large copying jobs, and it must have been he who helped Berlioz work out the principles of producing the thousands of pages of excellent copy that still exist. He often entered German and English translations into the vocal parts in preparation for Berlioz's foreign appearances and personally transcribed nearly all the revisions when it was necessary to bring parts up to date. The separate parts are nonetheless far from what we would today consider flawless: rehearsal letters are widely separated, there are no measure numbers, and indications of nuance are often less complete than in the score. There is not much annotation by the musicians, except for the dates and signatures routinely left in their parts by brass players and percussionists. The separate parts strongly suggest that most rehearsals were nonstop affairs, without opportunity for much attention to niceties of performance. They suggest, too, the numbers of performers Berlioz probably had in mind. Several instructions to the copyists of his orchestral songs have been preserved, and these usually demand parts on the order of five first violins, five seconds, four violas, four cellos, and three basses (that is, ten, ten, eight, eight, and six players, respectively)—though many of his orchestras were less well endowed with low strings.

The paperwork for the Paris concerts has likewise been preserved: the contracts with artists; Berlioz's own tallies of expenses for his musicians, the theater personnel, heating and lighting, and the printing of everything from handbills to tickets; and the invoices and receipts sent by the various comptrollers and business managers.[18] In a letter of 1856,[19] Berlioz outlines for the singer Charlotte Helen Dolby the costs she should expect from a concert in the Salle Herz, a small affair in a modest hall, but with nonetheless formidable expenses: 300 francs to rent the hall and have it lighted; 800 francs for an orchestra of fifty-four; 250 francs for the printing of handbills and tickets; 32 francs to rent the large instruments; 100 francs for the management; and a fee to be negotiated with the conductor. Not to be forgotten, either, was the inevitable *droit du pauvre,* the tax for the poor of 12.5 percent, perhaps 100 francs more. But Berlioz's own expenses were considerably greater, quite apart from his preference for larger halls and need for multiple rehearsals. He dealt heavily, for one thing, in large and unusual instruments, which had to be found, rented or (preferably) begged, and moved; these include the bells in the *Fantastique,* which came from the Opéra, and even the tambourines in *Harold,* which on one occasion were borrowed from the prince of the dance-hall orchestras, Philippe Musard. Harps and a piano had to be transported and tuned for nearly all his performances. Then there was the added expense of the elegant touches the public had come to expect of a Berlioz concert: they would find waiting in their seats, for example, a handbill for the next performance in the series.

Of particular interest are the seating plans for the Berlioz concerts, showing the names of the invited artists, family and friends, and the inevitable pack of journalists. Paris was bursting with periodicals: a half-dozen devoted uniquely to music, a dozen or more theater reviews, the daily papers, the illustrated journals, the satirical papers, and the foreign press (notably the Brussels papers and *Galignani's Messenger*). Names of more than fifty journals appear in lists of complimentary tickets in the archives of the Société des Concerts; Berlioz counted on distributing a minimum of thirty press tickets. He was in the habit of giving away dozens more to influential guests.

The proceeds were thus compromised from the start. The Salle du Conservatoire held just over a thousand people at best, and easily two hundred of the seats produced no revenue. That Berlioz cleared as much as he did is testimony to his skill at predicting expenses, balancing books, and programming to fill the house. Complications that would have staggered a normal musician he managed with dignity and apparent enthusiasm, always—until the late 1840s—willing to take the gamble. Others were neither so daring nor so successful at it, and Liszt writes with unveiled annoyance of the difficulties of presenting new music in Paris:

The multiplicity of obstacles to the technical organization of a concert, and the paucity of usual receipts, lead most artists to renounce the enterprise. What, then, will Berlioz do? What will the best of the young composers do—serious and conscientious men whose situation is virtually identical to his? . . . It is said that the answer is clear: they will write *romances, chansonnettes, pastiches*—or better yet *contredanses* and *galops* on the favorite tunes from new operas. *Vive Musard! Vive Tolbecque! Vive* the Louis-Philippes and the Aguados of music! *Aux grands hommes la patrie reconnaissante!*[20]

Berlioz, once disillusioned, puts the situation more strongly still in the *Mémoires:*

The composer who would produce substantial works in Paris outside the theatre must rely entirely on himself. He must resign himself to sketchy and tentative and thus more or less misleading performances, for want of the rehearsals he cannot afford; to halls which are inconvenient and uncomfortable from the point of view of both performers and audience; to the numerous difficulties raised, quite reasonably, by the opera houses, whose players one is obliged to employ, and who naturally have the needs of their own repertory to think of; to the bare-faced appropriations of the poor-house tax-collectors, who take no account of what a concert costs, and contribute to the deficit by walking off with one-eighth of the gross receipts; and to the hasty and inevitably erroneous judgements pronounced on large and complex works which are heard under these conditions and rarely heard more than once or twice. He must, in the last analysis, have a great deal of time and money to spend—not to mention the exhausting expense of will-power and spiritual energy required to overcome such obstacles. The situation of the artist who possesses these qualities to the full is like that of a loaded projectile which goes straight for its objective, sweeping aside everything in its path; it undeniably makes a mark, but is shattered to pieces in the attendant explosion.[21]

For all that the 1830s were in some ways the golden days of concert giving. There was an efficient system of princely patronage which the republican government before and the imperial government later never matched. The Salle du Conservatoire was regularly available. The concerts were protracted affairs, to be sure, lasting three hours or longer and sometimes including more than a fair share of what by modern standards seems trivial music: display pieces, transcriptions and arrangements or all sorts, countless *airs italiens*. But that was the taste of the time, and it must be remembered that Berlioz and even Habeneck were competing with masked balls and the infamous Concerts Musard, founded in the mid-1830s. Musard's hall, wrote an anonymous reporter for the *Gazette musicale,* was a "place of *rendez-vous,* where one walks about chatting while the orchestra plays the works of Weber, Meyerbeer, and Beethoven; you only quiet down for a moment to listen to the quadrille *La Brise du matin* or the galop *La Chaise cassée*."[22]

Fashionable Paris revolved around the Opéra, of course, and the two lesser opera companies, the Théâtre-Italien and the Opéra-Comique, to which would eventually be added the highly successful Théâtre-Lyrique, first producer of the Gounod operas and *Les Troyens à Carthage*. These enterprises were in constant flux: their houses would burn down, the directors and administrative structure changed at least as frequently as the government did, and the companies were habitually altering their working relationships with each other and with the houses they occupied. Each new development in this turbulent world affected Berlioz's aspirations and to some degree his creativity.

He was rather less affected, after Harriet's decline, by the night life elsewhere on the boulevards, that broad expanse from the Madeleine to the Temple quarter, with its uninterrupted succession of theaters of greater or lesser artistic significance though unwavering popular appeal: the Funambules, the Petit-Lazari, the Délassements-Comiques, the Cirque-Impérial, the Gaîté, and so on. (Much of this area was razed by Haussmann to achieve the Place de la République and its surroundings, completed in 1862.) And he was affected hardly at all by that other traditional pursuit of the artistically inclined: the literary and musical salon. This may explain why he seems to have known little about the recent developments in chamber music and the other salon genres.

Berlioz had established himself as a serious music critic with *Le Rénovateur* and the *Gazette musicale;* this led to his appointment with the *Journal des Débats,* where his first article appeared on 24 February 1835, signed H***; from 20 June 1837 he signed his full name. The criticism had its advantages, chief among them that the work was paid for on delivery: composition pays

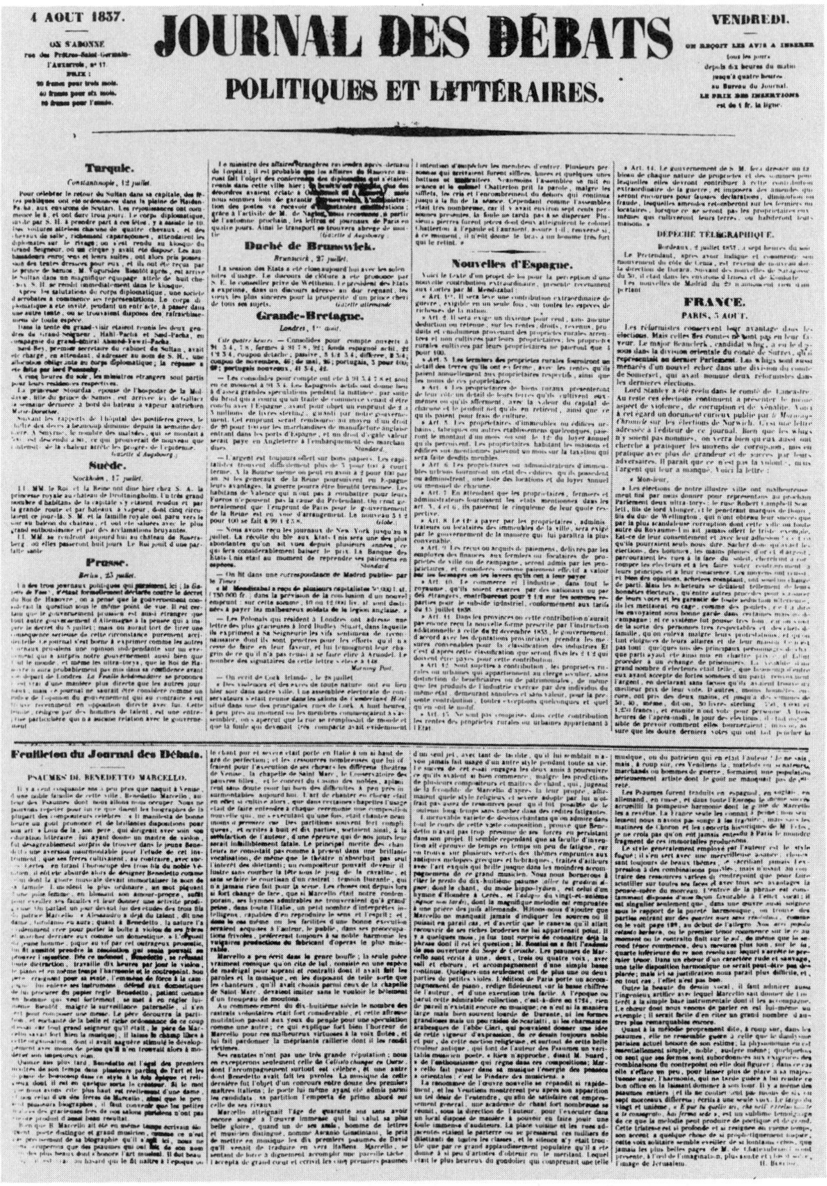

4 AOUT 1837.

ON S'ABONNE
rue des Prêtres-Saint-Germain-l'Auxerrois, n° 17.
PRIX :
10 francs pour trois mois.
20 francs pour six mois.
40 francs pour l'année.

JOURNAL DES DÉBATS
POLITIQUES ET LITTÉRAIRES.

VENDREDI.

ON REÇOIT LES AVIS A INSÉRER
tous les jours
depuis dix heures du matin
jusqu'à quatre heures,
au Bureau du Journal.
LE PRIX DES INSERTIONS
est de 1 fr. la ligne.

Turquie.
Constantinople, 12 *juillet*.

Suède.
Stockholm, 17 *juillet*.

Prusse.
Berlin, 25 *juillet*.

Duché de Brunswick.
Brunswick, 27 *juillet*.

Grande-Bretagne.
Londres, 1er *août*.

Nouvelles d'Espagne.

DÉPÊCHE TÉLÉGRAPHIQUE.

FRANCE.
PARIS, 3 AOUT.

Feuilleton du Journal des Débats.
PSAUMES DE BENEDETTO MARCELLO.

FIGURE 7.5 *Journal des Débats*, 4 August 1837. Berlioz's article on Benedetto Marcello appears in his customary space at the foot of p. 1.

late dividends, if it pays at all. Berlioz enjoyed the newspaper work, I think, more than he was prepared to admit, and it did give him a sweeping view of the musical scene. It was the necessity of doing it that vexed him: from an artistic point of view, as he was quick to point out, one symphony was worth ten times the articles of a year. But it is rather later that the incessant grumblings about "the pale work of criticism, without redeeming value" and "dog-work"[23] would begin to dominate his thoughts on the trade.

He knew more than most and prepared himself better than any. His *feuilletons* nearly always demonstrate a knowledge of the score that can come only from having studied it; he was in the habit of borrowing scarce manuscripts and visiting composers, nervous anyway about their forthcoming premiere, to mull over their autographs. When invited, he would willingly attend rehearsals and dress rehearsals. In the theater, he scrawled penciled impressions—on the plot, the mise-en-scène, and the other attributes of the performance—in his pocket notebooks, very like a modern reporter. "The expression is always true," he writes of an orchestral mass, then remarks on "the precision with which Dietsch [the chorus master] followed the motions of Girard [the conductor]." The entry concludes with an idea Berlioz expressed more than once: "the value of not seeking applause."[24] As an author he displayed a wry wit and an awesome command of both the French language and the language of music. His writing was admired for its spirit and followed, not least of all, for its mordant negatives. Here, too, he was an avid self-borrower: the meat of nearly every sentence of the published books is to be found in the newspaper articles.

The trials of a critic were many. Debutants wooed him; temptations of the basest sort were set in his path. Berlioz sometimes fell victim to favoritism or its reverse, unwarranted hostility. He probably used his influence to get Marie Recio an appointment at the Opéra—though, it must be said, while that company was in fact short of talent. He shamelessly manipulated the press in support of his compositions and was not above reviewing his own concerts from time to time. Yet especially for the *Débats* he would decline to write about works over which he would have to pass severe judgment. Such reviews, often watered down, would appear not in the *Débats* but in the *Rénovateur,* as for example the articles on Bellini's *I Puritani* and Halévy's *La Juive.*

Just as in the music, there are motives that run through the essays: the poor tax, the egocentrism of opera stars, musical grotesqueries of every kind. Berlioz's scorn for the poor tax—a curious attitude for one who considered himself a liberal—is exceeded only by his distaste for correctors, arrangers, mutilators of the great masters. Here there is irony, for despite his philosophical purism, in practice Berlioz was not above adjusting a masterpiece of Shakespeare, Gluck, Goethe, and Weber, when he found some "inspired discovery, incomparable in its pathos" to enhance it.[25] The difference, as he saw it, lay in his own nobility of concept and honesty of purpose, for neither _Freischütz_ nor the Gluck works could have been played at all in Paris without adjustment. He instinctively felt what he could not rationally admit: that the purpose of dramatic music is not to replicate but to recreate and reexamine.

He carped unnecessarily about criticism and its degradations. He surely knew that he did it well. Yet his sputterings have their comic value, and their hint of truth:

> Are we supposed to light up all of Paris because M. Sauzay, who is a bright, talented boy with a 97-year-old imagination, gave a dog of a concert in which he performed three or four pretty little playthings for violin with two-fingered piano accompaniment? Should we fire off a cannon at the Invalides to celebrate the appearance of M. Delsarte, who chose to sing—with a voice like a boat full of holes—some scraps of measured recitative based on old poetry? What in God's name is so extraordinary about that?[26]

$\mathcal{T}$he Italian sojourn was clearly more significant to Berlioz in terms of impressions garnered and ideas filed away in his memory than in terms of works he actually composed there. A few brilliant passages jotted down at the time seem to have been resurrected later in different guise, but the most obvious debts to Italy are in the masterpieces of a few years later, _Harold en Italie_ and _Benvenuto Cellini_ and _Roméo et Juliette_. The work completed in Rome or just afterward includes the refurbishings of earlier pieces (_Quartetto e coro dei Maggi_, the _Resurrexit_, and the music of the _Mélologue_), some vocal works that have not survived, and the overtures _Le Roi Lear_ and _Rob-Roy_. _Le Roi Lear_ is the more sophisticated of the two; I cannot explain why Berlioz offered _Rob-Roy_ to the Société des Concerts and not _Lear_, unless the orchestra had expressed specific interest in one of the _envois_. _Le Roi Lear_ would seem to be a programmatic work on the order of the _Tempest_ fantasy, but without the descriptive note: the composer writes in a letter, however, of its allusion to the old king's entry into his council chamber toward the end of the introduction,[27] where he cites a timpani flourish associated in Paris with appearances of Charles X. There are surely other suggestions of Lear's character, and presumably Cordelia's as well. But I think _Le Roi Lear_, like the _Francs-Juges_ overture and _Waverley_, more interesting as a stage in his maturation than as a compositional success: only some of its disjunctures can be written off as evocation of the mad Lear. Berlioz does not get a true feel for the proper scope of a concert overture until _Le Corsaire_ and _Le Carnaval romain_.

Easily the most important of the Roman works is _La Captive_, a bagatelle, as first cast in Subiaco, designed to fit a single album page. Though not his first attempt to set a poem by the great Victor Hugo—that was the lost _Chanson des pirates_, presumably equivalent to the _Scène des brigands_ in

Lélio, where the prosody is almost identical—*La Captive* is the first Hugo setting to have been preserved. As a rule, Berlioz was more interested in the musical allusions of potential song texts than in their literary merit; he was especially attracted to poems subtitled *chanson* or those with the admonition "à mettre en musique." (The text of *Le Jeune Pâtre breton,* in many ways a companion piece to *La Captive,* was appealing for precisely that kind of reason, but the poetry is saccharine and to a degree absurd.) Yet he had a good ear and decent luck in finding poems of merit, and he moved in the right circles. His 1834 setting of another of Hugo's *Orientales, Sara la baigneuse,* is splendid, too, and within a few years he had discovered the superb poetry of Théophile Gautier. It will be worth arguing, in fact, that *Le Spectre de la rose* from *Les Nuits d'été* is among the most perfect expressions of French Romanticism, summing up, in a way, everything that style was about.

Romantic poet and Romantic composer, in any event, enjoy in *La Captive* a meeting of minds with regard to orientalism, the affection for exotic subject matter that was fast becoming the rage. Hugo's text—Berlioz gives four of the nine strophes that appear in the *Orientales,* the first three and the last— consists of the reveries of a young woman captured for the harem of some Turkish pasha. She sits on a beach idly pondering her lot, guarded by a saber-wielding eunuch—an altogether useless companion and a poor con-versationalist. Not a few attributes of her situation might be pleasant enough, she reasons wistfully, if only she had her freedom and a virile young man with whom to share her thoughts. The sonority of the text is languid, and the setting magnificent: it is nightfall, with stars and a gentle evening breeze; the sea laps at the maid's feet. This is precisely the sort of imagery that tended to seduce Berlioz, and his music for *La Captive,* particularly its wide melodic intervals, markedly foreshadows Hylas's song from a quite similar perspective in *Les Troyens.* Berlioz would not have failed to notice the allusion, at the beginning of the second strophe, to the maiden's guitar, the instrument he had at his side as he wrote the music, and on which he doubtless first tried it out. One of the several preserved autographs seems to have been sent to his sister Nanci, also a guitarist.

The 1832 setting could be no simpler. Over the course of its two dozen bars, the right hand of the piano does little more than undulate on the chord progression, while the left merely supports the other voices with measure-long triads, open fifths, and at the end a cadential figure in octaves. The harmony, wandering through VI to V and touching on major II, is essentially straightforward. It is the melody that carries such power: a pair of matched phrases growing at first toward a striking peak, the high F♯ as caress of tonic E; all the points of subsidiary arrival have been deflected through feminine endings or equivocal harmonic direction. There follows a dramatic fall in the voice to low C♯ and the threefold cadential sequence that approaches tonic through the lowest note of the song, the dominant B. It is a breathtaking

a. Phrase structure of the melody:

b. The cello obbligato:

EXAMPLE 7.13 *La Captive.*

design in both shape and dramatic implication, naive yet impassioned, quite as fine as the more celebrated *idée fixe* and admirably suited to the prosody of the text (ex. 7.13a).

Berlioz was pleased to program so charming a *mélodie* for his Paris concerts, but not without the first of the rewritings in what became a long

c. The climax:

EXAMPLE 7.13 (continued).

and, on the whole, rather glamorous saga. By the concert of 30 December
1832, *La Captive* had a new cello part, *ad libitum,* written for the cellist
Desmarest, a member of Berlioz's coterie. This obbligato, too, is simple, at
first merely arpeggiating chords, with emphasis on the interval of the sixth,
for the even-numbered measures (ex. 7.13b)—a seemingly effortless touch
that nonetheless adds measurably to the scenic effect. (Berlioz relies on this
sort of arpeggiation in his "rustic" and "alpine" modes, too: it is the interval
pattern of open brass he pursues.) At m. 12 the cello joins in the melodic
climax, first supporting the high F♯ with a rising scalar figure of its own,
then, for the singer's approach to the low C♯ and B, with double-stopped
tremolandi (ex. 7.13c, mm. 15–16). This is very much on the order of the
delicious cello part in the second of the *Strophes* from *Roméo et Juliette.*
Berlioz was fluent at superposing such obbligati on preexisting material:
recall, in addition to these two passages for cello, the long oboe solo in the
Fantastique, movement I (mm. 358–409), and the French horn part, *ad
libitum,* in later versions of *Le Jeune Pâtre breton.*

The more important orchestration was prepared in 1848 for the celebrated
Mme Viardot to sing in London. For a subsequent performance by Mme
Widemann (who had premiered the *Strophes* in 1839), and for publication
in both full and piano score, Berlioz transposed the Viardot version down a
step to D. The fully orchestrated *La Captive* is a much-expanded, very free

Berlioz first orchestrated *La Captive* in 1834 for the soprano Cornélie
Falcon, just then achieving her short-lived stardom at the Opéra. This version
is lost, though what may be its ending appears in the 1832–36 sketchbook,
set forth as though for strings (ex. 7.14). The sketches also include an effort
to set Hugo's fifth stanza, which paints a canvas of vermilion towers, bright
fabrics, mansions of gold like children's playthings, and tents on elephants'
backs. It seems likely, though, that the new strophe was never finished, and
that what Mlle Falcon sang was an orchestral version of the setting with
cello.

variation of the original song. The cello part has been developed and redistributed, largely to the winds, beginning in bar 2 with a sprightlier version of what was the cello's first countermelody (ex. 7.15a).

Berlioz obviously enjoyed the added possibilities of orchestral accompaniment. Note, for example, the idiomatic, unpianistic climax of the instrumental close to the first stanza (ex. 7.15b). For the texture of the second strophe, Berlioz took the line about the maiden's guitar to heart, with staccato sixteenths in wind quartet and pizzicati in the strings (ex. 7.15c). The third strophe returns to the style of the first, with sustained chords in the wind. For the fourth, Berlioz set, for the first time, Hugo's eighth stanza, which makes reference to "a Spanish song." The accompaniment, accordingly, is in bolero rhythm, *pianissimo,* along the lines of *Zaïde*—the bolero he composed in 1845, and which was also sung in London in June 1848 (though not by Mme Viardot). Here, in the bass, one of the 1834 sketches finds good use (see ex. 7.15d).

The setting concludes with a fifth stanza like the first and third. What is ravishing here, and emphatically the stuff of Romanticism, is the way Berlioz has his scene wind down: the charming appearance of a second string orchestra (the remainder of the strings on stage), *con sordini;* the arrival of the double basses, following instructions to tune down their E-strings, on a low D; the four strokes of the bass drum and cymbal fading off into the distance; and the generous sprinkling of restless fermatas. The quintessential touch, however, is the captive maid's last sigh, "Ah!"—possibly the most successful of Berlioz's many dramatic Ah!'s—and the quiet reminiscence of her melody that draws the reverie to its close.

La Captive illustrates Berlioz's creative world in microcosm. It underwent, on a small scale, the same kinds of transformations as the great dramatic symphonies. The composer lavished on it the same attention—the same need to return to a good idea and elaborate on it, the same disinclination to let a promising accomplishment lie fallow—as was given to many a more exalted work. *Le Jeune Pâtre breton* has a very similar history: it was first sketched as a simple strophic song in 1833 (for the attempt to resurrect portions of *Les Francs-Juges* as *Le Cri de Guerre du Brisgaw*), then published with the solo part for French horn (1834), orchestrated for the 1834 concerts, and cast in more elaborate orchestral dress (1835). As *La Captive* was to serve Mme Viardot, so *Le Jeune Pâtre breton* became a vehicle for Marie Recio, in the 1840s. The difference between the two compositions is that one is timeless and the other ephemeral, largely because of the text: Brizeux's portrayal of a simple Breton peasant boy, for all its flavor of common glory, strikes the modern ear and eye as naive at best and very probably ridiculous. ("Oh, nenni da!," he says.) The captive maid, from whatever walk of life she was abducted, shames this dusty though noble savage with her intellectual clout.

Berlioz scored the piano versions of *La Belle Voyageuse, Hélène,* and *Sara la baigneuse* along rather similar lines, and all of these settings enjoyed success in the concert hall. The solo vocal works with orchestra are an important component of his oeuvre, and they have suffered from the demise of the *partie vocale* that was common in nineteenth-century concerts but which is no more. *La Captive* and the other individual songs are seldom performed in their full orchestral dress, and that deprives us of virtually all the solo-voice-and-orchestra music before *Les Nuits d'été* of the 1850s. Even the Gautier songs were meant to be freestanding, and when sung as an orchestral cycle are not, strictly speaking, authentic.

The individual movements of the *Mélologue, Le Retour à la vie,* are elegant; the Brigands' song and *Tempest* fantasy are particularly admirable ventures. *La Tempête,* moreover, had been composed in mid-1830 and thus is the first of Berlioz's Shakespearean works. It is a clear effort to capitalize on the rhetoric of the *Fantastique:* a program published at the time of the first performance[28] describes its sections, which concern Ariel, Caliban, Prospero, and the rest. The adventurous style of orchestration, with four-hand piano and emphasis, for the airy music, on high wind and *divisi* solo violins, is likewise in the mold of the first symphony. (The chorus of women and tenors, reconfirming the high tessitura, sings in rudimentary Italian, presumably Berlioz's.) What is surprising about *La Tempête* is that Berlioz left the promising but uneven work unrevised and undeveloped: after its premiere, it was heard only during the performances of the *Episode de la vie d'un artiste* and was never excerpted.

The exceptional feature of *Le Retour à la vie* is its text, an eruption in the mixed voices of poetry, drama, and song of the Romantic experience, a graphic self-portrait that endeavors to explain the meaning of the composer's Italian adventure to the Paris public. The complete *Episode de la vie d'un artiste* may well be the significant statement that nonmusicians like to make of it, perhaps even an artistic manifesto of sorts. There can be no denying the admiration of contemporary Paris for it. But the genre of the *Mélologue* is a false path, like Liszt's operatic fantasies and transcriptions, that will not suffice to arouse the listener's sympathy. It achieves little coherence in the twentieth-century concert hall.

*I*t is with *Harold,* the Requiem, and above all *Benvenuto Cellini* that Berlioz takes a leap forward in sophistication of style and technique—where, in short, his composition begins to reflect both true maturity and the sort of consistency of quality, grandeur of vision, and forthright intelligence that merit the summary term "great."

Harold en Italie, which consciously tries to follow Beethovenian practices, is on the whole the most conservative of his symphonies. It is the only one

EXAMPLE 7.14 Sketch for orchestral cadence, *La Captive*, sketchbook, fol. 34ᵛ (edited).

a. The cello obbligato orchestrated:
   cello version: orchestral version:

b. Climax of the first stanza:

c. Guitar stanza:

EXAMPLE 7.15 The orchestrated *La Captive*.

d. Bolero stanza:

EXAMPLE 7.15 *(continued)*.

to have but four movements, and they are, on the surface at least, cast in traditional molds: a sonata, a slow march, a scherzo-like movement, and a finale that begins with reminiscences of the earlier movements patterned obviously after Beethoven's Ninth. The symbolism, though, is decidedly non-Beethovenian: Chateaubriandesque, rather, as Harold—the physical presence of the violist as well as the part he plays—observes the action from a distance, a splenetic wanderer, perhaps somewhat aloof, whose recurring musical motive is square of form, unobtrusive, studiedly passive (ex. 7.16a).

The autobiographical elements are understated and more sensible than in the *Mélologue,* for *Harold* recalls not so much the Romantic agony as the pleasures of Italy: carefree wandering in the Abruzzi, the distant procession of a confraternity of monks, an evening spent in impromptu serenade,[29] and a wild to-do at the encampment of brigands Berlioz never actually saw, but was certain must be lurking somewhere about. Though he never directly says, "I drew on this and that incident for my *Harold* symphony," the intersection of memories and program is certain, as is shown by this citation from the *Mémoires:*

> . . . Then the rows of shrines to the Madonna along the tops of high hills where at evening, returning late from the plain, the reapers pass, singing litanies, while from somewhere comes the sad jangle of a monastery bell.[30]

Harold en Italie teems with imaginative ideas, displayed at a level of technical mastery not reached by either *Rob-Roy* or *Le Roi Lear:* here, in fact, is the true return to compositional life after the *Fantastique.* The opening is as strict a fugue as the century produced, curiously ahistoric in purpose— the fugue as evocation of wandering, rather than erudition; otherwise the parallels with the overture of Mendelssohn's *Elijah* are many. The most brilliant stroke is surely the three-way *réunion des thèmes* in the *Sérénade,* the spot that Narcisse Girard found impossible to get quite right (ex. 7.16c). Contortions of meter as the orgy draws to an end show that Berlioz's demonic impulse is not yet spent and display the vigorous terms he can now summon to vent it (ex. 7.16d).

a. Harold's theme, movt. I, mm. 38–45:

b. Variation procedure in the *Marche de pèlerins*, movt. II:

EXAMPLE 7.16 *Harold en Italie.*

Yet *Harold* is pointedly less complex than either the *Fantastique* or the later symphonies. The documents suggest a less labored, freer genesis for this symphony than for all the others. The overall tonal design, though appealing, is simple, with the key scheme of the four movements articulating third relations, Beethoven fashion: G minor–E major–C major–G minor, with the movements in G minor concluding in the major mode. The phrase structures are correspondingly direct.

The nineteenth-century public admired the Pilgrims' March most of all; our late-twentieth-century ears, grown accustomed to the approach of Roman legions in Respighi and in the movies, tend to find that movement

c. The *réunion des thèmes* in the *Sérénade d'un montagnard des Abruzzes à sa maîtresse*, movt. III, mm. 166–75:

EXAMPLE 7.16 (*continued*).

repetitive to the point of ennui. But the Pilgrims' March is Berlioz's first rigorous experiment with the use of space and distance as compositional variables. The great crescendo and diminuendo of the passing parade amounts to a musical version of the effect described by Christian Doppler in 1842, for the main theme does not simply grow in volume as the procession approaches, but broadens in style of attack and in tone quality—the composer is very clear on this point in the score. Note, too, the sublety of the variation procedure: in each of the first four statements, the march tune is altered to end a degree higher than before, only to be wrenched back to E in time for the new phrase (ex. 7.16b). The fragmentation at the end is *Eroica*-like; the chanted litany becomes a hallmark of Berlioz's style.

d. The *Orgie de brigands,* movt. IV, mm. 519–35:

EXAMPLE 7.16 *(continued).*

Berlioz still struggles, in *Harold,* to create the connective tissue between primary ideas that by contrast appear to come to him effortlessly. Things seem especially strained at the elisions between the G-minor brigands' music and the B♭ triumphal march that was the germ of the movement, and what passes for development in that movement (mm. 231–69) is diffuse, perhaps superfluous. And however timely the idea of a symphony with distant viola, the balance problem is hard to overcome. The soloist must be content with his symbolic identity in the last movement, where there is nothing to play after the catalogue of past visions and before the reminiscences. Otherwise he will succumb to the temptation of thinking that Paganini was right.

The vicissitudes of *Benvenuto Cellini*'s history, its shabby treatment at the hands of those who performed it in Paris and those who went to see it in London, and its several flaws of dramatic construction cannot hide the dazzling genius, the vivid color, or the commanding technique of a work that is, on the whole, very much on a par with the other fine compositions of the 1830s. Like Verdi's *Don Carlos* and Mussorgsky's *Boris Godunov*, *Cellini* has a confusing history of revisions, many of which owe their adoption more to practical than to aesthetic requirements; but in Berlioz's work the changes usually amount to quick fixes, patches acceptable only when the alternative is not to have one's work performed at all. The condition of the sources is such that no single authoritative version can be established, and as of this writing you cannot buy either a score or parts that could result in a decent reconstruction. But it is a disservice to dismiss *Cellini* from the repertoire, for Berlioz is right when he declares that it is "endowed with all the qualities which breathe life into works of art."[31]

The 1838 Paris *Cellini* was an opera in two acts and four tableaux: Monday before Mardi Gras at Teresa's house; Mardi Gras, commencing with the tavern scene and ending with the Roman carnival; Ash Wednesday at dawn in Cellini's studio; and Cellini's foundry in the Colosseum at four that afternoon. The primary difference between the original two-act version and the three-act versions for Weimar in the 1850s is in the latter tableaux, which were originally longer, with a number of incidents—a duel with Fieramosca, a strike at the foundry—designed to impede Cellini's progress on his statue. The Meyerbeerian sextet with the pope, which concluded the third tableau, was in the Paris version nearly twice as long as it is in the published scores. (In the Paris version, the pope gave Cellini the rest of the day to finish his work. In the Weimar version, Cellini asks for an hour, then spends nearly ten precious minutes singing his aria of despair, "Sur les monts les plus sauvages.")

Only in the Paris version does the action have much chance of seeming coherent. The Weimar version, by separating the first act into two, emasculates the grand curtain fall at the end of the carnival; in an attempt to make it brief and serious, Berlioz cut a great deal of the comic material. The original second act can be profitably amended by some excision and by using a few of the discoveries of the 1850s, and the whole can benefit from readings in the manuscript performance materials that have yet to be published. A successful step in this direction was taken with the Covent Garden production of the mid-1960s, recorded by Philips as part of the Colin Davis Berlioz Cycle. Its most controversial aspect is the introduction of spoken dialogue, as recitative had been sung in both Paris and Weimar. But there was talk in the 1850s of *Cellini* with spoken dialogue, which had been the composer's own intent when he undertook the work in the early 1830s, and the Choudens vocal score of 1864 suggests his final approval of the idea.

The large mound of performance material from 1838 and a dossier on the mise-en-scène, which includes an early libretto from the period when the work was in rehearsal,[32] show, however, that the content of *Cellini* was never particularly fixed, even as it approached performance. (A five-volume conductor's score, with the vocal line, a line for each of the strings parts, and a cue line for the winds—a primitive makeshift where it came to difficult music, but one still recommended later in the century as ideal for opera conductors[33]—was not done until after the "original" *Benvenuto Cellini* was covered over.) The early libretto and the orchestral parts show an original *Cellini* different in many details from the published versions. The opening scene, for example, began in D♭, with Balducci singing a *bon serment* to his daughter, warning her to stop her pointless daydreaming. A melodic motive was associated with Fieramosca: his appearances in the second act were accompanied by references to his fencing aria. Teresa's original cavatina was replaced, at the request of Mme Dorus-Gras, by the completely new aria "Entre l'amour et le devoir." There were any number of different readings in the carnival scene, from a considerably more offensive mimicry of Balducci in the puppet show to the use, for one of the choral passages, of the falling-fifths motive from *Le Ballet des ombres,* a reading that showed up later in the Queen Mab scherzo from *Roméo et Juliette.*

The Paris version changed still further after its premiere. Cellini's aria for the beginning of the second tableau, "La gloire était ma seule idole," was written between opening night and the second performance and therefore is not given in the original published libretto. (It was likewise at this chronological juncture that the sextet was abbreviated for the first time.) By the last of the complete performances, the old innkeeper had been excised from the opera altogether.

For all its uncertain ancestry, the *Cellini* left to posterity has its share of remarkable features, chief among them a pervasive vivacity of motion. The power of the temporal drive Berlioz harnesses here is foreshadowed only by a spot or two in *Lear,* perhaps, and the orgiastic portions of the *Harold* finale. It is largely a matter of studied eccentricity of rhythm and meter and of reinterpreting accent patterns, sometimes as early as the opening bars of a movement. The overture begins with just such an ambiguity, one that portends anything but the solemn goings-on of traditional grand opera (ex. 7.17).

This same rhythmic verve informs every bar of the goldsmiths' chorus, the opera's philosophical centerpiece, one of the strongest scenes in the literature. The smiths have been drinking rather heavily and continue to do so as the scene develops; this offers a convenient motivation for metric and harmonic lurching, and their lubricated condition only confirms them in the conviction that theirs is the noblest of pursuits. The merriment begins with the orchestral introduction, a fanfare during which the timpani figure and tagged-on endings based on it convey the good humor. The hymn itself finds in $\frac{3}{8}$ ample opportunity for ambiguous beat patterns, the result as witty a disregard for the barline as I know (ex. 7.18a). I do not mean to suggest that rhythm is the only special thing about this great scene. The orchestration is brilliant, the key structure attractive, especially in the abrupt tonal shifts between stanzas of the hymn. Part-writing and counterpoint seem especially assured (ex. 7.18b). A powerful entr'acte, too, is based on the *chant des ciseleurs:*

EXAMPLE 7.17 Metrical ambiguity in the opening of the overture to *Benvenuto Cellini.*

there, given in the minor mode, it wends its way toward the rise of the curtain with lugubrious, almost Wagnerian chromaticism.

The carnival scene opens with foreshadowings of the wild abandon of the Piazza Navona at nightfall. Berlioz stitches together three disparate elements to suggest the confusion (ex. 7.19a). This introduction is one of the better Weimar additions; the Paris version opened with the brass fanfares (m. 21 of the Choudens score). What follows is an elegant confusion, with the thoughts of Teresa, her father, and Cellini and Ascanio running in quite dissimilar directions (ex. 7.19b). The vicious difficulty of the chorus parts— it is as though, with "venez voir," Berlioz purposely shoves the singers past their limits—completes the sparkling atmosphere (ex. 7.19c). The ladies become overexcited and cannot seem to heed the admonitions of their gentleman friends to settle themselves for the puppet show (ex. 7.19d). Berlioz's sense of perpetual motion set down over a chain of character vignettes is altogether evocative of the opening tableau of Stravinsky's *Petrushka,* nearly eighty years later.

The other significant step forward in *Cellini* lies in Berlioz's creation of memorable characters, something at which he had not so far enjoyed particular success. (Not that he had tried particularly hard, but of *Les Francs-Juges* one recalls only the evil Olmerik and figures drawn from stock.) Fieramosca's bumbling apostrophe to his own swordsmanship leaves no doubt as to his overriding idiocy: "Vive l'escrime, c'est mon fort, oui, c'est mon fort," he sings, then shadow-fences, as though counting ballet steps, in patterns of $\frac{7}{4}$, $\frac{6}{4}$, and $\frac{5}{4}$. Balducci, the oversolicitous father and miserly papal treasurer, is made the brunt of a puppet show with blustering ophicleide solo and donkey's ears. Teresa's adolescent innocence becomes virginal devotion after the carnival, when she and Ascanio pray for Cellini's protection (ex. 7.20). The stage setting, with the heroine at her *prie-dieu* and her confidante looking on, is not so unusual: Agathe in *Freischütz* and Desdemona in Verdi's *Otello* come to mind. What give the scene its freshness are the Berliozisms: the litany of the passing procession (different choristers—

still nattering—but singing lines we have encountered before and will encounter again), the obvious affinities with the Romeo and Juliet story, the
mingled memories of Italy and La Côte.

Cellini is as well-conceived a hero as Teresa is a heroine, though the
admixture of artist's passion with brigandly bravado proved difficult for the
singers cast in the role. On the whole, though, it is the minor characters
who are most memorable: Ascanio, for example, an apprentice of boyish
enthusiasm but overly ethical concern for propriety. The pope, whose aria
was contrived to be comic and nevertheless to slip past the censors with its
apparent gravity, is a prototype for Père Laurence and King Herod, the

a. Mm. 80–88:

b. Mm. 145–53:

EXAMPLE 7.18 Tavern scene, no. 6 of *Benvenuto Cellini.*

a. Introduction:

b. Mm. 84–88, the *réunion des thèmes*:

c. Mm. 160–69:

EXAMPLE 7.19 The Roman Carnival, no. 8 of *Benvenuto Cellini*.

d. Mm. 357–64:

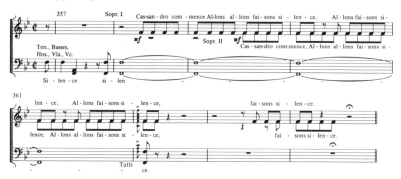

EXAMPLE 7.19 (continued).

EXAMPLE 7.20 Duo of Teresa and Ascanio, no. 12 of *Benvenuto Cellini*.

Méphistophélès of "Voici des roses," and most especially the grave Narbal of *Les Troyens*. My own favorite character is the crochety innkeeper, reeling off his account of wine consumed, a list nearly as long as Leporello's tally of Don Giovanni's conquests; cross but often funny, the *cabaretier* and Berlioz of the 1860s have a good deal in common.

There are many other things that make *Cellini* a work overflowing with genius: its lavish and original orchestra, with English horns, the ophicleide solo, guitars, anvils, and the rest; the play-within-the-play of the puppet show; the furious pace of the denouement as the gigantic Perseus is cast. Berlioz behaved gracefully at each of its failures; in Weimar, as we shall see, *Cellini* even enjoyed a degree of success. But his last word on the opera, penetrating as usual, reveals the depth of his disappointment over the lack of public enthusiasm for *Cellini:* "I cannot help recognizing," he writes in 1850 or so, "that it contains a variety of ideas, an energy and exuberance, and a brilliance of color such as I may perhaps never find again, and which deserved a better fate."[34]

With the Requiem—the *Grande Messe des morts*—Berlioz attempted to recover Le Sueurian ideals of imperial musical practice and to release his own pent-up Napoleonism. With it, he earned for himself the nation's laurels as its preeminent composer of ceremonial music, and it was doubtless the Requiem's success that led to the commission for the *Symphonie funèbre* and eventually to the Te Deum. Of the numberless contemporaneous French masses, funeral marches, triumphal marches, and cantatas of occasion—composed by virtually everybody, from Cherubini to Adam and Dietsch—none approaches in artistic merit Berlioz's three great national works. To that tally we should probably add *L'Impériale*, the cantata for Napoleon III which, though composed for another reason, was played in his presence during the closing ceremony of the 1855 Exhibition.

The Requiem is tightly controlled in its structure. The materials of composition—most notably, in this case, text, form, harmonic procedure, and orchestration—are interlocked to evoke a sequence of reflections on death and life, wherein contrasts of scene and viewpoint are made to cohere by pointed musical cross-reference. Edward Cone's analyses of the Requiem,[35] to which I am indebted for what follows, posit a dialogue between the hellish and the celestial, the personal and the universal, in a carefully ordered progress.

What the listener first perceives, however, is the size of the thing: it remains one of the two or three most apocalyptic works in the repertoire. It was with the brass fanfares and especially the percussion of the Dies irae that Berlioz had begun to conceive his vision, in the Et resurrexit of the 1824 Mass. (Both the published score of 1838 and the first Ricordi edition of 1853, in fact, erroneously give the text of the *Resurrexit* for the first choral entry after the fanfares as "Et iterum venturus est," instead of "Tuba mirum spargens sonum," doubtless an error in the transmission and regeneration of manuscript.) The moment of apocalypse cannot, however, sustain a ten-movement composition, and it is thus important to go beyond the matter of size as rapidly as possible, for much of the best music lies elsewhere.

The centerpiece of a Latin Requiem mass is the medieval prosa, *Dies irae, dies illa,* a rich pictorial poem of seventeen three-line strophes with rhyming final syllables, an eighteenth strophe of four lines, and a coda-like prayer of supplication ending in the words "Dona eis Requiem, Amen." Half the work, including all three of the grandiose movements (Dies irae, Rex tremendae, and Lacrymosa), is devoted to setting that text. The images are not pretty, dealing mostly with the wrathful nature of last judgment and the hapless supplication of poor sinners for absolution before a just but avenging judge.

Berlioz chose to set much of the rest of the traditional French liturgy, as well. (The government does not seem to have made specific provisions in this regard.) He combines the Introit and Kyrie in a single movement; separates the Offertorium and its versicle into two separate movements (Domine Jesu Christe, called at one point "Chorus of Souls in Purgatory," and Hostias et preces); sets the Sanctus as a single movement without Benedictus but with both Hosannas, and, after some abbreviating of text, joins the Agnus Dei and Communion. He sets neither the Gradual nor the Tract and makes but a brief allusion to the "Requiescant in pace, Amen" with which the funeral service concludes.

The very free treatment of the traditional liturgy recalls the kind of treatment Berlioz accorded the *prix de Rome* texts. The liberties allow him to cultivate relief from the terror of judgment and find comfort and asylum from dogma in the spirit of the individual believer. In the introspective Quid sum miser, for example—that haunting dialogue of tenors, woodwind soloists, and lower strings which follows the big Dies irae—he constructs from verses 7, 9, and 17 of the prosa a new, gentle prayer:

> What, then, shall I say, wretch that I am,
> What advocate entreat to speak for me?
> When even the righteous may hardly be secure?
>
> Remember, merciful Jesu,
> That I am the cause of thy pilgrimage;
> Do not forsake me on that day.
>
> I pray in supplication on my knees,
> My heart contrite as the dust,
> Take care of my end.

The *Dies irae* tune drones away in the lower instruments, reminding us of the promised doom. But the countermelody woven around it by the English horn and voices, likewise drawn from the previous movement, offers the sinner time for introspection and gives the horror time to subside.

Much of the more frightening imagery, including a line from the Offertory, is moved into the Rex tremendae. The Offertory is thus allowed to approach its end with a ray of hope, the word "promisisti," cast as an uplifting D-major triad, the tonic with *tierce de Picardie* spread across six bars (ex. 7.21). The conflation of Agnus and Communion paves the way for the restatement of the introit psalm-verse "Te decet hymnus" ("A hymn, o God, becometh thee in Sion")—the kind of textual allusion to music that always attracted Berlioz. This and similar ideas were suggested to him by the reminiscences embodied in the Latin liturgy and by the musical structure he had shaped. When Berlioz says of the Requiem, in mid-April 1837, that he has finally dominated his subject, he almost surely means that he has arrived at this version of the text, one that involves numerous other details of textual rearrangement.

Berlioz's music is broad of gesture, slow in harmonic rhythm, and ample in its structural repeats, from the restatements of passages first heard in previous movements to the prominence of B♭–A as a motivic reference point. The exquisite sparseness of the introspective movements balances the movements with brass and percussion. This is what is meant by "architectural," a term Berlioz tells us is applied properly to only the Requiem, the Te Deum, and *L'Impériale*. It is an outgrowth of the considerations of musical space essayed in the *Fantastique, Harold* (especially, but not exclusively, in the placement of the viola soloist), and the carnival scene in *Cellini*. The idea is evident in any number of passages where the point is for the performance venue itself to participate in the musical meaning: in the opening, for example, where the rising cello line simply grows out of a spatial void, or in the shattering emptiness following the explosion of the Tuba mirum, where pale vestiges tremble in the violas and cellos as the echo retreats naturally back into the void.

One of the most unifying devices of the Requiem is the strong reliance on chromatic relationships, a tactic suggested when the opening melody of the first movement is inverted to become the countersubject of the choral exposition and then the subject of the closing "Christe eleison" (ex. 7.22a). From these chromatics grow a number of significant relationships, including A–B♭ choral ostinato in the Offertory; this possibly explains, as well, the shape of the strange chords at the beginning of the last movement (ex. 7.22b). At the close of the work is a strong reference to the chromatic cadence of the first movement (ex. 7.22c).

That is but one of many allusions in the last movement to previous events. The trombone-and-flute chords from the *Hostias* occur early in the movement, leading to the reminiscence of the "Te decet hymnus." And the note of affirmation with which the work concludes, the cadence at "quia pius est" (m. 179), was first heard, to the similar text "fons pietatis," at the close of the *Rex tremendae* (m. 106). Like *Faust* and *L'Enfance du Christ*, the Requiem ends in Heaven.

I think, too, that it is with the Requiem that Berlioz perfects his sense of framing, a concept very much at issue in *Roméo et Juliette*. Concentric frames add shape and balance to the multimovement works; they become more important the bigger the work and the farther removed it is from Classical symphonic practice. The outside frame of the Requiem is of course the similarity of content and purpose between the first and last movements. The introspective movements frame, and are framed by, the apocalyptic ones. There are other levels of framing as well: the four brass choirs, at the extremities of the mass of performers, give the ensemble its physical frame. And the flute-and-trombone chords provide a curious frame of the musical space, when the hairpin dynamic marking draws the mind from the trombones to the flutes and back again.

Berlioz's Grand Army—of brass choirs (with, in at least one performance, an *ophicléide monstre*), ten timpanists, tuned bass drum, and more than a dozen suspended cymbals and tam-tams (these last struck once in the Dies irae and once in the Lacrymosa) plus the usual full orchestra and chorus— is by no means unprecedented: any number of works in the French ceremonial tradition call for similar effects. The novelty lies in the restrained deployment. The brass choirs are heard but three times; the English horn appears only in the Quid sum miser; the *cornet à pistons* only at the very end of the Sanctus. The two strophes of the Sanctus are splendidly subtle of orchestration, the celestial effects with flute solo and *divisi* solo violins not unlike those of the *Tempest* fantasy, though considerably more assured. The strokes of bass drum and cymbal in the second stanza, *sempre* **pp,** add elegant nuance to what would otherwise be a direct repeat, as does the cello part, which provides a bass line only implied in the first stanza. The graceful scoring has an ironic effect: it is in the Agnus dei and not the Tuba mirum where one can actually hear the chord progression in the timpani.

EXAMPLE 7.21 Cadence of the Offertoire, movt. VII of the *Grande Messe des morts.*

a. Movt. I:

b. Movt. X:

c. Close of movts. I and X:

EXAMPLE 7.22 Structural unities in the *Grande Messe des morts.*

Berlioz prefers his choruses in six parts, at least until later in his career. The three- and six-part texture, with corresponding emphasis on the tenor, is a norm of French tradition, doubtless a descendent of the male-only *maîtrise;* the later French four-part chorus, of balanced gender, has as much to say of the status of post-Revolutionary women as of compositional preference. The six-part chorus offers an interesting array of possibilities, not just when tenors II and basses I, for example, join forces to cover vocal breaks, but also in the overall increase in possibilities for pairing. Some striking uses of this kind of chorus occur in the Quaerens me, m. 31ff., where the unisons separate into harsh dissonances, and in the *promisisti* cadence of the Offertory, given above in example 7.21.

Berlioz proclaimed on several occasions that the love scene from *Roméo et Juliette,* the most intimately personal of his compositions, was his favorite work. But he was just as proud of the Requiem, as is shown by a number of public declarations to that effect and the frequent citations of passages from it in the *Traité de l'instrumentation.* A letter to Humbert Ferrand of 11 January 1867 confirms this passion: "If I were threatened with seeing my entire *œuvre* burned, less one score, it would be for the *Messe des morts* that I would beg mercy."[36]

 ot the least vexing problem of *Roméo et Juliette* is the inability to know which passages are the fruit of Berlioz's earliest ruminations on the subject, during the *Cléopâtre* and Shakespeare years. The work as it was offered in 1839 cannot be fully reconstructed. *Roméo et Juliette* is, on the one hand, the jewel of the golden decade; it remained, on the other, a work in progress for most of Berlioz's active life.

Berlioz began by conceiving a Romeo and Juliet symphony based on the incidents in Shakespeare that most inflamed his sensibilities: the swordplay between the quarreling families, Mercutio's Queen Mab soliloquy, the ball at the Capulet's house, and the balcony and tomb scenes. He was taken by the character of Friar Laurence, as well, and early on saw him as the key to ending the work. (All these he mentions in his review of the Bellini opera[37] as fitting for the attention of a composer; here he also mentions the buffooning of Juliet's nurse and the stark evil of Tybalt, though neither character appears in the finished symphony.) Three incidents in the symphony are not found in Shakespeare: the funeral march for Juliet, this particular tomb scene, and the scene of reconciliation between Montagus and Capulets. These ideas are borrowed from various corrupt traditions of the play, largely descended from the performances of the great English actor David Garrick. Garrick's version has Juliet awaken in the tomb for a few moments of shared anguish before the lovers' simultaneous deaths. Garrick's idea for a funeral procession, adopted in Deschamps's later French translation as well, was especially attractive to Berlioz because of its implicit invitation to repeat the successes of the *Marche au supplice* and the *Marche des pèlerins;* the image of strewn flowers alone is from Shakespeare. Berlioz seems to have thought that the reconciliation scene came from Shakespeare's era (see his remarks below), though I do not know where he came upon that notion.

The work was to be Beethovenian, as well, with a scherzo and a choral finale. What little more we know of the original formulation suggests a relatively conservative work, perhaps on the order of *Harold en Italie.* But once he got started, Berlioz could not resist the temptation to add movements and refer to other parts of the play, and with *Roméo et Juliette* he began to abandon the old symphonic ideals and broke altogether with sonata-inspired organization. He came to prefer strophic forms and free sectionality, procedures more useful to his dramatic purposes. Balance and coherence are achieved by the sort of framing he had worked out for the Requiem: there is a reprise of the opening swordplay for the quarreling of the rival families at the end, and a clear formal balance between the strophes at the beginning and Friar Laurence's aria in the last scene. In the first version, parallel recitatives commenced each half.

"There can be no mistaking the genre of this work," writes Berlioz in his five-paragraph foreword to *Roméo et Juliette:*

Even though voices are often used, it is neither a concert opera nor a cantata, but a choral symphony.

If there is singing, almost from the beginning, it is to prepare the listener's mind for the dramatic scenes whose feelings and passions are to be expressed by the orchestra. It is also to introduce the choral masses gradually into the musical development, when their too sudden appearance would have damaged the composition's unity . . .

[The] last scene of the reconciliation between the two families is the only one that falls into the domain of opera or oratorio. It has never been performed on any stage since Shakespeare's time, but it is too beautiful, too musical, and it concludes a work of this nature too well for the composer to dream of treating it differently.

If, in the famous garden and cemetery scenes the dialogue of the two lovers, Juliet's asides, and Romeo's passionate outbursts are not sung, if the duets of love and despair are given to the orchestra, the reasons are numerous and easy to comprehend. First, and this alone would be sufficient, it is a symphony and not an opera. Second, since duets of this nature have been handled vocally a thousand times by the greatest masters, it was wise as well as unusual to attempt another means of expression. It is also because the very sublimity of this love made its depiction so dangerous for the musician that he had to give his imagination a latitude that the positive sense of the sung words would not have given him, resorting instead to instrumental language, which is richer, more varied, less precise, and by its very indefiniteness incomparably more powerful in such a case.[38]

This is a significant manifesto, with more implications than he realized at the time for his later amalgamations of dramatic and symphonic elements in the same composition. The question was how to deal with the narrative mise-en-scène. Berlioz had been dissatisfied with the printed program of the *Symphonie fantastique,* thinking that readers had conceived "exaggerated and ridiculous notions" about it. It is probably for this reason that he was content with simple descriptive headings to the movements in *Harold.* His reservations about such programs, and a possible solution, are embodied in a note added to the *Fantastique* leaflets in 1836:

If the few lines of this program had been the sort that could have been recited or sung between each of the movements of the symphony, as the chorus of ancient tragedy did, their meaning would not have been misunderstood. But instead of hearing them one must read them.[39]

For *Roméo et Juliette* he thought to try sung choral recitative, with the incidents and characters of the drama summarized at the beginning of each half.

Berlioz was not happy with his prologues in the Greek style, however, and these underwent more intense scrutiny than any other passages save Friar

Laurence's monologue. His dissatisfaction with the recitatives is clear from the earliest stages of work, when the strophes and scherzetto appear to have been laid in, as though to append some further musical interest to a section that threatened to become monotonous. In performance the chorus failed to offer the intimacy he had envisaged, and because of the arias and finale a printed libretto was in any event necessary. Though the finished product works nicely—with the long second prologue deleted, musical foreshadowings added to the remaining one, and a return of the prologue singers for the end of the finale—Berlioz shied away in later works from such solutions. The settings of *La Damnation de Faust* are described briefly in the program; *L'Enfance du Christ* calls, with mixed results, for a *récitant*, or narrator. The idea that a series of musical tableaux might be connected in the listener's mind by his or her own prior knowledge of the story became an entrenched principle of Berlioz's composition. It was his way of pruning long texts into manageable shape.

Roméo et Juliette is a work in seven movements. All the original sources agree on this singularly misunderstood point; Berlioz's correspondence is quite clear about it. It is one of Malherbe and Weingartner's grosser manipulations of the facts to try to make of *Roméo et Juliette* a four-movement symphony, and their effort has managed to confuse most of the available performance material. The movements are as follows:

1. Introduction

   Combat, Tumult, Intervention of the Prince (orchestra alone)
   Prologue (prologue chorus)
   Strophes (contralto aria)
   Continuation of the Prologue
   Recitative and Scherzetto (tenor, with chorus)
   Conclusion of the Prologue

2. Capulet's House

   Romeo Alone: Sadness; Distant Sounds of Ball and Concert
   Great Festivity at Capulet's House
      (Andante and Allegro, for orchestra alone)

3. Balcony Scene

   Serene Night: Capulet's Garden, Silent and Deserted
   The Young Capulets, leaving the party, pass by while singing reminiscences of the ball (male chorus and orchestra)
   Love Scene: Juliet on the Balcony; Romeo in the Shadows (orchestra alone)

4. Queen Mab Scherzo

   Queen Mab, or the Dream Fairy

5. Funeral Cortège

   Funeral Procession for Juliet: Fugal March, at first instrumental, with psalmody on a single note in the voices; then vocal, with the psalmody for orchestra (chorus of Capulets and orchestra)

6. Tomb Scene

   Romeo at the Capulets' Tomb:
   Invocation
   Awakening of Juliet
   Delirious joy, despair, last anguish and death of the two lovers (orchestra alone)

7. Finale

   Finale for two choruses, prologue chorus, and Friar Laurence:
   The Crowd Rushes to the Cemetery
   Recitative, Statement, and Aria of Friar Laurence
   Quarrel of Capulets and Montagus in the Cemetery
   Invocation of Friar Laurence
   Oath of Reconciliation (all three choruses)

Berlioz calls for an intermission after the scherzo, an interval to be used for removing the harps and bringing on the chorus of Capulets for the funeral march. Throughout *Roméo et Juliette* there is an impressive visual element in the arrival and departure of the soloists, chorus, and harps and even the progress to the forestage of the antique-cymbal players. The intermission is equally important to the dramatic effect: *Roméo et Juliette* contrasts the ecstasy of the lovers with the tragedy of their death, and the interval serves to separate the tragic from the festive.

Perceived as Berlioz saw it, the work is simply Beethovenian in design, with the narrative elements overlain. Its core approaches a five-movement symphony with the choral finale and, as in the *Fantastique*, both a scherzo and a march:

   I. Fête chez Capulet
   II. Scène d'amour
   III. La Reine Mab
   IV. Convoi funèbre
   V. Finale

The "extra" movements are thus the introduction with its *potpourri* of subsections and the descriptive tomb scene. Berlioz in fact passed through a period of thinking the tomb scene should be omitted before all but the most learned audiences—ninety-nine times out of a hundred, he says—and he left a huffy note to that effect in the published score.

Our attention must be limited to the *Scène d'amour* which, with the septet from act IV of *Les Troyens*, is the best of Berlioz's night-musics. As Verona goes off to sleep, with the sounds of Nature at their most soothing, the star-crossed lovers have their famous dialogue. The scene is unashamedly pictorial: the movement, in the tranquil key of A major, is part duet, part orchestral fantasia, with four very free sections made up of paired strophes that spin themselves out ever further as the lovers' passions grow. It is unified by the celebrated refrain.

Though Berlioz suggests beginning the work at the Adagio (m. 124) when a chorus is unavailable, it is the departing Capulets, exhausted but jolly, who so aptly set the scene. They are heard to pass by, *à la Harold* and *Cellini,* thus letting the cloak of nocturnal solitude descend over Romeo; their tune is a transformation of the ball music (ex. 7.23a). More extraordinary still is the meandering chord progression that evokes serene night, governed by the chromatic wanderings around the low tonic A in the bass line. The resolutions of dissonance are buried, in this thicket of sound, in the under-voices, and the whole is articulated by the sultriest of wind qualities, flutes in the low register, with low horns. The Capulet boys sing two strophes of their song: "Allez, allez," they tell each other, "Dream of love until daybreak." The break of day portends for Shakespeare and Berlioz, as for Wagner in act II of *Tristan,* the tragedy to follow. So it is that at the cadence of the second strophe, at the word "jour," the double basses alight, sharply, on the dissonant G♮. They wind back to the cadence point via G♯ as the Capulets' song extends itself in drowsy codetta.

The curtain is thus raised on the orchard over which Juliet's balcony looks. (Note the soaring effect of the entry of violins I, where the tonic grows outward to the major third, a high C♯.) The gurgling of contented avian creatures in their nests perfumes the setting. The strophes are constructed around recurrences of the principal love themes, the first associated, as the composer explicitly states, with Romeo. Its response is probably to be associated with Juliet, and the refrain is identical (ex. 7.23b). As in the tomb scene, the voice of Romeo is identified with the tenor instruments (cellos and violas here, to which are added bassoon and English and French horn in the invocation at the tomb); that of Juliet, of course, with the violins and high winds.

The surprising return of the opening statement at measure 155, after the first statement of the love theme, seems a clear indication that Juliet has not yet appeared: the night reasserts its presence. The shift, at measure 168, to anxious, irregular, rising chromatics—an established Berlioz device, these pantings—in transition to the full-bodied statement of the refrain in C major (♮III) must treat Romeo's mounting excitement as Juliet appears.

Her willowy presence is suggested *Allegro agitato* (m. 181), in $\frac{2}{4}$. The lovers' first recitative ensues, Juliet responding tentatively at first, then in a full strophe of her own. This evolves well past its presumed ending and into another strophe, with ever-mounting passion: the third large section bears most of the weight of the movement.

Love scenes never end easily. The ear expects closure soon after the arrival at dominant in measure 300, particularly with the prolongation of cadence by an Italianate outburst in mm. 304–5. At measure 308, with syncopations and crescendo, the final drive to cadence and tutti recapitulation of the love theme seems clearly to have been reached. But this dissolves, too, into a quiet statement of Juliet's response (m. 322ff.), extended lyrically by the clarinets and interrupted by outbursts of increasing vigor and heavy reliance on the weak beats in $\frac{6}{8}$. The grand pause interrupts forward motion, yet the work lingers still more in its slow dissolution: the lovers cannot bear to part, nor can the composer leave them to their sad destinies. In measure 358, the frenetic drive to conclusion begins in earnest, with the love theme surrounded by some of Berlioz's most exquisite filigree work (ex. 7.23c). The parting is indeed difficult, with allusions to the lovers' reluctant exchanges of "goodnight" in the music (clarinets and violins, m. 383ff.; flutes, m. 384ff.). The movement dissolves.

Even if one chooses to ignore the blissful imagery of this movement, there can be no denying the artistry with which the composer asserts his principles: the association of tessitura with character, for example, heard for the first time at the "intervention of the Prince of Verona." The Queen Mab scherzo is full of elfin orchestration, notably at the trio with harmonics in strings and harps. The metric effect, with simultaneous $\frac{3}{4}$ and $\frac{9}{8}$, is similar to that of the notorious spot in the third movement of *Harold,* but here the notation is simpler. The notation, in fact, is strong throughout *Roméo et Juliette:* the score is peppered with all manner of nuance, expression marks, and helpful suggestions from composer to performer. Berlioz achieves a perfection of acoustic balance in the work, clearest in the *serment de réconciliation* of Père Laurence, whose part is placed carefully in both metric position and vocal range: the line "de tendre charité, d'amitié fraternelle" (mm. 419–24), gently underscored by the first identifiable reentry of prologue chorus, is among the most ravishing in the score. Elsewhere the reconciliation bears strong similarity to the Lacrymosa: the brass articulation with the $\frac{9}{8}$ meter is virtually the same, as are the exclamation points from the percussion and the obbligato figures in the strings.

In contrast to the Requiem, however, *Roméo et Juliette* is a work of profound difficulty—not so much technically, as *Cellini* is, but in terms of the care needed to mount an authentic and effective production. It requires two full choruses, nearly a third of whose members, as in the Requiem, must be tenors. (The Montagus must not sing the *Convoi funèbre,* but rather be saved for the eruption of the quarrel in the finale. Berlioz wanted the Montagus and the Capulets dressed in different colors, but I do not think he ever managed it.) The prologue chorus should consist of only twelve to fifteen singers, with emphasis on women to produce the mezzo-soprano qualities of which Berlioz was already growing fond.

Berlioz intended for the choruses to be arranged in front of the orchestra, descending on scaffolds from a theater stage. It is a dramatic effect, but it requires at least two assisting conductors, or today, perhaps, the aid of television. The soloists are to be near the conductor, presumably on the apron of the stage.

Berlioz demands of the listener both a knowledge of the drama and a conscious effort to recreate it in the mind's eye. It is only then that the composer can invite his audience to share his love for Shakespeare in general and these characters in particular. The experience should be shattering, especially as *Roméo et Juliette* approaches its conclusion. The hypnotic procession of stunned Capulets, strewing flowers along their course; the summary V–I of the cellos at the end of the tomb scene, announcing that the lovers are no more, Friar Laurence's too-brief lament, *"Pauvres enfants que je pleure"*—all these participate in a wonderful drive to peroration. The last panorama, of the families swearing friendship over the bodies of daughter and son "by the holy crucifix," is a strange but successful mingling of the values of Elizabethan drama, eighteenth-century English theatrical tradition, and nineteenth-century French Catholicism. What has emerged, during the evening-long symphony, summarizes Berlioz's decade of experiment, discovery, and achievement.

*T*he period includes two other major works: the *Symphonie funèbre et triomphale,* composed in the early summer of 1840, and *Les Nuits d'été,* probably composed that summer, too, but so quietly that almost nothing is known of their genesis. Important as the piano-vocal version is, the songs achieve their greatest stature in the later orchestrations: first *Absence* in 1843, then *Le Spectre de la rose* in late 1855, then the rest in March 1856 for publication.

The *Symphonie funèbre* shares, in many ways, the compositional concerns with time and space that are the rhetoric of the Requiem. The funeral march achieves the same solid, slow motion, both in its formal structure—a languid march-and-trio/sonata movement with the long first theme repeated (ex. 7.24a)—and in its ponderous harmony. The extended melody, in the composer's meandering idiom, denies closure for more than a dozen measures (ex. 7.24b).

The funeral oration may not be one of Berlioz's major accomplishments, but I cannot share Hugh Macdonald's clear disdain for the *Apothéose,*[40] which I find so far superior to the banal grand marches of French band practice as to be assured an important place in that repertoire. The addition of parts for strings and chorus is skillfully executed, and the big cadence at the end is among Berlioz's grandest.

The *Symphonie funèbre et triomphale* pleased for the same reason that, fifteen years later, *L'Enfance du Christ* would please: it was music that could be understood on one hearing. The key is in Adolphe Adam's remark that "in sum, there is a great progress, for the phrases are divided squarely, four-by-four, and are easily understood."[41] Paris audiences were not in the habit

a. The *Fête chez Capulet* theme transformed:

b. Love themes:
Romeo:

Refrain:

Juliet: Refrain:

EXAMPLE 7.23 Love scene from *Roméo et Juliette*.

c. Last statement of love theme:

EXAMPLE 7.23 (continued).

of having to think about music. "This time," observed Berlioz, "I wrote so big that even myopic people could read me."[42]

*B*erlioz's music of the 1830s, though full of experiment, is not, then, a matter of effect piled upon effect or miscellaneous assembly of orchestral devices. Rather it constitutes a studied progress from the untamed rhetoric of the *Fantastique,* with further refinements of style to be discovered in each new work.

Of the many maturations of the 1830s, the most profound are in what Berlioz calls the vast and fecund avenue of rhythm. Thoughts on rhythm, in its broadest sense—surface rhythms, harmonic rhythms, and long-term meaning of meter—occupied him throughout the 1830s. In 1837 he wrote a brilliant essay on the subject in the *Journal des Débats*[43] and returned to the matter, all too briefly, in the *Mémoires.* His central thesis appears today to be a simple truth, but at the time it was novel: that considerations of rhythm are as important to musical interest as melody and harmony. Audiences of his era, he thought, appreciated only the octaves and unisons of rhythm; most composers and virtually every instrumentalist failed to understand its possibilities. It was the most neglected aspect of French musical education.

Nothing in musical grammar was more platitudinous, he wrote, than the "phrase carrée," the square phrase of four or eight measures. Rhythmic combinations must certainly be as numerous as melodic ones, and the links between them could be made as interesting as for melody. "Nothing can be more obvious than that there are rhythmic dissonance, rhythmic consonance, and rhythmic modulation. Ingenuity in rhythm is even more difficult than finding beautiful melodies."[44]

He preached the need for greater sophistication in rhythm: alternation of binary and ternary, placement of recurring events at irregular intervals, episodic uses of ringing bells and harp glissandi, and rhythmic growth and decay. He practiced what he preached. As proof of the new sophistication, compare the fanfares of the *Tuba mirum* with the original version of the

a. Formal structure:

March as Th. I	March Repeated	Developmental Transition	C Pedal		Deflected to D♭
4	25	48	70		88	93
F minor		I	V		IV	V
					III	III

Trio as Th. II	Development (Return)	Recapitulation of March (and Dev. Trans.)		Recapitulation of Trio	Coda
95	125	156		207	240
III		i		I	

b. Phrase structure of melody:

EXAMPLE 7.24 *Marche funèbre*, movt. I of the *Grande Symphonie funèbre et triomphale.*

Resurrexit, or consider the tranquilizing effect of conventional rhythmic patterns after the sprung opening of the *Lacrymosa.*

Otherwise, Berlioz's growth in the 1830s was not so dissimilar from that of other maturing composers. Berlioz mastered not just instrumental range and practicality, but tone color and texture as well. He discovered the many opportunities a composer has to establish musical perspective and viewpoint. And he became more comfortable with the troublesome matter of dealing with text. Many of his solutions remained difficult to understand, however, and the resulting music was difficult for most everybody to remember. He was still further ahead of public taste than we can easily imagine.

Chapter Eight

Vagabondage
(1840–46)

From mid-August to mid-September 1840, Berlioz visited his father in La Côte-St.-André and called, elsewhere in the region, on his sisters and their husbands. Dr. Berlioz, at sixty-four, was in his ultimate decline. This is one of perhaps two occasions on which it appears that Berlioz and his father conversed intimately about his music, untroubled by thoughts of the past. Dr. Berlioz elicited from his son the promise to return for a month with Harriet and Louis, yet they parted with the tenderness of those who do not expect to meet again. Berlioz returned to Paris bearing for Louis a letter from his grandfather and slippers from his cousin Mathilde Pal. But little boys of six have other passions: the brioches and jam from the devoted maid, Monique, made a better impression.

In lieu of a concert series that fall, Berlioz hoped to produce a single concert on a scale commensurate with the grand design of his recent work. It was the first of his mega-concerts of the 1840s, announced as a "Festival de M. Berlioz." The term *festival* was ill-advised, as it turned out, for it was too suggestive of merrymaking; Berlioz had meant it in the sense of *fête musicale,* a musical festivity. The public preferred to think of such an event as a *concert monstre* and delighted in this new confirmation of its suspicion that M. Berlioz was veering beyond mere eccentricity.

The Opéra undertook the production as one of the annual benefits offered its administrative director, Léon Pillet. Berlioz negotiated for himself a fee of 500 francs, with the other financial obligations and the bookkeeping to be handled by the company. All this had to be presented to Habeneck, still the resident conductor, as a *fait accompli,* for fear he would otherwise insist on his privilege of conducting. Four hundred fifty performers were thus more-or-less secretly engaged to appear in a program consisting of the Dies irae, Quid sum miser, and Lacrymosa from the Requiem; orchestral excerpts and the finale from *Roméo et Juliette;* and the *Symphonie funèbre et triomphale,* along with selections by Palestrina, Handel, and Gluck. "The performance will end, by popular demand," gloated the *Charivari*, "with an ascent by M. Berlioz in a bass drum."[1]

The technical preparation for so large a concert was a daunting task even for Berlioz and the indefatigable Rocquemont. The existing chorus parts had to be doubled and in some cases quadrupled. To accommodate the large number of musicians, carpenters built a platform and ramp from the stage of the opera house over the pit and down as far as the *parterre*. Berlioz's first experience with that kind of stage setting, which he designed for himself, was entirely positive; he went on to describe it as ideal for *Roméo et Juliette* (in the *Observations* at the head of the published score), and it is the arrangement he specified for the 1855 *Lélio* in Weimar.

Sectional rehearsals for the chorus were held in the several music rooms of the quarter, including at the Opéra, Théâtre-Italien, and Salle du Conservatoire. Orchestra sectionals proceeded along similar lines, and toward the end consecutive four-hour rehearsals for strings and winds took place in the lobbies of the two opera houses.

The drawback of Berlioz's system of sectional rehearsals is that the conductor, alone of the performers, must be at virtually all of them. Berlioz's fatigue and his irritability grew alarmingly as he struggled through day after day filled with practice after practice. In the course of this ordeal the members of the Opéra orchestra, whose participation in benefits was required by the terms of their salaried contract, insisted on a remuneration commensurate with that of the supplementary players. Frightened of what they might otherwise do during the performance, Berlioz contributed his own modest fee in an effort to make up the difference.

For economic reasons and because of the exigencies of scheduling so large a force, a single full rehearsal was held, on Saturday, 31 October, at 11:00 A.M. There it was discovered that *La Reine Mab* was unworkable with an orchestra of that dimension, and the movement was withdrawn from the program. (Pondering later on the problem of Queen Mab, Berlioz decided to move the antique cymbals closer to the front and to reduce the number of strings invited to play the movement. A direction to that effect appears in the published score.) For reasons I do not know, the first two movements of the *Symphonie funèbre* were canceled as well. The general level of confusion at the dress rehearsal left Berlioz in a state of profound unease.

Neither Habeneck nor his lieutenants had taken news of the festival well; the atmosphere at the house was decidedly hostile. Rumors reached Berlioz of plans to sabotage the instruments and music. Rocquemont, accordingly, stood guard over the stage between the dress rehearsal and the performance the next day (Sunday, 1 November). Berlioz fretted all night, then before the concert went around his orchestra checking the crooks of the trumpet and horn players to assure against "accidental" tunings in the fanfares of the Dies irae. In the event all went beautifully: he entered a full house; stood before his host of musicians enjoying the unaccustomed luxury of full theatrical lighting; then proceeded to conduct what was by all accounts a superb performance. He reports frenzied applause from the musicians after the Requiem excerpts and a near riot of excitement during the *Apothéose*.

Not that the claque failed to make its presence known. A *siffleur* hissed the end of the Dies irae and was just as ostentatiously hushed by the audience, then thrown out by the police. Others among the hired rabble began to cry for the *Marseillaise*, a notion found attractive by the audience at large; they took up the chant and had to be quelled by the chief of police and the composer/conductor himself. Later, as though that were not disruption enough, an editor of the *Charivari*, one Bergeron, sought out the owner of *La Presse*, Emile de Girardin, to provoke a duel.[2] *La Presse,* it seems, had insinuated that Bergeron was guilty of the 1832 attempt on Louis-Philippe's life. Mme de Girardin cried of murder from her box, and pandemonium ensued.

The inflated payroll amounted to 130 francs more than the 9,000 taken in at the box office, with the difference, of course, paid by the composer.[3] But despite the monetary loss, and above the din in the house, Berlioz had managed to give what was widely believed to be the biggest concert ever presented.

His own euphoria confirms a remarkable success. The festival/concert was a fitting conclusion to a twelve-month period that had already seen the glorious first performances of *Roméo et Juliette* and the acclaim granted the *Symphonie funèbre* in July. Berlioz was pleased with himself for having managed the concert all alone, and after a single full rehearsal. To be seen at the Opéra before its formidable company of artists was the more significant in view of the fact that everybody knew Habeneck's days to be numbered. The consequences, he thought, would be of incalculable value.

Soon enough, indeed, there came inquiries from organizers of the festivals in Lille, talk of another Paris festival for early 1841, and an invitation to come to London for two months of promenade concerts. None of these plans developed much momentum, and Berlioz's disinclination to follow his countryman Louis Jullien in conducting the London proms earned disdainful remark in the English papers.

The Paris papers thought they had identified more sensational fodder. For his monster concert Berlioz had given acts from Handel's *Athalia* and Gluck's *Iphigénie en Tauride*, and Palestrina's madrigal *Alla riva del Tebro*. (This last, known already in Paris from performances led by Girard, Valentino, and Fétis, was thought the epitome of gothic art.) A detractor seized the opportunity to attack the well-known attacker for colossalizing Gluck and Handel and orchestrating Palestrina, and the press hostile to Berlioz staged a full assault. His vigorous response appeared in the *Revue des deux mondes:* despite the large number of performers, he wrote, Gluck's work had been performed exactly as notated—without ophicleides—and the Palestrina had been rendered as it was meant to be, *a cappella*.[4]

*F*rom noon on 13 November Berlioz was for twenty-four hours a bemused inmate of the prison on the quai d'Austerlitz. He had missed National Guard duty on 30 July, two days after the grueling service to his country of conducting the *Symphonie funèbre* in the streets of Paris. (He had reported for duty on the 29th, but found he was too exhausted to carry on.) He rather enjoyed the notion of going to jail and was happy enough to pass the time by writing a long letter on the festival/concert to his sister Nanci and sleeping the next day until noon.[5]

There was a tamer concert on 13 December, featuring the first four movements of *Roméo et Juliette* and the *Symphonie fantastique*. Balzac, an infrequent guest, came specifically to hear the *Fantastique*. But the receipts were poor, and Berlioz lost another 1,320 francs just as he was on the verge of figuring his annual accounts.

The ship bearing the mortal remains of Napoleon had arrived on French shores, a *retour des cendres* to be marked by their enshrinement in majesty beneath the dome of the Invalides. To capitalize on the public excitement, Berlioz resurrected his Napoleonic cantata, *Le Cinq Mai*, for his December concert. Under the circumstances he was pleased to retitle the work, or subtitle it, *Chant sur la mort de l'empereur Napoléon*.

He had expected the authorities to invite him to join Auber, Adam, and Halévy in writing music for the Napoleonic cortège, and an invitation was indeed proffered—two short weeks before the ceremonies. He declined that dubious honor with the observation that it was not the sort of enterprise one undertook during one's evening nap: time was too short. In truth, he fancied the idea of standing by as the work of the others failed by comparison with his own work of the previous July. At the dress rehearsal on the evening of 13 December—one reason the crowd was poor for his concert earlier in the day—the musicians duly pronounced the funeral marches flat and lifeless. The same players had, after all, played the *Symphonie funèbre* and were in a position to make comparisons. Only Halévy's march was applauded, and that without much enthusiasm.

Tuesday, 15 December, a frigid day, saw the slow procession of the rococo catafalque from the docks in Courbevoie to the Invalides. Berlioz had imagined a splendid national event, with cannonades of five hundred rounds and majestic funeral marches by grand ensembles. What he witnessed was pale and prosaic. He could hear only disjunct snatches of the music as the bands passed by, and Mozart's Requiem as played in the church seemed anything but Napoleonic, unsuited even to the scale of the coffin, let alone the magnitude of the myth. He wept at the ceremony for "our sublime emperor" and felt his tears freeze—not from the cold, he thought, but from shame.[6]

FIGURE 8.1 The *Retour des cendres* of Napoleon I, 15 December 1840: the Place de la Concorde, looking up the Champs-Elysées.

The absence of the Berlioz touch was noted. Antoine Elwart, a fellow composer and later the chronicler of the Société des Concerts, observed that "everybody missed him, friends and opponents alike."[7]

Les Nuits d'été, Berlioz's great contribution to the literature of song, were quietly born during 1840 and 1841. Gautier's poems doubtless came to his attention shortly after their publication in 1838, when he had little time to undertake another project on the spur of the moment. Six of the fifty-six poems in *La Comédie de la mort* seemed, however, ideal candidates for musical setting, and he returned to them when he was able. The title was Berlioz's own, though neither the image of the summer night nor the allusion to Shakespeare was especially original. *Absence* is somehow related to the incomplete cantata *Erigone* of 1839, the manuscript text of which contains the refrain "Reviens, reviens." The *Villanelle* was composed, according to a dated autograph, in March 1840; *Absence* and *Le Spectre de la rose* were intended for a *soirée* of the *Revue et Gazette musicale* on 8 November 1840, though neither appears to have been sung there. Perhaps the other three songs were sketched out during the visit to La Côte-St.-André in the late summer of 1840; the set was complete by the next year, 1841, when it was published without fanfare by Catelin. The songs went unperformed and, but for one review, unnoticed: their public life did not really begin until the foreign concerts of 1842–43, during which at least one of them was first orchestrated.

Similar quiet surrounds the composition of the *Rêverie et Caprice* for violin and orchestra. It began as a reworking of Teresa's original act I cavatina in *Benvenuto Cellini*, "Ah, que l'amour une fois dans le cœur," which had been replaced at the time and was never performed. The violin fantasy must have been nearly finished by March 1841, when rights to the score, parts, and piano reduction were sold to Richault.[8] (There was a nearly simultaneous edition by Pietro Mechetti of Vienna.) The program about a man suffering from a troubled heart and transformed by the music into a state of voluptuous passion, printed in Malherbe and Weingartner's edition, is the work not of Berlioz, however, but of Julien Tiersot, who later confessed to the ruse.[9] The *Rêverie et Caprice* often served as a vehicle for the local concertmaster or visiting soloist during Berlioz's foreign appearances of the 1840s and 1850s, and thus it was eventually played by most of the century's noted violinists, including Ernst, Joachim, and Wieniawski. Its dedicatee, the Paris violinist Alexandre-Joseph Artôt, may have been the prime mover of the project.

Liszt's arrival in Paris that March to secure subscriptions for the Beethoven monument in Bonn went all but ignored by the Société des Concerts. Instead, another Berlioz-Liszt concert, like the ones of the old days, was arranged for 25 April to benefit the Bonn project. An all-Beethoven program seemed proper, with sonatas played by Liszt and the "Emperor" Concerto and Sixth Symphony conducted by Berlioz. Both artists waived their customary fee; nevertheless the 7,000 francs collected in revenue was barely enough to pay the musicians. The *droit des pauvres* was ruthlessly levied, and members of the royal family who came made no contribution to the Beethoven monument.

*T*he failure of *Cellini* had at the time considerably dampened its composer's enthusiasm for writing opera. Now, after three years, the memories were no longer quite so bitter, and the festival/concert at the Opéra had gone well enough for Berlioz to begin to consider another work for the theater. The tentative first steps in 1841 toward this new goal were given particular direction by the fact that the great librettist Eugène Scribe, arguably the most powerful man in the theater, had at last indicated a willingness to work with him. So far their ideas for a libretto were of the most tentative sort, though by early 1841 it had been agreed that a text would be developed jointly by Scribe and Frédéric Soulié, a celebrated novelist of the day held in some quarters to be the equal of Balzac. Léon Pillet, the director of the Opéra, seemed favorably disposed.

In view of these plans, Berlioz must have been confronted with a real dilemma when Pillet approached him with a proposition as intriguing as it was distasteful: to render Weber's *Freischütz* acceptable for production at the Opéra. House tradition dictated sung recitatives in lieu of the spoken text and called for ballets in the second act. Knowing that this was the only way anything approaching a true *Freischütz* might be produced at all, and fearful of the damage a less sympathetic hand might do, Berlioz agreed to the task. He set one condition: that otherwise no changes would be made in libretto or score. There were to be no *castilblazades,* and the printed libretto would not bear his name. He deftly turned aside the well-meant but absurd suggestion that the *divertissement-ballet* be danced to the waltz from the *Fantastique* and the *Fête chez Capulet.*

He spent the month of May composing some dozen passages of recitative, including music for the spoken text in the Wolf's Glen scene, to a translation prepared by the house librettist, Emilien Pacini. For the ballet he conceived the altogether brilliant notion of orchestrating Weber's *Aufforderung zum Tanz,* calling it *L'Invitation à la valse,* to be given in succession with or-chestral music from *Preciosa* and *Oberon.* He gently modified the orches-tration of *Freischütz,* calling, for example, for much of the hunting-horn music to be played by eight players. The arias for Mme Stoltz as Agathe and Duprez as Max, both venerable singers having passed their prime, required transposing down into more comfortable keys.

The Paris *Freischütz,* a critical episode in Berlioz's career, was quickly, perhaps desperately, put together. The production got under way in mid-May; general rehearsals began as early as the end of the month. The house was pleased to draw again on Berlioz's considerable talents as an opera coach, but he found it as difficult to achieve the spirited delivery of what he called *Singspiel*—with which he had no former experience—as it had been three years before to breathe sprightliness into *Cellini.* The singers, more comfortable in graver styles, did their usual complaining. Duprez, whose once-golden voice was now exhausted, had to be replaced: "dead, very dead" was Berlioz's summary of his condition.[10] Mme Stoltz had become Pillet's mistress—the "directrice du directeur"—and thus felt free to behave in imperial fashion toward Berlioz and any other underling in her path.

Habeneck was ill. Had either reason or justice prevailed, Berlioz would have been invited to conduct. Instead the regulations took precedence, and the resident nonentity Pantaléon Battu was to be found in the pit for the general rehearsal on 5 June and the opening two nights later.

Though the principals were below par, the orchestral and choral forces performed well enough to warrant a respectable reception, and *Le Frey-schutz,* as it was called, went on to have an initial run of sixty-one perfor-mances through 1846 and several later revivals.[11] For Berlioz it was a substantial victory, sweetest of all because he was granted the composer's royalty of 230 francs for each performance—a tidy sum over the years. The clear success of his coaching was also a matter of record: demand for his services as opera coach lies at the heart of the series of events that led him in 1847–48 to the London stage.

Just how many knew, at first, of Berlioz's true role in the composition of the recitatives is less clear. It seems unlikely, in view of the typical Paris gossip, that word would not have got around. On the other hand, the orchestra and singers seem for a time to have attributed the recitatives to Weber himself.[12] Wagner's first notice of the forthcoming production, in the *Revue et Gazette musicale* of 23 and 30 May, says a great deal of Berlioz. He predicted that Weber's score would be disfigured, and in the event found Berlioz's recitatives "intolerably wearisome." Schlesinger's vocal score of March 1842 distinguishes Weber's music from Berlioz's recitatives by a series of Ws and Bs. Saint-Saëns thought of the affair positively, admiring the discretion and propriety Berlioz had shown in dealing with Weber's masterpiece.

"The full score of these recitatives," Berlioz later wrote, "can be had only from the copying service of the Opéra."[13] Eventually his autograph went to London for the 1850 production of *Il franco arciero*, though the recitatives were not in fact put to use. Then it was spirited by some functionary to Italy, where it remains. The recitatives may have been used for a Boston production, also in Italian, in 1860.

Except for the *Invitation à la valse*, Berlioz's contribution to *Le Freyschutz* was, as he intended it to be, rather pallid. The recitatives were the most suspect particular of what he regarded to be, in principle, a bastard staging. With all its compromises, however, the production was on the whole the closest thing to true Weber ever to have been seen in Paris.

The fees from *Le Freyschutz* modestly delayed but did little to avert another financial crisis in the Berlioz household. He was anxious, for a variety of reasons, to get on with his tour of German-speaking nations, where the promise of financial gain interested him only slightly less than the opportunity to introduce new audiences to his works. At the same time he feared any prolonged absence from Paris. Cherubini's expected death, for one thing, was certain to prompt a reshuffling of every critical position in French music-making. Habeneck was thought the likely successor to Cherubini at the Conservatoire, but as a conductor he was no longer able to manage at the Opéra with any distinction; sooner or later he would be forced to give up the Société des Concerts as well. The directorate of the Conservatoire was an appropriate pasture for the infirm, Berlioz reasoned: "If I become old and incapacitated, the direction of the Conservatoire will devolve naturally on me."[14] Still young and vigorous, he imagined himself a prime contender for both conducting posts and so simply stayed in Paris, waiting.

He was too optimistic. Berlioz could have had but little chance of becoming first conductor at the Opéra, and in pinning his hopes on the podium of the Société des Concerts he betrayed a curious naivete with regard to its government and internal politics. It is true enough, however, that opportunities were routinely lost during the time it took news to travel across Europe and back, at least until after a network of rail and telegraph lines was in place. On at least one occasion Berlioz did indeed miss a golden opportunity when a letter from Germany failed to reach Paris by a specified deadline.

Berlioz's monetary embarrassment was for a variety of reasons more awkward now than when he was younger. Given his stature he was generally thought to be well-to-do. He was surprised when people tried to borrow *his* money. He could no longer think seriously of committing himself to a spiral of loans and debt retirement. Accordingly, he wrote to La Côte and Grenoble to secure his share of the estates of his mother and his brother Prosper, an amount he believed to be on the order of 6,000 francs. (Nanci responded with self-righteous inquiries about his personal habits.)[15] On 27 April he signed a receipt for his inheritance, intending to deposit it with the Rothschild bank and add the 4 percent interest to his annual income. Though called an inheritance, he knew the money was really his father's, and this brought on a seizure of anxiety over his remaining dependence on the Isère. A period of depression set in, perhaps the germ of the unhappy resignation that would plague the second half of his career.

Might his fortune be made with the new grand opera? He settled, ill-advisedly, on an opera to be called *La Nonne sanglante* (The bloodied nun). It was a fantastic tale based on a gothic novel, *The Monk,* by Matthew Gregory (called "Monk") Lewis. Scribe was to do the libretto, assisted not by Soulié but by the brothers Casimir and Germain Delavigne—though Casimir soon died. Berlioz had the text of the first act in hand by the summer of 1841 and was at work on the music by July.

By August, although he was nearly done with the first act, he had begun to lose interest in the story. Yet developments at the Opéra could not, he imagined, have favored him more: Meyerbeer, who had set aside *L'Africaine* when Mlle Falcon's voice gave out, was now withholding *Le Prophète* until the matter of Duprez and *his* voice could be resolved. The Opéra would soon be short of new works to premiere, so for a time Berlioz kept at *La Nonne sanglante.*

If indeed he was attracted by more than the opportunity to have any Scribe libretto at all, the lure of *La Nonne sanglante* must have lain in its similarities, largely of nocturnal mystery, to *Les Francs-Juges* and *Freischütz.* The nun carries a dagger; there are Bohemian peasants, stone tablets and benches, bells striking at midnight, and a full-scale explosion—all the kinds of dramatic situations that had delighted him in his Black-Forest period. Berlioz kept *Les Francs-Juges* and *La Nonne sanglante* together in his *armoire* (as did his executors, and for that reason today the manuscripts have come to have successive shelfmarks at the Bibliothèque Nationale); set into the manuscript of *La Nonne sanglante* is the autograph remnant of *Sardanapale.* The implication seems strong that for his new opera Berlioz intended to use as much material as he could salvage from the two earlier, forgotten works. And that does not bespeak the molten flow of ideas that led to the much worthier *Faust* and *Les Troyens*.

The setting of *La Nonne sanglante* is a castle on the Moldau. The story concerns two lovers, Agnès and Rodolphe, whose dreams of future bliss are shattered by her father's decision to marry her to Rodolphe's brother. Rodolphe's confidant is the monk Hubert, the only other character to appear in the portion Berlioz completed. The Nun, also called Agnès, is an apparition who roams the castle parapets at midnight, dressed in a blood-stained white habit—a splendid theatrical effect this, with the moon's rays illuminating a play of red and white against the greys and blacks of the set. Castle doors open magically before her. The lovers plot to elope: the true Agnès will appear on the ramparts, Rodolphe will join her, and before them the doors

FIGURE 8.2
Madame Stoltz
as Léonore
in Donizetti's
La Favorite (1840).

will open for their escape. But it is the Nun who meets Rodolphe at the appointed hour, and he is swept away into the hereafter.

It seems likely from the autograph fragments and the testimony of his correspondence that Berlioz did serious work on two of what he assumed would eventually be three acts. Four sections of the music have been preserved, all of them from act II, where the *légende* of the Nun is recounted. I do not know what became of act I.

La Nonne sanglante was probably doomed from the beginning. Composer and librettist, for all their celebrity, shared few affinities. The story never kindled the inner fire Berlioz needed to do his best work, and he found himself less comfortable than ever in dealing with strict metered verse of the sort Scribe supplied. Scribe, for his part, was overworked and unwell. Not especially fond of Berlioz to begin with, he seems to have had little personal interest in the project. It may be true that he offered his new associate what he knew to be a lesser work.

The state of things at the Opéra, moreover, was dreadful. What Berlioz first perceived as a great opportunity was in fact symptomatic of general malaise. The repertoire was unarguably poor, with Rossini gone and, for all anyone could tell, Meyerbeer having exhausted his creative genius. The aging singers, though no longer reliable, were indisposed to retire. The chorus was in decline. Mme Stoltz, in her new role of dominatrix, wove webs of intrigue that quite surpassed the customs of a house already known for that sort of thing. So *La Nonne sanglante,* though she gasped for several more years, was soon left to die: her lamp, said Berlioz, had no more oil.[16] Gounod set a version of the same libretto in 1853, and the 1854 production of his opera was successful enough to merit publication of a score. But it did not survive the fall of Nestor Roqueplan's administration at the Opéra.

*T*he Opéra was not the only Paris institution to have lost the luster of its heyday a decade before. The euphoria that had for so long gripped both artists and their public had somehow dissipated. The most obvious reason is middle age—of the Société des Concerts as an institution just as much as of the personnel at the Opéra. In his correspondence Berlioz reels off dozens of other negative trends: dwindling government interest, for example, in staging monumental civic works; the lack of a decent hall for such enterprises; the burgeoning bureaucracy; the antiquated system of privileges accorded resident conductors.

He was also troubled by French indifference to the plight of Spontini, now cast off by a forgetful government and a fickle public. A Paris performance of *Fernand Cortez* had just triggered in Berlioz one of his violent spasms of emotional upheaval; shortly thereafter he learned of Spontini's dismissal from Berlin, which he was unable to comprehend. Spontini returned to Paris in July 1842 and spent most of the rest of his life there, but though he and

Berlioz renewed their affection for each other, he was otherwise left mostly to himself, embittered and increasingly irrational.

Then there was the matter of the widow Weber, living with her children in poverty. Wagner forwarded Berlioz a letter from her in which she quite naturally inquired of the financial arrangements for the Paris *Freyschutz*. Berlioz was sympathetic to the notion of a benefit performance in her behalf—he must have been embarrassed to consider the implications of his royalty agreement—and proposed such an event to Pillet. But Mme Stoltz, who had withdrawn from the production and was angry with Berlioz for publishing unflattering remarks about her girth, saw to it instead that the *Freyschutz* performances were suspended altogether. He declined into a yet profounder melancholy:

> The widow and children of the sublime [Weber] are terribly poor, as if by logic! Just try being a poet! Auber has horses, town houses, country houses, all the burdens of luxury. He will not die of a broken heart; neither will he write an *Oberon*. He will die without having lived. He sees not, hears not. He doesn't like music—yet it pays him well in return.[17]

By contrast there was mounting evidence of warmer artistic climates elsewhere in Europe. In August, for example, came news of a regal St. Petersburg performance of the Requiem, organized and conducted by Heinrich Romberg. It had apparently been easy enough for Romberg to secure the choruses of the imperial chapel, the two opera houses, a military chorus, and all the orchestras in the city. He had cleared for himself a handsome fee.

Berlioz was led to conclude that music in France had somehow become disinherited from her noble origins and prerogatives; she had become a public charity. There was no contemporary art left; Romanticism was dead. Yet he sensed—though he would vacillate on the issue—that "to abandon France completely . . . would be virtually impossible."[18] So he was left, for the moment, with his melancholia and his periodic outbursts on Paris as a city where art was boring at best, and most likely dying.

Since the late 1830s Berlioz's journalism had been limited for the most part to routine reports on opening nights in the theaters and the annual season of Conservatoire concerts. His articles were eagerly anticipated, both in Paris and, increasingly, abroad: translations of some of them had been appearing in the *Neue Zeitscrift für Musik*, under the heading "Berichte aus Paris von H. Berlioz." Now, for the first time since the Beethoven analyses of 1838, he embarked on a sweeping literary project: the essays on orchestral instruments, first published serially in the *Revue et Gazette musicale* as "De l'Instrumentation." It would be his longest serialized effort, dominating the pages of that periodical from November 1841 through the following July.

He wrote with vigor. He would eagerly anticipate the daily visits to his apartment of the Paris virtuosi, invited to spend the afternoon demonstrating their instruments.[19] He was just as diligent in his own visits to instrument makers and their shops, where he familiarized himself with the latest developments in design and construction—of the conventional orchestral instruments as well as the novelties of the day. When he was done, he had emerged as one of the two or three most learned authorities in all Europe. But for the *Mémoires*, the orchestration treatise is his most influential book; at the time, of course—more than two decades before anybody knew much about the *Mémoires*—the treatise had greater impact and more immediate purpose than anything he had ever written. It contributed to his growing stature as a savant and, I think, quite broadened his literary skills. The revisions to the serialized version took the better part of 1842, and the treatise was duly published the following year.

*T*he concerts of 1 and 15 February 1842 in the Salle Vivienne fulfilled the agreement for four concerts concluded during the July 1840 rehearsals of the *Symphonie funèbre*. He programmed his new *Rêverie et Caprice* for the first time, with the violin solo played not by its dedicatee Artôt but by the young virtuoso Delphin Alard. The *Invitation à la valse* made the first of its many appearances on Berlioz's concerts, and there was an unusual work, the Beethoven Triple Concerto, with Alard, the cellist Desmarest, and Charles Hallé at the piano. Both concerts featured the *Symphonie funèbre*, of course, with new parts for strings in the *Apothéose*.

At the first of the performances, a full house—including Liszt, Marie d'Agoult, and the young César Franck—cheered the peroration of the *Apothéose*, and the *parterre* surged forward toward the stage in rapture. Berlioz, however, was not at his best. He was ill again with tonsillitis, and a persistent ringing in the ears obstructed his hearing. A sudden muscle spasm in his right hand, moreover, forced him to conduct the better part of the concert with his left. Stephen Heller left a vivid description of the second February concert, wherein he writes of the bitter cold of the theater and of the confusion of the artists' entry and backstage, lit by a smelly candle and littered with overcoats, ophicleides, cases, and account books. Berlioz was agitated because three of his musicians had so far failed to appear.[20]

The precise sequence of events leading to the failure of Berlioz's marriage is impossible to establish—so sensitive a development is naturally shrouded in mystery—though by February 1842 it is clear something was afoot. His liaison with a mezzo-soprano named Marie Recio, offspring of a French father and a Spanish mother, probably began in mid- to late 1841, though even the date of her arrival in Paris cannot be established with certainty, much less when their dalliance began. By the start of the 1841–42 season, she had secured a year's engagement at the Opéra, possibly through Berlioz's intermediation. Her debut there on 30 October 1841, as Inès in Donizetti's *La Favorite*, was noted briefly, and anonymously, in the current-events section of the *Revue et Gazette musicale;* the author may well have been Berlioz himself. A friendlier notice appeared in Berlioz's column for the *Débats* of 14 December: "Mlle Recio is gifted with a pure and extended soprano . . . She sang the solo 'Rayons dorés' well, despite the nervousness that the first view of the blazing footlights and the fear of the *parterre* (that famous *parterre!*) imparts to all *débutants*." Her role, he says, was too small. "Why not give her the role of the page in Rossini's *Le Comte Ory;* what are they waiting for?" Mme Stoltz, after all, was too portly for it.

The part was given Recio in due time—though Mme Stoltz did not soon forget the slur—and she failed in it. Berlioz was forced to limit his review of 30 January to generalities about her "good intentions" and her "striking appearance." This championing of Recio is one of his few lapses of critical judgment, but it must have damaged his credibility, especially at the Opéra, and surely dampened whatever enthusiasm may have been developing there for *La Nonne sanglante*. Given her vocal limitations, Berlioz could not have done much to help Recio in any case.

The first reference in the correspondence to Harriet's growing unhappiness over her husband's frequent absences from the house occurs on 5 February 1842.[21] She was concerned most of all for Louis: though he had learned to read and enjoyed singing and playing the piano, he had begun to feel abandoned, too, and talk of sending him away to school only increased his anxieties. If a certain letter from Félix Marmion to Nanci comes from 26 May 1842, as seems likely, the household was in disarray by the spring. Harriet, who had been to the country to take a cure, was upset on her return to find that her husband had neglected his "domestic duties." For an hour she complained to Marmion, giving, he said, one of her most original performances. "But the poor woman! Her youth and her beauty are gone forever, and she has no illusions about it."[22] The situation declined rapidly from there.

After abruptly resigning his post at the Conservatoire, grand old Cherubini died on 15 March. Auber was elected, without substantive opposition, to succeed him, but there was at least the possibility that Cherubini's seat at the Institute might fall to Berlioz. Such elections required of the candidates an organized campaign and careful maneuvering. Spontini agreed to mobilize efforts in Berlioz's behalf and to make the appropriate introductions, after which it would be up to the candidate himself to make the exhausting round of courtesy calls on the incumbent members. The election was not to take place until the end of October.

Shortly before, Berlioz formally declared himself by preparing the requisite *curriculum vitae*.[23] In it he lists each of his works, then gingerly broaches the journalism with which he had probably offended most of the electors, expressing the hope that the academy would consider this "modest work" on its merits and without prejudice for his presumption in bringing it up, on the one hand, or his temerity about its worth, on the other. He claims membership in the Euterpe Society of Leipzig, an honorary society of Stuttgart, the Society of St. Cecilia of Rome, and the Society of Sciences and Arts of Grenoble.

In late November George Onslow of Clermont-Ferrand, considered in some circles *le Beethoven français,* was elected over Adolphe Adam by a vote of 19 to 17. Berlioz repeated this process of candidacy for the Institute three more times before he was successful: he had written, by the time he was done, as many petitions of candidacy as he had composed *prix de Rome* cantatas.[24]

Six weeks after Cherubini's death came the demise of the inspector of singing for the primary schools of the Paris region, Guillaume-Louis Wilhem. Berlioz pursued that position as well, for it carried an annual stipend of 2,000 francs; he was even successful in securing a recommendation from the Duc d'Orléans. But numerous objections to his candidacy were forwarded from other quarters: the job was beneath his dignity, he would not do the work, and—the most annoying of the old saws—he did not need the post, for he was wealthy. A functionary was given the job.

On 14 April, at a concert of the amateur composer Mortier de Fontaine and his wife, a singer, *Absence* had its first performance.

Sometime during the summer of 1842, Berlioz decided to undertake, at last, his advance on Germany. He began quietly to investigate travel arrangements and, more significantly, arranged with Schlesinger to have his symphonies published, beginning with the *Symphonie funèbre.* The Duc d'Orléans accepted the dedication of this first Berlioz symphony to reach print, an honorific that recognized his various endorsements of Berlioz and not inconsiderable monetary patronage over the years. That promising relationship—the duke was, after all, the future king of France and would surely express the royal satisfaction most generously—was snuffed in a trice when he was killed that 13 July in a carriage accident. The duchess, his widow, later sent Berlioz a paltry bronze trinket in gratitude for what turned out to be a posthumous honor.

When an invitation to offer the *Symphonie funèbre* in Brussels arrived from the bandmaster there, Joseph-François Snel—he and Berlioz probably met during Snel's visit to Paris in August—Berlioz seized the opportunity to arrange his first concerts abroad. He proposed to give his performances in Brussels and then go on to Frankfurt for a pair of concerts of which there had been talk for some time.

He summoned Rocquemont to assemble the necessary performance material. In his haste he forgot to beg formal leave from his duties at the Conservatoire library, an oversight for which he was later reprimanded. Marie for her part secured a leave from the Opéra, to no one's regret, presumably with the specific intent of accompanying her lover. On the morning of 20 September, he and she left Paris by stagecoach; after stopping for the night en route, they arrived in Brussels at noon the next day. They checked into the Hôtel du Domino on the majestic place de la Monnaie, near the theaters.

Fearing Harriet's "insane jealousy," Berlioz had not discussed his plans with her. She read of his departure in a terse note he left with the maid.

*B*erlioz had waited half his career to undertake his first concert tour, and then when the time came he acted too abruptly. The reasons are obvious: the decision to publish his symphonic works, for instance, lent considerable urgency to his resolve to conduct them throughout Europe before they became common stock. His marriage was in disarray; a mistress had entered the picture. There was also the opportunity to prove something to the Parisians, just before the elections at the Institute. But for all its promise, the trip was not a success.

After having engaged Mme Widemann for the contralto solo in *Roméo et Juliette,* Berlioz invited Marie to sing *Le Jeune Pâtre breton* and two duos—from *Cellini* and *Norma*—with her. This arrangement was indelicate enough that the notices he left behind for the Paris press, announcements Harriet would surely see, described the vocalists as "Mmes *** de l'Académie Royale de Musique." Ernst, the celebrated violinist, was to play the solo part in *Harold.* The concert would conclude with the military symphony, played by Snel's bands, a force of over two hundred players. It was the first performance of any of these works outside France.

For the *Apothéose,* Antoni Deschamps, brother of the librettist of *Roméo et Juliette,* had written a new text for chorus:

> Gloire et triomphe à ces héros;
> Ils sont tombés aux champs de la patrie:
> Gloire et respect à leurs tombeaux
> Venez, élus de l'autre vie!
>
> Changez, noble guerriers,
> Tous vos lauriers
> Pour des palmes immortelles;
> Suivez les séraphins
> Soldats divins
> Dans les plaines éternelles;
> A leurs chœurs infinis
> Soyez unis;
> Anges radieux,
> Harmonieux,
> Brûlants comme eux,
> Entrez, sublimes
> Victimes!

(Glory and triumph to these heroes. They fell in the fields of the fatherland. Glory and respect at their tombs; come, elect to another life! Noble warriors, exchange all your laurels for immortal palm branches. Divine soldiers, follow the seraphim to the eternal plains. Be united with their boundless choruses. Blazing, harmonious, like the radiant angels, enter, sublime victims!)

I suspect the chorus part had been added more for the impending publication than for the Brussels concerts. In any event, the revisions were now so heavy as to require a new manuscript copy, which Berlioz had along with him in Belgium.

Ernst wrote to Liszt that the rehearsals quite gripped the musicians in waves of enthusiasm.[25] The large public, on 26 September, was not so impressed, in part because the hall of the Royal Brussels Military Band was cavernous and echoey. The press was confused:

> The compositions of M. Berlioz resemble nothing heard here before; it is an entirely new system . . . One aspect of M. Berlioz's music particularly struck us: its almost total lack of melody . . . M. Berlioz's orchestration is sometimes so complicated that it is impossible to catch its rhythm or meaning. We freely confess to not having understood anything in certain of the works. Nevertheless in the *Symphonie funèbre,* we thought we fathomed beautiful and great things within this nebulous music, buried somewhere amidst the deafening racket of the orchestra.[26]

Mlle Recio was true to her reputation:

> There is little to be said about the voice and the singing of Mlle Recio.

> Mlle Recio, of somewhat frail soprano voice and a still-defective technique, sang her *romance* with a most appropriate sentiment, and was duly applauded for it.[27]

Meanwhile, she and her consort enjoyed the sights of Brussels by day; one evening they heard a Mass composed by their host, Snel. At his first opportunity, Berlioz had left his card at the royal court; on 5 October, he was presented to Leopold I, king of the Belgians, and offered the monarch in homage a manuscript copy of the *Marche des pèlerins.*[28]

Another concert followed on 9 October in the hall of the Augustinian Temple, a church used since its deconsecration in 1830 for expositions, festivals, and public ceremonies. The repertoire included the *Fantastique, Harold,* the *Francs-Juges* overture, and the *Invitation à la valse,* as well as some of the works from the first concert. Marie sang *Le Jeune Pâtre breton* and operatic airs accompanied by Théodore Döhler, a rival of Liszt and Thalberg; Döhler then played a display piece of his own. Fewer people came to this concert than to the first, and the trivial gross of 1,120 francs was reduced by a poor tax of 25 percent, twice the going rate in Paris.

The Paris *Revue et Gazette musicale* reported some "ill will" expressed toward Berlioz in Brussels, but Fétis's son Edouard, in the Brussels *Indépen-*

dant of 20 October, observed that he had been treated rather well. The minister had lent him the halls after denying them to others, along with enough music students and other musicians that he had only had to pay a few outright.

The stay in Frankfurt was frustrating. A letter from Meyerbeer, who was supposed to have paved his way, apparently went astray, and the colorful but wily Kapellmeister Karl W. F. Guhr was caught unaware, having made no preparations at all for the concerts. He did his best to rectify the embarrassing situation, promising Berlioz two splendid concerts—on Christmas Day and New Year's—with a guaranteed income of 1,200 florins. Berlioz left parts for the first two symphonies and the Requiem with Guhr before returning to Paris in the third week of October, more than a little dejected but better aware of the demands of musical tourism than he could have been before. In that respect, as an experiment, the Brussels trip yielded some good results.

Harriet had been ill with worry, and Berlioz doubtless told her nothing of the plans for returning to Frankfurt at Christmastide. He went on to make detailed arrangements for an immediate tour of the major German capitals, including Leipzig, Weimar, and Berlin. His farewell to the Parisians came in the form of a performance at the Opéra on 7 November: a "festival" offering of the complete *Symphonie funèbre*, wedged into the interval between an act of Auber's *Gustav III, ou le Bal masqué* and Adam's ballet *Giselle*. Habeneck conducted from the pit, while Berlioz led the hundred-piece band and the large chorus onstage.

In mid-December, perhaps on the 12th, Berlioz and Marie Recio left for Brussels once again, this time on a protracted journey. He expected to give two concerts each in Frankfurt and Stuttgart, then go to Munich, Vienna, Berlin, Hanover, Pest, Brunswick, Dresden, Hamburg, and Amsterdam—an itinerary that changed considerably as they went along. This time, Berlioz remembered to beg leave from his supervisor at the Conservatoire, Bottée de Toulmon. For spending money, he took an advance on the *Traité d'instrumentation*, which he had just sold to the publishing house of Schonenberger.

The wanderings of 1842–43 began a new period in the composer's life. Touring of this sort presented its share of problems he had not so far encountered. Chief of his concerns was the music itself, usually packed in two trunks weighing more than 500 pounds. The ruinous cost of its transport, the major expense of his expeditions, soon came to argue strongly in favor of published parts: they were lighter and more compact by half, and anything lost in transit could, in principle, be replaced in a few days' time.[29] Engraved materials were easier to read, particularly where the foreign-lan-

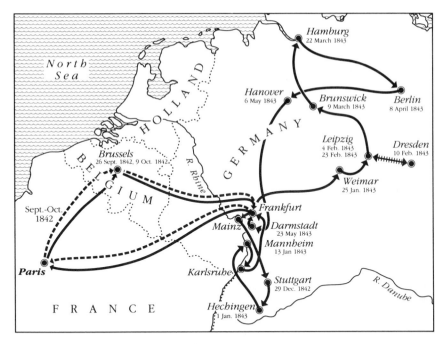

FIGURE 8.3 Berlioz's journeys of 1842–43.

guage translations were printed rather than added in some hurried foreign
hand. Moreover, it was as easy to have two sets of published music as one:
a set could be sent ahead to the next city on the schedule while the local
orchestra worked with another. Berlioz and his music would travel by the
most convenient public transportation, usually postal coach or steamboat.
Later they relied heavily on the railroad.

He generally took lodging in an excellent local hotel. (Over the years he,
and particularly Marie, left a good deal of property behind in hotels; the
correspondence is full of efforts to retrieve it.) He received his mail *poste
restante*, but his addresses changed so frequently, and his plans were so
informal, that a good deal of it must have been lost in the shuffle.

Language was seldom a problem, for French remained the language of
civilized people everywhere. Nearly every city, moreover, enjoyed the service
of musicians trained at the Conservatoire, or at least a French-speaking
amateur de musique. In not a few unfamiliar places he found old acquaintances: Hiller in Frankfurt and elsewhere, Meyerbeer in Berlin, Mendelssohn
in Leipzig, the Müller Quartet in Brunswick. Where there were no old friends,
new ones were soon made. There is no indication that Berlioz ever mastered
German, though like all tourists he could muster up a few elementary
phrases.

Errands at home were run by Rocquemont, Auguste Morel, the cellist Desmarest (who seems to have been privy to Berlioz's secrets and attended to the most delicate of his affairs), and any number of other friends. They were given a broad spectrum of tasks: to avoid, for example, troubling Harriet and yet to assure her well-being; to see that the public was saturated with news from Germany without being bored by it; and to tend to his other business and professional enterprises.

The relationship with Marie was now more or less public, and as of the first Brussels trip she was in the habit of adding thank-you notes to Berlioz's letters. Yet her presence demanded considerable attention to social propriety: Berlioz's letters call her at first by a code name—"the black eyes"—though abroad she was widely thought of as Mme Berlioz. The lovers obviously thought of themselves as equals in spirit to Liszt and his paramours, or, more prosaically, as no more shocking than Pillet and Mme Stoltz. Marie did what she could to assist in the practical details of their daily life, but her resentment of other composers, particularly French rivals encountered en route, was a constant liability.

The next concert in a tour was often arranged from the previous venue. The triumphant visit to Mendelssohn in Leipzig, for example, was arranged from Weimar; the very first letter concerning the possibility of a concert that took place in Leipzig on 4 February was posted on 23 January. Most often there was genuine excitement that he might come: "Venez! Venez!," wrote Lobe concerning Weimar, and Mendelssohn responded to Berlioz, on short notice, "I [hereby] engage you to come to Leipzig . . . I'll be delighted to shake your hand and bid you 'Willkommen' to Germany."[30]

From time to time there were long waits for an appropriate opening in the season or a vacancy at the right theater. Berlioz owed his success in Hamburg, for example, to a side trip taken during a two-week delay while Meyerbeer's Berlin opera company wound up its other obligations. The Frankfurt concerts, which in one sense motivated the touring to begin with, did not come to fruition until 1853. By contrast the crown princes and electors had the power to summon their court orchestras on the spur of the moment, something that was unthinkable in Paris. Berlioz was generally given excellent rehearsal time, once he arrived, and there was nearly always a large, curious public.

His attention to detail through this often confusing progress is remarkable. Long letters are devoted to the specifics of the required instrumental and choral force, or to changes needed in a score to accommodate the local orchestra; there is a detailed letter, for example, on how to go about readying the modest little Chant sacré. ("Only take care that the horn in C doesn't play me B♭s there where I have put stopped B♮s and that the stroke of the bass drum at the end is not given forte but a good third less forcefully, just a tiny bit more sonorously than the piano before it.")[31] Most often the difficulty was in finding correct instruments in sufficient number, especially the English horn, ophicleide, and harp, which were not widely encountered outside Paris.

Among the most provocative of Berlioz's many discoveries in Germany was that of the concertmaster, a usually genial factotum who attended to the parts, assembled the appropriate players and instruments, and accomplished, in general, much of the work Berlioz was accustomed to doing for himself at home. As an institution the concertmaster was superior to the French *garçon d'orchestre,* on the one hand, and *premier violon* on the other. To the end of his days, Berlioz was taken aback to arrive at a rehearsal and find everyone in place, respectfully awaiting his downbeat. Where possible he used the services of the local Kapellmeister, engaging him to play the *Rêverie et Caprice* for violin or the solo part in *Harold.* The rank-and-file musicians were on the whole courteous, and some of them went out of their way to cultivate lasting acquaintances. It was the theater intendants, business managers of the local monarch, with whom negotiations could prove most grueling: their role, after all, was to ensure the fiscal soundness of houses where practices and repertoire were dictated by the sometimes whimsical pleasure of the local prince.

Perhaps the most substantial contribution to Berlioz's artistic growth during this period came from the long roster of intellectuals he met along the way. He encountered any number of the best music critics in Europe: A. W. Ambros, J. C. Lobe, Wilhelm von Lenz, and, later, in England, Henry Chorley, J. W. Davison, and Edward Holmes. He met publishers like Härtel and Novello and Rieter-Biedermann, the intendants Lüttichau and Dingel-stedt, the geographer Humboldt, and the poet Hofmann von Fallersleben. He visited the homes of the local music lovers, where talk of Beethoven and Mozart was common stock: these *mélomanes,* as Berlioz thought of them, were sometimes confused, but they invariably found his music *important.* From the most progressive players he was able to learn of new developments in instrumental technique and construction, and he made last-minute changes in the *Traité d'instrumentation* as a result. He discovered the artistic and financial advantages of a kind of princely patronage that well outdistanced the token offerings of the French monarchy. He saw any number of opera houses play their native repertoire. He found enthusiasm, nobility of purpose—the very qualities that seemed to him lacking in Paris. All the while he was sketching musical ideas and recording his impressions of the places he had visited, documents to which he invariably returned when he got home.

He sent long letters to his friends and family in France, written between rehearsals or late at night in the afterglow of some exhilarating performance. He remembered, of course, to send notices of his triumphs, *bulletins de la Grande Armée,* to the Paris papers; that these eventually became the butt of the satirical press is a mark of the interest they stimulated. Once home he would amalgamate his observations in the form of open letters for publication, the foundation of his autobiography.

The travels of the forties and early fifties mark the pinnacle of Berlioz's international acclaim. He was at the peak of his social, conductorial, and compositional forces. Yet the trips were curiously dissatisfying, too, and as he discovered abroad, year after year, what he yearned for at home, he developed a discontent with his lot that was as unwarranted as it was unhealthy.

*T*he repertoire for the 1842–43 journey of six months included the *Symphonie fantastique* and *Harold,* the overtures *Le Roi Lear* and *Les Francs-Juges,* and the easier excerpts from the Requiem and *Roméo et Juliette*—with a very few additions, the staples of all his concert tours. On this particular tour, however, the *Symphonie funèbre* was uppermost in his mind; he was doubtless carrying proofs of the orchestra parts and score that were soon to be published. Once under way, he orchestrated *Absence* from the *Nuits d'été* and *La Belle Voyageuse,* to give Marie something to sing and, possibly, to provide a reason for having brought her along.

Things did not begin well. They approached Frankfurt via Brussels, where a third concert had been planned. It was canceled because of the indisposition of Mme Nathan-Treillet, Mme Stoltz's successor at the Opéra, who was to have offered the *partie vocale.* Mme Nathan-Treillet had roots in Brussels, where her rise to stardom had begun, and the players and potential public were so disappointed that no alternative seemed to promise a decent house. Berlioz simply left town, not to return to Brussels for more than a decade.

In Mainz he stopped to inquire after the military band that had played his works and to try to induce the publisher Schott to help arrange a concert, all to no avail. Schott, who gave "the impression of having been, like the Sleeping Beauty, asleep for the last hundred years," complained that there was no money in it.[32] They went on to Frankfurt in time for the holiday concerts.

In Frankfurt Guhr had seen to it that Berlioz would have no free night to give his concert. The Milanollo sisters, Teresa and Maria, prodigious violinists and the talk of the circuit, were dominating the Frankfurt stage. Guhr was unwilling to compromise the income from these appearances with the risky business of the Berlioz concerts, promised or not. He left Berlioz and Marie with any number of cheerful suggestions for the future but for the moment nothing more than the promise of an unhappy Christmas in his fair city.

The next day they went on to Stuttgart, where a concert had been prepared for them by Peter von Lindpainter. Lindpainter was quick to disabuse Berlioz of the notion that Stuttgart's stature as a royal city gave it any musical importance. "But since you are here, it's certainly not going to be said that we let you leave without performing some of your works, which we are so curious to know." (A version of this story was repeated many times over as the tour gained momentum; a recurring motive through this first trip is how curious the little German orchestras were to know his music.) The concert on 29 December was presented before the king and the court in the Redoutensaal, the royal theater being imperfect for the event; the program consisted of the two symphonies, the *Francs-Juges* overture, and some songs with piano for Marie. The tickets were too cheap for much of a receipt at the gate, and Berlioz thought the orchestra and hall too little, the whole enterprise "misérable." Nevertheless, he liked the players, the performance was good, and he was able to write to Paris, at last, of a warm welcome. Before they left they went to hear performances of *Freischütz* and Auber's *La Muette de Portici* at the court theater.

From there they went south to Hechingen to give a private concert for the Prince Hohenzollern-Hechingen, a jolly monarch who proved over the years one of Berlioz's most loyal patrons. They arrived on New Year's Eve, in time to be led away to the holiday banquet at court and to the ball the next evening. Täglichsbech's orchestra, with only fifteen strings, was hardly sufficient, but by virtue of considerable rescoring and the enthusiasm of the players, they managed well enough, and Marie had the occasion to encore her songs. Afterward there was a dinner party at the castle in Berlioz's honor.

A last preparatory concert before assaulting the great cities of central Germany—Weimar, Leipzig, Dresden, and ultimately Berlin—took place in Mannheim in another inadequate theater with another inadequate orchestra. The weather was intolerably wet and cold, the orchestra incapable of the brigands' orgy in *Harold*. Worst of all was Marie Recio's insistence on singing, rapidly becoming an obstacle to the success of the trip. They went as far south as Karlsruhe, but were unable to arrange a concert there.

They needed to return to Frankfurt in order to collect scores and parts left behind; there, on 16 January, Berlioz saw Beethoven's *Fidelio* for the first time since 1830. And at the opera house he and Marie by chance encountered Ferdinand Hiller. Hiller, whom Berlioz had not seen in over a decade, was giving a performance the next day of his cantata *Die Zerstörung Jerusalems* (The fall of Jerusalem) and invited Berlioz and Marie Recio to attend as his guests. Berlioz, however, had other plans: he was going to abandon Marie. "She sings like a cat . . . and the worst of it is that she wants to sing at all my concerts."[33] Moreover, there was a French ambassador in Weimar, their next stop, who Berlioz feared might send compromising gossip to friends of Harriet back in Paris. He led Marie to understand he was dining with the Baron Rothschild; instead he took a reserved place on the postal coach, having left his bags earlier in the day, and set out for Weimar at 7:00 P.M. on 17 January. But Marie was not so easily cast off. She went to the ticket office and ascertained Berlioz's destination from the passenger manifest, then set out in hot pursuit, pausing only to fire off an angry letter to Hiller. Berlioz was philosophical about the outcome: "We neither trapped nor retrapped one another, but rather found ourselves reunited."[34]

*W*eimar was a civilized city, second only to Leipzig in its cultural sophistication. His hosts had gone out of their way to offer Berlioz a large, accomplished orchestra. The *Fantastique* was done in full, for only the second time on the trip, and Marie sang her pieces "attractively." It was possibly for Weimar that he orchestrated *La Belle Voyageuse;* Marie had been singing the piano version for some time, and it could be that the orchestrated *Belle Voyageuse,* with its suggestive title, represents some sort of apology for the *contretemps* of a few days before.

They enjoyed Weimar from the first. The "excellent" grand duke and his duchess Maria Pavlovna of Russia, formidable patrons of music, made them feel unusually welcome. Later, when Liszt and his princess had established themselves there, Berlioz would consider Weimar a second home.

Arriving in Leipzig on 28 January 1843, Berlioz was led at once to the Gewandhaus, where Mendelssohn was rehearsing for the first performance of his Goethe cantata, *Die erste Walpurgisnacht.* Mendelssohn was eager to show off the accomplishments of his musicians, the incontestably distinguished orchestra of the Gewandhaus, to his old acquaintance from Rome; the idea was for Berlioz to attend the subscription concert, meet the orchestra, and then be at leisure to make the final arrangements for his concerts there and in Dresden. The orchestra, though overcommitted, willingly added new rehearsals and a Berlioz concert for 4 February to their schedule. Ferdinand David was to play the *Rêverie et Caprice,* and, for the first time on his trip, Berlioz would conduct his *Le Roi Lear* and, more significantly, the Offertoire of the Requiem. Mendelssohn's players were charming and competent, able to master Berlioz's difficult music in a pair of rehearsals. Mendelssohn himself was the epitome of old-world courtesy in welcoming Berlioz as a lost comrade, though he must still have harbored reservations over the music about to be offered. He held his tongue when he was not enthusiastic about what he heard and warmly complimented Berlioz on what he did like, the orchestral songs. Berlioz was perceptive enough to understand what went unsaid and to appreciate both halves of the proposition.

On 2 February he discovered firsthand the astonishing implications of the railroad for musical vagabondage, when he took the train to Dresden in the morning—a distance of 70 miles, covered in a mere three and a half hours—completed doing his business and then returned that afternoon in time to hear the premiere of Mendelssohn's new cantata. Railroads had sprung up all over France, too, notably the old *rive gauche* line from Paris to Versailles, but this is the first time Berlioz appears to have profited from this new mode of transportation.

At his dress rehearsal the next day, he and Mendelssohn exchanged batons—his a long, thin stalk of wood, and Mendelssohn's a more formidable, leather-covered marshal's baton, held at the center (fig. 8.5). The instrument of trade, a famous letter, reads as follows:

To Chief Mendelssohn:
Grand Chief:
    We promised each other to exchange our tomahawks; here is mine. It is rude and yours is simple. Only squaws and palefaces prefer ornamented armor. Be my brother! And when the Great Spirit sends us hunting in the land of souls, may our warriors hang our tomahawks crossed over the door of the council-hut.[35]

Though one of the more picturesque ceremonies in the history of conducting, its Mohican symbolism was lost on Mendelssohn, and Fanny Mendelssohn Hensel later indicated that her fastidious and somewhat pious brother took offense at the various double entendres.[36]

The Leipzig concert on 4 February was Berlioz's first unqualified triumph in Germany. The single crisis—failure of the harpist to arrive—was resolved

FIGURE 8.4 Mendelssohn in 1840.

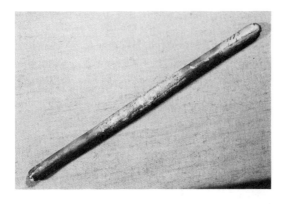

FIGURE 8.5
Mendelssohn's leather-covered baton, given to Berlioz in February 1843; note how it is worn shiny at the center by Mendelssohn's grasp.

by Mendelssohn's covering the simple part at the piano. The public and the musicians, delighted by the Offertoire, made known their hope to hear the full Requiem as soon as it could be scheduled. Mendelssohn had already arranged, moreover, for Berlioz to return after his Dresden concerts to offer a charity performance for the needy of the city, where it was hoped they might give all or a major part of *Roméo et Juliette.* His cordial treatment of Berlioz in 1843 is among his great legacies, for it turned the tide in what had so far been a mediocre tour.

It was also in Leipzig that Berlioz's long friendship was kindled with Mendelssohn's concertmaster, Ferdinand David. As violin teacher at the new Leipzig Conservatory (among his first students were Joachim and Wasielewski), David was to have considerable influence on its repertoire and attitudes, and he must have conveyed to his students a certain fondness for the Berlioz style.

Two days after the Leipzig concert, Berlioz and Marie left for Dresden to begin the eight rehearsals agreed to before his concerts of 10 and 17 February. His closest contact there was the Polish violinist and concertmaster Karl (or Karol) Lipinski, in his time a rival of Paganini; Berlioz had known Lipinski since his visit to Paris of 1836. Like David, he was an influential teacher, possibly the one who introduced both Joachim and Wieniawski to the *Rêverie et Caprice,* which he played on 17 February. Among the other new acquaintances to be made in Dresden were the great *Heldentenor* Joseph Aloys Tichatschek—the first Tannhäuser and an obvious candidate for the role of Cellini—and Wächter, the bass. Berlioz was also fond of Karl Gottlieb Reissiger, the co-Kapellmeister, who acted as assistant conductor for the larger works but whose prestige at court was falling as fast as Wagner's star was rising.

Wagner was enjoying the first days of his appointment as Royal Kapellmeister "for life." Berlioz found him self-satisfied but warm and for his part greatly enjoyed the last three acts of *Rienzi* and the fourth performance of *Der fliegende Holländer,* with Frau Schroeder-Devrient. Wagner appears to have kept his distance. In his Autobiographical Sketch of 1842 he had written unkindly of Berlioz's music as "lacking all sense of beauty" and of Berlioz as spoiled by his admirers and laughed at by the rest of the world. These remarks appeared in the *Zeitung für die elegante Welt* while Berlioz was in town. In a letter of April 1843, Wagner regretted the course events had taken: "He is an unhappy man, against whom I certainly would not have written anything if I had previously been to the concerts he gave here: I was sorry for him."[37]

Both Dresden concerts pleased their audiences, however. *Le Cinq Mai,* with Wächter as soloist, was the particular triumph of the evening, deemed the equal of the symphonies.

Berlioz and Marie left Dresden in time to be in Leipzig for the benefit concert of 23 February. The success of the first Leipzig performance was repeated at the second. The triumph was further enhanced by the obvious enthusiasm of Schumann, who—to the wonder of the Leipzigers, since he had not had anything to say for several weeks—grasped Berlioz and shook his hand warmly, crying "This Offertoire: it surpasses everything!"[38] It was, apparently, their only meeting, though they must have considered themselves old friends.

It was at this performance, too, that Marie sang Berlioz's breathtaking new orchestration of Gautier's *Absence*, which so attracted Mendelssohn.[39] Like *La Belle Voyageuse,* the text had come to have a special meaning for the composer and his mistress. She had sung the piano version at most of the recent concerts, and perhaps it, too, had come to be identified with their misadventure and reconciliation of the month before. He gave the original autograph to an admirer in Berlin that April; for Marie he prepared a

FIGURE 8.6 Albumleaf, 3 February 1843, from the notebook *Souvenirs—Bêtises—Improvisations.* The caption reads "after the rehearsal where Marie sang so well."

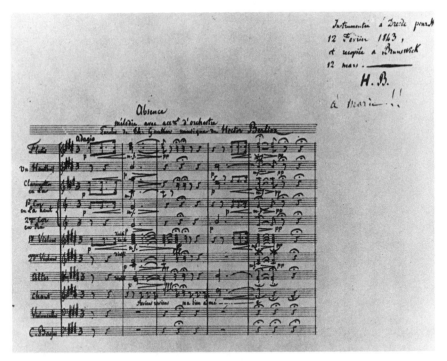

FIGURE 8.7 *Absence,* autograph fair copy for Marie Recio, 12 March 1843.

handsome fair copy on ornamental album paper headed by the remark "Orchestrated in Dresden for M. on 12 February 1843 and recopied at Brunswick on 12 March. H. B. To Marie!!" (fig. 8.7).

$\mathcal{T}$he situation in Paris was not good. Berlioz had endeavored to assure the well-being of his wife and son by sending frequent bank drafts in the amount of several hundred francs each, and to that sum they were to add all the proceeds from the *Freyschutz* performances. His pension income from his mother's estate was forwarded directly to Harriet by his brother-in-law in Grenoble, though she had to be reminded how to go about negotiating the drafts.[40] On 18 February he wrote to Morel inquiring of his wife in terms of considerable agitation. Three days later came the tragic letter from Louis to his aunt Nanci, containing the astonishing implication that his father had not so far written home at all:

Maman is very sad because she has not had any letters for a month. Since the twentieth of September, when my Papa left for Brussels without saying anything to us, my poor Maman has not been able to sleep. Every day she waits for a letter which never arrives. I don't know where my Papa is.[41]

Adèle offered to have Harriet and Louis stay with her at their home in St. Chamond, but Harriet could not bring herself to respond to the invitation. The discreet reports reaching Paris from abroad—"Mlle Recio, then located in Dresden, consented most graciously to sing two *romances* with orchestra, and the public thanked her handsomely"[42]—could not hide the situation for long.

Berlioz had fallen ill in Dresden and after the second Leipzig concert stayed in bed there for a week. He had planned to go on to Berlin, but Meyerbeer was occupied with a command performance and begged him to delay his arrival for ten more days. In the interval, more or less by chance, Berlioz arranged to visit the tiny town of Brunswick, which was to be over the years the site of some of his most satisfying musical experiences.

The excellent orchestra in Brunswick was built around the Müller brothers' quartet, whose 1837 Paris performances Berlioz remembered fondly.[43] Georg Müller was the Kapellmeister to the Duke of Brunswick; his brother Carl was concertmaster and first violinist in the quartet. They welcomed Berlioz heartily, and Carl Müller readily agreed to play both the *Rêverie et Caprice* and *Harold*. They offered him four rehearsals for a concert on 9 March, though the orchestra was able to manage his scores with ease.

Berlioz arrived on stage on the evening of the 9th to find his scores and desk bedecked with laurel crowns. The *Marche des pèlerins* was wildly applauded and encored; Marie sang *Absence* again. After the concert, the *amateurs* of the town offered him a banquet with toasts in Latin, more crowns, and the presentation of a silver baton.[44] Despite the low price of the tickets, receipts were reasonably good and a profit of 1,500 francs was split with the theater intendant. It was in some respects his most successful concert of the tour, where nothing of the sort had been anticipated. Berlioz harbored particular affection for Brunswick and its artists for the rest of his life.

Because Berlin was still not ready to receive him, he went on to Hamburg to give on 22 March his only concert in that city. He knew no one there, but was welcomed nonetheless and encouraged to present a long concert: all the works in his trunk, in fact, except for the *Fantastique*. The major discovery of this stop was the bass Joseph Reichel, who sang the solo part in *Le Cinq Mai* better than it had ever been done before; Reichel's brilliant interpretation may have been one of the factors behind Berlioz's decision to publish the work in 1844. The local principal players took the solo parts in *Harold* and the violin *romance*, Marie sang her two songs, and the wife of the theater intendant, Mme Cornet, sang Teresa's cavatina from *Benvenuto Cellini*. They were in Hamburg long enough—ten days—to be able to hear its famous opera company in three productions: Mozart's *Die Zauberflöte,* Rossini's *Moïse,* and Donizetti's new *Linda de Chamounix,* a work with which Berlioz would in a few years' time be intimately familiar.

There was enough to do in Berlin, when he finally got there, to occupy him for nearly a month. He especially wanted to cultivate the acquaintance of the German branch of the Schlesinger family, whose Berlin publishing house was headed, since the death of their father Adolf Martin, by Heinrich Schlesinger, younger brother of Maurice. Also he hoped for an audience with Frederick William IV, king of Prussia, to offer him the dedication of his *Traité d'instrumentation.* There was Meyerbeer's opera company to be heard—they saw Meyerbeer conduct Gluck's *Armide* and his own *Les Huguenots*—a St. Matthew Passion, and of course Berlioz's two concerts to be rehearsed and presented.

Meyerbeer had for some time been a diligent proponent of Berlioz's music, having on one occasion, for instance, secured the services of all four hundred bandsmen from Berlin and Potsdam for the *Symphonie funèbre.* He managed to summon two hundred performers for Berlioz's first concert, on 8 April in the Royal Opera House, so that the larger movements of the Requiem might be heard to best advantage. Leopold Ganz was given the solo part in *Harold,* and the capable bass Boetticher sang *Le Cinq Mai.* Fifteen days later the second concert featured the entire first half of *Roméo et Juliette.* The king, deeply moved, came backstage afterward to ask Berlioz for a souvenir of the work for the royal library. A manuscript copy of the *Fête chez Capulet* was hastily prepared for him.[45]

Meanwhile, Marie Recio—whose standard pair of songs had been edged off the first Berlin concert—gave her own recital on 18 April, in the Hôtel de Russie, with a local French tenor named Edouard Martinet. Little attention appears to have been paid them.

Berlioz on the other hand was a popular guest. At a luncheon concert in his honor, the royal military band surprised him with the *Francs-Juges* overture arranged for winds. He got along well with the royalty, who were reputedly standoffish with foreign visitors. The Berlin musicians, he thought, were not only more diligent than any of the other players he had met so far but also more gifted. He took care to thank them in an unusually warm note just before he left.[46]

Not all the concerts he had hoped to give in Germany could be arranged: Breslau, Meiningen, and Saxe-Coburg had to be forgone, and return engagements in Brunswick and Weimar were postponed. It was time to begin the long journey back to France. In late April Berlioz set out for home, pausing en route for concerts in Hanover (6 May) and Darmstadt (23 May). In Hanover he discovered an enthusiastic pamphlet about his recent visit to Brunswick, only a few miles distant, written by one Robert Griepenkerl: *Ritter Berlioz in Braunschweig.* In Hanover, too, he attracted the keen interest of the crown prince. But the main novelty of the visit there was that he conducted his *Waverley* overture for the first and only time in his career: he had been ill for the November 1838 premiere, where Habeneck conducted. The travelers paused briefly in Frankfurt, once more, and were back in Paris on 4 June.

*F*ifteen concerts and three times as many rehearsals in the course of what would have been a taxing journey for the common tourist had adversely affected Berlioz's health. He had lost considerable weight and was suffering from his throat disorder, colic, and headaches. He had consulted physicians in Dresden, Leipzig, and Brunswick. There had been little time to recuperate on the road, and there was no rest to be found in Paris.

Yet if the trip had taken its toll, it was nonetheless excellent for Berlioz's reputation. In some ways it was, as he boasts, "without precedent in the history of art."[47] (In other ways it was not: virtuoso soloists were always on the road; any number of them logged many more miles than he.) He had learned, moreover, how (and how not) to conduct his business affairs. The first German tour did not make much money. In the future he would demand that all the costs be borne by the producers and that he receive 50 percent of the gross, not net, receipts—conditions that he placed on invitations he now received from London, The Hague, Copenhagen, and Milan.

There were those in Paris who doubted that the ecstatic remarks on the German concerts which had appeared in the *Revue et Gazette musicale* and the *Débats* could possibly be accurate. The *Ménestrel* deduced from its scan of the German papers that Berlioz and his compositions had been a failure.[48] In fact, although the foreign critics were sometimes left puzzled and occasionally put off, their reactions were for the most part resoundingly positive. For them to have heard Berlioz's work at all, and for many of them to have met and been charmed by the man, represented a major step in the internationalization of the Berlioz style. He had brought, as he observed for himself, honor to his country.

Berlioz was at once swept back into his frenzied Paris life. A new Association of Artist-Musicians, founded by Baron Taylor for the specific purpose of offering large-scale festival concerts of the type Berlioz had pioneered, required his support. The proofs of the *Traité d'instrumentation,* in which he had identified many errors during his travels, needed attention, as did the projects for its translation into German (by J. C. Grünbaum for the Berlin Schlesinger and by J. A. Leibrock for Breitkopf und Härtel) and Italian (by Alberto Mazzucato, first in serial format, then as a book published by Ricordi). An English translation, in which he was most interested from the first, was not published until after the second French edition of 1855. Appearances in London seemed the logical outgrowth of the German tour, and these demanded lengthy negotiation. Most important, after nearly three years without a major composition, his thoughts began to be haunted by images of another huge work. Like Gulliver in Lilliput, he was being bound to Paris—again—by thousands of tiny threads.

He spent the summer readying superb essays on his recent journey for the *Journal des Débats*. The *Voyage musical en Allemagne*, as his open letters were called, began to appear in the *Débats* on 13 August and continued through the rest of the year. These were translated into German by J. C. Lobe as they appeared, then gathered into a Leipzig edition, *Musikalische Reise in Deutschland*, which preceded their appearance in book form in France. German readers found the letters sensational.[49]

The satirical press in France made the most of Berlioz's *voyage musical*. One caricature of the celebrities of 1843 shows him staring out the back of a coach charging eastward; in his left hand he holds a quill to record his observations of it all (fig. 8.8).[50]

Marie Recio's debut in Auber's *L'Ambassadrice* that August was a failure; the only two notices agree that she was dreadful. "They say she is a pupil of M. Berlioz," one complained. "My God, he would be capable of it."[51] The song *La Belle Isabeau*, which Berlioz composed that fall to a text of Dumas *père* about a woman's eloping with the man she loves, is presumably thick with autobiographical associations. It was published in the Christmas album offered subscribers to *Le Monde musical*, where it carried a dedication to Marie.

Berlioz's domestic situation had by now passed the point of no return. He found it next to impossible to accustom himself to the renewal of tensions at home on the one hand and to the unyielding demands of his quotidian duties on the other. While he was trying to organize his life around new projects in which he had little interest, Harriet was shrilly opposing his intention to travel again, thereby promoting the very thing she feared most. They disagreed over Louis's education, though under the circumstances it was clear he would need to be sent away to a boarding school. Berlioz missed the exhilarating chaos of rehearsals, chores, and diplomatic negotiations now that the level of his activity on that front had subsided. He began to daydream again of distant places, seriously now of England, more romantically of Tahiti.

During the summer he thought over the possibilities for a large festival in September at the Théâtre-Italien, something to involve over a hundred players and an appearance by Spontini himself to conduct excerpts from *La Vestale*. He mused on a short opera; he attended to his proofs. Czar Nicholas of Russia wrote to ask Berlioz to arrange ancient chants of the Russian church, and for this he proposed a setting for chorus of sixteen parts. This commission, announced in the *Revue et Gazette musicale* of 13 August, was never fulfilled, but it turned his thoughts toward Russia; eventually he set two choral works of Dimitri Bortniansky for unaccompanied chorus, and the *Symphonie fantastique* was dedicated to the czar.

Short of new work for the concert season, he undertook in September the

FIGURE 8.8 "The Main Composers of 1843." Berlioz, on his journeys, is fifth from the left.

fashioning of a concert overture on themes from *Benvenuto Cellini*. The result was *Le Carnaval romain*, based on the Mardi Gras saltarello and Cellini's strophe "O Teresa, vous que j'aime plus que ma vie" from the act I trio. The adoption of these materials into an *ouverture caractéristique*—he had as yet no idea that *Cellini* might ever be heard again—represents a recomposition on the scale of the orchestral *La Captive*. *Le Carnaval romain* proved one of his most useful and popular concert works, a cornerstone of his repertoire for the succeeding two decades and the work by which many listeners remembered Berlioz then, and remember him now, most fondly.

Though there was nothing really new, the concert of 19 November in the Salle du Conservatoire was nonetheless memorable. Duprez, Massol, and Mme Dorus-Gras sang the trio from *Cellini* for the first time in several years; Duprez introduced the orchestral *Absence* to French audiences. The *Rêverie et Caprice*, with Delphin Alard, had not been given in Paris since its premiere in February 1842. Louis came to the concert and was thrilled by the volume of it all. More thrilling for Berlioz was that Spontini, now returned to Paris, was there. In a letter written the next morning Spontini raved "Vivat! terque quaterque vivat!" and offered advice on his conducting technique.[52] Berlioz himself thought the concert wonderful, a *tremblement musical,* and was still excited about it two days later. Louis wrote to his aunt of a great financial success.

It was the last concert he was ever to give in the Salle du Conservatoire. A governmental edict of 1843, announced at the annual prize-giving at the Institute, forbade further use of the hall by outside parties. Berlioz assumed he was the intended object of the resolution, and this may have been at least partially true.

*H*e spent the end of the year finishing with the proofs of the *Traité d'instrumentation,* adding a new essay on the harp and altering substantially the chapters on the brass instruments. With the publisher Labitte he engaged to publish a two-volume book called *Voyage musical en Allemagne et en Italie,* incorporating his German essays, the long treatments of the Italian journey that had appeared in *Italie pittoresque* and elsewhere, and two novellas. The edition, which appeared in 1844, enjoyed brisk sales and was eventually exhausted. Later he drew on the historical narratives for the *Mémoires* and put the novellas into *A Travers Chants.*

Another financially attractive venture was set in motion when Thalberg asked to arrange the *Symphonie funèbre* for solo piano. The publication rights were sold to Schlesinger for 1,000 francs, 500 each for Thalberg and for Berlioz, and ultimately Thalberg's arrangement of the *Apothéose* had good sales and broad exposure. Proofs for *Le Cinq Mai,* the first of his works to be published with both French and German text, began to cross Berlioz's desk during this same period.

The denial of the Salle du Conservatoire was a crushing blow that forced Berlioz to undertake a grueling, bitter search for a new venue. The concert of 3 February was given in the little Salle Herz at number 38, rue des Victoires, one of the few halls available for the high season at such short notice. The new music on the program consisted largely of arrangements and rewritings of earlier works: the Irish melody *Hélène* for male chorus and orchestra, the *Chant sacré* arranged for six instruments manufactured by Adolphe Sax, and *Le Carnaval romain.* This last, a premiere, was apparently offered with no general rehearsal, the wind players having been elsewhere at the time; it was, miraculously, successful nonetheless. Despite having been thrown together from the most miscellaneous of repertoires, the February concert was in two respects noteworthy indeed. It marked, so far as I can tell, the public debut of the saxophone, as well as of a number of other new instruments built by Sax: the piccolo valved trumpet in E♭, piccolo valved bugle in E♭, valved bugle, and bass clarinet. Moreover, a "scene of Marguerite alone" (that is, "Une amoureuse flamme," the seventh of the

Huit Scènes de Faust, with soldiers' chorus) shows almost indisputably that Berlioz's imagination was now focused on *Faust* for the great new symphony we know him to have been pondering for some months. Marguerite's scene, however, was canceled: Mme Nathan-Treillet was once again indisposed.

Adolphe Sax arrived in Paris in 1842, just after Berlioz had finished his treatise—of the Sax instruments only the saxophone is considered in the first edition—but while his interest in the manufacture of orchestral instruments was still at its peak. Berlioz's exhaustive promotional activity on behalf of the Sax enterprise was critical to getting it well established in Paris. Sax returned the favor by offering Berlioz his showroom for rehearsals and, from time to time, the storage of his music. In addition to using saxhorns in the arrangement of the *Chant sacré,* which is no longer preserved—or is it merely that each of the instruments took one of the vocal lines?—Berlioz called for them in both the Te Deum and *Les Troyens.* His relationship with Sax was on the whole very similar to his friendship with Jacob Alexandre and his son Edouard, the organ makers. All three became intimates of Berlioz, and at the end Edouard Alexandre served as his executor.

Presentation copies of the *Traité de l'instrumentation,* a volume that had been endangered by an alarming shortage of subscribers, came off the press in early December. Berlioz sent an unbound copy to Spontini, one to Hugo, one to Meyerbeer, and another to the Berlin Academy. A third *Traité* went to Berlin as well: the formal dedication copy for the king of Prussia, printed on fine paper and handsomely bound at the establishment of the engraver Lard. The king sent a gold snuff box in appreciation.[53] The first edition was released to the public in February.

Berlioz's repeated hurling of himself after trivial government appointments in the mid-1840s is less unseemly than it may first appear. Apart from his modest job at the Conservatoire library and the occasional demand for his services at times of national celebration, he had little by way of recognition from a governmental system that often went out of its way to support national heroes. To survive freelance appeared to him the most absurd of dreams: what little he had so far earned by selling his compositions could hardly be considered regular income. In a gesture reminiscent of earlier times, he wrote to yet another minister of the Interior, the Comte du Châtel, outlining his many embarrassments and pleading to be named, by administrative fiat, to a chair in orchestration at the Conservatoire. He implied, moreover, that the post had been promised him by the previous minister, Montalivet. (What had in fact been essentially promised him was the privilege of the Théâtre-Italien.) His epistolary outburst is as confused in its reasoning as in its factual account, for Berlioz manages to ask for more work in order to find more leisure to compose. "I'm a composer," he complains, "and I have no time to compose . . . I have no time to work, and thus I have done none of the things I am most capable of accomplishing."[54] Teaching positions at the Conservatoire rewarded modest responsibility with good pay, it is true; nevertheless it is difficult to believe, despite the French penchant for pluralism of appointments, that he would have been able to compose, write for the *Journal des Débats,* and teach at the same time. And it is hard to imagine that he could have managed the patient dealing with students for which professors like Baillot and Reicha were held in such high esteem. What is most interesting about the episode is his frank admission of the conceptual mediocrity of his recent works.

The ministry responded with a one-time "encouragement" in the form of some cash but no commitments for the future. The bureaucrats, he said, failed to understand his reasoning at all. Berlioz wrote once more to the minister to summarize his disappointment, but this time there was no answer.

His *concert spirituel* at the Opéra-Comique was scheduled for Palm Sunday, 6 April, a day the national theaters were to be closed. The religious centerpieces were the motet *In media nocte* of Le Sueur; the Sanctus from the Requiem, with the solo part rewritten for tenor and soprano so that Marie Recio would have something to sing; and, through a wonderfully Berliozian turn of association with the Easter story, the *Apothéose* from the *Symphonie funèbre. Le Carnaval romain* was given a second time, and *Le Roi Lear* resurrected again. An arrangement of some Meyerbeer for Sax instruments was doubtless programmed for promotional considerations. The large performance force numbered 180; the conventional ticket prices were, accordingly, doubled.

The featured soloist was Gustave Roger, a tenor from the Opéra-Comique and heir apparent to Duprez at the Opéra. He went on to be the first Faust and to sing in many another Berlioz production, the tenor most prominently associated with Berlioz's mature work. It was for Roger, too, that Meyerbeer finally finished *Le Prophète.* Roger was a high-spirited and intelligent singer, gifted with acute powers of observation and a fetching sense of humor, especially in matters concerning food. (He imagined that the reason oysters were out of season during the months lacking an R was to give them time to make love, a process he was certain exhausted them and made them tough.) Roger's delightful memoirs, in which Berlioz figures from time to time, are quite superior to those of Duprez; his saga therein of a fantastic tour of the British isles with Jenny Lind, singing every night before rabid audiences, bears close comparison with Berlioz's accounts of his own travels, where the *vivats* and *hourrahs* are roared rather less frequently. One cannot escape the conclusion that the virtuosos had an easier time of it.

Liszt returned to Paris in April, in part to visit his children and arrange for the education of the eight-year-old Blandine at the boarding school of Mme Bernard. He was greeted by an adoring public keen to offer a hero's welcome. Berlioz, too, was delighted to have him back and did his share of the errands necessary to assure Liszt's success. Liszt gave two solo recitals in late April, and Berlioz was at least at one of these, though so troubled with violent pain in his left arm that they did not at first meet. Together they gave on 4 May the sort of concert they had perfected in the mid-1830s. There is a certain nostalgia for days gone by in their choice of program, which included the first two symphonies, the *Francs-Juges* overture and the *Carnaval romain,* and Liszt playing his arrangement of *Un Bal,* a Weber concerto, and his own *Réminiscences de Don Juan* and Hungarian melodies of 1840. The concert, at the Théâtre-Italien, was well played by an orchestra that Berlioz thought outshone those he had led in Germany. The immense profit of perhaps 12,000 francs he split with Liszt. The promoters were delighted, and at least one reviewer remarked that it was the most interesting concert of the season.

The cornet obbligato heard that evening in the second movement of the *Fantastique* was doubtless written for the occasion for the cornettist J.-J.-B. Arban.[55] Arban had come to Paris in 1841, at the tender age of sixteen, to study with Dauverné at the Conservatoire. He played alongside his teacher at the demonstration of Sax instruments during Berlioz's concert of February 1844; after the May concert and another year of studies at the Conservatoire, he went on to become the century's most celebrated brass virtuoso and author of the tutor modern players know as *Arban's Famous Trumpet Method.* His path crossed Berlioz's repeatedly, notably in London in 1852 and during the summers in Baden-Baden from 1853.

Berlioz's relationship with Harriet reached its nadir between May and October 1844, when they separated once and for all. The progress of Harriet's illness was now measured in terms of the frequency of her episodes of aberrant behavior. In one fit of despair, for example, she sold all her costumes.[56] She had deduced the truth about Marie Recio. But the cruelest blow to Berlioz was to discover from the servants her darkest secret, the consumption of vast quantities of *eau de vie* in the evenings after he had retired for the night. She would interrupt her husband's sleep with fits of rage and pitiable weeping, to which he eventually became indifferent. In mid-June he rented an apartment in the country for her, where he hoped she might find a cure. Instead, she returned worse than ever; the cries and maledictions came to be expected every night. His tragic letter of 23 June, the existence of which has been known for only a short time, summarizes the situation for his sister Nanci:

> If you could only see the disorder, the neglect and abandonment of all care for herself! She cannot even keep the accounts of our household. She gets up in the middle of the night when she knows I am asleep, comes into my room, closes the doors, and hurls invective at me for three solid hours—sometimes until sunrise. In the morning, she begs forgiveness, swears that she loves me, that I could trample her under foot without her affection for me changing. At night it starts again. O, truly, this is intolerable.[57]

Louis, home for the summer, would cry out during the tantrums that he needed his sleep. Félix Marmion was turned away by Harriet when he came to call and made no further attempts to visit; Berlioz asked his friends to keep their distance. "Pity me," he writes. "I don't know how all this will finish, but finish it must."[58]

Berlioz's sisters appear to have been relatively supportive through the worst of this new drama, and they cooperated in keeping Dr. Berlioz from hearing of it. Berlioz saw eventual escape from the situation in new concert tours, but the preparations were certain to take several months, and this time he could not simply leave Harriet to her own devices. He could only wonder, like everyone else, what the future was to bring.

The domestic unrest caused him to neglect his professional responsibilities. Invitations to appear in Milan, Lyon, and Baden-Baden—the first in a series of offers that ultimately had great consequence—faded away without his attention. Proofs for the *Symphonie fantastique,* the *Carnaval romain,* and the *Voyage musical* lay on his work table. Happiness was to be found only in his imagination: during the spring and summer he wrote *Euphonia,* a novelette on the musical utopia where everyone was a musician. It gave him collateral when he once again needed to borrow money, which this time was advanced by Schlesinger against the payment for the completed work.

Marie, still struggling to establish her career, sang that June in a benefit concert to raise money for the reconstruction of the old monastery on Mount Carmel. The work was a cantata by Carafa to a text by Emile Deschamps. A cosmopolitan public attended the event, which Berlioz may have helped organize. It was one of her last appearances.

Meanwhile Berlioz and Armand Dartois, an impresario and sometime playwright, approached the government for permission to organize and sponsor a third lyric theater, a second home for comic opera. Since the 1820s it had been generally held that Paris should have three opera companies. The arguments forwarded paralleled those contained in Berlioz's similar initiative in 1838: the public and young artists were expecting a venue for contemporary work, the theater would cultivate unique opportunities for the nation's young composers, and so forth. As if to forestall an obvious objection, the self-proposed directors promised not to present works of their own. All this they set forth in the usual formal petition, but it was left undealt with by the government until the momentum had died.[59]

The government was rather more occupied that spring with its preparations for an international Festival of Industrial Products, which ran from May through July 1844. A conversation between Berlioz and Isaac Strauss, encountering each other by chance in a cafe one afternoon, turned first to the festival and then to the idea of a spectacular public entertainment to coincide with the end of the fair. As they talked over their tea, a three-day series took shape in their minds: a ball, a banquet, and a monster concert in the pavilions occupied by the exhibition, just after they had been vacated.

Berlioz was squeamish early on over engaging in the battle to secure the venue, but together they set out to ascertain what might be done. There was no difficulty with the bureaucrats at the ministry of Trade: a certain Sénac readily agreed to the proposal that Strauss had envisaged. The police commissioner, however, declined to sanction the volatile combination of eating, drinking, and dancing, fearing the riot that was likely to ensue.

Never one to resist, once engaged, a good squabble with the bureaucracy, Berlioz invoked the aid of the Bertins and succeeded in gaining access to the minister of the Interior himself, with the result that Strauss was authorized to give promenade concerts—without the dancing—and Berlioz was allowed his concert of serious music. The series was set for the end of July.

His own contribution was a patriotic *Hymne à la France,* written that June and July to a text of Auguste Barbier. Another text had been proposed to him by Adolphe Dumas, a *Chant industriel,* but Berlioz was in no frame of mind to finish two new works and left that composition to Dumas's brother-in-law, the composer Amédée Méreaux. The *Hymne à la France* is another strophic hymn, much like *Le Cinq Mai.* In this case the strophes given tenors, sopranos, basses, and full chorus are variations of the same material (ex. 8.1a); the choral parts in the refrain are unchanged from stanza to stanza. The orchestration, however, grows more lavish with each refrain (ex. 8.1b). (Another stanza, originally the third, was for sopranos and tenors; it was deleted after the first performance.) The five-part chorus—sopranos I–II, tenors I–II, and basses—is unusual and unusually set forth in the score. Otherwise the *Hymne à la France* is a simple work in the manner Berlioz cultivated for occasions of ceremony.

The *Apothéose* was given a new text in order to end the extravaganza with a sentiment appropriate to the venue:

Gloire et triomphe à l'Art vainqueur!
Qu'il règne en maître sur notre patrie;
Gloire et respect à votre ardeur;
Venez, héros de l'Industrie.

(Glory and triumph to conquering art! May it reign as master over our land. Glory and respect to your ardor: come, heroes of Industry!)

And so on.

The concerts were to take place on 18 and 21 July in one of the exhibition halls. Berlioz took the 18th, leaving the later date for Strauss. He circulated published invitations to participate in his festival to all the orchestral and choral musicians in the city, offering each one 15 francs for his or her trouble. Supplementary choral forces were convened from as far away as Lille; a thousand performers were expected altogether. A few singers from the Opéra sent their regrets, and the Société des Concerts as an institution was ill-disposed to support the venture, but generally speaking the response of the invited artists was favorable.

The ambitious program consisted of, in addition to his own music, works by his favorites: Gluck, Spontini, Meyerbeer, even some Halévy and Auber. A huge run of parts was drawn specifically for the occasion. Two full rehearsals, nine sectionals, and a dress rehearsal took place in what must have been an exceedingly cramped Salle Herz. Meanwhile the concert was postponed until 19 July, the day after the awards ceremony, and then until 1 August, after the official close of the Festival.

a. Varied strophes:

b. Refrain:

EXAMPLE 8.1 *Hymne à la France.*

Paris was keen with anticipation of the concert, for Berlioz was now noted for such events as these. Even the aristocrats were intrigued, so much so that Berlioz was invited to the Louvre to watch the fireworks at court on 29 July—the fourteenth anniversary of the July Days—and was questioned closely by the nobility about his plans. The advance sale of tickets was slow and therefore alarming, in view of his own financial exposure. When the day appointed for constructing the platforms arrived, the exhibits had yet to be moved away. The workmen were lethargic and uncooperative, with but a single afternoon left to do their work. Berlioz and Rocquemont thereupon lent themselves to the back-breaking labor of arranging the seating and finished with only a few hours to spare.

The slow pre-sale proved to be a false alarm: more than 8,000 people came to hear by far the largest of Berlioz's concerts to date. There were 1,022 performers—quadrupled and octupled wind sections, solo voice parts sung by groups of twenty and eighty—an assistant conductor, Tilmant, and five chorus masters. The very size of the aggregation hypnotized the audience. The scene of the blessing of daggers from *Les Huguenots* was wildly popular, as were the orchestral pieces: the overtures to *La Vestale* and *Freischütz* and the third and fourth movements of Beethoven's Fifth Symphony. The scenes from *Armide,* Rossini's *Moïse,* and Auber's *La Muette de Portici* appear to have pleased Berlioz, though how they could have been intelligible in such circumstances I cannot say.

There was, however, one unforeseen development. At the last minute, too late to advertise, Berlioz added a scene from Halévy's *Charles VI* to the program, largely as a favor to Schlesinger, who had the score on sale. To be heard in the text was the line "Never shall the English dog be lord in France." There was an unexpected eruption of patriotic fervor, with loud cheering and the throwing of hats. This angered the ministers, trying as they were to improve political relations with England, and offended Halévy. The result was that within a few weeks more stringent censorship was invoked for public gatherings of the sort.

Berlioz was lucky not to have lost his shirt, but in hindsight he could only see that he had been robbed of the rightful profits of a great triumph. Of the 66,000 francs brought in through ticket sales, more than half went to pay the artists' expenses. Of the remaining 32,000, 4,000 francs (the usual 12½ percent) went for the poor tax, 1,200 francs went to the police, and another large amount was applied to a deficit incurred by Strauss's promenade. Berlioz had given the largest concert in history and netted for himself the grand total of 800 francs.

Knowing that he was already exhausted before the concert, Berlioz had dismissed feeling ill during the first half as a symptom of the nervous agitation to which he was prone. By intermission he had developed alarming chills and sweats. A makeshift dressing room was fashioned of the harp trunks, and there his assistants led him to change his clothes and drink punch. Dr.

Amussat, the physician from whom Berlioz had briefly studied anatomy, was summoned from the audience for a consultation. He diagnosed typhoid, then did Berlioz the inestimable service of letting his blood—all this still during the intermission. Directly after the concert, he ordered, Berlioz was to go south on a protracted holiday.

Instead of going on to Germany, then, Berlioz went to Nice, where once before he had recovered his health and spiritual outlook. Finding his former rooms occupied, he took lodging near the old lookout tower perched in the rocks. He sojourned there for a month, from perhaps 22 August to 20 September, swimming in the Mediterranean, wandering along the shore, and in general reliving his 1831 adventure and spending what little the festival concert had brought him. He began, at last, to compose again, drafting an overture called, in honor of his stay nearby, *La Tour de Nice. Le Corsaire*, as it was retitled by 1851, is one of the few substantial works between *Roméo et Juliette* and *Faust*. Its quality quite confirms his oft-stated belief that if only he had a little leisure, he could accomplish as a composer all that he was capable of doing.

*D*uring the preparations for the festival concert, Berlioz had left Harriet for the last time. She and Louis were sent to a country house in Sceaux, and he permanently vacated the apartment in the rue de Londres. She promised to mend her ways, but Berlioz, surprising her in Sceaux on his way back to Paris from Nice, found her too drunk to talk, with the strong smell of her *eau de vie* permeating the room. He had come to discuss the necessity of their living apart—one of the purposes of his trip to Nice, he later said, having been to accustom her to the idea—but conversation was impossible. The doctors feared they could do little more to help her. Though she was to spend much of the rest of her life "in the country," Berlioz at length agreed to her pleas and took for her a much smaller flat at 43, rue Blanche, which he used as his own legal address.

His own personal arrangements are veiled, as he surely intended, in secrecy. I think it unlikely that he moved into Marie Recio's rooms right away: he was too conscious of nuance for so obvious an announcement of the collapse of his marriage. Before the August concert he seems to have lived in a hotel room, and as late as October told his sisters, at least, that he was lodged in a hotel in the rue de Richelieu. He had his mail directed, for a time, to 31, rue de Londres, where he retrieved it from the concierge; after November only his official mail was delivered to the rue Blanche. By December he had moved into Marie Recio's apartment at 41, rue de Provence. There is little in the return addresses he lists to suggest he had been living there much before, but on the other hand his acquaintances had known for some time to call on him in the rue de Provence between eleven and noon. To an intimate friend like Emile Deschamps, he acknowledged the situation: "It is not my official address, but my true one."[60]

Old Dr. Berlioz, who would only be troubled by it, never knew of the separation. Louis, surely, suffered the most. Once again the boy wrote in distress to his aunt:

> Papa causes me great anguish by not writing me at all. He wrote us that he was in Nice but that we should write him in francfort posterestante and when passing through marseille he would give concert [sic] and that he would return at the earliest the 15th of october, dear aunt, you will write to my grandfather that I have written him ten letters or so and that papa didn't put a single one in the post because I found them all in the place where we usually put letters and cards . . . Maman tells me to write to you that she is very sad over papa.[61]

Berlioz was already the sole financial support of a fading wife and a child who would require at least six more years of boarding school. To these responsibilities he now added, presumably, at least half the living expenses *chez* Marie Recio. Armand Bertin offered to help secure a purse for Louis's schooling at a nearby college, perhaps in Versailles. Eventually Louis was granted a half scholarship to the preparatory college in Rouen, the port city on the Seine, where his interest in naval affairs could be encouraged.

That autumn the directors of the Odéon theater, scene of Harriet's greatest triumphs, invited Berlioz to compose incidental music for a production of *Hamlet* in the translation of Léon de Wailly. In view of the author, translator, and venue involved, it was not the sort of project he could well refuse. By November he was hard at work on this unexpected task. A manuscript inventory of his compositions prepared in late 1845 lists three *morceaux d'Hamlet:* a *Scène de la comédie,* the *ballade sur la mort d'Ophélie,* and a *coronach* (funeral procession). The first of these was presumably incidental music for the dumb show in act III, scene 2, and is lost or was never finished; the *ballade* was a reworking of *La Mort d'Ophélie* of 1842; and the procession is the *Marche funèbre pour la dernière scène d'Hamlet.* Berlioz refers again to his *morceaux pour l'Hamlet de Shakespeare* in a published catalogue of his works from 1846 and in an autobiographical sketch of 1847. But he was unable to complete the music by the time the production opened.

Under the circumstances, however, the *Hamlet* pieces were shattering in their biographical associations. Already of fragile spirit, Berlioz was thrust into any number of unwelcome reveries as announcements of a new Shakespeare season of *Hamlet, Macbeth,* and *Othello* were posted about town. Seeing the *Hamlet* poster, he began to cry in the streets, his thoughts fixed on Hamlet and Ophelia and most of all poor Yorick—of the wonders in his life that were no longer. He could not avoid poignant reference to Shakespeare in the *Débats* of 6 December. And the haunting funeral march for *Hamlet,* one of his glorious accomplishments, was in a few years' time to have a more melancholy association still.

His other composition as the year drew to a close included the final touches on *La Tour de Nice* and, for a holiday album of songs called *La Mélodie*, a little work for bass voice and piano titled *Le Chasseur danois* (The Danish huntsman). This shortly earned considerable attention in its orchestrated version; for the moment his primary interest in the work was its sale to the publisher Bernard Latte, for 200 francs. Additionally he was induced in those weeks to complete three short keyboard works to demonstrate the capabilities of a harmonium organ built by Jacob Alexandre.

Alexandre's *orgue mélodium* was a portable, foot-pumped harmonium that Berlioz thought had great promise for the concert hall. In 1842, a portable one-manual organ had been patented by Alexandre Debain, who jealously contested any other use of the term "harmonium." The instrument built by the firm of Alexandre *père et fils* was an imitation, probably preferred by Berlioz simply out of affection for its manufacturers. He wrote a promotional *Notice* on the instrument in 1844, drawn in part from a laudatory column in the *Débats*,[62] and over the years endorsed it as often as he could. The collection of pieces for *orgue mélodium* published by Alexandre in 1844 was promotional as well. Volume one consisted of Berlioz's three bagatelles and one by Meyerbeer; the second volume contained three *mosaïques* by Adolphe Adam. Alexandre's melodium went on to garner a first prize at the Paris Industrial Exhibition of 1855, the same year Berlioz's chapter on it appeared in the second edition of his orchestration treatise.

*T*he 1844–45 season is memorable for its strong emphasis on repertoire evocative of exotic lands. The vogue began when Félicien David, in a private concert at the same Salle du Conservatoire to which Berlioz was now denied access, gave the premiere of his *ode-symphonie*, *Le Désert*. David was one of the St.-Simonian disciples who had journeyed in 1833 to Constantinople, Smyrna, Jerusalem, and Egypt in search of a lady messiah, and *Le Désert* that 8 December was his souvenir of oriental images culled during the trip. Paris, moreover, was full of Arabs, for six Algerian chieftains and their large retinues had been invited by the government to absorb *la civilisation française*. With their exotic names and unusual garb, they captured the French imagination and provided material for everyone from legitimate writers to the cartoonists in the *Charivari*.

Berlioz's ecstatic review of David's cantata helped launch both the work and a more traditional career for its author: "A great composer has just appeared; a masterpiece has been unveiled . . . David writes like a master: his movements are carved out, developed, and transformed with as much tact as science and taste, and he is a great harmonist. His melody is always distinguished, and he orchestrates extraordinarily well." Those left of the St.-Simonian movement were delighted, and Duveyrier wrote once more to

Berlioz: "By the way, you must go see [Enfantin] . . . he would be delighted to shake your hand."[63]

At the same time, Berlioz was himself pondering the exotic. The new Cirque Olympique was an enclosed hippodrome off the Champs-Elysées, descended from a venerable edifice erected by the Franconi family, founders of the modern European circus. The Cirque was begun in 1843 in the course of the civic renewal that also saw the opening of rail lines to Rouen and Orléans, the electrification of the Place de la Concorde, and useful experiments in Paris with the telegraph. The manager of the equestrian palace, a certain Gallois, had been impressed with Berlioz's concert after the Festival de l'Industrie, and particularly with its receipts. He persuaded Berlioz to give a series of six events along the same lines in his arena. The alliance—or misalliance—in Berlioz's life of music, theater, and circus was, just as his parents had suggested it would be, now complete.

The concerts were scheduled for 2:00 to 4:30 on Sunday afternoons that winter. The handbills focused on the magnificence of the room, with modern lighting and heat and with its 6,000 seats raked so sharply that those who wished might admire the costumes of fashionable women from head to toe. Too large to be lit sufficiently from the outdoors, the circus was artificially illuminated even during midday. There was always the possibility that the prospect of trudging as far as the Place de l'Etoile through the mud (and, that winter, snow) might discourage audiences; still, the general idea of Sunday afternoon concerts was well enough established and well enough patronized elsewhere that the "Festival Franconi" seemed assured of a good profit.

Berlioz assembled some 350 players and singers; he had to do without members of the Société des Concerts, as it was midseason for them and they were discouraged from accepting other engagements. Each Cirque Olympique concert was, however, purposefully scheduled for the week after a subscription concert of the Société des Concerts. The chorus was made up of students of the singing teacher Michel-Maurice Lévy, a valiant supplier of choral forces once Berlioz's *entrée* with the Conservatoire students was effectively ended. The rehearsals were in the Salle Herz.

Berlioz's first concert, on 19 January, was the usual mixture of Beethoven (the "Emperor" Concerto, with Hallé as soloist), Gluck (excerpts from *Alceste* and *Orphée*), and his own work, including the *Carnaval romain* and, for the first time (and the only time in its original version), *La Tour de Nice*. All six concerts ended with the Dies irae and Tuba mirum, trademarks of the festival.

The second concert, on 16 February, was more interesting, for with that program the repertoire began to be organized around themes; this one was a *séance orientale* in honor of Félicien David and the Arab fever. *Le Désert* was heard a second time, as was a chorus of Janissaries David had composed. The Austrian virtuoso Léopold de Meyer, the "lion-pianist," played his

Marche marocaine, op. 22, subtitled "War-song of the Turks." The *Francs-Juges* overture was exotic if not precisely oriental. An engraving made of the first concert, incidentally, shows two Arabs prominently in the foreground (see fig. 8.9); the chieftains left town two days later.

Meyer was in the process of taking Paris by storm. He arrived from a triumphal European progress, instantly became the bright star of the season's salons, then was off, as abruptly as he had come, for a voyage to the New World. His *Marche marocaine,* offered for the first time at a *soirée* of *La France musicale* on 8 January, was the centerpiece of his recitals. Berlioz wrote of its "charming originality," and that the *Marche,* having electrified the audience, was furiously encored.

The third of the Cirque Olympique concerts, on Palm Sunday, 16 March, was a *séance russe* built around the works of Glinka. Glinka had been in Paris since late 1844, but there is little indication that he and Berlioz spent much time together until shortly before the March concert. (They remembered each other, vaguely, from their meeting at the Cafe Greco in Rome in 1831.) Berlioz programmed excerpts from Glinka's *A Life for the Tsar* and a ballet from *Russlan and Ludmilla;* a Russian bass sang the role of Père Laurence in the finale of his own *Roméo et Juliette.*

FIGURE 8.9 "Concert given by M. Berlioz in the hall of the Cirque Olympique, on the Champs-Elysées."

Berlioz was smitten with this taste of the Russian repertoire. A week later he wrote Glinka: "It is not enough to play your music and to *tell* lots of people that it is fresh, lively, charming in verve and originality: I must give myself the pleasure of *writing* several columns on it."[64] Thereupon he invited Glinka to furnish biographical information and to teach him the opera scores, especially the new *Russlan* (1842). In his column of 16 April Berlioz wrote:

> Glinka's talent is essentially supple and varied. His style has the rare ability to transform itself according to the will of the composer, according to the exigencies and the character of the subject he treats. It can be simple and even naive, but without ever descending to vulgar tricks. His melodies have unforeseen accent, in periods of charming oddity. He is a great harmonizer and writes for the instruments with a care and an understanding of their most secret resource, making of his orchestra a modern ensemble as new and vivacious as one could imagine.[65]

That spring, then, the seeds of Berlioz's Russian tour of 1847 were well sown.

Glinka, likewise, was delighted with the music of Berlioz. After a concert of his own in early April, he set off for Spain, determined to write *fantaisies pittoresques* in the Berlioz style.

The last of the Cirque concerts, on 6 April, was a *séance Berlioz*, with excerpts from *Harold*, *Roméo et Juliette*, *Freischütz*, Mlle Bertin's *Esmeralda*, another work by David (a nonet for brass), two more selections from *A Life for the Tsar*, and the ever-popular prayer from Rossini's *Moïse*. The queen and members of her household may have attended, for her secretariat asked for ten tickets and sent an honorarium of 100 francs. The novelty of the program was Berlioz's orchestration, with a new coda, of Meyer's *Marche marocaine*. It was another in his growing list of unimportant occasional works, but it proved useful to his repertoire for the rest of that year. It was, moreover, an audience favorite. Bourges wrote that Meyer was "cast in bronze" by Berlioz's pen, which, said he, gave to the short work "a brevet of long life."[66]

With that the concerts at the Cirque Olympique came to an abrupt conclusion. Although the house had been nearly full for the first two, the novelty quickly wore away, and the audience dwindled. The winter weather was too unpredictable, they said, and by late spring the arena was needed for the equestrian displays it was meant to house.

Monster concerts never failed to arouse the best in the satirists. This latest round prompted Louis Reybaud to incorporate a thinly disguised Berlioz as "l'artiste" in his roman à clef called *Jérôme Paturot à la recherche d'une position sociale* (1846). If there was any doubt about the identity of the mad conductor, Grandville's illustration therein of a "concert of gunfire" (see fig. 8.11), with its unmistakable caricature of Berlioz at dead center, erased it. ("Happily the room is solidly built," says the caption, "and withstands.")

CIRQUE OLYMPIQUE DES CHAMPS-ÉLYSÉES.

DIMANCHE 6 AVRIL, à 2 heures précises,

QUATRIÈME

GRANDE FÊTE MUSICALE

SOUS LA DIRECTION DE

M. HECTOR BERLIOZ.

Les Exécutants seront au nombre de 400.

PROGRAMME.

PREMIÈRE PARTIE.

1° Ouverture du *Freyschutz*. WEBER.

2° *Prière des âmes du purgatoire*,
Chœur sur deux notes pendant une fugue instrumentale; fragment du *REQUIEM* de M. BERLIOZ.

3° Air avec chœur de Quasimodo,
d'*Esmeralda*, de Mlle Louise BERTIN.
Chanté par M. MASSOL.

4° *Marche de Pèlerins* chantant la prière du soir,
Fragment de *HAROLD*, symphonie avec un alto principal de M. BERLIOZ.
L'alto-solo sera joué par M. LANDORMY.

5° *DIES IRÆ* et *TUBA MIRUM*,
du *REQUIEM* de M. BERLIOZ.

DEUXIÈME PARTIE.

6° Premier morceau et final du nonetto pour instruments à vent, de FÉLICIEN DAVID,
Exécutés pour la première fois.

7° Cavatine et rondo de l'opéra (*la Vie pour le Czar*), de M. GLINKA,
Chantés en langue russe par Mme SOLOWIOWA,
Artiste du Théâtre de Saint-Pétersbourg.

8° *La reine Mab, ou la Fée des songes*,
Scherzo de *ROMÉO ET JULIETTE*, de M. BERLIOZ.

9° *Marche Marocaine*, de Léopold de MAYER,
Instrumentée avec une coda nouvelle, par M. BERLIOZ,
Exécutée pour la première fois.

10° *Prière de Moïse*, de ROSSINI.

CHEF D'ORCHE STRE, M. H. BERLIOZ.

MAITRES DE CHANT : MM. LATY, DIETSCH ET TARIOT.

Prix des Places { STALLES D'AMPHITHÉATRE NUMÉROTÉES. 10 FR.
{ SECONDES PLACES D'AMPHITHÉATRE. . . 5

Les Bureaux de Location sont établis chez MM. les Éditeurs de Musique : SCHLESINGER, *rue Richelieu*, 97; TROUPENAS, *rue Neuve-Vivienne*; BERNARD LATTE, *passage de l'Opéra*; CHABAL, *boulevart des Italiens*; au BUREAU CENTRAL, *place de la Bourse*; *chez* HEUGEL, *rue Vivienne*, 2 bis; MEISSONNIER, *rue Dauphine*; LAUNER, *boulevart Montmartre*; *chez* GUILLEMIN, *au café du Cirque aux Champs-Élysées, et à l'*ADMINISTRATION DU CIRQUE, *boulevart du Temple.*

PARIS.—IMP. DE E.-B. DELANCHY, FAUB. MONTMARTRE, 11.

FIGURE 8.10 Handbill for the Cirque Olympique concert of 6 April 1845.

Funnier still is a cartoon from the *Charivari*'s series called "The Arabs in Paris" (see fig. 8.12). The Arabs are seated on a beach, hands over their ears, in what appears to be great pain. Behind them is a Berliozian force of drums and brasses and a lion-maned conductor. The caption reads: "Having come to France to see everything and hear everything, the Arab chieftans were too courageous to retreat before the announcement of a grand concert. They went to a *festival Bédouino-musical.* Nearly all the works appeared to impress them vividly, and they promised always to savor the memory." The cartoon appeared on 18 January, on the eve of Berlioz's first concert but after the handbills had appeared.

Léopold de Meyer sailed in September 1845 for his tour of the United States. He took with him the manuscript score and parts to the *Marche marocaine,* which, with the New York performance of 10 November "as instrumented by the great Berlioz, with an original Coda, and executed in

FIGURE 8.11 "Concert of Gunfire." The caption (not pictured) reads: "Happily the room is well-built, and withstands."

FIGURE 8.12 "The Arabs in Paris." *Charivari*, 18 January 1845.

Paris under his direction with astonishing effect," probably became the first Berlioz to be heard in America. Following Meyer on a later vessel were both an Erard piano and another of his marches as orchestrated by Berlioz: the *Marche triomphale d'Isly,* played for the first time on 2 October 1846 in New York as "expressly arranged for the Orchestra by the celebrated Berlioz in Paris."[67] This was certainly a world premiere.

The notion of a *voyage musical en France* had considerable appeal, and for the summer of 1845 Berlioz made arrangements for festival concerts in Marseille, Lyon, and Bordeaux. The advantages of a trip to Lyon included not just the opportunity for Berlioz to visit his family, but also the possibility that his father might actually be able to attend, at last, one of his concerts. Then Liszt suggested the Requiem for the unveiling of the Beethoven monument in Bonn during midsummer, and it thus appeared that Berlioz would be on the road again for the better part of ninety days.

The concert in Bordeaux was put off for several years, but by early June, perhaps on the 6th, he was ready to depart for Marseille to give his two concerts there. Of his recent works he took the *Carnaval romain* and *Hymne à la France,* along with movements from the first two symphonies, the *Apothéose,* and the usual Gluck and Weber. Because his friend Alizard, the first Père Laurence, was resident at the Théâtre-Italien in Marseille, he programmed *Le Cinq Mai,* with its bass solo. We know little of the reception of these concerts or of Berlioz's reaction to them—even the dates are but surmises. But he must have enjoyed renewing his acquaintance with the city where he had first seen the sea: he lingered there for several days. Then he wended his way by coach on through Avignon to Lyon, there to establish himself for concerts on 20 and 24 July. He arrived early on purpose: it was his intention that the Lyon concerts be large and splendid, and that would require time to court the local press.

On 9 July he hired a carriage for La Côte-St.-André and spent the day with his father, sister Adèle, and her husband, returning to Lyon in the middle of the night. It must have been well nigh impossible for the siblings not to discuss Harriet in front of their father, but they agreed to put off that particular subject until they met again in Lyon.

The conductor at the municipal theater in the bustling city of Lyon, second largest metropolis in France, was the energetic François George-Hainl, a gifted cellist and conductor and an old friend from the Conservatoire days. He was happy to be Berlioz's host and had made preparations with a diligence to which his guest was unaccustomed. A large orchestra supplemented by local amateurs and choruses had been well rehearsed, handbills had been posted everywhere, even on the Rhone steamers, and Liszt, who had passed through just beforehand, had taken care to stir up the public—including Berlioz's sisters—for his arrival. Hainl had even mastered the harp part in the march from *Harold* when a competent player could not be found. This vivacious, shaggy music master would eventually accede to the podium of the Paris Société des Concerts, defeating Berlioz in the process.

The concerts played to full houses in the very small theater—too small, actually, for the number of players involved. Nanci, Adèle, and their husbands came to Lyon and occupied a loge together for the first; they talked of Harriet and met Marie, who had come down from Paris.

The welcome accorded Berlioz, like Liszt's in Paris the year before, befitted a returning hero: he was elected to both local musical societies and applauded in a long article in the local paper, *La Clochette.* The essay, probably by George-Hainl, talked of the Conservatoire days and of *Sardanapale,* but mostly it called proud attention to his birthplace nearby: "He is one of our glories."[68] As Berlioz never gave a concert in Grenoble, the two festival performances in Lyon were as close to home as he ever came to conduct.

Away from Paris for almost exactly eight weeks, he returned to find two important letters waiting. The first was a formal invitation from the master

FIGURE 8.13 François George-Hainl.

of the Russian Imperial Chapel, Alexei Lvov, to come to Russia. There had been talk of this possibility for some time, for Berlioz had discussed it both with Glinka and with Léopold de Meyer earlier in the year. He imagined he would leave as early as November or December on a trip he was more anxious to take than any other.

The other was a formal invitation to the unveiling of Ernst Hähnel's Beethoven monument in Bonn, a three-day festival of concerts and ceremonies organized by Liszt and Spohr and scheduled for 11–13 August. By insisting on conducting his Requiem if it was to be given at all, Berlioz had attached one too many conditions to interest the organizers, but the trip could not be passed up on that account. There was his devotion to Beethoven to consider, and the hundreds of German-speaking musicians he was sure to encounter, both friends from 1842–43 and those who could be of value to his future enterprises. He decided to go as a foreign correspondent, intending to write a major article for the *Débats* and perhaps to sell a series to some other French journal or review.

He left on 8 or 9 August in a train crowded with the French delegation: George-Hainl from Lyon, Janin, Félicien David, Elwart, Sax, Mme Viardot, and such instrumentalists as Massart, Seghers, and Vivier. Bonn was bursting with aristocracy, such heads of state as the king and queen of Prussia and Queen Victoria and Prince Albert, chapelmasters from hither and yon, and, as onlookers, the finest players of the era. Berlioz catalogued the delegates he recognized in a list that reads like a roster of the most prestigious figures of the nineteenth century. The absence of Auber and Halévy was noted, however, and Berlioz regretted that neither Schumann, Mendelssohn, nor Wagner had been able to come.

At the head of the orchestra, as they worked their way through the symphonies and concertos and the *Missa solemnis,* stood old Spohr. Berlioz had never heard the Ninth Symphony led by anyone but Habeneck and was surprised to find the recitatives in the finale taken at a breakneck clip. Nor had he ever heard the double basses in the scherzo of the Fifth and the repeat in the last movement, as both had been suppressed in Habeneck's performances. Liszt conducted the Fifth Symphony, and although Berlioz's published article handles his appearance tactfully, he wrote to his sister that Liszt conducted like Musard—that is to say, he did not conduct at all.

In his imagination Berlioz saw what grand ceremony might have been made to occur, just as he had daydreamed over the proper return of Napoleon's remains. The Bonn festival orchestra had been summoned by twos and threes, apparently with little advance notice, from the smaller cities and towns in the area, whereas he would have organized—and been highly qualified so to do—an opulent ensemble composed of the great European virtuosi.

The rehearsals suggested some debacle brewing, or at best some very pale performances.

FIGURE 8.14
The Beethoven monument in Bonn.
L'Illustration, 9 August 1845.

That was not the case: during the three concerts and the church performance of the Mass in C, with a single exception, there were only tiny errors. The chorus acquitted itself admirably in precision and ensemble, and the orchestra, though weak, to be sure, in several respects, maintained itself at that medium level which is as far from the inferior orchestras as it is from those heroic phalanges of players on whom one can rely in Paris, London, Vienna, Brunswick, and Berlin. It took the center course: between a Florentine or Roman orchestra and the Paris Société des Concerts.[69]

Otherwise Berlioz found Bonn provincial and unpleasant. Following the festival the king of Prussia gave at his chateau in Brühl a large reception and concert, led by his chapelmaster Meyerbeer. Liszt played; Jenny Lind and Staudigl, whom Berlioz much admired, sang. The king recognized Berlioz from his previous visit to Berlin, and they conversed amiably together. Later the absentminded princess chatted with him, too, not remembering Berlin, then rebuked Meyerbeer for having failed to introduce her to the celebrated M. Berlioz.

He repaired across the Rhine to Königswinter to compose his articles on the ceremonies and concerts and to consider the several invitations he had had from the Viennese delegates to return with them to Austria. His decision was to cancel the Bordeaux concerts, return to Paris to collect his scores and parts and arrange for the Vienna trip, do some preliminary work on behalf of the large composition he was now pondering, and depart without further delay. He returned via Frankfurt, arriving in Paris on 28 August.

The seven weeks from the beginning of September until his departure were a time of hurried preparation for a trip he had not expected to take quite so soon. He saw to it that his regular income would be disbursed to Louis and Harriet. He tried, as well, to deal with Louis's unhappiness at school. (More and more, however, his sisters were concerning themselves with Louis's interests, in the manner of mother hens.) As yet he had little new music to offer the Austrians: there were the *Carnaval romain* and the *Marche marocaine*, and he took along the *Scène de brigands* and *Le Cinq Mai* for Staudigl to sing, but *La Tour de Nice* could not be given until he had finished the necessary revisions. It appears that he arrived in Vienna with the *Chant sacré* from the Irish Melodies already orchestrated, with ideas for scoring *Le Chasseur danois* for Staudigl and orchestra, and with the text and possibly sketches for a bolero for soprano and orchestra called *Zaïde*. Orchestra parts for all these were first extracted that November by Viennese copyists, who also prepared a set of parts for Cellini's aria "Sur les monts les plus sauvages."

In fact the long hiatus from serious composition had come to an end with the euphoria of the summer festival concerts, the Beethoven celebration, the promise of invading other capitals of the civilized world. *La Damnation de Faust* began, as so many other projects had begun, with the idea of rewriting an early work—the *Huit Scènes de Faust*—to fill out his concert programs. But he had grown immeasurably as a composer since the *Huit Scènes*, and on sober reflection he saw that the *Huit Scènes* could serve only as the starting point for a new *Faust*. In September he contracted with a librettist named Almire Gandonnière to provide recitatives and other passages of an expanded text, though it is clear that the poet had not finished much by the time Berlioz left. In mid-October he gathered up his scores and parts, albums of notes, loose sketches, and texts and made ready to assault Vienna.

He left on 22 October with Marie Recio, who had promised not to sing, traveling by slow coach through Nancy and Augsburg to Regensburg, where they hoped to catch a Danube steamer. In Nancy, he suffered a frightening attack of pain in his side, and they were forced to pause for some time. By then there were no steamers to be had in Regensburg, and so they made their way in yet another carriage, though the mud, to Passau and Linz. A luxury vessel took them on to Vienna, where they arrived on 2 November, two weeks before his first concert.

The 1845–46 journey, which was expected to last six months, was conceived on different principles than the foray into Germany three years before. Vienna served as a hub from which Berlioz made radial excursions into Hungary, Bohemia, and present-day Poland. Because of the greater distances and more rigorous terrain, the trip ran longer by over a month. Travel, however, had become easier, at least between the major capitals: passage by steamboat on the rivers was convenient and included meals, and railways now connected the major cities. The sojourns in the central European capitals were long and thus afforded him more leisure to respond to the local predilections and to prepare coherent offerings of his works. But because the projects were bigger and the calendar more complicated, the recalculations necessary at every stage were of greater magnitude than anything he had so far managed.

He heard a great deal more new music and, Vienna being the equal of Paris as a mecca for intellectuals, met dozens of the music world's most influential citizens. He was obviously busier than before, such that the correspondence from this journey is sparser and on the whole less interesting; the same is true of the letters he later published, but their breezier tone may have been encouraged by his publishers, who feared that the public was tiring of his essays. Berlioz and Marie traveled as husband and wife, and she began to sign her name as Marie Berlioz.

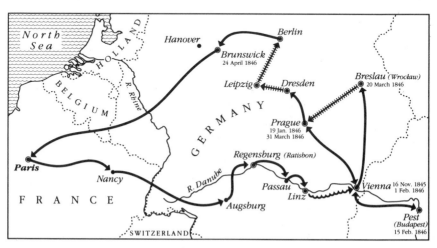

FIGURE 8.15 Berlioz's journeys of 1845–46.

The greatest difference from the earlier voyage is that Berlioz was engrossed in the composition of a masterpiece. On every leg of the journey he plugged forward with *Faust:* in postchaise, steamboat, and railway coach; in the common rooms of various inns by night; and, during moments of spare time, in hotels in Passau, Vienna, Prague, Breslau, and Pest. When he ran out of Gandonnière's text, he began to fashion his own, beginning with the pointedly autobiographical lyrics of the *Invocation à la nature.* Once he had finally begun, it came more easily and quickly than he had ever imagined it might. *Faust* is as much a product of Passau as it is of Paris.

*H*e was expected in Vienna; even the customs agent knew he was coming. The arrangements for his concerts in the Theater an der Wien had been made by Joseph Fischof and by a French-speaking civil servant and devoted *amateur* with the decidedly un-French name of Johann Wesque von Puttlingen. (His pen name, Hoven, was in homage to Beethoven.) Berlioz conducted his first three concerts, on 16, 23, and 29 November, in a state of high euphoria. His orchestra, of the Theater an der Wien, was a younger, more liberal ensemble than that of the Kärntnerthor, which was doubtless to his advantage. Berlioz stood on Beethoven's podium—or so he thought—and his music rested on Beethoven's rack.

He presented most of his major repertoire, though not the fifth movement of the *Fantastique* or, so far, any of *Roméo et Juliette.* At the third of the concerts, the great bass Joseph Staudigl, who had already sung *Le Cinq Mai* and the role of the brigand chief in the *Mélologue,* gave the first performance of the newly orchestrated *Le Chasseur danois.* Its companion work, *Zaïde*—the sprightly bolero with castanets—was also heard, sung by Henriette Treffz. Both were received with a favor they well merit, though so far his most popular work with the Viennese was *Le Carnaval romain.*

Between concert appearances, Berlioz was the most intrepid of tourists. He seems to have attended nearly all the concerts and operas playing: Weber's *Oberon* in a concert version, Nicolai's *Il Proscritto,* Lortzing's *Zimmermann,* Bellini's *I Puritani,* a performance by the Kärntnerthor orchestra, concerts by Alexander Dreyschock and Josef Dessauer. There was a Mass by Joseph and Michael Haydn at the Imperial Chapel, a *concert spirituel* in the Redoutensaal, a ball or two with quadrilles by the orchestra of the elder Strauss. He babbled to his Viennese admirers of Gluck, whom they had forgotten, and visited his tomb. He met the ancient Metternich (apparently in the early days of January) simply by presenting himself, without an introduction. Sometime in December, he sat—stood, actually—for a pair of fine portraits by August Prinzhofer. A few weeks later, in early 1846, the prolific court painter Joseph Kriehuber published his lithograph of a *Matinée chez Liszt,* a superb illustration of the pianist seated at a Graf piano, surrounded by the artist, Berlioz, Czerny, and Ernst, his gaze fixed

FIGURE 8.16 Berlioz in Vienna, December 1845.

over the top of the Beethoven sonata on the music rack at some distant paradise. (I doubt this depicts any particular meeting of the five, but rather constitutes a reminiscence of the 1845–46 season.) Berlioz, in short, was a brilliant guest in concert hall and salon alike. With the aristocracy, he was thought to be *à la mode*.

In early December Berlioz went to Prague to arrange his concerts there. One concert already scheduled was postponed until he could return in more leisurely circumstances.

In Vienna, a banquet was offered him on the eve of his forty-second birthday. The Viennese musicians gave him a baton in silver and gilt on which were engraved the names of the forty subscribers and the titles of his works. The emperor sent a gift of 100 ducats, worth more than 1,000 francs. On the evening of the birthday party, or just afterward, the idea for a better honorific took root: the presentation, for the first time since 1839, of a complete *Roméo et Juliette*.

Berlioz spent much of December on preparations for *Roméo et Juliette* and the composition of the superb seventh scene from *Faust,* Méphistophélès's "Voici des roses" and the *Ballet des sylphes.* On 2 January 1846 *Roméo et Juliette* was born again before a glittering house in an excellent rendition. It drew Berlioz's creative attention back to one of his masterpieces, in part because, for reasons that are not clear, the work was led by a conductor named Groidl, and thus the composer had the unusual opportunity to experience his work as a member of the audience. Problems of balance and scale suddenly became clear to him, as did their solutions, and he forthwith set about some major revisions which would be ready in time for Prague.

Ernst arrived in Vienna soon enough to play *Harold* at a Redoutensaal concert of 11 January, Berlioz's *concert d'adieu.* Afterward, a Hungarian nobleman invited him to come to Pest, with the intriguing suggestion that he consider setting a national march for the delectation of his countrymen. Berlioz agreed to both proposals.

A presence in Vienna less felicitous than Ernst was Félicien David, who Berlioz and Marie both suspected had come to profit from the Francophilia engendered among the Austrians by the Berlioz concerts. (Indeed, David had taken for his concert the first date available after Berlioz left, but his veiled purpose had more to do with proselytizing for a canal in the Suez than

FIGURE 8.17 *Matinée bei Liszt,* Vienna 1846.
From left: Josef Kriehuber (who did the drawing), Berlioz, Czerny, Liszt, Ernst.

challenging Berlioz.)[70] Marie sent a shrewish letter about David to Desmarest in Paris, and David soon faded from Berlioz's biography.

A few days after selling *Zaïde* to the firm of Tobias Haslinger, taking care to send manuscript copies to France to protect his ownership there, Berlioz set forth toward Prague, where he arrived in mid-January and stayed for two weeks. This was the first of two sojourns in Prague during 1846. He was drawn there in large measure by the enthusiastic analysis published by A. W. Ambros of *Le Roi Lear,* which the orchestra had attempted some years before. And indeed, the January concerts and the three that followed in March and April were the triumphs of this tour. There were good singers, including the baritone Karl Strakaty and the soprano Katerina Podhorska and an excellent amateur choral society. The director of the thriving Conservatory, J.-F. Kittl, brought his students to study Berlioz's style of conducting. The excerpts from *Roméo et Juliette* were popular enough that Berlioz was invited back, as soon as he could manage it, to perform the whole work. This he was anxious to do, having nearly finished his round of major revisions to the score.

The press, it must be said, was mixed. "True Czech musicians," claimed one review, "can never take pleasure in the composition of M. Berlioz, even if the German critics consider him the *ne plus ultra* of music."[71] Others were a great deal more enthusiastic. One paper compared him favorably with their idol Mozart, an especially apt formulation in view of the fact that Berlioz had expected to "fall into a population of antiquarian pedants who will recognize only Mozart." The young Hanslick, who wrote a long appreciation of the concerts, got along well with Berlioz, who shortly afterward recommended him to Liszt as "a charming young man, full of enthusiasm, . . . [with] a soul, a heart, and intelligence."[72]

He left Prague on 28 January 1846 and arrived in Vienna just in time to rehearse for his last concert there, in the Redoutensaal on 1 February. On this occasion the new prologue to *Roméo et Juliette,* with its musical foreshadowings, was heard for the first time, but with the recitatives spoken in German by a local *régisseur.* Berlioz spent the next week putting the last touches on the revised symphony and, as the Hungarian count had suggested, orchestrating the popular Hungarian national march *Rákóczy indulŏ* for his concerts in Pest, scheduled for 15 and 20 February.

To the innocent Frenchman abroad, Prague, Pest, and Vienna were all in "southern Germany." Berlioz had not been aware of the fierce nationalism stirring in the Austrian empire, nor had he realized how sympathetic the Hungarians would be to a French citizen. France, after all, had two revolutions to her recent memory and the growing possibility of a third. It was precisely because "the French know how to write revolutionary music" that the Hungarian count had drawn Berlioz's attention to the *Rákóczy* march. Berlioz had intended to "raise the popular passions" with his march, but

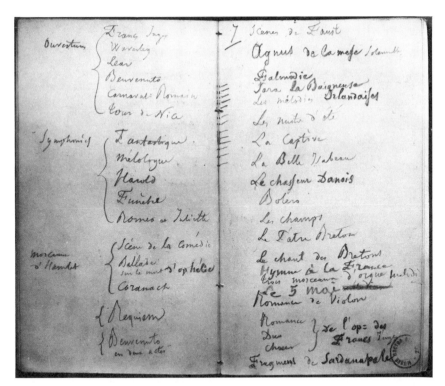

FIGURE 8.18 Autograph inventory of works, found in a pocket notebook of 1845.

the frenzy that ensued on the evening of 15 February took him entirely by surprise. Cheers and foot-stomping drowned out the orchestra, and at the drum strokes, which the audience perceived as the cannon fire of revolution against the Austrians, a full-scale demonstration broke forth.

This was one of several experiences during his travels that elevated Berlioz's social conscience. In the gypsy dances at his banquets and balls, and likewise at a performance of Erkel's *Hunyady,* he discovered the racial pride of the Hungarians and thereby achieved a refined understanding of what was meant by a nation. The autograph of the *Rákóczy* was sold to Count Casimir Batthianyi for 500 francs; Berlioz took away a manuscript copy. He left Pest something of a national hero, and he is still held in affection there today.

Berlioz and Marie were in Vienna again by 24 February. They were looking forward to a rest, but instead found an invitation to come to the Silesian capital of Breslau (Wrocław, now in Poland) for three concerts. Pausing only to attend to monetary transactions, they left to cross Czechoslovakia once more on their way northeast. Thus their departure from Vienna, when finally it happened, was without fanfare and as if by accident. By the end Berlioz no longer found Vienna particularly attractive. The critics were harsh, and the Viennese seemed on the whole antipathetic. He returned again toward the end of his life but, despite the birthday party, never had as spirited memories of Vienna as he did of Brunswick, Berlin, Weimar, and later London and Russia.

By the time he reached Breslau on 10 March, he was exhausted. He was also preoccupied with *Faust,* particularly with the students' drinking song. Breslau was home of a century-old university (with a sumptuous concert room, the Aula Leopoldina);[73] it may have been this ambience that turned his attention to Latin drinking songs. In any event, he was simply too tired to prepare his concert, so he left it to others. He was able to attend a concert in his honor on 14 March, where he was as moved by Mendelssohn's *Midsummer Night's Dream* as Mendelssohn had been moved by *Absence.* ("I've never heard anything so profoundly Shakespearean in my life," he wrote to Leipzig. "I would gladly have given three years of my life, leaving the theatre, to be able to embrace you . . . I love you as much as I admire you, and that is greatly.")[74]

Where three concerts had been scheduled, he conducted a single time, on 20 March, when he offered the first four movements of the *Fantastique* to a public so far unfamiliar with it. The nobility and wealthy citizenry had come from miles around to hear him, and they greeted the superb performance with a respectful silence that at first shocked him.

A direct rail connection to Prague delivered him there in a single day, 23 March, for his remaining three concerts. He was pleased to be back among friends, and the Bohemians in turn were fanatic in their zeal. At the concert on 31 March he resurrected the *Rêverie et Caprice* and gave the complete *Fantastique;* much of the program was repeated on 7 April at a concert to benefit the monastery of Mount Carmel—the same charity for which Marie had sung in June of 1844. Kittl and his cohorts agreed to schedule the complete *Roméo et Juliette,* so he extended his stay in Prague, despite the fact that his succeeding schedule for Brunswick and Hanover was thus thrown into question.

Liszt came to Prague expressly to hear *Roméo et Juliette,* with which he was so far familiar only by reputation. At the dress rehearsal on 15 April he translated Berlioz's French and grew flushed with enthusiasm for the score. For his part Berlioz was pleased with the changes in the work: the new musical foreshadowings added character to the recitatives; the shortened scene of Père Laurence and a sprightly new ending to *Queen Mab* worked as he had hoped they would. Knowing that the Czechs were unlikely to be familiar with the Garrick denouement, he suppressed the tomb scene and suggested in the published score that that should be done much of the time. It was with the Vienna and Prague performances of *Roméo et Juliette* that Berlioz first comprehended the magnitude of his achievement, and these performances instilled in him his deepest affection for the love scene.

The dinner party after the general rehearsal was in the restaurant Trois Tilleuls, where the players offered him crowns, a goblet of silver and gold, and the usual toasts. Liszt delivered a fine discourse, then drank too much and had to be carried home. Berlioz toasted the local critics, whom he complimented for, unlike his Paris colleagues, covering his concerts fairly and without carping.

After five and a half months in the Austrian empire, Berlioz and Marie turned westward. From Dresden, they took the railway to Berlin, where they arrived on 21 April. The concert in Brunswick on the 24th repeated the brilliant and productive performances of March 1843, and the entire *Fantastique* was offered: he could not have asked for more. The hiatus for *Roméo et Juliette* in Prague had meant canceling the Hanover performance, and so they went directly home and were established once again in Paris by

FIGURE 8.19 Berlioz in 1846.

the beginning of May. Berlioz returned richer by several thousand francs, a diamond ring sent by the czar for the dedication of the *Fantastique,* a golden cigar box from the Prince Hohenzollern-Hechingen for the dedication of *Le Carnaval romain,* and numerous presentation batons and crowns. They were short Marie's fur muff, which she had left in Brunswick and never recovered.

*I*t had been a taxing journey, especially toward the end when he was more interested in *Faust* than in traveling:

> I have worked assiduously this year, if not in composition, then at least on exterior refinements of diverse works which were already nearly done. I am broken, exhausted, and feeling sadder and sadder: the cold is overtaking my heart. It's the beginning of the end: I've suffered too much, endured too much not to be extinguished soon. And yet I've never felt more the master of my musical faculties than now. But I don't have the time to compose.[75]

In Vienna, there was more than idle interest in the possibility of his accepting an appointment as Kapellmeister to the Austrian court theater, succeeding Joseph Weigl who had died in February. Moreover, everybody knew that Donizetti, who was Hofkapellmeister for court chamber music with conditions of appointment that allowed him six months' annual leave, had retreated to Paris in declining health. Berlioz was more interested in Donizetti's sort of appointment, and Liszt, too, had written to inquire of the succession. D'Ortigue argued fiercely against the idea of Vienna, reminding Berlioz—naively—of the certainty of future posts in Paris, greatest of all European cities. Now Berlioz formulated for himself a principle that had in fact guided his actions for some time: Paris, or at least the promise of Paris, held his heart. His friends, the ferment of ideas, the vigorous intelligence of the artistic community drew him inextricably home. He declined the Vienna initiatives, but took care to place news of them in the Paris papers. By the summer's end, he had been elected a corresponding member of the Gesellschaft der Musikfreunde.

The first order of business in Paris was to attend to the commissions with which he had been entrusted in the Austrian empire, such as the purchase of two Vuillaume violins for friends in Prague. He hoped, meanwhile, to finish *Faust* in time for performance in the autumn, orchestrating what he had written and writing what he had sketched. Gemmy Brandus had purchased Maurice Schlesinger's enterprises, including the *Revue et Gazette musicale,* on Schlesinger's retirement in January, and so Brandus now had to be cultivated.

There was also urgent demand for his services to lead another performance of oriental fare, similar to the *séance orientale* at the Cirque Olympique, for the state visit of Ibrāhīm Pasha, military hero and crown prince of Egypt. The pasha arrived in state on 24 April, when Berlioz was still in Germany.

Lodged at the Elysée Palace, he was received by Louis-Philippe on the 27th. On 9 May there was the command performance of the *Marche marocaine* and *Le Désert* at the Théâtre-Italien; the pasha then went on a sight-seeing trip to the chateaux and finally was decorated with the *grand croix* of the Legion of Honor and honored by a full-dress military review in the Champ de Mars on 25 May.

In late May a breathless and confused ambassador from the municipality of Lille, underwritten by the Baron de Rothschild himself, arrived on Berlioz's doorstep with a commission for a cantata for the opening of the Northern railroad line, stretching from the Paris Gare du Nord to Lille at the French border and then on to Brussels. Jules Janin was asked to write the text. There was promise of good food and drink, and it was argued by the promoters that a little music might aid the digestion.

They were asking the near-impossible, for by the time it was clear just what was happening, there remained just over a week to complete the work, organize the concert, and have the parts prepared. Berlioz was nevertheless titillated by the idea; he sketched out the melodies in three hours and orchestrated the work the next night.

At the outdoor ceremony in the public promenade on the evening of 14 June, the royal princes representing the king arrived, an archbishop blessed the endeavor, and 150 musicians drawn from the military bands of Douai, Valenciennes, and other outlying areas—the excellent bandsmen of Lille having been given other duties—played the *Apothéose* from the *Symphonie funèbre*. The concert organizers had gone to elaborate lengths to arrange a fusillade of cannon fire on the last chord, set off by the choristers, but the ramrods and lighters were left behind in the arsenal, and a deafening silence ensued, the penultimate in a long series of failed conflagrations of Berlioz's career. He then hurried to the Hôtel de Ville to conduct the choral society and local theater orchestra in his cantata.

The general tenor of this event was one of utter confusion. Too many people had come, it was hot, and there was too little to quench their thirst. Thievery was pandemic: Janin lost one of his diamond-studded decorations, worth nearly 9,000 francs, and after the concert, while Berlioz was accepting the congratulations of the king's two sons, the Duc de Nemours and the Duc de Montpensier, an *amateur d'autographes* took his hat and every scrap of his music: full score, parts, and all. "Voilà un ouvrage perdu," he wrote to Nanci philosophically.[76] The music was later recovered, but not the hat. The grateful townspeople serenaded him four times, however, and the city fathers later sent a gold medal inscribed with thanks from the city of Lille on one side and a portrait of Louis-Philippe on the other.

The *Chant des chemins de fer* is an unhappy wedding of text and music. Janin was asked to embody in verse the miracle of industry, the future come true—promising stuff, possibly, but the sort of thing that took better poets than he more time to work out. His result is, in the words of Léon Guichard, "a bewildering platitude."[77] The chorus, a sort of collective, bourgeois Dido, proclaims the glories of hard work:

> We, the witnesses to the marvels of industry,
> Must sing to peace, to the king, to the worker, to the country,
> And to commerce and all its benefits.

Berlioz daintily sidestepped the issue of the text in his account of the adventure, writing that it was "tailored in a certain manner, which I shall not endeavor to characterize."[78] He adopted his strophes-plus-refrain technique, as in his other works of ceremony. The cantata thrashed out in three days, he knew, might embarrass his reputation for forty centuries. "But in pressing and unforeseen circumstances, like the inauguration of a railroad, an artist need not expect forty centuries, more or less, of attention to his work. And the nation has the right to ask of each of its children an absolute commitment. And so I said to myself: 'Allons, enfant de la patrie!'"[79]

He went back through Rouen to visit Louis, now twelve years old, on the occasion of his first communion. Louis, though still a slow learner, was well established in his school and reasonably happy, pleased by his father's visit and gifts from Paris and Prague. From Rouen, Berlioz went to the chateau in Normandy of the Baron de Montville, where he spent four tranquil days composing the duo and chorus, "Ange adoré," that concludes part III of *Faust*. The end was in sight, but the summer was advancing, and he was far from done. The main business of July and August was clearly to attend to the troublesome conclusion of *Faust*.

Harriet's condition deteriorated still further with the onset of the inevitable by-products of alcoholism, stomach and liver disorders. That Berlioz's visits to the rue Blanche, where until leaving for Vienna he had collected his mail, were now reduced to practically nothing is indicated by his remark to Nanci that "my address is now rue Neuve-St.-Georges, no. 10."[80] This was the address of Sax's showroom; it had doubtless become necessary to halt correspondence to the rue Blanche once letters from central Europe began to be addressed to a different Mme Berlioz. He continued to rely on the good offices of Sax for several months, particularly as he made plans to visit Russia without Marie Recio. She, too, was in poor health, under treatment by Dr. Amussat, possibly for a heart condition.

The extent of Harriet's distress is shown in her letter to Louis of 22 October 1846, written in her lamentable French. It reads in part:

> Alas, my dear son, I could certainly never endure my profound chagrin without the promise of your future. Your father has not come to see me since you left, nor written either. Tell me *everything* he said to you when you left, *everything, the truth,* and all your own news, and believe me to be your poor affectionate mother . . . I couldn't return your paper because I would have had to pay sixteen *sous* to put the package on the train . . . Write me as soon as you have heard from your father. *You must write him soon. He's about to leave.*[81]

He found that the tireless Baron Taylor and his Association of Artist-Musicians, the same society that had needed him on his return in 1843, had more plans for him. On 24 July at the open-air hippodrome near the *rond-pont* on the Champs-Elysées, Théophile Tilmant conducted a rendition of the *Apothéose* by 1,800 players, the largest ensemble to have so far played his work. Berlioz was uninspired, writing in the *Journal des Débats* as he had of the *Scène héroïque* years earlier: "Open-air music is a chimera; 150 musicians in a closed building produce more effect than 1800 in the Hippodrome scattering their harmonies to the wind."[82] Three days later, the hippodrome burned to the ground.

The society's next project was a performance of the Berlioz Requiem at St.-Eustache, billed, rather feebly, as in memory of Gluck's death. (This may have been Berlioz's idea, for in Vienna he had heard, or perhaps instigated, conversations about a proposed monument to Gluck.) Together he and Taylor signed and distributed circular letters inviting five hundred musicians to participate. Gustave Roger was engaged to sing the tenor solo, and Michel Lévy's singers were convened, as they had been for the Cirque Olympique concerts, to serve as the chorus. Taylor attended to the more tedious details; Berlioz had only to conduct. The general rehearsal was on 18 August, with the memorial ceremony and performance on 20 August at 11:00 A.M.[83]

A large crowd flocked to the performance, and, despite the fact that there had been a single rehearsal with the orchestra, this second complete performance seemed to its composer decidedly better than the first. Louis, home from school for the summer holiday, probably heard it; Spontini came backstage to observe how important Michelangelo must have been to the conception. And, just as the previous December Berlioz had been drawn sharply back to *Roméo et Juliette*, he now returned to this masterpiece. "My thoughts keep coming back to the Requiem. Those sinister harmonies wail in my brain. Yesterday it seemed as if I were at some apocalyptic scene: [today] I can only hear fearful cries, explosions of thunder, the sound of worlds collapsing at the *clangor tubarum*."[84] He altered some details in the work immediately afterward and soon began to see the need for a second published edition.

Performance of the Requiem led to gossip and a certain degree of excitement over the new *Faust*, now announced as an *opéra de concert*. The pressure of the calendar led him to turn aside an approach in October from the Ministry of War, acting on behalf of the Duc de Montpensier, to write a military symphony for a performing force of 3,000, an outgrowth of a conversation with the prince about his 1832 project for a symphony commemorating Napoleon's Italian Campaign. It seems likely that whatever new thoughts he had on the subject came to be embodied in the Te Deum, which he undertook within a few months.

Producing a work the length of *Faust* entailed an enormous financial risk, for it was barely likely that the income would cover rental of a hall, fees for a long sequence of rehearsals, and the cost of a new mountain of hand-copied parts. Petty hostilities, not to mention sheer jealousy, had grown within the establishment during his long absences, due in no small measure to his incessant harping over the decline of musical life in Paris. That consisted, he had written, of "bad works, peppered with bad melodies,

FIGURE 8.20 *Faust:* Pandemonium. Frontispiece in *La Damnation de Faust* (Paris: Richault, [1854]).

FIGURE 8.21 *Faust:* "Le Ciel." Autograph of *La Damnation de Faust*, vol. 4, p. 131. The fourth and fifth staves were originally allocated for saxophone parts.

accompanied by a bad orchestra, sung by bad singers, and heard by a bad public" who would listen to a new work twice and then forget it completely.[85] Such railings against mediocrity, particularly the mediocrity at the Opéra, did little to help his recruitment of singers.

He took the Opéra-Comique, a hall to which the public was unaccustomed to coming on Sunday afternoons but the only one available that could accommodate the huge performing force. The rental fee was so great as to force him to double the usual ticket price. On 19 October he finished and dated the autograph.

Then he set about orchestrating the publicity, which surpassed anything he had done before. He sprinkled countless notes in the press on the conception of the work, its composition in Germany, its evocative color. He offered the score for examination, and at least one writer took him up on the offer. In mid-November he sent the published libretto to the king and queen and Duchesse d'Orléans, begging them to come to "a veritable opera without costumes or sets"; they indicated that the Duc and Duchesse de Montpensier would represent them and sent 200 francs. (The libretto he forwarded, incidentally, includes the first careful listing of all his works—called, after its publisher, the Labitte catalogue.) "Good or bad," said one of the papers, *Faust* "will make a splash."[86]

The rehearsals went tediously, partly because the work had so recently been finished. Cuts and other changes were demanded, and the bass engaged to sing Méphistophélès, Herman-Léon, found relearning the changes all but beyond his abilities. Gustave Roger, though a capable and cooperative tenor, by his own admission could not understand the part. The other soloists— Mme Maillard as Marguerite and a bass named Henri as Brander—were accomplished but not fashionable. The instrumentalists, who were at last comfortable with the *Fantastique* and *Harold,* found the music extremely difficult. The premiere was postponed from late November until 6 December, after a dress rehearsal on 27 November.

The performance was apparently brilliant, and a few of the movements were encored. But *Faust* was an utter failure at the box office. At neither the premiere nor the second performance on 20 December was the small house more than half full, and those who did come seemed bewildered by the unusual form and epigrammatic treatment of the story. By then it was clear that Berlioz had incurred a gross financial loss, by far the greatest of his career. The third performance was canceled: the theater was needed for an opera, and the other houses were in use or forbidden him. Too much money had already been lost.

Baron Taylor and the performers, anxious to assuage him, offered a subscription dinner on 29 December and arranged for the casting—not finished until three years later—of a gold medal commemorating the work. Knowledgeable artists saw that *Faust* was his best composition to date.

Gautier praised the work's originality and its lack of concession to philistinism; he elevated Berlioz, with Hugo and Delacroix, to the trinity of romantic art. Spontini, unable to come, begged for a copy of the libretto.

But there was no erasing the pain of the worst failure he was ever to endure. "Nothing in my career as an artist wounded me more deeply than this unexpected indifference."[87] Berlioz's morale was permanently affected, his urge to compose stifled for years. He was never again to have confidence in the Paris public and seldom to risk his own purse again in presenting a new masterpiece. He would leave town at once, migrating, like a bird, in search of a better climate.

Faust was a catastrophe.

Chapter Nine

Portrait in 1846
La Damnation de Faust

n Vienna during Berlioz's visit of 1845–46, August Prinzhofer prepared two pen-and-ink portraits of him which circulated widely at the time in lithograph and which remain among the best likenesses we have of Berlioz in his forties. "H. Berlioz non dandy," he signed one copy, for in truth, Prinzhofer's illustrations portray a man of decided rakishness, extravagantly dressed, carrying a cane, and sporting two rings on his right hand. He wears an under-the-chin beard, Wagner style, white pantaloon trousers, and a waistcoat with buttons to the collar. One of his decorations hangs from the lapel of his frock coat. His hair, though bushy, is shorter than in most of the other portraits. Whereas the Signol portrait of 1830 captures the young artist during the peak of the Romantic flowering, Prinzhofer evokes a citizen of midcentury, recognized and well established, enjoying his measure of celebrity. Berlioz liked the more restrained of Prinzhofer's pair, and his publishers tipped it in as a frontispiece in several editions of his music.

In his apparent effort to evoke the fashion favored by Paris Romantics, Prinzhofer was out of date by more than a decade. Modern French society was defined less by extravagance than by industry. For the middle classes, and for people of Berlioz's responsibilities, the twelve-hour workday was common. There was a new sobriety to the night life, with laws that required most *spectacles* to be done by 11:00 P.M. and the cafes and restaurants to close by midnight. The pace of life became perceptibly faster toward midcentury: the streets, noisy with barrel organs and itinerant entertainers, were always congested. Whatever contribution the omnibus and the steam train made to the public convenience, their augmentation of the traffic problem was cause for widespread wringing of hands. Louis-Philippe's policy of cordial détente with England had more to do with domestic tranquility than the public realized, but, as in the years before 1830, there was more social

FIGURE 9.1
Berlioz in Vienna,
December 1845.

unrest than the government seems to have identified. The king was losing his grip.

Berlioz still rose early when rehearsal schedules or business affairs demanded. Otherwise he found it increasingly difficult to bestir himself before 9:00 A.M. and preferred to get up at noon to begin his round of calls at one. The passions, the agony of the 1820s and 1830s—"both comical and diabolical," according to Legouvé[1]—were over; his dignity was widely noted, and that alone was a real change. He was careful of his public image, recording in his monthly expense accounts the costs of appropriate tailoring,[2] coiffure, and transport by carriage. Where once he had been pleased to contemplate theater works from the *parterre,* now he was guaranteed a stall or box for the asking. His income remained about 500 francs per month.

The life of the *boulevardier* still held its allure, and he continued to enjoy, when he was in Paris, stops at favorite cafés by day and a fine cigar with friends by night. Partly from distaste for the situation with Harriet, he shunned much by way of strong drink, but he enjoyed coffee and, after his 1847 journey to St. Petersburg and Moscow, good Russian tea.

Adolphe Boschot, Berlioz's definitive biographer of the first decade of this century, thought the early 1840s the *années mystérieuses* in Berlioz's life. He could find but sparse documentation of these years, and the *Mémoires,* which are out of kilter at this point, seemed to him to have been artificially manipulated to avoid dealing with some unpleasant truths. (The confusion in the *Mémoires* is much simpler to explain: Berlioz merely conflated the

Salle Vivienne concerts of 1840 and 1842.) What is true is that nearly every detail of Berlioz's personal and professional life changed a good deal between 1839 and 1846. The three turning points were his rupture with Harriet and *ménage* with Marie, his being denied access to the concert hall of the Conservatoire, and his decision to leave Paris in search of global recognition. As a result, in large measure, of these developments, ceaseless travel replaced composition, conducting elsewhere replaced appearances in Paris, and long narratives on the musical life of the foreign capitals replaced, for the most part, his biweekly treatments of the Paris season.

The way Berlioz handled his marital crisis is a sorry episode in his biography. At a certain point he seems simply to have dismissed both his wife and his son from his day-to-day concerns. Harriet's repertoire of noble tragic roles, to be sure, did not extend to that of the wronged wife. Between them they succeeded in confusing poor Louis to the point of serious mental distress. She is said to have followed the newspapers, early on, for traces of her husband's infidelity; later she simply retreated into an alcoholic stupor and an endless sequence of profitless cures and takings of the waters. She was sent to Montmartre, in 1848, to finish her days, and there almost immediately had the first of the strokes to which she eventually succumbed.

Marie Recio, once she agreed not to sing in his concerts, was by traditional measures a more satisfying helpmate than Harriet could ever have been. She taught Berlioz much-needed economic prudence about the house: there is not a word of servants, for example, until after her death, and their lodgings appear to have been the model of simplicity.[3] She, and later her mother, managed his household well. She was too jealous on behalf of her mate, casting herself without invitation as his protectress and business agent. This was not appreciated by Berlioz's associates. (The Wagner camp, with which Berlioz was having increasingly more to do each year, was particularly sensitive to Marie's clear dislike of their idol. This situation manifested itself most obviously during the London visit of 1855, when both Berlioz and Wagner were conducting there and inevitably became the focus of comparison.) She earned a reputation for shrewishness.

Legouvé's account of Marie Recio's cruelty to Harriet Smithson-Berlioz is, however, suspect. There is no confirmation of his story that Marie paid a visit to Harriet during which she called her "the old Mme Berlioz, the abandoned one" and referred to herself as the young one, the pretty one, the preferred one. (She did, however, call herself Mme Berlioz well before their marriage; during the European travels it was occasionally deduced that she was the famous English actress.) It is true that each of the very few remarks about Marie by contemporaneous observers is negative; it is equally true that Berlioz continued searching—indeed, until his death—for the magic, forbidden romance that Romeo and Juliet shared and that he had once conceived for Harriet. He never, so far as I can tell, developed the romanticized estimation of Marie that he held of half a dozen other women in his life. But of her great contribution to his well-being there can be no doubt.

Simply keeping his tangled domestic life under control was one of Berlioz's major concerns during his periods of residence in Paris. The other overriding concern through the better part of the 1840s was to see his works through their publication, first negotiating sales with Richault, Schlesinger, and Schlesinger's successor Brandus, then reading and correcting the proofs, often succumbing to the temptation of last-minute changes of mind. His proofreading was anything but flawless, but the worst of the errors came to light as he prepared concerts from the proof copies. The Paris editions of his works, at least those published during his lifetime, remain superlative sources, more than a few of them having profited from the careful attention of his associates.

From the earliest days of the *Revue et Gazette musicale* Maurice Schlesinger was Berlioz's publisher of first choice; during the 1840s Simon Richault gradually encroached on that preeminence, and by that time Berlioz was happy to take full advantage of their modest competition. Schlesinger was himself a brazen individualist; he and Berlioz always got along well and remained close friends to the end of their days. By contrast the relationship with his successor Brandus (later Brandus, Dufour, & Cie), though warm, was never quite as close.

*T*he government gave any number of reasons for its decision to close the Salle du Conservatoire to all but its own orchestra and instructional programs. The most persuasive—and honest—of these was a situation Berlioz had helped to create: the city had seen a proliferation of successful, rival concert series, they observed, and there was no compelling argument in favor of housing the competition. Berlioz was thus probably overreacting to consider the gesture a personal affront, but it was nonetheless true that in some respects precedent was squarely on his side: he had, after all, begun to give concerts in the hall almost simultaneously with the orchestra that was now exerting complete hegemony over it. His worst suspicions were justified by the selective enforcement, within the year, of the new policy: privileges of the hall were extended to Félicien David for *Le Désert,* and then to César Franck, Ernest Reyer, and J.-B.-T. Weckerlin. Later Jules Pasdeloup, whose Société des Jeunes Artistes could claim at least some affiliation with the Conservatoire's teaching goals, was allowed use of the hall twice each week. But I doubt that Berlioz's concerts were the only reason behind the promulgation of this edict.

Still, the gesture erased forever for Berlioz the comforts of an assured venue and—at least by comparison—relatively risk-free financial exposure. The public had to pay attention merely to learn where he was about to offer his latest work: he was adamant in his view that presenting *Faust* in an unfamiliar hall contributed to its downfall. The tiny Salle Herz and Salle Ste.-Cécile became the only rooms readily open to him, and these were already occupied most Sunday afternoons by long-term clients. To a composer who had turned to him for help, Berlioz outlines the situation of 1850:

> Here is what you absolutely must submit to in Paris these days to have a work like yours performed.
>
> You must give the concert yourself if you want it performed completely.
>
> If you give a concert on a weekday, during the day, there will be no public. If you give it on Sunday at 2:00, you will be scheduled simultaneously with the Conservatoire, or the Société de l'Union [Musicale], or the Société Ste.-Cécile. If you wish to give your concert in the evening (as is the case with the Société Philharmonique, which I conduct), it will still be very difficult to have an orchestra because of theater services, inasmuch as the Société Philharmonique has gathered nearly all the musicians who can secure leave at night.
>
> If, however, you succeed there, a combined orchestra and chorus of 200 people would cost you at least 3,000 francs for three rehearsals and the performance. For the vocal soloists the difficulty is still greater, since in general they are not paid, but will only sing for themselves—that is, sing cavatinas appropriate to show off the talent they think they have.
>
> The hall would cost 350 francs in the evening and 300 francs during the day. I speak of the Salle Ste.-Cécile, which is the only possibility in Paris. It is taken every Sunday during the day.
>
> The posters, tickets, and programs would cost you still another 250 francs at least. Then comes the *droit des pauvres,* which claims eleven percent of the gross income from concerts. Beyond that, the public's indifference to music surpasses anything you can possibly imagine.
>
> There, dear sir, is the exact truth, which I tell you without adornment, assuring you nevertheless that if you decide to come to Paris, I am at your service to help you out in any way I can.[4]

In place of the one-man concert came cooperative ventures: the Cirque Olympique series of 1845, for example, and the Société Philharmonique of the early 1850s. The income though small was guaranteed, but as the risk disappears so, too, in some measure does the magic. That proposition is proved by the euphoria that surrounded the first performances of *L'Enfance du Christ* in late 1854 and early 1855, the only exception after 1846 to his new policy of avoiding personal monetary risk.

In place of the Salle des Concerts, too, came the magnificent journeys abroad. The Vienna trip of 1845–46, or possibly the foray into provincial France that just preceded it, was the first to have much polish; after that came the advance on Russia in 1847, the English ventures of 1847–48 and following, and the almost continual peregrinations of the early 1850s. Like Liszt, Moscheles, Joachim, and Ernst, Berlioz was well suited to the life of a vagabond. That much was clear from the early 1830s in Italy. (The implications for his promise as *père de famille* were not so positive.) His apathy toward politics and his natural fondness for practicing musicians made him adaptable to the broad array of conditions he faced on arriving in new places. The German princes must have been relieved to find that a Frenchman of his obvious iconoclasm was never heard to espouse threatening political views.

The conditions of travel improved with every trip. Alongside the rail networks were built systems of telegraphic communication. (So far as I am aware, no telegrams sent by Berlioz have been preserved, but there is reference in his correspondence to a telegram urgently requesting money, as well as to any number of congratulatory telegrams sent by admirers on such occasions as his birthday.) The postal and parcel delivery services were radically improved by the dawn of modern transportation; during the 1840s their speed approached and in some cases surpassed that of the mail 150 years later.

Brunswick was the high point of 1842–43; Prague and *Roméo et Juliette*, of 1845–46. His music, though puzzling, was admired in sympathetic surroundings such as these; it is true that listeners often wrote of its "strangeness," but they were more frequently apt to use the words "color" and "rhythm" to focus their reactions. Just as his conducting style affected European practice in general, his other musical attitudes began to make their mark on the younger generations. His influence on the future culminated in the trip to Russia in 1847 and the five visits to England from 1847 to 1855— and, doubtless, in the half-dozen annual visits to Weimar, once Liszt and his admirers were settled there. Weimar came to replace London as his most congenial home away from home, and there is considerable merit in the view that Berlioz's regular presence among the Futurists watered the most fertile intellectual soil of midcentury.

Overtures to determine Berlioz's interest in a permanent post—at one of the German courts, or in Vienna, London, or possibly St. Petersburg—were routine and in several cases became quite serious. This issue came to a climax in 1846 with the matter of the Hofkapellmeister's post in Vienna. Similarly he expected his first trip to England would set the stage for a permanent appointment there. He was sorely tempted by such possibilities, and between 1846 and 1848 his inclination to leave France forever is palpable.

At home he could see only heartbreak in his path. Carafa, for example, was a third-rate composer and a foreigner, yet was considered by many the logical heir to Cherubini and was already a professor at the Conservatoire, director of the Gymnase, and a member of the Institute. Parisian taste, just as Berlioz maintained, could have its dreadful episodes. Read the reaction of any distinguished musician to his Paris stay—Meyerbeer, Wagner, or Hallé—if you think he overstates his case. Consider, for instance, Hallé's account of an 1837 concert where the order of trios by Mayseder and Beethoven was inadvertently reversed: "The consequence was that Mayseder's Trio, passing for Beethoven, was received with acclamation, and Beethoven's very coldly, the newspapers also eulogizing the first and criticizing the length and *dryness* of the other severely."[5]

Berlioz's campaign to improve Paris musical life is measured in terms of his continuing efforts to establish a third lyric theater company, his advocacy of new concert halls (Barthélémy's elliptical hall, for example), his experiments with existing spaces, his determination to see the Conservatoire offer classes in orchestration and conducting. These and other efforts were rebuffed. He would eventually have his successes—the Gluck revivals of 1859 and the 1860s and the establishment of a universal pitch standard in 1859— but there was no such comfort to be found in 1846.

Yet, when he stopped to ponder the foreign offers, he would be drawn inexorably to the intellectual climate at home: "Paris is an electric city which attracts and repels in alternation, but to which one must definitively return when in its grasp, and especially when one is French."[6] "It would be impossible," he wrote elsewhere, "for me to live anywhere but in Paris."[7]

What might be called the Paris problem exacerbated the melancholy of his later years. The crossness and the outrage over this one subject mar his later writings; the onset of illness, which made him crabbier anyway, drew a veil of morosity over the slightest remark about music in what remained, after all, a thriving musical capital. At times his attitude had its picturesque qualities:

> We continue in Paris to make such [trivial] music—we have become so prodigiously Spice Merchant, so National Guard, so Deputy, so ill-bred, so stingy, so greedy—that during my absence I will rest easy on the question of being homesick. From that I shall not die.[8]

He never found his Utopia, the Polynesia of his dreams, though he never stopped searching for it.

*T*he exchange of batons with Mendelssohn in February 1843 is an appropriate symbol of Berlioz's growing importance as a professional conductor, both of his own compositions and, increasingly, of the works of others. By midcentury there had flowered in Paris the very notion of the virtuoso conductor, the development of a theory of his art, and a vastly improved standard of measure for the quality of orchestral performance.[9] Berlioz could claim much credit for this development, in part because of the dialectic that had been engaged between his attitudes and those of the musical establishment.

Habeneck and nearly all his successors at both the Opéra and the Société des Concerts almost invariably rose to fame through their virtuosity on a stringed instrument: they were descendants of, to use British parlance, the leader, or first violinist, rather than of that courtly jack-of-all-trades, the *maître de chapelle*. The last of the great nineteenth-century *chefs* of the

Société des Concerts, E.-M.-E. Deldevez, in fact conducted with his violin bow from his seat at the head of the violin section. Berlioz saw things quite differently.

Once he broke company with Narcisse Girard in 1835 over the performances of *Harold en Italie,* Berlioz began seriously to ponder the philosophy of orchestral conducting. A synthetic view of musical direction began to evolve in his mind. Between 1835 and 1846 Berlioz conceived of sectional rehearsals, perfected the production of flawless orchestral parts, began to expand his repertoire, and started to think of a systematic study of the orchestral instruments. A child of the new century, unlike Habeneck, Berlioz took for granted the new orchestra, the new repertoire, and above all the new demands of the job in terms of production and management. Familiar with the advances of Spohr, Weber, and the others only, so far as I can tell, by reputation, he was left to work out the rudiments of effective conducting technique for himself—much as, for that matter, he had worked out the rudiments of composition for himself.

Like the composer who first writes a text because he cannot find an ideal librettist and then sees that he is himself that librettist, Berlioz virtually stumbled on the advantages of a composer's conducting his own works. "Unhappy composers!" he writes: "Learn to conduct [for] yourselves . . . for conductors, never forget, are the most dangerous of all your interpreters."[10] The danger to music posed by poor conductors is a theme that runs throughout his writings. The *Mémoires* argue: "We often complain of there being so few good singers, but good conductors are rarer still and in the great majority of cases far more necessary and potentially dangerous to the composer."[11] The conducting treatise opens with a warning to the same effect.

Only in the matter of conducting (and not, I think, in his composition) does Berlioz's lack of virtuosity on an orchestral instrument appear to distinguish him from the competition—and for the better. It seems not to have occurred to him that this experience *should* be a prerequisite for conducting; indeed, his own orientation to the job tended to give him a useful distance from the day-to-day trials of instrumentalists, thereby freeing his imagination for more important ruminations on effective leadership—and leaving him time for detailed analysis of full scores.

The 1839 performances of *Roméo et Juliette* were the most demanding on his conducting skills thus far, and their great success marks the progress from tenuous first steps in conducting to a lifelong mastery of and passion for it. Charles Hallé attended the rehearsals for *Roméo et Juliette,* where he admired Berlioz's imperial control of the orchestra during the long gestation of the work—a control that he said "resulted in a magnificent performance, stirring the public to enthusiasm."[12] From then on, Berlioz was praised, imitated, and occasionally ridiculed as much for his conducting as for his composition.

His conducting career flourished in the 1840s with the foreign concert tours and reached its pinnacle in the spring of 1852 with the London performances of Beethoven's Ninth, which apparently taught the work for the first time to the English public. During these tours he mastered the business of the traveling conductor, learning, as I have noted, to carry along double copies of the difficult works so that they could be performed in one city and rehearsed in another simultaneously. He supervised, often while en route, the production of elegant lithographed and engraved parts for his works, and put them directly to use for performances (as, for example, in the case of *La Fuite en Egypte* in 1854). He studied and admired the conducting of many of his contemporaries—Mendelssohn, Otto Nicolai, Lindpainter, and Reissiger, among others—and his conducting style, in turn, was embraced by a new generation of European conductors: Seghers and George-Hainl in France, for example, and Adolphe Samuel in Brussels. Nearly all the Parisian conductors after Habeneck played under Berlioz's baton, most of them repeatedly.

In Paris, Berlioz's most substantive exposure as conductor came during his seasons with the Société Philharmonique in 1850 and 1851, and it is in the course of those that he offered his most interesting repertoire.

*O*f all performance practices, the nature of a conductor's conducting may be the most difficult to document. Much of Berlioz's genuinely significant conducting must have been done at rehearsals and away from public scrutiny. Orchestral musicians are not, by and large, remembered for their written memoirs of their leaders, and the daily press of the era was not much interested in describing precisely what conductors did. (The constitution of the Société des Concerts specifies the privileges of the conductor, but so indirectly as to be positively tantalizing: "He will direct the performance and will be the only one to mark the beat.")[13] The documentary evidence of how Berlioz conducted is limited to one photograph, a silhouette, some lithographs, and a few cartoons; a few eyewitness accounts; and a half-dozen batons, including ornamental and ceremonial cudgels never intended for concert use.

The evidence shows, primarily, that Berlioz conducted in what we now conceive to be the ordinary fashion, with baton and full score, and right-handed. (The baton is in his left hand in two of the lithographs, but this has to do with the mirror images involved in the process of engraving.) He stood on a podium, often in the midst of the performing force, and generally seems to have been constrained in posture by the near-perpendicular design of the music rack. The pictorial sources and the eyewitnesses agree on one point in particular: his arresting sense of command.

The baton, according to Berlioz's conducting treatise, should be about half a meter long—a shade over 19½ inches, compared to the conventional

Mais si au milieu d'un morceau d'un mouvement lent, est introduite une forme nouvelle dont le mouvement est vif, et si le compositeur, soit pour rendre plus facile l'exécution du mouvement vif, soit parcequ'il était impossible d'écrire autrement, a adopté pour ce nouveau mouvement la mesure brève qui y correspond, il peut alors y avoir deux et même trois mesures brèves superposées à une mesure lente.

La tâche du chef est de faire marcher et de maintenir ensemble ces mesures diverses en nombre inégal et ces mouvements dissemblables. Il y parvient dans l'exemple précédent en commençant à diviser les temps dès la mesure Andante N.º 1 qui précède l'entrée de l'Allegro à $\frac{6}{8}$, et en continuant à les diviser ensuite, mais en ayant soin de marquer encore davantage cette division. Les exécutants de l'allegro à $\frac{6}{8}$ comprennent alors que les deux gestes du chef représentent les deux temps de leur petite mesure, et les exécutants de l'Andante que ces deux mêmes gestes ne représentent pour eux qu'un temps divisé de leur grande mesure

Ceci, on le voit, est assez simple au fond, parceque la division de la petite mesure et les subdivisions de la grande concordent entre elles. L'exemple suivant où une mesure lente est superposée à deux mesures brèves, sans que cette concordance existe, est plus scabreux.

Ici les trois mesures Allegro assaï qui précèdent l'Allegretto, se battent à deux temps simples comme à l'ordinaire. Au moment où commence l'Allegretto, dont la mesure est le double de la précédente et de celle que conservent les Altos le chef marque deux temps divisés pour la grande mesure, par deux gestes inégaux en bas et par deux autres en haut:

Les deux grands gestes divisent par le milieu la grande mesure et en font comprendre la valeur aux hautbois, sans contrarier les Altos qui conservent le mouvement vif, à cause du petit geste qui divise aussi par le milieu leur petite mesure. Dès la mesure N.º 3 il cesse de diviser ainsi la grande mesure par quatre, à cause du rhythme ternaire de la mélodie à $\frac{6}{8}$ que cette division contrarie. Il se borne alors à marquer les deux temps de la grande mesure. et les Altos déjà lancés dans leur rhythme rapide le continuent sans peine, comprenant bien que chaque mouvement du bâton conducteur marque seulement le commencement de leur petite mesure.

946

FIGURE 9.2 Conducting patterns from *Le Chef d'orchestre* (Paris: Schonenberger, [1855]). The second excerpt shows the troublesome metric modulation in the third movement of *Harold en Italie*.

14 inches of the present. It is a simple instrument, of "heavy oak," he said to Mendelssohn, and "rough-hewn." Berlioz seems to have used a baton from the beginning: he mentions one in the description of his 1827 debut.

He was apparently flamboyant on the podium, leaping hither and yon, yet nearly every account of his "energy"—the word most frequently associated with his leadership—also mentions control. Anton Seidl, in a rather questionable account, writes: "Now he was high in the air, then under the music rack; now he turned to the bass drum, then he was coaxing the flutist."[14] Spontini admonished Berlioz for his conducting at the concert of 19 November 1843: the performance would have been equally good, he writes, "with signals from a conductor's baton *not white* and a foot *shorter,* which would then circumscribe in its rotations a narrower and shorter space, and would be less fatiguing for your arm, your head, and your body." This would have made his "excessively varied motions more certain, more precise, and clearer." Yet according to Rimsky-Korsakov, his gestures "were simple, clean, [and] beautiful"; and E.-M.-E. Deldevez writes that "Berlioz himself argues for small gestures, since they are done so quickly."[15]

Berlioz seems to have been studiously unpretentious in costume—a simple frock coat and perpetually tousled hair were his uniform—and manner. He acknowledged the public as little as possible, feeling that bows provoked unwarranted applause. "He was the most perfect conductor that I ever set eyes upon, one who held absolute sway over his troops, and played on them as a pianist upon the keyboard," writes Charles Hallé.[16]

It was this very image of playing *upon* the orchestra, as it were, that so intrigued Berlioz. (Deldevez, incidentally, applied the same image to Habeneck.) "How well I conducted," says Berlioz of the performance of *Roméo et Juliette* in St. Petersburg in 1847. "How well I played upon the orchestra."[17]

His tempi were usually spirited, and they were always flexible. "I do not wish to say that [the conductor] must imitate the mathematical regularity of the metronome," he writes in the conducting treatise; "music played in such a manner would be of glacial rigidity." Wagner, however, says Berlioz ignored metronome marks, and Saint-Saëns implies that he ignored his own tempo indications. Berlioz's Beethoven was correct to the point of seeming to some, including Wagner, austere and cold. Yet Moscheles, who began the evening with a need to be convinced, writes of the 1852 Weimar concerts that "Berlioz's conducting inspired the orchestra with fire and enthusiasm; he carried everything as it were by storm."[18]

He saw the many roles of the *chef d'orchestre* as inseparable: "conducteur–instructeur–organisateur" are terms he tends to summon in the same breath, and in *Les Grotesques de la musique* he likens the job to being captain of a ship. When he admires conductors, it is invariably for their combination of organization, intelligence, and keen rhythm—and it stands to reason that what he admired in others he strove for in himself. He dismisses poor conductors either for their lack of feeling or for their stupidity. One Russian conductor he simply calls "an oyster"; Wagner, he says, "conducts, in fact, *in a free style,* as Klindworth plays the piano," which he had described earlier in the same letter as "like dancing on a slack wire for an hour."[19] Berlioz admired Wagner, at least at first, but later removed a complimentary remark about his conducting from the final version of the *Voyage musical.*

Reminiscing about his work in 1827 as conductor of his own Mass at St.-Eustache, Berlioz inadvertently summarizes his view of the craft:

> Yet how far I was from possessing the many varied qualities—precision, flexibility, sensitivity, intensity, presence of mind, combined with an indefinable instinct—that go to make a really good conductor, and how much time and experience and heart-searching have I since put into acquiring two or three of them.[20]

"Quel orchestre! quelle précision! quel ensemble!" he once remarked,[21] and this is typical of his feelings for competent instrumentalists. He was careful of their feelings as well; the correspondence includes dozens of notes written to assuage wounded egos. His natural didactic skills were useful when it came to introducing orchestral players to difficult new music in a few rehearsals; several observers remark on the confidence he imparted to his musicians. Sympathetic to their goals and protective of their needs, Berlioz was a step closer to being their advocate than the more class-conscious Parisian *chefs* who insisted on aristocratic reserve and distance from their players. The players seem to have returned the affection, often playing for him better than for others—though the Société des Concerts would never elect him their permanent *chef.* Berlioz was as proud of his conducting abilities as of any other accomplishment of his career: "I can direct an orchestra," he writes, "and give it life."[22]

Conducting was for Berlioz a life-sustaining proposition. He found that he was nearly always healthy when he conducted. He missed few engagements because of illness, though on several occasions he conducted while unwell. The "uplifting fatigue" of long rehearsals sustained him through the rigors of the most difficult performance. He would gladly, he said toward the end, conduct every day of his life.

*I*t is no coincidence that both Kastner and Berlioz added remarks on the art of conducting to revised editions of their orchestration treatises. Virtually nothing had so far been written about the trade, and by midcentury it had come of age, such that there was widespread interest in the observations of accomplished conductors. Though they both came to use the term *conducteur,* which has never been widely adopted in France, Berlioz and Kastner took radically different positions on the qualities to be expected of the ideal musical director. At issue was the question of the *chef d'orchestre–compositeur* versus the *chef d'orchestre–violoniste*.

The election in 1860 of Théophile Tilmant to succeed Girard at the Société des Concerts was deemed, with some justification, the triumph of the *chef d'orchestre–violoniste* over the *chef d'orchestre–compositeur*. Deldevez, George-Hainl's successor, as late as 1878 wrote a powerful conducting treatise in the course of which he argues that "the violin is the natural instrument of the conductor" and attacks Berlioz's advocacy of the baton as "naive, elementary [and] insufficient by comparison with the countless resources at the disposal of the violinist-[conductor]."[23] That view held sway for most of Berlioz's lifetime. It is the main reason Berlioz was never seriously considered for a major conducting post in France. Candidates for the succession were traditionally to be found within the orchestra, and the players (whose position Kastner argued) suspected the motives of the composer with a baton. And indeed Berlioz wielded his baton largely in service of his own works: as far as the work of others is concerned, though circumstances led him to master what was by the end of his life a considerable repertoire, when left to his own devices he would always return to a corpus of perhaps two dozen works by Beethoven, Weber, Gluck, and his other favorites. More fundamentally, his concept of composer-conductor was doomed by the demands of the modern styles on both performer and composer. The virtuoso professional conductor was, on the whole, more suited to the task and certainly more suited to the fancy of the time.

*H*is travels afforded Berlioz exposure to a wide variety of performance spaces: hippodromes and riding schools, assembly halls, proscenium theaters and opera houses, and now and then a proper concert hall. Having amassed copious experience with such rooms and having tried any number of solutions to the problems he found there, he began in the 1840s to develop systematic ideas about the most effective placement of the performing force and committed his notions to print with increasing frequency. Here, too, he was witness to the forging of traditions that continue to govern practice today. Every performance custom from the number of players to the distribution of parts in a chorus—not to mention the ever-vexing issue of where to put both an orchestra and a chorus—was subject to great variation from city to city. His observations on performing *Roméo et Juliette* take the differing practices of the major European halls into account, mentioning many of them by name. The *Traité d'instrumentation* and the later conducting treatise devote similar attention to this matter of orchestral placement.[24]

Berlioz argues that the ideal arrangement of an orchestra is in a semicircle, with the back rows raised on platforms or risers. (His concert preparations regularly involved a staggering amount of carpentry. It is a tribute to French *métier* that there was, so far as I know, no accident with any of the makeshift amphitheaters he erected.) The semicircular deployment was relatively unusual for the time; the Conservatoire, for example, had lateral bleachers, which he disliked. The violin sections occupied the forestage, facing one another, with violas between. Cellos and contrabasses were arranged behind the second violins; woodwind and horns, behind the firsts, as in some modern opera pits. The brasses and percussion were in the back rows at the center; harps were always in the foreground. With his back to the public, the conductor stood close to the desks of his principal strings, in what has since become the customary position.

Berlioz tried a number of different arrangements for the chorus, usually with the women seated in the front rows and the men standing behind them. Often platforms for the chorus were built down in tiers from the theater stage over the orchestra pit. For control by a single conductor, these would be arranged in a wedge, so that the singers, by slightly turning their heads, could see his baton. Most often, however, Berlioz engaged assisting conductors to stand in front of the chorus and follow his gestures. This practice of placing the choral force in front of and below the orchestra, though uncomfortable for musicians of today, lends both the timbre and the text of the singers a stunning presence, notably in such movements as the finale of *Roméo et Juliette*.

A Berlioz concert presupposed a good deal of moving about on stage. The chorus, for example, was expected to leave when not needed, so that "this large number of human bodies might not detract from the immensity of the instrumental force";[25] the same was true of the harpists. In *Roméo et Juliette* the appearance of the chorus of Montagus at the very end is part of the dramatic effect, and likewise in *Faust* the children are not to enter until the closing tableau. Berlioz calls for offstage players in all three dramatic symphonies, and in each case the players leave the stage during the performance and later return.

His concern for proper deployment of performing force is reflected in the detailed specifications of the published scores. The numbers he requires tend to vary, but there are some constants. Less than four bassoons will not do for a large Berlioz work, for instance, and one properly needs two cornets and two trumpets. Most of Berlioz's music requires just over 100 in the orchestra and a chorus of 150 to 200 distributed in equal parts among women, tenors, and basses.

Outside Paris it was often necessary to replace the harp with a piano, or find an alternative for the English horn or for a feeble tenor trombone soloist who could not manage the *Symphonie funèbre;* some of these solutions are proposed in both the published scores and the parts, suggesting that Berlioz was not particularly troubled by necessity's sometimes capricious demands. The published editions are mindful of the particular needs of the conductor as well, with tempo relationships carefully explained, as at the end of the serenade in *Harold,* and admonitions on countless other details of performance. A note in the score of *Roméo et Juliette,* for example, tells the conductor that the antique cymbals for *Queen Mab* may be rented from Brandus's shop.

He had, too, a flair for summoning armies to delight his public. Concern for the public and its perceptions was never far from the center of Berlioz's thought; it lay behind, for example, his preoccupation with programs and narrative. He often grumbled of them, as when he began the long epigraph before the scene at Capulet's tomb with the remark "The public has no imagination." But it was for the public, after all, that the concerts of 1,200 were envisaged and performed, the public who gave him his triumphs, with few enough interruptions, year after year.

*B*erlioz's orchestration treatise was not the first important one of the era: Georges Kastner's *Traité général d'instrumentation* (1837; revised in 1844) and *Cours d'instrumentation* (1839; revised in 1844), a companion volume designed to show how instrumental forces might be combined, have that distinction. Moreover, Kastner's work, examined and certified by the Institute and put directly to use in classes at the Conservatoire, had official imprimatur. Kastner and Berlioz follow remarkably similar strategies, basing their observations on full pages of engraved score, for which in several cases the same plates were used: it is almost as though Berlioz were attempting to outdo Kastner at his own conception. It was Berlioz's book that became the benchmark of the genre, partly because of his name and reputation and partly owing to his success in promoting foreign translations. The treatise, which remained in more or less continuous print during his lifetime, was never bettered, but simply went out of date.[26] It was Berlioz's love of the orchestra and feeling that it was generally misused, added to his unquenchable curiosity, that led to this maze of tables, technical observations, score pages, and suggestions of what and what not to do. The plan of the *Traité* is simple enough: the instruments are considered one after another by family, with their ranges and other specifications, observations on their most effective use, and nearly always an example of good usage from the hand of a great master. Berlioz is modest to the point of archness when he cites his own works, speaking of the *Fantastique* as "a certain symphony" and referring to the work of "one composer, in a mass"—that is, his own Requiem.[27]

The first edition of the *Traité* predates most of his published scores; therefore several of the examples represent first engravings. (Kastner's treatise had included examples from the Requiem and *Roméo et Juliette,* the first passages of those works ever to be published in full score.) I doubt if before this time Berlioz's larger scores had been seen by more than several dozen people: these pages certainly introduced the musical world at large to the appearance of his music.

To musicians of the period, especially provincials intrigued and perplexed by the latest innovations even as they conducted plainchant to the accompaniment of serpent and strings, the treatise was most important for its consideration of the newer instruments: the E♭ clarinet, the ophicleide (a French product of the 1820s), valved brass, harps, percussion, and the like. To modern eyes the more important feature is the distinction Berlioz draws between instrumentation, the art of correctly and effectively manipulating the individual orchestral instruments, and orchestration, the art of treating the aggregation as a unified ensemble and creating beauty in terms of that conception. The distinguished treatment of color, voicing, and registration in orchestral music is held to be the mark of special genius; the rest, says Berlioz, is simple craft.

The *Traité* is written in a rather dry, academic style, though occasionally it slips into Berlioz's more familiar modes of expression, as in this passage:

> Viola-players were always taken from among the refuse of violinists. When a musician found himself incapable of creditably filling the place of violinist, he took refuge among the violas. Hence it arose that the viola performers knew neither how to play the violin nor the viola. It must even be admitted that, at the present time, this prejudice against the viola part is not altogether destroyed; and that there are still, in the best orchestras, many viola-players who are not more proficient on that instrument than on the violin. But the mischief resulting from forbearance towards them is daily becoming more felt; and, little by little, the viola will, like other instruments, be confided only to clever hands.[28]

The second edition of the *Traité* adds, in addition to the conducting treatise, treatments of the saxhorns, Alexandre's *orgue melodium,* and the other keyboard instruments of the new generation. If there is an overriding theme of the *Traité*, it is that the new instruments must first be welcomed, then experimented with, and finally used as appropriate to the ends of art music. Each of the two editions captures a moment in what is doubtless the most dramatic half-century in the evolution of the orchestra.

In the *Traité* Berlioz was of course speaking largely from personal experience. The organ pieces he wrote for Alexandre and the *Chant sacré* for Sax instruments are, however, only curiosities, merely indications of his flush of interest in the new inventions. It is where he takes his own advice and uses new instruments to dramatic ends that his work with orchestral sonority becomes seminal. What he had already done with the E♭ clarinet, English horns, cornets, percussion, and harp in the period of aggressive experimentation, say 1824 to 1837, he was now prepared to do with these later inventions, but with more assurance and dignity. The small harmonium organ finds its most significant use in *L'Enfance du Christ*, where, with eerie, distant sonority it accompanies the offstage celestial chorus. A Sax instrument makes its first appearance after the 1843 demonstration in the Te Deum, where Berlioz calls for a single saxhorn *suraigu;* in *Les Troyens* he

FIGURE 9.3
Tenor saxhorn,
designed by Adolphe Sax
and made in France,
mid-nineteenth century.

requires a double quartet of saxhorns and a saxhorn *suraigu* for the *Marche troyenne* and entry of the Trojan horse (no. 11); and in the Hunt and Storm he writes a colloquy of hunting calls for a quartet of saxhorns. In the postscript to the *Mémoires,* in fact, Berlioz reacts to criticism of his "excessive use of Sax's instruments" with the not-quite-accurate claim that they were used only in one scene of *La Prise de Troie,* "of which no one has yet seen a note." Berlioz called for a saxophone only once, in the unusual (and unpreserved) setting of the *Chant sacré.*

Another new sound in the Berlioz orchestra of the 1840s and 1850s was that of the bass tuba, an instrument whose timbral superiority over the ophicleide must have become clear to him during the course of his German concerts. When, in the 1840s, his major works of the 1830s were published, he simply renamed the original ophicleide parts "ophicleide or tuba," without changing their texts; *Faust,* the Te Deum, the later editions of the Requiem, and *L'Impériale*—his Napoleonic cantata of the early 1854—call for ophicleide *and* tuba, with, in the Te Deum, the addition of lower octaves for the tuba. This interest in tubas was a logical outgrowth of his interest in trombones, which stemmed from his interest in Gluck. He experimented, for example, with the alto valved trombone and was often to be found worrying about fatigue in trombone players.

During his Russian journey and more especially his visits to London, he became intrigued by the question of how to use a pipe organ in an "architectural" work. It was a natural issue to confront: the building of the century's colossal instruments was in full swing, and there were fine players and a good repertoire in both France and England. In France, however, the pipe organ was nearly always to be found at the rear of the church; thus fashioning such an arrangement presupposed careful working-out of antiphonal principles. Berlioz gradually developed a theory of the matter and put it to work in the Te Deum. To Saint-Saëns, however, would be left the distinction of first working the organ into a true symphonic composition.

By the same token, Berlioz's ongoing concern for choral textures led him to seek out and study the practices of the choirs he encountered along his way. He was most moved by the noble sonorities of the Russian imperial choir, a smallish group of eighty males singing *a cappella,* but the effect he

FIGURE 9.4
Ophicleide. French,
mid-nineteenth century.

put to use in both *Faust* and the Te Deum was that of the massed unison children's chorus added for emphasis to the prevailing orchestra-and-choral texture. This approach appears to have been born of his attendance at a Berlin performance of J. S. Bach's St. Matthew Passion, with its great opening chorus with *soprano in ripieno,* and a concert in St. Paul's Cathedral in London where a vast chorus of orphans sang the Old Hundredth. In France, the flourishing Orphéon movement had other implications for his choral writing. He adapted the broad, strophic style favored by these ensembles for the *Hymne à la France* and *L'Impériale* and a number of shorter compositions such as *Le Temple universel.* What is perhaps most interesting about the choral writing of the 1840s and 1850s is Berlioz's gradual adoption of the four-part style. *L'Enfance du Christ* is almost entirely in four-part textures; *Les Troyens* and *Béatrice et Bénédict* mingle the new style with the old six-part sonorities.

FIGURE 9.5
Pavillon chinois.
German, nineteenth
century.

Not all of Berlioz's orchestrational tactics hit their mark. But the fizzles were minimal compared to the masterly successes: the low F♭ for a female voice in *Le Spectre de la rose,* the distant bass drum strokes in the *Rákóczy,* the castanets in *Zaïde,* the antique percussion in *Les Troyens.* These are Weberesque touches, on the whole, not Beethovenian ones.

*J*n 1846, Berlioz was so firmly established at the *Journal des Débats,* and the power of the *Débats* was so strong, that not even the 1848 Revolution, with all its devastating effects on newspapermen, could diminish his stature. No other music critic in Paris approached Berlioz in influence or importance, or had so many knowledgeable readers. Everybody knew what he thought of things.

Yet to its author the task of the criticism was fast losing its appeal. The great flights of critical attention to Gluck, Beethoven, Rossini, and even Meyerbeer were over. From time to time, now, some jewel of new music attracts his attention—the best article of his wandering years was on Meyerbeer's *Le Prophète* in 1849, and of his last years was the treatment of Wagner in Paris from 1861—but otherwise it was the *grotesquerie*s of musicians and their craft that caught his eye. These he ridiculed: a consulting service for composers, for instance, and a method for tuning without recourse to the ear. But in general there was nothing to get one's teeth into, just as he complained. And every autumn it began again.

The great majority of Berlioz's criticism is concerned with new theatrical productions, most of which were ephemeral. Here his approach is formulaic: he first assesses the dramatic strength of the libretto, then evaluates the composer's success at setting that text to music. The dominant theme of this portion of his work is the need for unity of dramatic purpose built from materials—scenic elements, numbers, voices both human and instrumental, movement, and dynamic expression—of the richest variety. "Variety wisely ordered," he wrote, "is the soul of music."[29]

Certain practices, many of them all but universal, were sure to set him off. He disliked even a hint that a work was parodying serious feelings or purposes. Any flashy device he suspected of lacking motivation earned his scorn; one of the things he liked least was the unwarranted introduction of low brass and percussion. (By extension he poked fun at Mozart's use of a single trombone in the Requiem, where he would have found a hundred too few.) His horror of unwarranted decoration by singers was not so different from that of many another composer. What was unusual was his memory of the specifics of their sins: an added trill, a roulade, a superfluous cadenza were peccadilloes he was pleased to remember in print long after their perpetrators had forgotten them. His objections lay in any hindrance to the fusion of music and poetry, his highest ideal. "Their power is doubled when they express a passion, a lovely sentiment . . . The two arts reinforce each other."[30]

Berlioz's appreciation for Rossini was selective, and even in the case of composers he genuinely admired, like Meyerbeer, he felt free to voice strong reservations. He was guarded on the subject of Mozart, in part because until midway through his life he had seen only a bastard *Zauberflöte*.

Berlioz's understanding of the history of his art, a field then in gangly adolescence, was spotty. Though conversant with the efforts of Fétis, Bottée de Toulmon, and the other French-speaking historians quietly establishing a remarkable body of scholarship, Berlioz shared with his circle a general confusion and much misinformation about the musical practice of earlier times. Anything before the Revolution of 1789 was held to be antique (except, of course, for Gluck), and he had little sense of how the music of earlier times differed by century or nation. (Le Sueur's passionate but flabby notions of music history may well have had something to do with the flaws in his own conception.) His curiosity was undaunted, however, and he willingly participated, for example, in the fads for Palestrina and Clari. He programmed old music when he could, and as the learned tomes of music history were published, he reviewed them favorably in his columns. What he knew of Bach, Handel, and Lully seems grossly limited by modern standards—he thought Lully wrote *God Save the Queen*—and he cared little or nothing at all for the music of the *trouvères,* Machaut, or the Burgundians.

Yet to read his essays is inevitably to be struck with both his command of factual detail and the breadth of his concerns. Much of what he collected into his essays, especially in the case of Gluck, presupposes monumental study. On relatively recent history he was nearly always well informed. The spectrum of subjects that attracted his interest is, moreover, staggering, especially when he escaped from the limitations of the single-performance notice. He darted freely from the acoustic qualities of cast bells to the latest promise of electricity, the compositions of Stephen Heller, the biographies of Bortniansky and Glinka, and new treatises on the anatomy of the hand and the metaphysics of beauty.

His journalism is a sometimes idiosyncratic admixture of autobiography, analysis, and true criticism. It is liberally sprinkled with personal musings that typically begin: "I recall, not without feelings of tenderness" or "When I first came to Paris, in 1820 . . ." It is eclectic to the extent that conversations overheard in the lobby often made their way into his column the next day. His musical analysis, practiced without much by way of precedent, can be penetrating, as when he studies the last movement of Beethoven's Ninth. Here he revels in the chord structures, taking particular pleasure in the second fanfare, where he discovers that the pitches added in the string choir constitute a "terrifying" chord, F–A–C♯–E–G–B♭–D, embracing all the pitches of a minor scale.

And he was funny. In a civilization enamored of the *bon mot* and the *raconteur,* Berlioz was an aristocrat. His pet names are withering; Fétis, for example, he merrily calls the "boar of Brussels," and the guardian of Paris after the 1848 Revolution, a man who saw fit on one occasion to occupy the royal box at Versailles, he calls Marrast o. His review of Carafa's *La Grande Duchesse* reads, *in toto:* "Madame se meurt! Madame est morte!"[31] The puns are rampant: the need to service autograph collectors he considers an *albumination;* the reestablishment of Nestor Rocqueplan's administration at the Opéra is its *Nestoration;* much is made of the French *Ruinepublique.* Having landed himself in trouble for asking the students in *Faust* to sing of their sweethearts "Veni, vidi, vici," he went on to contrive any number of references to the fondness of the French for their spas—he was soon to become a celebrated spa figure himself—just so he could say: "Veni, vidi Vichy!"

Berlioz continued his journalism for just over fifteen more years, until late 1863. From the mid-1840s on, with a few exceptions, the essays of greatest interest originated not in Paris but from his experiences elsewhere. It is these, by and large, that he assembled for his books of the 1850s and 1860s: *Les Soirées de l'orchestre, Les Grotesques de la musique, A Travers Chants,* and of course the *Mémoires.* The long dispatches from Germany and Austria are matched by his vivid letters on Lyon and Marseille, on the inauguration of the railroad in Lille, and, later, on the spas of Plombières and Baden-Baden. These letters, titled variously "Diplomatic Correspondence," "Academic Correspondence," and "Dispatches of the Grand Army," became the main focus of his journalism.

*T*he life of the itinerant musician so hypnotically upturned his spirit, so conveniently offered escape from the tragedies of Harriet and Louis, that the cost in creative time lost seemed well worth paying. It was not that he was idle, but rather that composition of any sort came less often within the prevailing climate of frantic planning for the next step and constant attention to hotel accommodations and baggage. After the *Grande Symphonie funèbre et triomphale* and the *Nuits d'été* at the beginning of the decade, the great works simply came less often.

This is not to say that there was no fine composition between the *Symphonie funèbre* and *Faust.* Both overtures, *Le Carnaval romain* and *Le Corsaire,* are works of quality, as is the wonderful funeral march for the last scene of *Hamlet,* begun in 1844 and apparently not put to rest until 1848. *L'Invitation à la valse,* too, merits respect for its seemingly effortless crossing of medium (piano to full orchestra) and aptness for the ballet, not to mention its great popularity with the public.

For the most part, however, song was the one genre in which there was time to accomplish something memorable, despite the hectic schedule. The songs began, most of them, as works for specific occasions, and for that reason are rich in personal allusions and the more poignant for it. Because there was no end of appropriate occasions, most of the songs were orchestrated early on and put into the concert repertoire. In fact, it was two songs, *Zaïde* and *Le Chasseur danois,* that ended the compositional hiatus of 1842 to early 1844.

La Mort d'Ophélie, written in 1842 and drawn into the plans for the *Hamlet* production of 1844, is a work in the tradition of the Irish Melodies, very like *Hélène.* Legouvé's text, closely following Shakespeare, is Queen Gertrude's account in act IV of the death of fair Ophelia in the rippling brook, a garland of "dead men's fingers" in her hands, her lovely garment first lifting her up, then dragging her under. Berlioz's haunting lament is dominated by the refrain of repeated ah's, a sequence of appoggiatura figurations in a long fall of an octave and a half (ex. 9.1a). The melodic idiom is otherwise open-intervaled, natural-horn style, and in barcarole rhythms, and the watery accompaniment consists of simple undulations and arpeggiations in continuous sixteenth-note motion. The strophes are freely varied: bits and pieces of a countermelody peek through from time to time, but it is never quite complete. Berlioz expanded the one-line vocal part for a two-part women's chorus when he orchestrated *La Mort d'Ophélie,* probably for the Musical Shakespeare Night planned in London in 1848. (Though the plan was never seen through, one of the autographs carries the date "Londres, 4 Juillet 1848.")[32] What appears first to be an almost routine rendering in close-harmony thirds and sixths becomes strikingly beautiful at the exchange of sighs in the refrain, especially during the long dissolution at the end (9.1b); note the prominent ♭6 (E♭–F♭–E♭) cadential figure in the upper voice. Berlioz associated *La Mort d'Ophélie* with Harriet and her decline; the dedication to the countess Marie d'Agoult, herself facing a cruel separation, cannot be coincidental. It is also worth reviewing Delacroix's *La Mort d'Ophélie* of 1843 in conjunction with Berlioz's song: all this merely hints at the ongoing effect on French art of the performances of Harriet and her company in 1827.[33]

La Belle Isabeau, too, concerns a lovely young woman and is likewise in the developing strophes-and-refrain style. It was composed to a poem of Alexandre Dumas for piano, voice, and chorus, though the chorus part was deleted for publication of the song in a holiday album. The poem is a kind of ghost story told by an old wife during a terrible storm, a *conte pendant l'orage.* At the end of each verse the howling wind and rain assert themselves, and the woman exhorts her listeners to fall on their knees and pray to God (ex. 9.2). Isabeau's father, so the story goes, has confined her in a cell, away from her knight-lover. One evening, during a similar hurricane, the paladin appears at her door while her father is at prayer. "Come," says the knight, "we shall be back before dawn." With two *Erlkönig*-like lines, Dumas abruptly concludes his story:

Hélas son père encore
L'attend depuis ce jour.

(Since that day, alas, her father still awaits her.)

La Belle Isabeau is, in its turn, a song of the escape of lovers from their confinement. His liaison with Marie Recio preoccupied the composer as he read the proof, curiously admonishing the engraver "to print after correcting, but change nothing in either the title or the dedication."[34]

Both *Le Chasseur danois* and *Zaïde* are connected, at least in their orchestral versions, with the Vienna concerts of November and December 1845, as is the orchestrated *Chant sacré* from the *Neuf Mélodies irlandaises*. *Le Chasseur danois* had appeared in a holiday album at the close of 1844 and was hurriedly orchestrated for Vienna; *Zaïde* seems to have been composed especially for the Vienna concerts. Both are orchestrally rousing, the *Chasseur danois* in a rollicking, strophic $\frac{6}{8}$ with trombones, and the bolero with a continuous castanet part that appears in the piano reduction as well. Berlioz was justly proud of the evocative color of *Zaïde*, in which a young girl sings of Granada, Aladdin's palace, the court of sultans, and their shimmering pools; she begins to cry in thus remembering her homeland, and a handsome knight shows up to share her sorrow and presumably to lead her home again. The vocal writing is especially vivacious: not since Teresa's and Ascanio's *cavatines* had Berlioz written so brilliant a song for soprano, with fine passagework in the refrains and cadences with high B♭ at the end of the first and last strophes (ex. 9.3). *Zaïde* is *La Captive* of the middle period, oriental in the Hugo fashion, a spirited return to compositional life that whetted Berlioz's appetite for the sustained work of *Faust*.

The jewel of the orchestral song of the 1840s is surely *Absence*, composed to Gautier's text in perhaps 1840 and orchestrated for Marie in Dresden in February 1843. *Absence*, as both poem and piano-vocal song, was profound to begin with, but it is the orchestral setting that makes the song so haunting, so agonized in its longing. Berlioz's growing preoccupation with progressively detailed variation is here epitomized: note especially, at mm. 53–54, the rescoring of the last refrain to emphasize the A♯s (ex. 9.4). The orchestral crescendo surges toward "loin" and subsides again with the lingering clarinet line. This famous passage is marked by unorthodox part-writing and a blatant violation of the rules of the $\frac{6}{4}$ chord—between the $\frac{6}{4}$ at "loin" and the correct V–I resolution there are two full bars of prolongation, with a root-position tonic intervening—that raised eyebrows but also served in the long run to broaden the function of such chord patterns.[35] More significant even than the harmonic freedom is the panting parlando of the episodes, finely varied and with a prominently higher climax in the second verse than in the first;

a. Refrain in the piano version:

b. Refrain in the orchestral verson:

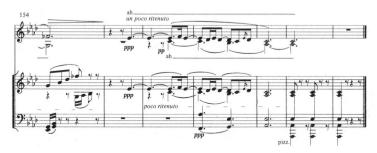

EXAMPLE 9.1 *La Mort d'Ophélie.*

the effect can be compared with a very similar and equally dramatic one in *Le Spectre de la rose* (ex. 9.5). *Absence* had a life of its own, separate from the rest of the *Nuits d'été*. The orchestral version was published in 1844, and there were some nine public performances before the appearance of the fully scored *Nuits d'été*—a cycle that was, so far as I know, never performed in its entirety.

Generally speaking the most prominent organizational concern of the music of the 1840s is with freely varied strophes-and-refrain forms. In the longer and more imaginative symphonic works there is a growing emphasis on the peroration, a summary drawing together of all that has come before, often called a coda but in truth anything but a tail. Often there is a Beethovenian dissolution, as in the spectacularly tragic close of the *Hamlet*

EXAMPLE 9.2 Refrain from *La Belle Isabeau*.

EXAMPLE 9.3 Refrain from *Zaïde*.

Mm. 1–4:

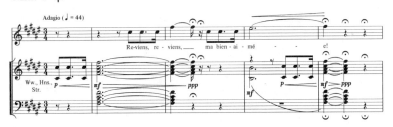

EXAMPLE 9.4 The orchestral *Absence*.

Mm. 53–56:

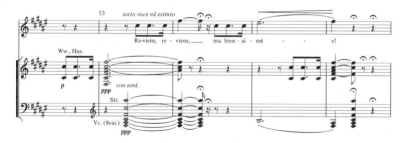

EXAMPLE 9.4 *(continued)*.

a. *Absence:*
Mm. 21–25:

b. *Le Spectre de la rose:*
Mm. 22–28:

Mm. 46–49:

EXAMPLE 9.5 Climaxes in *Absence* and *Le Spectre de la rose*.

march, closely associated in Berlioz's mind with the Napoleonic march in Beethoven's Third (ex. 9.6). Not one of the major works so far, incidentally, lacks a prominent march or procession, and this trend continues to the end: the *Rákóczy*, the nocturnal march in *L'Enfance du Christ*, the great processionals in *Les Troyens* and of course the *Marche troyenne*, and the wedding march in *Béatrice et Bénédict*.

*A*lthough Berlioz returns again and again to certain well-tested ideals, his assured style also incorporates a pronounced antipathy for repeating himself. Large-scale formal design, for one thing, is from *Faust* on quite different and fresh for each new work. The unusual phrase lengths, the experiments with rhythm and meter, and the splashes of apparently nonfunctional harmony continue unabated, but there are some new surprises in store.

The most substantial symphonic compositions of the years leading up to *Faust* are the two splendid overtures, *Le Carnaval romain* and *Le Corsaire*. They are similar in formal design and harmonic structure, both investigating soft, third-related key areas. Both evolved in stages, the one drawing on material from *Cellini* and the other progressing from *La Tour de Nice* to *Le Corsaire rouge* to the work we now know as *Le Corsaire*. Both are evocative settings, for *Le Corsaire* had to do with nautical brigandry.

Le Carnaval romain, which enjoyed a total of twenty-six public performances even before it was adopted in 1852 as the "second overture" for the Weimar and London productions of *Cellini*, was subtitled by its composer an *ouverture caractéristique*. The work bursts forth with the motto of the carnival saltarello for its initial gesture in A major, but this thrilling material is forced into C, after reaching the dominant, by the languorous English horn theme, a melody as characteristic of the Berlioz melodic style as the *idée fixe* (ex. 9.7a). Notice how effortlessly the consequent of this seemingly square phrase—the passage from *Cléopâtre*—is expanded, first by two measures, then by another four. The restatement lifts from C major up a third to the dominant E, with richer decoration, and there follows a third strophe in the tonic A, a brilliant display of canon at the quarter note, with rich string sonorities, and, in the winds and percussion, Mediterranean filigree (ex. 9.7b). This passage has a precedent in the first movement of *Harold en Italie*, where both the decorative style and the contrapuntal tactic are similar.

The main Allegro of the "exposition" follows *Cellini* virtually measure for measure (though transposed from F major to A major) for nearly two hundred measures, embracing the lengthy written-out repeat in the opera. The "development" consists of a brief fugato over an ostinato figure in the second violins, a pro forma departure and regrouping during which the English horn figure from the slow section asserts itself (ex. 9.7c). All this merely sets the stage for the peroration, where saltarello, canon, slow theme,

EXAMPLE 9.6 Dissolution of *Marche funèbre pour la dernière scène d'Hamlet.*

a. English horn solo, mm. 21–37:

EXAMPLE 9.7 *Le Carnaval romain.*

b. Mm. 53–56:

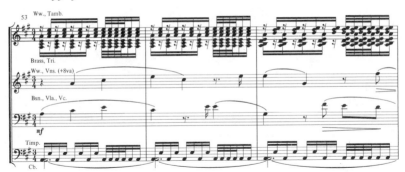

c. Mm. 304–18:

EXAMPLE 9.7 *(continued)*.

and the various phrasal and metric tricks work themselves together into a frenzy. The brass assume an increasingly prominent role, with a fantastic circle of dominant sevenths before the last arrival in tonic (mm. 428–39; the measures just previous, again, repeat material from *Cellini*). The final chord is sustained by woodwinds, as the brass sustain the last chord of the *Rákóczy* in a last salute. But it is the relentless speed of the work that lingers in the memory. Few orchestral pieces move so fast, in a $\frac{6}{8}$ of one tactus to the bar, for so long as does this one.

Le Corsaire, too, opens with a brash motto and passes by with relentless propulsion, though the duple meter gives it a very different sensation. The spasm of woodwinds at the beginning skews the meter to the right by an eighth note, in hemiola at two levels (ex. 9.8a). There follows a slow, lyric theme in A♭ major (♭VI) to be used again as contrastive material in the succeeding Allegro. From here on, the tonal progress is much as in the first

a. Mm. 6–9:

b. Mm. 91–106:

c. Mm. 374–400:

EXAMPLE 9.8 *Ouverture du Corsaire.*

movement of the *Fantastique,* passing through E♭, G, and B♭ and at length resettling in A♭ to prompt a ♭VI–V transition to C over a tonic timpani roll.

The main theme of the Allegro, a downward arpeggiation of the C-major tonic triad that merely wiggles right back to where it was, is, in view of the rich opening gambit, a curiously hollow idea, apparently chosen because it allows a rather good inversion (ex. 9.8b).[36] A vaguely contrastive second theme in G major (V) is followed by the lyric theme from the slow section in white-note values, with winds and strings exchanging their material over static E♭ harmonies. In effect the overture is all but "monothematic," for no other material has the significance of the C-major theme. The opening motto recapitulates (mm. 266–83), but this nod to sonata form is overshadowed forthwith by the long, stunning progress toward peroration, with scalar figures descending stepwise to reach V (ex. 9.8c). In *Le Corsaire* Berlioz gives up thematic interest for rhythmic ploy and contrapuntal device, rather as in the *Cellini* overture but with the spare, bare instrumental colors of the *Francs-Juges. Le Carnaval romain* is in that respect the more interesting work, for its capital combination of tunes with technical elan. Yet the lively metric character of *Le Corsaire* has made Berlioz's last concert overture as welcome in the concert hall as any of the others.

In certain respects the *Marche hongroise* is structurally similar to both *Le Carnaval romain* and *Le Corsaire.* The rousing fanfare fades into the march theme, which one first hears as from a distance. Berlioz proceeds methodically through successive strains until he reaches the "trio," where a dogfight-like wedge-and-canon figure in the brass bursts in (ex. 9.9). Here begins the summoning of forces to peroration: the celebrated hints of distant battle from the bass drum serve again less as a development than as a structural upbeat to the extravaganza at the end. The formal progress of all three works (themes—brief development—peroration) is thus much the same.

*F*aust was woven together in 1845 and 1846 out of the excellent and by then forgotten *Huit Scènes de Faust,* combined with settings inspired by the central European capitals and musical depictions of landscape, the images of *forêts* and *rochers* that had captivated him since his wanderings

EXAMPLE 9.9 Wedge and canon in *Marche hongroise.*

in the mountains of Italy. Of the late works, only *L'Enfance du Christ* has so multifaceted a genesis; *Les Troyens* and *Béatrice et Bénédict* each adhere to a more systematic plan. *Faust* was another of those masterpieces composed in passion during a period of great adventure, when musical ideas sprung from the most diverse wells were apt to be swept right into the work at hand.

If the rather dramatic introduction of a Hungarian March into the *Faust* legend seems a purposeful flaunting of the source, that was in the spirit of the conception, too. It was not to Goethe that Berlioz was trying to do particular justice, but to the more general concept of Romantic longing. The Germans would hold anyway—and did—that no Frenchman could possibly succeed with so Teutonic a legend. It may well be, however, that no other musical *Faust* so successfully captures Goethe's spirit. In any case the freedom of form and concept seems to have released Berlioz to pursue unfettered his affinities for musical tableau: no previous work of his fits so effortlessly together, goes by so quickly, or seems so lean and carefully trimmed. *La Damnation de Faust* can be taken on its own terms: derivative of its sources but not reliant on them; Germanic in tradition but French in musical style, a souvenir of the wandering years, yet equally the product of Romance language, reason, embellishment, and above all *paysage* and *panorama*—on the printed page, on canvas, and in the theater.

Berlioz justifies his views with an *avant-propos* in the printed score based on his experiences of the public reaction to his *Faust* thus far. His first remark is to the effect that by its very title, *La Damnation de Faust* calls attention to its difference from Goethe, where Faust is redeemed. The story of Faust, he says, is in the public domain. Far from "mutilating a monument," as his accusers declared he was doing, he was merely performing the usual operations musicians effect on their poetic sources—without which, he reminds us, we would be deprived of masterpieces by Mozart, Rossini, and Gluck. (As for the scene in Hungary, he confesses outright that he simply needed a motive to introduce the Hungarian March, which he already knew to be superb.) The *avant-propos* is as well-reasoned a defense of the process of forging a libretto as may be found in much longer treatments. It shows how sincerely Berlioz took the accusations of his lack of respect for Goethe's genius. That would have violated, on the contrary, "the religion of [his] artistic life."

In organizational concept, *Faust* is not so different from *Roméo et Juliette*: an evening's worth of symphonic music devoted to a single story. As in the dramatic symphonies, there is a series of related tableaux with relatively little connective tissue. Yet from the beginning Berlioz had intended to incorporate in *Faust* elements of opera; three of the soloists (Brander, Méphistophélès, and Marguerite) and the chorus were predetermined by the use of the *Huit Scènes*. To these Berlioz added solo arias for Faust, a love duet, and the three big scenes at the end of the story. For the orchestra alone there were the march and the two ballets (the *Ballet des sylphes* and the *Menuet des follets*), as well as the military music at the beginning of part III. For a time Berlioz considered his work an *opéra de concert,* but in its finished form *Faust* was not that at all, but rather a *légende dramatique,* a panoply of scenes assembled into four distinct parts.

Berlioz's version of the story centers on the three main characters: Faust, pretty obviously a self-portrait in his propensity to attacks of *isolement* and in his nostalgic regret at losing his innocence in pursuit of passion; a malevolent but seductive Méphistophélès; and the sultry Marguerite, who first creeps into the story after its midpoint, just before she becomes its major focus. Another significant character is Nature herself, and Berlioz's wonderful panoramas here often recall the spirit behind *Harold en Italie.*

Part I is Faust's, a treatment of his isolation, his splenetic uncertainty, his Harold-like detachment from the events that pass by his ken on the Hungarian plain. At the beginning of part II, back in his workroom and still suffering, he takes a drug that will either illuminate his mental process or kill him. His first vision is of an Easter procession, which attracts him in its naive piety. In a blaze of brass, Méphistophélès appears; he is, he says, the spirit of life, and he promises happiness, pleasure, and the fulfillment of one's most ardent desires. Faust, like Simple Simon, asks for a sample and is thereupon whisked to the fine scene in Auerbach's cellar. The drinking chorus is as merry as the one in *Cellini,* and Méphistophélès joins in with a song of his own, but Faust finds it all ignoble and vulgar. Méphistophélès thus transports him to a riverside grove inhabited by sylphs and gnomes of his acquaintance, and these induce in Faust hallucinations of Marguerite. Faust falls asleep; the sylphs dance their ballet. He wakes abruptly with visions of Marguerite and insists on being transported to her house. Outside her door students and soldiers cross paths, much as the Capulet youth do in the love scene of *Roméo et Juliette,* and go their separate ways singing of their exploits. In part III, Faust enters Marguerite's room and tries to absorb its atmosphere, then hides in the curtains as she enters and sings her wistful ballad of the king of Thule. From the street, Méphistophélès summons his will-o'-the-wisps, and together they enchant the surroundings. Marguerite discovers Faust, and they sing their one duo, "Ange adoré." Their song, Méphistophélès is pleased to observe, rouses the locals, who now call to Marguerite's mother that she is entertaining a gallant in her house. The act ends in confusion, with the lovers refusing to leave each other as the nosy townspeople knock at the door and Méphistophélès grows certain he is on the verge of success in his campaign.

Marguerite's ravishing *romance* of longing for Faust (see ex. 4.8d) begins part IV. Faust has gone to some locus of forest and cavern where, during his *Invocation à la nature,* he discovers in Nature the perfection for which he has so long been pining in life. Méphistophélès appears with the news that Marguerite has been imprisoned for murdering her mother, who has succumbed to the "innocent" draughts with which Marguerite intended merely to induce her to sleep through the lovers' trysts. To save Marguerite's life, Faust signs the parchment at last; the wild Ride to the Abyss follows, then the plunge into Pandemonium, and, finally, Marguerite's arrival and redemption in Heaven.

The sources for Berlioz's version of the story are quite varied, for in addition to Goethe's he had encountered any number of other Faust stories, extending to the most miscellaneous of melodramas. The eight scenes, spruced up and otherwise gently adapted, come from part I of Goethe's *Faust;* as I mentioned, these were the passages given in verse by Nerval. Certain ideas come from Goethe's part II, notably the imagery of Méphistophélès's *Voici des roses.* The other details appear to constitute a free assemblage of bits and pieces from the Faust stories in common circulation at the time. I suspect Berlioz knew only generally of Christopher Marlowe's *Doctor Faustus,* which was widely played in German translation and in which there is a fantastic voyage like the Ride to the Abyss. (The Wild Ride, of course, has dozens of exemplars in the Romantic lore.) He did know Spohr's *Faust,* the scenario of a Faust ballet by Heine, and Mendelssohn's *Die erste Walpurgisnacht,* of which he had heard the first performance. The idea of Marguerite's apotheosis was apparently an afterthought,[37] added to the libretto late in the process of composition.

The strong unity that informs *Faust* is imparted by recurring motives of orchestration, a pervasive tonality of D major inflected with B♭, and above all the most pronounced control of thematic foreshadowing, recall, and transformation that Berlioz ever practiced.[38] This foreshadowing is evident at the very beginning, where the pastoral calm of Faust's reveries is interrupted by presentiments of the *ronde des paysans* and military fanfares of the *Marche hongroise,* the latter a full forty pages before the march finally bursts forth (ex. 9.10). Méphistophélès first appears to a brilliant trombone figure with *Freischütz*-like exclamation point in the flutes and piccolos (ex. 9.11), an effect that nearly every observer from Saint-Saëns forward has thought one of Berlioz's most inspired strokes. (This figure is not fashioned from thin air, but rather is a gloss on the main melodic gesture of the *Chanson d'une puce,* which Berlioz had at hand when he came to set up Méphistophélès's first entry.) It occurs twice more, after the "Amen" fugue and at the beginning of the scene in Marguerite's room, to introduce Méphistophélès. His solo work, moreover, is nearly always supported by the deep brass, as in the rich trombone underpinning of his aria *Voici des roses.*

There are other motivic identities, too, as when Marguerite's first entry is foreshadowed by the opening figure from her aria *Le Roi de Thulé* (see ex. 4.8c) at the beginning of scene x; the same melody is heard again later, before the duo "Ange adoré," as a reminiscence.

Thematic transformation is practiced on much grander scale. Méphistophélès's silly serenade in part III—his "moral song, the better to mislead

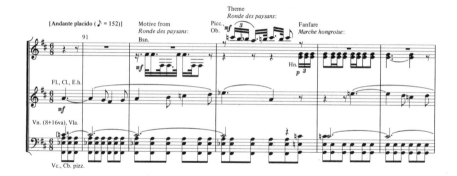

EXAMPLE 9.10 Foreshadowings in scene i of *La Damnation de Faust.*

EXAMPLE 9.11 Appearance of Méphistophélès in part II, scene v.

her"—is foreshadowed, for example, in the coda of the will-o'-the-wisps' sprightly minuet just before (ex. 9.12a; the order of composition is irrelevant to the effect, of course, but the autographs show that every case of musical foreshadowing was a retroactive adjustment: to be foreshadowed, that is, a passage must already have been composed).

Brander's tipsy song of a kitchen rat, roasted during its dying delirium, is followed by the drunken "Requiescat in pace, Amen," with the fugue subject drawn from the song of the rat (ex. 9.12b). The effect is tamer than it was meant to be—the fugue is too good—until the pedal point, where the parody becomes clear.

The most sustained essay in thematic transformation is in the scene by the Elbe, which commences with *Voici des roses,* a through-composed aria that, like Père Laurence's *Pauvres enfants,* is over just as the listener begins to swim in its beauty. The entire scene is made up of versions of the melody first fashioned for the chorus of sylphs (ex. 9.12c). The ballet, over a D pedal, serves as a long dissolution.

a. *Sérénade de Méphistophélès:*

Coda of the *Menuet des follets*:

b. *Chanson de Brander:*

Fugue sur le thème de la chanson de Brander:

c. *Chœur [Concert] de sylphes* (composed 1828–29):

Air de Méphistophélès:

Ballet des sylphes:

EXAMPLE 9.12 Thematic transformation in *Faust*.

Though *Faust* is not one of the works Berlioz terms "architectural," he brings his advanced sense of musical space to bear in a number of the scenes. When the paths of the soldiers and the rowdy university students cross, Berlioz composes a stylized *réunion des thèmes,* with the soldiers' march in $\frac{6}{8}$ and B♭ major, the students' Latin song in a modal D minor and $\frac{2}{4}$. Both texts celebrate women and the glories of seducing them, thus commenting indirectly on Faust and Marguerite, and the D-minor flavoring of the B♭ acts in some respects as the inverse of the dramatic inflection, at the very beginning of the work, of the D-major melody with a prominent B♭.[39]

Faust's signing of the old parchment, done in a trice, is followed by his and Méphistophélès's frantic ride, on two black steeds named Vortex and Giaour, to the abyss. This exceptional movement represents another masterly treatment of musical space. As Faust and Méphistophélès tear through the countryside with thundering hooves and an eerie oboe theme, we are presented with a succession of passing scenes: a litany of peasants at devotion by a roadside cross, quite similar to effects in *Harold* and *Cellini,* and a *Freischütz* world of hideous howling beasts, flapping night birds, and dancing skeletons. All this ends with Faust's great cry and plunge into the abyss, to the delighted cries of demons and the damned in their "infernal" language— *Ha! Irimiru Karabrao: Has! Has!* and so on. The idea of the language of the damned was first used in the "ancient Nordic" of the Chorus of Shades in the *Mélologue;* I think it is also a souvenir of the many languages Berlioz had heard around him but failed to understand in the months just preceding.

Faust concludes with another movement that dwells on issues of space, Marguerite's apotheosis in Heaven. All three of his celestial settings—this one, the Sanctus of the Requiem, and the final tableau of *L'Enfance du Christ*—share high-pitched consonance, slow, simple chord progressions; and hymn-like chorales. The rich key of D♭ is unique to the work. But Berlioz is more successful with wine-cellar scenes and the giddier happenings on this side of his pastel Heaven; I doubt that he spent much time, after the rustic Catholicism of his youth, considering what Paradise was like.

He spent a good deal of time, by contrast, considering rocky, cavernous landscapes, and Faust's *Invocation à la nature* is surely one of his most memorable accomplishments. It comes at the dramatic peak of the work, the Alexandrine text, which we know to be by the composer himself, embodying his most elemental feelings toward the world around him:

> Nature immense, impénétrable et fière,
> Toi seule donnes trêve à mon ennui sans fin;
> Sur ton sein tout puissant je sens moins ma misère,
> Je retrouve ma force, et je crois vivre enfin.
> Oui, soufflez, ouragans! criez, forêts profondes!
> Croulez, rochers! Torrents, précipitez vos ondes!
> A vos bruits souverains ma voix aime à s'unir.
> Forêts, rochers, torrents, je vous adore! Mondes
> Qui scintillez vers vous s'élance le désir

D'un cœur trop vaste et d'une âme altérée
D'un bonheur qui la fuit.

(Vast Nature, impenetrable, proud, you alone give pause to my endless boredom.
At your all-powerful breast I feel my misery the less; I regain my strength, and
think myself alive at last. Yes, blow hurricanes, cry, deep forests; crash down,
o rocks; waterfalls, let your waves tumble down. My voice desires to mingle
with your sovereign noise. Forests, rocks, waterfalls, I adore you! Glittering
worlds, toward you comes the desire of a heart too vast, of a longing soul, of
a fleeting happiness.)

The fifty-five bars are built over a chord progression that mutates almost
entirely by stepwise motion, beneath which is the ebb and flow of a surging
figure in the bass (ex. 9.13a). The movement is in C♯ minor, moving enhar-
monically through D♭ to allow a brilliant cadence in F major at "Je retrouve
ma force, et je crois vivre enfin." We know from a variety of sources that
this point was central to Berlioz's concept of *Faust*. (The pair of scrupulous
sketches for this movement in some respects opened up the entire field of
research into Berlioz's compositional processes.)[40] The carefully forged fluidity of this movement, symbolizing Nature's vast mysteries and perfections,
sets up with its surge into F major the last significant tumble of the work,
downward from F into B as Faust moves ever closer to the abyss. Note, too,
that this mystic relationship had introduced Méphistophélès's evocation (ex.
9.13b,c).

There is much more to the tonal relationships in *Faust* than can be
demonstrated here. That the work is principally in D, for example, is only
the most general point of reference. Within that framework, quite a number
of other identities come to prominence: the F major of Marguerite's scenes,
the plunge from C♯ minor through C minor to B major at the abyss, and the
hellish clash of B major and F major at the end (ex. 9.13c). The play of third
relationships, familiar from Berlioz's other recent works, dominates this
harmonic fabric as well. Finally, note the pervasive fugal textures in *Faust,*
where both parts I and II commence, for example, with elegant displays of
contrapuntal craft; the strong reliance on pedal points for stasis, looking
both backward to the Offertoire of the Requiem and forward to the septet
in *Les Troyens;* the artful stitching together of the seams between the movements. There is, in short, little question that Berlioz arrived in *Faust* at the
achievement of an altogether mature musical language.

La Damnation de Faust has nothing to lose from comparison with the
work of any composer anywhere in Europe during those years. It is concep-
tually superior to Wagner's *Tannhäuser* (1845) and Glinka's *Russlan and Ludmilla* (1842) and technically more secure than either; it makes Mendelssohn's
wonderful *Elijah* (1846) seem a relic of the distant past; its concision shames
Verdi's *Nabucco* (1842) and *Macbeth* (1847); and its sense of pace surpasses
that of every single product of the Paris stage for more than a decade. Yet
Faust, though not Berlioz's last major work, is his last forward-looking one.

a. Analysis of the *Invocation à la nature:*

Mm. 1–9:

Analysis of voice-leading:

Reduction:

Freely adapted from Julian Rushton, *The Musical Language of Berlioz* (Cambridge, 1983), pp. 244–52.

b. Harmonic progression from *Invocation* to *Pandaemonium:*

c. *Evocation de Méphistophélès:*

EXAMPLE 9.13 Tonal relationships in *Faust.*

Chapter Ten

The Paris Problem
(1847–52)

ith feelings bruised and purse emptied by the failure of *Faust*, Berlioz hurried to force the arrangements for his Russian trip into shape. He needed to be well established in St. Petersburg by the beginning of Lent, the traditional time for daily and sometimes twice-daily recitals by foreign virtuosi during the annual closure of the theaters. After his Russian appearances, when the ice had melted, he might sail for England or possibly return to Prague, searching for a city hospitable to his art. He took a brief holiday to hunt at his dentist's country house near Beauvais, then spent a month preparing with his copyist and other associates for his departure. Of particular urgency was contracting for a good German translation of *Faust;* because of the prevalence of German-speaking musicians in Russia, it had been agreed to do the texted works in that language. He took the other symphonies, too, all of them at last in published form, with the instrumental parts for *Roméo et Juliette* just reaching proof. He packed *Le Carnaval romain,* but none of the excerpts, songs, and arrangements that had filled his repertoire before. It is as though his specific intent, in this trip to recoup spiritual and financial standing, was to present only the major works, complete if possible: to reassure himself of their merit. Above all, Berlioz was anxious for the Russian nobles to hear the *Fantastique,* for it carried a dedication to the czar.

For capital, he had to borrow money and negotiate advances on his writings: 1,000 francs from the coffers of the *Journal des Débats,* thanks to the continuing largesse of the Bertins; 2,000 francs from the writer and publisher Pierre-Jules Hetzel, an advance against his memoirs of the trip (the advance was repaid; the Russian letters did not appear until 1855–56); 1,200 francs from Sax; and 1,200 francs from Ferdinand Friedland, an *amateur* Berlioz had met in Breslau and Prague and who made frequent visits to Paris. The spontaneous loan from Hetzel, whom he barely knew, touched him deeply: "He is one of those rare souls of the sort one is only too happy to find and which we artists appreciate better than anyone."[1] Just before leaving, he borrowed Balzac's greatcoat.

Marie was not told of the details. His instructions to Rocquemont—to have the wrapped performance material delivered to Desmarest and to send the leftover parts to Harriet in the rue Blanche—end with a plea for absolute secrecy: "I want to leave for Russia *alone*."[2] He apparently succeeded—though Marie joined him at the end, probably having taken the train to meet him in Berlin. The first mention of her being along is in a letter written from Berlin the following June, on the last leg of the return trip.

The trip began, as it was to continue, in the bitter cold. When he left Paris on 14 February, six inches of snow had accumulated. There was a stopover, possibly of two or three days, in Brussels, then a long wait in Tienen (that is, Tirlemont, between Brussels and Liège) for the railway to be cleared. The papers that week were filled with news of the snow, which had interrupted traffic and was beginning to cause shortages of vital supplies all over western Europe.

In Berlin, he stopped briefly to procure a letter of introduction from the king of Prussia to his sister, the czarina. (The king reminds his sister that they had already talked of Berlioz and that the *z* is pronounced; he writes partly in baby talk, referring to "bum-bum Berlioz," and signs his note "your faithful, fat Fritz.")[3] Berlioz proceeded eastward by postal coach and then, for the last four days and nights, by iron sled over rutted, frozen terrain, reaching St. Petersburg on 28 February. Visions of Napoleon's Russian campaign naturally dominated his thoughts.

On his arrival, Berlioz was whisked to the palace of the counts Wielhorsky for a musical *soirée* given by Count Michael. There he met his sponsors: Heinrich Romberg, music director of the Italian Opera; Alexei Feodorovich Lvov, a major general and chorus master of the imperial chapel; Alexander Mikhailovich Guedeonov, the intendant of the imperial theaters, likewise a general; and the German violinist and conductor Ludwig Maurer. Plans for his first concerts were confirmed on the spot, including the location, ticket prices, and probable performers.

Berlioz was but one of a long succession of composer-conductors and virtuoso instrumentalists to make the difficult winter journey to St. Petersburg. Liszt had already been twice; Schumann and his wife came the next year; Wagner would come in 1862. St. Petersburg was on the verge of a virtual explosion of musical accomplishments, much as Leipzig had been a decade before; so far the only well-known Russian composer of nationalist tendency was Glinka, though while he was there Berlioz met another avatar of Russian nationalism, Alexei Verstovsky. By the time Berlioz returned in 1867–68, Anton Rubinstein's Russian Musical Society and Conservatory were well established, with the Mighty Five—Cui, Balakirev, Borodin, Mussorgsky, and Rimsky-Korsakov—and Tchaikovsky launched on their careers. In this context, Berlioz's pair of visits to St. Petersburg, separated by two

FIGURE 10.1 St. Petersburg: the Imperial Theater. *L'Illustration,* 5 May 1849.

decades, can be seen as a most seminal legacy: the legend of Berlioz, and possibly much more than that, helped shape the golden age of Russian music. The time was ripe for precisely what he could offer. His conducting was admired, works were dedicated to him, his opinions were given a wide forum.

His sponsors lodged him in a private house on the Nevsky Prospect and in general treated him splendidly. The elegance of these surroundings greatly exceeded what he had found in the little principalities of Germany, or even in the court of the Prussian king. It suggested to him how royal France, now faded from glory, must once have been.

The orchestras were made up largely of foreigners. Berlioz noted among his performers three Russians, an Englishman, and a Frenchman—Dominique Tajan-Rogé, an old acquaintance from Paris; the rest were Germans. The musicians seemed excited by his presence, willing to expend extra effort on behalf of his music. He found the choruses to be splendid, superior, even, to his fine French ones.

The announcement he placed in the local newspapers rather exaggerated the success of the Paris *Faust:*

> M. Berlioz, who has just arrived in St. Petersburg, intends to give several concerts where he will offer major excerpts from his most important works, if it proves impossible to give them complete. Among the numerous musical works he would like to have us know is his latest composition, which sustained in Paris this winter such enthusiasm that the author, despite his being French, received an unaccustomed ovation. Artists and writers, chaired by Baron Taylor, gave a

banquet in his honor, and it was decided to gather by subscription a sum of money, soon completely raised, to cast a medal in memory of the first performance of this musical work.[4]

In St. Petersburg he was able to find a capable translator, one Minslaff (or Münzlaff), for the German text of *Faust.* Although not finished in time for the first Russian performances, Minslaff's translation was done shortly afterward, and it is the one that appears in the published scores.

The Berlioz concerts were given in the Assembly Hall of the Nobility, a traditional venue for events of the sort. The first, on 15 March, featured a bilingual performance of parts I and II of *Faust,* with the tenor Ricciardi singing in French and the noted bass Versing singing the role of Méphistophélès in German. Complementing the selections from *Faust* were Juliet's funeral procession and the Queen Mab scherzo (with the two local conductors, Romberg and Maurer, playing the antique cymbals) and *Le Carnaval romain.* At the end of the program, the imperial bandsmen joined the ensemble for the *Apothéose.*

At the intermission, fatigued and not looking his best, Berlioz answered a summons from Count Michael Wielhorsky to meet the Czarina Alexandra, formerly Princess Louise Charlotte of Prussia. Czar Nicholas I was suffering from gastritis and was unable to attend Berlioz's concert; it appears that he and Berlioz never met. Among the high nobility, Berlioz's closest contacts were with the czar's brothers, the grand dukes Alexander and Constantine.

The public was taken with the new works and called for encores of movements from *Faust* and the Queen Mab scherzo. Berlioz regretted that the published vocal scores of *Faust* had yet to appear, for they would have sold well to the Russian audiences.

The excitements of the first concert were repeated at the second, on 25 March, where the czar was represented by his three children, for whom the eldest, Marie, duchess of Leuchtenberg, acted as spokeswoman. When Berlioz remembered to inquire after the receipts, he discovered that a large profit had been cleared, something on the order of 15,000 francs.[5] The empress had sent a diamond ring and Duchess Marie a jeweled brooch, with a combined value of 600 rubles, or over 2,000 francs. In one stroke, Berlioz had recovered the money to pay back his debts and rebound from the Paris *Faust;* it may have been the most he ever earned from a single concert.

On 27 March, at the invitation of Grand Duke Alexander, he conducted the *Apothéose* at a festival to benefit the needy.

The other mandatory stop in Russia was, of course, Moscow. He left his St. Petersburg forces to prepare their full performance of *Roméo et Juliette* for the Imperial Theater and in early April made another cold journey by sleigh, inland to Moscow. The Lenten concerts there were offered by visiting artists in yet another Assembly Hall of the Nobility, where an ancient grand marshal, unable to grasp that Berlioz was a composer-conductor and not the usual virtuoso instrumentalist, refused to waive the traditional requirement of a private recital for the nobles. After prolonged negotiation, this obstacle was overcome by an exceptional ruling based on the visitor's apparent stupidity.

Rehearsals for the concert, to be built around parts I and II of *Faust,* were unusually painful. There was a language barrier for one thing, and for another the chorus appeared at their rehearsal without a pianist. Finally, the censors found offensive a passage from the students' chorus in *Faust:*

> Nobis subridente luna, per urbem quaerentes puellas eamus, ut cras fortunati Caesares dicamus: Veni, vidi, vici.

> (While the moon winks down on us, let us search the town for girls, so that tomorrow, like fortunate Caesars, we can say, "I came, I saw, I conquered.")

(This same passage was deemed unsavory in Germany, where the citizenry professed doubt that proper German students might ever be found carousing in such fashion.) For all that, the concert on 10 April failed to satiate its public, who clamored for another performance. Again a large fee was cleared, perhaps as much as 8,000 francs.[6]

It proved impossible, for lack of a suitable hall, to present a second concert, so Berlioz occupied the rest of his three weeks in Moscow with the usual tourism, viewing the Kremlin from without and slogging through streets made nearly impassable by the spring thaw. Everywhere there were reminders of the French defeat at the hands of the Russians: cannons captured from the Napoleonic legions, plaques and monuments commemorating the victory. There were courtesy calls to pay and musical establishments to visit; one evening he attended a complete performance of Glinka's *A Life for the Tsar,* conducted by Verstovsky.

In late April he returned to St. Petersburg, crossing the melting Volga this time by boat, in order to be on hand for the last rehearsals of *Roméo et Juliette.* Ernst having arrived in St. Petersburg, the first two movements of *Harold en Italie* were added to the program, which was to conclude with *Le Carnaval romain.* The gala performance on 5 May was repeated a week later, with part II of *Faust* in lieu of *Harold.*

Here it is worth leaving the description to Berlioz himself. He posted this account to Morel for insertion in the *Revue et Gazette musicale:*

Our St. Petersburg correspondent writes:
Berlioz has just returned from Moscow, where his music excited the most lively enthusiasm. We saw him day before yesterday in the great theater at the head of his admirable musical army. This solemn occasion was the most brilliant yet, more grandiose than any Berlioz has so far organized here. *Roméo et Juliette* was heard complete, along with the first two movements of *Harold.* The enormous room was filled, glittering with uniforms and jewels. The ovation accorded the composer upon his entry must have proved to him again how popular he has become in Russia. Through the entire evening the most sustained attention,

the frenetic applause, the encores called for by the whole audience—all these welcomed the performance of his colossal work in a rendition which was moreover flawless in every respect. Ernst played the viola solo in *Harold* in a style as simple as it was poetic and with the rarest of expression. Versing was Frère Lorenzo, Holland sang the scherzetto with chorus concerning Queen Mab, Mme Walcker sang the delicious *Strophes* from the prologue with soul and great purity of style. The choruses were particularly distinguished; the orchestra, under the direction of Berlioz, had already accustomed us to its ability to do marvelously. We noted the excellent manner with which the master had deployed his groups of voices and instruments. The orchestra was elevated on three risers on the stage. The soloists sang from the forestage; the fifteen voices in the prologue chorus, from a lower platform placed over the pit used by the orchestra in dramatic performances. To the left and right were found the two large choruses, Capulets and Montagues. The whole was of excellent tone quality and produced the most imposing sounds.[7]

This is typical of the many reports Berlioz placed in the Paris papers from abroad, glossing over the defeats—there is no mention of the rigors of Moscow, for example—to portray the most glamorous of victories. What it only hints at is the depth of his own response to the full *Roméo et Juliette*. Overcome with the work, he had to force himself to keep conducting it; during the final *serment*, he began to cry.

*J*t was no accident that Berlioz was traveling alone, nor that he would go by himself to London that fall, for he was longing to find a new romantic attachment—the kind of exalted love he had conceived for Harriet and which he had not so far enjoyed with Marie. In St. Petersburg he found to share his affections a member of the chorus, an artisan seamstress who knew the rudiments of five languages. They embarked on a "true if grotesque love," a *véritable grand amour poétique,* an affair that was "poetic, atrocious, and perfectly innocent" for "a young fool of forty."[8] They walked late at night through the streets of St. Petersburg, hand in hand, oblivious to their surroundings and not caring who might see them. They shed tears together over *Faust* and *Roméo et Juliette.*

The Russian visit ended in a swirl of parties and receptions. At one of these Berlioz met for the first time Carolyne, the Princess Sayn-Wittgenstein, only a few weeks after she had been captivated by Liszt in Kiev. She and Berlioz were, likewise, taken with each other, and the woman who by year's end would be Liszt's mistress remained over the years one of Berlioz's staunchest confidantes.

The memory of Russia that lingered longest in his mind's ear was the celestial sound of the imperial chapel choir: their strange sublime harmonies were precisely what he had hoped to hear in the Sistine Chapel nearly two decades before. He was invited there by the czarina for a private mass; the grave music of the Russian Orthodox ritual, stark and unaccompanied, left him trembling with emotion. In late 1852, when he submitted a plan for the organization of an imperial French chapel to the new emperor, Napoleon III, he based much of his vision on the possibility of recreating in Paris the sounds he had heard from "the best choir in the world": "the unbelievable power of emotion that lies in a mass of voices exercised in the imperial surroundings such art demands" governs his conception. The Te Deum, too, aims to achieve something of the Russian pomp, and in the *Soirées de l'orchestre* of the same period Berlioz remembers again his experiences in St. Petersburg:

> The eighty singers in their rich costume stood facing each other in two equal groups on either side of the altar. The basses were farthest from the center; in front of them were the tenors, and in front of these again the child sopranos and contraltos. Motionless, with downcast eyes, they all waited in profound silence for the time to begin, and at a sign doubtless made by one of the leading singers—imperceptible, however, to the spectator—and without anyone's having given the pitch or indicated the tempo, they intoned one of Bortniansky's biggest eight-part concertos. In this harmonic web there were complications of part-writing that seemed impossible, there were sighs, vague murmurs such as one sometimes hears in dreams, and from time to time accents that in their intensity resembled cries gripping the heart unawares, oppressing the breast, and catching the breath. Then it all died away in an incommensurable, misty, celestial decrescendo; one would have said it was a choir of angels rising from the earth and gradually vanishing into the empyrean.[9]

Lent was over, the sun had come out; the nobles would now leave St. Petersburg for their country estates. The love affair, the bittersweet associations provoked by *Roméo et Juliette,* the arrival of spring and its call to leave Russia—all these combined to thrust Berlioz into a state of deep melancholy. "The tone of his [recent] letter," wrote Liszt to Marie d'Agoult, "is as hopeless as a funeral knell: poor, great genius, at odds with three-quarters of the impossible."[10]

At a court concert to bid farewell to the bass Versing, Berlioz finally offered his *Symphonie fantastique* and bid his own farewells, amid rumors that the czar was soon to offer him an exalted post. Meanwhile, he had accepted the invitation of the king of Prussia to come to Berlin for a full production of *Faust,* so he would not return via Copenhagen and Hamburg as originally planned.

On the way back, he paused in the Latvian capital of Riga for a concert arranged for him by Lvov. Riga, site of Wagner's 1837–39 sojourn, had a small but competent orchestra of fifty, and he chose a program in keeping with those forces: *Harold,* with the local concertmaster, Löbmann, as soloist; *Le Carnaval romain;* two songs sung by a local soprano, and two excerpts from *Faust,* including the *Concert des sylphes* without its chorus. It was a matinee concert, and as the men of Riga were occupied with their marine and agricultural concerns, the audience consisted mostly of women and the elderly. The profit was a mere 3 rubles, but Berlioz enjoyed working with the orchestra, as well as the opportunity to see *Hamlet,* in German, with the great actor Baumeister.

*T*he month of June 1847 he spent in Berlin, at first preparing his *Faust,* scheduled for the 19th. It was not a happy experience. Although the producers had offered him virtually unlimited rehearsal time, the musicians were unsympathetic to the foreign *Faust,* they said, and hostile over certain remarks about them—asides, really—he had made in the letters from Germany. For his part Berlioz was ill-tempered with the soloists, whom he found passable at best and insufferable where it came to his Méphistophélès; at one point he summoned the intendant to have him rebuke the orchestra for its behavior.

The concert was set, following the king's wishes, for 6:00 P.M., though the early curtain time resulted in a loss of half the audience—and half the proceeds. And during the performance, Berlioz failed to understand the cries of "Da Capo" from the house and refused to grant an encore, a gesture that offended the public. The proceeds were just over 400 francs.

Berlioz remained, nevertheless, a favorite of Frederick William IV. He decorated Berlioz with the Red Eagle of Prussia, an award the composer took care to note in his biographical sketches for the rest of his life. At a dinner party at Sans Souci, he and the king were seen on a long promenade through the orange groves; the guests, who included Count Matthew Wielhorsky and Baron von Humboldt, the naturalist, were duly impressed with a man who laughed with the king and could make him laugh, and afterward were excessively deferential. (The French ambassador, on the other hand, seemed indifferent to his presence.) He took tea with the absentminded princess on several occasions, and of course paid Meyerbeer the appropriate respects. Marie had by that time joined him, and there followed an unexplained hurry home, with concerts in Hamburg and Bremen abandoned. One has the sense that she went to fetch him back to Paris.

They reestablished their living arrangement in the rue de Provence during the early days of July, discovering in the process that though he had been gone for just over eighteen weeks, his stipend from the Conservatoire had been suspended for a full half year. For more than two years, Louis had been promised a trip to La Côte-St.-André, and to that promise was now added more than idle discussion of accompanying his father to England, the better to absorb that portion of his ancestry for himself. Father and son were on the verge of leaving for the Isère when a series of precipitous turns at the Opéra demanded Berlioz's continued presence in Paris.

The director of the Opéra, Pillet, had at last fallen—victim of his mistress, Rosina Stoltz, and her swift decline. Berlioz suddenly found himself a central character in a drama defined by the tangled politics indigenous to that troubled house. The need to restore the former distinction of the Opéra, especially in terms of rejuvenating conductors, chorus, and soloists, was felt nationwide, and it was held in many quarters that Berlioz was the man to do it. This possibility was complicated by the matter of his unfinished opera, *La Nonne sanglante,* the libretto of which the new administration wished to assign to someone else; and by his strained relationship with Narcisse Girard, Habeneck's powerful assistant conductor and heir apparent. At the same time the new directors of the Opéra, Nestor Roqueplan and Edmond Duponchel, imagined that their success hinged on support from the *Journal des Débats* and its influence with the government. So for a variety of reasons, few of them especially wholesome, the new administrators offered Berlioz the post of director of singing at the Opéra. Here was his long-sought invitation to assume a permanent, formal post, one that had been held by the excellent composer Halévy. He was asked to begin work on 1 September.

Halévy or no, it was a shabby offer, for Berlioz was worthy of the post of general music director. The proposed position, though it involved the kind of work for which he had shown, during *Esmeralda, Cellini,* and *Freyschutz,* a considerable gift, was time-consuming and would leave little opportunity for composition. Berlioz declined the offer on 19 August, in elegant, restrained language—all the parties to the discussion knew the exchange would be published—"releasing you from your verbal commitment."[11] The directors responded with "surprise and regret" and the traditional assurances of esteem and devotion. Yet it was a genuine rupture; how severely Berlioz's feelings were hurt by what he concluded to be the insincerity of it all is clear from his account in the *Mémoires,* written soon afterward.

*B*erlioz had meanwhile received what seemed a much more attractive offer. Louis Jullien, the audacious but gifted showman given to conducting Beethoven in white gloves, had conceived the idea of resurrecting an opera company at the Drury Lane Theatre and saw fit to invite Berlioz to be its music director. Berlioz had for some time hoped to visit England, and the position seemed as attractive as any of those sorts of jobs might ever be. A six-year contract was developed between Jullien on the one hand and Berlioz and one of the Escudier brothers, acting as his agent, on the other. This document was signed on 19 August, the very day Berlioz declined the invitation from the Opéra.[12]

The contract provided that Berlioz would conduct the first season of the opera company, give four orchestral concerts to his own benefit, and—a clever touch—compose for the company an opera in three acts to a French libretto by Alphonse Royer and Vaës. He might engage for these enterprises the artists of his choice. Compensation for the new opera was to be 10,000

FIGURE 10.2 Louis-Antoine Jullien.

francs; for the three-month season from December through February his fee would be £400 (another 10,000 francs or so). The public concerts might well bring in another third, such that Berlioz's yearly income from this project would approach 30,000 francs, a princely sum, minus 15 percent in commission for Escudier. The terms seemed unbeatable; they might even allow him to retire from the *Débats*.

In mid-September Berlioz and Louis made their long-delayed visit to La Côte-St.-André. The boy and his father went hunting in the countryside, as Louis's father and grandfather had done before him, and he was to remember these as the happiest days of his life. (Berlioz later gave Louis the rifle that had belonged to his brother Prosper, partly as a souvenir of this trip.) Louis returned to the college in Rouen. He was miserable there, forty-fifth in a class of forty-five. He promised to squander his scholarship money to assure that he would no longer have to go to school. "Tell me at least," he writes petulantly to his father, "if you *might consent* to tell me how *maman* is doing."[13]

Berlioz spent the autumn correcting proofs of *Harold en Italie* and *Roméo et Juliette* and writing the letters on his trips to Vienna and its surrounding capitals. The published materials for the symphonies were needed for the London season, and the last corrections would have to be done there; both publications in fact appeared while he was out of town. *Roméo et Juliette* was not dedicated to Liszt, as he had written to ask; Berlioz chose instead to dedicate to him the more fitting *Faust,* and in return Liszt eventually dedicated his own *Faust-Symphonie* to Berlioz.

Berlioz reached London for the first time on 4 November 1847 and took lodgings in Jullien's large house at 76, Harley Street. That same day, in Leipzig, Mendelssohn died. The conversation during Berlioz's first visit to England would often have turned to Mendelssohn's recent sojourn there in any case; as it was, the memories of the Leipzig master were all-pervasive, and in the succeeding weeks Berlioz attended the memorial service and the many commemorative concerts, from *Messiah* to *Elijah* and, for the first time in his experience, the Scotch Symphony. The British seemed prepared to treat him as Mendelssohn's successor in their affections.

Berlioz had made this trip, too, without Marie, anticipating liberty and an unfettered bachelor existence. Instead he missed her and felt cast adrift in London, where, though his spoken English was found to be acceptable, he was unable to understand much of what was said to him. The "few steps" reported to be between Jullien's house and the Drury Lane Theatre took three-quarters of an hour to walk, and he was at first put off by the great distances involved in negotiating the city. London's size amazed him.

Jullien had redecorated his theater in blue and white and engaged a good orchestra and a chorus of 120 voices. It was up to Berlioz to summon and deploy the force. Mme Dorus-Gras, his prima donna, would open in *Lucia di Lammermoor* and was expected to continue with Donizetti's *Linda di Chamounix* and a new opera by the Irish composer Michael Balfe called *The Maid of Honour.* The fee promised her for three months' work was 50,000 francs. Sims Reeves, just returned from his La Scala debut and on the verge of his best singing, was the tenor; Staudigl, not yet arrived, had been engaged as the resident bass. The chorus master was Max Maretzek, who in a year would embark on a brilliant career in the New World; the director and manager was Frederick Gye, associated from the first with Jullien's Prom Concerts at Covent Garden and later to be general manager of the Theatre Royal there. On the governing committee were Sir Henry Bishop and Sir George Smart. This assemblage of talent bordered on the stellar: with a conductor of Berlioz's accomplishment and some good management on the part of the producers, their ambitious repertoire might well be proffered with memorable result.

Whatever Jullien's merits as a conductor of popular entertainments, he had little experience in the rigorous, competitive world of the dramatic stage. Berlioz saw signs of mental imbalance in his extravagant ways and his disinclination to govern their affairs by any measure of ordinary practicality. To complete the season, for example, he proposed to do *Robert le diable,* though without the slightest idea of where the music, scenery, costumes, or translation might come from. He accepted Berlioz's suggestion that they do *Iphigénie en Tauride,* which he did not know, but only on the condition that they send straightway to Paris for a particular helmet he had once admired. For opening night, he asked Berlioz to arrange the tame anthem *God Save the Queen* on the order of the *Marche hongroise.*

The English welcomed Berlioz with the warmth they were accustomed to extending foreign artists, and of course his marriage to Miss Smithson lent extra mystique to his presence. He was invited, for instance, to dine at the home of the great actor William Macready, opposite whom Harriet had once played Lady Macbeth. Within a few weeks he had met Thackeray and Mrs. Charles Dickens, daughter of the music critic George Hogarth, as well as many other writers and musicians. He was made an honorary member of an English gentlemen's club. Of the composers he most favored Julius Benedict, with whom he developed a lasting friendship, and Vincent Wallace, peripatetic composer of *Maritana,* the highlight of the 1845–46 season, to whom Berlioz was attracted by the whiff of his escapades in Asia, the Americas, and Australia, including a putative expedition against the Maori in New Zealand. There is a good deal of secondary evidence, though little primary documentation—he himself seems to have taken it as a matter of course—that he was swept into both the salon and the exalted intellectual sphere of Vincent and Mary Novello and their dynasty: their son Alfred, founder of Novello & Co., the *Musical World,* and the venerable *Musical Times;* their daughter Mary, who among her several literary accomplishments was soon to number a translation of his orchestration treatise, and her husband Charles Cowden Clarke; their protegé Edward Holmes, whom Berlioz identified early on as the best of the English critics. The younger sister Clara Novello was pursuing her musical, amorous, and political fortunes in Italy; she knew Berlioz in London and enjoyed the height of her career there at a later date. These luminaries were to vie with one another for the honor of having discovered Berlioz. Edward Holmes, for example, boasted in 1857 that "I . . . introduced him into England."[14]

$\mathcal{T}$he season opened on 6 December, after barely a month of rehearsals, with *Lucia di Lammermoor.* It was treated fairly by the press, who singled Berlioz out for praise as a conductor of "promptitude, decision, and intelligence."[15] Because *Lucia* had no formal overture, he had chosen to begin the *soirée*—doubtless after *God Save the Queen* in somebody else's version—with the *Leonora* Overture No. 2, and his brilliant performance of the Beethoven work appears to have had formidable results in terms of subsequent invitations to conduct in London. (Afterward he introduced

Lucia with *Leonora* No. 3, which he preferred.) He left it to Balfe to conduct the first performance of *The Maid of Honour,* partly as a courtesy and partly out of distaste for the work. It was probably a poor choice for so early in the season, for it attracted little public interest and caused unrest among the performers. By the end of December the financial affairs of the new house were already in the first stages of disarray. Meanwhile Jullien left town on a concert tour of the provinces, hoping to boost his capital, and he took with him the best players in the company's orchestra.

Berlioz was now faced with his contractual obligation to compose an opera for the troupe. The matter of *La Nonne sanglante* figured into his deliberations; it was at least possible that it could be refitted for the occasion, and the work was still wanted back in Paris by Duponchel and Roqueplan. An approach to Scribe to supply an outline for finishing the libretto yielded the response that he would have nothing ready before 1850, and with that the long saga of *La Nonne sanglante* was, as least so far as Berlioz was concerned, suddenly ended. There was no sign of a libretto, either, from Royer and Vaës. At the latest, Berlioz would need a new opera for the beginning of the second season, scheduled to commence on 1 December 1848, and a year was little enough time to finish a work of magnitude.

It was within this context that his thoughts turned to expanding *Faust* into a three-act opera called *Méphistophélès,* a project there is reason to believe may have been lurking in his thoughts all along. Such a work could feature Pischek, the baritone he had first heard in Frankfurt and whose appearances with the Philharmonic Society had made him a favorite of the London audiences. That Berlioz turned again to Scribe, offering him a fee of 4,000 francs to add forty-five minutes' worth of text to the existing two and a half hours of *Faust,* seems on the face of it almost unfathomable, but I suppose we must take Scribe's continued celebrity into account—what today we would call his name-recognition value. In any event Berlioz ordered up texts for a new grand air of Méphistophélès and for several additional incidents, instructing Scribe to keep the other characters, Marguerite in particular, essentially unchanged. Jullien, who at first opposed the idea because he wanted to present Spohr's *Faust,* at length agreed to it and from then on pestered Berlioz daily to complete his *Méphistophélès.* The exchange of correspondence with Scribe was as haphazard as their former intercourse, and it does not appear that Berlioz did any serious composition for the new version.

Jullien's company had another problem to resolve, this with regard to its so far unsatisfactory *corps de ballet.* It was decided to approach Théophile Gautier for a scenario on Goethe's *Wilhelm Meister,* and Berlioz, who knew Gautier better than did any of the other officers, was assigned the negotiations for this boondoggle as well.[16] Their turning to Paris for a ballet is indicative of the sort of problem that plagued Jullien from the beginning. He had no roots in London, nor particularly close connections with anyone there, and always thought first of all of sending away to France for provisions. His natural instinct for the grand touch was offset at every turn by his lack of experience. And his venture was not overstaffed.

The pace was exhausting, even for so energetic a figure as Berlioz. His daytime rehearsals lasted from noon until 4:00 P.M., and at night he conducted from 7:00 until 10:00 or 11:00; he was at home to callers only between 4:00 and 4:30 in the afternoon. The third in a succession of severe colds developed into bronchitis, and an attack of grippe in late January was debilitating enough for him to cancel, most unusually, his engagements, leaving the baton on 28 January and following to his concertmaster, Tolbecque. After a few days in bed, he tried to return to work but suffered a relapse and was out of commission through early February.

By that time Jullien's enterprise had nearly disintegrated, sooner than even the most pessimistic had expected. The expenses of the company were grossly in excess of its receipts. At first it was merely the soloists and management who were asked to accept a reduction of 33 percent of their admittedly high fees; the orchestra, chorus, and stagehands were paid as before. Berlioz in fact was never given a farthing, and by February Mme Dorus-Gras, fearing the worst, refused to appear one evening in *Lucia;* she waited, costumed, in her dressing room for Jullien to come discuss the matter of her payment.

It was in this confused and melancholy climate that Berlioz, still unwell, presented the first of his four promised "grand vocal and instrumental" concerts, on 7 February. This splendid affair featured parts I and II of *Faust* in the English of Henry Chorley, the Offertoire from the Requiem, and the latter two movements of the *Symphonie funèbre et triomphale,* with the solo played on an alto valved trombone. Mme Dorus-Gras sang her cavatina from *Cellini,* and Miss Miran, who in a few days' time would become Berlioz's prima donna when Mme Dorus abandoned ship, offered an Englished *Jeune Pâtre breton.*

For the musicians, the concert offered respite from Balfe's opera and the opportunity to work with a man they already admired on music that intrigued them more than anything they had so far done with him. *Faust* was a favorite of the English artists from the very beginning: Sims Reeves, for example, said, "It was his *Faust* music that left upon me the deepest impression."[17] The sylph's scene was encored; the *Marche hongroise* was soon to be heard played by the street musicians. The representatives of the British press, who on the whole give the impression of being more cosmopolitan and better informed than their Parisian counterparts, were mostly enthusiastic. They had come with the traditional doubts; they went away with memories of the public crying for more and a jubilant admiration of conducting skills they had never before witnessed. Morris Barnett, who had gone to four of the rehearsals, praised Berlioz as "the natural exponent of the loftiest aspirations and the deepest passions of the poet."[18] Hogarth of the *Daily News* allowed that he had never been so excited by a concert;

FIGURE 10.3 Poster from the Theatre Royal, Drury Lane, London, for Berlioz's concert of 7 February 1848, his first in London.

Charles Lewis Gruneisen wrote a long biographical account of Berlioz, illustrated with the Prinzhofer lithograph.[19] (This essay tells the whole story of Harriet and includes the anecdote of Berlioz's shouting in 1827 "This woman shall be my wife.") Julius Benedict said simply that it was the most important concert of the season. The pride Berlioz took in all this is demonstrated by his systematic collecting and pasting up of the newspaper clippings.

With this concert, Berlioz became the star of the season, his attendance either invited or expected at morning concerts, private recitals, and affairs of court—sometimes to conduct, sometimes as guest of honor. On 18 February the palace band played portions of the *Symphonie funèbre* in the presence of Prince Albert and its composer. (It was announced that the queen would attend, and possibly she did, but I do not think they ever met.) He was toasted at a banquet of the Royal Society of Musicians and was forced to improvise a response, according to some accounts, in his halting English. For the moment, his way seemed clear to a brilliant season lasting through the spring.

Only gradually does it appear to have dawned on him that he was adrift in London without serious work or promise of reimbursement. The seizure and sale of Jullien's music shop for £8,000 in January had not stemmed the tide of his bankruptcy; he neglected to turn over the proceeds of Berlioz's benefit concert. It was Berlioz who suggested *The Marriage of Figaro* as an inexpensive but viable masterpiece to rescue the company. This opened on 11 February, to a certain public esteem. It was Berlioz's first serious exposure to conducting Mozart, and we know too little about it.

*L*ouis-Philippe had ruled in France for eighteen relatively stable and prosperous years when the rising price of food, notably bread—together with an overextension of industrial capital to such ambitious enterprises as building the railroads and a similar overcommitment of public capital to the subjugation of north Africa—toppled his government. The specific cause was banal, as sparks to the powder keg usually are: a dispute over the right of a dissident group in the twelfth *arrondissement* to assemble for a banquet. Street fighting erupted in the last week of February, and on the 24th Louis-Philippe, unable to form a government and unwilling in his old age—he was seventy-five—to face a long period of civil unrest, abdicated in favor of his grandson, the nine-year-old count of Paris. On 26 February the Second Republic was officially proclaimed; on 9 March Armand Marrast, a journalist, was elected mayor of Paris and interim protector of the public tranquility.

The Revolution of 1848 brought certain changes that had a good deal more effect on Berlioz, and on French music in general, than anything that had happened in 1830. The government, lacking legitimate Bourbon successors to whom the centrists might turn for leadership, simply disappeared, and with it went many of the career bureaucrats who had so long governed the institutions of French art. Elected by universal male suffrage to the new assembly, on the other hand, were any number of professional artists, among them Hugo and Lamartine and Victor Schœlcher and Eugène Süe. The 1848 Revolution was widely believed at the time to be more epochal than 1830 had been, harking back to the spirit of 1789: it was held to be "socialist, romantic, utopian; it was believed that things would never be the same again."[20] Yet for its several promises, the events of 1848 caused Berlioz a pair of major personal setbacks: the suppression of his sinecure at the Conservatory library and the grave fiscal discomfort of the *Journal des Débats,* formerly his two sources of regular income. In the turmoil he did not at first notice one of the more interesting developments of the earliest days of the revolution: on 24 February the *droit des pauvres* was reduced to 1 percent.

Berlioz watched all this from London, understandably frightened by the confluence of financial uncertainty at home and the running dry of his English income. Whatever republicanism he had conceived in his youth had faded; he had come to admire the enlightened despots of Germany, and they, too, were falling, one by one, by the end of the year. His old friend Augustin de Pons committed suicide in despair over it all. Mail from home was erratic and very likely censored; no one in France could predict, anyway, where events were leading. What was clear was that he had suffered monetary loss. When the banks failed, he appears to have lost 4,000 francs outright and the value of a note due him; at the same time he was being pressed to pay a personal note of his own and to resolve his obligation to the Escudier brothers, whose various enterprises had also failed. Louis had lost his financial support at the college of Rouen, and Harriet's expenses, though she moved in February or March to a yet more modest apartment in the rue Blanche, Montmartre—her second address in the same street—were mounting. Berlioz resigned himself to the prospect of permanent residence abroad, where he would cling to his liberty like a savage. "I have struggled enough," he wrote; "I have suffered enough; I have waited long enough."[21]

England, too, was suffering her share of political unrest, with ramifications that affected the financial health of the arts. The Drury Lane was by no means the only company facing bankruptcy; until Berlioz learned of the upheavals elsewhere in Europe, he thought he might do better in Germany or go to Prague to stage a complete *Faust.* London's hospitality was strained to the limit by refugees both artistic and political, from his friend Charles Hallé to such notables as both Louis-Philippe, the deposed monarch, and Louis-Napoleon, the future emperor. Louis-Napoleon and Berlioz encountered each other in London more than once, and Berlioz later enjoyed remembering how he had addressed his prospective imperial highness as "monsieur."

What little opportunity he had left to make money in London seemed to rest on the forthcoming publication by the firm of Cramer and Beale of several editions of his works; in an 1846 parlor edition—"Les Concerts de Société: Wessel & Co.'s Choice Series of German Songs"—the strophes from *Roméo et Juliette,* titled "First Love's Pure Vows," had sold reasonably well. Sales of Julius Benedict's arrangement for piano, four-hands, of the *Marche hongroise* were brisk from its appearance in early 1848; by April it was said to be "on every piano in London." Berlioz hoped Benedict would arrange the *Ballet des sylphes* and the *Marseillaise* for the same force, but the *Sylphes* went unfinished, and Berlioz arranged the *Marseillaise* himself, for solo tenor, chorus, and piano. He prepared a similar *Apothéose* for voice and piano, published without its dedication to Duc because of some *contretemps* regarding the architect's association with the Bastille. (It is obvious, however, that the spate of patriotic music being considered for publication was intended to capitalize on the revolution.) The translator, listed as J. de Vere, was probably Isabelle Duchène de Vère, a young Englishwoman who had married his French acquaintance Adolphe Duchène de Vère and with whom Berlioz maintained a considerable correspondence.

He agreed, as well, to arrange two other French patriotic songs, the *Chant du départ* and Rouget de Lisle's *Mourons pour la patrie,* but commercial interest in the revolution subsided before he got around to the task. There was less demand than he had hoped for published translations of his prose: *Euphonia* appeared, in the *Mirror* of June and July 1848, but the letters from Germany and Austria did not, and there was only faint interest in his projected autobiography. It was, however, in the course of reasoning out such commercial possibilities that he first came upon the notion of a series of tales told each evening by members of a theater orchestra. To these would eventually be given the title *Les Soirées de l'orchestre.*

He had little recourse but to milk whatever he could from the last performances of his opera company. The hurry of a few weeks before had dramatically subsided into an existence that was just short of lazy. He writes ironically of an "absorbing" schedule that leads him to rise at noon, chat with company from 1:00 to 4:00 P.M., work from 4:00 to 6:00, dine and read the newspapers, sit through concerts until 11:30, then go out with musician friends to public houses, where he would smoke until 2:00 A.M. It was in truth a combination of simple boredom and anxiety—two conditions that often lead people to begin keeping diaries—that gave birth to the *Mémoires.* They were assembled from his published travel pieces, with much of the connective tissue composed during his remaining weeks in London. The preface, dated 21 March 1848, is a gloomy reflection on the limitations of the French public, the hostility of the Société des Concerts, the ignobility of the press.

Most of his personal property, including his music, he had already caused to be removed from Jullien's house, not wishing it to be seized when they came to throw his landlord into debtors' prison. (Jullien did not, in fact, spend any time in jail; instead he gaily sailed for the United States in search of a fatter bank account, Berlioz's *Le Roi Lear* in his repertoire.) On 28 April Berlioz left Jullien's apartments for the last time and took simpler rooms at 26, Osnaburg Street in Regents Park. A few days later Marie arrived in London to join him and, like many others, to escape from the trials of Paris. Her presence improved his spirits considerably; together they enjoyed Jenny Lind in *La Sonnambula* and a performance of *Hamlet.* Gustave Roger was also in London, following his tour of the provinces as a sort of warm-up act for Jenny Lind, "the Swedish nightingale." He and Berlioz dined together on more than one occasion and once went to the country house of the critic Morris Barnett to *polyglotter*.

The London Philharmonic Society was for reasons unclear to him hostile to Berlioz's presence, such that he was not extended the usual invitation to appear in their concerts. (It is likely that the principal conductor Michael Costa, jealous and threatened by the thought of another opera conductor in town, was the culprit.) Because the failure of the Drury Lane company had robbed him of his three remaining benefits, Berlioz and his supporters elected to offer a public concert at their own risk in the Queen's Concert Rooms, Hanover Square. The program was to include the first part of *Faust*, the first three movements of *Harold*, his orchestral songs, *Le Carnaval romain*, and *L'Invitation à la valse*. Mme Viardot, who was in town to challenge the Swedish nightingale with a *Sonnambula* of her own, agreed to sing a reorchestrated and expanded *La Captive;* Louise Dulcken, Ferdinand David's sister, would appear in two movements of a Mendelssohn piano concerto. He summoned the best London musicians by printed invitation, and they, privy to the details of his financial circumstance, responded by offering to volunteer their services without fee.

The concert, on Thursday, 29 June, at 2:30 P.M., went well enough, despite the fact that the *Marche hongroise* was denied its bass drum and cymbals by house rules designed to spare the neighbors any sonic discomfort. (He apologized for this inconvenience from the stage—apparently in English.)[22] The four encores the audience desired could not be granted either, as the musicians needed to be at their regular jobs by early evening.

Roger describes the concert as magnificent of enthusiasm and short of purse. Mme Viardot, just on the verge of her debut as Fidès in *Le Prophète* and preoccupied with mastering the role, was, however, not at her best. And there was an air of melancholy surrounding the assemblage so far from Paris of so many notable French citizens—the horn player Vivier and the bass Massol in addition to Berlioz, Roger, Hallé, and Viardot. It was, said Roger, "a true gathering of exiles."[23]

Berlioz could well have stayed longer in London—many refugees did— but his longing for home overcame him. This homesickness was due at least in part to what he sensed as the growing English resentment of the wave of foreign artists who had appeared to be invading the nation. The queen herself supported engaging native artists in preference to the visitors. Yet the letter of farewell he published in the *Morning Post* of 10 July is tender:

I am going away, back to the country which is still called France, and which after all is my own . . . But whatever be the term of the ordeal in store for me, I shall retain to the end the most grateful remembrance of your excellent and skilful artists, of your intelligent and attentive public, and of my colleagues on the Press for their ungrudging and constant support. I am doubly happy to have been able to admire in them the fine qualities of good feeling, talent, intelligent attention, combined with honest criticism; these afford clear evidence of a real love of art and an assurance to all the friends of music for its future.[24]

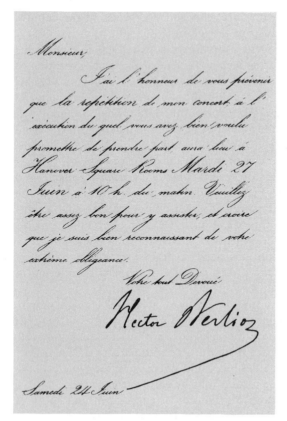

There was no question but that he would return. Already he had begun to organize a Musical Shakespeare Night at Covent Garden for the following season, where in one evening *Le Roi Lear, La Tempête, Roméo et Juliette,* and *La Mort d'Ophélie* were to be given together. For this same occasion, I think, he completed and reworked that summer his *Marche funèbre pour la dernière scène d'Hamlet.* The finished autograph is dated 22 September 1848, just a few weeks after he returned home, and the piano-vocal score was turned over to Richault late in the year.

Berlioz and Marie Recio left London on 13 July and were in Paris the next day. His travels continued for two more decades, with frequent return visits to London, but the London venture of 1847–48 represents his last conquest of a major European capital.

They had little idea of what they might find at home. New violence had erupted in northeastern Paris during the last weeks of June, a reaction to the government's reluctant suppression of the National Workshops for unskilled laborers, held by liberals to be a symbol of the right to work. Barricades had sprung up from the faubourg Saint-Denis on the northern boundary of Paris, south past the Conservatoire and Hôtel de Ville, and on into the Left Bank. Harriet, walking in her garden at dusk on the 27th, was fired upon. Berlioz's frantic appeals to Réty for news of all this had, in the confusion, gone unanswered.

On their arrival Berlioz and Marie took a year's lease on a small apartment at 15, rue de La Rochefoucauld. What they found was their civilization in complete flux: institutions in transition—the Gymnase Musical, for example, was moving to Strasbourg—alongside radical lifestyles and fashions for which the newspaper accounts had not prepared them. On the positive side were several new opportunities, including the possibility of a chair in orchestration when the Conservatoire was reorganized and the likelihood that Berlioz's services would be required by one or more of the theaters. Still, there was little certainty of anything. The *Débats,* for example, could only afford his articles twice a month, where before he had had a weekly column. So far there was no interest in his letters from Russia nor, because the book publishing trade had suffered heavily, in his first initiatives to secure a publisher's backing for the idea of the *Soirées de l'orchestre.* The *Revue et Gazette musicale,* for a change, was offering higher fees; this explains why his columns on the Société des Concerts appeared in that journal during the winter and spring. His letters on Prague, Marseille, Lyon, and Lille likewise appeared there during the fall.

Hugo was able to regain for Berlioz his chair at the Conservatoire library, as well as some of the back pay due him; Stéphen de La Madelaine, highly placed in the new administration, could protect his interests with the bureaucracy. He began to write again for the *Débats* in late July, with an article on the reopening of the Opéra, now renamed, as it had been with every change in the rule of France. His sense of humor had not vanished: his piece carried the sassy title "Opening of the Theater of the Nation, or the National Theater, or, Old Style, the Opéra."[25]

In the first days of August Berlioz received news of his father's death in La Côte-St.-André on 28 July. Nanci and Adèle had stayed by his bedside during the five days of his last delirium; it was left to Adèle's husband, Marc Suat, to close Dr. Berlioz's eyes, a traditional duty of the eldest son. A long cortège, made up largely of the poor and sick to whom his life had been dedicated, followed the coffin to the cemetery.

Toward the end the grand old man had asked repeatedly after his famous son. Berlioz regretted not having been at the bedside, though the decline was so rapid he would not have been there in time even had he been notified at the first sign of impending death. The need to please his father, even if subconcious, had long governed Berlioz's actions and impulses; it certainly explains not a few of his adjustments of the facts in his letters to La Côte. Both were acutely aware that his father had never heard any of Berlioz's music. That is one of several reasons the *Hamlet* funeral march, completed within a few weeks, has such tragic associations.

In the confusion, no one bothered to tell Louis of his grandfather's death; he learned of it from a friend who saw an obituary in the papers. Louis, who had refused for several months to correspond with anyone in his family, had simply been forgotten.

Berlioz went to La Côte-St.-André in late August to join his sisters in their grieving and his brothers-in-law, both solicitors, in disposing of the estate. His share of the inheritance amounted to the rent on the farm at Les Jacques, which brought in about 600 francs monthly, a portion of the large wine cellar, his father's library, and perhaps some furniture. It was Berlioz's intention to sell the library and use the proceeds to support Louis's upbringing; within a few years he had Suat sell a portion of the farm as well. The family had an obligation, too, to the maid, Monique Netty, whom they set up (at her suggestion) in the tobacconist's trade; she soon grew unhappy with it.

Inevitably it was a trip tinged with the pangs of nostalgia and regret. At the house he found his father's watch still ticking in a drawer of his desk; after a few last moments of reflection, he gathered it up and strode from the room. The watch was among his own effects when he died, and it has since been returned to the house in La Côte-St.-André.

From La Côte, still dwelling on his past, he went to Grenoble and Meylan. In London he had written for his *Mémoires* the description of Estelle and of his adolescent love, fixed in his memory as purer, simpler than anything he had otherwise known, an ideal love that transfigured the experiences of real life, a passion he knew to be the fantasy of a splenetic forty-five-year-old. Some of the neighbors remembered Estelle and gave him her address. Then he searched out the farm where they had had that first encounter he could picture so clearly. He could not find her rock, but the rest was about the same:

> Time has left my shrine as I remembered it. Only, strangers live there now; other hands cultivate your flowers. No one in the world could have guessed why a solitary man, with a sad, preoccupied air and the marks of toil and tribulation imprinted on his face, went there yesterday and walked about the secret haunts and by-ways of the place—no one, not even you. O *quante lagrime!*[26]

That was on 5 September. The next day, thinking better of visiting her, he penned the lyric outburst.

Louis, nearing his fourteenth birthday, decided that October definitely to abandon his studies, he hoped by the end of the academic year, in favor of a sailor's life. Simultaneously, Harriet suffered the first of her strokes. For some weeks she had shown the symptoms that often precede cerebral accidents, more than once having taken to her bed, unable to talk. The stroke

FIGURE 10.5
Berlioz in September 1848,
as seen by a citizen of
La Côte-St.-André.

caused a paralysis of her right side, and her speech was permanently im-
paired. After more than six weeks, Harriet had attempted only a few English
words. The primitive treatment prescribed by her physicians consisted of
daily emetics and multiple bleedings. Berlioz called on this dreadful scene
twice daily, but there was little he could do to help. Under the circumstances
he barely noticed his election to the Dutch Philharmonic Society, and he saw
Emile Deschamps's *Macbeth* at the Odéon with the heaviest of hearts.

Mostly to distance himself from the sickroom, he organized and conducted
a concert on 29 October, a sublime combination of the old and new orders,
sponsored by the Association of Artist-Musicians to benefit their depleted
emergency fund. It was a festival event with 450 performers, as many before
had been; the repertoire of Mozart, Gluck, Beethoven, Rossini, and Berlioz—
one reviewer took the effortless grouping of Mozart, Beethoven, and Berlioz
for granted[27]—not so different from earlier times. But this very public concert
took place in a remarkable theater, the king's private opera house at Versailles. In the royal box, sitting in the king's seat, was the citizen-mayor of
Paris, Armand Marrast. Mme Widemann gave the French premiere of the
new *La Captive,* transposed down a step from Mme Viardot's key to her
own, and with the introduction toward the end of a second orchestra, as
though from a distance. The *Marche hongroise* was heard for the first time

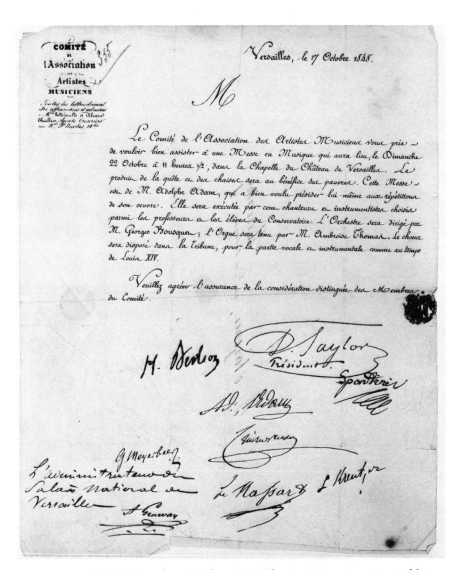

FIGURE 10.6 Invitation of 17 October 1848. The musicians are summoned by the Association of Artist-Musicians to play in Versailles for a concert to benefit the needy. Signed by Berlioz, Baron Taylor, Spontini, Adam, Niedermeyer(?), Massart, Meyerbeer, and Léon Kreutzer.

in France since the fatal performances of *Faust* in 1846. The rest of the program consisted of other works of proven public appeal, clearly chosen with republican taste in mind.

*B*erlioz cannot have been in anything other than frail condition after nearly a year of debilitations. At the beginning of November he succumbed to the first attack of the intestinal disorder from which he eventually died. Everything we know of this problem suggests a diagnosis of ulcerative colitis, a condition aggravated by emotional stress.

Meyerbeer had also been ill for a month, just as the production of *Le Prophète* was reaching the stage. To celebrate Meyerbeer's return to health, Gustave Roger gave a holiday dinner party on 23 December. Celebrating the guest of honor were Berlioz, Dumas, Halévy, Adam, Fiorentino, and Méry. It was maladroit, the host confessed, to have so many men "of spirit" at one table, even spaced comfortably to encourage conversation. Each politely waited for the others to start, and Berlioz had to be prodded with Shakespeare and Gluck to start the discussion; thereafter he and Dumas had little difficulty dominating the evening. The *pièce de résistance,* Roger reported, was a *salade Meyerbeer.*[28]

By the beginning of the new year, Berlioz was composing the Te Deum, his first major work since *La Damnation de Faust.* We know little of the circumstances that led him to begin the project: there was no commission, no literary thunderstroke to induce him, no dramatic turn of events to commemorate. Probably the Te Deum had its roots in the unfinished projects of 1831–32, *Le Dernier Jour du monde* and the military symphony. In 1846 Berlioz had discussed with the Duc de Montpensier the idea of following through on the Napoleonic symphony, and the listing of his works at the end of the *Faust* libretto—the Labitte catalogue—includes the Te Deum, as though it was already taking shape in his mind. In Russia he had pondered the issue of using the pipe organ in symphonic music. As he envisaged it in 1849, the Te Deum was a work in seven movements for two three-part choruses, organ, and orchestra. Initially he allotted himself three months to complete it. The sketches and drafts were finished by September 1849, and he announced the Te Deum as "done" in October. But works of such dimension require an appropriate ceremonial event to achieve their maximum effect, and Berlioz accordingly sought such a circumstance for the next several years by proposing his composition for every major ceremony that came up. Not until 1855 did his offer take root, and even then the excuse was trumped up. That was the single complete performance of the Te Deum during Berlioz's life.

His spirits and possibly his health were mended by the composition of the new work. Harriet, however, grew worse. Her second stroke, in mid-February, was more severe than the first. This time the bloodlettings offered no relief, and her nighttime bouts of vomiting made the doctors fear for a time that she had fallen victim to the new cholera epidemic as well. Harriet's were not the only frailties of the flesh to demand his attention: his sister Nanci's illness proved to be cancer, and she survived for only a few more months.

And the great Habeneck, who for more than three decades had controlled a substantial segment of Parisian musical life, died on 2 February. His successor at the Société des Concerts was Narcisse Girard, with whom Berlioz had had so little to do since the mid-1830s that the tensions of their relationship appeared to have dissipated through simple neglect. Within a few weeks, Girard and the governing committee of the Société sent to ask permission to program excerpts from *Faust*—their first gesture in his direction in sixteen years. At the time it seemed a barrier fallen.

So it was that Berlioz had the unfamiliar experience of waiting backstage with the firemen, trembling like a debutant, while Girard conducted the sylphs' scene and *Marche hongroise* from *Faust* that 15 April. The selections were wedged between a Beethoven symphony and a long excerpt from Spontini's *La Vestale,* but both the movements were greeted with warm applause and calls for more—a good sign from what he regarded as "a difficult public, generally ill-disposed to living composers."[29] Girard conducted well, Berlioz was forced to admit, but refused to grant encores, pleading that he could not find his place again in the thick score. This *contretemps* rekindled their old hostilities: Berlioz's description of the concert for his *Mémoires* is decidedly sour, and Girard programmed no further Berlioz during his long tenure at the head of the Société des Concerts.

The headline of Jules Janin's review for the *Débats,* on the other hand, trumpeted "Berlioz au Conservatoire, enfin!"

> These compositions that in recent days so delighted the Conservatoire's public have been long familiar to the *amateurs* of London and St. Petersburg. Must Berlioz make a circuit of 1200 leagues to arrive in the rue Bergère? . . . Now that Berlioz doesn't give any more concerts, they play his music everywhere. Tired of moving toward the mountain, he quit; now the mountain has begun to move toward him.[30]

The most electrifying event of the 1848–49 season, however, took place the next day. This was the long-anticipated opening on 16 April of Meyerbeer's *Le Prophète,* the Opéra's first major creation since Halévy's *Charles VI* of 1843. The lethargy of the past five years vanished with Roger's accession to the place too long occupied by Duprez; the entrance that night of Mme Viardot, for whom Meyerbeer had written the part of Fidès, was eagerly awaited. Berlioz knew he would have to write a major article on the work, his most serious analysis since long before *Faust,* and he did not fancy the task. Meyerbeer badgered him to attend the rehearsals; Berlioz refused, just as aggressively, to set foot in a place he had come to loathe on any other terms than as a member of the public. At length he appeared for one dress rehearsal, though his article bespeaks scrupulous study of the score. Meyerbeer's courting was effusive—"Cher et illustre Maître!" his notes usually begin[31]—because he was frightened about what Berlioz might say: "I love you immensely, as you know. But tonight I fear you more than I love you—from the hope that my score will impress you well."[32]

Berlioz could not hide his envy, tinged perhaps with resentment of the lengths to which Meyerbeer was willing to go to guarantee a victory:

> What an undertaking, today, to make an opera succeed! What intrigues! What seductions to be concluded, what money to spend, what dinners to give! It makes me sick at heart. It is Meyerbeer who caused all this, and who forced Rossini to give in.[33]

The other critics amused themselves by creating their usual *bon mots* (Méry: "if only it were music"; Janin: "a theological treatise minus the faith"),[34] but to Berlioz *Le Prophète* was an accomplishment seldom before equaled on the Paris stage. This review alone, given his disgust with the politics of the situation, is enough to prove him capable of maintaining fastidious critical distance. He talked proudly of Roger and called Mme Viardot "one of the greatest artists it is possible to cite in the history of music, past or present." He summarized the production as follows:

> First of all, the success of *Le Prophète* was of matchless magnificence. The music alone would have seen to that. But every conceivable richness—of decor, costume, dance, and staging—came to its support. The dance of the skaters is the sort of lovely thing that assures a vogue for an opera. The settings of the interior of the church in Münster and of the prophet's palace are of incomparable beauty. The musical performance hasn't reached this level, at the Opéra, for many long years. The chorus sings *and acts* with admirable verve; the tenor voices were fresh and vibrant—and even noticed, for the first time. The orchestra was beyond praise: in subtlety of nuance, technical perfection, cleanliness of the most complicated passage-work, learned discretion of accompaniment, impetuousness and furious verve at the moments of violent action, and in the trueness of the pitch and the exquisite tone quality—evoking that of the Conservatoire orchestra, and which tastelessness and lassitude have often rendered unrecognizable at the Opéra. Animated by its enthusiasm for the new work, and by the firm, precise, warm, and ever attentive direction of M. Girard, [the orchestra] easily proved that it is one of the greatest prides of European music.[35]

He wrote this enthusiastically on precious few occasions.

Louis came to Paris on 7 April for his spring holiday. He could not be left alone for any length of time with Harriet and the maids, though it seems clear he stayed in the Montmartre apartment and not with Berlioz and Marie Recio. He accompanied his father to *Le Prophète* and often tagged along to dinner and other theatrical events, both that spring and during his summer vacation. On 16 July, Berlioz and Marie installed themselves in an apartment at 19, rue de Boursault (now the rue La Bruyère), between the rue Pigalle and the rue Blanche, not far from Harriet. Berlioz tried to visit her daily, a trip made easier by a new stairway up the hill.

That summer she had two strokes. Her mobility never returned, and, though she lingered for four more years, her death was expected at any moment. In mid-October, just before Berlioz took Louis back to Rouen for one last year of school, they shared the terrifying experience of trying to find the doctor for Harriet after yet another attack, her fifth. She was unconscious and pale—they were certain she was dying—and Berlioz and Louis wandered throughout the quarter for two hours on their unsuccessful search.

With Louis about to become a sailor, Berlioz yielded to obsessive day-dreams of foreign lands, his *mal des pays lointains*. He would willingly go to some tropical island, or South America, or Australia. "Oh! la mer!," he cries out in a letter to Nanci in July: "The sea, a good boat! A good wind! To flee this old continent, to go be among naive and primitive savages, to hear no further of our own hide-bound, ferocious, rotten savages."[36] More realistically, he tried for a time to organize concerts in new lands: Sweden, Denmark, and Holland. He considered retiring to the farm at Les Jacques. He seemed on the verge of some drastic change of life.

He began, too, to organize himself for the definitive publication of all his remaining works, as though sensing the termination of his artistic career, or the beginning of the last chapter in the novel of his life. This process began with his assembling the piano-vocal versions of the *Méditation religieuse* and *La Mort d'Ophélie* into a collection called *Tristia* (version I, 1849), very obviously associated with Harriet's melancholy condition and bearing what may have been intended as an idealized portrait of her as title vignette.[37] Shortly afterward he gathered piano-vocal versions of the *Hymne à la France* and his new march and chorus, *La Menace des francs,* into a publication called *Vox populi,* dedicated to the Philharmonic Societies of France and sold to Richault in November. A third edition of the Irish Melodies, now called *Irlande,* was ready shortly afterward. Much of this amounted to routine ordering of old work, but it was encouraged by his publishers, and the longing titles they dreamed up attracted the public eye.

With the same goals in mind, he began to weave some of his better essays and tales into a new book-length collection, tied together by the nattering gossip of old musicians in the orchestra pit of an opera house: the concert-master, cast in the brigand mold and named Corsino; the brothers Kleiner the younger and Kleiner the elder; horn players, strings players, a second bassoonist; an *habitué* of the *parterre* who volunteers his comments from time to time; and the author. Few of them are French; all of them enjoy tale-telling to pass away the hours during operas that are too long. These, of course, are the *Soirées de l'orchestre,* the *Evenings in the Orchestra.* For the time being, the fiscally troubled publishers were not interested. The delay in publication until 1852 left Berlioz considerable leisure to refine the conceit.

$\mathcal{H}$e was rescued from the malaise that characterized much of 1849 by Baron Taylor's idea of organizing a new orchestra. Here was a project he could get his teeth into, and with some luck the enterprise might rival not just Seghers' Union Musicale but even the Société des Concerts. He threw himself, heart and soul, into organizing the Société Philharmonique de Paris. From the beginning he was its guiding light.

The Société Philharmonique de Paris was formulated as a cooperative enterprise of some 90 instrumentalists, 110 choristers, and perhaps a dozen

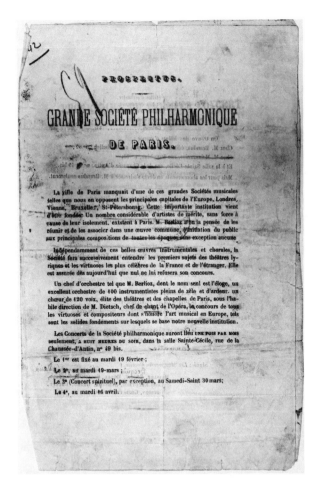

FIGURE 10.7
Prospectus for the
Société Philharmonique,
January 1850.
"M. Berlioz had the
idea of uniting
[artists of merit]
and associating them in
a common undertaking."

guarantors and patrons. The financial risk was shared, and the profits distributed, among holders of the 220 shares, with Berlioz as conductor entitled to four shares. On the patron list were to be found the names of Liszt, Meyerbeer, Spontini, and of course the indefatigable Taylor, who served in his customary roles of patron saint and general manager. The concertmaster was Lambert Massart, professor of violin at the Conservatoire since 1843 and close friend of Berlioz from the monster concerts of 1844–45 and *Faust* in 1846. Massart and his wife, the pianist Louise, née Masson, formed with Stephen Heller and Ernest Reyer Berlioz's most intimate post-Harriet circle, their association stemming at least in part from the heady excitement of organizing the Société Philharmonique and making it work.

Among the interesting musicians in the group were Waldteufel (violin), Jules Offenbach (viola), Tajan-Rogé, and the composer-critic Léon Kreutzer at the triangle. The society was successful in inducing the best Parisian singers to appear on its programs, among them Mme Viardot (to offer her increasingly admired renditions of Gluck), Roger, and the aging bass Levasseur. The limp, unprepossessing Pierre Dietsch, who tended to wreak havoc on his undertakings, was engaged as chorus master, assisted at the keyboard by the young pianist-composer Justin Cadaux. Berlioz chose as his own assistant the able cellist Seligmann. It was imagined that the group would travel to such outlying cities as Rouen, Angers, and Versailles, and from the beginning Berlioz had the fond hope that they would offer the first performance of his Te Deum. The Paris concerts were given in the Salle Ste.-Cécile, in the rue du Mont-Blanc off the Chaussée d'Antin. A season of three Tuesday evening concerts and a Saturday *concert spirituel* was announced.

Of course Berlioz brought a seasoned hand to this sort of concert-giving. A printed prospectus was distributed in the right circles; the musicians were notified of their rehearsals and performances by lithographed announcements. The rehearsals, most of which took place in Sax's rooms in the rue Neuve-St.-George, were largely sectionals. The routine was tried and true, but the myriad details—cultivating the press, coping with the vast antipathy of the Société des Concerts and the competition from the Union Musicale—consumed as much of his time as they ever had.

The Société Philharmonique was, in its studied democracy, given to noisy convocations and a tendency to infighting, particularly over questions of repertoire. Though Berlioz's predilections are clearly reflected in the programming, there was also new music he might not otherwise have considered: works of Dietsch, David, Vogel, Gastinel, and Niedermeyer. The fantasies and *solos de concert* on motives from the operas in vogue were cleverly balanced with Berlioz's familiar repertoire of Gluck, Spontini, Beethoven, Weber, and Meyerbeer. All things considered, there was very little of his own music.

They opened on 19 February 1850, after rehearsals on the 14th, 16th, and 18th, with a strong program of excerpts from *Faust* with Roger and

Levasseur, Mme Viardot in scenes from Gluck's *Iphigénie en Tauride* and *Echo et Narcisse,* and Joachim, just in from London, in Ernst's *Fantaisie brillante* on Rossini's *Otello.* After expenses were deducted from the gross receipt of 4,119 francs, 2,772 francs were left to be divided among the shareholders.[38] Berlioz's share would have been less than 100 francs.

Receipts for the remaining three concerts of the season, on 19 and 20 March and 23 April, steadily declined. At the second, Massart gave a splendid performance of *Harold;* at the third, the *concert spirituel,* sacred works by Dietsch and Niedermeyer stood alongside offerings by Mme Massart, in the Weber *Konzertstück,* and Wieniawski, in a solo of his own composition. Featured for the last concert of the season were the overture to Mendelssohn's *Athalia* and Gustave Roger in a selection of arias from *La Donna del lago* and Méhul's *Joseph.* Curiosities programmed for the delectation of the wider public included a caprice for violin, called *Pizzi-Arco,* by one Apollinaire de Kontski; selections from *Robert le diable* on the monochord; a solo by the noted Belgian cellist François Servais; and the *Marche des Hébreux* from Félicien David's 1846 oratorio, *Moïse au Sinaï.*

On 16 April news reached Paris that 219 soldiers of the Eleventh Artillery Regiment had drowned in the river Maine when a bridge at Angers collapsed after they failed to break step. The Société bogged itself down in tempestuous discussion over whether Berlioz's Requiem or a mass by Dietsch would be the more appropriate memorial; the chorus, loyal to its master, grumbled that "M. Berlioz's music tires artist-singers."[39] A motion favoring the Requiem finally carried; Dietsch promptly resigned from the society and was heard from no more. Thus it fell to Massart, Kreutzer, and Berlioz to divide the work of assembling an expanded ensemble of four hundred. This aggregation, after three rehearsals, gave a moving commemorative performance at St.-Eustache on Friday, 3 May, at 11:00 A.M. Berlioz had touched up the musical text; these readings appear in the Brandus choral parts of February 1852 and the Ricordi edition of 1853. (It was shortly after this performance, I believe, that Doré drew his famous cartoon of the seemingly left-handed Berlioz conducting a sea of studious singers; see fig. 10.8.) The performance netted 726 francs.

Nanci Berlioz Pal succumbed to breast cancer, following a week of agony, the next day; Berlioz received the news on the 8th. Adèle had kept much of the worst of it from her brother, doubtless out of the conviction that he had quite enough on his mind. Surgery, for example, had been considered, but was then deemed useless. He went to Montmartre to tell Harriet, and she, seeing her own fate ahead, could but weep profusely.

Adèle proposed a family holiday at the spa in Plombières as a gesture of collective escape from suffering. Attractive as this notion was, Berlioz was forced to decline. He had succeeded to Bottée de Toulmon's position at the library of the Conservatoire, though at no increase in his 125-franc stipend, and was hesitant to beg leave. Then there was the matter of Harriet's

FIGURE 10.8 A Concert of the Société Philharmonique in the Jardin d'Hiver. *Journal pour rire,* 27 June 1850.

uncertain condition and the need to attend to Louis during his vacation; in March he had been called to Rouen when Louis broke his clavicle. Fearing to aggravate her health problems, Berlioz had kept this development from the boy's mother entirely. The Société Philharmonique could not be left alone for long, either, with rehearsals scheduled for the summer and the possibility of mutiny if he were gone for any length of time.

Another good reason not to go to Plombières was that he could not afford to squander the necessary several hundred francs. Not only were Harriet's medical bills astronomical, but the charges for Louis's last year at college were well past his means, and there was the threat of substantial costs for marine training; already Berlioz was drawing regular advances from Marc Suat on his income from the farm at Les Jacques. A revival that April of the Paris *Freischütz* was bringing in a few francs, and he had earned a few more by selling the recitatives to a London production that had opened on 31 March. (There is no evidence that his recitatives were used.) But these and the receipts from the Société Philharmonique of a few hundred francs here and there did little to stabilize, much less improve, the situation.

On 12 September Berlioz and his son arrived in Le Havre to put Louis aboard a training vessel, though for six days they had little to do but wait in the hotel for the lading of the ship. Louis, determined to succeed at this activity after having failed at so many others, dismissed the discussions they overheard in the dining room to the effect that eight out of ten abandoned the sea after their maiden voyage. Instead they paid attention to more romantic talk: of California and Mexico and the tropics, the very subjects certain to induce daydreaming in father and son alike.

Louis's ship was bound for the French West Indies, calling first at Guadeloupe, then Havana, and possibly American ports. Reconciled at last to the notion that his son had been irrevocably seduced by the lure of the sea, and prone since his own childhood to such yearnings, Berlioz nevertheless feared for Louis's safety and health. Tropical disease, for example, headed the list of causes of death for European merchant mariners. A waiting train spared him the agony of seeing the ship pass the distant lighthouse and disappear over the horizon, but he took time to post a letter to Port-au-Prince with an English steamship. It was there when Louis arrived.

*T*he cost of Louis's marine training was not inconsiderable, and Berlioz had no recourse to the kinds of scholarships that had been available for the college in Rouen. The candidate's family bore the expenses of the first eighteen months; after that, upon successful completion of a preliminary examination, he was qualified for a three-year apprenticeship at 480 francs annual compensation. After five years, it was possible to become captain of a merchant vessel, with a decent salary attached. In the most optimistic projection, then, Louis would be twenty-four before he (or his family) could count on his financial independence. Outfitting him for his first voyage had cost his father 600 francs, all of it borrowed.

Adèle, having begun to emerge from the shock of Nanci's precipitous decline and death, now turned an eye to her brother's affairs. She took it upon herself to pose penetrating questions about his style of life and the matter of his maintaining two residences, and his testy response gives us a detailed picture of his finances. As of 24 September he listed debts of 1,762 francs:[40]

900 francs	borrowed for Louis's trip
300 francs	owed to Harriet's doctor in Montmartre
350 francs	owed to his tailor
180 francs	owed to his copyist
32 francs	owed to his hatter

His monthly income, he said, consisted of 118 francs from the Conservatoire library, 100 francs for each column for the *Journal des Débats* (now back to an average of four a month), 500 francs in pension from his mother's estate, and 84 francs from the Société Philharmonique. This amounts to something over 12,000 francs annually, twice what he had lived on in the 1830s. Certainly he was not poor, but by then one needed 18,000 to 20,000 francs annually to exist comfortably in Paris.

He carried on that autumn with his song collections and his preparations for the forthcoming season, though he would not pause to set either a text sent by Ferrand or a cantata for men's voices and orchestra that had occurred to him. *Feuillets d'album* (Albumleaves) includes the piano reduction of *Zaïde;* a slightly retouched version of *Les Champs,* the little song he composed in 1834 for a fashion magazine; and the piano-vocal setting of his Lille cantata, the *Chant des chemins de fer.* (Though not a bad souvenir of a memorable occasion, this last hardly seems an albumleaf.) *Feuillets d'album* appeared in September 1850. Later, in 1852, he would ask the prospective customer to append to this collection some other individually published bagatelles: the *Prière du matin* to a text of Lamartine (1846), the 1843 Dumas song called *La Belle Isabeau,* and *Zaïde*'s companion, *Le Chasseur danois.*

Richault continued mining this vein of recyclings with a collection called *Fleurs des landes* (roughly, Wildflowers), published in November. These five songs center around *Le Jeune Pâtre breton*—a rustic youth is pictured on the title vignette—and its companion piece, the *Chant des bretons* of 1835, each of them slightly revised. (The *Chant des bretons* went on to enjoy something of a vogue in the Galin-Paris-Chevé singing school, where it was performed and in 1853 published in Chevé's figured notation, the so-called *musique en chiffres.*) Three newer works complete the set of rural delights. Berlioz had composed *Le Trébuchet,* a "scherzo" for two matched voices and piano, in the 1840s; it was cited in the Labitte catalogue of 1846. When he came to add it to *Fleurs des landes,* he could find only the autograph of the first stanza, which lacked the subsequent text. Unable to reconstruct for himself where the original text had come from, he begged Emile Deschamps for three new stanzas, a week later thanking the author "forty thousand times," in four languages, for a canzonetta "very charming and perfectly *taillata per la musica.*"[41] The other two songs in the collection, *Le Matin* and *Petit Oiseau*, are different settings of the same poem by Adolphe de Bouclon (ex. 10.1). We know nothing of the reasons for this musical joke.

What we know of Berlioz's arrangement of two short works by Dimitri Bortniansky for four-part chorus, the *Chant des chérubins* and *Pater noster*, suggests that his role was largely limited to the preparation of Latin texts. The anthems were introduced at Société Philharmonique concerts of late 1850 and early 1851, probably prepared from a source he had brought home from Russia, where the music of Russian liturgy had stimulated Berlioz by its *douce et grave inspiration.*[42] Rights to the pair were sold to Richault in September 1850 for 100 francs. The *Chant des chérubins*, known in English as the Cherubim Song, enjoyed a considerable vogue in the nineteenth century and was anthologized in a large number of English and American octavo editions for church choirs—a circulation, in short, that well exceeded that of most of his other publications.

a. *Le Matin:*

b. *Petit Oiseau:*

EXAMPLE 10.1 Two settings of the same text for *Fleurs des landes.*

The documentation of 1850 is almost exclusively devoted to the new season of the Société Philharmonique, in an expanded schedule of one concert a month starting in October. Berlioz now had firm control of the choice of repertoire, which included substantially more of his own music and several first performances. At the opening concert on 22 October, for example, he offered a new arrangement of *Sara la baigneuse* for three choruses and orchestra, the Bortniansky *Chant des chérubins,* and, for the young bass virtuoso Paul Barroilhet, *Le Cinq Mai*—a work that just afterward disappeared entirely from his repertoire. The profit of 1,658 francs was enough to satisfy the *sociétaires.*

In matters of artistic quality, however, the second season of the Société Philharmonique was less impressive than the first. The increased dosage of Berlioz's own music carried with it a pronounced increase in technical difficulty. The second concert, scheduled for 12 November, was meant to include the *Symphonie fantastique,* but after seven rehearsals the orchestra was still not up to the task. The embarrassed musicians persuaded him not to cancel the concert, but rather to call an extra rehearsal for the afternoon of the performance; in the event they played better than ever before. After the symphony, moreover, the ladies of the chorus materialized with a crown of oak, laurel, and privet branches intertwined, as though to make amends with their leader. He thought it *fantastique.*[43] The new version of *Sara la baigneuse* was given for the second time.

Slipped into the 12 November program was a seemingly inconsequential morsel. At a boring party the previous September, Berlioz had scribbled out a four-part Andantino for organ in the album of the architect Duc, signing it "Pierre Ducré." In view of the turbulence surrounding the preparations of the *Fantastique* that November, he withdrew the long *Hymne à la France* and substituted in its place Duc's albumleaf, rewritten for four-part chorus. This was the lovely *Adieu des bergers à la Sainte Famille* (The shepherd's farewell to the Holy Family). It was one of his more elaborate ruses: the autograph calls for *flûtes douces, oboë di caccia* [sic], and *chalumeaux,* and the little *mystère* was attributed, in both the program and the parts from which the artists played and sang, to "Pierre Ducré, master of music to the Sainte-Chapelle, 1679." He told the performers and the press he had discovered the manuscript in a cupboard at the Ste.-Chapelle during the renovations there, and that the "old notation" had been difficult to decipher.

He gave the work twice that season (the second performance was most likely on 17 December) to a reception that quite amazed him.[44] Those who heard it praised the "pure and simple style," and only a few suspected the attribution of authorship. That he already imagined the *Adieu des bergers* might lead to something more is clear from the manuscript materials and lithographed parts used for the performances, which make a point of suggesting a larger work. "Fragment," they say, "de la Fuite en Egypte, mystère en 6 actes." *L'Adieu des bergers* is the first stage in the long and circuitous

FIGURE 10.9 *La Fuite en Egypte,* autograph. "Overture and excerpts from *La Fuite en Egypte,* a mystery in the old style . . . attributed to Pierre Ducré, imaginary chapelmaster."

genesis of *L'Enfance du Christ,* finally completed in 1854. Berlioz kept his silence for two more years, then made a good deal of the story. If the confluence of a seventeenth-century composer, Baroque-sounding instruments, the Ste.-Chapelle, and mystery plays seems unlikely, it merely underscores the era's confused perceptions of music of the past.

The fourth Société Philharmonique concert, on 28 January, offered the first four movements of *Roméo et Juliette* (through the Queen Mab scherzo), more of it than had been heard in Paris since the first performances in 1839. Alexis Dupont declined to recreate the Mab scherzetto, and the role was given to Roger; Mme Maillard sang the strophes. The long excerpt from *Roméo et Juliette*—before which the orchestra took a half hour, it was said, to tune—overshadowed the rest of the program, which included a Polyphemus-and-Galatea cantata by a *sociétaire* named Membrée and a fantasia on *La Favorite* played by Alard. Berlioz's setting of the Bortniansky *Pater noster* had its first performance.

The excerpts from *Roméo et Juliette* were so popular that they were repeated at the fifth concert, on 25 February, with the *Marche hongroise* from *Faust* and the sentimental air from Dalayrac's *Nina, Quand le bien-*

aimé reviendra, of which Berlioz had been fond since his childhood and which he had now copied out in full score. Two women from the chorus came forth during the February concert to present him with another gold crown.[45]

Spontini's death on 24 January was not unexpected. "I loved him, this unlovable man, because I had admired him," Berlioz wrote. "And besides, the very asperities of his character attracted me to him, doubtless because they intersected with the asperities of my own."[46] He published his long necrology of Spontini in the *Débats* of 12 February, under the title "Spontini: His Life and Works"; this appears, with revisions, as the thirteenth of the *Soirées de l'orchestre.* He supplemented his personal wealth of knowledge about Spontini with diligent research, at one point sending Pierre Erard, the piano manufacturer and Spontini's brother-in-law, to go through the composer's belongings and catalogue his manuscript scores; this listing appears in Berlioz's essay.

It is a disciple's obituary, of course, with sentimental paragraphs on *Cortez* ("there is a religion of beauty; I subscribe to it"), a long analysis of *La Vestale,* and as accurate a history of the composer and his works as Berlioz could construct in two weeks. There is a rather surprising apostrophe to the Conservatoire for its fostering of Spontini and his work. Writing the essay rekindled his admiration for the spectacle, characterization, orchestration, recitatives, and all the rest of what he loved about Spontini's work. Spontini's family and followers were touched; Erard sent him a new piano in gratitude.

Nothing would have satisfied Berlioz more than to accede to Spontini's chair at the Institute. On 6 March Berlioz wrote his letter of application, dutifully outlining his works and qualifications. The list includes the Te Deum and the new collections: *Vox populi, Tristia, Fleurs des landes,* and *Feuillets d'album,* along with the new version of *Sara la baigneuse.* He points proudly to the Société Philharmonique, "which is now prospering and which renders true service to art and to artists,"[47] then goes on, as usual, to cite his awards and decorations, this time including the Red Eagle of Prussia. But on 22 March Ambroise Thomas was elected to Spontini's chair; Berlioz's name was third on the list.

The Société Philharmonique struggled on through the spring, offering on 1 March a Mass by Niedermeyer in memory of the victims of the cholera epidemic and to benefit their orphans. The sixth concert, on 25 March, was an all-Berlioz program, with the *Fantastique,* Mme Dorus-Gras singing her *cavatine* from *Cellini,* and a new version of *La Belle Voyageuse* for female chorus and orchestra. This version was fashioned by alternating the vocal line of the 1843 setting for mezzo-soprano and orchestra between the two choral parts and by adding, from measure 21, a new contralto part (ex. 10.2). The orchestral parts were unchanged, and Berlioz merely had the new version added by his copyist to a copy of the 1844 published score. This is to be compared to the similar orchestral setting of *La Mort d'Ophélie* (see ex. 9.1).

FIGURE 10.10
Berlioz in 1850.
Oil on canvas; Courbet.

On the same program was the first performance of *La Menace des francs,* which had already appeared in a published piano-vocal score. The mystery surrounding its composition is greater even than for *Les Nuits d'été,* as the author of the strange text goes unidentified, and, but for an albumleaf dated in London on 28 April 1848, there is no documentation whatever of its composition. It seems clearly to be a response to the February revolution, with a text proclaiming the certain rising up of the French people against the oppression of tyrants:

Ah! si le sceptre en main,
Trop fier d'un pouvoir surhumain
Roi tu prétends éclipser notre gloire
 A la victoire
On nous verra marcher soudain.
Malgré ta couronne, tu trembleras
Et de ton trône tu redescendras.
 Les bras, les âmes
 Enfants et femmes
Tout combattra pour nous, tout s'unira.
Et contre toi sur nos pas entraîné
Armé du fer et des flammes
Le peuple entier marchera.

(Ah, king, if, with your scepter in hand, too proud of your exalted power, you dare cloud our dignity, then shall you see us on the march to victory. Despite your crown you'll tremble, and be toppled from your throne. Bodies, souls, children, women—everyone will unite with us in the combat. And, borne along in our path, armed with lance and torch, the very populace will march against you.)

The setting is for small chorus of men in four parts, large six-part chorus, and full orchestra with two pairs of timpani. The work is a through-com-

EXAMPLE 10.2 The orchestral *La Belle Voyageuse*.

posed march of the ponderous sort, prevailingly syllabic, and with copious doublings. Its studied simplicity suggests a conception for massed choirs, perhaps with a gathering of the Orphéon movement in mind. *La Menace des francs* is technically clever, especially in the chromatic coloration of the thick, Protestant style homophony, and rousing toward the end. Yet it is a routine piece of work, on a par with the railroad cantata and not so elegantly crafted as the *Hymne à la France*. He was in better form for his tribute to Napoleon III, the cantata *L'Impériale*.

*L*ouis Berlioz returned from his first voyage late in March, "in good form, large, and strong, and full of enthusiasm for his rude career."[48] He had thrived on the journey and been seasick only at night; swabbing decks in the sun had left him bronzed and muscular, and he had developed a passion for tropical fruit. Berlioz could not contain his excitement; he rushed on the night train of 26 March to Le Havre and was at the docks at 6:00 A.M. to wake his son. The necessary arrangements for a second voyage were made with the ship's owner and the captain, and Berlioz and Louis were back in Paris by 5:00 P.M.

Dressing Louis from head to foot "en gentleman," cost him 1,000 francs in two days. But that was scarcely noticed: Louis had grown in maturity and appearance, though his hands were badly calloused, and he had discovered for himself that his father was famous even in distant lands. He had found, too, that he was capable of his work, good enough at it that his company was prepared to pay him a salary as of his third voyage. Harriet was well enough to have been overjoyed to see her son, though her condition is usually reported as "about the same."[49] He was home for two weeks or so, and gone again by mid-April. Berlioz's letter of the following June is full of fatherly advice based on what he had gathered of Louis's shipboard life: "Try to dress well; do your duty without imprudence. I beg you not to expose yourself to as much sun as last year. Beware of the fever. Don't eat too much fruit."[50]

The last formal concert of the Société Philharmonique de Paris was on 29 April, with works by two minor composers: an overture by Berlioz's friend Morel, the director of the Marseille Conservatoire, and *Le Moine,* a cantata by Henri Cohen, who had purchased the services of the society for 1,000 francs. The vestiges of the Société Philharmonique offered promenade concerts in the Jardin d'Hiver for a few more weeks, but Seghers's rival Union Musicale, now called the Société Ste.-Cécile, had the better following, and Berlioz's group was disbanded by the end of the year.

The third Festival du Nord in Lille was to take place that summer, including on its programs the Lacrymosa of the Requiem and the *Chant des chérubins.* (It was at the second festival, in 1838, that Habeneck had conducted the Lacrymosa to such acclaim.) Berlioz helped prepare the program annotations for his work and was making ready for the short trip northward when, to his complete surprise, he was named a member of the French delegation to the Great Exhibition in London, a world's fair soon to open in Hyde Park. Specifically, it seems, he was expected to oversee the interests of the French instrument builders: Vuillaume, Sax, Alexandre, the organmaker Ducroquet, and so on. After a certain degree of confusion over departure times and arrangements for lodging in London—sure to be overcrowded—and the usual quibbling over reimbursement for his personal expenses, Berlioz crossed the channel on 8 May. He had little idea of what awaited him in London, or of how long he was expected to stay.

He reported to the rooms of Adolphe Duchène de Vère, at 27, Queen Anne Street, just north of Cavendish Square and perhaps ten blocks from Hyde Park. The proprietor of the building, an English musician named Francis Soutten, offered him for the duration of his stay an apartment close enough to the main staircase that he could leave his door ajar and hear rehearsals and performances of the Beethoven Quartett Society in the large drawing room on the ground floor. After a day or so of calling on his London friends, he ventured out to Hyde Park to examine, for the first time, the Great Exhibition—more properly, the Great Exhibition of the Works of Industry of All Nations—housed in a Crystal Palace built there for the occasion.

*T*he Crystal Palace: no more fitting temple to industrial progress, to the fruits of revolution, could have been built. ("Look well on these, my dear," Prince Albert had said to Queen Victoria of the designs, "for you may be seeing the architecture of the future.")[51] Joseph Paxton's greenhouse run amok—inspired, he said, by the structure of the Amazon lily—occupied an area of more than 75,000 square feet; the facade was more than a third of a mile across. It was the first great prefabricated edifice, the first temple of metal and glass. Nearly 300,000 panes of glass had been cast for the roof and walls. Berlioz was gazing on the imagination of the age, a monument to all that had happened between the *Symphonie fantastique* and the Te Deum: a celebration of suspension bridges and tunnels and the cast-iron pavilions that housed handsome locomotives. Likewise, he thought, he was seeing a future in which his own participation would be much smaller.

The adventure continued within, where the handiworks of peace lay alongside and overshadowed the engines of destruction. There were Chinese vases, lacquered work, silks, even a junk; Hindus from India with "primitive" instruments whose functions he could not understand; Scots in kilts with bagpipes. The American inventions, especially in music, were deemed pretentious and silly: there was a "piano-violino," "a mammoth double-action grand pianoforte, to be used by three or four performers simultaneously," and "a very ingenious little instrument for turning the leaves of music."[52] In the music rooms he first understood that the task of assembling written reports on the instruments would be harsh and much longer than he had imagined.

He was one of a ten-man committee chaired by Sir Henry Bishop, with Thalberg, Sterndale Bennett, Sir George Smart, Henry Wylde, and delegates from the United States and Germany. Together they adopted a grueling agenda of six-day work weeks during which they would audition, one by one, every instrument in the exhibit, from the tiniest piccolo on through to the pianos and organs. "You have no idea what an abominable forced labor I have been charged with," he writes to his sister. "I have to *hear* the wind

FIGURE 10.11 Exterior of the Crystal Palace in Hyde Park: the so-called aeronautic view from the northwest.

FIGURE 10.12 Interior of the Crystal Palace in Hyde Park: the eastern nave, looking west into the exhibits of foreign nations.

instruments, both woodwind and brass. My head is splitting from having to listen to these hundreds of vile machines, each more defective than the next, with but three or four exceptions."[53] And Class X-A, as it was known, was small by comparison, for instance, with industry's contributions to modern homemaking displayed in adjoining rooms: churns, chandeliers, and soaps in abundance. Berlioz was conscientious in his duties, however, and well prepared for them. Once the auditions were done, it was necessary to prepare the reports, of which duty he was naturally assigned a large share.

By 15 July the French government had grown edgy over the expenses of the open-ended stay and ordered him home. Berlioz stayed on, at his own expense, and was the last of the French to be done. The jury reports appeared over the next year or so, and Berlioz was the principal author and editor of the French edition drawn from the chapter on musical instruments.[54]

He reported the wonders of the Great Exhibition to the readers of the *Débats* in letters that appeared through the summer. He wrote, too, of the Beethoven concerts in his building, of George Osborne's annual *soirée musicale* (the same George Osborne who had helped with the piano-vocal version of *Les Francs-Juges*), the activities of the English choral societies, Thalberg's new opera *Florinda*, and so forth. But the experience to have the most impact on his composition was the concert of the Charity Children in St.

FIGURE 10.13 Berlioz in London, 1851.

Paul's Cathedral that he heard in early June. This was an annual event of a hundred years' standing, and Berlioz, curious to see what it was like, managed through the good offices of the organist to get admitted by agreeing to sing in the seventy-voice male choir. From his seat he watched with mounting excitement as 6,500 orphans in bright uniforms filed onto sixteen levels of bleachers. The church was bedecked in banners; the Archbishop of Canterbury and the Lord Mayor were dressed in their ceremonial regalia. He was transported by the visual spectacle even before they began to sing the Old Hundredth in unison.

He left in a daze, analyzing in his mind the explanations for the superb effect (the superior tone quality, he reasoned, must have had something to do with the better diet of the English working classes) and dreaming up ways to imitate it in his own music. In due course he resolved to add a part for unison children's choir to his unperformed Te Deum. He raved of the Charity Children to his friends and wrote for the *Débats* the beautiful account that appears as the twenty-first *soirée*. "Berlioz says that it is the finest thing he has heard in England," wrote George Eliot, who was convinced to go herself the next year. "I was not disappointed—it is worth doing once, especially as we got out before the sermon."[55]

He tried, unsuccessfully, to organize for the Crystal Palace a monster concert of the Te Deum and *Hymne à la France*. The rest of his time in London was occupied with social functions and talk of future plans, though he dabbled aimlessly with the notion of setting some Joan of Arc poems by a canon in Poitiers. He went to the London *Freischütz, Il franco arciero,* to verify for himself that they were not using his recitatives. By the time he left, though few knew of it, he had taken a London apartment for the following season. A New Philharmonic Society was to be formed, and Berlioz was to be appointed its director. He sailed for France on 28 July, having missed the festival in Lille.

*W*ith the Société Philharmonique and the London trip, Berlioz's life had gradually regained the hectic pace on which he thrived. In Paris he learned from Belloni that Liszt was planning a Weimar production of *Benvenuto Cellini.* Liszt proposed to stage the opera essentially as it had been done in Paris, though divided into four acts. This was the start of developments that would occupy Berlioz for many months; in late 1851 it was merely a question of sending Liszt the manuscript scores and parts, published materials for the two overtures, and questions on the forces at his disposal. Louis was home for a time in the autumn, between his second and third voyages. Again there were expenses for his clothes and the next period of training.

Berlioz spent the last months of 1851 touching up an orchestral version of *Tristia,* his Shakespearean work, which for its forthcoming publication was to include the *Marche funèbre pour la dernière scène d'Hamlet.* This edition was dedicated to Prince Eugène Sayn-Wittgenstein, sculptor and cousin of Princess Carolyne. Now Berlioz had three scores of which he had not heard a note: *Tristia;* the revised overture *La Tour de Nice,* just delivered to Richault for publication under the title *Le Corsaire;* and of course the Te Deum.

Louis-Napoléon dissolved the Assembly on 2 December and issued warrants for the arrest of his opponents, including the republican deputies; Hugo, for one, fled the country. This anticlimactic coup d'etat, having encountered only minimal resistance in the streets of Paris, was done by the 5th, and a plebiscite on 20 December confirmed Louis-Napoléon's presidency for ten years.

Berlioz conceived reasons to be optimistic over these developments. He had met Louis-Napoléon from time to time in London in 1847–48, and since then they had enjoyed pleasant encounters in the Paris streets, when the "prince-president" paid calls on an aunt in the neighborhood. Berlioz convinced himself that his Te Deum was certain to be chosen for Notre Dame on New Year's Day, in conjunction with a service of thanksgiving for the turn of events in December. Failing that, a coronation was sure to take place and, in all probability, a state wedding—each of these an ideal occasion for his work. What Berlioz did not yet understand was the new Napoleon's complete antipathy toward music of quality. In fact Napoleon III proved a good deal less supportive of the better French composers and their work than Louis-Philippe and his family had been.

Berlioz's schedule for early 1852 approximated the whirlwind of earlier times. He was due in London at the beginning of March and in the meanwhile hoped to give a concert in Bordeaux; the Weimar *Cellini* required his presence, and by year's end he had also considered and declined an attractive invitation to travel to the United States. (There is some indication that *Much Ado About Nothing* attracted his attention again during this period; scrawled on the cover of a primitive manuscript scenario, in Legouvé's hand, are the words "Bénédict et Béatrix.") *Cellini,* it seemed as late as 1 February, was to open in Weimar on the 15th, and Liszt wanted him there beforehand to conduct a concert of *Roméo et Juliette* and *Harold en Italie.* Berlioz accepted this invitation, though refusing the offer of a room at the Altenburg. He would be traveling with Marie Recio, and joint residence there would be thought unseemly at court. (Liszt's relationship with the princess was never recognized by the court, either; his official correspondence was sent to the Hotel Erbprinz in the city.)

In Weimar, however, things were developing poorly. There was a crisis in mid-February with a recalcitrant tenor, and some of the other singers were genuinely ill. The Berlioz festival was postponed until the autumn; only *Cellini* was to be heard that spring, in what amounted to a preview performance, and in the interval it was to undergo decided change. The press, which had got wind of the difficulties, pestered Berlioz, who did not know the reason for the delay, and Liszt, who did; together they managed to convince the public that illness was the cause.

Heinrich Ernst was in Paris, and in gratitude for his many previous services on behalf of *Harold* and those surely to come, Berlioz assisted him in organizing and presenting two public concerts, which he conducted on 14 January and 4 February. Ernst, too, had become a London habitué, leading a string quartet that eventually included Joachim, Wieniawski, and Piatti; he settled there permanently in 1855 and was involved in several of Berlioz's London concerts.

Berlioz's *feuilleton* of 3 February 1852, complaining of the audible "tacks" by conductors at the Opéra and other bad habits there, created a brief citywide diversion. The prince-president/emperor-"elect" had taken the health of the Opéra under his wing, and his censor had forbidden publication of Berlioz's review. Bertin printed it nonetheless—inadvertently, Berlioz imagined, as it contained nothing political—and was hauled before the commission of censure. It fell to Berlioz to make a pale apology to Louis-Napoleon's private secretary. ("As for my sentiments toward the prince who has saved France and all civilization from the frightful morass in which they were drowning, these may be summarized in a grateful admiration.")[56] He was fearful that the government would again try to abolish his modest post at the Conservatoire during his English sojourn, for he knew he would not be missed.

Shortly before leaving for London on 3 March, he saw to the publication of an advertisement in large folio, printed front and back, of all his published works. It begins with an explanatory paragraph:

M. Hector Berlioz, wishing to revise his works at leisure and preserve them from poorly conceived or incomplete performances, long refused to have them published. Now the advancement of these grandiose and hardy works, brought about by massed performances of instrumentalists and vocalists, is widespread: the author has had them heard under his direction in most of the capitals of Europe, where he has left his conceptions behind as tradition. The old habits have been broken. Moreover, he has profited from these many experiences to introduce improvements to which these works seemed susceptible and to remove the faults he discovered in them. Thus he decided, several years ago, to publish them all. Many artists and *amateurs,* however, and foreigners especially, are unaware of this. Thus his Paris publishers deemed it necessary to give the public the list of the major works of M. H. Berlioz which they own, even including those so far unpublished—but which will appear presently—and his salon works, written in such originally poetic style, so lively and novel of coloring.[57]

The catalogue itself shows the several changes made in the works since publication of the Labitte catalogue of 1846, especially with regard to the new collections of songs. *Sara la baigneuse* is described, for example, as a "ballad for three choruses and orchestra," where formerly it had been a "madrigal-quartet, for soprano, two tenors, and bass, with chorus and orchestra." The 1852 catalogue also indicates that before Berlioz left for England, he had intended to round off the *Adieu des bergers* of 1850 with a fugal overture and a tenor solo, *Le Repos de la Sainte Famille* (The Holy Family at rest). This was the finished work *La Fuite en Egypte,* "attributed to Pierre Ducré, imaginary *maître de chapelle,* and composed, both the words and the music, by M. Berlioz." The "Richault catalogue" appeared in Paris in February or March 1852 and in the *Monthly Record* of the London Musical Union at about the same time.

The *Mémoires* fail to note the extraordinary brilliance of the foreign concerts that ensued between 1852 and 1855: the autobiography was all but finished, and the new round of travels was simply wedged into the existing fabric of the book, summarily and fragmentarily. If the tours of the 1840s seemed to him rigorous while they were under way, in retrospect they must have seemed relaxing compared to those of 1853 and 1854. Over the next few years there were a half-dozen different visits to Liszt in Weimar, three major summer series with the New Philharmonic Society in London, and another extended invasion of Germany. In Baden-Baden the impresario Bénazet offered him a fresh new outlet for his formidable skills, free of risk. He witnessed during these years both his greatest triumph as conductor, his

FIGURE 10.14 Berlioz in 1852.

London performances of Beethoven's Ninth, and (arguably) the worst failure of his career, *Benvenuto Cellini* at Covent Garden. Every appearance, it seems, was the occasion for another banquet or toast or crown, and when, in the course of it, the idea for a new symphony in A minor came to him, he was too busy to tax himself by attending to it and let it slip away. There was but a single masterwork composed in the rush of things: *L'Enfance du Christ*.

The peregrinations would, for the most part, come to an abrupt end in 1856, with Berlioz's election to the Institute; thereafter there would be only sporadic adventures abroad, and the long saga of *Les Troyens* would come to dominate his life. But for the better part of the five years until then, he was in Paris for less than twenty weeks at a stretch. In fact, 1852–55 were more the *années de pèlerinage* than the 1840s had been.

The New Philharmonic Society was established by Henry Wylde and a committee of wealthy industrialists to compete with the historic Royal Philharmonic Society, at the time under the autocratic control of Michael Costa and hamstrung by a repertoire consisting almost entirely of Mendelssohn and his predecessors, nearly always rescored in some fashion by Costa himself. The prospectus of the new society promised "more perfect performances of the great masters than have, hitherto, been attained"[58] and a season of six concerts from March to June, with an emphasis on the contemporary repertoire. The concerts were to be given in Exeter Hall, a three-thousand-seat auditorium in the Strand, large enough to assure cheap tickets.

(A. W. Ganz notes, from a contemporary illustration, the quaint juxtaposition of the word "Philadelpheion," chiseled into the lintil above the great doors, with the "No Popery" placards resting prominently in the street.)[59] The orchestra of 110 numbered among its members Sivori as concertmaster; Henry Hill, John Loder, and William Ganz as violinists; Piatti as principal cellist; Bottesini as principal double-bassist, the clarinettist Henry Lazarus; the cornettist Arban; the timpanist Thomas Chipp; and Eduard Silas as a percussionist. The chorus of two hundred was led by Frank Mori. Frederick Beale, of the publishers Cramer and Beale, was the manager of the enterprise.

The repertoire was solid if typically Berliozian in its heavy reliance on Gluck, Beethoven, Weber, and Mendelssohn. After the opening concert, which featured the first half of *Roméo et Juliette*, there was relatively little Berlioz: the *Francs-Juges* overture, some *Faust,* and the *Chant des chérubins* and *Invitation à la valse.* Among the moderns to be heard were Wylde, Smart, Silas, and Edward Loder. The orchestra greeted an excellent house on 24 March with the Jupiter Symphony, a scene from *Iphigénie en Tauride,* the Beethoven Triple Concerto, the movements from *Roméo et Juliette,* a double-bass solo composed and played by Bottesini, and the overtures to *Oberon* and *Guillaume Tell.* The press, using words like "acme" and "faultless," was unanimous in its praise, with the quality of Berlioz's conducting singled out as it had been in 1847–48. Berlioz himself used the superlative "pyramidal" to describe the results and was seen the next day walking down Regent Street with a poetical look of satisfaction on his face.[60]

What he did not yet know was that *Cellini* had, likewise, passed muster at its three Weimar performances. It had opened on 20 March and played again on the very night of his first London concert. Liszt's report arrived in London on the 29th:

> *Honneur aux ciseleurs!* Glory to beautiful things, and opportunity to them. *Benvenuto Cellini,* performed here yesterday, is still standing, and at his full height. It is *sans puff* that one can announce its success to London and Paris. I thank Berlioz deeply for the noble pleasure that attentive study of his *Cellini* has brought me. It is one of the strongest works I know, at once a splendid sculpture and an original, living statue.[61]

During his London season Berlioz was stymied by the English manner of rehearsal, which is to say that there was very little of it. He had been hard pressed to deliver a polished *Roméo et Juliette;* now for his second concert on 14 April, he was faced with the first performance of Edward Loder's masque on the Telemachus story, *The Island of Calypso.* There was little enough time to do the work whatever justice was due it, and the antipathy toward their responsibilities of the tenor Sims Reeves and his wife, the soprano Emma Lucombe, was contagious. The critics, who enjoyed Beethoven's Fifth and the *Chant des chérubins,* drew attention to faults in the performance of the masque. Berlioz replied to the editor of *The Musical*

World that "the non-efficiency of the performance of Mr. Loder's masque must be ascribed to the non-attendance of Mr. and Mrs. Sims Reeves at a single rehearsal with orchestra."[62] He wrote in a similar vein to Loder, complaining that at all three rehearsals with the instrumentalists he had had to sing both parts while trying to conduct. Reeves complained that he had received no notice of the first and third rehearsals and was indisposed for the second.

> M. Berlioz says that the only *grave error* was not committed by the orchestra, but with due deference I must observe that it appears to be a very *grave error* to perform a work from first to last without any successful attempt at accent or colouring, and this was certainly the case with the execution of Mr. Loder's *Calypso,* and will be so whenever a conductor (however excellent his merits) consents to give a new and *bel ouvrage* to the public with only one full band rehearsal.[63]

Things went on like this for the remainder of the season, with performances admirably delivered under the circumstances, but inevitably betraying the lack of careful preparation. Berlioz went so far as to alternate halves of the orchestra for the smaller works in order to double the rehearsal time.

The third concert featured excerpts from *La Vestale,* to which Berlioz was of course keenly attached, with Staudigl as the High Priest, Clara Novello as Julia, and the young Alexander Reichardt as tenor. Mme Spontini and her brother Pierre Erard came to London for the concert, and she had Spontini's "bâton de commandement" delivered to Berlioz, the one "my dear husband used to conduct the works of Gluck, Mozart, and himself. Where better could it be placed than in your able hands?"[64] And on this same program his former fiancée Camille Pleyel played the Weber *Konzertstück* under his baton and, by herself, Liszt's *Illustrations du Prophète,* a fantasy on themes from Meyerbeer's opera. To Liszt alone did he write of "*Elle* (The Queen of the Pianists)," dismissing their curious reencounter in a few words.[65]

With its fourth, fifth, and sixth programs (12 and 28 May and 9 June), the New Philharmonic Society achieved a certain stride, such that these "altogether extraordinary" concerts began to rival his great successes in Germany and even Russia. By the end of the season the orchestra had so grown in capability that Berlioz began to consider it the best he had ever led. On 12 May and again at the last concert, his performances of Beethoven's Ninth sealed his reputation in England as the world's greatest living conductor. Again there were fine soloists: Clara Novello, Miss Williams, Reeves, and Staudigl; again the press acknowledged the magnitude of the occasion. The Ninth, it was said, had never been fully understood in London, and for several weeks thereafter it was the talk of the at-homes. Berlioz was called back to the stage many times that night, both excerpts from *Faust* were encored, and after the Ninth a crown was thrown to him from the galleries. The New Philharmonic Society had survived its first season and, thus established, showed every promise of a long and useful existence.

During his quieter moments at 10, Old Cavendish Street, Berlioz was approaching the end of his new volume of musical anecdotes, now provisionally titled *Les Contes de l'orchestre* (Tales of the orchestra members); the complete *Soirées* were almost ready for delivery to the publisher by the time he reached France. He had also proofread Richault's edition of *La Fuite en Egypte* and in London attached to the dedication to John Ella a long epistle on its true genesis. Berlioz took Marie when he went for a second time that spring to hear the Charity Children, and to the usual concerts and plays.

To Louis, who wrote that he had spent all his money—including 15 francs of duty charged by a Cuban official for bringing cigars into the country— he fired off an unusually hostile letter. "Why didn't you throw them in the sea?" he asks of the cigars, and encloses half a 100-franc note, promising the other half in due course. Then comes some strong advice: "I urge you to measure your language when you write me: that style doesn't suit. If you think life is a bed of roses, you'd better begin to see the contrary."[66] Louis had been home for six weeks by the time Berlioz and Marie Recio returned to France on 20 or 21 June.

Once more there was a letter from Liszt, this one resurrecting the idea of Berlioz's coming to Weimar for a complete *Roméo et Juliette* before the new performances of *Cellini*, possibly in the late fall. Liszt enclosed a long series of cuts and changes he thought might improve the second half of the opera, and Berlioz spent the better portion of the summer effecting painstaking revisions to the score, both to satisfy the German taste and to rectify the Paris shortcomings. By summer's end the plans for a Berlioz festival in Weimar, a *Berlioz-Woche,* had taken pleasing shape.

*J*oseph Girod de Nienney, baron de Trémont, died on 1 July in Paris at the age of seventy-three. Berlioz had known him since the early 1820s. The baron's long career of service to the governments of France had always included patronage of musical events, and in his will he bequeathed a handsome annuity to the five associations of Paris artists, among them the Association of Artist-Musicians. Thus it seemed fitting to Baron Taylor and his administrative committee to ask Berlioz to conduct the Requiem for a memorial service at St.-Eustache. This was the largest Requiem he ever conducted, with an orchestra of 180, a chorus of 250 assembled from the choruses of the various opera houses, and an *orphéon* of 250 further voices for the Tuba mirum and Lacrymosa, among them a chorus of children. Roger, again, agreed to appear for the tenor solo.

Meanwhile Berlioz declined the widow Le Sueur's invitation to write something for the unveiling of her husband's statue in Abbeville, pleading

FIGURE 10.15
Caricature of Berlioz by Nadar.
Journal pour rire,
18 September 1852.

physical and spiritual exhaustion. His fatigue was in fact alarming enough for Dr. Amussat to step in and prescribe a period of rest at the sea. He went to St.-Valery-en-Caux, on the Normandy coast, for what appears to have been something over a week, and returned to Paris in better health and good spirits. (Dr. Amussat's latest therapy for Harriet, incidentally, was electric-shock treatment of her paralyzed arm. Her condition went unchanged, but she was relatively happy and from time to time seemed even optimistic about the future.)

Just before the memorial performance of the Requiem on 22 October, Roger was forbidden, in view of a conflicting engagement at the Opéra, to appear; the solo part in the Sanctus was given on short notice to Mlle Lefebvre from the Opéra-Comique and four tenors from the chorus, apparently using the version composed for Marie Recio and Roger in 1844. Roqueplan also forbade the participation of the Opéra chorus, but Baron Taylor and Berlioz, in a sweet victory, had his veto overridden by the Ministry of the Interior. It was the chorus of the Opéra-Comique, however, that thus bore the brunt of the hard work. They were doubtless at the center of the five hundred voices arranged that morning on a massive scaffold constructed especially for the event, a structure that probably lent the performance its memorable acoustic qualities. It was one of those events that attracted hordes of listeners, many of whom were moved to tears. In the audience were Meyerbeer and Saint-Saëns; Saint-Saëns was for the first time seeing Berlioz conduct.

The prince-president returned in mid-October from his campaign in the provinces—where his gracious response to challenge was that he was prepared to govern "under whatever title might be given me"[67]—and established himself in the royal palace of St.-Cloud. While the decrees necessary to promulgate a new empire were being rendered in draft, Berlioz was lobbying to assure the adoption of his Te Deum for the ceremonies of coronation. He wanted a large budget—"We don't crown emperors every day, and Notre-Dame is not a village church."[68] But splendor was not the sort of thing that appealed to this Bonaparte, and Berlioz's negotiations with the government to that end were fruitless. He left for Weimar on 12 November.

Liszt's study of *Cellini* had been attentive, and the performances in March had led him to an idea for resolving the troublesome conclusion. It fell to the twenty-two-year-old von Bülow, the most capable of Liszt's young disciples, to analyze and review the first Weimar *Cellini* for the *Neue Zeitschrift für Musik,* and his long essay of 2 and 30 April surely reflects Liszt's sentiments: "I would recommend the complete omission of the fourth act or tableau, and would include only the very last thing, the casting of the statue, [for the end of] the third act." They had separated each of Berlioz's two acts into two halves for their four-act version; what von Bülow and Liszt were recommending, then, was the compression of all of the Paris act II into a shortened Weimar act III. Von Bülow also attacked the German translation of A. F. Riccius, with whom he enjoyed sparring, as pale and tasteless, with the result that for the 1856 revival a new version by Peter Cornelius was used.

Berlioz, preoccupied in London and Paris, was only too happy to accept the proposals of an intimate whose instincts he trusted implicitly. Liszt and his followers, in the course of what must have been heated discussions of *Cellini,* were able to develop the kind of artistic advice a composer too seldom gets. Berlioz did the recrafting himself, cutting the original scenes 10 through 20 of the second act and rearranging much of what was left in his second act. The workmen's chorus "Bienheureux les matelots" was retained, with the dialogue given to Francesco and Bernardino; Ascanio's aria "Tra-la-la-la-la . . . mais qu'ai-je donc" followed; then Cellini's "Sur les monts" and the sextet and finale. "You were the one to set me right," he tells Liszt.[69]

In neither of its 1852 versions was *Cellini* a particular success. The audiences were polite and that November called for the composer after every act, but nothing was encored. Where the Paris *Cellini* was diffuse, the compressed Weimar version was illogical and thus equally graceless in its denouement. And Berlioz was not the sort of individual to leave a work to posterity in a configuration largely molded by others. There would be still further revisions before the Weimar revival and Brunswick publication of 1856.

The *Roméo et Juliette* of 20 November, however, and parts I and II of *Faust* (of which Liszt was the new dedicatee) were quite another matter. The orchestra and chorus, pleased to have him back, decorated his desk in laurel. He outdid himself that evening, and the orchestra responded with fire and distinction. Moscheles, who had made the pilgrimage to Weimar with his share of doubts about Berlioz, was stunned. "Berlioz's conducting . . . carried everything, as it were, by storm. I am glad to have made his acquaintance, both as a composer and as a conductor."[70] He had liked the melodic style of *Cellini* and the delicate instrumentation and was much impressed with the depth of thought he saw in Berlioz's work.

The next night, after another performance of *Cellini,* there was a sumptuous dinner at court hosted by the grand duchess, where Berlioz was decorated with the order of the White Falcon of Saxe-Weimar. On 22 November, a ball was given in his honor. Probably most gratifying of all, on 23 November the artists gathered *chez* Liszt and his princess at the Altenburg to lionize him. It was a breathless week, ending with a rush back to Paris for Berlioz to sign for his monthly stipend: he had not taken a formal leave. There was nothing waiting at home that concerned the imperial ceremonies.

The Weimar *Cellini* was a pivotal event in Liszt's effort to establish Weimar as the center of the futuristic spirit. The aesthetic tenets of the Futurists were rather vague: witness the too-easy pairing of Berlioz with Wagner as their avatars. Wagner let it be known that he did not like *Cellini,* though he could

FIGURE 10.16 Liszt, c. 1841.

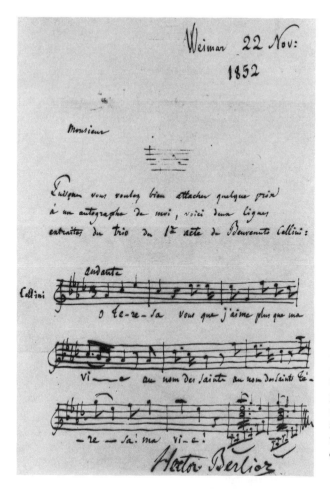

FIGURE 10.17
Albumleaf for an
autograph collector,
prepared in Weimar,
22 November 1852,
showing the start of
the trio from act I
of *Benvenuto Cellini*.

not have seen a score. But whatever he knew of that particular work, he understood better than either Liszt or Berlioz the need for a kind of perfection of dramatic structure that *Benvenuto Cellini* manifestly lacked. The other disciples—von Bülow, Peter Cornelius, Raff, and Richard Pohl—were at least respectful to and for the most part enthusiastic over Berlioz. They rendered him useful service as well: Cornelius and his sister as translators of his musical texts, Pohl in his translations of the prose, and Mme Pohl as ever-willing harpist. (Berlioz thought Cornelius intolerably slow in his work, but always liked the results.) The Grand Duchess Maria Pavlovna did not know quite what to make of all this, but there could be no denying the gravitational pull of her "music master in extraordinary," Liszt, or his serious efforts to become an important composer; if nothing else, she sensed that the busy intellectual climate gave Weimar a renewed stamp of international significance in music. It is true that Weimar in the 1850s was the Olympus of Futurism.

The Weimar experience, as it began for Berlioz in 1852 and continued through 1856, signals the commencement of his last creative period. He fit easily into the Weimar circle, moving therein with a charm uncommon in his Paris existence. Liszt and he were both older and arguably wiser, but they were able to rediscover their former intimacy with little effort. Berlioz admired Princess Carolyne Sayn-Wittgenstein, Liszt's mistress of some five years, with a passion he had never felt for Marie d'Agoult. The princess was a voracious reader and writer, fluent in French, and wealthy; the daughter she had borne her husband Nicholas in 1837, Marie, was herself becoming an engaging young woman. The princess returned Berlioz's sentiments. They fell easily into soulful musings on art and truth; he felt welcome, indeed obliged, to return as often as he could. It was at the Altenburg that his enthusiasm for composition was rekindled, and there that *L'Enfance du Christ* grew to maturity and that *Les Troyens* was born and in successive visits fostered.

FIGURE 10.18
Carolyne Sayn-Wittgenstein,
c. 1848.

Chapter Eleven

The Princess Carolyne—The Fair Ophelia
(1852–59)

erlioz's vain efforts to attract the emperor's attention to his Te Deum, perfect though it was for imperial ceremony, began to confirm his worst suspicions of the new regime. But the emperor let it be known he would require a chapel, and accordingly Berlioz volunteered a plan for its organization, based largely on his impressions of the Russian chapel and emphasizing the need for a composer-conductor of the highest qualifications and celebrity. There is no evidence that this document was ever seen by the emperor; it is, however, a well-reasoned, carefully written manifesto, recounting from memory and personal experience the lessons of the Tuileries Chapel and ending with some prescient remarks:

> The Emperor's superintendent [of music], if he is laced with the love of his task, of the beauty of his mission, and if he is endowed with the necessary knowledge and instinct—not to say the genius—could complement His Majesty's purposes and give birth to an institution both great and admirable. If, however, he is but a mediocre artist, or tired, without the flame of excitement, a foreigner to true religious style, or preoccupied with his personal interests (in the most common sense of those words), then despite the Sovereign's will and his most precise instructions, his goal will obviously never be achieved . . . In the last analysis it is to the Emperor to wish it and to his *maître de chapelle* to achieve it. For all this is do-able. The resources of France are immense: one need only put them to work.[1]

But Auber was named *maître de chapelle,* and the imperial progresses through Paris and ceremonies of thanksgiving at Notre Dame, such as they were, came and went without the benefit of Berlioz's hand. The best he could hope for was a role in the emperor's forthcoming wedding ceremony.

The *Soirées de l'orchestre* appeared in December 1852, published by Michel Lévy frères, a prestigious firm which, though Michel Lévy was only thirty-one, was already the preferred publisher of Janin, Hugo, Alexandre Dumas, and George Sand. (Lévy published two of Berlioz's three subsequent prose works and acquired the *Grotesques de la musique* when he purchased Bourdilliat's Librairie Nouvelle in 1861.) In the crush of holiday publications the *Soirées* were scarcely remarked by the papers, but the collection sold well and was reprinted in 1853 and in 1854. Perhaps 1,500 copies were sold during Berlioz's lifetime.[2]

Gautier, when he finally got around to publishing his review, remarked that "Berlioz, in addition to being a great composer, writes with a fantasy, verve, and spirit that many professional authors, incapable of writing the shortest fugue, might find enviable. The *Soirées de l'orchestre* are there to tell them so."[3]

The 1854 edition purported to be "entirely revised and corrected." In fact only three passages were changed: Berlioz toned down negative asides concerning Spontini and Costa and a "diatribe in poor taste" on Castil-Blaze about which Escudier had complained in the pages of *La France musicale*.[4]

 Early in the new year Berlioz was summoned by the emperor's secretary and told to ready the Te Deum for the rather sudden marriage—as though for the good of the empire—of Napoleon III to Eugénie de Montijo, the Spanish countess of Teba. There was to be a civil ceremony on 29 January followed the next day by a Catholic wedding at Notre Dame. Berlioz had already ordered his copyists to work when he discovered that the Ministry of the Interior had at the same time directed the staff of the Conservatoire to provide the music. A pale program was chosen, in part by rummaging through Berlioz's own Conservatoire library for the old standbys. The minister sent for the director of Fine Arts, who sent for Auber, who sent for Girard, who sent for the venerable *chef de copie* Leborne to do the legwork necessary to have the parts ready in time for a single rehearsal. Excerpts from the sacred music of Cherubini, Adam, and Le Sueur were offered, plus a "plain-chant," *Domine salvum fac Napoleonem,* orchestrated by Auber. The full Te Deum chosen was Le Sueur's. For a grand march they selected something from a recent ballet of Schneitzoeffer. "What do you think of that omelette?" Berlioz asked Chorley.[5]

The emperor's secretary, in his embarrassment, promised Berlioz both reimbursement for whatever expenses he had incurred and a full performance for the coronation—a ceremony that never took place. Sensing the obvious parallels with the Requiem, Berlioz did not believe a word of it: "They'll arrange a quadrille by Musard, if they can't find anything worse."[6] As late as the first performance, in 1855, he suggests that he was never paid even the 1,200 francs for the copying.

The impetus to mount *Cellini* at Covent Garden seems to have come from Henry Chorley, music critic of the *Athenaeum,* who had been in Weimar the previous November. "We are glad to hear a rumour," his paper tattled in January, "that the *Benvenuto Cellini* of M. Berlioz may be one among the novelties given at Her Majesty's Theatre during the coming season."[7] Berlioz's strong desire to be presented at one of the Italian houses was more than a rumor, and he was optimistic enough over the possibility to have had the libretto translated into Italian. He did not accept reengagement by the New Philharmonic Society for 1853; Henry Wylde, who controlled the purse strings, insisted on sharing the podium, and Berlioz thought little of his abilities. Moreover, he expected to be otherwise engaged.

It was a routine winter, made memorable only by the definitive signing over to Gounod early in 1853 of the libretto to *La Nonne sanglante*. The debut of the season was that of Pasdeloup's Société des Jeunes-Artistes on 20 February. Jules Pasdeloup and his young artists began their remarkable nine-year tenure as a protest over what was perceived to be studied neglect of young composers by the Société des Concerts; by 1856, under Auber's patronage, Pasdeloup's charges too were a Société *du Conservatoire,* and they did more than their fair share of premieres by the next generation of French composers. The Société des Jeunes-Artistes, moreover, was but the first of Pasdeloup's distinguished ventures. Throughout his long career, he was an ardent advocate of Berlioz's music; it was Pasdeloup, in fact, who kept the central Berlioz repertoire before the public in the late 1860s and 1870s, and who deserves much of the credit for carrying his torch into the modern era. On the program of Pasdeloup's first concert was *Le Carnaval romain,* and among the critics present was, of course, its composer.

The very favorable terms of his contract with Richault for *La Damnation de Faust,* signed on 30 March, foresaw the simultaneous publication of a full score, orchestral and choral parts, and a piano-vocal score. But of the several reams of proofs that occupied him that spring, the most unusual were for a second edition of the Requiem, being prepared by Ricordi in Milan. He had submitted the revised text in mid-1852, after the two performances of the early 1850s, out of the need for a score that would incorporate the revisions made then and, more urgently, match the chorus parts already published by Brandus in 1852. Late February 1853 found Berlioz absorbed in work on the new edition, complimenting Ricordi for the quality of the engraving and asking for the addition of a line to the title page: "2me Edition revue par l'auteur, et contenant plusieurs modifications importantes."[8] (The listing of the Requiem in his catalogue of 1859 notes: "Ricordi's edition is the only correct one, differing in several essential details from the earlier edition done in Paris by Schlesinger and now out of print.") He returned the last proofs to Milan on 17 April.

Among these "several essential details" were revised declamation for several passages of the Latin text, a good deal of redistribution of material among the various choral voices, and the inclusion of the subtitle he had used in 1848 for a performance of the Offertoire: Chœur des âmes de Purgatoire (Chorus of souls in Purgatory). These deceptively modest changes, entered so long after first composition, had a marked positive effect on the score. Most notable is the systematic change of declamation, in the Rex tremendae, of the words "salva me" (ex. 11.1a). This process led in turn to the inspired addition of the ethereally dissonant C♯s in oboes, clarinets, and sopranos in mm. 97–98, where originally there had been only B♮s (ex. 11.1b). Three other significant revisions to the Requiem were not published until Ricordi issued a new edition in 1867. These were the deletion of ten measures in the Quaerens me (a passage still to be found in some popular vocal scores) and seventeen bars in the Offertoire and the substitution in the second movement of the words "Tuba mirum, spargens sonum" for "Et iterum venturus est" at the moment of apocalypse. This reading must have been customary for some time, however, as Berlioz refers to the passage as the "Tuba mirum" in portions of the *Mémoires* written as early as 1848.[9]

In Le Havre Louis was spending a great deal of his father's money and failing his hydography courses, in grave danger of being ejected from the one career for which he had shown any promise. The Admiral and Count-Senator Jean-Baptiste Cécille, highly placed in the administration of the imperial navy, took Louis's situation under advisement as a favor to Berlioz, and now suggested enlisting Louis on a military frigate for a term of three years. Berlioz was confused and frightened by the proposal, troubled though he was by Louis's lot and by his ceaseless demands for money. He feared he had aggravated Harriet's condition by recounting his worries to her. She now had to be lifted in and out of bed, which required paying for the services of a third nurse. His cousin Alphonse Robert, attending her of late, had curtailed the electric-shock therapy and announced that there was nothing further to be done.

Berlioz himself was ill with bronchitis during the three weeks in late March and early April when negotiations for *Cellini* reached their climax. The Italian Opera at Covent Garden offered him a substantial fee (£2,000, apparently) and reimbursement for the copying, which they agreed should be done under his supervision in Paris. His demands included the return of the manuscript materials in time for use that fall and winter in Germany and the participation of the best of the company's singers: Tamberlick as Cellini, Mme Julienne as Teresa, and Tagliafico as Fieramosca. He hinted at his desire to conduct; whatever their decision on that matter, the company was to pay his travel expense and take care to call him to London the moment the rehearsals got under way. To Frederick Gye, the manager of Covent Garden, he wrote insisting on the need for a spectacular production. "For this score to produce the appropriate effect, it must be staged with verve, fearlessly and without hesitation, in order to arrive at a performance dazzling with these qualities—a performance insolent, so to speak, with brio."[10]

His conditions were met on 8 April, and that very afternoon he summoned his copying staff and gave them a week to prepare the solo and chorus roles. (The bill came to 1,110 francs.) The solo parts were in London for the

a. Original: Revised:

Revised:

EXAMPLE 11.1 Changes in the Rex tremendae of the Requiem (1852–53).

singers to begin their studies on 20 April; the necessary adjustments to the orchestra parts could be made once he was there. After agreeing to appear at a concert of the old Philharmonic Society and dealing with a few remaining details at home, he departed for London on 13 or 14 May, cautiously optimistic: "Let's hope for the best."[11]

Berlioz had not meant to appear in public before the opening night of *Cellini,* but the Philharmonic Society scheduled him to conduct their fourth concert, on 30 May. It was his intention in accepting the engagement to present the *Symphonie fantastique,* so far unheard in London under his baton, but he would not consent to it on the single rehearsal offered him. Instead he chose *Harold en Italie* and, to whet the appetite for *Cellini, Le Carnaval romain.* More significant was the first performance of his new biblical scene with tenor and orchestra, *Le Repos de la Sainte Famille.* Portions of the aria had to be revised to accommodate the tenor, Italo Gardoni, but the result was a satisfying rendition that earned an encore. That was enough to delight Berlioz with the piece and to send a number of his admirers, notably Eduard Silas, into ecstasy. "No one can deny," wrote the *Morning Herald,* "the presence of a musical poet, one burning with rapid and exacting passages."[12] This offering of concerts with the Philharmonic

FIGURE 11.1 Check for ten guineas, 22 June 1853, payable to Mons. H. Berlioz, for the (Old) Philharmonic Society Concert of 30 May 1853.

Society on one rehearsal was nevertheless a risky business, and for the negligible fee of 10 guineas.

The *Fantastique* was never to be heard in London under the baton of its composer.

The rehearsals for *Cellini* went promisingly. Berlioz found Tamberlick well suited to the title role, able to reach the highest notes with an ease that was fast making his abilities legendary. Costa, for a change, seemed positively self-effacing in his errands on behalf of *Cellini*. Adopting a Meyerbeerian strategy, Berlioz nurtured his friendships with those who might positively influence the outcome, dining with the critics Henry Chorley (17 June) and J. W. Davison (18 June) and as many other music journalists as he could. But the press was chafing over new house rules that required them to secure invitations before coming to rehearsals, a policy Berlioz thought counterproductive; he had, moreover, exhausted his own supply of complimentary tickets for opening night long before his three dozen petitioners were accommodated.

Cellini opened before a glittering audience that included Queen Victoria and Prince Albert, the blind king of Hanover and his queen, and, sharing a box with Victor Schœlcher and Edward Holmes, Mme Viardot. It closed the same evening, his supporters powerless to compete with the well-organized, loud, and very angry claque. *Cellini* was hissed from the first note to the last; not even the Roman Carnival overture, so well received at the Philharmonic Society concert the week before, was spared. "Don't you think, sir, it is very wrong to hiss an opera like this?" Mme Viardot inquired of her hosts. Marie Recio had been alarmed from the time she entered the house. "To see the generous work of Berlioz so crushed," wrote Edward Holmes, "the labour of months and years destroyed in a few hours, quite overpowered me."[13]

This rowdiness could not be permitted to recur, and Berlioz withdrew his work the next day:

> I must . . . beg of you to consent that it shall not be repeated, as I cannot again expose myself to such acts of hostility as those which we had to undergo last night, to the great amazement of the impartial public, and the like of which can scarcely have been witnessed in the annals of civilized theatres. I regret infinitely to have exposed you, and the distinguished and kind artists who took part in the execution, to so much trouble and annoyance by accepting your offer to produce my work.[14]

It was the single failure of all his visits to England.

The claque had been summoned and its services reimbursed by parties protesting the encroachment of foreign works and foreign artists on a proper Italian house. Of the members of the cast Mme Julienne, Mme Didiée, and Tagliafico were French; Formes and Stigelli [*sic*] were German; and there was a Belgian. A chilly reception had already been accorded *La Muette de Portici,* which opened the season that April as *Il Masaniello.* (Yet, ironically, the true Italian work to be heard that year, *Rigoletto,* likewise failed to ignite the public.) Berlioz's was the third production of the season, and it is probable that any work in that position, other than something of Bellini or Donizetti, would have met the same fate. Berlioz suspected that Costa was at the bottom of it all, exacting retribution for his published complaints over Costa's consistent mutilation of the great masterworks. If that was so, then Costa had been shameful in his dissembling, cheerfully helping out with the production and offering Berlioz countless services while at the same time working behind the scenes to assure its defeat.

It is difficult to deduce, in view of these circumstances, just how well the work was performed. Berlioz, as late as when he entered the pit that night, was pleased with the performers, though the press was rather less enthusiastic than he about Tamberlick. Four excerpts were published shortly afterward in *The Pianista,* the "Italian Opera and Promenade Concert Magazine," and

FIGURE 11.2
"Tra-la-la:
the favorite Comic Song"
from *Benvenuto Cellini*.
At the foot of the page
is the comment
"This Song was
enthusiastically encored."

at the foot of the first page of Ascanio's aria appears the remark "This Song was enthusiastically encored." But nobody remembered much about *Cellini* beyond the cabal.

The artists, anxious to demonstrate their sympathy, secured the patronage of the piano manufacturer Broadwood for a large subscription concert to be given at the Exeter Hall early in July to benefit the composer. When this proved impractical, Beale brought Berlioz a gift of the money collected thus far, and it was agreed to apply this sum toward the publication of an English piano-vocal score of *Faust*. Noble and well timed, the gesture enabled Berlioz to leave London in decent spirits, though there was not an English edition of *Faust* during his lifetime. Talk of reviving *Cellini* in 1854 was soon abandoned, and it was not heard again in London for more than a century. Berlioz was in Paris by 9 July; he had been away for only fifty-seven days.

And he stayed for only three weeks. He was engaged already to conduct a festival concert in early August at the casino in the spa city of Baden-Baden,[15] and waiting in Paris was an invitation for him to conduct, at last, in Frankfurt. (K. W. F. Guhr, who had been of little use in Frankfurt, had died in 1848; the concert was sponsored by his successor as Kapellmeister, Gustav Schmidt, a champion of Futurism.) Berlioz paused at home just long enough to work through the proofs of *Faust*, attend to Harriet, and correspond, after a long hiatus, with Louis. His son was now on board the *Corse*, a vessel of the French Navy, earning a salary of 40 francs a month; to him Berlioz writes, before leaving town, that Harriet is "about as well as she can be."[16] On 1 or 2 August, he set forth for Germany.

The casino in Baden was managed by an imaginative impresario named Edouard Bénazet. He had studied at the Conservatoire; his father was the *fermier général*—a sort of inspector—of gambling in Paris. By familial experience and education, then, Edouard Bénazet was well equipped to sponsor elevated vacation concerts at his gaming house. These were presented in the Salon de Conversation, a lounge where guests met to take the waters—what the English would call a pump room. Bénazet was an ideal manager: sympathetic to the needs of artists, anxious to please his audiences, full of bright ideas for ever grander undertakings. Berlioz liked him from the first, and the association developed into an annual August engagement for the six years beginning in 1856.

Musicians to supplement the spa orchestra were hired from the ducal chapel in Karlsruhe. Every morning at seven, for several days, Berlioz and the Baden musicians journeyed by train to Karlsruhe for a rehearsal followed by lunch set for them in the public garden. There was a single full rehearsal in Baden, where the main order of business was to incorporate the contribution of Ernst, who had come to play his variations on the *Carnival of*

FIGURE 11.3 Edouard Bénazet.

Venice. It was a timely coincidence that the Karlsruhe musicians made the acquaintance of Berlioz, for the following October Liszt led them in a festival performance of portions of *Roméo et Juliette,* and by that time they knew what they were about. So far they had had difficulty with Berlioz's music; but after working on the *Faust* excerpts with Berlioz for a few days, their conductor, another Strauss, had begun to comprehend. "It was so new that my thoughts were still confused until this evening," he wrote, "but now the light has been cast, I see everything, I understand everything, and upon my word of honor, it's a masterpiece."[17]

There was in Baden neither a competent tenor nor a German translator for *Le Repos de la Sainte Famille,* so that work was removed from the program. Otherwise Bénazet's fondest dreams were realized. The room was bedecked for the event with shrubbery and flowers and lit as though by daylight; the public of elegant ladies, diplomats, and curious German musicians, though much too large for the room, found it all "most satisfying." The Cruvelli sisters, Sophie and Marie, showed in their duet from Rossini's *Semiramide* why they were the rage of Paris. Berlioz regretted the absence of the Princess Alexandra, wife of the future Wilhelm I of Prussia; she was unable to attend because she was in mourning. Otherwise the only disappointments voiced came from the gamblers, who found the tables closed for the day.

Apropos of the gaming tables, Berlioz's indignant remarks in a letter to Adèle—the "spectacle of addle-pated gamblers makes me sick: this one reasons with chance, that one does his calculations, and they're all ultimately fools"[18]—strongly suggest the tone of his moralizing over Louis's spendthrift ways. Louis must have been losing heavily at the tables, or at least his father suspected as much. His very next letter to Adèle contains the mysterious remark "as he is occasionally in port in France and Scotland, I fear he'll start up again with the Le Havre escapades—which, however, he assures me he has seriously renounced." And when, in 1862, he urges Louis to come to Paris after Marie Recio's death, he writes: "I fear to have you come to this city of gaming and gamblers, but if you give me your word of honor not to risk even a florin . . ."[19]

The two identical Frankfurt concerts, probably on 24 and 29 August,[20] were in the Municipal Theater. Ernst played yet another *Harold en Italie;* the concert continued with *Le Repos de la Sainte Famille* in the German of Peter Cornelius and ended with the first half of *Faust.* The public was small, but the musicians welcomed Berlioz with a supper in his honor, the typical speeches and laurel crowns and honorary verses, and, outside the windows, a serenade by the Prussian military band in the overture to *Les Francs-Juges.* The earlier, abortive visits to Frankfurt could now fade from memory, and before Berlioz left Schmidt expressed the hope that he would come back for a *Hamlet* staged with his incidental music.

He was not destined to give a concert in Munich. Efforts to secure an engagement failed on this occasion, just as they had every other time he set them in motion.

It was not so much the taking of the waters as the sun and open country surrounding Baden-Baden that brought Berlioz back to Paris relaxed and in good health. That was a good thing, for a full calendar of engagements was taking shape at home. George V, king of Hanover, wrote from London to invite Berlioz to visit his royal city, and Berlioz hoped to combine this long overdue and obligatory concert with a return visit to nearby Brunswick and perhaps even Prague. September and early October were thus devoted to arrangements for a new excursion (which, however, had to be postponed until the king returned from England to Hanover) and to negotiations for an unnamed but significant London appointment, presumably the permanent conductorship of one of the Philharmonic Societies. If these failed, he wrote, he would go to Russia and "raid the ruble supply."[21] There were *feuilletons* waiting to be written on Halévy's *Le Nabab* and Adam's *Le Bijou perdu*.

Just at the moment Berlioz was ready to leave, Liszt and his entourage descended on Paris. The scene is vividly described by Jules Janin, explaining to his wife why he had not written the day before:

> What devil do you think stopped me? The devil and his din in person, Franz Liszt—the great Liszt, who fell on my house like a bomb: yelling, smoking, singing, beating on the piano in such formidable fashion that the poor old instrument, awakened for a moment under that all-powerful hand, scarcely knew which saint to invoke. Thus he came, and with the princess his wife and the prince his brother-in-law, and all the household including the children . . . Liszt remains a fine, rollicking, obstreperous boy, pleased with his glory and blissfully ignorant of everything that's gone on in Paris since he left.[22]

There was another member of Liszt's entourage: Wagner. They had crossed paths in Baden after Liszt's Karlsruhe concerts, and though Wagner was "afraid of Berlioz" and ashamed of his French, they went on to Paris together so that he could finish reading the text of the *Ring* to his partisans. Liszt's party was gathered at the Hôtel des Princes: Wagner, Carolyne Sayn-Wittgenstein, her cousin Eugène (the sculptor), her daughter Marie, and Liszt's two daughters Cosima and Blandine. Cosima was sixteen; it is not clear whether she and Wagner were meeting for the first time. There Wagner was declaiming his libretto on the evening of 10 October when Berlioz walked in. What could have been an embarrassing situation was eased by Berlioz's gracious manner and Liszt's prodigious memory: they began to play and sing *Cellini*, and Berlioz insisted that Wagner come around for lunch the next day.

On the evening of the 11th, Berlioz joined Bertin, Janin, Victor Cousin, Ludovic Vitet, and Count Daru at the Café de Paris for Meyerbeer's latest press conference on his forthcoming *L'Etoile du nord.* He left for Brunswick the next day.[23]

*F*or his third tour of Germany, the pièce de résistance was *Le Repos de la Sainte Famille,* which had gone well in London and Frankfurt and for which there was now a good translation. It was heard at every major concert on the journey. Berlioz also took parts I and II of *Faust,* the first four movements of *Roméo et Juliette, Harold en Italie, Le Carnaval romain,* and *Le Roi Lear.* By 16 October he was in Brunswick to rehearse for his concerts of 22 and 25 October, benefits again for the musicians' widows-and-orphans fund. For the second of the pair the twenty-three-year-old Joachim came from Hanover, where he had just been engaged, to play a concerto of his own and a Paganini caprice; though they had met when Joachim was concertmaster for the Weimar *Cellini,* this was their first opportunity to work closely together. "C'est un talent superbe" was Berlioz's summary impression.[24]

It was Berlioz himself, however, who was the returning hero, and Brunswick's musicians built a three-day festival in his honor. The tiny orchestra of Brunswick played the *Carnaval romain* in the city park; after one of the concerts there was a supper for a hundred notables where Berlioz was given a ceremonial baton in gilt, inscribed in his honor.[25] The orchestra attendant brought the leftover laurel crowns to him in his hotel room. In gratitude for his efforts on their behalf, the musicians named the pension fund after him.

Among the many attending these festivities was a stranger who urged Berlioz to write an opera on *Romeo and Juliet.* He replied in his melancholy

FIGURE 11.4 Joseph Joachim.

fashion that there would be no one to sing or stage it, that he would be dead before the first performance. That night at his concert he overheard the stranger in an adjoining box relating the encounter; another voice replied, "All right, let him die—but let him write the opera."[26]

The stranger was Baron Donop, chamberlain to the prince of Detmold-Lippe, who went home to rave about Berlioz and to arrange a complete *Roméo et Juliette*, with his prince, Frederick of Lippe, as Père Laurence and the princesses in the chorus. Berlioz was not there to hear it.

Arriving in Hanover at the first rehearsal for his concerts of 8 and 15 November, he was greeted with applause and trumpet flourishes, and his scores were covered with laurels; during the break, Joachim introduced him to his twenty-year-old friend Brahms, who was enjoying *Le Repos de la Sainte Famille* and who later came to number *L'Enfance du Christ* among his favorite works. Goethe's Bettina von Arnim, seventy-two years of age, came not to see him, she said, but to look at him. The Hanover newspaper considered him on a par with Mozart, Weber, and Beethoven.

The blind king and his queen were already admirers. "I cannot see you," he said, "but I sense how you do it."[27] They showered him with compliments and diamond-studded trinkets and demanded his return in a year's time for a leisurely production of *Roméo et Juliette*.

In Hanover Berlioz learned of the death the previous month of George Onslow, which had left vacant a seat at the Institute; on 10 November he posted his letter of candidacy. But it arrived too late: the nominations had been closed on the 6th, and Henri Reber was elected over Louis Clapisson on 13 November, after five ballots. The closeness of the election virtually assured that Clapisson would be elected to fill the next vacancy.

Joachim played *Harold* for Berlioz's concert in Bremen on 22 November, the Frenchman's sole appearance in that city, and they were off together the next day for Leipzig. This was Berlioz's first visit since Mendelssohn's death, and he was reticent about it. The Gewandhaus orchestra could be hard on visitors, the Leipzig public cold. Yet they could not have been more courteous to their guest, filling most of a regular subscription concert with his music and offering him their house and services, *gratis*, for a benefit. Ferdinand David, Mendelssohn's successor, turned out to be at least as supportive of Berlioz as Mendelssohn had been.

For the Leipzigers he drew from his trunks a new work: his complete "biblical legend," *La Fuite en Egypte,* which now consisted of an overture as well as the *Adieu des bergers* and *Le Repos de la Sainte Famille.* (The other works on the program were excerpts from his symphonies and Beethoven's Eighth, conducted by David.) *La Fuite en Egypte* came to life at the rehearsal of 30 November. The next evening Berlioz conducted his charmingly anachronistic creation in a house packed with distinguished listeners and the historic performing groups that had been assembled: the celebrated Gewandhaus orchestra; the chorus of the Leipzig Conservatory, which Men-

FIGURE 11.5 *La Fuite en Egypte,* title page (Leipzig: Fr. Kistner, 1854).

delssohn had built; and the Thomaner-Chor and Pauliner-Sänger-Verein, both with roots extending back to J. S. Bach. Liszt and all his circle came from Weimar and Dresden.

La Fuite en Egypte became, in fact, Berlioz's homage to Leipzig and its formidable history: in addition to first being performed there, the work was dedicated to its great choirs, translated into German by Cornelius, and published in a lovely illustrated edition by Julius Kistner (who had also handled the ticket sales and publicity for his Leipzig concerts). It was with regard to the Leipzig performances of *La Fuite en Egypte* that Cornelius put Berlioz with Bach and Beethoven (and later von Bülow) at the head of his alphabet of masters.

The cluster of musical celebrities who had come to hear Berlioz took the opportunity, once the public had dispersed, to make merry. At an evening of chamber music at Karl Brendel's on 5 December, Jeannette Pohl played her harp and Brahms gave portions of his F-Minor Sonata. Brahms noted that

> Berlioz, Pohl, and all were there . . . and all the literary notables (or nonentities?) of Leipzig. Berlioz's praises were so exceedingly warm and hearty that the rest meekly followed suit. Yesterday evening at Moscheles's he was just as friendly. I have much to thank him for.[28]

Liszt gave a *soirée* for Berlioz at Ferdinand David's house, perhaps on 9 December. Gathered around him as he played, apparently for the first time, his *Bénédiction et Serment: deux motifs de Benvenuto Cellini* was virtually the whole of the Weimar contingent: Cornelius, Pohl, Klindworth, Reményi, Pauchner, Raff, and Joachim. The *Bénédiction et Serment,* though not published until 1854, was a souvenir of the 1852 Weimar production of *Cellini.* So, too, I imagine, was von Bülow's four-hand arrangement of the *Cellini* overture first played that night. *Cellini* fever had given birth to the idea of a new edition of the work, and before Berlioz left Leipzig in 1853 he gave Liszt carte blanche to arrange with the publisher of his choice for a piano-vocal score with French and German text.

For his benefit concert on 10 December, Berlioz chose the first half of *Roméo et Juliette* along with the first half of *Faust* and the new cantata, and his earlier triumph was repeated. Afterward the Pauliner singers came to his hotel and serenaded him beneath his window; the morrow was his fiftieth birthday.

One unpleasant aspect of his otherwise pyramidal Leipzig visit was the hostility of certain elements in the Leipzig press. It explains his eruption in the last chapter of the *Mémoires* over the petty and abrasive "pupils of the Leipzig Conservatoire, who, without knowing why, look upon me as a scourge, a kind of musical Attila, and cultivate a fanatical hatred of me, making faces at me in the corridors of the Gewandhaus when my back is turned." But these harsh words were mostly repercussions of a disagreement some weeks later concerning the Paris *Freischütz.* The review by Otto Jahn was decent, and Lobe published a twenty-page, laudatory biographical sketch in the *Fliegende Blätter für Musik* late in the year.

From Leipzig he took the most direct connection back to Paris, arriving late on 16 December or early the 17th. His eye fell on a handbill announcing a performance of his little *mystère* at Seghers's Sunday concert in the Salle Ste.-Cécile. (Seghers must have been using parts obtained from the collection of the defunct Société Philharmonique, as all the rest of the materials were in Berlioz's possession.) Berlioz managed to find Seghers and prevail on him to do the expanded version, turning over to him in time for the rehearsals on the 17th his bundles of parts fresh from the baggage compartment, all this within a few hours of arriving in the railroad station after a journey across Europe of several days' duration. Seghers, then, gave the first complete Paris performance of *La Fuite en Egypte* on Sunday, 18 December. But the chorus was not the equal of the superb German choirs Berlioz had just led, and the performance was disappointing.

*B*erlioz had for some time intended to expand his biblical cantata yet further; in Leipzig he had been urged to add a scene on the Holy Family in Egypt and promised so to do. Just after the Paris concert, once he had caught his breath, he began the music for *L'Arrivée à Saïs*—Sais being an ancient Egyptian city on the Nile delta where Berlioz imagined the Holy Family had sojourned. What became the final third of *L'Enfance du Christ* was thus composed in late 1853 and January 1854.

He had a huge backlog of errands. Music had to be sent to his German admirers, as for example the Requiem and *Sara la baigneuse* to David in Leipzig; and Baron Donop needed advice on his performance in Detmold of *Roméo et Juliette*—the Detmolders were probably the first to use his new published edition. Donop was the male counterpart of Carolyne Sayn-Wittgenstein in his relentless badgering of Berlioz to keep composing; Berlioz countered that since he had not heard a note of *Tristia,* the Te Deum, or the revised *Le Corsaire,* he would just as soon focus his attention on having the existing works known.[29]

He was also forced to focus on a quintessentially Parisian squabble over Weber's *Freischütz.* The Polish count Thaddeus Tyskiewicz, editor of the Leipzig *Allgemeine musikalische Zeitung,* had attended the revival of what he assumed to be "Berlioz's edition" on 7 October. Shocked by the dismemberment of Weber's masterpiece, he filed suit against Roqueplan, demanding an uncut performance and a fine levied for every day it was not mounted. He had not seen Weber's work, he said, although he had paid for a ticket. A lawyer representing management saw fit to blame the cuts on Berlioz, who was most conveniently out of town—in Leipzig. It was the sort of thing the press loved most, and they sensationalized the incident to the point of confusing many of the facts. The court ordered a refund of the 7 francs the offended party had dispensed for his ticket, and it was left to the merry Auber to wonder: "How can one sympathize with anybody named Tyskiewicz?"

Berlioz took it all quite seriously, however, and attempted to explain things in a formal letter to the editor of the *Débats*.[30] He had heard of the suit while in Germany, but had not known until arriving home that he was being held to blame. The original cuts had been made while he was away in Russia in 1847: *L'Invitation à la valse* and its ballet had been the first to go, followed by much of the last finale, then the bridesmaids' chorus. Later he had been summoned to hear that his own recitatives were to be cut and had been asked to be so kind as not to respond. Damage was being done to his own reputation by the reports in the German press, and having the German audiences turn against him was one of the last things he wanted.

Berlioz was still brooding—it was he, on the contrary, who had been responsible for the work's first integral performance in Paris—when an offensive letter on the subject arrived from a Leipzig law student named Wisthling. Berlioz responded by having his side of the story translated and sent to the major German papers, then fired off a strong remonstrance to Herr Wisthling:

> Be informed that I am as blameless in all of this as you yourself. Be further informed that I have shown more proof of my religious respect for the great German masters than you could do in your whole life, and that I am therefore above this sort of perfidious accusation and superficial judgment.
>
> You have thought it your duty to write your second letter in the name of *messieurs* your colleagues of the Leipzig student body; I trust you will likewise consider it your duty to communicate my answer.
>
> As for my works and as for your musical opinions, I have nothing to say: I am not disposed to discuss their worth.[31]

*H*arriet died on Friday, 3 March 1854, in Montmartre, attended only by her nurses. She had been suffering from progressive paralysis, breathing irregularities, and skin disease. Over the five years since her first stroke, in October 1848, she had never fully regained her mobility or her powers of speech. Berlioz and Louis were together during her ultimate decline: Louis had been on leave from Calais[32] and was with her during the last days of February. He returned to port on Wednesday, 1 March.

Berlioz slowly mounted the steps of Montmartre to view the body and collect his racing thoughts. At her bedside was a portrait of Harriet in her prime, a gift of the fond husband to the doting wife. He kissed the still corpse and bid Harriet a last adieu.

There was no family to help him take care of her final arrangements. A Protestant pastor was required; on the trip to call on him in the rue Monsieur le Prince, Berlioz passed through the Place de l'Odéon, where he could not ignore the vista of the theater at the top of the shallow hill. There he had seen her act for the first time; there he had stood at the stage door to watch her arrive for her rehearsals of *Othello*. Now, in her death certificate, she was identified as "Harriet Smithson-Berlioz, sans profession."[33]

Baron Taylor—later to be a pallbearer for Berlioz—led the funeral procession to the smaller of the two Montmartre cemeteries, called the cimetière St.-Vincent. D'Ortigue, Brizeux, and de Wailly came, along with enough other literary figures to make the farewell appropriate though small. The gravestone identified her as Henriette-Constant Berlioz-Smithson, born in Ennis, Ireland. She rested on the north side of the hill, facing England.

Too distraught to witness the burial, her husband stayed in the Montmartre flat, gazing at the likeness from happier times and fondling a lock of her hair. There, too, was a daguerreotype of the absent Louis, taken when he was twelve. Berlioz's thoughts turned to Juliet and Ophelia and Desdemona, then back again to the troubled woman and her wasted life. Pity and black recollection caused him to shrink in horror. Then the pulsing rhythms of his music for the deaths of Cleopatra and Juliet came to mind, and thoughts of *Othello* left him trembling.[34] He visited her grave every morning for the three weeks he stayed in Paris.

Harriet was by no means forgotten. Jules Janin, who always wrote vividly, now produced perhaps his best prose:

> How sadly, how swiftly they pass, these legendary divinities, frail children of Shakespeare and Corneille. Alas, it was not so long ago—we were young then, filled with the thoughtless pride of youth—that Juliet, one summer evening on her balcony above the Verona road, with Romeo at her side, trembling with rapture, listened—and heard the nightingale, and the lark, the herald of the morn . . . When she moved, when she spoke, her charm mastered us. A whole society stirred to this woman's magic.
>
> She was barely twenty, she was called Miss Smithson, and she conquered as of right the hearts and mind of that audience on whom the light of the new truth shone.[35]

He closed his *feuilleton* with the simple image of the flowers strewn over Juliet's bier.

Dumas and Gautier both wrote of Harriet in their *feuilletons*. Liszt's gentle reaction, in a personal letter, was both informed about the truths of the relationship and indicative of his view of mates: "She inspired you, you loved her and sang of her; her task was done."[36]

From Brunswick a few weeks later, Berlioz tried to organize his thoughts in a letter to his uncle Félix Marmion, of his relatives the one who had known her best. They had remained friends, he wrote, or at least so it seemed in retrospect; an artistic sympathy had always allied them. "She was so greatly intelligent in things of the poetic world, this poor Harriet! She divined what she had never learned." He was acutely conscious of her impact on his art, especially where Shakespeare was concerned: "C'est incalculable . . .

C'est l'infini."[37] When he comes to write of Harriet's death in the *Mémoires,* he does not conceal their separation, but there is deep affection in his account of a love that

> came to me with Shakespeare in my manhood, a voice out of the burning bush, among the lightning flashes and thunderclaps of a poetry that was new to me. It struck me down; my heart and whole being were possessed by a fierce, desperate passion in which love of the artist and of the art were interfused, each intensifying the other.[38]

Adèle wrote to ask about the estate, wondering if a legal marriage had actually taken place. If not, with Louis just short of majority, there was some legitimizing to be done. It was at this juncture that Berlioz's neuralgia recommenced, affording him little respite for the remainder of his life.

His grief could best be managed, he expected, by carrying on with his engagements to return to Hanover and Brunswick. It was to be a short trip, for he did not wish to outlast his welcome. Yet the queen of Hanover, who said she knew all his works by heart, had specifically requested her favorite parts of *Roméo et Juliette,* which he had not programmed the previous November, and the king wanted to hear *Le Roi Lear* again. (With the Hanover and Brunswick performances of 1853–54, *Lear* receded—but for a single offering a decade later—from the Berlioz repertoire.) He left Paris for Hanover on Sunday, 26 March.

They had told him to bring the complete *Roméo et Juliette* and that they would fetch whatever extra musicians were needed, but Berlioz regarded such a venture as inappropriate to chapels of modest size; instead he offered the love scene and scherzo and ended the program with the first four movements of the *Fantastique,* which he had not yet played in Hanover. Joachim played the violin fantasy, now retitled *Tendresse et Caprice,* almost surely in Harriet's memory. The royal couple sat with rapt attention through the entire dress rehearsal.

All was perfection at the concert, the orchestra offering him precisely the nuance and color he demanded. Joachim was "daring and impulsive" in his interpretation, and Berlioz was taken once again with the "elevation and profundity" in so young a performer.[39] It was, moreover, his first opportunity to compare in performance the *Scène aux champs* with the *Scène d'amour* from *Roméo et Juliette,* whose aesthetic motivations had been altogether similar. He was overwhelmed with the love scene, his thoughts flooded with memories of Harriet. It took a couple of days, and the letter to Marmion, for him to regain his composure.

He called on the king the next morning and at the monarch's urging spent some hours recounting his biography. The king insisted that the complete *Roméo et Juliette* be offered in Hanover in a year's time, and in return he promised Berlioz the Order of Guelphs, his third German decoration after the Red Eagle of Prussia and the White Falcon of Saxe-Weimar.

FIGURE 11.6 Berlioz's decorations: the Red Eagle of Prussia (left)
and the White Falcon of Saxe-Weimar (right).

From Hanover Berlioz wrote to Reissiger in Dresden, hoping to arrange
for two concerts; instead Reissiger proposed three, with the rehearsals commencing immediately, so he had to refuse the invitation of the duke of Gotha
to attend the premiere of his new opera, *Santa Chiara,* conducted by Liszt.
In Brunswick on 18 April, for a subscription concert of Müller's orchestra,
he conducted a single work, *Le Corsaire.* This was its first performance in
the finished version, one of only two times he ever conducted it.

He was nervous about the Dresden concerts, as he was unsure of the
allegiance of either Reissiger or Carl Krebs, Wagner's successor at the Dresden Opera, unfamiliar with the singers, and unknown to the new grand
duke, Carl Alexander. He had, moreover, forgotten his decorations, and was
certain to be presented at court as a *chevalier* of the late duke. In fact the
three weeks in Dresden were exceeded in quality and glamor only by the
1852 Berlioz Week in Weimar. The three concerts became four, when a
second *Damnation de Faust* was demanded; Reissiger turned out to be warm
and accommodating. Krebs, admittedly hostile to Berlioz, had the good
manners to stay in the background, though von Bülow wrote Liszt that he
later rebuked the orchestra for playing foreign music so well.[40]

In the course of his four Dresden concerts—22, 25, and 29 April and 1
May—Berlioz offered much of his best music: the complete *Faust* at the first

two and at the second pair both *Cellini* overtures, the complete *La Fuite en Egypte,* and a good portion of *Roméo et Juliette.* The rehearsals were complicated somewhat by editorial problems. In order to conduct *Faust,* for the first time, from his advance copy of the new full score, he had to do what amounted to a forced march of proofreading through stacks of flawed material. Every evening he would correct the mistakes found the day before, trying to control his irritation. (Later, in Paris, he gave the proofread score of *Faust* to the conductor Deldevez for review, and Deldevez found yet another hundred errors before he was halfway through.) Likewise, Berlioz had wanted to use the parts for *La Fuite en Egypte* newly engraved by Kistner of Leipzig, but these were found to have too many errors. The corrected parts arrived from Leipzig on 27 April, in time for the dress rehearsal. Meanwhile he had all but completed *L'Arrivée à Saïs,* which was orchestrated in Dresden and sent forthwith to Cornelius to translate.

Dresden was, then, the next victory in his heroic progress of 1853–54. Berlioz found the orchestra a virile aggregation of young virtuosi, much better than the personnel he had encountered there in 1843. He was touched by their sympathy and respect: "what love of art; what rapid comprehension!" Von Bülow, who was in Dresden, confirms Berlioz's ecstatic account and says that he shared his own enthusiasm with Lipinski, the concertmaster.[41] The kind intendant Lüttichau was enraptured, first coming backstage during *Faust* in a state of spiritual elevation, then offering a banquet for the artists after the second performance, and finally approaching Berlioz with the notion of succeeding Reissiger, whom he disliked, as court Kapellmeister.

The players seemed devoted to Berlioz, whom they hoped might help make Dresden once again, as it had been under Schütz, the musical center of Germany. One of them wept at his feet at the beauty of it all. Berlioz himself often said that the three weeks in Dresden were the most gratifying of his career. Four concerts in ten days was, in any event, some sort of record.

At the general rehearsal on 28 April, an artist of whom we know nothing more prepared an excellent silhouette of Berlioz conducting (fig. 11.7). It shows the music stand with candle rack, the conductor's stance, the baton, the height of the podium, and most notably what I take to be a mirror, conveying his image to the performers behind his back.

The critics, inevitably, took him to task for the liberties in his treatment of *Faust.* This he shrugged off with the observation that "there are rascals everywhere"; they liked *Roméo et Juliette,* which took similar liberties, and no one would argue that Shakespeare was less respectable a writer than Goethe. Meanwhile, he penned his own self-congratulatory bulletin to the *Revue et Gazette musicale.*[42]

He had thought to go home via Karlsruhe and Darmstadt, but he had had enough concert-giving and feared that little money could be made in either place anyway. Instead, he decided to pay a quiet visit to Liszt—if the word "quiet" can properly be used to describe any meeting of those two—and

FIGURE 11.7
"M. Berlioz, orchestra conductor from Paris, done at the Dresden Court Theatre on 28 April 1854 at the rehearsal for the concert."

Carolyne Sayn-Wittgenstein in Weimar. The Dresden orchestra musicians accompanied him to his train to bid him farewell, and a welcoming party was, likewise, at the train station in Weimar when he arrived at 1:00 A.M. From one point of view, there is little to say of this restful stopover. Liszt asked Berlioz to check on his children, studying in Paris, and see to their upbringing in artistic matters; Berlioz looked over Liszt's new score of *Mazeppa*. There was a courtesy call on the new grand duke and, surely, the dowager grand duchess, Maria Pavlovna. They sent him away with the reminder that their theater was always at his disposal.

From another point of view, however, a very great deal must be said of this visit to Weimar and of the one the following year. For Carolyne Sayn-Wittgenstein made it clear to Berlioz that she expected him to undertake something majestic, something of vision and scope, something equal to capacities he had not lately taxed. She brought her inexhaustible powers of persuasion to bear: it was undeniable that he had completed nothing of lasting value since the Te Deum of 1849, and for nearly a year he had not written a note. They touched for the first time on the notion of a "vast opera," to which Berlioz alludes in the (first set of) closing pages of the *Mémoires,* prepared a few months later. Nor could he deny that he had enjoyed the euphoria of writing the bits and pieces of his biblical legend and was looking forward to completing *L'Enfance du Christ*. For the moment he remained convinced of the futility of an opera for Paris, and the more fruitful discussions took place during the next year's visit.

It was also during this visit that Marie managed to sow the first seeds of discord ever to exist between Liszt and Berlioz, when she took it upon herself to make several indiscreet observations concerning Wagner to the princess.

Another significant project grew out of this visit, the plan for a complete edition of all Berlioz's works in full score. He had begun to think in these terms as early as 1852, when he prepared the listing of his compositions for Richault; the preamble of that broadside advertisement remarked on his decision to publish every work. In an undated note on his copy of *Harold en Italie,* probably from this period, Berlioz wrote in a similar vein with the idea of a complete edition in mind:

> I should like for my complete works to be sent to the chapels or philharmonic societies of Brunswick, Hanover, Karlsruhe, Berlin, Vienna, Weimar, Munich, Bremen, Hamburg, Dresden, Leipzig, Amsterdam, London [and] St. Petersburg.

As an afterthought he noted, "Griepenkerl [the Brunswick savant] already has the scores of *Le Roi Lear, Waverley,* and the *Fantastique.*"[43]

Back in Paris that June he wrote of his dream for "a careful German edition by Kistner of Leipzig of all my works" (a remark later doctored by Breitkopf & Härtel, publishers of the first complete edition of Berlioz, to read "a carefully executed German edition, to be published in Leipzig, comprising the whole of my works").[44] Kistner, it will be recalled, had just published his edition of *La Fuite en Egypte* in score, piano-vocal score, and orchestral parts, and—at least after the proofreading stage was past—Berlioz was pleased with their elegance.

The cost of this project Berlioz reckoned to be something on the order of 20,000 francs, nearly two years' earnings. Liszt would oversee the business arrangements in Leipzig and sponsor the edition with his considerable prestige. There was an added advantage in a foreign edition, for Berlioz would again own proprietary rights to it—rights ceded in France "for a paltry sum."[45] Berlioz volunteered to sustain a portion of the engraving costs, and he wrote to Marc Suat to find out if the value of his share of the farm at Les Jacques might somehow be made to support the venture.

On 4 March 1855 he asked Suat for an advance of a quarter of his annual revenue of 8,000 francs, a sum that would enable him to have 350 plates engraved, starting with work not yet published.[46] They might do that much again each year for four years, or until the end was reached. By that time Liszt was dealing with Breitkopf & Härtel, in the hope that their edition could look like that of the Bach-Gesellschaft, which had begun to appear in 1851. Failing there, they eventually turned to Hofmeister, who already owned the German rights to some of Berlioz's works. As late as April 1856,

Berlioz mentions to Liszt a systematic review of his works, obviously with the complete edition still in mind.[47]

The idea died away without gaining any momentum. But it did cause Berlioz to ponder the overall scope of his work once again, and in so doing he no doubt refined his aesthetic principles yet once more. Indirectly these deliberations yielded Litolff's handsome edition of *Benvenuto Cellini* in piano-vocal score (Brunswick, 1856), for Berlioz had always intended to start with that work. Its dedication to Liszt's patroness, the dowager grand duchess, was likewise a foregone conclusion.

He reached Paris on Sunday, 7 May, in time to learn of and then attend a subscription banquet on the 15th to benefit Baron Taylor's enterprises. A sense of personal debt demanded his presence at this two-hundred-place affair in the Jardin d'Hiver in the Tuileries: Taylor had long been one of his bulwarks, notably and most recently at the time of Harriet's death.

By June he had before him an uninterrupted period of time to compose. He would not go to England again in 1854, but for the coming months live off his German earnings, which had been considerable.

The first of his new projects was an imperial cantata for presentation in August. The national holiday under the empire—republic, monarchy, or empire, there was always a patriotic summer holiday—was the *fête de l'Empereur* each 15 August. The third of these, in 1854, was to be celebrated with particular energy owing to the outbreak of war with Russia in the Crimea. (France and Britain had allied themselves with the Ottoman empire that March to defend it against Russian claims on Turkey.) A warship was to be anchored in the Seine, from which the emperor would view a naval regatta; Te Deums were ordered to be sung at the end of high Mass in every Paris church; there would be free entry to the theaters, military reviews on the Champ de Mars, fireworks, and an illumination that night of the city's historic buildings. Berlioz's contribution was to be a monster concert involving 1,200 musicians in the new Palais de l'Industrie, a *palais de cristal* under construction at the river end of the Champs-Elysées. It was meant to house an industrial exhibition in 1855, but from the moment the foundation was laid Berlioz saw it as a venue crying out for a concert.

L'Impériale was indeed finished in early July, well in time for the *fête de l'Empereur*. It is a 300-bar hymn for two choruses and large orchestra, to a text by another vagabond of his acquaintance, the poet known as Captain Lafont. Berlioz had worked quickly, borrowing a page or two from *Sardanapale* and perhaps other works, in order to be done in time. What was not finished was the roof of the Palais de l'Industrie, and as it happened, on 15 August Berlioz was elsewhere and *L'Impériale* was not played. The concert that night was given by two hundred bandsmen, playing in the Tuileries gardens "with the most beautiful effect" to an audience that did not include the emperor after all. He was in England, visiting Queen Victoria.

That summer Berlioz also finished *L'Enfance du Christ*. He had completed and orchestrated *L'Arrivée à Saïs* in Dresden and appended it to *La Fuite en Egypte*. In June and July the scene of Herod's troubled kingship dominated his spirit as he worked passionately, barely eating or sleeping. *Le Songe d'Hérode* (Herod's dream), envisaged as a prologue, now became the first of three equal portions. The autograph of *La Fuite en Egypte* was with Cornelius in Germany, so he combined his manuscripts of the outer movements with a copy of the printed edition of *La Fuite* and on 27 July titled his new sacred trilogy *L'Enfance du Christ*. At the time he had no idea that he had just completed what was to be his most popular work. He delivered his materials to the pianist-composer Amédée Méreaux, who was to prepare the piano-vocal score, though Méreaux's work later had to be simplified by a young pianist named Théodore Ritter.

Each third of the biblical oratorio is headed with a significant dedication: the first, to his nieces Joséphine and Nanci Suat, suggesting the innocence he attached to the work; the second, to John Ella, in whose *Musical Union* the story of Pierre Ducré had first been set straight and who had convinced Berlioz to expand it; and the third, to the choruses of Leipzig, who had sung so well for him in 1853, serenaded him, and later asked him to write something for them.

*P*lans to premiere the Te Deum first began to take shape not with an imperial ceremony but when the organ builder Ducroquet started to look toward the unveiling of the instrument he was finishing at St.-Eustache. The relatively sparse role of the organ in Berlioz's work gave him little pause: the inaugural concert could begin with a fancy solo by Hesse, Lemmens, or "that pretty little organist with his rings, cameos, and gold-handled cane, who *beautifies* the themes that he plays, and that they call Lefébure-Wély."[48] The empress, patron of an orphanage, might be induced to offer the services of seven or eight hundred children to sing the simple lines Berlioz had added to the Tibi omnes and Judex crederis. If all the artisans involved met their schedules, the premiere of the Te Deum would just coincide with the grand opening of the Industrial Exhibition.

Throughout July and the first week of August it was Berlioz's intention to conduct a series of concerts in Munich while Lachner was on vacation, then be back for the *fête de l'Empereur*—or the other way around, depending on the precise course of events. Then, suddenly and unexpectedly, a chair at the Institute was vacated on 29 July when Halévy became perpetual secretary, following the death of Raoul Rochette earlier in the month. Thinking he finally had a fighting chance—the only other serious candidate was the altogether mediocre Clapisson—Berlioz canceled the trip to Munich in order to be in town for the necessary campaign of letters and courtesy calls. His letter of candidacy is the most scrupulously presented of the five he composed over the years, headed with a listing of his great works for chorus and orchestra and dwelling for the first time on his journalism for the *Débats*. "I think I have constantly shown, while fulfilling these duties, a real and devoted love of art."[49] His effort had positive results in that he and Clapisson were presented to the Institute as candidates of equal merit—with Berlioz's name coming first, moreover, in the alphabetical listing. But it was Clapisson who had been edged out of the previous election, and thus he was elevated, as if by foregone conclusion, to Halévy's chair on 26 August. The music section now consisted of a single distinguished composer, Auber; the others were Adam, Carafa, Clapisson, Reber, and Thomas.

Berlioz was not only discouraged but also quite ill. The doctors feared from his symptoms that he might have cholera or its less sinister twin, cholerine, and he was sent for a week—after his candidacy was announced on 10 August but before the election—to St. Valery-en-Caux, where once before he had vacationed. What surely brought on this attack was worry over Louis, a *volontaire aspirant* in the French fleet somewhere in the North Sea. (His last letter had come from Denmark.) The allies were preparing, in disorganized fashion, to invade Russian territory by simultaneously blockading the enemy fleet in both the Black Sea and the Baltic. Louis's ship, the *Phlégéton,* was engaged in the bombardment and siege of Bomarsund, a Russian fortress on the tiny island of Åhland between Sweden and Finland, then later in the siege of Kronstadt on the coast near St. Petersburg. While Uncle Félix was able to tolerate this uncertainty with all the iron of a professional warrior, Berlioz could not stand the tense waiting around for news in an isolated Norman village. He rushed back to Paris to be nearer the papers and the post. The siege of Bomarsund was, in fact, victorious, and Louis was safe and sound. It was like that for the rest of the year: engagement after engagement, bulletin after bulletin, with the battle of the Alma River on 25 September, Balaklava on 25 October, Inkerman on 5 November. Not a little of the news-mongering was flawed; the city rejoiced, for example, at news that Sevastopol had fallen without resistance, but that was only the beginning of the longest of the sieges.

Roqueplan had not been able to make ends meet at the Opéra and was relieved of most of his duties in late June; he finally resigned in November. Control of the house reverted to more businesslike agencies of the imperial government; among their first and most senseless decisions that summer was to revoke the free passes traditionally enjoyed by professional critics. On opening night of the new season, upon meeting in the lobby, they elected to respond by not mentioning the event at all. This decision was all the more dramatic in that the *soirée* marked the return to the stage, in *La Favorite,* of none other than the venerable Mme Stoltz. Berlioz devoted his *feuilleton de silence* of 6 September in the *Débats* to a long dissertation on his trip to Normandy, a book about Rossini, and the like, and ended with a sly quotation from *Hamlet:* "The rest is silence." Mme Stoltz cried, fainted, and demanded 30,000 supplemental francs for her shame, threatening otherwise to break her engagement. The free passes were restored.

In mid-September he went to La Côte-St.-André for a reunion with his sister Adèle and her daughters, and to sign the papers necessary to sell the farm at Les Jacques. This was a complex matter, involving notarized letters, payments in several directions, and the negotiation of a long-term mortgage to be extended to the buyers. Louis's inheritance had yet to be regularized, and this had become urgent in view of Berlioz's intent to remarry at the first suitable moment; the customary six months of mourning had just elapsed. He had completed the major portion of the *Mémoires* before he left for La Côte-St.-André; on his return in October he wrote chapter 59, his moving description of Harriet's death and funeral, a summary of the cabal at Covent Garden, and notes on his recent trips to Weimar and Dresden. He dated the last page 18 October.

The next day, 19 October 1854, he married Marie Recio.

J remarried; it was my duty" is the simple explanation in the *Mémoires;* the singular woman who became the second Mme Berlioz is barely mentioned there at all. He told Legouvé he deserved to be relegated to hell for the early chapters of their life together. He would now make amends. With some notable exceptions Marie was content to live quietly in his shadow, and that was, in fact, what Berlioz needed. He now had a stable home, a semblance of domestic quietude, and a mother-in-law of whom he was genuinely fond. He tried to explain all that in a tender letter to Louis.

What with the *Mémoires* and the wedding, he was unable to attend the opening night of Gounod's *La Nonne sanglante,* though he went to a dress rehearsal and wrote Gounod (misspelling his name) to wish him good luck and to express his regret should the composer "feel even a moment of embarrassment over her or over me."[50] Within the week he went to a subsequent performance; Scribe renewed his subscription to the *Journal des Débats* specifically to read Berlioz's review, which he assumed would be shocking and require response. But the article of 24 October was pale and routine, and there was nothing much to respond to.

Louis landed briefly at Cherbourg in early November, visited Paris (more on the repercussions of this visit shortly), then went by himself to visit his relations in the Dauphiné. Berlioz celebrated his fifty-first birthday without his son and with a case of the flu, and Marie had hives. Later in December Louis was in Malta, on board a new ship called the *Laplace,* bound for the Crimea.

Berlioz renamed his imperial cantata *Le Dix Décembre* for a performance to celebrate the accession to imperial status of both the Napoleons. (He— or else his printers—got the date wrong: it was actually on 2 December, *le deux décembre,* that Napoleon I was crowned in 1804 and from which date in 1852 Napoleon III's empire reckoned its formal beginning.) The festival performance was at length announced for 28 January 1855 at the Théâtre-

Italien, but canceled at the last minute by the directorate of Fine Arts, who argued that the grave concerns of national warfare precluded public merrymaking.

L'Enfance du Christ was given three splendid first performances in the Salle Herz, on 10 December and Christmas Eve 1854 and, in an encore offering, on 28 January 1855. These are the only exceptions to Berlioz's post-*Faust* rule of not risking his personal finances on public concerts. In fact he made a large profit, for *L'Enfance du Christ* was a crowd-pleaser from the beginning.

The first of the concerts included a movement from a Haydn symphony, the *Rêverie et Caprice,* again called *Tendresse et Caprice,* and a Mendelssohn piano trio; on Christmas Eve Mme Stoltz sang *La Captive.* His soloists were excellent, with M. and Mme Meillet as Joseph and Mary, the eminent bass Battaille as the *père de famille,* and Depassio as Herod. Students from the Conservatoire made up the chorus.

Verdi was there, as were Heine, Vigny, and Liszt's daughters Cosima (who was enchanted) and Blandine. Even the less sympathetic members of the press enjoyed the new work, and no one could help admiring the new restraint of *L'Enfance du Christ.* Adolphe Adam wrote of a "truly grand and beautiful thing";[51] congratulatory letters dominated his mail as they had for *Roméo et Juliette* in 1839. He cleared a profit of several thousand francs, enough to keep his household comfortable for another year.

Berlioz was now receiving more proposals from the capitals of Europe than he could possibly fulfill. Just after arrangements for another season with the New Philharmonic Society of London were settled, the more august Royal Philharmonic Society inquired if he would replace the retired Costa for their 1855 concerts, and he was forced to decline. (Next they asked Spohr, then settled on Wagner, so that Wagner and Berlioz were soon to be conducting rival London orchestras.) He accepted Liszt's invitation on behalf of the grand duke of Saxe-Weimar for a pair of concerts in February, acceded to Adolphe Samuel's pleas that he come to Brussels with *L'Enfance du Christ,* and refused the rest. Even so he had a daunting calendar before him for 1855: Weimar and Gotha in February, London in March (though this was postponed until the summer), Brussels later in the month, and the Te Deum in Paris in late April, after which he would need to be on hand for the Festival de l'Industrie. The king of Hanover reduced his burden somewhat by asking him to postpone for a year the visit they had discussed, in view of the disarray of his chapel; he enclosed the promised decoration of the Order of Guelphs.

Louis had, once again, become cause for great concern, but this time not so much for his personal safety as for his moral fiber. Berlioz had not been pleased with his conduct in Paris the previous November, which included at least one episode of drunkenness; perhaps this was a none-too-subtle protest over his father's remarriage. Louis then managed to miss the departure of his vessel in Cherbourg by waiting for it in Le Havre, in the meantime squandering a great deal of money at the gaming tables. Admiral Cécille ordered him arrested and imprisoned in Marseille, which prompted him to write an irate epistle articulating his hatred for both his father and the admiral. His base for the next several years was the huge naval installation at Toulon, from which he made several more voyages to the Crimea. Berlioz was left to piece together Louis's comings and goings from Adèle, who was closer to the news in the Mediterranean, and from the correspondents at the *Journal des Débats.* His comments on his "unhappy, badly formed" son are harsh and pitiful.

Berlioz left Paris on 8 February, spent a day in Brussels making plans for his performances there, then arrived in Weimar on 11 February. The main business at hand was the new oratorio, a pious work, followed by an impious performance of the *Fantastique* with its sequel, now slightly refined and within a few months' time retitled *Lélio.* His arrival had been arranged to coincide with the grand duchess's birthday on 17 February, for which their highnesses had commanded a performance at court. (The February 1852 *Cellini* had been a birthday performance, as well; he was also there for her birthday in 1856 and for a late celebration in 1863.) For this particular concert he gave short excerpts from *Cellini, Faust,* and *Roméo et Juliette; La Captive;* and a celebratory first offering, with the composer at the piano, of Liszt's revised and completed First Concerto, in E♭.

The big public concert on 21 February was to benefit the musicians' pension fund. Cornelius was done with the German text for *L'Enfance du Christ,* which was printed in a handsome *Textbuch* together with the program of the *Fantastique* and the libretto of the *Mélologue,* this last announced as a *monodrame* in first performance. Supplementary players came from Gotha, Erfurt, and Jena; the able Mme Pohl played the harp; an actor from the royal theater, Grans, declaimed the text of the *Mélologue.* The solo work was by the fine court singers, Feodor von Milde, his wife Rosa, and the tenor Caspari. For *Le Retour à la vie* the artist was costumed and equipped with pistols and the other appropriate properties; orchestra, chorus, and conductors were concealed behind a curtain until *La Tempête,* the result being an "oddly mysterious sound." Berlioz was called back twice after the oratorio, twice after the *Fantastique,* and four times after the *Mélologue.* There was another laurel crown.

Following this adulation, Liszt gave a supper for the Club Nouveau-Weimar with a Latin toast rendered into verse by Hoffmann von Fallersleben, the poet-philosopher, and set to music by Joachim Raff:

Vivas, crescas, floreas
Hospes Germanorum,
Et amicus maneas
Neo-Wimarorum.

(May you live, grow, and flourish as the guest of the Germans, and always be the friend of the Weimar progressives.)[52]

The musicians of Weimar were in high spirits and pleased to find themselves together again with Berlioz. He clowned with the eighteen-year-old Marie Sayn-Wittgenstein, leaving on 18 February a one-line composition in her album ("Liszt est prié d'écrire la basse").[53] He dined at court a half-dozen times, and before he left sat for a portrait in oils by Leuchert. Cornelius, who had become a disciple, wrote a long, enthusiastic report to the *Revue et Gazette musicale* where he declared (possibly with a hint of backhandedness) *La Captive* worth an entire opera. He bragged in his article, "Hector Berlioz à Weimar," that their city had become Berlioz's artistic fatherland, that he was a Frenchman animated by the German spirit, and that Weimar artists and public alike had little difficulty understanding the true meaning of his work. *La Captive* he called, citing Rückert, "a heavenly teardrop changed into a pearl, a triumph of landscape revolving around a figure of profound sadness"; he greeted the *Mélologue* as one of the most compelling things Berlioz had written, observing that the last notes were drowned by applause. Raff wrote his *Fantasie über Motive aus Benvenuto Cellini*, opus 65, sometime that year, possibly for the occasion. And the musicians, despite the bitter cold, could not resist singing Raff's little toast again beneath Berlioz's hotel window before he left.

As in 1854, private conversations between Berlioz, Liszt, and the princess yielded significant results, for they returned to the matter of his writing an opera. Gently he broached the one, theretofore secret, notion that could move him to write: a work on Virgil's *Aeneid*. He had been thinking about it since finishing his memoirs, where he had remarked on a "grandiose, magnificent, and profoundly moving" subject that was beginning to trouble him.[54] Once the princess heard this confession there was no turning back; he writes within the week of his fancy's beginning to take flight. A few literary and musical ideas were roughed out over the next months, but it took one further trip to Weimar, in 1856, to get him seriously to work.

He had written to Gotha that in view of the unforeseen magnitude of events in Weimar, his concert would have to be postponed; for one thing, his deliberations with Liszt and the princess had kept him considerably longer than he had anticipated. There was a *malentendu:* the duke was ill, Berlioz's letter may have gone astray, and in any event the theater season could not be rearranged to allow a later date. His quick stop in Gotha was thus devoted largely to apologizing, but he was received nonetheless warmly at court by the duchess and asked to dine, and she made him promise to come again in 1856—before going to Hanover or Weimar. It turned out to be a stroke of luck that he had gone first to Weimar, for the Russian czar died on 2 March, and the remaining concerts of the Weimar season were canceled during the mourning period of the dowager grand duchess, his sister.

*B*erlioz was in Paris at the beginning of March for long enough to collect himself and recover as best he could from his fatigue and increasingly sinister intestinal complaints. In two weeks he was off for Brussels, where Samuel had arranged concerts for 17, 22, and 27 March, with *L'Enfance du Christ, La Captive,* the *Fête chez Capulet,* and *Le Carnaval romain.* They would be held in the Théâtre du Cirque, which had replaced the Théâtre de la Monnaie as royal auditorium after a fire the previous January. Berlioz's memories of Brussels were not especially fond, and he was troubled by the certainty of encountering Fétis there.

The performers, though welcoming, brave, and patient with him, were nevertheless unable to sort out even the simplest passages of the new oratorio and floundered completely at the sight of measures in $\frac{7}{4}$. Barielle, singing the

FIGURE 11.8 Berlioz, c. 1855.

role of the *père de famille,* lost his way during the first performance and Berlioz sang his part from the podium; the strange, thin voice emerging from some unseen throat quite troubled the listeners. His other singers were mediocre and easily confused; the flutists in the trio played "like Spanish cowherds."[55] Only the third of the performances was acceptable.

Yet the Belgians did what they could, and their charm could not be denied. Berlioz and Marie dined with Fétis, who was surprised by how much Berlioz had aged but captivated anew by his irresistible spirit and lofty intelligence. Fétis wrote glowingly of *L'Enfance du Christ* in the papers, though in a note to Liszt confided that he thought Berlioz lacked imagination.[56] Edgar Quinet, the leftist French historian then waiting out the Second Empire in a self-imposed Brussels exile, was delighted to make Berlioz's acquaintance: "His good intentions, his energy, his pride are to my taste—the most beautiful of symphonies . . . What a beautiful work is the life of a true artist."[57] Quinet heard two of the performances and likened *L'Enfance du Christ* to a painting of Raphael.

A yet more fruitful association began when Berlioz met the Belgian Verbrugghen, inventor of a device for controlling massed forces in performance which he called his electric metronome. He would of course come to Paris to exhibit his wares at the Festival de l'Industrie, and Berlioz, already developing projects in his mind for concerts there, left Brussels determined to put the electric metronome to work.

It was soon Easter week, and for the *concert spirituel* of the Opéra-Comique on Holy Saturday, Tilmant invited Berlioz to conduct a portion of *L'Enfance du Christ.* The reviewer for *La France musicale,* who suggests that the entire oratorio was given, remarks that he had not seen the theater so full in many months.[58] But there had been better performances of the work: the room did not favor the tender music, giving it a "denatured" quality, and only Jourdain was up to his role. For Berlioz it was a profitable experience in that the soprano, with whom he had not so far worked, was Caroline Carvalho, née Marie Miolan, who, with her husband Léon Carvalho, was soon to be at the apex of his operatic ventures—and he at the apex of theirs.

He was vexed with both his publishers, partly because they were paying too little, partly because they were (properly) disinclined to cooperate with him on behalf of his Leipzig edition. Nevertheless it was foolish to deny the public its rightful opportunity to purchase *L'Enfance du Christ,* for which there was insistent demand, and accordingly he signed a contract with Richault to that end on 21 April. Richault reimbursed Berlioz for the engraving of the choral parts used in the performances and took custody of the plates. His handsome score, with the 1846 Prinzhofer portrait as frontispiece, appeared in September. A vocal score preceded it by a few weeks; the parts appeared a little later. The better indicator of the oratorio's popularity, however, was the appearance of a *morceau de salon* on the trio for two flutes and harp. This was by the sixteen-year-old prodigy Théodore Ritter, who had helped with the piano score of *L'Enfance du Christ* to such an extent that Berlioz commissioned a piano-vocal score of *Roméo et Juliette* from him, and sent in the same mail to Captain Nieper—translator of both *Absence* and Berlioz's rejoinders concerning the *Freischütz* incident—for a new German text.

The main work of April was to stage the Te Deum. The Festival de l'Industrie (officially, the Exposition Universelle des Œuvres d'Art et des Produits de l'Agriculture et de l'Industrie), Napoleon III's not entirely unsuccessful attempt to outdo the Crystal Palace exhibition, was expected to last from May until the end of October. Visits were foreseen from countless foreign dignitaries: Queen Victoria, the king of Sardinia, Arabs and Turks of all description. The huge palace on the site now occupied by the Grand Palais (built for the 1900 World Exhibition), along with an annex near the river called the Queen's Gallery, was expected to display the products of twenty thousand exhibitors. Berlioz and his consortium thought to capture the mounting excitement and entertain the distinguished guests by scheduling the Te Deum for 30 April. Ducroquet's organ at St.-Eustache, after all, was precisely the sort of thing the visitors were coming to see, and the tourists would already know of St.-Eustache's excellent reputation for programs of sacred music.

Three choruses were engaged for the performance, including the choir of orphans that, though a far cry from the Charity Children at St. Paul's, nevertheless numbered six hundred. At first Berlioz hoped that Liszt would come from Weimar for the organ solos; when that was found to be impractical, Henry Smart was engaged to come from England for the honor of inaugurating the instrument. The tenor was Perrier of the Opéra, just making his debut there and anxious to make a good impression on what promised to be an influential gathering. The high saxhorn part was for Arban, the instrument itself possibly making its public debut. A guest from Brussels, presumably Adolphe Samuel, was to be in the loft to conduct the choruses. Altogether the force numbered something on the order of nine hundred: one hundred in the orchestra, one hundred in each of the adult choirs, and the children.

There were the usual last-minute crises. Smart was ill and could not make the trip after all; Saint-Saëns was offered the job and declined it. At length the duties were given, as they probably should have been in the first place, to Edouard Batiste, titular organist at St.-Eustache and professor at the Conservatoire. On 27 April, a day before the dress rehearsal, the opening of the Festival de l'Industrie was postponed by imperial decree for what turned out to be a period of two weeks. This affected the Te Deum insofar as the idea of blessing the flags of the Catholic exhibitors as an excuse to play the *Marche pour la présentation des drapeaux* had to be abandoned. It is abundantly clear, however, that the *Marche des drapeaux* was in fact heard (as the third movement) during the performance on the 28th. What was dropped from the program was the Prélude, the dress rehearsal having revealed to Berlioz "unseemly modulations." Some judicious cuts were made in the Judex.

The substantial capacity of St.-Eustache was strained by a full house of spectators added to an already extended performing force. The musicians, who had been transported at the dress rehearsal, brought Berlioz's "Ninivan and Babylonian" effects to life with magnificent precision and without audible error. The Judex was, as intended, the climax of the proceedings. Berlioz was nearly crushed by admirers afterward, among them Lecourt and Rémussat, who had come from Marseille, and representatives of the emperor's family. After the bookkeeping was done, he was remitted a paltry sum; embezzlement was suspected, and Berlioz found himself barely able to cover the out-of-pocket expenses for the copying of the revisions to the parts. (Most of the copying had been done years before.)

He never heard the complete work again, but the one performance convinced him that he had given birth to a twin sibling for the Requiem. For many months he regarded the Judex crederis as the most imposing thing he had written. Brandus was immediately engaged to publish the work by a subscription arrangement very like that for the Requiem seventeen years before. The Prélude, which had failed to pass muster, remained unpublished. The *Marche* appears to have been born of Berlioz's vision of the battered standards of returning legions passing beneath the vaults of Notre Dame and was almost surely added to the work in anticipation of the festivity he wrongly expected on the accession of Napoleon III.

Verdi was in Paris for the opening of his own product for the fair, *Les Vêpres siciliennes,* rediscovering what it was like to conquer the Opéra—which he thought of as "la grande boutique"—and having the traditionally difficult time of it. Berlioz dined with him on 4 May, and during those weeks they got to know each other as well as they ever would. (In 1860, Verdi asked Escudier to "greet Berlioz for me warmly, warmly, whom I esteem as a composer and love as a man.")[59] Later in the month, just as he and Marie were on the verge of setting out for his concerts with the New Philharmonic, Berlioz was put in charge of the music for the closing ceremonies and distribution of prizes for the Festival de l'Industrie. This provided a fine opportunity for excerpts from the Te Deum to be heard again and for *L'Impériale* finally to be given a fitting premiere.

*T*hey reached London on 8 June and lodged in rooms let by Mary Pannier, dressmaker, at 13, Margaret Street, near Cavendish Square and just around the corner from his other London residences. It had been Berlioz's intention for his second set of appearances with the New Philharmonic Society to feature the *Fantastique* and *Roméo et Juliette,* the two major works he had not so far conducted in London. But it was impractical to attempt more than the first half of *Roméo et Juliette.* Completing the repertoire for the first concert were Mozart's G-Minor Symphony and overture to *Zauberflöte,* Beethoven's "Emperor" Concerto, showpieces for the soloists, and an overture by Henry Leslie called *The Templar,* this last added to the program when its composer called to explain how little of Berlioz's music he understood.

Berlioz sailed directly into his rehearsals, for his concert was in just five days. There were problems from the start. The postponement of the last two concerts of the season until June and July, at his request, had created irresolvable conflicts of schedule for some of the best wind players. The soloists, M. and Mme Gassier, turned out to be a baritone and high soprano, ill equipped in tessitura and therefore unacceptable for the solos in *Roméo et Juliette.* The prologue chorus had learned its role in French, but the new soloists were unable to sing in that language, and a fresh start had to be made with English texts for everyone. At the dress rehearsal the chorus of Capulets at the beginning of the love scene (those of them who had deigned to appear) was unable to coordinate itself with the orchestra and vice versa; in an unusual display of pique, Berlioz dismissed all the singers and offered on 13 June only the *Fête chez Capulet,* the love scene without the voices, and the Queen Mab scherzo.

Yet for all the vicissitudes leading up to the performance, Exeter Hall was filled to capacity with a public anxious to show its enthusiasm for Berlioz's return. The *Fête chez Capulet* was encored—though one distinguished member of the audience, Wagner, found the performance of *Roméo et Juliette* pitiable and the Mozart symphony flat and unbearably routine. Berlioz himself thought the concert to have been unusually spirited. But the papers, crowded with dramatic news of bloody engagements of the Russians, in different parts of the world, by both the English and the French, devoted little space to the New Philharmonic concert. Davison's review, for instance, was bumped from the *Times.* It was eventually published in the *Musical World,* but by then that journal was occupied with the rather more interesting exchange between Berlioz and his choruses over the cancellation of their part of *Roméo et Juliette:*

> On hearing that it was now usual [he responded] to perform choral works publicly without the singers having had a single rehearsal with the orchestra, I became extremely nervous . . . It was clear that those who were to sing at the concert, without ever having heard the orchestra (that is to say, the greater number), would for a certainty miss their cue. Could I expose them to such an annoying proceeding? Could I expose the (New) Philharmonic Society to such a serious disaster? And could I expose myself to seeing one of the principal pieces of my work compromised in making the attempt? . . . As far as I am concerned I do not think that such experiments ought to be made publicly.[60]

By other measures, the quick trip to London of 1855 was one of his most pleasant. Berlioz and Marie were swept up in social engagements for the duration of their month-long stay: a trip to show Marie the Crystal Palace as it had been rebuilt in Sydenham; an English-speaking weekend with Mr. and Mrs. Alfred Benecke and Karl Klindworth, the pianist, at the Beneckes' country house at Champion Hill, Camberwell; greetings to Meyerbeer upon his arrival for the Covent Garden production of *L'Etoile du nord*. Negotiations with Novello for an English edition of *L'Enfance du Christ*, called *The Holy Family*, were successfully concluded. And it was during those weeks that Berlioz and Wagner finally came to admire, if not precisely to understand, each other.

Berlioz was rehearsing his own orchestra during Wagner's command performance for Prince Albert of the *Tannhäuser* overture on 11 June; Wagner was in Berlioz's audience on 13 June. Berlioz called on him the next day, when they chatted amiably for several hours. A few days later they were together for dinner at the home of the violinist Prosper Sainton, future husband of the singer Charlotte Dolby, where again they conversed, in French, at great length and with obvious intimacy. They dined together before Wagner's last concert on 25 June, and after it Berlioz went home with him to drink, like the students in *Faust*, until three in the morning. Every indication suggests that they parted company on the closest of terms. Wagner, though annoyed at the language barrier, was as delighted with the quickness of Berlioz's mind as Fétis had been in Brussels. Berlioz promised him a copy of the *Soirées de l'orchestre* (and later sent it) and wished him the best of luck on the *Ring;* they promised to exchange scores. Liszt, who heard of the meetings from nearly everybody, must have smiled some fatherly, satisfied smiles in distant Weimar.

The sixth and last concert of the New Philharmonic's 1855 season was given, after a week's delay, on 4 July, a long program that included *Harold en Italie* with Ernst; a scene from *Le Prophète;* works of Mendelssohn, Mozart, Beethoven, Rossini, and Ferdinand Praeger; Henselt's F-Minor Piano Concerto with Klindworth; and a cantata called *Tam O'Shanter* by Howard Glover. The concert seems to have gone well enough despite the unfamiliar repertoire. Anna Bockholtz-Falconi sang so beautifully that Berlioz determined to fashion something special for her at his first opportunity; it is possible that he ended the season with his rousing orchestration of the *Marseillaise*.[61] William Ganz noted in his diary: "Meyerbeer was there: he sat right in front, he is a small thin man, with an interesting face, and attracted a good deal of attention."[62]

Two days later Berlioz conducted Mrs. Anderson's Annual Grand Morning Concert at Covent Garden, an event sponsored each year by Queen Victoria for the royal piano teacher, from whom she had taken lessons. The cast was regal, too: Viardot sang "her" version of *La Captive;* Mme Nantier-Didiée resurrected Ascanio's aria from *Cellini;* the London stars sang the quintet

FIGURE 11.9 Wagner (in Paris, February 1860).

from *Così fan tutte;* Ernst played his *Carnaval de Venise;* Mrs. Anderson herself appeared in Beethoven's Choral Fantasy. Berlioz opened the program with a brilliant *Euryanthe* overture and closed it with a volcanic performance of Rossini's *Stabat mater.* This exceptional concert was, though no one suspected it, his farewell to English audiences.

Berlioz and Marie left London that weekend, as he was anxious to be home to attend to his obligations for the Festival de l'Industrie. He took with him a commission for a theory of conducting, to be appended to the forthcoming English edition of the orchestration treatise (and, as it turned out, to a second edition of the French as well); he was, moreover, engaged to return in February with *L'Enfance du Christ* and the Te Deum. There was still talk of his moving permanently to England, but in a few weeks' time Berlioz was all but forgotten, eclipsed by the return to England of Jenny Lind.

In Paris he was, in addition to music master for the closing ceremonies, one of seven members of the jury for class XXVII of the Universal Exposition: manufacture of musical instruments. The others were Halévy, an acoustician named Marloye, and a retired piano maker named Roller, all French; the Scot George Clarke, president of the Royal Academy of Music; Fétis; and Joseph Hellmesberger, director of the imperial conservatory in Vienna and president of the Gesellschaft der Musikfreunde. Of this company only Fétis and Berlioz can have done much of the writing. He spent most of July and

August engaged in the herculean effort of hearing several hundred instruments, among them many pianos, each one given an identification number and carted to the Salle du Conservatoire for its audition. (He describes the process, with amusement, in articles for the *Débats* of January 1856.) Despite the supposed anonymity of the makers, Paris was declared by the judges to be of incontestable superiority in the manufacture of pianos of every kind, and medals of honor were given to Alexandre *père et fils,* Erard, Herz, and Pleyel. Similar honors were bestowed, as they had been in London, on the woodwind maker Boehm, the organ builder Cavaillé-Coll, Sax, and the great luthier Vuillaume.

The distribution of prizes and formal closure of the Exposition took place on 15 November at a large ceremony for invited guests only, presided over by the emperor. Additionally, there were to be two monster concerts offered to the public during the week of closure, each of them repeated later in the month as well. For the public events Berlioz settled on a program typical of his festival concerts of the 1840s: the *Freischütz* overture, Beethoven's Fifth, the prayer from Rossini's *Moïse,* a scene from Gluck's *Armide,* the blessing of the daggers from *Les Huguenots,* and the *Apothéose* from the *Symphonie funèbre.* This program was virtually identical to the repertoire of August 1844, for the previous industrial exhibition; perhaps the "industrial" text of the *Apothéose* was heard again. Additionally there were to be Mozart's *Ave verum corpus* and a chorus from Handel's *Judas Maccabeus.* As in 1844 the *Hymne à la France* had been given its first performance, for these concerts *L'Impériale*—from which Berlioz had deleted a stanza—would be heard for the first time (having been withdrawn from the concert of 28 January 1855). The concerts were to conclude with the Te Deum, Tibi omnes, and Judex crederis from the Te Deum. He had accepted the appointment on the condition that he would bear no financial responsibility; the physical arrangements were carried out by an entrepreneur named Ber.

Among his force of 1,250 were thirty harps for the Te Deum, a hundred wind players, and a chorus of seven hundred. This megaforce was led by Berlioz, five assistants (Tilmant, Bottesini, Hellmesberger, and chorus masters from St.-Eustache and the Opéra-Comique)—and Verbrugghen's electric metronome. Berlioz controlled this contraption by tapping a switch over a bowl of mercury with his left hand. Erected behind his music stand were a voltaic cell and a switching apparatus that carried the signal through wire to four large metronomes distributed among the ensembles. Though described with glee in the newspapers and made the brunt of some of the cleverest satirical cartoons ever to portray him, this unlikely product of the century's industrial imagination was soon widely adopted in the opera houses of Europe.

The music for the prize-giving on 15 November was limited to the imperial cantata and the *Ave verum corpus.* The musicians were arranged behind the rostrum, and what little of their work could be heard over the roar of the crowd was interrupted in mid-performance for the emperor to deliver, without amplification, his longwinded address to the assembled tens of thousands of nobles and exhibitors. On the 16th, however, the performing force was moved to the main floor. It is said that forty thousand people veritably flooded the turnstiles to hear his concert that day; the gate was 75,000 francs, of which Berlioz's share was the genuinely extravagant sum of 8,000 francs. The peroration of *L'Impériale* impressed the crowd, and the scene from *Armide* went over especially well; Berlioz himself enjoyed studying his so-called architectural works in close proximity. These were his last performances of the *Apothéose* from the *Symphonie funèbre et triomphale*.

I have remarked that the London performance of Beethoven's Ninth represented the peak of his prestige as a conductor. But this occasion must have been just as grand. A primitive photograph of the events shows Napoleon III before his hordes at the prize-giving; with some imagination you can picture the massed musicians in the bleachers behind the throne. There stood Berlioz, before what was arguably the century's most influential assemblage of personalities, and I cannot escape the feeling that it must have been one of the great thrills of his career.

The second of the public concerts, scheduled for 18 November, was a smaller event consisting of patriotic and religious works, among them *God Save the Queen* (who, incidentally, did make the trip) and a new *Vive l'Empereur* by Gounod. Gounod, Delaporte, and Félicien David conducted this concert; Berlioz did not appear. The ten-day closing ceremonies continued with repeats of the 16 November concert on the 24th and of the 18 November concert on the 25th. After this Berlioz took to his bed, exhausted and ill from his sustained labor of many months.

*S*ometime in late 1855, after the exhibition, he was asked to prepare a biographical sketch—invitations of this sort were becoming increasingly common—and to complete a list of all his works. In the curious manuscript document he produced,[63] he asks to be remembered as conductor, author of *Les Soirées de l'orchestre,* and disciple of Byron, Moore, Hugo, and Goethe. Most intriguing are the adjectival descriptions attached to many of the titles: *Sara* and *La Captive* are termed "gracious and even voluptuous"; the *Fleurs des landes* are "naive, rural, gay"; the *Fantastique* is "passionate, violent, and expressive." He calls *Roméo et Juliette* one of the best works he had done, and remarks of *Cellini:* "Never will I find again the verve and brio that there is there," a summation quite similar to that contained in the *Mémoires.* The Te Deum he describes as grander in form and style than any other work, especially in the shattering effect of the Judex crederis. Of his most recent work, *L'Impériale,* he says that the peroration, with unison voices over an immense orchestral tremolo, as the drums play "from the fields," is one of the most stunning effects he has discovered.

The 1855 autobiographical sketch suggests, in short, the composer's marked satisfaction with his career, a much more positive attitude than that found in his assessments of 1848 and 1850. *L'Enfance du Christ* and *Lélio* had appeared in excellent editions, the latter just retitled and with a vocal score by Saint-Saëns. The Te Deum had been performed; the essay on conducting was complete and about to be added to new editions of the *Traité d'instrumentation.* (A serialized version appeared in the *Revue et Gazette musicale* in early 1856.) In the recesses of his mind was beginning to stir the idea for his greatest work.

Indeed, the failure of the London *Cellini* excepted, there had been no serious reverses to his career since the horrors of 1848. (The decline and fall of the Société Philharmonique was unfortunate, but not unpredictable.) There had been an uninterrupted succession of laurel wreaths, banquets, and private and public recognitions of his genius. It began, perhaps, in Brunswick, and was repeated in Leipzig, Weimar, Dresden, Hanover, and again and again in London. Despite the emperor's lack of interest in serious music, Berlioz had been enjoying more than his share of official attention. He had not lacked interesting work, but rather had suffered from a pronounced overabundance of engagements.

Even his financial situation was stabilizing. Marc and Adèle Suat, in their provincial fashion, worried too much about him; after Harriet's death and Louis's enlistment in the navy, we hear relatively little from him concerning his finances.

In response to popular demand, he gave another performance of *L'Enfance du Christ* on 25 January 1856. Despite the small size of the Salle Herz and the large audience expected, he invited all the members of the Institute and a large contingent of the press, that they might better grasp the new direction of his recent work.

Keeping a year-old promise, he went directly to Gotha a few days later, taking for distribution to his admirers quite a number of copies of the imperial cantata as it had just been published. He arrived on the afternoon of 2 February and dined that evening with the duke, Ernst II of Saxe-Coburg-Gotha, himself the accomplished composer of *Santa Chiara. L'Enfance du Christ* was well prepared during the course of four leisurely rehearsals; he took time, too, to ready the overture to the duke's opera and the ravishing new orchestration of *Le Spectre de la rose.* The latter had been scored a few weeks earlier—the parts were copied by Rocquemont before Berlioz left Paris—specifically for its dedicatee, the mezzo-soprano Anna Bockholtz-Falconi, with whom he had been enchanted the previous summer in London and doubtless for whom he transposed the original version down a third.

FIGURE 11.10 *Le Spectre de la rose,* from Rieter-Biedermann's edition of *Les Nuits d'été* (Winterthur, [1856]). The dedication is to Anna Bockholtz-Falconi of Gotha, the mezzo-soprano who sang the first performance of the orchestrated version.

He programmed *Le Spectre de la rose* at least twice more, in 1857; but for *Absence*, it was the only one of the orchestral *Nuits d'été* that he heard.

He was decorated that evening with the cross of knights of the order of the Ernestine Saxon duchies and given the modest receipts of the house. Liszt had made the short trip to Gotha, and afterward they went on together to Weimar.

The Weimar concerts amounted to another Berlioz festival. Peter Cornelius's new translation of *Cellini* was used for the performances on 16 and 18 February. (Immediately afterward he sent the final revision of the troublesome last act to Litolff in Brunswick and thereupon authorized the publication of the new vocal score.) The 17th was Grand Duchess Maria Pavlovna's birthday, for which there was a private court concert quite similar to the one the year before and including, in addition to excerpts from *Faust* and *L'Enfance du Christ, Le Corsaire,* for the second and last time.

For the public concert on the 28th, again to benefit the musicians' pension fund, he gave a complete *Faust,* the first such offering since the full score and parts had appeared. It was the usual Weimar success.

Over the years the Weimar singers had mastered most of his great vocal roles. When the Swiss publisher Jakob Rieter-Biedermann, moved by the orchestral *Spectre de la rose,* invited him to submit the complete *Nuits d'été* in orchestral form, it seemed fitting to frame the set as a mark of gratitude to the Weimar court chapel.[64] The *Villanelle* was accordingly dedicated to Louise Wolf, his Ascanio; *Sur les lagunes,* transposed into his range, to Feodor von Milde, his Fieramosca, Méphistophélès, and St.-Joseph; *Au Cimetière,* to Caspari, his Cellini, Faust, and *récitant;* and *L'Ile inconnue,* to Rosa von Milde, his Teresa, Marguerite, Ste.-Marie, and, later, Béatrice. *Absence* was dedicated to Madeleine Nottès, who had sung it in Weimar in late 1853. One wonders how Marie Recio received the news of this last, as *Absence* had been hers to begin with.

The 1856 stay in Weimar did not mark Berlioz's final visit there, but it was the last time he was with Liszt at the Altenburg. The Liszt fever was subsiding; Liszt's own prestige in Weimar and the princess's favor at court were beginning their dramatic decline. Berlioz feared he did not like Liszt's recent spate of efforts at composition, and Liszt's increasing preoccupation with Wagner drew him away from Berlioz's artistic principles just as Berlioz was discovering his own conservative streak.

Yet this was his most important visit to Weimar, for Liszt and Carolyne Sayn-Wittgenstein now purposefully drew Berlioz out on the question of his Trojan opera. They talked of Classical antiquity and Shakespeare—she baited him to do operas on *Antony and Cleopatra* and *Romeo and Juliet* after *Les Troyens* was done, and gently but pointedly chided him for his procrastinative fear of lacking the necessary will and patience. She told him, indeed, not to come back if he shrank from the task. (In fact they met only once or twice more, notably in late 1859 when she visited Paris and heard a few bits of the work she had encouraged with such tenacity.) They sent him on his way with this strong message, and, calmly at first, he did set to work at last on *Les Troyens*.

*P*aris suffered in those months from a burst of inflation in the cost of living. When his landlord demanded a two-thirds increase in the rent at the rue de Boursault, Berlioz decided, for the first time in his life, to purchase a dwelling outright. At the rate things were progressing, it would double in value in ten years' time, and he could sell his remaining properties in the Dauphiné (which had long been his financial trump card) to raise the needed capital. The search for a suitable lodging to buy, however, was unsuccessful, and from 16 April he and Marie and Marie's mother, Mme Martin, had to content themselves with a sensible but ordinary fourth-floor apartment at 17, rue de Vintimille.

With Trojan warriors and a Carthaginian queen dominating his thoughts, he first cleared his work table of another matter—filling Rieter-Biedermann's commission for the *Nuits d'été*. This task he managed in just four weeks, shipping the autograph full scores and manuscript copies of the piano-vocal reduction to Winterthur on 1 April.

For the next twenty-four months he positively reveled in the composition of *Les Troyens*. Taking books II and IV of Virgil's *Aeneid*, he began to fashion his libretto, guided by his strong affinities for the vivid story and his previous experience with Shakespeare and Goethe. His name was Hector, after all, and he had spent his life with this race of demigods.[65] Seduced by the character of Cassandre, of whom there is scant mention in Virgil, he decided to erect the first half of his epic around her, giving her Laocoön's role as prophet of doom and allowing her to act as chief element of contrast in the otherwise festive proceedings surrounding the Greeks' apparent abandoning of Troy. Cassandre, a tragic heroine, would be a mezzo-soprano. Periodic dispatches to Liszt and the princess proudly reported each new idea: a barcarole for Laocoön's serpents, a mute tableau for Andromaque and Astyanax. The princess replied with unrelenting encouragement in what became a sheaf of testimony to her hortatory skills and must have been a bulwark of strength at countless critical junctures.

Non-Virgilian ideas came to him, too, just as external elements had flavored his versions of *Romeo and Juliet* and *Faust*. The image of Ascagne drawing the ring of Sychaeus from Dido's finger, around which act IV is constructed, for example, was to be found in a painting of Pierre-Narcisse Guérin, *Aeneas Telling Dido of the Misfortunes of Troy* (1815). The love duet is based on Jessica and Lorenzo's famous duologue, "On such a night as this," from act V of Shakespeare's *Merchant of Venice*. Louis, visiting from Toulon, brought tales of Athens and Tenedos, where his ship had called, and some of these were woven in as well. The ideas came effortlessly:

Les Troyens was not written for an impresario or a house—he never really expected to see a production—but for himself and the circle of his most understanding intimates. The libretto was signed and dated on 26 June and sent directly to Carolyne Sayn-Wittgenstein.

He was careful not to write the music until the poem was done; rather he jotted down sketches from time to time and experimented with evocative scale patterns and "oriental" effects. But he could not resist pausing to set the love duet in act IV, *Nuit d'ivresse,* over which scene the music "settled like a bird on ripe fruit."[66] Then he went back to the beginning to compose the rest.

Adolphe Adam's death on 3 May had left a chair vacant at the Institute. This time Berlioz put off his pro-formas as late as he could, assuming, for once, that he would be elected.[67] Halévy and Auber, both of whom were smart enough to be sensitive over the conspicuous absence of intellectual accomplishment in the music section, would probably support him; Carafa would not. (In fact, Carafa cast the only dissenting vote.) Ingres promised his support if his own candidate, Gounod, was not elected on the first ballot.

Berlioz's name led the list of nominees in 1856, and he was finally elevated to the Institute on 21 June over Elwart, Panseron, David, Niedermeyer, Louis Boieldieu, Leborne, Bazin, and the first candidacy of Charles Gounod. The irony of succeeding Adam, who detested his work, cannot have been lost on him, but for once he held his tongue. It was the emphatic success of the German, Russian, and English tours, he thought, that had tilted the scales in his favor, and not his music or his work for the *Débats.*

The election was proclaimed at the palace of St.-Cloud on 25 June in the form of a decree from Napoleon, "by the grace of God and the national will, emperor of the French."[68] The reading of the decree was the first order of business at the academy's meeting on Saturday, 28 June, after which Berlioz was ushered in, dressed in full academic regalia, to take his seat. He invited the music section to dine in his home on 1 July, and on 3 July enjoyed a victory celebration with the young pianist Ritter and his parents.

Like his winning of the *prix de Rome,* his elevation to the Institute had taken many tries, but Berlioz was luckier than Balzac, who was never elected, and no less victimized by the experience than Hugo, who stood four times. (Ravel's inability to garner the *prix de Rome* became a *cause célèbre;* he later declined the Legion of Honor and was never elected to the Academy.) From July 1856 until his death, Berlioz—rather proudly, I think—went each Saturday to the Institute to read in the elegant library, write his letters in tranquil surroundings, and, at 3:00 P.M., attend the weekly *séance* of the Académie des Beaux-Arts. He was remarkably regular in his attendance, missing successions of meetings only for his annual August trips to Plombières-les-Bains and Baden-Baden and for his last journey to Russia in 1867–68. This was at least in part because an annual stipend of 1,500 francs was payable in full to those who were scrupulous in leaving their *jetons de*

FIGURE 11.11
Berlioz in his
Institute regalia.

présence. He was present at well over 450 official meetings and activities of the Institute.

As his own health continued to decline, death claimed many of his friends: the pianist Adolfo Fumagalli, Dr. Amussat, Sax's child and only sister. Among the increasing references to his illness are complaints of involuntarily falling asleep in his carriage; he was not well when he conducted a mass of Niedermeyer on 16 July at St.-Eustache. He was cheered in August when Carolyne Sayn-Wittgenstein replied to his libretto with a sixteen-page critique; among his several responses was to add the text of the scene for the Trojan soldiers at the beginning of act V. They began to discuss titles for the work.

Victors deserve a long vacation. Berlioz and Marie extended his late-summer obligation at Baden-Baden into five weeks of travel to the summer resorts of the fashionable and eminent. Plombières, a spa in the Vosges which had long been favored by his family, could be construed as "on the way" to Baden-Baden. They found Plombières in full dress, for Napoleon III was taking the waters, and they lingered there for nearly two weeks, enjoying long strolls in relaxed surroundings and innumerable glasses of the health-giving mineral water. His *feuilleton* makes fun of Plombières—partly to set up, by contrast, the noble character of Baden-Baden—as "sad in the summer, frightful in winter," the populace made up of foreigners and indigents,[69] but I think he enjoyed himself immensely. In view of his august new rank, he found no difficulty in securing presentation to the emperor; he wanted to broach the issue of *Les Troyens,* but in fact they hardly spoke.

Bénazet had invited Berlioz back to try to establish in Baden something more formidable than the ubiquitous *Kur-orchester,* the tiny spa band that still today endeavors to induce holiday joviality in phlegmatic patrons. Dignified gentlemen and their illustrious though not always legitimate mates planned their rendezvous in Baden-Baden already. What Bénazet desired was nothing less than an annual music festival.

Berlioz came to look forward to the August visits to Baden: he liked the musicians, the freedom of programming, and the aristocratic audience. It amused him to take on the preserve of the salon artists. But above all it was the life-giving injections of excitement that rehearsals and concerts always induced in him, an excitement reminiscent of the Cirque Olympique concerts of 1845 and the Société Philharmonique of 1850–51, that kept him coming back. Though in a *feuilleton* titled "Petites misères des grands concerts" he does his share of complaining about the numerous changes of mind of the soprano, the lack of parts, the lack of musicians, the difficulties of printing and posters and paper supply, all of which he encountered in Baden-Baden, his prevailing tone is one of great enthusiasm.

Mme Viardot came in 1856 to sing Gluck and Bellini and her other favorite airs. Additionally the program for 14 August consisted of Beethoven's Fourth Symphony, the overture to Mozart's *Zauberflöte,* the barcarole from Verdi's new *Vêpres siciliennes,* excerpts from *L'Enfance du Christ, L'Invitation à la valse,* and numerous other selections. There was never much question but that the program would be well received. Reported *Dwight's Music Journal* to its American (largely Bostonian) readers: "A more brilliant and fashionable audience was never seen in the *Maison de Conversation,* which Mr. Bénazet has rendered so attractive that all the 'eaux' and 'spas' of Germany, France, and Belgium (including Austria and the Tyrol) put together sink into insignificance by the side of Baden-Baden."[70] The proceeds were to benefit victims of the floods of the Seine; to the receipts of the house, 4,690 francs, Bénazet added his personal gift of 5,000 francs and Mme Viardot added hers of 500.

"The next day, [I suffered] a re-eruption of gastritis brought on by various causes of which the most significant was excessive fatigue. Confident, not without reason, in the efficacy of the waters of Plombières, I went again to beg that relief for which one does not have to wait."[71] Berlioz and Marie stayed at the French spa for two more weeks, until the end of August, finding the atmosphere more relaxed and a great deal friendlier since the emperor left. In early September they were home, and by 16 October had purchased an apartment at their last address, 4, rue de Calais, between the rue Blanche and the rue de Clichy. It seems conceivable from the terms of Berlioz's will that his mother-in-law actually bought the place, a large dwelling of some five or six rooms. The furnishings belonged to Marie and her mother; Berlioz paid Mme Martin a small rent for them each month. The inventory taken after Berlioz's death suggests that his home was well equipped with pieces of furniture, draperies, and linens, though short on cooking utensils and place settings.[72]

The music for act I of *Les Troyens* took shape that fall, sketched, re-thought, and polished during the long Saturdays at the Institute. During September he began to accept invitations to read the poem aloud, quietly establishing the climate necessary for its production yet assuming early on that the personal intercession of Napoleon III would be necessary. It was for this reason that he began to insinuate himself onto the guest lists for court events and public ceremonies, easy to do now that he was a member of the Institute. It was difficult, as it always had been, to keep up with his ideas. They never ceased coming: he was at the peak of his compositional power.

This pinnacle of fame and artistic accomplishment intersected with phys-ical decline. Neuralgia slowed his forward motion considerably, especially when it came to the tedious work of orchestration. From age fifty-three on, he suffered recurrent bouts of intestinal trouble, taking to his bed for days

FIGURE 11.12 Berlioz, c. 1855.

at a time. He was put on a severe diet ("only sardines," he says), but could not avoid the public banquets to which he was invited several times each week. Ignoring the provisions of his diet became a habit.

Act I was finished at the beginning of February, with the most time—and the most euphoria—expended on the splendid pantomime of Andromaque and its exquisite clarinet solo. His momentum increased: pleased with the spirit of the act I pantomime, he turned again to Carthage and act IV, commencing a ballet-pantomime where Dido and Aeneas might discover their love, the Royal Hunt and Storm. Act IV occupied him for much of the rest of the winter and early spring.

Legouvé read the libretto in February and suggested major revisions to the finale, which had become the central artistic problem of the work: how, in short, to get out of the epic. In early March, at the home of Edouard Bertin, Berlioz read *Les Troyens* to a rapt audience of his friends and the men of letters associated with the *Débats*. Later in the month, on 22 March, he attended a *soirée* at the Tuileries given by the Empress Eugénie; during his thirty seconds of conversation with her, he asked permission to come back and read her the poem, and went home optimistic that he had made some impression. The readings had their purpose, for the greater the number of influential people who had heard and liked the libretto, the more easily pressure could be brought to bear if the time seemed ripe to push for a production.

The year flew by with minimal correspondence, virtually no public activity, and but one monthly article in the *Débats* to keep his followers abreast of the musical life about town. Act IV was finished on 7 April; then he returned to act II during the time remaining before the Baden concerts and another vacation in Plombières.

Berlioz and Marie left on perhaps 14 July for their second taking of the waters in Plombières. The emperor was to vacation on the Isle of Wight that season, so Berlioz was able to pursue his cure in peace. Ideas for *Les Troyens* kept coming to him, and at the fountain one lovely summer afternoon he conceived the marvelous, sunny opening of act III, prompted by the line "Vit-on jamais un jour pareil?" (Have you ever seen such a day?).

Now that he knew what he could count on in Baden, he chose more ambitious programs. Of his own works he programmed for 1857 *Le Spectre de la rose*[73] (for Mme Widemann, who had come along), the Judex crederis (with the organ parts scored for cornet and bassoon) from the Te Deum, excerpts from *L'Enfance du Christ,* the *Marche hongroise,* and, to open the program, the *Francs-Juges* overture. There were also excerpts from Verdi's *Il Trovatore,* now much in vogue since its Paris opening the previous January, passages from *Iphigénie en Tauride,* and the second and fourth movements of Beethoven's Seventh. The nobility was well represented that August: there were several royal and imperial highnesses in the forward rows.

Just as he had hoped, gossip of his new opera crept into the favorable press from Baden. "A setting of the story of Dido is among the rumors," they began to report. The rumors grew colorful, and before it was over there was considerably more fiction than fact in circulation. Berlioz paid these little heed: it was useful publicity. On 25 August, just after returning to Paris, he began and dated the full score of act III, work on which carried him through November. The rough draft of *Les Troyens* was done by year's end, though the bulk of the orchestration for act V and the vexing problem of its ending still needed attention. Sometime that winter he completed a routine correction of the errors in the published score of *Roméo et Juliette* and sent it to be issued as a "2me Edition corrigée par l'auteur / 1857"; the score appeared in 1858 and was soon followed by the piano-vocal edition of Rieter-Biedermann.

By the beginning of 1858 it was clear that *Les Troyens* would, indeed, be finished, and clear to its composer that it was a masterpiece. His public readings, of which the latest was on 22 January at the home of Jacques Hittorff, architect of the Gare du Nord, showed rather more abandon than before, a theatrical style which certain listeners found unbearably tedious.

*W*agner was in Paris in January, trying to collect himself and to unravel his knot of feelings for Frau Wesendonck and his wife, Minna. He was also feeling out the climate for a Paris production of *Tannhäuser* and was thus proposing a major new production to the very theaters that might soon mount *Les Troyens*. He and Berlioz met several times, including at dinner with Blandine Liszt and her new husband, Emile Ollivier. Berlioz read him the poem during a visit of several hours. Wagner could not hide his dismay at the "unspeakable absurdity" of the text, and he was one who reported Berlioz's style of delivery to be tedious. Berlioz sensed this, and from that meeting on the two grew apart again, though not quite so rapidly as they had grown together in London in 1855. Negatively affecting the relationship were at least two ladies: Marie, who had long been suspicious of Wagner, and Carolyne Sayn-Wittgenstein, patroness of *Les Troyens* and, though still secretly, another of his detractors.

In February there was a reading in his own home. But not one of these events drew the attention of Napoleon III, without whose patronage Berlioz imagined the work to be doomed. The Opéra was the only theater in France that could do the work justice, and there was precedent for imperial intercession there: Napoleon I, after all, had commanded the performance of Le Sueur's *Ossian, ou Les Bardes*.

Louis succeeded in becoming a more or less responsible adult during late 1857 and early 1858. Finding the disciplinary rigors of the navy not to his liking, and assuredly harboring a grudge over his imprisonment, he cast his lot with the merchant marine companies based in Marseille. After returning from India in August 1857, he was, with the help of Berlioz's Marseille friends Lecourt and Morel, appointed lieutenant on a vessel called the *Reine des Clippers.* In early 1858 the tone of Berlioz's letters becomes markedly more affectionate, and the pace of the correspondence considerably increases as he takes care to post letters on the 10th and 26th of each month to coincide with the dispatches for the Indies. He writes proudly to Louis of *Les Troyens,* and in February connects his son with one of the superb passages in the work, the song of Hylas, the young Phrygian sailor who sings himself to sleep as he longs for home from the crow's nest. It is one of Berlioz's best poems:

> Vallon sonore
> Où, dès l'aurore,
> Je m'en allais chantant, hélas!
> Sous tes grands bois chantera-t-il encore
> Le pauvre Hylas?
> Berce mollement sur ton sein sublime,
> O puissante mer, l'enfant de Dindyme!

(O, sonorous vale, where from daybreak I used to wander singing: alas, shall poor Hylas ever sing again under thy great trees? O, mighty sea, rock gently on thy noble breast the child of Dindyma.)

Les Troyens was finished, but for the ballets and the act V duo of Didon and Enée, on 12 April 1858, the day he completed the original epilogue. (When Mme Viardot criticized this rambling conclusion, he replaced it with the shorter passage that now concludes the work.) Cocky that the end was in sight, he wrote the emperor an ill-advised parody of the effusive epistles often sent forward to attract the attention of great princes to a work of art. "Despite its boldness and the variety of means employed," he wrote, "the resources available in Paris would be sufficient to perform it . . . Unhappily, it is not vulgar, but that is a fault which Your Majesty will pardon."[74] His associates convinced Berlioz that such rhetoric was likely to be lost on the emperor, and though he did not send the letter, he included it in the postface of the *Mémoires,* where it is dated 28 March. Nobody who mattered had so far the remotest intention of producing *Les Troyens.* In response to his formal notes of appeal he received only polite formulas.

Henry Litolff, who had published in Brunswick the fine vocal score of *Cellini,* came to Paris to give a series of concerts of his music in April and May, and Berlioz could not but support his efforts. He conducted the third of Litolff's concerts on 2 May, with a repertoire that included *La Captive,* sung by Mme Falconi, and the second movement of *Roméo et Juliette.*

Reducing *Les Troyens* to piano-vocal score, he knew, would reveal limitations and problems in the work. He undertook this task with the help of Mme Viardot; whereas the composition took two years, the polishing required five. On the whole, he was delighted with the music, most of all with the "great truthfulness of its expression."[75]

The growing *contretemps* with Wagner was smoothed over for the Congress of Artwork of the Future in Leipzig that June, an event organized by Liszt and A. F. Riccius, conductor of the Leipzig Euterpe concerts. The opening concert juxtaposed an aria from *Cellini* with works of Wagner (the *Vorspiel* to *Tristan und Isolde* and duet from *Der fliegende Holländer*), Liszt, and their spiritual ancestors Schubert, Schumann, Mendelssohn, and Chopin. There would be other performances in this vein before Futurism had run its course, before Wagner, Liszt, Carolyne Sayn-Wittgenstein, and Berlioz had gone their separate ways. He did not attend.

Nor would he go to Plombières before the summer concert in Baden-Baden, announced for 27 August. There Litolff was to play one of his own concertos; the featured works were *Sara la baigneuse* and the first four movements of *Roméo et Juliette*. The performing force, larger than any he had ever assembled there, included a contingent from Strasbourg as well as the usual players from Baden and Karlsruhe, and there were eleven rehearsals. Mme Charton-Demeur, rapidly becoming one of Berlioz's most trusted singers and most intimate of friends, came to sing the strophes in the prologue.

He was not well in Baden and was consequently unable to work on his vocal score, but on the podium he was at his most inspiring. His old friend Georges Kastner, a Strasbourgeois, made in his review of the concert one of the most penetrating of all the analyses of his conducting: "Berlioz has the three cardinal virtues of the orchestra conductor: faith, inspiration, and authority."[76] The review closed with the promise that plans to stage *Les Troyens,* under the patronage of the emperor, were soon to be announced.

Perhaps more important than the concert itself was a discussion with Bénazet concerning the composition of a new opera for Baden-Baden. It appears that Berlioz went to Baden with the idea already conceived; perhaps they had talked of the matter in more general terms before, and it was logical enough, in that Bénazet had already staged new theater pieces by several others. The first notion was for an opera on the Thirty Years War to a libretto by Edouard Plouvier—an unlikely choice for the composer of *Les Troyens,* but one that allowed for the appearance of a *franc-juge* or two and, presumably, the legend and some other passages from *La Nonne sanglante.* This notion was abandoned many months later in favor of *Béatrice et Bénédict,* Berlioz's last major work (though it was written, produced, and published before *Les Troyens* ever reached the stage). Plouvier's libretto was not wasted, either; Litolff set it for a first production in Baden on 10 August 1863, just after the revival of *Béatrice et Bénédict.* By then it had the uncomfortable title *Le Chevalier Nahel, ou La Gageure du diable.*

Berlioz and Marie returned to Paris via Strasbourg, where they spent a brief holiday at Kastner's family home. They were in Paris a few days before his long-awaited audience with the emperor, which took place on 6 September. The private reception he anticipated turned out to be a *soirée* for forty-two. Napoleon III, with his customary courtesy, took the poem and agreed to read it when he had the time. In fact he passed it on to his administrative director of theaters, who not only disliked the work but may have been responsible for some of the uglier misinformation about it—for example, that all twelve books of the *Aeneid* were to be portrayed.[77]

In September the *Mémoires* began to appear serially in Saturday issues of *Le Monde illustré*, preceded by an introductory letter to the editor on 18 September; they were of course edited and expurgated as he went along. But on the whole he was more interested in his latest idea for a book-length collection of essays. For some time, since the travel pieces had begun to lose their charm, his best articles had been woven together of satirical vignettes. These were now to become his *Grotesques de la musique*. Again he began to assemble and revise his clippings, as he had done before for the *Mémoires* and the *Soirées de l'orchestre*. His specialty in this case was his exalted sense of the *bon mot*, but to the amusing anecdotes he added his serious letters on the Marseille and Lyon concerts of 1845 (*Correspondance académique*), on Plombières and Baden (*Correspondance diplomatique*), recollections of his jury service for the Industrial Exposition of 1855, and the dedicatory letter to John Ella confessing to the authorship of *La Fuite en Egypte* (*Correspondance philosophique*). The preface to his musical grotesqueries and a few excerpts appeared in the *Revue et Gazette musicale;* these are presented in the form of an exchange between the author of the *Soirées* and the choruses at the Opéra, for the dedication of the *Grotesques* is "To my good friends the artists of the choruses at the Opéra of Paris, a barbarian city." (The *Soirées* had been dedicated "to my good friends the artists of the orchestra of X***, a civilized city.") *Les Grotesques de la musique* appeared on or about 1 March 1859.

The other absorbing project of 1858–59 was his participation in establishing a universal pitch standard for France and its dominions. On 17 July 1858 the minister of the Interior had appointed a commission to investigate the issue: in addition to ordering what the universal pitch should be, the commission was to suggest the measures necessary to assure its widespread adoption. The problem of inexorably rising habits of pitch had long vexed composers, performers, and instrument builders alike; interest in the work of the commission was expressed throughout Europe and from as far away as the Americas.

It appears that Berlioz did the majority of the legwork in gathering a large collection of modern tuning forks for scrutiny. They came from the cities he had visited and where he maintained close contacts: Brussels, Gotha, Weimar, London, Brunswick, and the like. Each fork was identified with a tag in his handwriting; the measuring of their frequency was of course left to the technicians. (Most of them are in fact quite high by modern standards;

FIGURE 11.13
Tuning forks,
labeled in Berlioz's
hand.

more than half are pitched in C, not A.) Berlioz began to reflect on the problem of a pitch standard in the *Débats* of 29 September 1858. The full report was presented early in January 1859, and a "diapason normal" was proclaimed on 16 February 1859, a pitch of 870 vibrations per second (A = 435) at 15° C. A complicated apparatus consisting of a large tuning fork housed in a weatherproof glass case was constructed and sent to the Conservatoire, where it remains.

He read *Les Troyens* to an informal gathering of friends on the evening of 12 October; among the guests was Thalberg, just back from his tour of the Western Hemisphere. The pressure on the emperor was likewise renewed, and it was arranged through an accommodating minister that Berlioz should be invited to the country palace in Compiègne in November, so that he might approach Napoleon in surroundings more tranquil than the crowded Tuileries palace. The Goncourt brothers were there, too; their journal reports that the emperor spoke to him once in four days, during a conversation about his failing eyesight:

"Monsieur Berlioz, is your tails-coat blue or black?"

"Sire, I should never take the liberty of appearing before Your Majesty in a blue tails-coat. It is black."

"Good," said the emperor.[78]

There is no mention of this holiday in Berlioz's correspondence.

It is not clear when he first considered abandoning Plouvier's legend of the Thirty Years War in favor of the Shakespearean opera *Béatrice et Bénédict*. By the end of 1858 he had agreed to write a three-act opera for Bénazet, to be ready in time for the opening of his new theater in Baden in 1860 or, if construction was not done, the following season. A contract was signed. Yet each step he took toward the Plouvier libretto was as dilatory and uninspired as was any episode in the history of *La Nonne sanglante*. As late as October 1859 he writes of needing to get on with a piece due in a few months. It seems reasonable to imagine that while the Plouvier piece was stagnating, ideas for *Béatrice* were collecting and coagulating.

Idle conversations, breathless reports of overheard gossip, and the ordinary Paris scuttlebutt all tended to reassure Berlioz that *Les Troyens* would soon find its way onto the Opéra's published agenda. Mme Viardot herself may have planted some of the gossip, as she fancied the mezzo role or roles. The director of the Opéra, since 1856, had been Alphonse Royer, one of Berlioz's earliest Paris associates and the brains behind *L'Europe littéraire*, and that was a decidedly promising development. The emperor's indications of support, though so far faint, were often rumored, and it seemed at least within the realm of possibility that he might command the production some afternoon when his whim happened to turn in that direction.

Berlioz was in no position to scheme or even to quibble, for his state of health was reaching a new crisis point. In August 1857, during an era rife with mesmerists, phrenologists, and sorcerers, a mulatto named J.-H. Vriès— calling himself "the celebrated Docteur Noir"—had arrived in Paris from the Caribbean. He had had his share of medical successes, it was said, having for example apparently cured Adolphe Sax of a lip cancer. In January or early February 1859 Vriès undertook Berlioz's care with his panoply of mystical treatments. The specifics of the cure were not made public, but almost immediately there was an improvement in his condition and some remission of symptoms. By 9 February Berlioz writes, with some surprise, "I'm relatively well at the moment."[79] In his gratitude he helped organize at the Louvre on 17 February a banquet for Vriès, where *Le Carnaval romain* was played.

It was also in gratitude to Vriès that Berlioz embarked on one of his more eccentric compositions, a *Hymne pour la consécration du nouveau Tabernacle*, privately printed that October with a lavish cover and fanciful engraving. Vriès believed himself divinely appointed to erect this remarkable edifice on the Champs-Elysées. He would build it "as a token of the reconciliation between God and man, between man and his future, as a symbol of universal peace." "When all men are united by the same religion," said the hymn's title page, "peace will reign on earth." There were but twenty bars of music, extravagantly reengraved for each of the eight strophes of text.

As for Vriès, he was condemned for quackery on 29 March by the Academy of Medicine—unanimously. The panel said that he had succeeded in none of his cancer treatments, that he could not, that his remedies distilled from tropical vegetation were largely inert substances or available at any pharmacy, and that, in fact, Vriès had no idea of what cancer was, or even of proper examination procedures for the sick.

The new theater season included the first performance of Gounod's *Faust* on 19 March at the Théâtre-Lyrique (a company of which there will soon be a great deal more to say) and, on 4 April, Meyerbeer's new opera *Le Pardon de Ploërmel,* which Berlioz covered for the *Débats* with a certain amount of enthusiasm. The first reviews of *Les Grotesques de la musique* were prevailingly positive—except for Scudo in the *Revue des deux mondes,* who was smarting from having been ridiculed by its author for confusing saxhorns and saxophones—and the sales were good. Later in the month, on 23 April, Berlioz conducted a Holy Saturday sacred concert at the Opéra-Comique with *L'Enfance du Christ,* the *Hymne à la France,* and excerpts from *Faust,* along with the Bach/Gounod *Ave Maria.* For the bass Charles-Aimable Battaille he had orchestrated Martini's popular *romance* called *Plaisir d'amour,* to a text of Florian, and this made its debut at the concert of 23 April; Berlioz sold it in June to Richault for 50 francs.[80]

In June he traveled to Bordeaux, an on-again, off-again journey that had been in the works one way or another for fifteen years. This particular event was a festival concert of the Bordelais Société Ste.-Cécile on 8 June. He was there for perhaps a week, to rehearse and conduct portions of *Roméo et Juliette* and *L'Enfance du Christ,* along with *Le Carnaval romain* and possibly the *Marche marocaine.* He enjoyed there the kind of success he had come to expect and was treated to his customary crowns, dinner parties, and *vivats.*

This trip was followed by the annual Baden concert. The first half of *Roméo et Juliette* had been popular enough the previous August to be programmed again, this time with Mme Viardot singing the strophes. There would be scenes from Meyerbeer's new opera and the overture to *La Vestale.* But the excitement in Baden had mostly to do with *Les Troyens,* for Berlioz had decided to present the two big duos there: that of Chorèbe and Cassandre, from act II (no. 3, "Quand Troie éclate"), and, from act IV, the great "Nuit d'ivresse" for Dido and Aeneas. He read the libretto once more at the home of Donon on the afternoon of 6 August before two dozen close friends; shortly thereafter Mme Charton-Demeur—Mme Viardot having gone for the summer to her chateau in Courtavenel—and the tenor Jules Lefort sang the duos and a few other excerpts for the first time in the Salle Beethoven, a tiny music studio in the passage de l'Opéra run by Théodore Ritter, who accompanied them at the piano. It was agreed that the music was magical; Berlioz wept, then shrank again in horror at the thought of seeing a production through.

The thrill to his admirers of hearing music from *Les Troyens*, especially after having heard so much *about* it, was repeated when Lefort and Mme Viardot sang in Baden on 29 August. (Now Mme Charton-Demeur was on her way to Russia; Mme Viardot, who had grown passionate about the work, had been engaged for the Baden debut many months before.) Never before had he premiered major portions of a new work in advance of its first performance, though he had thought of the possibility several times; having settled on this tactic, he orchestrated a barrage of publicity concerning the events in Baden-Baden. But it was true that the performance was brilliant, perhaps the best of his Baden concerts, and the reception enthusiastic. Mme Viardot was praised for the power she exerted over her listeners; the reviewers found in the new work highly original effects combined with great musical science. As it turned out, the duo from act I was the only excerpt from the Troy half Berlioz ever heard performed.

The autumn was devoted to a revival of Gluck's *Orphée*, with Mme Viardot in the title role. Berlioz was in charge of editing the text and preparing the performance materials. (The idea, however, was not his: it began with a suggestion Meyerbeer made to Viardot.) Saint-Saëns was to assist Berlioz in these formidable duties.

The 1859 *Orphée* was a project of the Théâtre-Lyrique, the promising new company overseen since 1855 by the young Léon Carvalho. Under his leadership it rose quickly to become one of the important theaters of Paris, numbering among its impressive accomplishments four premieres for Gounod, including *Faust,* and the Bizet/Daudet *L'Arlésienne.* Carvalho was a shrewd, rather daring impresario, as inclined as any of his colleagues to the position that tampering with theater pieces was his privilege. He was quick to see the inspiration behind the idea of Berlioz and Mme Viardot's collaborating on Gluck, to say nothing of its possible though so far uncertain commercial appeal. Berlioz was able to dissuade Carvalho and Viardot from modernizing the orchestration and making of *Orphée* a potpourri of the most popular airs from the chosen work, the *Iphigénie*s, and *Armide*.[81] (Saint-Saëns ultimately finished up some of the light rewriting Berlioz himself refused to do.) He was of course intoxicated by the opera, the only person in France who knew enough about Gluck to prepare such a production, and the version he fashioned for Mme Viardot remains well entrenched in the repertoire. Carvalho liked Berlioz and made clear his willingness to undertake *Les Troyens,* perhaps for the opening of his new theater to be built in the place du Châtelet. Berlioz did not dismiss that possibility, though he feared Carvalho would want his wife to sing the leading role and knew already that there were no suitable male singers in the company.

Adèle and a niece came to visit Berlioz in Paris in early September, when he was too busy to be hospitable. Marie took them to Fontainebleau, then established herself with friends in St.-Germain for a holiday. This made him lonely—and in mid-September he took the train to visit Mme Viardot in Courtavenel. They spent two days going over *Orphée* and the revised piano

FIGURE 11.14
Madame Viardot
as Orphée, 1859.

score of *Les Troyens,* the latter having occupied her attention from its earliest stages. Not a few indications suggest that his feelings for the great lady were fast developing into a romantic involvement, and that she returned the affection.

Most of all, however, she was appalled by his health:

> The sight of this man, suffering so much moral and physical pain, so much intestinal illness, so affected by our warm welcome, a prey to horrible emotional torments, the violence of his efforts to hide them; this burning soul that bursts from its casing, this life which hangs by a thread, the great overflowing tenderness of his gaze and of his slightest utterance—all this has shattered me . . .
>
> Alas, I fear that Berlioz will not be at the performance [of *Les Troyens*].[82]

Mme Viardot had—as Pauline Garcia—entered Berlioz's life in February 1839, when she sang an excerpt from *Orphée* at a salon concert. At the time Berlioz judged her harshly, both in a *feuilleton* and in a letter, where

FIGURE 11.15
Madame Viardot as
Orphée. Sepia, 1860.

he wrote of her "pretended talent" and dismissed her as a "diva manquée."[83] He changed his tune when she sang Fidès in *Le Prophète;* then he pronounced her among the greatest singers of all time. Now in her prime—she was thirty-eight and had borne her last child—she was admired everywhere for her intelligence and astonishing range of interests as much as for her singing. Berlioz was smitten with her from the first time she sang *La Captive;* in Baden-Baden her Gluck and the strophes from *Roméo et Juliette* had touched a tender string.

He returned from Mme Viardot's to begin electric-shock treatment from an English physician, writing to her that their next handshake would be shocking.

Orphée opened on 18 November and, rather to everyone's surprise, was positively welcomed. Berlioz had transmitted to Viardot and the others his feel for the 1820s style of Dérivis and Branchu, a magic memory still treasured by those in their middle age. The small size of a lesser theater helped matters, and, within its limited means, the production was faithful and animated. The costumes, for example, were of a severe simplicity that was deemed perfect for the work. Mme Viardot's rendition was memorable for its learned technique, elegant phrasing, and nobility of gesture—a sublime amalgam, they said, of discipline and spontaneity. In his own review, Berlioz praised her for all but one note that she sang, and she argued in turn that every pitch was exactly what she had been told to do. The music, though antiquated, clearly held its dramatic sway.

The Belgian singer Marie Sass was Viardot's Eurydice, and from this production began her rise to stardom—though once she reached the stage of the Opéra she was forced to change her stage name, Mlle Sax, as a result of a lawsuit brought by the instrument maker of the same name. But the triumph was Viardot's. It was an event on something of the same scale as Harriet Smithson's playing Ophelia and Juliet a generation earlier. The writers all agreed on this point. Jules Janin summarized the adventure well when he wrote of *Orphée:* "We cannot take up masterpieces anew: it is the masterpieces that take us up anew."[84]

Berlioz feared Gluck's becoming modish and therefore vulgar or, worse still, merely *charmante,* but that did not dampen his pleasure. The production went on to have 138 performances between 1859 and 1863, and he doubtless received a small stipend for each. It was still Mme Viardot's most popular role when she retired from the stage.

Late in 1859, all but certain of a production, he composed the ballets for *Les Troyens* and was, for all intents and purposes, done with it.

Berlioz cannot have been unaware that Wagner's renewed presence in Paris—he had taken a three-year lease—was for the purpose of having an opera of his own staged at one of the very houses that were grappling with the question of *Les Troyens.* But the work was there for posterity, and it was moreover fast becoming the talk of Paris. Now he could turn his attention to accomplishing other things in the few weeks or months he thought remained to him.

Chapter Twelve

Portrait in 1859
Les Troyens

*I*n 1859 Berlioz, though only just beginning to suspect it, was nearly done with composition. *Les Troyens* was complete; his last great work, *Béatrice et Bénédict,* was taking shape in the recesses of his mind. The triumphs of Weimar and elsewhere, the decorations of grateful princes, and the affection of many publics confirmed his reputation among the German-speaking peoples. *L'Enfance du Christ* confirmed it with the French, if indeed there was any question of his standing in view of the other events of 1854–55. It was common knowledge that *Les Troyens* was finished, and even though few yet knew anything about the music, a journalistic ground swell was forming in support of that work. Despite the fact that his efforts as a composer were nearly done—or perhaps because of it, for composition now taxed his limited resources severely, and it was necessary to conserve his strength—he remained in splendid form. Over the past decade or so he had written, at least in terms of duration, between a third and a half of his greatest work: the Te Deum, *L'Enfance du Christ,* and *Les Troyens,* with *Béatrice et Bénédict* soon to follow.

Of the many technological advances the nineteenth century witnessed, perhaps none so excites the biographer as the advent of photography and the rapid development of the new art form of photographic portraiture. In France, one of its most skillful practitioners was Félix Nadar, who turned to photography in the early 1850s after a disastrous career in medicine and a highly successful one as caricaturist, balloonist, and spy. (For one of Nadar's cartoons of Berlioz, see fig. 10.15.) In 1856 he took a three-quarter-length photograph of the composer (fig. 12.1), one of the triumphs of his career. It is among the earliest photographs of Berlioz, taken against a bare background with the composer's face turned just enough away from the camera to evoke distance and vision. He is dressed in a traditional business suit—which is not the case in either the Signol or the Prinzhofer portrait—and wears an enormous greatcoat; his hands are tucked in the sleeves, just

FIGURE 12.1 Berlioz, c. 1856.

as described by Russian observers in 1867. (Otherwise the greatcoat is suspicious, for we know that Berlioz went without one in Paris whenever he could. It is surprisingly large. Did Berlioz never return Balzac's coat after the Russian journey of 1847? Is he, in this picture, on his way to or from wintry Weimar?) Neither cane nor jewels nor Wagnerian beard adorns the artist here, as they had in 1846. Despite his declining health, he appears robust and vigorous. The photograph is illuminated by an arresting depth of gaze, a fire in the eyes; the bushy mane of hair, now apparently dark russet instead of flaming red, is still prominent, as is the aquiline nose.

He looks older and sicker in four photographic *cartes de visite* (figs. 12.3–12.6) made at a sitting with Pierre Petit six years later, during the period of *Béatrice et Bénédict* and *Les Troyens à Carthage*. Berlioz was delighted with these pictures, however, particularly the one where his head droops on his fist, and thought them his best likenesses.[1] He wanted this favorite pose to serve as the frontispiece for the German editions of the *Traité de l'instrumentation,* and it falls in that position in the Malherbe and Weingartner complete edition. He wears a dark, three-piece suit with waistcoat, a watch chain draped across the front. In his lapel is one of his decorations, around his collar the traditional black tie. (This must have been pretty much how he appeared, in his critic's armchair, to the theater-going public.) His hairline seems to have receded slightly; his jowls have fallen; more wrinkles appear around his eyes. Yet a certain warmth pervades the pensive, reflective pose. The general effect accords well with Judith Gautier's description of "a man

FIGURE 12.2 Berlioz, c. 1860.

FIGURE 12.3 Berlioz, c. 1863.

of original and striking appearance. He was small, lean, with bony cheeks, a nose like an eagle's beak, a great forehead with piercing eyes, a ravaged, passionate look."[2]

Liszt's description of the Berlioz he encountered in 1861, however, suggests a more sinister spiritual condition:

> Berlioz's voice has sunk deeper. He speaks with a bass voice anyway—so his whole being seems to tend toward the tomb! I don't know how he has managed to isolate himself in this way. In fact he has no friends, no supporters—neither the bright sunshine of the public nor the sweet shade of intimate friends.[3]

This assessment is not entirely accurate, for the part about the friends—and even the public—is simply wrong. (This meeting took place at the height of *Tannhäuser* fever, when the allegiances of both Liszt and Berlioz were sorely tried.) Something about the photographs reinforces what the other evidence strongly suggests: that in the briefer and briefer periods between his attacks of neuralgia, he retained the remarkable energy and volcanic intellectual qualities that had enabled him to accomplish his many endeavors thus far.

Berlioz's home life, by 1859, was tranquil and relatively comfortable. His primary financial concern after Harriet's death and Louis's accession to paid ranks was his son's tendency to spend an entire six months' wages on a single extravagant shore leave and then unexpectedly arrive in Paris, needful of lodging, food, and new clothes. But Berlioz's income was steady, and there was no longer any question but that his expenses and fees, when he conducted abroad, would be more than met. Unlike Liszt, he traveled in first-class carriages; the provisions for his 1867–68 trip to Russia can appropriately be termed princely.

He rose late in the morning to attend to his letter writing and other personal business. He ran his errands in the early afternoons and attempted to be at home to callers by 4:00 P.M. His duties at the Conservatoire library, even after Bottée's death, were minimal, requiring what seem to have been weekly visits, if that, mostly to acknowledge gifts to the library. He paid a little attention to developing the collection, at one point systematically acquiring Liszt's scores and often donating publications sent to him in which he had no interest. (Among these are the quartets of the Müller brothers in Brunswick.) On evenings when he was not engaged, he would compose for several hours, then relax by the fire until he was ready for bed. Nights at the theater would be longer, extended by dinners that often lasted until well past midnight.

Saturdays he went to the Institute, where he took on his rightful portion of such responsibilities as judging the *prix de Rome* competition, assessing learned treatises, and so forth, in general seeing official musical life from the other side of the table. It was not just the financial incentive that drew him there, for he was interested in much of the work. He went to the Institute nearly every Saturday he was in Paris, and on more than one occasion appears to have timed a homeward journey from abroad in order to be back by Saturday afternoon.

He had apparently become something of a gourmet, for references to good food crop up frequently in writings from the later years. We know him to have been fond of a partridge-and-egg stew he had discovered in Germany,

FIGURE 12.4 Berlioz, c. 1863.

for example, and one writer testifies—somewhat questionably, in view of Berlioz's weakness for lady singers—that he preferred dessert to the attention of a vivacious young woman. One evening after dinner, the story goes, Adelina Patti committed the *albumination* of asking Berlioz to leave his autograph. If only he would sign, she said, he could choose for dessert between a kiss and a pastry by her chef; he need only write two words. The two he wrote, "*Opportet pati*," could be interpreted either way.[4] Saint-Saëns regretted Berlioz's obstinacy in not following the diet his physicians prescribed to alleviate his gastric distress. The abdominal cramps invariably subsided when he abstained from rich food and stimulants.

*L*ouis was by now twenty-five years old. His life as a seaman, centered around Le Havre, the several large ports near Marseille, and later, when his voyages took him frequently to the Americas, the Atlantic port cities. After the rigors of the Crimean War and his dispute with Admiral Cécille, he led the life of a journeyman-officer, for a time taking cargo ships to and from India and the French West Indies. Later he was conscripted, with his ship, to serve Napoleon III's ambitious though ill-conceived Mexican adventure. There is every indication that Louis could be exceedingly difficult, his poor behavior and spendthrift ways reaching their peak in the years that

Marie Recio was married to his father. Berlioz bore all this relatively well, although I find it surprising that he failed to note the parallels, especially concerning fathers and money, with his own young manhood. Berlioz did vicariously enjoy Louis's tales of the sea, and Louis had, for his part, moments of wisdom and insight: "I know I have sometimes been a trial to him, but I am very young, dear aunt, and young people go through terrible times . . . God willing he will someday be proud of his son."[5] After Marie's death in 1862, the relationship took a decided turn for the better, and for an all-too-brief five years Louis was a source of abiding satisfaction. Louis had liked his father's music since he was a small child; now he was old enough to be proud, no longer embarrassed by his father's reputation. He appears to have been one of the most devoted followers of *Les Troyens.*

There is virtually no documentation of Marie Recio's life after she became the legitimate Mme Berlioz. Months pass with no mention of her; during the worst times with Harriet and Louis, she maintained a discreet and deliberate distance. She does not seem to have appeared in public at all during the formalities surrounding Harriet's death and burial. It seems, in those circumstances, an extraordinary stroke of luck that her photograph, which must have been made in the late 1850s, has been preserved (fig. 12.7). There she is seen to be a handsome woman indeed.

The great, all but coincidental dividend of his marrying Marie Recio was the acquisition of her mother, Mme Martin, née Solera Villa-Recio. I cannot tell when she became part of the *ménage;* surely it was not before their

FIGURE 12.6 Berlioz, c. 1863.

FIGURE 12.7 Marie Recio.

marriage, and possibly it was not until their move to the rue de Vintimille, in 1856. Much of their furniture was hers, and she paid her share or more of the leases and mortgage; after Marie's death she took remarkably patient and good care of Berlioz and offered a degree of domestic companionship. At the end, she saw to it that he was never left alone. Berlioz, who obviously was attached to her, made generous provision for her in his will, leaving a good deal more to her than, for example, to Estelle Fornier. A single negative remark about her in the Berlioz correspondence seems to be in jest: he would give two *louis d'or,* he writes the Massarts in 1865,[6] to hear French spoken around him. His mother-in-law chatters at him in Spanish, his maid in German, and his friend Asger Hamerick in Danish.

His ties to La Côte-St.-André deteriorated quickly with the deaths of his father in 1848, Nanci in 1850, and Adèle in 1860. Nanci's survivors in Grenoble were her husband, Camille Pal, and their daughter, Mathilde. Adèle left behind her husband, Marc Suat, and two daughters, Nanci and Josephine; they lived in Vienne and had a country house nearby. Each of the brothers-in-law helped administer Berlioz's business affairs, especially those having to do with his properties in the Isère, and they advanced him money when his need was greatest. Berlioz grew away from Camille Pal as the years wore on and the family became resigned to Nanci's loss. After the death of Adèle, on the other hand, who had met and loved Harriet and was Louis's godmother, Berlioz cultivated his ties to Suat and his daughters and visited them frequently. It was an easy journey by train, and for a time Estelle Fornier lived nearby. He delighted in all three of his nieces, the Suat girls especially; he asked after them frequently and saw to their musical interests, shepherded them through Paris, dedicated part of *L'Enfance du Christ* to them, and, when they were grown, tried to like their husbands. The girls became his heirs after Louis's death and dispersed such of his estate as was left to their attention.

The bizarre tale of Estelle, she of the pink boots, the nymph of Meylan, crops up once again in his last years, to such an extent that for a brief period both parties considered the possibility of there being a third Mme Berlioz. It was the writing and expanding of the *Mémoires,* between 1848 and 1854, that brought Estelle again to mind; with Harriet's death and, not so long afterward, Marie's, Berlioz's thoughts turned more and more frequently to his purest attachment, the one identified in his mind with the first stirrings of his adolescence. Berlioz was often a woeful failure at romantic love, but he went on looking for it until nearly the end of his life. In 1854, "burned up, yet burning," he writes in the postscript of the *Mémoires:*

> Those to whom all this [that is, Estelle, Harriet, and Shakespeare] is incomprehensible will understand me still less when I mention another idiosyncrasy of my nature: the vague feeling of ideal romantic love that comes over me when I smell a beautiful rose. For long I used to have a similar sensation at the sight of a fine harp; when I saw one, I wanted to go down on my knees and embrace it.
>
> Estelle was the rose "left blooming alone"; Harriet the harp whose strains were part of all my concerts, my joys and sorrows—of whose strings, alas, I broke many.[7]

Before Estelle's reappearance several other women must have sensed that they were becoming the focus of Berlioz's longing. No one could have sensed it more than Mme Viardot, by this point in her career more than a little experienced with adulation of various sorts. Those excessively long hours spent with the piano-vocal score of *Les Troyens* surely had much to do with romance.

The revival of *Orphée,* and Viardot's complete triumph over the role, only complicated Berlioz's feelings. His long, impassioned letters to her during the late 1850s and 1860s are, to use words Berlioz once applied to Louis, just barely wise. It was doubtless she, moreover, who first sang to him the arias of the three great women in his last two operas, who first brought them to life. Mme Viardot saw him through *Béatrice et Bénédict* as surely as Carolyne Sayn-Wittgenstein—an infinitely less attractive woman, though Viardot's equal in intelligence—had seen him through *Les Troyens.*

*A*t home and abroad, perceptions of Berlioz were often confused, but his activities never failed to interest a variety of people. The American press, notably *Dwight's,* took particular pleasure in its accounts of "Mon-

FIGURE 12.8
Caricature of Berlioz, c. 1863.
The scroll in his hand
is entitled *Les Troyens*.
The names of his other works
are chiseled into the wall
behind him.

sieur Berlioz, the genial Frenchman," or, more often, "Monsieur Berlioz, the eccentric Frenchman." In nearly all the papers the rumors flew: that he was rich, that *Cellini* had required twenty-nine general rehearsals, that *Les Troyens* had twenty-two roles and would last eight hours. Misconceptions about the size of his works were widespread, even among those who should have known better. Berlioz was especially disheartened, for instance, by Heine's characterization of him as a "colossal nightingale." But it was only natural that what people remembered best were the big works and the monster concerts. It was for this reason that *L'Enfance du Christ*, for Heine as well as many others, seemed such an unexpected announcement of a new style.

The satirical press was at its best when it came to Berlioz, poking more and better fun at him than at either Meyerbeer or Wagner. Berlioz's hair and beak-like nose made for a good caricature, and the monster concerts were ideal fodder for the cartoonists. The events of 1855 in the Palais de l'Industrie, with their 1,200 performers and electric metronome, prompted the funniest cartoons of all. One of them, published just afterward, shows persons "of delicate eardrums" listening to the concert from the Place de la Concorde, a half mile away (see fig. 12.9). Two weeks later the *Charivari* showed Berlioz conducting a global event, with electric wires strung round the world. Another cartoon shows a "grand concert" in which "M. Berlioz will conduct with a telegraph pole" (see fig. 12.10).

Berlioz was sensitive, perhaps overly so, to the public's tendency to think of him merely as a colossalist or breaker of the rules. In a letter to Peter Cornelius of 9 April 1862 he writes:

What makes me the most impatient is when people attribute to me musical opinions which are precisely the contrary of my own, and that they think me prone to flawed theories that I have always fought against. A consequence of these errors is to have my works, even the simplest, considered as monstrosities. You can say to certain people: "How do you like this progression of Berlioz?":

And they would respond with indignation: "Oh, how frightful!"[8]

Asked to annotate proofs of his biography in the *Dictionnaire musical des contemporains,* he penned in the margin a vehement defense against the familiar charges of eccentricity, expression purely by means of effect, and delusions of grandeur:

> What grandiose means are employed in *L'Enfance du Christ?* In the legend of *Faust?* In *Roméo et Juliette?* In *Harold?* In the *Fantastique?* In my overtures? In *Cellini?* It is the Dies irae of the Requiem that has given rise to this notion. It is as ridiculous as the assumption of the Englishman who, having seen some goitrous women in Savoy, wrote: "on the Continent, all women have goiters."[9]

He cannot have been displeased at the regular inclusion in the 1850s of his name with Liszt's and Wagner's as one of the trinity of the Artwork of the Future. (Some added Meyerbeer to the list.) Yet he barely understood what Liszt was attempting in Weimar and was insensitive, largely because

FIGURE 12.9
"For Persons with Delicate Eardrums." The caption reads: "Reserved seats to hear the next monster concert to be given by M. Berlioz in the Salle de l'Exposition."
The listeners are seated in the Place de la Concorde.
Cham, in *Charivari,* 18 November 1855.

M. Berlioz donnant prochainement un concert européen en battant la mesure avec un poteau du télégraphe électrique.

of his poor German, to the crosscurrents there. He saw von Bülow and Cornelius, for example, mostly as amanuenses, useful in arranging and translating his works and purveying them to the German-speaking world. He had little to say of the opera that brought Liszt's Weimar experiment tumbling down, Cornelius's *Barbier von Baghdad,* and seems never quite to have grasped the reasons for the radical changes in Liszt's life after 1858. He took it as a matter of course that Liszt, in his labored but proud attempts to write important music, turned to his own symphonies for models of what to do. He did not see the irony of that's transpiring just as Wagner was churning up the world of music as he knew it, nor did he ever feel himself, as he should have, the spiritual godfather of the Symphonische Dichtung.

Berlioz's royal patrons abroad—the blind king of Hanover, the dowager grand duchess of Saxe-Weimar, the prince of Hohenzollern-Hechingen, and the various Russian nobles—maintained their admiration and support. It was only because he did not give concerts in Berlin after 1847 that his friendship with the king of Prussia evaporated. He went abroad more than a dozen times between the great journey of 1853–54 and the long trip to Russia in 1867–68, but the terrain was familiar and the faces mostly those of old friends. The repertoire consisted largely of the works since *Faust,* though by special request he would include *Harold* and *Le Roi Lear* and the *Fantastique.* The *Symphonie funèbre* and *Le Cinq Mai,* for example, were dismissed.

Berlioz's accession to the rank of national treasure is reflected in the role he played in the Gluck revivals that began with *Orphée* at the Théâtre-

Lyrique in 1859. His expertise on the subject of Gluck's life and works was recognized by all; there can have been no greater artistic satisfaction than watching the success of *Orphée* lead to *Alceste* at the Opéra in 1861 and to both *Armide* and a revival of *Alceste* in 1866. Something of the depth of his accomplishment in this regard is shown by two particular incidents of the period. Challenged on a correction he had made to a passage for trombones in *Alceste,* he defends himself by saying that after having heard the work a dozen times, he went to the chief copyist at the Opéra and had the correct manuscript reading certified. ("The music of a score is the music one *sees,*" writes Berlioz to François Delsarte; "the music of the separate parts is the music one *hears*—and what I am sending you are the chords that Gluck *heard* and *designed to be heard.*")[10] Supporting an effort by Charles Hallé and his associates to introduce Gluck to the English, Berlioz writes:

> There are no other orchestra parts of *Armide* except those at the Opéra, and you may be certain these would not be lent you. Besides, they contain a mass of alterations made long ago by Gardel and others, as well as additions of instruments by God knows whom, that you would certainly not want to follow. Your intention is to produce Gluck *as is.* Hence you can do no other than have the parts copied from the full score which, incidentally, is one of the least faulty and confused Gluck has left us. The composer, no one knows why, does not employ any trombones in it; the same is true of *Iphigénie en Aulide.* In *Orphée, Alceste,* and *Iphigénie en Tauride,* on the contrary, the trombone plays a very important role.
>
> In *Iphigénie en Aulide* Gluck has changed a few passages and written some *ballet music* which is to be found only in the manuscript score at the Opéra. You will therefore not be able to make your English edition accurate without coming to Paris. If it is only a piano and vocal score, the harm will be less. I don't believe there ever will be a more remiss composer than Gluck or one who took less care of his works, though he seemed proud enough of them. They are all in the worst disorder and disarray imaginable.[11]

Berlioz was asked by Alfred Dörffel to prepare the Heinze edition of *Orphée* (1866), and he did read the proofs; later he was the guiding spirit behind a modern French edition of Gluck.

In his capacities as critic, impresario, and, later, member of the Institute, he watched the whole of the next generation of French composers pass in review. He welcomed the exoticism of Félicien David and Ernest Reyer, whose *Sélam* of 1850 attracted his close scrutiny; Reyer went on to become his most direct spiritual descendent. Berlioz's other great admirer was Camille Saint-Saëns, who shared, in his broad intellectual and technical accomplishments, many affinities with Berlioz beyond composition. Saint-Saëns prepared the 1855 vocal score of *Lélio,* then after Berlioz's death left a number of evocative if factually suspect cameo portraits of the composer. Berlioz knew Gounod only slightly, at first from crossing paths, not swords, over *La Nonne sanglante;* by 1857 he thought highly enough of Gounod to offer him a hardbound, autographed copy of *L'Enfance du Christ*. By and large, the other younger composers, the less good ones, found him frightening and aloof, and succeeding generations trod gently, if at all, in the direction of the Berlioz style. By 1870 royalty and empire were all but things of the past, as was their ceremonial music; for French composers of that generation the most engrossing issue was the Wagner problem. Their dominant genre, on which Berlioz had decided impact but which he did not practice at all, was the symphonic poem. The reflourishing of the *mélodie* at the century's end shows rather more of the Berlioz spirit.

The Revolution of 1848 and accession of Napoleon III, coupled with the deaths of Dr. Berlioz and Nanci and the rapid decline of Harriet, had triggered radical changes in Berlioz's life and lifestyle. The new emperor cared little for music, certainly less than the family of Louis-Philippe. The new French attitudes were stodgy and predictable: one could gamble on a bold stroke in the 1830s, he noted, but no longer. The Second Empire was dangerously aggressive in international affairs; Berlioz, remembering with the rest of the populace the devastating economic distress of 1848 (which had been brought about in part by Louis-Philippe's adventures in Africa), was thus prompted to reflect on his intellectual estate and to gather his artistic affairs together as though the end of the life he knew might come at any time. He developed marked nostalgias and melancholies as his mind dwelled more and more on his past, as he lingered over the tinted memories of his childhood.

The *Mémoires,* the original parts of which were written in large measure over the years between *Faust* and *Les Troyens,* is by no means his only (or even his most coherent) autobiographical essay. It was the age of encyclopedias, and the editors of these works were disposed to include a sketch of his life—though not, they would remind him, too long a sketch. Publishers demanded that he prepare for them the lists and catalogues that have served diligent research ever since. And then of course there were the recurring elections for the Institute, for which the candidate was obliged to number all his accomplishments, always pondering his shortcomings as he compiled the list anew for each freshly vacant chair. He added not a few autobiographical remarks when he collected his best essays, between 1852 and 1862, for the three engaging volumes of criticism he left behind. It was a tall order, this tidying up of one's life's work, and it occupied a major portion of his time between 1848 and 1865.

Berlioz on Berlioz is a delightful combination of self-esteem, frank admission of weaknesses, and subtle manipulation of the factual evidence in his own defense. His particular satisfactions were with his conducting, his writing (he valued the *Soirées* above the others), and his mastery of Shakespeare, Byron, Moore, Hugo, and Goethe. His reflections nearly always mention the role of Nature in his works. The rest is almost offhand: "I begin to know French, to be able to write a decent page of music, of verse, or of prose."[12]

Spiritual skepticism and physical and mental exhaustion gave rise to the *Mémoires* and became the unfortunate theme that unites an otherwise positive autobiographical account. He was fed up with metaphysical speculation: "Life is a lottery," he says simply in a letter of the time. In the final portions of the *Mémoires* that motive occurs again and again: "the orbit of emotions, aspirations, and frustrations within which I am fated to turn until I turn no more." And, "How meaningless are all these questions of fate, free will, the existence of God, and the rest of it: an endless maze in which man's baffled understanding wanders helplessly lost." His expectation as he completed the *Mémoires* was to finish his life in a whirlwind of frustration, dashed hopes, and deep spiritual vexation. "I feel that my faculties have never been so great; but material obstacles prevent me from using them. This [usurpation of my creative impulses] makes me literally ill."[13] Yet if Berlioz chose to paint his self-portrait as a tragedy, he also gave in the *Mémoires* a trove of useful facts, brilliant *aperçus*, and experiences that opens a window on the civilization's way of life. His descriptions of individuals—Guhr, Mendelssohn, Jullien, Habeneck—are second to none and have formed our overriding impressions of these people. The beautiful chapter on Harriet's death is as moving as anything a composer ever wrote. The *Mémoires* must be numbered among the great autobiographies.

*T*he period of magnificent achievement from the Te Deum to *Béatrice et Bénédict,* so reminiscent of the glorious days of the 1830s, embraces, as did the earlier days, its share of shorter works, rearrangements and recastings of existing pieces, and the like. The more important project of the 1840s and 1850s was, however, not so much composing new songs as assembling the piano-vocal sets, those publishers' collections with such titles as *Tristia, Vox populi,* and *Feuillets d'album, Fleurs des landes,* and the new *Irlande.* The titles surely came from Berlioz himself. Whether this spate of publication was the result of some commercial inspiration of Richault or part and parcel of Berlioz's systematic attention to his artistic legacy is hard to say.

Whatever the explanation, the effort of collecting these works for engraving and reengraving offered Berlioz the opportunity to update and delicately rewrite them. In *Irlande,* for example, he transposed and expanded *Adieu, Bessy* and added, before the *Elégie en prose,* the long discourse on the Irish nationalist Robert Emmet, a story he had picked up in England. In the little (and decades-old) songs *Les Champs* and the *Chant des bretons,* he made modest changes to the accompaniments and text settings. *Le Chant des chemins de fer* was offered for the first time in any edition when it appeared in *Feuillets d'album*. Had he waited a couple of years to publish *Vox populi*, two of his big ceremonial works in more-or-less simultaneous full and piano-vocal scores, he might have fashioned a splendid collection of that pair along with the cantata *L'Impériale* of 1854–55 and *Le Cinq Mai*, which he seems temporarily to have forgotten. The D-major piano reduction of the orchestrated *La Captive* was important enough to have had separate publications in Paris and Berlin and so was not included in the collections.

The larger works from *Faust* on all have prominent vocal and choral parts, so a major concern in publishing them was the preparation of the piano-vocal scores. In some respects the need for the full scores was less urgent: the vocal scores had greater market value, and in multiple copies they could be put straight to use for performances where he himself might use the autograph score. The publications of *Faust, L'Enfance du Christ, Lélio,* and the Te Deum went smoothly and resulted in near-definitive and quite lovely texts, though with regard to the first two of these Berlioz was extended beyond his limited capacities as a proofreader. (In both cases, a second reader found hundreds more mistakes after he was done.) For all of these, Berlioz insisted in his contract that full score, parts, and piano-vocal score appear simultaneously; generally he had his way, and they were published within a few weeks of each other.

Second editions were issued of two major works, the Requiem and *Roméo et Juliette,* during the period, in both cases because the first edition had been depleted. Why Brandus, Schlesinger's successor, had no interest in the new, revised edition of the Requiem, with the result that Berlioz had to turn to Ricordi in Milan for a complete reengraving, is a mystery. In short, except for the lamentable mess with the full scores of his operas, the state of his published editions, when he died, was exemplary. What he left for posterity was in better shape than posterity has been inclined to admit.

The 1840s and 1850s were the decades of the fine foreign editions. Berlioz's flirtation in 1847–48 with the London firm of Cramer and Beale had resulted in three patriotic curiosities for piano and voice, and there were plans for more. The more important British connection was with Novello, who contracted with Berlioz for the *Treatise upon Modern Instrumentation and Orchestration,* a piano-vocal score of *The Holy Family,* and an English edition of *Faust.* In Vienna Pietro Mechetti published *Le Trébuchet* and *Les Champs* in his collection of favorite parlor tunes, and *La Captive* had an elegant Leipzig edition as *Die Gefangene,* by the firm of C. F. Kahnt. A number of other significant prints were issued by the venerable Leipzig presses, under agreements that were in some measure similar to his earlier arrangements for copublication in Berlin by the German Schlesingers. The 1856 *Cellini* vocal score, which embodied the Weimar revisions, was a product of Henry Litolff's firm in Brunswick, which succeeded Leibrock's, and was perhaps the most important of the several homages made by that excellent city to Berlioz. The fine *Béatrice et Bénédict* by the Berlin firm of

Bote und Bock is virtually a clone of the Paris vocal score; doubtless the connection was through Richard Pohl.

Of all the foreign publishers, the most important was Rieter-Biedermann of Winterthur, in Switzerland. The relationship apparently began when the publisher was captivated by *Le Spectre de la rose* in Gotha in February 1856. The *Nuits d'été* in piano-vocal and full scores were Rieter-Biedermann's plate numbers 2 and 3 of 1856; later he published von Bülow's piano score of *Le Corsaire* (1857) and the superb piano score of *Roméo et Juliette* (1858), then became interested in the new work of promising younger artists, most notably Brahms. Rieter-Biedermann's editions are masterpieces of the printer's craft, crisp and clear, and correct to the point of provoking in Berlioz the one admission of true delight with a publication he is known to have expressed. There was talk of other projects, perhaps a *Cinq Mai* or a *Roi Lear,* and Rieter-Biedermann did issue new editions of Liszt's transcriptions, but mostly he was interested in *Les Troyens,* publication of which Berlioz would not allow.

Rieter-Biedermann provided Berlioz with the impetus to seize the momentum of *Le Spectre de la rose* and go on that year to complete the set, adding to it, of course, the splendid 1843 setting of *Absence.* The orchestral *Nuits d'été* are Berlioz's peroration in (as he put it) fields of song, displaying a perfection of craft that strongly foreshadows the technique of *Les Troyens* and *Béatrice et Bénédict.* Nowhere before in Berlioz's work had poetry, song, and orchestral color achieved so effortless a union. The languid, sultry world of these summer nights outdistances Gautier's already superb poetry: it is the aesthetic sphere, especially in the four center songs, of the *Troyens* septet and the *Marche nocturne* from *L'Enfance du Christ. Les Nuits d'été* prove Berlioz's oft-stated adage that the union of music and poetry redoubles the force of each.

The *Nuits d'été* as published by Rieter-Biedermann are, like the *Huit Scènes de Faust* and *Irlande,* intended for different singers and nowhere purport to be a true cycle. Berlioz intended that they be extracted from the collection by the artist and used in the *partie vocale* of a concert, just as *La Captive* and *Zaïde* had been. The dedications before each song show that the set was not a vehicle for a specific singer but rather a gift to a musical establishment, the "chapel" in Weimar, where, with the same singers time and time again, Berlioz's great works were given their fairest hearing. No studied unity of melodic or harmonic design informs the *Nuits d'été* in the way that, say, the disparate elements of *Faust* were subsequently tied together by the addition of foreshadowings and recollections. In other circumstances Berlioz might just as well have given birth to a true cycle of orchestral songs; in this case it is clear he simply did not think of it. The performance of a cycle of songs had little place on his kinds of programs, anyway.

There are nevertheless some identities to be noted. Ian Kemp writes of the only Berlioz collection which can legitimately be regarded as a song cycle. When performed as published the orchestral version undoubtedly presents a coherent unit, since many of the unifying features of the original version are still there, and the inconsequence of the initial key relationships (A to B, B to F minor, F minor to F sharp) is disguised by the unexpected and dramatic sequence of voices. All the same, performances of the orchestral version in the original keys (A, D, G minor, F sharp, D and F), with a single voice, and possibly omitting the introductory bars in *Le spectre de la rose,* constitute a legitimate attempt to restore his original conception.[14]

However that may be, their arrangement, with the airy, major-keyed songs at either end and *Absence* in more or less the dramatic center, framed by the two most somber movements, is demonstrably purposeful, for we know the original order of the songs to have been changed to that effect. With the confluence of the three slow, relatively morbid songs—*Le Spectre de la rose, Au Cimetière,* and *Sur les Lagunes*—at the center, relieved only by the shimmering textures of the refrain in *Absence,* the dramatic scope of the work argues strongly, if not exactly historically, for performance as a group. Berlioz must have come around again to that view when he marked all six songs in the 32 *Mélodies* "mezzo-soprano or [failing that, I believe he means] tenor."

In 1856 Gautier's poetry was decidedly old-fashioned, and thus the orchestral *Nuits d'été* are also poignant reminders of the spirit of the 1830s, full of the haunting images (unsurpassed, I think, in the literature of song) of what Berlioz thought of as true Romanticism: the shadow of a yew tree ("l'ombre d'un if"), the spirit of a rose blossom, distance from a rose-colored smile. This is poetry of exotic places and climes, perceived through the mists of revery. The spring song and final barcarole, for all their sprightliness, share in the exoticism: this last song, foreshadowing Baudelaire's famous invitation and its several musical settings, calling us to Java and Scandinavia and the Pacific with its gallant musical question mark, a seventh-chord with haunting D♭ (♭6) in the orchestra (m. 123), is surely to be savored as the best of the many armchair voyages Berlioz took, an efficacious antidote to his *mal de pays lointains.*

The most exceptional of all Berlioz's orchestral songs, however, is *Le Spectre de la rose,* here set down into B major expressly to suit the voice of Mlle Falconi, and therefore of Mme Charton-Demeur and Mme Viardot; the new key also thrusts the accompanimental figuration into the most erotic range of the viola. It is not merely the delicate strokes of the orchestrator's pen that attract here, the elegance of the opening cello arpeggio or the languid pairing of flute and clarinet in octaves in the long tune at the beginning— added, certainly, to make of the Gotha performance a more memorable appearance of the soloist. Nor is it even the wandering tonal idiom: the stunning progress from B major to B♭ major (m. 43), the restless intrusions of the minor mode, the subsequent reckoning of a tense and uneasy truce at the end. It is the studiedly through-composed shape of the vocal line and its radical dissolution into a free declamatory style that make this song critical to the mutation of the French *mélodie* (ex. 12.1a). This recitative-like declamation is a vital component of the other tragic songs as well (ex. 12.1b–c), but here the opening melody is never fully recapitulated; there is no *da capo*. The imagery, dramatic situation, and marriage of compositional materials render *Le Spectre de la rose* among the most splendid things in all of Berlioz.

The *Villanelle* has attracted a good deal of analytical attention, partly for its several levels of dramatic tonal rise and exemplary free-strophic style, partly for the allusion to the Allegretto scherzando of Beethoven's Eighth, where "the wind accompanies the violins' and basses' dialogue with eight *pianissimo* chords in each bar, like two children picking flowers in a field one spring morning."[15] Ultimately, however, it is the tragic songs that exert the strongest allure, with their incessant ♭6–5 inflections and prolonged dominance prompting the unbroken, panting melancholy that leaves its stamp even on the uneasy final cadence of *L'Ile inconnue*. The lower-strings ostinato of the other barcarole, *Sur les Lagunes*, undulates rhythmically in suggestion of a barque afloat; a second, more important ostinato (C–D♭–C) maintains both pitch and rhythmic identity in an effect not dissimilar to that of the vocal lines of the funeral marches. Of that motive is born the main thematic material of the song (ex. 12.2). At the swooning phrase "Ah, sans amour s'en aller sur la mer," even the alliterative sibilants inform the orchestral texture. The end of *Au Cimetière* is made exquisitely painful by the dissonant clarinet B♭ clashing against the A of the tonic D-major triad, persistently delaying resolution; it is this song that profits most from its orchestral resetting. Note, in all the songs, the pronounced downward drive of the melodies: the inevitable conclusion of nocturnal revery is sleep.

Both Martini's *Plaisir d'amour* and Schubert's *Erlkönig* were arranged by Berlioz during this period to give specific singers vehicles for his Baden-Baden concerts. (Roger's *Erlkönig* may well have been in German, although the Paris publication, *Le Roi des aulnes,* has only French text.) The Schubert setting, routine on the whole, adds a countermelody at the Erl-king's entry (ex. 12.3).[16]

Berlioz's late style, which begins with the Te Deum, is best defined as a new embrace of Classical, ultimately conservative ideals, reflected not just in the subject matter but also in the composer's disciplined restraint of musical materials and pronounced terseness of design. It was in Berlioz's best interests to declare, after *L'Enfance du Christ,* that his style had not changed, but this is true only to a point. What Berlioz saw in Beethoven and Weber had long been absorbed into his working methods and his imagination. (We see the last of the Wolf's Glen in *La Damnation de Faust;* the cave where Didon and Enée take refuge is a locus of Arcadia.) Wagner's new paths and Liszt's new forms were so uninteresting to him as to have had little import to his own work. It was, of course, to Gluck and Spontini that he ultimately returned: to their dramatic vision and economy of means. A new *hauteur* is to be seen in the music, a loftiness, a detachment.

Two modernisms stimulated his imagination as well: compound meters and modal scalar patterns. Both devices are used gently, mostly in connection with oriental or antique subject matter. The flamboyant meters occur but twice, in the soothsayers' scene in *L'Enfance du Christ* and in the *Combat de ceste* ballet in act I of *Les Troyens*. The most extravagant metric device is found at the peroration of the Royal Hunt and Storm (ex. 12.4). Berlioz's most systematically derived modal patterns are for the Trojan women (where he writes out the scale at the top of each page of sketches), the ballet and song of the Nubian women, and, in *L'Enfance*, the overture to *La Fuite en Egypte*, though Herod's air is in a semi-Phrygian mode (see ex. 12.8). Berlioz knew little enough about the historical modes, though he had a vague sense, probably garnered from Bottée de Toulmon, of how their scalar patterns were arranged.

A significant element of the late works is the slow, steady marshaling of force that informed their genesis. None of the last masterpieces was rushed. (*L'Enfance du Christ* was, however, pieced together; though the birth was lengthy, the planning cannot have been particularly rigorous.) Berlioz wrote the entire libretto of *Les Troyens* before doing much of the music; when he went back to compose it, he sketched in great detail and set up its best effects in advance of the drafting process. Overall the genesis of *Les Troyens* was decidedly more systematic than were those of *Faust* and the symphonies.

A colossal Te Deum seems on the face of it an unlikely work to herald a newly refined style. It was conceived for an event of pomp (Berlioz called it "ceremony"; the papers usually described the ceremonial trappings of imperialism as "pomp"), in keeping with the nineteenth-century French view of a Te Deum as the fitting gesture of thanks for God's having showered particular grace upon the nation in the form of military success, the birth of a royal heir, the accession of a monarch. Only the Judex crederis at the end, however, is of particularly grand proportion; only there, for example, does the chorus of children make its dramatic presence really felt. What governs the structure is more an essay in cerebral counterpoint than a study of spatial architecture. The role of the organ is carefully limited to setting things in motion and to participating in short dialogues; it could have no other, because of the distances between the organ and the rest of the performing force.

The first movement is an imitative treatment featuring the motive "proposed," as Berlioz put it, by the organ in the beginning bars. The second movement, Tibi omnes, represents progress in vision from personal medi-

a. *Le Spectre de la rose:*

Mm. 42–46:

Mm. 63–65:

b. *Absence,* mm. 17–22:

c. *Au Cimetière,* mm. 52–66:

EXAMPLE 12.1 Parlando declamation in *Les Nuits d'été.*

EXAMPLE 12.2 *Sur les Lagunes.*

EXAMPLE 12.3 *Le Roi des aulnes.*

EXAMPLE 12.4 *Chasse royale et orage,* from act IV of *Les Troyens.*

tation to celestial vision, a small-scale version of the conceptual world of the Requiem. The improvisatory organ passage at the beginning resembles those played in Catholic churches to call the faithful to prayer. What follows is a series of three strophes, each serving as a long structural crescendo toward the ancient cabala: "Sanctus, sanctus, sanctus."

The Dignare is built on a succession of third-related pedal points in the bass, rising from low D in minor thirds, wrenching briefly into E♮, then receding by major thirds back to the original D. Berlioz described the plan in a letter to Liszt of 1 January 1853, and gave a chart (ex. 12.5).[17] Above these pedals, the upper voices weave a prevailingly canonic counterpoint.

The Te Deum progresses thus, through a Christe, rex gloriae, and a worshipful Te ergo quaesumus, toward its climax, the Judex crederis. This Judex is a triumph of construction, in its striking fugal entries by semi-tone, the easy coexistence of $\frac{9}{8}$ and $\frac{3}{4}$, and the very length of the fugue subject. The key is B♭ minor lifting at the end into B♭ major, with a contrasting center section in D♭, the harmonic fabric quite radical indeed in its enharmonies and ambiguities of triadic construction (ex. 12.6).

The Te Deum is one of those works on which we have enough information that we need not guess at what the composer was about. His letter to Liszt is straightforward about its aims: after describing the Dignare and his hope that it might work beautifully if well sung, he goes on to admit, "It might also be quite boring."[18] Because the Te Deum was a splendid work by a splendid composer offered for a splendid occasion, it got a great deal of attention from the press, and much of that was quite obviously fed by the composer himself. There exists, for example, an autograph in the composer's hand of the long, unsigned piece that appeared in *La France musicale* on 22 April 1855. It is from this kind of press coverage that we know of the origin of the Te Deum in the 1832 Military Symphony. The article for *La France musicale* emphasizes his search for variety and contrast, his joy at finding a *miserere* in a text of jubilance; he talks of "prayers whose humility and melancholy offer contrast to the majestic solemnity of the hymns."[19] And for all his pride at having created in the Judex crederis a "younger brother" to the Lacrymosa, he thought of the work as an intimate composition. "There is no need," he writes, "for 1,000 performers."[20] Where the Requiem is awash in memorable brass and percussion, here the most intriguing sounds, aside from the texture of the large choral forces, are those of a single soprano saxhorn (in the *Marche*) and a bass clarinet.

L'Enfance du Christ, although it took years instead of months, came to Berlioz rather as *Harold* had: first in one part, then in another, and finally another. It thus provides an excellent example of Berlioz's way of approaching his compositions as organic entities, which grow and increase in wisdom and stature, as it were. The tenor arioso was added to the shepherd's chorus with a subtle transformation of the head-motive from the one into the broad theme of the other. Note the several constants: the paired upper voices, the bass lines offered by the clarinet, and the pastoral rhythms (ex. 12.7). A solo after a chorus might, the composer then thought, be balanced by a fugal, modal overture. This process of adding on and then framing was repeated at a higher formal level when *L'Arrivée à Saïs* was balanced, ultimately, by *Le Songe d'Hérode*. Berlioz cannot have been unaware of the three-in-three symbolism. Here, operating on a grand scale, is the same kind of concern for retroactive balancing and composing out of freshly discovered implications that I showed to be at issue in the sketches.

The wonderful discovery of *L'Enfance du Christ*, however, lies in its characters, notably Herod and, almost as powerfully, Joseph and the Virgin Mary. Only with Père Laurence and perhaps Marguerite had Berlioz previously defined characters of such depth in such short order. With Herod

EXAMPLE 12.5 Tonal scheme of the Dignare, movt. III of the Te Deum.

a. Fugue subjects:

b. Tonal plan:

F = Fugue subject (or allusion)

EXAMPLE 12.6 Judex crederis, movt. VI of the Te Deum.

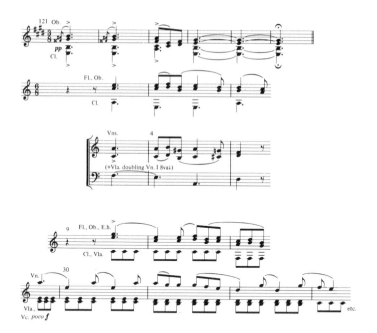

EXAMPLE 12.7 Linkage of the *Adieu des bergers* with *Le Repos de la Sainte Famille* in *La Fuite en Egypte*, part II of *L'Enfance du Christ*.

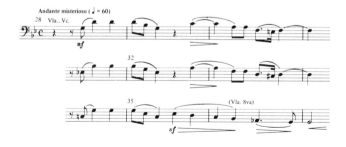

EXAMPLE 12.8 Countermelody of Herod's air in part I of *L'Enfance du Christ*.

EXAMPLE 12.9 Duo of Ste. Marie and St. Joseph in part III of *L'Enfance du Christ*.

Berlioz manages in a few minutes what Wagner takes hours to accomplish for Wotan. The air "O misère des rois" is one of Berlioz's profound creations, with its eerie bass timbres and exquisitely painful text stressing such words as *misère* and *ravagé* and *stérile*. Berlioz tints his portrait of the mad monarch with a haunting, open-ended countermelody of restless wandering, incessant suspension, and certain fall (ex. 12.8). Here, too, the framing is tight, with the nocturnal march before and the useless soothsayers after.

The Virgin Mary is similarly striking (stronger on the whole than St. Joseph, who, like Aeneas, takes second place to the lady). Gentle but alarmed, motherly but tried to the breaking point, she conveys an urgency that is poignant and even heartrending, especially when she and her husband arrive in Saïs from Judea exhausted, their feet bleeding, and with still no place to rest (ex. 12.9). Both Ste. Marie and Herod were good practice for *Les Troyens*, for they begot Cassandre and Dido, and Chorèbe and Narbal.

Berlioz found in *L'Enfance du Christ*, almost by accident, a workable solution to his dramaturgical problem of how to convey to an audience the narrative between the set pieces: the deceptively simple device of having a narrator, or *récitant*. It is to this point that the written programs and the recitative choruses led. The narrator's free rhetoric takes flight from the style of, say, the opening lines of *Faust* and helps thread a somewhat diffuse drama together into a convincing whole.

The simplicity of the performing force did not preclude Berlioz from some experimentation, especially in scene vi. The unseen angels there come from earlier French tradition, but the harmonium organ and the living swell box, where a door is slowly shut on the offstage chorus, are new. In the Herod scene, there are other experiments—somewhat tentative, I think—with such "archaic" devices as organal chant and mock-Phyrgian cadences with urgent ♭2. Berlioz is muddled, as everybody else was in those days, in his notion of biblical antiquity; the medieval and Renaissance practices he thought he was imitating, especially with regard to the old instruments, are in fact figments of his imagination. He was more familiar with the corridors of ancient Troy and Carthage.

*I*t is fitting that *Les Troyens*, regarded by its composer as the summary of his life's work, should be one of his most nearly perfect compositions. In breadth of dramatic concept, visual grandeur, and compositional technique, it ranks easily with the best French opera from any era. The vicissitudes the work endured were for the most part due to problems inherent in any work of its length and complexity. *Les Troyens* is a difficult and expensive work to stage; many of its best effects, for example, depend on a large *corps de ballet*. Yet by any measure, even the number of performances in the composer's lifetime, the opera is the jeweled crown of Berlioz's career, just as the Ninth Symphony was for Beethoven and *Parsifal* was for Wagner.

Les Troyens—here I will consider the work as a single entity—demonstrates a majestic control of form and scope with a subject of far greater depth than any he had treated but *Romeo and Juliet*. He embraced the traditions of the grand opera with seeming ease, finding that delicate and seldom-achieved balance of spectacle on the one hand and serious dramatic development on the other, while never discounting (as the symphonic settings purposefully do) the need for displaying the talents of the vocal soloists. The spectacle is unsurpassed: nothing in Meyerbeer can compare with the bimodal (C major/minor) march and hymn of the Trojans, so carefully paced to its climax, or the finale of act I, the Trojan march with its three groups of offstage brass (including a band of saxhorns) and a fourth of oboes and harps. If the spectacle has a fault, it is that it surpasses the technical limitations of any ordinary theater: you feel the building bulge at the seams.

The poetry is excellent from the first lines, where the Trojans rejoice in the simple freedom of fresh air:

> Après dix ans passés dans nos murailles,
> Ah! quel bonheur de respirer
> L'air pur des champs, que le cri des batailles
> Ne va plus déchirer.

> (After ten years confined within our walls, what joy to breath the pure country air, no more to be sullied by battle cries.)

The emphasis is on the second and third lines. There is a very similar, balancing sentiment at the beginning of act III, in Carthage, a world away:

> De Carthage les cieux semblent bénir la fête!
> Vit-on jamais un jour pareil
> Après si terrible tempête?
> Quel doux zéphir! Notre brûlant soleil
> De ses rayons calme la violence.
> A son aspect la plaine immense
> Tressaille de joie; il s'avance,
> Illuminant le sourire vermeil
> De la nature à son réveil.

> (The Carthaginian sky seems to smile on our festival: have you ever seen, after such a terrible storm, such a day? What sweet breezes! Our burning sun calms the violence with its rays. Beneath its gaze the great plain quivers with joy. The sun advances, lighting the ruby smile of Nature at its awakening.)

Again, the musical emphasis is on the half lines concerning the beautiful day and the sweet breeze: "Vit-on jamais un jour pareil" and "Quel doux zéphir!" Note, too, the freshness of the line lengths and rhyme patterns and, in that same context, the freedom with which the poetry arranges itself into verse.

Berlioz had feared the rigor of composing *Les Troyens*, but the actual composition—including, as in all the works after *Faust*, that of the libretto—

went relatively quickly. Many of the tableaux certainly occurred to him long before he set to work. He must have dreamed of its fundamental character for many years. Yet before he began, he stopped to consider the whole at the greatest possible leisure: "I am amassing myself," he wrote, "as cats do before they make a desperate leap."[21]

From books I, II, and IV of the *Aeneid* and from details gleaned elsewhere in the epic he distilled his narrative of the episode of the Trojan horse and the sack of Troy and the love story of Dido and Aeneas in Carthage. Many of the lines are direct translations from the Latin. The most notable development of the libretto-forging process was that of the character of Cassandre, daughter of Priam and Hecuba, born of some half-dozen references in Virgil. His opera thus evolved into a study of the two women and the antique people: Aeneas himself is only a little less wooden than in Purcell. And it is a study of a vision: "Italie! Italie!"—one of which he spoke from considerable experience.

The substance of *Les Troyens* is an amalgam of all he knew to harness in support of his concept of antiquity. Shakespearean situations, especially, work their way into the Virgilian fabric, notably at the paraphrase in the love duet of Jessica and Lorenzo's duologue in act V of *The Merchant of Venice*. The scene with Dido and her laborers has a great deal to do with the annual *fêtes nationales* of the Republican calendar—Le Sueur had written music for such occasions—with overtones of the various utopian movements Berlioz had encountered during his life. The tableau of the Trojan women contemplating mass suicide is very close in dramatic situation to that of the court of Sardanapalus preparing to set itself afire in the *prix de Rome* cantata *Sardanapale;* in musical materials, it bears a strong similarity to the prayer of the *Scène héroïque,* as I have already noted. I also noted that the *Marche troyenne* which closes act I is, by the composer's own acknowledgment, fashioned on the grand march in Spontini's *Olimpie,* both in length and in metric design. (Spontini, however, had no electric metronome at his beck and call.) Any number of other passages from the opera may have been consciously or unconsciously related to Spontini,[22] and the scale of the work is decidedly Meyerbeerian. The tactic of dispensing with the overture specifically to allow the first three dozen pages to be accompanied by winds alone, delaying any substantive writing for strings until Cassandre's entry, is Gluckian in ancestry, for *Iphigénie en Tauride* had no overture. The last tableau is quite similar to that of act II of Rossini's *Le Siège de Corinthe,* and the vision of the dying hero and apotheosis finale are from French operatic lore.[23] Finally, I suspect *Les Troyens* embodies a special tribute to Harriet and Louis, for the pantomime of Andromache, widow of Berlioz's namesake Hector, is the ultimate mute role: surely that slow progress across the stage is of his wife and son, in memory of their Hector—the composer's own epitaph.

Though he worked rapidly and comfortably, he was also unusually careful: many more sketches have been preserved for *Les Troyens* than for all the

FIGURE 12.11 Sketches for Iopas's song in act IV of *Les Troyens*.

other works put together. To be sure, that is partly an accident of preservation, but we must take seriously some of the implications of his remark that the opera came together "like stalactites in humid caves."[24] The sketches are especially detailed for Iopas's song and the love duet, for passages from the lament of the Trojan women, for Aeneas's fearful report of the Laocoön incident, and for Cassandre's laments, as well as for some of the ballets. They show, for various movements, nearly all Berlioz's typical stages of work, from first to last. Among these are what must be an early idea for the ⅝ *Combat de ceste;* some discarded fourth-act ballet music, also in 5, clearly replaced by the *Pas d'esclaves nubiennes;* and some experiments with harmonizing a single chanted pitch (as when the specters appear) and with bizarre scale configurations.[25]

A sketch for Iopas's aria, for example, shows how carefully the strophes and their departures were fashioned. Berlioz was quick to discard his own text when he thought it did not fit: the primary concern was for rightness, concision, formal balance (ex. 12.10). The love duet was composed in very similar fashion, with one of the comparisons in the long exchange abandoned altogether. It was sketched in D♭; we must assume that it was raised to G♭

both for the natural warmth of that key and to allow the stunning modulation from the F major of the septet.

Berlioz borrowed as he went, though it is not possible to ascertain just how much. Possibly the borrowings from *La Nonne sanglante* and *Les Francs-Juges* were extensive; all told, however, I rather doubt it, for *Les Troyens* does not often feel like that sort of work. The brief passage we know to have come from *Sardanapale* is shown in example 4.3. After completing a short-score draft, he went back to polish, recast, and reject, dealing with problematic areas as they occurred to him.

After the opera was completely done, while he and Mme Viardot were at work on the piano version, he began to worry about the ending. He had always hoped to end with an apotheosis: a version of the Trojan March transformed by oral tradition into the Roman national hymn. It would be a vision of Rome, the triumph of Aeneas. Here he introduced a new character: Clio, history's Muse, who brings out in succession Hannibal, Scipio Africanus, Julius Caesar, Caesar Augustus, and finally the divine Virgil himself. It was unwieldy and very likely unstageable. The replacement ending is somewhat better: Dido the queen foresees Hannibal, the Carthaginians curse Aeneas and his band in "the first battle cry of the Punic Wars." Yet upstage of the Carthaginians, as the victorious strains of the Trojan March drown out their curse, the audience sees a tableau of the forum of ancient Rome, where Aeneas is surrounded by the great military and political leaders of the empire.

Scenes were recast or removed as Berlioz rethought the scope and pacing of the opera. One of the last major cuts made by the composer to the five-act version was in response to Royer at the Opéra, when in mid-1861 the work was accepted for production there. Berlioz had included a scene in which the Greek Sinon, a spy who claims to have escaped from the Greeks, attempts to persuade the Trojans that the horse has been left as an offering to Pallas Athena. Berlioz saw that act I could proceed just as well from Andromache's pantomime (no. 6) to Aeneas' account of Laocoön and the serpents, so Sinon's scene was abandoned and later references to him rewritten.

Strophic and rounded forms predominate in *Les Troyens*: act III, for example, embraces a structure based on alternating stanzas of Dido's aria with repetitions of the national anthem. (Aeneas, on the other hand, has a long, through-composed aria, "Ah, quand viendra l'instant des suprêmes adieux.") Procession is fundamental to the opera, for it relies heavily on the goings and comings of a large chorus: the Trojan march, which runs through the work, and the introductory procession and hymn in Troy are elegantly balanced by the much happier Carthaginian national anthem. All of these bloom from simple triadic arpeggiation (ex. 12.11). Juxtaposition of the major and minor triads in the bittersweet Trojan procession and of major and minor modes in the two versions of the Trojan march gives the marches a certain interrelationship; the contrast of these with the confidently major-mode national anthem allows the one to comment on the others. The scene of the sentinals in act V bears several similarities to the nocturnal march in *L'Enfance du Christ*.

There are any number of interesting, usually understated, fugal textures, as, for example, at the beginning of the Hunt and Storm. The most powerful of these is at *Châtiment effroyable* (no. 8), where the people react in horror to the description of Laocoön's death (ex. 12.12).

Berlioz's command of orchestrational device is evident from the opening tableau. One of his principal goals is to introduce in his orchestra, but more importantly onstage, suggestions of the musical instruments of antiquity. Youths sit on the tomb of Pallas playing "ancient double flutes"—aulos, one would suppose from the scoring; the Nubian slaves play on a drum called the tarbuka. The Trojans carry an antique sistrum and a set of tuned bars Berlioz calls a *jeu de triangles*. The saxhorns, a curious example of the ultimate in modern living used to evoke the past, serve to suggest primitive military and hunting horns and have a great deal to do with the spatial effects. The triple strokes of the tam-tam at the appearances of Mercury cast a new spell over spellbound proceedings. All of this is engaged with the same subtlety as in the Requiem: the effects make their presence known and then quickly disappear.

The best orchestral device is subtler still. The decorative woodwind, with which Berlioz had such success in the *Scène d'amour* of *Roméo et Juliette* and in *Nuits d'été*, here outdoes itself, as, for example, in the languid trio of the *Pas des almées*, where the melodic consequent is announced with the most delicate of filigree work (ex. 12.13a). There is a very similar effect in the *Entrée des matelots* (ex. 12.13b). The trombones are used, as Berlioz frequently tells us they must be, to articulate extraordinary events: the suggestion of serpents, for example, and the night music of example 12.13a. Dominating the tone quality of the opera is the mezzo-soprano timbre of the heroines, with its dignity and suggestion of reserve. Not a single cadenza sullies *Les Troyens*, not one shriek. That, too, says a great deal of the composer: of his fondness for dignified lady singers, of his passion for the low voice, of his distaste for the ornamentation practiced at the Opéra.

Les Troyens is united, as well, by any number of thematic identities and recurring melodic contours. Within a few seconds of the opening, we hear the boys playing on their antique flutes, and this little turn of phrase recurs many times, notably in both the *Marche troyenne* and the *Chasse royale* (ex. 12.14a). Cassandre and Dido are each defined by thematic contours, Cassandre with a rising, foreboding scalar figure (ex. 12.14b) and Dido with uncertain, undulating sixteenths (ex. 12.14c); these figures are related to each other because of the premonitions with which both ladies are concerned.[26] The climax of Cassandre's duo with Chorèbe, her betrothed, is foreshadowed early on (ex. 12.14d).

The individual melodies, of which Berlioz was proud enough to hope they would be sung in the streets, are in the drawn-out, long-phrased style he had pioneered (ex. 12.15). The harmonic fabric is complex and sometimes ambiguous, modally flavored in Troy, broadly G major in Carthage, with the most radical passages saved for the supernatural events. *Les Troyens* has no overriding key scheme.

Virtually every detail of the stage setting is specified in the score, from the presence of Achilles' abandoned armor to the placement of Dido's throne. The character groupings of the choruses are always indicated. At Andromaque's pantomime, the composer leaves in the score a long description of the mourning traditions of Trojan women. In the Hunt and Storm, the stage action that is to transpire during dozens of musical details is carefully noted (ex. 12.16).

To my way of thinking, the second tableau of act IV, the scene in Dido's garden by night, is the most perfect of all Berlioz's dramatic settings, the succession of numbers an effortless progress from one superlative to the next. The scene begins with the duet of the two subsidiary characters, Dido's maid Anna and her minister Narbal, then continues with the entry of the queen, the three ballets whose purpose is to rouse her from her restless unease, and an effort by her court poet, Iopas, to calm her spirit and distract her attention with a pastoral hymn. Dido retreats from her queenliness and becomes for the first time a woman of human passions. But that alone will not do: there follows the crux of the matter, the image from Guérin's painting, with Dido's unforgettable line as she suddenly loses sight of her problem (for Ascagne has drawn the wedding ring from her finger):

> Tout conspire
> A vaincre mes remords, et mon cœur est absous.

> (Everything conspires to make me overcome my remorse, and my heart is absolved.)

Then come the ineffable septet, the quintessence of musical stasis, and the G♭ love duet. The tableau takes forty-five minutes; it seems to last ten or twelve.

The duo of Narbal and Anna, in G, discusses their queen's troubled spirit. Narbal is one of those big Berlioz basses whose voice is associated with gravity and wisdom. Anna sings her strophe, a sprightly cavatina to the effect that Troy must be rescued from this misery. So far it is a rather typical duet, giving the secondary figures their moment on the stage, but then something radical occurs: the $\frac{3}{4}$ and the $\frac{9}{16}$ of the two portions are heard simultaneously, and the air and the cavatina interlock. Narbal and Anna are not so unimportant, after all: it is they who set the grave tone of the scene that follows.

a. First sketch

Ò blon - de Cé - rès,   Quand à nos gué - rets

b. Second sketch

Du vieux la - bou - reur   Du jeu - ne pas - teur   La re - con - nai -

c. Third sketch

Du vieux la - bou - reur   Du jeu - ne pas - teur   La re - con - nai -

d. Fourth sketch, near-final reading

Ob.

Du vieux la-bou - reur Du jeu - ne pas - teur___   La re - con - nai -

e. The *beau papillon* strophe (abandoned)

Le beau ___ pa - pil - lon   Et l'hum - ble ___ gril - lon

EXAMPLE 12.10 Summary of sketches for Iopas's aria, no. 34 of *Les Troyens*. (For more on the *beau papillon* strophe, see NBE, IIc, 939.)

a. *Marche et Hymne,* no. 4:

Allegro moderato e pomposo (♩ = 112)

Chorus:

Dieux pro - tec - teurs de la ville é - ter - nel - le

b. *Marche troyenne* in the major mode, no. 11:

[Allegro non troppo (♩ = 138)]

C.à p.

c. *Marche troyenne dans le mode triste,* no. 26:

[Allegro non troppo (♩ = 126)]

C.à p.

d. Carthaginian *Chant national,* no. 18:

[Maestoso non troppo lento (𝅗𝅥 = 66)]

Chorus:

Gloi - re, gloire à Di - don,   no - tre rei - ne ché - ri - e!

EXAMPLE 12.11 National hymns in *Les Troyens*.

EXAMPLE 12.12 *Châtiment effroyable*, no. 8 of *Les Troyens*.

a. *Pas des almées*, no. 33a:

b. *Entrée des matelots*, no. 21:

EXAMPLE 12.13 Decorative figuration in the ballets of *Les Troyens*.

a. "Antique flute motive":
   In the opening chorus:

In the *Marche troyenne:*

In the *Chasse royale et orage,* mm. 185–90:

EXAMPLE 12.14 Thematic identities in *Les Troyens.*

Dido, queen of Carthage, enters, her spirit troubled not with affairs of state—her capital city has been completed, the war with the Numidians has been won with the help of the band of Trojans sojourning there—but with an affair of the heart. The wandering figures in the violin, a counterpoint to the national hymn as quietly stated in the winds, show her distress. It is the hope of her court that an entertainment by her dancers will raise her spirits, and so the three ballets of her servants follow. The first two have splendid contrasting trios. In the first, lyric main material in the cellos is succeeded and offset by a sprightly, bouncing trio. The second ballet is just the opposite (see example 12.13a). This second ballet is the most sustained and riotous of all Berlioz's movements for the dance.

Then the Nubian slaves, with their tarbukas, open fifths, and racing violin figuration, sing in an imaginary language,

Amaloué, midonaé,
Fai carimé, Dei caraimbé. Ah!

one closer in "grammar" to the language of Queen Aimata Pomaré than to the earlier languages of the damned; all of this is delivered over an ostinato pedal. The spirit of Spontini's Aztecs and Mexicans is to be felt as well.

These joyful entertainments, however, will not do: Dido turns to her poet Iopas and entreats him to sing his song of the fields. (The rest of the act is static, as pose succeeds pose with little other action.) Iopas is an Orphée-like character, with a harp and a high tenor voice. After a great orchestral sigh, a confirmation of Dido's spiritual condition (ex. 12.17a), Iopas begins what seems to be an elegant but guileless apostrophe to Ceres, god of the harvest, with the simplest of accompaniments (ex. 12.17b). But in fact there

b. Cassandre's motive:

In no. 2:

In no. 3:

c. Dido's motivic contour:

In no. 19:

In no. 24:

d. Climax of the Cassandre-Chorèbe duo, no. 3:

Its foreshadowing:

EXAMPLE 12.14 (continued).

a. Cassandre's aria, no. 2:

b. *Pas des almées*, no. 33a:

c. *Chanson d'Hylas*, no. 38:

EXAMPLE 12.15 Melody and phrase structure in *Les Troyens*.

is nothing simple about his song: the departures grow in excitement and in the detail of the text painting, spinning themselves out further and further. The second strophe is highly decorated, with canonic responses in the clarinet (ex. 12.17c). Iopas finishes with an extravagant rise, melodic and harmonic, to high C, before his cadence (ex. 12.17d).

Dido, unmoved and still unsettled, interrupts his song and proceeds to fret; Berlioz merges into his great quintet without a seam. This noble movement centers on Dido's refrain (ex. 12.18). She sings her strophe; Anna draws Narbal's attention to Ascagne and the ring, and Iopas and Narbal respond. This is complicated business, and a ring is a tiny thing to see in an opera house. But Berlioz sets it up carefully, and the effect, especially if one knows what to look for and if the actress playing Ascagne mimes artfully, can be riveting.

The impediments to the love between Dido and Aeneas are now gone. The stars have come out, a gentle breeze is blowing, and the harmony is thrust upward. Dido's subjects are delighted with this state of affairs and encourage the lovers with a lullaby. Sounds of night are pervasive: a throbbing upper pedal point on high C, interrupted only with the caress of D♭, dominates the piece, the C reinterpreted in each of its possible harmonic guises. This searching ostinato and the reminiscences of the Capulets' garden are not, however, the crux of the matter. This is Dido's movement, drawing attention to her through her softspoken passage-work, heard across the full orchestra, full chorus, and all the principals as surely as is Père Laurence in the *Serment de réconciliation,* and more elegantly still.

All of this was composed to lead up to the love duet, which was already done, and I suppose the relative simplicity of this *sicilienne* might be construed as something of an anticlimax. But the long poetic conceit from Shakespeare is handled with such conviction and delicacy that it seldom seems as complex as it is. The structure is very similar to that of Iopas's aria; the refrains, *Nuit d'ivresse,* are separated by the Shakespearean comparisons of the great loves of old, each refrain varied and ornamented and

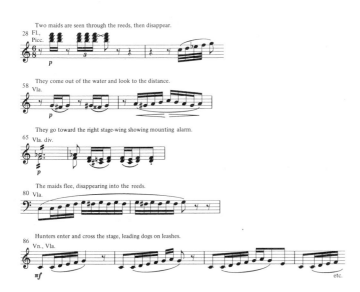

EXAMPLE 12.16 Stage action in the *Chasse royale et orage.*

a. Orchestral sigh:

b. First strophe:

c. Second strophe, varied:

d. Final cadence:

EXAMPLE 12.17 *Chant d'Iopas*, no. 34.

EXAMPLE 12.18 Dido's refrain in the Quintet, no. 35.

EXAMPLE 12.19 Refrain and strophe structure of the Duo, no. 37.

rising in ecstasy (ex. 12.19). Aeneas works himself into fever pitch at the end: he gets a high C♭, and Berlioz proves that such notes can in fact be motivated. During the coda, the lovers retreat from the stage, still singing of love—much as in the love duet of Puccini's *La Bohème*. But the lovers cannot be left to their bliss, and suddenly Mercury appears, thumping on Aeneas's breastplate, to remind Aeneas once more of his destiny. It is a spectacular harmonic event, tumbling headlong from G♭ major to E minor in a cascade of redirected seventh chords.

I said that act IV is a perfect act, but the spell continues in act V, with Hylas's song of longing for home (like the sailor's song in *Tristan,* undulating of melody and sung from the crow's nest), the departure of the sailors, Aeneas's dramatic leave-taking ("Debout, Troyens"), and Dido's farewell ("Je vais mourir; Adieu, fière cité"). Or one could back up and argue for the perfection of act II, with Cassandre and the Trojan women. To argue of perfections is merely to recognize the masterpiece of a career.

Les Troyens requires a loving production, an open pocketbook, a willingness to let time pass slowly. It has had one or two such productions, an excellent recording, and a fine edition. Great singers of progressive bent have shown what can be done with the roles. But *Les Troyens* still lives most grandly in the mind's eye.

*W*riting *Les Troyens* so roused Berlioz that he cast about for another opera topic, largely at the insistence of Carolyne Sayn-Wittgenstein, for much of 1858 and 1859. The issue of a new opera vexed him, as in the 1820s; numerous ideas were proposed to him, his attention was attracted, and then it faded away. (This situation was different from the one that had kept him from writing the Symphony in A Minor in about 1852; in that case, Berlioz refused to begin out of the certainty that he would never have the time to finish.) He looked first to Shakespeare's *Antony and Cleopatra* and then to *Romeo and Juliet.* But both of these involved recasting earlier work, which he was reluctant to do: he had, in a way, already said his piece on these subjects. Then he considered *Christophe Colomb,* with its images of the sea, perhaps as a tribute to Louis. He was careful not to rush into anything. Both the long ruminations over dramatic content and the reluctance to commit to a project until it was perfectly framed in his mind are characteristic of the period.

He did, indeed, turn to Shakespeare, though not to epic tragedy but rather to *Much Ado about Nothing. Béatrice et Bénédict* is a Shakespearean coda,

a. Overture:

EXAMPLE 12.20 Scherzo figures in *Béatrice et Bénédict.*

b. Benedict's Rondo, no. 7:

c. Beatrice and Benedict's *Scherzo duettino*, no. 15:

EXAMPLE 12.20 (*continued*).

EXAMPLE 12.21 Somarone's *Improvisation*, no. 9.

in comic vein, to *Les Troyens*. It is light and funny, one long essay in triplets and triple meters and guitars and the other joys of Italy, dominated from the opening bars by scherzo-like music (ex. 12.20). Berlioz reduced Shakespeare's play to a few vignettes and did not hesitate to add his own character, Somarone ("a big donkey"), or his own text. There are autobiographical elements, including allusions to Spontini as well as to Gluck and Thomas Moore. (There is no autograph text of the spoken dialogue, which does not appear in the published vocal score; the most authentic text of the dialogue comes from manuscript libretti used in 1862 and 1863.) The guitar in the drinking song in act II follows a pattern found in *Benvenuto Cellini* and invokes more memories of Rome in 1831–32.

Like all Berlioz's major works, *Béatrice et Bénédict* mutated as it was composed, from a one-act version to a version with a long first act and a short second act. After the first performance, other movements were added, drawn into the work in time to be produced in Weimar and again in Baden-Baden. Otherwise it was a quick, almost private little accomplishment. The result, in view of all the spoken dialogue, is a curious blend of the comic stage and light opera.

Where *Les Troyens* focused on breadth of melody and grandeur of scope and sound, *Beatrice et Bénédict* dwells naturally on its good humor. There is a grotesque fugue, in the style of the Amen from *Faust* though double and correspondingly more complex; some excellent drunken stammering, reminiscent of Brander's cellar (ex. 12.21); and any number of other comic devices. The rhythmic vivacity aims to recapture the spirit of *Cellini*.

The great movement is again a nighttime garden scene, the Duo-Nocturne of Héro and Ursule. In this very popular duet, the two women meet and the bride complains of sweet restlessness, soon pacified by serene and peaceful night. The refrains are surrounded by contrastive departures, and the orchestra reflects the night, as it had done so well in *Les Troyens*. During a long, dissolving fade, the women disappear as the curtain falls.

Gounod, in short, was wrong to say of *Les Troyens:* "It finished him . . . He died beneath the walls of Troy."[27] Berlioz's lightest, most carefree work was still to come.

Chapter Thirteen

Parnassus
(1860–63)

or a few months, between the completion of *Les Troyens* and start of *Béatrice et Bénédict,* Berlioz enjoyed that exhilaration, born partly of freedom from care and partly of the opportunity for retrospection, that comes with finishing a chapter in one's life. The work of reducing the piano score gave him the welcome opportunity to review and polish his composition at leisure, a luxury he had seldom before enjoyed.

Early in 1860, Berlioz and Carvalho reached the first of at least two separate agreements by which *Les Troyens* would be produced by the Théâtre-Lyrique. (It was rumored, without foundation, that a wealthy patron of Berlioz had offered Carvalho 50,000 francs to come around.) *Les Troyens* would be a fitting inaugural for the company's new theater in the Place du Châtelet, one of the pair built, facing each other, by the architect Davioud. Opening night was projected for 1861 or perhaps 1862; the same season would include the premiere of Bizet's *Les Pêcheurs de perles* and a *Rigoletto*. Berlioz, like Wagner, was titillated by the idea of being involved in the design and decoration of a major house and had often written in support of bright ideas in theater construction. Accordingly he went on to volunteer more than his share of suggestions: he thought the frescoes in the lobby, for example, should venerate both native Frenchmen and the great foreign artists Paris had harbored. (A version of this idea was adopted.) Of his other suggestions a few were useful and the rest tolerated, if reluctantly, by the management. Neither he nor anyone else seemed able to influence the speed of the construction.

Among the local opera singers there began to be a certain amount of jockeying for the roles in *Les Troyens*. All three of the leading French mezzos, Mesdames Viardot, Charton-Demeur, and Stoltz, craved the parts of Cassandre and Dido and soon enough conceived for themselves the obvious glories of appearing in both roles at once. On 12 August 1859 Berlioz had given Stoltz the manuscript libretto—"with his profound affection, to save for the rest of her life"—as though in consolation because there would be nothing more for the faded star. (The hint was too subtle for her.) Publishers, including Rieter-Biedermann, were likewise beginning to vie for the rights, and there was some discussion of a prompt staging in Vienna. Berlioz would have done better to follow up on these possibilities, but instead he insisted on saving both the production and the publication for Paris.

During a performance of Meyerbeer's *Les Huguenots* on 15 January, Narcisse Girard was stricken in the orchestra pit and conveyed home, where he died the next morning. In some circles Berlioz was considered his obvious successor as principal conductor at the Opéra. Berlioz, however, had simply lost his will for this sort of thing; he would have refused, he says, even 30,000 francs for the taxing position: "It's dog's work."[1] He was rather more interested in the less fatiguing and on the whole more prestigious post as director of the Société des Concerts, and that idea enjoyed a certain measure of official support. Auber opposed Berlioz's notion of taking over the imperial chapel, saying (properly) that the position was not worthy of him. With the appointments of Dietsch at the Opéra and Tilmant at the Conservatoire, both mediocrities, Berlioz's quest to be named head of one of the great Parisian institutions of music-making finally came to an end. In 1863, when Tilmant retired, Berlioz was thought too old for the job.

It was during this confused reorganization of the Parisian musical establishments that Louis Jullien burst into his apartment, tried to pay him back for the long-forgotten debacle at Drury Lane, and asked to buy the rights to *Les Troyens* for 35,000 francs. Berlioz could see that Jullien was quite mad, but did try to help him organize one last Paris promenade concert. Jullien was found dead, in an insane asylum, on 14 March.

*T*he relationship between Wagner and Berlioz in 1860 and 1861 has been widely misunderstood. The overriding fact is that Wagner was anxious for Berlioz's approval and respect. (He would have thought adulation appropriate.) He knew Berlioz would cover his three concerts at the Théâtre-Italien on 25 January and 1 and 8 February. On 21 January he sent Berlioz one of the first copies of Breitkopf's full score of *Tristan und Isolde*—an admirable feat of the engraver's craft, given that he had finished it only the previous August. The score was graciously inscribed:

Au grand et cher auteur de
    Roméo et Juliette
l'auteur reconnaissant de
    Tristan et Isolde.

This gift must have been timed to arrive just before Wagner's first concert, and enclosed with it were four of the hundreds of complimentary tickets

Wagner apparently distributed—though not to other members of the press—preceding the *soirée*. Berlioz was for his part eagerly anticipating the concerts, pondering anew the issues of Artwork of the Future and his relationship to it. Like the good critic he was, he took several days to reacquaint himself with Wagner's music, not just *Tristan und Isolde* but also the earlier works on the program, scores of which he borrowed from Mme Viardot. After the first concert he wrote one of his significant essays, which appeared in the *Débats* of 9 February under the title "Concerts de Richard Wagner: La Musique de l'avenir."

The Wagner camp was quick to believe Berlioz hostile: he did not thank Wagner for the score of *Tristan* for three weeks; the *Débats* article did not appear for two weeks; Berlioz had not sought out Wagner socially; and von Bülow had what he held to be a similar experience with Berlioz's lack of civility shortly afterward. Yet there is little in the documentation of 1860 to suggest that Berlioz did other than his best for Wagner, and under trying circumstances. He was, after all, critically ill, and doing precious little receiving of anyone. He went to all three of Wagner's concerts. He had for some time been scrupulous to avoid improper influence when it came to writing a major piece of criticism—witness his refusal to be drawn into Meyerbeer's net before *Le Prophète*. Finally, Berlioz's first allegiance had always been to Liszt, and at the time he was greatly concerned for his friend's well-being. (Liszt's son Daniel had died only a few weeks before; and he was stricken by the loss. His artistic establishment, moreover, was under attack in Weimar.) The nature of the relationship between Wagner and Liszt was no longer clear to Berlioz, and not wanting to be drawn into dangerous discussion gave him yet another reason to keep his distance.

Marie Recio's hostility to Wagner in London a half decade before cannot be denied, but I think her influence on her husband's opinions in this matter has been much exaggerated. Berlioz, of course, knew the emperor to be in favor of authorizing *Tannhäuser* at the Opéra, and everybody knew that Wagner had *Tristan und Isolde* waiting if *Tannhäuser* proved a success in Paris. Berlioz knew, too, better than anyone else, that his own opera was a masterpiece. If there was rudeness or slight to Wagner by Berlioz in 1860, it was surely inadvertent; if there was a certain conflict of interests, it was in the nature of the profession.

It is not hostile, cruel, or devious when a master composer so manifestly at the end of his career as was Berlioz simply fails to understand a work so shattering of tradition as was *Tristan*. Berlioz had after all done his homework and tried to understand the selections he heard at Wagner's concerts. (In returning Mme Viardot her scores, he said he had feared that the diminished sevenths would escape and nibble at his furniture.)[2] The more progressive elements simply left him cold. Of the *Tristan* prelude he writes, "I have read and reread this strange page; I have listened to it with the most profound attention and a healthy desire to discover its sense. And now I must confess that I have yet to discover the least idea of what the author wishes to do."[3] The *Débats* essay on the Music of the Future, later included in the collection *A Travers Chants,* is one of the most revealing of Berlioz's manifestos. (It was his first essay of 1860, no further delayed than many another.) It is a savage attack on neither Wagner nor Futurism. Berlioz had himself been proclaimed, time and time again, a Futurist, and he was anxious to set the record straight:

> If by futurism is meant that music, now in the strength of its youth, is emancipated, free, and does what it wants; that many of the old rules no longer apply; . . . that certain forms are too overworked to be useful; . . . that the master remains master, and it is up to him to command . . . etc., etc. If this is the musical code of the school of futurism, then we [Wagner and I] are of the same school, body and soul, with the most profound conviction and the warmest of attraction . . .
>
> But if futurism means to say that one must contradict what the rules teach us; that we are weary of melody, of melodic design, of arias, duos, trios; . . . that the ear is to be scorned; . . . that the point of music is no longer to please it; . . . that the witches in *Macbeth* were right: fair is foul and foul is fair—if this is the religion, and a new one at that, then I am far from confessing it. I never have, am not about to, and never will. I raise my hand and swear: *Non credo!*[4]

It seems a fair, even wise, assessment of his dilemmas.

Wagner fired off a "tangled and turgid" response, printed in the *Débats* on 22 February without comment from Berlioz, who feared that the letter did Wagner more harm than good. Wagner begins by blaming someone else for the idea of Futurism: Hans Bischoff of Cologne. He then reminds Berlioz of the impossibility that he could have read Wagner's true opinions—a jab at Berlioz's lack of proficiency in German by one who was consistently shamed by his French—and alludes to feeling hurt by "an artist so uncommonly gifted, a critic so honest, a friend so sincerely valued." And, still cloyingly courteous, he offers Berlioz his best wishes for *Les Troyens.* Berlioz answered Wagner with a personal letter to the effect that while Wagner was ready for battle, he, Berlioz, was ready but to die, to sleep, perchance to dream. He begs Wagner to address him by some other appellation than *maître.*[5] He later attended, with great interest, a private rendition of *Tristan,* act II, at Mme Viardot's.

*A*dèle Berlioz Suat was near death, and late in February Berlioz was called by her family to come to their home in Vienne. She had been ill for three years, though her suffering was never so great as Nanci's. He returned to Paris at the end of the month after reassurance from her physician that her convalescence was soon to begin. She died that week, on 2 March, at the age of forty-five.

Under the circumstances it came as a rude shock; in any case the death of his favorite sibling, the last remaining, was certain to be the occasion for melancholy reflections. "We loved each other like twins; she was an intimate friend." "Poor Adèle! She was a person of such spirit and warmth of heart. She bore so tenderly the asperities of my nature and was ready to indulge my most childish whims."[6] Louis, preparing in Dieppe for his captain's examinations, rushed to Vienne to be with the family of his late godmother.

Berlioz retreated into a life of routine, and for long periods little was heard from him. Evenings in the concert hall and theater on behalf of the *Débats* continued, of course, as did his near-religious attendance at meetings of the Académie des Beaux-Arts. Each morning he wrote a few letters, usually on pressing business details, and worked quietly on his *feuilleton* or such little musical composition as he was doing. As for *Les Troyens,* he reported to Félix Marmion in April: "My opera is finished, retouched, revised, twice corrected; I have finished the ballet." Arriving at the conclusion to the majestic work was the hardest task of them all; in January he replaced the original finale and added the duo and chorus, no. 44. Carvalho, having difficulty balancing the bankbook, was removed for a time in 1860–61 as director of the Théâtre-Lyrique, thus throwing the fate of Berlioz's opera further into question. But Berlioz was too old, too tired to care: "I wait with quasi-indifference."[7]

When the Théâtre-Lyrique offered Beethoven's *Fidelio* in May, Berlioz took the opportunity to relearn that great work. Again, he borrowed Mme Viardot's copy, a piano-vocal score, then went to the Conservatoire to examine the full score. His essay for the *Débats* appeared on 19 and 22 May. It is an important one, tracing the history of Parisian performances of *Fidelio,* relating his own encounters with the opera during the course of his travels, comparing the versions of the score, and lamenting the atrocities he thought were being perpetrated on the Parisian public. Carvalho had thrashed out a version of *Fidelio* set in Milan in 1495 (before pistols, Berlioz observed), this to overcome Beethoven's purported chastity and lugubriousness and to permit a "brilliant" closing tableau. "In France, we cannot abide a translation, pure and simple, of a foreign opera."[8] Berlioz's case is familiar: abominations had been visited on a masterwork to accommodate the presumed requirements of a public that in fact would have been happy to see the work as the composer had written it. His article is full of the old fire.

In July he had the news that Louis had passed his captain's tests and would soon command his own vessel.

The program he chose for Baden-Baden that summer was not particularly novel. He thought it inappropriate to offer selections from *Les Troyens* two years running, and in view of that belief instructed Liszt not to bother to come. Mme Viardot appeared in scenes from her still-admired *Orphée;* Mme Carvalho sang the *cavatine* from *Benvenuto Cellini.* The overtures were those to *Les Francs-Juges* and Weber's *Euryanthe,* and there was the familiar scene from *Faust* with Méphistophélès and the sylphs. Only one Prussian princess was to be found in the audience.

The new work on the program that 27 August was Berlioz's orchestration of Schubert's *Erlkönig, Le Roi des aulnes,* presumably done for and at the suggestion of Gustave Roger, who sang it. Roger's *Erlkönig* was famous: he delivered it without body gestures, using only eye movements and changes of vocal quality to achieve his effects. In Baden he had just sung four performances of Gounod's *Colombe,* then valiantly showed up for what he later remembered as the "magnificent festival of Berlioz." (Roger had that year been wounded in a hunting accident and had an arm amputated. This effectively ended his career at the Opéra: despite his having been fitted with an artificial limb, his carriage had been permanently affected. He took to excessive gambling and thus accepted every opportunity to appear in Baden.) The new *Roi des aulnes* was dedicated to Francilla Pixis, daughter of Berlioz's old friend Pixis, the pianist, then living in Baden.

Bénazet, who had already approved in principle the substitution of *Béatrice et Bénédict* for the Plouvier legend, was now positively enthusiastic about the new opera, and Berlioz returned to Paris in late August roused from lethargy by the excitement of new work. The summer vacation and the soothing waters had, as usual, improved both his spirits and his digestion. He began to compose with his old abandon, scarcely giving a thought to the proposition that he was now waiting for two different opera houses to be constructed.

Béatrice et Bénédict was well under way by November, when he wrote both to Louis and to Cornelius of his pleasure in the work and the improvement of his physical condition. He had planned nine short numbers for a single act and was already done with four, the music coming, one last time, faster than he could write it down. "It amuses me greatly, and I am writing *con furia,*" he writes to Cornelius. "It is gay, mordant, and at times poetic; it brings a smile to both the eyes and the lips."[9]

At first he had thought merely to borrow the general plot of Shakespeare's *Much Ado about Nothing.* To Louis he remarked that reducing a five-act play to a one-act opera was easy: it was merely a matter of "persuading Béatrice and Bénédict . . . that they are in love with each other."[10] Little by little it became heavily Shakespearean. The spoken dialogue was borrowed in large measure directly from Shakespeare; the final story is more or less a simplification of the play. The sung texts, of course, are by Berlioz, the character of Somarone his invention. *Beatrice et Bénédict* was nourished by his August holidays in Baden-Baden and composed largely in Paris; in the *Mémoires* he says that the words of the Duo-Nocturne, which became its most popular number, were written during a long-winded speech at the Institute.

He reused one of his earliest works, the little song called *Le Dépit de la bergère,* as the *sicilienne,* heard twice in the opera. But there is no evidence of other self-borrowing, or of much relationship between this *Much Ado* and the plans of 1833 and 1852. Possibly the borrowing of the early song was meant as a symbol, a statement that he knew this to be his last work. The pointillism, mordancy, and capriciousness are the stuff of rebound from Troy. Sketches were done by late 1860, after which came a hiatus of five months.

Though Berlioz's massed performing forces had much in common with the ideals of the Orphéon movement, he had never written a composition specifically for such a society or received one of their frequent commissions. In June 1860 J.-F. Vaudin, guiding spirit of the Orphéons, led an expedition of his troops to join similar glee clubs in London for a joint performance. While there they formulated plans for a second London trip, to culminate in a monster concert at the Crystal Palace. A chorus of ten thousand voices, half French and half English, each man singing in his own language, would celebrate universal brotherhood in rather belated recognition of the efforts of Queen Victoria and Napoleon III toward a permanent alliance of their two nations. This intriguing event was to take place in September 1861.

Vaudin accordingly wrote a text he called *Le Temple universel* and invited Berlioz to compose the music. This double chorus was finished in February 1861 and put into rehearsal, at least in France. But then some unbrotherly dispute caused the enterprise to be abandoned, apparently before the English parts were done, and the trip was canceled.[11] In 1867, almost surely with the new industrial exhibition in mind, Berlioz rearranged his composition for simple four-voice chorus, shortened it, and removed the dialogue between the two peoples. It appears that this version, too, went unperformed, but parts were acknowledged to have been published when they were deposited with the government in 1868.

Le Temple universel is a substantial work: longer, more complex, and considerably more refined than the twenty-bar *Hymne pour la consécration d'un nouveau tabernacle* with which it is often paired. The poetry is rather too typical of the patriotic hymn—it makes one grateful for the more elevated conceits of the *Battle Hymn of the Republic,* also of 1861—with some gruesome doggerel:

O jours splendides,
Riants matins,
O jours limpides,
De nos destins,
A nous le monde!
La foi profonde
Doit nous unir.

(O splendid, limpid days, laughing mornings of our destiny: the world is ours! Deep faith shall unite us.)

The greeting of the French choir to the English is so general as to suggest that a second text was substituted for the publication; the English hail the

French (in French, as published) with imagery of which Berlioz surely approved and may have been the author:

Salut à toi, France héroïque,
Héritière de Rome antique,
Foyer d'amour, terre de feu,
Non, tu n'es plus notre rivale
Dans notre marche triomphale.
Soyons les vrais soldats de Dieu.

(Greetings to you, heroic France, heir of ancient Rome; home of love, land of fire, no more are you our rival in our triumphal march. Let us be true soldiers of God.)

Berlioz's setting is based on a twenty-bar march tune in $\frac{3}{4}$, in a highly inflected F major. Trio-like sections alternate with the march in what becomes, because of the greetings of the two choruses, a freely sectional work, centering on the dramatic trio in A♭. The part writing is clever and well conceived, the effect one of finely wrought, vigorous patriotism in the Rouget de Lisle tradition from someone who presumably sensed rather intimately the difficulties of marrying England and France.

I cannot say precisely why the revised version was preserved as it was. The title implies an unaccompanied performance; the rearrangement is for single four-voice male choir. Yet there are empty bars at the beginning and end of the only source, which amounts to a vocal part drawn for some specific occasion. I think it reasonable to suppose that Berlioz intended to underlay a grand orchestral accompaniment in the style of the *Hymne à la France* or *L'Impériale*—his pieces for the other two expositions—then was prevented from doing so by the devastating turn of events in his life.

Tannhäuser opened at the Opéra on 13 March 1861. Six months had been devoted to this production by imperial command, and over 160 rehearsals, nearly all of which were supervised by the composer. Things progressed well enough in the early stages, with Wagner optimistic, Alphonse Royer and the government politically supportive, and the technical possibilities of the house seeming almost inexhaustible. The singers were intrigued by the difficulties they found in the music and willing, with Wagner's help, to master it. They clearly had the professional ability to do so—though Wagner went through stages of thinking *Tannhäuser* unperformable—and the orchestra appeared ready for the challenges as well.

The same cannot be said, though, for the new conductor, Pierre Dietsch, facing his first major premiere. Dietsch was short of memory, devoid of technique, and wedded to the notion of conducting from a violin part— Wagner, from a violin part! On no other point in the history of the Opéra is there such unanimity of opinion, from the French as well as the Germans, as there is regarding Dietsch's ineptitude with Wagner's score. Fauré remembered (and dismissed) him as "cold in nature, . . . of methodical and reactionary mind." Von Bülow thought him "the most asinine, thickest-skinned, most unmusical" conductor he had met.[12] Wagner did his best to have Dietsch removed from at least one general rehearsal and a few of the first performances, but the traditions of the house were as incorruptible as they had been for Berlioz with *Esmeralda, Cellini,* and *Freischütz.*

There was, too, the problem of the ballets. Wagner adamantly refused to add a ballet in the conventional position at the beginning of the second act, assuring everyone that a late curtain time (8:00 P.M.) and the expanded Venusberg music in act I would meet the public demand. He was not taking into account the Jockey Club, a ruffian band of opera-for-pleasure aristocrats who refused to arrive until 10:00 P.M., just in time for the second-act curtain and ballet. In any event they had made no secret of their intent to disrupt the performance of a mad work by a mad foreigner, so the issue of the ballet music quite fueled their hot young tempers.

The reception accorded *Tannhäuser* in Paris makes *Cellini*'s shabby treatment at Covent Garden seem tame indeed. The white-gloved dandies went to work beginning in the second scene, as early as they could get there; those interested in hearing a Wagner opera in Paris hushed the claque and tried to argue them down—all in the face of a production as spectacular as any that had been mounted at the Opéra, and in the presence of the emperor, his court, and the German-speaking diplomatic corps. Wagner held out for three performances, though he did not go to the third, and then, like Berlioz in London, succeeded in persuading the authorities to retire the work. (Unlike their genteel British counterparts, the French authorities had the audacity to suggest that a composer did not have the right to retire his own work.) *Benvenuto Cellini,* with four Paris performances, had survived longer.

Berlioz had resolved early on not to review *Tannhäuser*—like a prejudiced judge, he disqualified himself; like Caesar's wife, he meant to stay above suspicion. It cannot be denied that he was jealous of the ease with which Wagner's opera had been accepted at the national theater of France, or that he found the reception accorded Wagner another in the long list of indignities he had had to face, or that he was offended by the amount of money lavished on the affair. But his modest gloating over Wagner's failure was limited to personal correspondence, mostly to his son, and much of what he reports in the letters—the laughter in the house, the unanimous negativism of the press, the weary dissatisfaction of the officials—is simple fact, easily corroborated. Judith Gautier's account of the "small, lean man with bony cheeks, a nose like an eagle's beak, a great forehead with piercing eyes, a ravaged passionate look"[13] stopping her famous father in the streets with a gleeful report of disaster at the dress rehearsal has its share of inconsistencies. Moreover, she told a rather different version of the story later in her life, and was but eleven when the encounter took place. Berlioz's public reactions to *Tannhäuser* seem best described as those of studied neutrality.

The failure of *Tannhäuser* left an unexpected vacancy in the calendar of the Opéra and an urgent need, from a financial perspective, for a certain success. So it was that the directors, without the slightest sense of the several ironies inherent in their action, engaged Berlioz to produce Gluck's *Alceste* at the Opéra with the hope of duplicating his triumph with *Orphée* at the Théâtre-Lyrique. In return, though there were loose commitments to Gounod and the Belgian F.-A. Gevaert, they broadly hinted of their willingness to consider *Les Troyens* for the next season. By this time the Théâtre-Lyrique was virtually in receivership, its new building scarcely begun. Berlioz's agreement with the Opéra became more or less official in June.

In April Tilmant, Girard's successor at the Société des Concerts, programmed the sylph's scene from *Faust* for his concert on the 14th. It was *faustissimus*, Berlioz wrote Janin,[14] and from then on Berlioz's music was once more to be found, occasionally, in the offerings of that august orchestra.

By May Trojan fever had the community of artists in its grip. Edouard Bertin gave on 3 May a *soirée* for the sort of influential assemblage he alone, of Berlioz's advocates, could muster. There Mme Charton-Demeur and Lefort, with Ritter at the piano, presented the major excerpts from the opera, much as they had done in 1859. The power of the *Débats* was now engaged: "Donnez-nous les Troyens!" barked d'Ortigue from his column.[15] Royer, despite his reservations as to the length, the liaison between the two halves of the story, and the suitability of the *Aeneid* to the public taste, was resigned to the necessity of taking it on. The Opéra was, after all, "the only institution capable of doing it properly, of producing, whatever the result, a great work of á talented man, a member of the Institute, a very honorable and honored man, one who has on his side both public opinion and the entire European press."[16] Berlioz, meanwhile, began to lobby overenthusiastically, and with decided prematurity, to have detailed control of the production, from the singers to the ballet dancers to the carpenters.

For the last concert he was to conduct in the Salon de Conversation at Baden-Baden, he chose to amuse himself by having "people of pleasure come to Baden to hear a mass for the dead."[17] Besides the Dies irae and Offertoire he programmed the complete *Harold en Italie*, Beethoven's Choral Fantasy, and the usual scattering of opera scenes and symphonic selections. For the Requiem excerpts he assembled the chapel musicians and philharmonic societies of Baden, Karlsruhe, and Strasbourg, with extra brass from the Prussian band in the nearby military garrison of Rastatt. Rehearsals were in Karlsruhe, three each week for two-and-a-half weeks—an unusually comfortable total of eight. In the interim Berlioz wandered among the ruins of the castle and there polished the libretto of *Béatrice et Bénédict*, notably the poetry for the Duo-Nocturne.

But the vacationers were not interested in thoughts of the hereafter, and the crowd on 26 August was poor. (*Béatrice et Bénédict* would be the sort of bonbon they could admire during their holiday.) Nonetheless, the performance of *Harold en Italie* struck Berlioz as the best of any he had conducted. He sent Richard Pohl a souvenir:

> Liszt told me that you wanted a triangle. Here is a Saxon one which has just been used for the first time in the introduction to *Harold*. It is cast in the image of God, as are all triangles. But more than other triangles, and certainly more than God, it is well tuned.[18]

Between July and November, *Béatrice et Bénédict* grew into two acts. It profited from Berlioz's sojourn in Baden, and during the autumn he was able to finish the draft. By the end of the year the orchestration was complete.

The work of September and October was to produce *Alceste* at the Opéra. Berlioz had declined, despite considerable financial incentive, to have anything to do with the "modifications" to *Alceste*, but he agreed to supervise the mise-en-scène:

> I went to many of the rehearsals, and I conveyed to the singers and directors of the various enterprises all I remembered of the performances of this work. The intense study that I had made of the composer's style allowed me to make useful observations. I have reason to believe that the performance of *Alceste* will be as good as is possible.[19]

He overcame his scruples long enough to transpose some material into keys more comfortable to Mme Viardot, in the title role; otherwise the version they performed was relatively true to Gluck. *Alceste* opened on 21 October and was considered by the press the most important event of the season; it was indeed, but for the scandal of *Tannhäuser*, the only remotely interesting theatrical of the year.

Alceste, like *Orphée*, was a substantial artistic and financial victory; again Mme Viardot triumphed. The grateful administration granted Berlioz the composer's royalties, 127 francs for each performance, and he was content to smile to himself at having conquered the Opéra, a second time, with another composer's work.

*W*ithin the week, on Sunday, 27 October, Berlioz attended the first concert of Pasdeloup's newest society, the Concerts Populaires de Musique Classique. Pasdeloup had for nearly a decade sustained his young-artist concerts by making up the deficits from his own purse. Now he engaged the newly refurbished Cirque-Napoléon, the winter circus at the end of the boulevard du Temple, for a series of Sunday afternoon concerts for the common people. The Cirque-Napoléon, one of the few buildings to escape

Haussmann's 1860 demolition of the historic theaters in the boulevard du Temple as he reshaped the avenues, seated more than four thousand. Sunday after Sunday huge crowds flocked to the circus to hear Pasdeloup's hundred-piece orchestra offer the German repertoire and the easier new music of the French masters. At the second concert, on 3 November, he gave *L'Invitation à la valse,* and thereafter the Concerts Pasdeloup, as they came to be called, kept Berlioz's music before the public in multiple performances each year. (Pasdeloup's favorites were the Weber arrangement, the three orchestral excerpts from *Faust,* and, later, the Duo-Nocturne from *Béatrice et Bénédict.*) It was thus Pasdeloup who cultivated the popular interest in Berlioz by playing his works again and again, and not, as it should have been, the Société des Concerts.

Berlioz's notice in the *Débats* of 12 November was ecstatic: "M. Pasdeloup has the joy and merit of having founded a lovely institution which we had lacked: his bet is won." One could not truly appreciate music of value in so large an arena, he wrote, but he acknowledged that the crowd was carried away with enthusiasm nonetheless. The Concerts Pasdeloup were in fact so successful that the Cirque-Napoléon was signed over to the enterprise each Sunday in perpetuity, and today the site is called the Place Pasdeloup.

FIGURE 13.1
Rehearsal of the Pasedeloup Orchestra at the Cirque d'Hiver, c. 1876.
Oil on canvas; Sargent.

The year ended with some grave problem concerning Louis, who I think must have fathered a child,[20] and with Berlioz's forced march to complete *Béatrice et Bénédict* in time for its production eight months hence.

His work was slowed in January when he took to his bed for a week. His illness was soothed by a new diet and visits from Mme Viardot, who had a few last suggestions for the piano score of *Les Troyens* and was surely angling for the title role in *Béatrice et Bénédict*. But in this case his fancy for Mme Charton-Demeur took precedence, and it was she who was cast as Béatrice, with the tenor Montaubry named her opposite.

The piano readings of the completed portions of *Béatrice et Bénédict* may have begun in late January. On 25 February Berlioz finished and dated the autograph orchestral score—writing "the end" in English—and soon thereafter began to convene regular Monday and Tuesday afternoon rehearsals in his apartments.

From early 1862, then, the concerns of readying *Les Troyens* and *Béatrice et Bénédict,* simultaneously approaching their first performances, dominated his life. The lively Shakespearean work was guaranteed production and would almost certainly succeed; it seemed reasonable to Berlioz, in that light, to step up his campaign to assure the staging of *Les Troyens*. He spent another evening in February, for example, unsuccessfully trying to attract the emperor's attention long enough to get him simply to command the performance, following the precedent of *Tannhäuser.*

The continued uncertainty over the fate of *Les Troyens* forced him to stay in Paris when he would have liked to accept invitations to travel. The Gesellschaft der Musikfreunde, for one thing, was pressing him to come conduct his symphonies in Vienna, and this attractive offer he felt obliged to refuse, lamely pleading to Peter Cornelius his ignorance of the Viennese taste. The Gesellschaft went on to present that season the *Fantastique, Harold,* and *Le Carnaval romain,* anyway, and although the *Fantastique* failed—with repercussions Berlioz felt when he did go to Vienna, in 1866— the viola symphony was held in esteem.

Halévy died in Nice on 17 March, vacating the permanent secretary's chair of the Académie des Beaux-Arts. Berlioz was not asked to provide music for the funeral on the 24th—the job was left to Auber and his charges at the Conservatoire—though he attended it with the other members of the Institute. He declared himself a candidate for the post of perpetual secretary and spent the next week campaigning for the job. No more qualified person could have been elected than Berlioz, and he was indeed nominated on 5 April, but his name fell in the fourth position on the list. He lost the election on the 12th to Charles-Ernest Beulé by a vote of 19 to 14, after four ballots.

By then the negotiations to secure a decor and costumes appropriate to old Sicily were well under way. There were garlands and tambourines to be found, bottles, wheelbarrows, fresh roses, and signs.[21] The singers had to work hard to seem at ease in the vivacious style, as their impulse was to declaim their spoken lines like French tragedians. At the home of Escudier on 7 April, the first excerpts of *Béatrice et Bénédict* were presented alongside some selections from *Les Troyens*. The choruses began to rehearse in Strasbourg, where in midsummer Berlioz would go to prepare the orchestra himself. Perrin, the director of the Opéra-Comique, tried to interest Berlioz in the possibility of a *Béatrice et Bénédict* in his house that season, but Berlioz remained adamant that *Les Troyens* was to be done in Paris before the lighter fare.

Although he continued to refuse publication of *Les Troyens* before it was produced, enough influential people were interested in the fate of the work that the production of multiple copies soon became unavoidable. Some months earlier Berlioz had delivered his manuscript piano-vocal score to his favorite engraver, the widow Ris, the artisan who had prepared the plates for many of his later works. Perhaps a half-dozen copies were drawn that winter and spring, at the composer's expense, by the firm of Thierry. Some of them were presented to his closest friends; the others served as proofs. At least three stages of corrections in the known proof copies suggest a long period of revising and reengraving of the plates. The earliest datable copy was presented to Georges Kastner on 8 February, marked "épreuve correcte";[22] two more presentation copies, with (like Kastner's) an extra leaf included at the front for the autograph *envoi,* were prepared for Mme Stoltz and for Louis, and there were surely several others. In addition to the proof copies, some fifteen corrected copies were drawn after the first half year of proofreading, again at the composer's expense; these were for the rehearsals, which he hoped would start in July. Seven copies of the original piano-vocal score of *Les Troyens,* in various stages of textual revision, have been preserved; they represent the only printing of the full opera during Berlioz's lifetime. The subsequent issues of *Les Troyens à Carthage,* though drawn from the original plates, are badly flawed by cuts reflecting the eccentricities of the production.

A rehearsal for *Béatrice et Bénédict* in the composer's apartment on 13 June was interrupted by a telegram announcing that Marie, who was visiting her friends the Delaroches in Saint-Germain-en-Laye, had suffered a heart attack at about noon. Berlioz left his singers[23] and rushed to St.-Germain, expecting to find his wife merely ill, but by the time he reached the outlying suburb she had succumbed to the heart condition from which she had been suffering for several years. She had turned forty-eight three days before.

Meanwhile, Mme Martin, Marie's mother, had returned home. The musicians offered a pretext for the composer's sudden absence, but she became suspicious when he was not home for dinner. A cross-examination of the maid, Caroline, produced the truth about the telegram, and Mme Martin left at once for St.-Germain. Berlioz and the Delaroches, however, by then had left for Paris to sign the death certificate and arrange for the funeral. The two carriages crossed in the night, and the fragile Mme Martin found her daughter's lifeless body attended only by a priest. The shock was too great: Mme Martin collapsed and herself hovered near death for four days.

Berlioz, too, was overcome. Marie, it turned out, had had some prior inkling of her fate, but her death—unlike Harriet's or that of either of his sisters—came as a surprise to Berlioz. The necessity for him to deal with the formalities of a death was as repellent to him as it had been eight years before when Harriet died. In view of his mother-in-law's sad condition, Mme Barroilhet, a friend of the family, did her best to help with the details.

Marie was buried after a quiet ceremony at the larger of the two Montmartre cemeteries in a cheap plot—the cost of the long funeral convoy from St.-Germain having used all Berlioz could afford by way of *pompe funèbre*.[24] Neither Louis nor Berlioz's nieces nor Mme Martin attended the funeral; the tiny gathering consisted of his cousin Jules and Marie's circle of intimates.

Louis came from Le Havre two or three days later and tried to deflect his father's grief. They got along well, and from this point Louis seems to have offered Berlioz nearly constant support and friendship. When he left again, Berlioz gave him a bound copy of *Les Troyens,* inscribed

My dear Louis:

Keep this score, that in reminding you of the harshness of my career, it may make the difficulties of your own appear more bearable. Your father who loves you,

H. Berlioz
Paris, 19 June 1862[25]

The "brusque and violent separation" from his second wife threw him into a bout of *isolement* typical of his youth, a condition he describes as of "the most profound chagrin."[26] He was attended by a doctor who offered him no particular relief. For some months his correspondence, particularly to his niece Mathilde, is full of references to his "cruel loss."

Les Troyens and *Béatrice* could not be left for long, however, and by July rehearsals were again under way. The pace quickened with the start of staged rehearsals for the soloists at the Opéra-Comique. After a last general rehearsal on Saturday, 26 July, the Parisian members of the company set out together for Baden. Berlioz left behind him a relationship that had flowered during his long daily walks in the Montmartre cemetery, an idyll with a woman named Amélie, probably a recent widow visiting her husband's resting place, and he had in his pocket as he conducted in Baden a love letter from her. He had not sought this attention, he later wrote, but was willing

FIGURE 13.2 The new theater in Baden-Baden, 1862. *L'Illustration,* 23 August 1862.

to let himself be loved. Allusions to the romance continue through the following March; then, apparently, that lady died as well.

*T*he new theater in Baden was ready in time for its appointed opening, and the forces for *Béatrice et Bénédict* had been well prepared both in Paris and to the east. Bénazet had already expended a considerable sum, not just for the costumes and decor and to secure the best singers available, but also on a princely fee for Berlioz: 2,000 francs each for words and music of both acts, a total of 8,000 francs. *Béatrice et Bénédict* opened on 9 August, with the composer conducting. Mme Charton-Demeur, his Béatrice, was thought charming in her role; he had had some prior qualms about Montaubry as Bénédict, but the results were deemed both elegant and distinguished. The role of Béatrice's cousin and confidante, Héro, was played by Mlle Montrose, a young singer who Berlioz thought lacked musical instinct, but whose delivery, it could not be denied, was fresh and natural, befitting the part. The supporting characters were at least adequate—Prilleux as Somarone was noteworthy—and the chorus from the Strasbourg opera house was excellent. *Béatrice et Bénédict* played again on 11 August, preceded on this second occasion by *La Servante maîtresse,* a French version of Pergolesi's *La Serva padrona.*

The audience cheered rabidly after the act I nocturne, and this was enough to carry Berlioz through the performance, despite his being quite ill; he reflected later that he had conducted the better for it. The multinational public seemed to consist primarily of wealthy Germans and Russians on vacation, but there were not a few who had made the journey specifically to hear the new opera. The Parisian claque stayed at home, and for once a Berlioz opera was first performed in French before a dispassionate, fair-minded audience: *Béatrice et Bénédict,* so far from home, was granted the kind of reception that should have gone to *Cellini.* Certainly there were faults in this performance by what was after all a provincial and largely borrowed company, to the extent that the closing duettino, "L'amour est un flambeau," for example, had been more successful in the piano rehearsals. There were suggestions of petulance from the orchestra players, overtaxed by their parts. But the reviews merely noted the difficulty of the music, especially of the overture, and congratulated all the musicians. Everybody knew that *Les Troyens* was still in his portfolio, and it seemed possible that before the next year's revival of *Béatrice et Bénédict* the public would be richer by still another Berlioz opera.

While he was out of town, his last collection of essays came off the presses: *A Travers Chants.* An initial run of 1,500 copies went on sale in September. It is the most serious of Berlioz's books and, in general, contains the best of his criticism. Perhaps half of it comes from the critical essays in the two-volume *Voyage musical* (1844); these had been appended to that volume to flesh out his autobiographical sketches and had not been used for the *Mémoires.* For the new book they had been updated in light of later experiences—the Paris productions of Gluck, for example—and spruced up and made to cohere by the addition of connective passages of various sorts, which quite fill the margins of the pasted-up clippings.[27] *A Travers Chants* includes his complete Beethoven, Gluck, and Weber cycles; the essays on the standardization of pitch from his project of 1858–59; the article on Wagner and Futurism; and notes on Henri Reber, Stephen Heller, Joseph d'Ortigue, and the Paris version of Bellini's Romeo and Juliet opera.

The appearance of a new book by Berlioz was duly noted in the Paris journals of music and literature, whose critics dwelt, for the most part admiringly, on the concept of the "compositeur-écrivain," though they lamented the occasional violence of his opinions. Richard Pohl, already preparing his German *Béatrice et Bénédict,* began work on the German translation as soon as he received the French. The shorter items in *A Travers Chants* served European music publishers for many months as fillers for their periodicals, as similar passages in both the *Soirées* and the *Grotesques* had done.

In Paris that autumn Berlioz attended involuntarily to the transferral of the library of the Conservatoire to a new, poorly conceived room where the rare manuscripts were in a glass case exposed to the sunlight and the most valued scores on shelves accessible to passersby. The disarray of the Conservatoire library and the large and obviously historic collection of performance material belonging to the Société des Concerts is a story that stretches well into the present century. The worst of it came after Berlioz's tenure as librarian;[28] at least he was able to maintain the status quo. Remodeling problems also plagued Berlioz at home; he and his mother-in-law were forced to move out of their apartment in the rue de Calais that summer while their building, which had been constructed as recently as 1856, was restored.[29]

Louis, again dissatisfied with his lot, had quit a position with the imperial cargo service and was seeking other employment. A "big boy of 28," as his father described him,[30] he came to Paris for several months to roost with what was left of his family. Berlioz was not sure what to make of this development, but Carolyne Sayn-Wittgenstein tried to draw his attention to its poetic aspects: "There must be, between the sailor and the musician, some serious affinities, as between the ocean and the symphony: tempest, chaos, grandeur and power, divine serenity, adorable sweetness."[31]

Shortly afterward she wrote on Liszt's behalf, calling Berlioz "cher et bien Maître," in gratitude for the sympathy he had expressed to Liszt after the tragic death of his daughter Blandine. She took the opportunity to remind him to keep working, perhaps on a *Cléopâtre,* and threatened to visit Paris in person, expecting to find him there, pen in hand, at work covering music paper of thirty-two staves. She wrote from Rome, where the previous October her long idyll with Liszt had reached its abrupt termination.

Just after the Baden premiere, Berlioz composed two new movements for the second act of *Béatrice et Bénédict:* the trio for Béatrice, Héro, and Ursule (no. 11) and a chorus from the wings (no. 12), both intended for inclusion in the published score and future performances of the work. They had been suggested to Berlioz in the review by Félix Mornand that had appeared in the *Illustration de Bade* of 18 August. Negotiations for a production at the Paris Opéra-Comique were, on the whole, positive, but ultimately unresolved for lack of a competent Béatrice—Mme Charton-Demeur was abroad—and because *Les Troyens* was still at issue. The Paris vocal score, with its piano reduction by the composer, was the work of three months toward the end of the year; it was engraved in late 1862 and published the following January or early February, with a dedication to Bénazet. Berlioz declined to underwrite the cost of a full score.

In mid-November Richard Pohl wrote from Weimar to secure permission to produce *Béatrice et Bénédict* there in his own German translation. Berlioz consented to the plan and arranged the loan of performance material, most of it still in Baden-Baden, on the condition that he be allowed to conduct the last rehearsals and first performances. An agreement was reached in January, the parts were lent from Baden, and the first copies of the new vocal scores were readied for shipment to Weimar, where the German texts would be underlain. A very similar vocal score, with French text and Pohl's

translation, was issued by Bote & Bock of Berlin in early 1864, exactly a
year after the Paris edition.

To Emile Perrin of the Opéra-Comique, who must have seen and been
impressed by much of the rehearsing for *Béatrice et Bénédict* in his theater,
Berlioz wrote a long letter in early January asking him to reread *Les Troyens*
and bring his influence to bear on the negotiations for a production in Paris.
Berlioz sought to separate the fact from the gossip: "People say there are
twenty-two roles; there are only nine; people say that it will last eight hours;
. . . it lasts only as long as the *Huguenots*." He expected that his work would
be successful and popular, that the tunes would be hummable. "Why keep
doubting? Why keep neglecting it? Why trust only idols of clay or wood, or
pray to deaf gods, to old, predictable icons?"[32] By February it was clear that
Les Troyens had no future at the Opéra, and that Berlioz was not to be
named its administrative director, though there had been discussions to that
effect; almost immediately a final contract to produce his opera was reached
with the Théâtre-Lyrique. Neither Mme Stoltz nor Mme Viardot would have

the role of Didon, for it was evident that both were past their prime: Mme Charton-Demeur would have it when she came back from America.

For nearly ten months Berlioz experienced a new burst of physical energy and high spirits as the momentum gathered toward opening night. It began with his emergence to conduct performances of *La Fuite en Egypte* from *L'Enfance du Christ*, *Le Carnaval romain*, and *L'Invitation à la valse* at concerts of Félicien David's musical society on 8 and 22 February. Looming ahead in April was *Béatrice* in Weimar; in June he was expected in Strasbourg for *L'Enfance du Christ* at the Lower Rhine Music Festival, then in Baden for the revival of *Béatrice*. Finally, *Les Troyens* would reach the stage of the Théâtre-Lyrique, it was all but certain, by the end of the year: Mme Charton-Demeur was back in France, so there was the possibility of a half year's worth of rehearsals. She wanted a fee of 6,000 francs a month, however, and was stalling to get it, so her final contract, and thus the start of serious rehearsals, was long delayed.

On 22 March the Société des Concerts programmed the Duo-Nocturne from the end of the first act of *Béatrice*, with Mmes Viardot and Vanden-heuvel-Duprez, daughter of the tenor Gilbert Duprez. Berlioz thought the performance "thunderous," and the public considered the piece his most popular *morceau* since "The Shepherd's Farewell." The rich, shimmering barcarole enjoyed the kind of vogue that the *Marche de pèlerins* had two and three decades before. The same ladies sang it often at the Conserva-toire—according to the programs "at the general demand of the public."

It cannot be a coincidence that three days later Berlioz made the dramatic offer of his entire collection of performance material to the Société des Concerts:

> I own a rather lovely musical library of separate parts for orchestra and chorus and of scores, both manuscript and engraved, representing virtually the whole of my work. I have often anxiously considered what would happen to this costly collection after my death: there is every reason to believe that it might be dispersed or improperly used, or even left intact without being used. The Société des Concerts is the only musical institution in France whose promise for the future inspires confidence in a composer, and I would be happy if it would accept this music as a gift, adding it to its own library. One day these works may possibly have some value to the Société des Concerts. I only ask, *messieurs*, that if you accept my offer I be allowed to use these parts and scores during my own lifetime, for concerts in Paris or trips abroad, agreeing to return them all according to the inventory you will have made.[33]

Berlioz's offer was accepted by the governing committee of the Société des Concerts on 31 March—that is, immediately—and his gift was announced at a general meeting of the society on 17 May, the announcement followed by "numerous indications of approval."[34]

Berlioz had on 30 March left for Weimar to conduct the two performances of *Béatrice et Bénédict* for Richard Pohl. It was his last trip to Weimar: Liszt and Carolyne Sayn-Wittgenstein were in Rome, trying to lay the foundations for their new, separate lives. (Her legitimate husband died in 1864, leaving her free to marry, but by then their romance had run its course.) It was the dowager grand duchess who had called for *Béatrice et Bénédict,* as a late birthday present. Even without Liszt Weimar was bustling with musical activity: *Béatrice* attracted royal guests including the Prussian queen and artists from all over north Germany. There was a supper given by the musicians for Berlioz, and a gala dinner for three hundred at court, during which a band played the *Marche hongroise* from the gallery. On 6 April there was a performance of *Tannhäuser,* and under circumstances more refined than those in Paris Berlioz was able to see "truly beautiful things in the score," particularly in the last act.[35]

The production on 8 and 10 April of *Béatrice et Bénédict,* at which its two new movements were heard for the first time, came as an agreeable surprise to its composer. The artistic level of the performance was considerably higher than in Baden, though the Teutonic Mme Milde—who had seemed the epitome of "dove-like beauty" when she sang Elisabeth in *Tannhäuser*—was incapable of meridional sentiment and appearance. She was "charming," Berlioz wrote, "but she made of the Sicilian lioness a German Beatrice, and her dove's eyes never succeeded in shooting off flames—another genre of truth." She was, however, a seasoned performer, "deliciously beautiful, and a true artist,"[36] and that was qualification enough for the part. He was not fond of the German translation, but found Pohl, as usual, "an excellent chap." During the prolonged curtain calls, the royal couple sent a huge bouquet to the stage. On 15 April he read his Weimar admirers the libretto of *Les Troyens.*

He had arrived in Weimar to find a letter from the prince of Hohenzollern-Hechingen demanding a concert in Löwenberg; in a few days a personal emissary showed up to repeat the invitation and to wait patiently until Berlioz consented to it. The Hechingen concert of 1843 had been memorable, and Berlioz was happy enough for the opportunity to visit the old prince once more. His territory in Baden-Württemberg had passed to Prussia in 1850, seven years after Berlioz's visit, but he still maintained a small orchestra in his retinue, now resident in Löwenberg, between Dresden and Breslau in Silesia. Max Seifriz had become Kapellmeister, succeeding Täglichsbech.

The passage of time and the misfortunes of 1848 had left the prince with physical infirmities, but failed to dampen either his spirit or his hospitality. Berlioz was lodged in private apartments in the castle, from which each day at 4:00 P.M. he was summoned to greet an assembled and well-tuned orchestra of forty-five waiting in respectful silence. The concert room seated several hundred, with the vast music library the prince had gathered over the years arranged in cupboards behind the orchestra. The performance on Sunday, 19 April, was warm and precise, among the best of Berlioz's last decade. Seifriz played *Harold en Italie;* he wept over the work and vowed that "there is nothing finer in all music." Mme Pohl, the harpist, had come to do the solo parts in *Harold* and *Roméo et Juliette,* and her husband, though he had meant merely to accompany her to Löwenberg and hear the concert as a member of the audience, was put to work as cymbal player. Berlioz had virtually forgotten *Le Roi Lear,* which he had not heard since 1854; *Le Carnaval romain* and scenes from *Roméo et Juliette* completed the program. He was applauded by the players after each of the rehearsals, which he found at once exhausting, uplifting, and agitating. *Béatrice* in Weimar, by comparison, was child's play.

The prince was confined to his chambers with gout, but messengers were sent to and from the sickroom to report on the rehearsals and concert, and during one dinner a lackey brought Berlioz a jolly note timed to arrive between fresh pears and *baba au rhum.* At the first intermission of his concert, Berlioz was decorated with the cross of the order of Hohenzollern-Hechingen; at the end the orchestra presented him a crown. The next day a banquet and ball were given in his honor, and the prince bade him a tender farewell: "Goodbye, my dear Berlioz. You are going back to Paris, where you have friends who love you. Tell them I love them for it."[37] He did just that. From Paris, Berlioz included in his thank-you's a solicitous inquiry as to the prince's gout and heartfelt gratitude for his "lively and noble sentiment for art."[38]

He left Löwenberg on the 21st, behind schedule, and was thus obliged to cancel his planned stop in Strasbourg,[39] where he had been expected to rehearse the choruses for the forthcoming festival performance of *L'Enfance du Christ.* (I think his concern must have been to be back in Paris for the *séance* of the Institute on Saturday, the 25th.) In May and early June he simply waited while Carvalho and Mme Charton-Demeur worked out exactly what she was worth: she was still demanding 6,000 francs a month against an offer of 4,000. He read all five acts of *Les Troyens* to the assembled company of the Théâtre-Lyrique on 1 June, then left two weeks later for Strasbourg to supervise three chorus rehearsals, 16–18 June, and three general ones, 19–21 June, before the performance of *L'Enfance du Christ* on the 22nd.

Berlioz's Strasbourg concert was but a small part of a great Franco-German festivity to inaugurate the bridge across the Rhine from Strasbourg in France to Kehl in Germany. The annual Lower Rhine Music Festival had been scheduled to coincide with the festivities. The performance of *L'Enfance du Christ* and other works on 22 June took place in an iron and glass pavilion erected for the occasion in the broad Place Kléber at the center of town. The performing force numbered 450; 6,000 or more came to listen and were appropriately moved by what they could hear of the oratorio in this unusual venue. There were fanfares and cannon fire that night. The night before there was a banquet with its inevitable long-winded toast in his honor, to which Berlioz responded, "Today France and Germany intermingle. The love of art has united them. That noble love will do more good even than this noble bridge."[40] The day after the concert, the honored guests visited Kehl and were again received by bands and cannon fire. Berlioz was cheered, then given the place of honor for a performance of sacred music in the town church.

Only in late June—he was back in Paris on the 25th—did he let Carvalho persuade him to drop the first two acts of *Les Troyens* in favor of a more careful staging of what would henceforth be known as *Les Troyens à Carthage.* Berlioz had long foreseen this eventuality and does not seem to have objected too much. He wrote the new prologue, in which a *récitant* summarizes the Troy half, at the end of the month.

The spirited rehearsals revived him: the music was thrilling, and neither the artists nor the journalists could contain their enthusiasm. He came home from his rehearsals exhausted beyond measure, barely able to speak, a symptom Mme d'Ortigue interpreted as despair, but which was in fact a mixture of fatigue and euphoria.

*T*hat summer Berlioz authorized Richault to release a *Collection de 32 Mélodies,* a compendium of most of his smaller vocal works. It begins with the *Nuits d'été* and *Irlande* and continues with the works first published as *Vox populi, Tristia, Fleurs des landes,* and *Feuillets d'album* and the individual songs never published in a collection—*La Captive, Sara,* the *Prière du matin, Le Chasseur danois,* and *La Belle Isabeau.* The version of *La Mort d'Ophélie* for female chorus and orchestra represents a first publication in piano-vocal score. There is also a piano-vocal *Chant des chemins de fer.* The publication appeared in late November, during the run of *Les Troyens à Carthage.* The following year a reprint included *Le Cinq Mai* at the end, so the collection became *33 Mélodies* (1864).

What seemed to be the greatest coup of his publishing career turned out in the end to be his greatest failure: on 21 July he sold rights to the score of *Les Troyens* to Antoine de Choudens, publisher of Gounod's *Faust* and later of *Carmen.* The enormous fee of 12,500 francs changed hands, with Choudens contracting to release the full score a year after the vocal score appeared.[41] The vocal score of *Les Troyens à Carthage* was on sale by the time the production opened, but work on the full score was lethargic, and though at length it was completed, the score was never published. Berlioz sold foreign rights to the opera to a London publisher, and sometime that summer the ministry guaranteed a further 100,000 francs to the Théâtre-Lyrique against the costs of the forthcoming production.

Louis came to Paris in late July and went with his father to Baden-Baden for *Béatrice et Bénédict.* The cast had changed with the naming of Jourdan, the *récitant* in the Paris *L'Enfance du Christ,* to the role of Bénédict. Mme Charton-Demeur, her worth established to her satisfaction, was now prepared to outdo herself, at least in part to advertise the Paris *Troyens*. Berlioz, who was paid 1,000 francs to conduct *Béatrice,* was too ill to appear at the first dress rehearsal but managed to lead the second and at least the first of the two performances on 14 and 18 August. His heart was with the production about to occur in Paris, however, and he left Baden as soon as he could get away. (Louis, too, was off, as a member of Napoleon's expeditionary force to the New World: he went to Mexico and back between *Béatrice et Bénédict* in August and *Les Troyens* in November.) Berlioz quit Baden-Baden for the last time almost stealthily, all but unnoticed. Responsibility for the musical edification of that bejeweled community, like so many of his other duties, passed on to Ernest Reyer.

*D*espite their subsidy from the government, Carvalho and his company had neither the funds, the artistic standard, nor the space to stage so complex a production. Berlioz's concept of the vast settings for the Hunt and Storm and the other grand tableaux had to yield to the clear necessity for thrift. (The sketches for the sets, on the other hand, are glorious. These were done by Philippe-Marie Chaperon, designer in those years of *Don Carlos* and *L'Africaine*.) Berlioz himself paid for the extra orchestral players he deemed indispensable. Carvalho insisted on directing the work, and though genial and of obvious goodwill, he, like Jullien and many another impresario Berlioz had dealt with, had his own somewhat stereotyped notions of what the infamous Parisian public "required"—and what it would find, for one reason or another, offensive or, worse, risible. He was quick to demand a measure of music added here and a passage subtracted there.

The Théâtre-Lyrique was not the Opéra: it was not fashionable; it did not stamp on a work the promise of notoriety. Nevertheless Berlioz was carried away with a "boyish sense of excitement." Mme Charton-Demeur was taken with her role and went so far as to decline a much more attractive offer from Madrid in order to remain in the production. The libretto went to the censor on 29 September and was passed without comment. The chorus master, Léo Delibes, delivered his charges with the same panache as, earlier in the same year, he had delivered them for Gounod's *Faust* and Bizet's *Les Pêcheurs de perles*. Moreover, the production kept to its announced schedule—indeed, it was forced along, as the ticket income promised to keep Carvalho's company solvent for a few more months. The general rehearsal on 2 November encountered few problems, and the cast, even if Berlioz thought they could have used a little more rehearsal, was well prepared for the opening on 4 November.

Les Troyens à Carthage, though it did not light the sort of wildfire a Meyerbeer opera usually did, enjoyed a favorable response. Berlioz saw tears in his listeners' eyes, and there was endless applause. The septet and the love duet were the most popular, as they deserved to be, and the septet was

FIGURE 13.4 Setting for the death of Dido, in act V of *Les Troyens*.

encored. Mme Charton was a regal queen; like Mme Viardot in *Orphée*, she reminded old-timers of Mme Branchu. The vast majority of the press— d'Ortigue, Fiorentino, Damcke, Escudier, Léon Kreutzer, and others less well known—praised *Les Troyens à Carthage*. Berlioz said that more than fifty articles were devoted to it. D'Ortigue found it amusing that one who had declared himself a Romantic so early on had now turned to such pure, Classical subject matter. He did not suggest that the work was faultless, finding the recitatives and airs too often run together for his taste, the accompaniment too thick, and the harmonies harsh enough that the tonality was sometimes obscured. He would have preferred a simpler treatment of the antique subject. "But what accent! what elation! what respect for the truth! what beautiful declamation! what an orchestra!"[42] Gasperini said that the work was perfect from start to finish.

The outpouring of affection expressed in congratulatory notes at least equaled the response to *Roméo et Juliette* and *L'Enfance du Christ*. Gustave Roger, who had wanted the role of Aeneas, wrote tenderly, as did Mme Spontini (who said she felt the same *frisson* she used to sense at first performances of her late husband), Ambroise Thomas, and other admirers, young and old alike. The best of the letters was from Auguste Barbier, penned on 9 November:

> Well roared, Lion! It is great, it is beautiful, it is magnificent, it is above all tender! The flames of Virgil have been completely conveyed by your songs.

What ravishing duos of Dido and Anna, of Aeneas and Dido. Then the hunt, the utterly original dance music, the divine song of the Trojan by the sea, the air of Montjauze, the cries of passion, and finally the powerful choruses framing the poem. All of this moved me to the last instance. The father of *Benvenuto Cellini, Béatrice,* and *Les Troyens* can present himself to posterity with pride. The scepter of dramatic music in France has not been cast aside. It is valiantly carried by Hector.

Hourrah for Hector!

Farewell. A thousand congratulations, and a firm shake of the hand from your old friend and admirer

Auguste Barbier[43]

Meyerbeer went to twelve performances; Davison came from London just to see it. But perhaps the most gratifying feature of the production from Berlioz's own point of view was that Louis was there to witness it. He attended all of the performances and collected clippings of the reviews.

Les Troyens à Carthage, though it ran for twenty more performances— far longer than any of his other stage works—was played complete only on the first night. As was so often the case in Paris, it was vitiated, little by little, night after night. While Berlioz was ill at home, they began to cut it. Because of the fire restrictions, the thunder-and-lightning effects had been amateurish from the beginning; the ballet seemed mediocre. It had taken an hour to break the set after the Hunt and Storm, so that scene was abandoned entirely. Then the rest of the ballets were abbreviated, the exquisite scene between Anna and Narbal deleted; after that came the arias of Iopas and Hylas, the duo of the sentries, and Didon and Enée's great scene of parting: "Errante sur tes pas." The spineless conductor, Deloffre, did not object. As Choudens and Carvalho had agreed that the published vocal score should correspond to what was actually performed, successive issues of the published version were cut more and more. It was this treatment of the vocal score that caused a century-long confusion over the correct placement of the *Chasse royale,* which is properly the first tableau of act IV.

Berlioz likened the treatment to that of "the carcass of a calf on a butcher's block,"[44] but was too sick to complain. He had contracted severe bronchitis during the rehearsals in the drafty theater and was able to attend only half the performances before having to take to his bed.

The mutilated vocal scores sold well, and that certain mark of popular esteem, publication in the form of popular excerpts and *potpourris,* was conferred on *Les Troyens* with the appearance early in 1864 of twelve "favorite airs," the ballets, and a "brilliant fantasy." Orchestral parts of the *Chasse royale et orage* and the March for the Entry of the Queen were put on sale, and Berlioz, as one of his last serious ventures in composition, revised the published *Marche troyenne* to serve as a concert piece.

Abruptly on Christmas Eve, Mme Charton quit her post with the Théâtre-Lyrique to accept her better offers from the Théâtre-Italien and from Madrid. She had fulfilled her responsibilities admirably and professionally, however, and could not be blamed. *Les Troyens à Carthage* was over.

At the end of the 1863 season of the Société des Concerts, Théophile Tilmant was allowed to take a graceful retirement after a long and useful though undistinguished career. Berlioz was suggested as successor, and he nominated himself in a letter of 13 December, promising to consecrate to the duty all his time and his total attention.[45] But this time, though the artistic climate favored his election, his age and obviously poor health did not. His friend George-Hainl, already principal conductor at the Opéra, garnered forty-nine votes on the first ballot of the *sociétaires,* E.-M.-E. Deldevez—Hainl's eventual successor—was in second place with thirty-two, and Berlioz had but ten. On the second ballot he was eliminated.

After *Les Troyens* he appeared in public no more than a dozen times. His review of *Les Pêcheurs de perles* for the *Débats* of 8 October proved to be his last. But for a few measures here and there, he composed no more music.

Chapter Fourteen

Marche funèbre
(1864–69)

The productions of *Béatrice et Bénédict* and *Les Troyens à Carthage,* led Berlioz into all but total retirement. The periodic bursts of his creative energy had for years been growing further and further apart. The composition simply petered out. "No more of that," he says on a couple of occasions, "Othello's occupation's gone." He retired from his other two careers with grand gestures: the donation of his performance material to the Société des Concerts and his formal resignation as music critic of the *Journal des Débats.*

In spite of its studied formality, his disappearance from the front page of the *Journal des Débats* was not intended to be dramatic. At first he merely intended to give up the drudgery of the performance review and devote *feuilletons* to more musical issues at his leisure. Three decades was long enough for the dog's work: it had cost his career dearly in terms of encouragement and support from the Parisian community of musical institutions, performers, and composers, and of late it had seemed almost impossible to accomplish with dignity and discretion. On 12 February 1864 he begged of Edouard Bertin an unspecified period of leave from his duties; by the end of the month he was informing correspondents that he would do no more *feuilletons.* "Do not reproach me for having given my resignation," he begs Louis; he simply cannot bring himself seriously to confront such successors to *Les Troyens* as Gounod's *Mireille:* "Carvalho and all his world are furious that I do not offer them their usual crown of praise, and d'Ortigue is not happy that they are unhappy. It wounds him, and he is right."[1]

The review of Bizet's *Les Pêcheurs de perles* at the Théâtre-Lyrique had been his last, a routine piece with a touch of humor—"M. Bizet, laureate of the Institute, made the trip to Rome and came back without having forgotten music"—and a bow to Bizet's gifts as a reader of full score at the keyboard. He closed his journalistic career—he could not have done better had he planned it so—with a barb: "The score of *Les Pêcheurs de perles* bestows the highest of honors on M. Bizet, whom we shall be forced to accept as a composer, despite his unusual talent in score reading." "After thirty years of slavery," he says in the *Mémoires*, "I am free."[2]

He had not been dependent on the income from his journalism since Marie's death, and his mother-in-law was self-sufficient. He could rely on the monthly payments from the Isère to support his needs, several hundred more francs of stipend from the Institute and the library of the Conservatoire, comfortable savings from the sale and performances of *Les Troyens*, and the income from the Gluck productions. Gifts from sovereigns and similar forms of unexpected income raised his annual earnings to something over 12,000 francs per annum. Though not large enough to guarantee his heirs much of an estate or to rescue Louis from some fiscal *bêtise*, this was a comfortable retirement income. Such negotiations as he had with Choudens now were for the purpose of seeing the Paris vocal score of *Benvenuto Cellini* through the press and, if possible, arranging for the publication of full scores of all three operas—more to preserve the proper texts for posterity than for the money.

Louis left to go back to Mexico on 6 January, while Berlioz was ill in bed, spending his few useful hours on the *Cellini* vocal score and the revised *Marche troyenne*. His son was not, therefore, in Paris when Berlioz was notified that the ten-year concession on Harriet's plot in the St.-Vincent cemetery would soon expire. The body had to be moved to the larger plot in the cimetière Montmartre where Marie Recio lay. The exhumation took place in early March, possibly ten years to the day after her death on 3 March 1854,[3] and Berlioz found he could not stay away. He arrived in time to see a gravedigger wrenching open the old coffin and removing first Harriet's head and then her body to the new one. The cortège moved slowly down the hill into the larger cemetery, where she was laid once more to rest, alongside Marie, in the family vault. It was not the first time he had been present at an exhumation: some months earlier Edouard Alexandre, thinking Marie's resting place too humble, had given Berlioz a more suitable location in the cemetery, and he thus witnessed the digging up and reinterment of both his wives.

*H*e could not withdraw entirely from his artistic affairs. Gasperini, self-appointed herald of the "new" school, was giving a public lecture on *Les Troyens* and required coaching; Humbert Ferrand needed help with a French translation of something by Gluck. (The lively correspondence with Ferrand, which had slacked off in the 1840s, resumed in 1858, from which point there are more than sixty preserved letters.) And his works were being played, or sometimes played at, throughout the world; these often required his attention in one way or another. In 1864 he learned of major performances of his symphonic work from Basel to New York, and of productions of *Béatrice et Bénédict* in Weimar and in Stuttgart; in January 1864 there was a reading in Weimar of the act II duet from *Les Troyens*. In Paris it was the vogue to sing excerpts from his operas after dinner and during the salons. Admirers offered selections from *Béatrice et Bénédict* at Louise Bertin's on 25 February after rehearsing them on the 23rd; similar proceedings seem to have been customary at parties given in Passy, where the Erards lived with Mme Spontini. Carvalho wanted to give the septet from *Les Troyens* at a Lenten *concert spirituel* on 27 March, but Berlioz was for a variety of reasons opposed, and the work, though announced on handbills and in the press, was dropped.

Pasdeloup's insistent programming of Berlioz continued, too, and George-Hainl, now conductor of the Société des Concerts, asked to offer a major, though (he cautioned) short performance during his first season, perhaps the first four movements of *Roméo et Juliette*. Berlioz suggested instead that Mme Charton-Demeur should sing excerpts from *Les Troyens* and even went so far as to write her in Madrid inquiring about her return date. At length they settled on *La Fuite en Egypte* for the seventh concert of the season, on 3 April.[4] Among the ironies of the event was that Bizet, for whom Berlioz had just promised a future better than the accompanying of singers, was praised in the papers for his skills as an accompanist during the chorus rehearsals.

The concert version of the *Marche troyenne* was fashioned from the act I finale (no. 11) of the full opera, altered to approximate the version heard during the prologue to *Les Troyens à Carthage*. It was not put on sale until mid-1865 —Choudens had grown lethargic over several outstanding matters, chief among them the full score of *Cellini*—but as early as January 1864, Berlioz was trying to have the *Marche troyenne* programmed alongside the *Chasse royale et orage*. It must have been finished and sent to the publisher early in the year.

Whether or not the full scores of the operas appeared during his lifetime, *Les Troyens* and *Béatrice et Bénédict* were safe for the future, and that was reason enough to pursue at least the ideal of a private life. His mother-in-law cared for him and fretted over his well-being, to the point of refusing to take vacations herself unless Louis was in town. He spent much of the day in bed and, except for his trips to the Institute, left home rarely. When he did go out in the evening, it was nearly always to the homes of close friends nearby: the Massarts; Berthold Damcke and his wife; Mme Charton-Demeur and her husband, the flutist Demeur; Kreutzer; Stephen Heller; and Edouard Alexandre. These hosts would cater to his whims and had accustomed themselves to his tendency suddenly to stretch out on a sofa and demand to be left alone. (His boots were at times covered in mud, and the Damckes, "the personification of order and propriety" according to Heller, found that part difficult to endure.[5]) From time to time he would join the whist, charades, and other pastimes, or weep while hearing Mme

Massart play Beethoven. One evening, for example, he went with the Massarts to Bertin's, where the ladies worked at crochet and the men played chess and dominoes. Sooner or later the talk always came around to Shakespeare, and on at least one occasion the Massarts urged him to read *Hamlet* aloud. This he did, and then *Coriolanus,* over a five-hour period, the tears streaming down his face.

The Massarts had been in the inner circle of the Société Philharmonique; Berlioz had long advocated the instruments of Edouard Alexandre and his father and had on more than one occasion, including once in the recent past, come to the aid of the firm in coping with the ever volatile climate of patent wars and lawsuits over just who had invented what. The long relationship with Stephen Heller blossomed anew in 1861 with a fond article in the *Débats* of 23 July on Heller's *Préludes*, opus 81. Heller had been ardent in his support of *Les Troyens;* he was one of the admirers who, as the librettist Ludovic Halévy grumbled to his diary, had been proclaiming the work a masterpiece for "ten years."[6] Berlioz considered Heller a member of the tiny family of musicians committed to love and respect the arts: "He writes quietly, lives tranquilly, and sees his reputation grow." D'Ortigue, in the short time he had to live, belonged to this inner circle, as did Janin, the two of whom now shared Berlioz's former duties at the *Débats.* The Viardots, too, were intimates, taking care to include him in their activities when they were in town.

The newcomers were the Damckes, who resided just around the corner. They had moved in 1859 to Paris, where Damcke wrote on Parisian life for the German press, composed a great deal, and taught at the Conservatoire. Their formidable salon specialized in welcoming foreign musicians, and there Berlioz renewed his friendship with Joachim and his acquaintance with Moscheles and may have seen Clara Schumann and Anton Rubinstein. It was Damcke who finally paid attention to Berlioz's repeated insistence on a complete edition of Gluck. Damcke assisted Fanny Pelletan, the principal financial backer, in the editorial tasks leading up to the spectacular Richault edition, in regal format, of the two *Iphigénie* operas. Though published after Berlioz's death, the edition is a monument to his passionate study and advancement of Gluck, a more important and more fitting memorial, indeed, than any of the insignificant statues hidden away in ill-traveled squares in Paris and the French provinces.

This coterie, along with Ernest Reyer, became Berlioz's legatees, executors, and pallbearers. Several of them were present at his deathbed, and it was they who inherited the mission of preserving his memory and his interests for posterity. There was no widow Berlioz to do for him what Mme Le Sueur and Mme Spontini did on behalf of their late husbands.

In his more lucid and contemplative periods, Berlioz returned to his reading, for which there was now ample time. Though he tried to cover the new literature sent him by the heirs of Romanticism, he was no longer intimately involved with the moderns. Most of his writer friends were past the age of their greatest accomplishment; Vigny had died in 1863. Berlioz's preoccupation was with his two favorites, Virgil and Shakespeare, and he read and reread their complete works, committing hundreds more lines to memory and peppering his correspondence with more citations than ever before.

He often writes of excruciating suffering, lasting for periods of twelve hours and more; even on better days, the pain would commence at eight in the morning and continue into the midafternoon. To Ferrand, also ill, he writes, "I cry toward you as one is always tempted to cry toward loved ones."[7] He took progressively larger doses of laudanum, an easily obtained tincture of opium, which not only failed to offer much relief but also left him feeling dazed and stupid. At least it let him sleep. Adherence to his diet gave him some relief, but we know from several sources that he could not resist coffee, champagne, or his favorite Havana cigars, all forbidden. He shared, in sum, in the sentiments of Auber's *bon mot,* offered at one of the many ceremonies at the Père Lachaise cemetery that demanded the presence of members of the Institute: "Dear chap, I sense myself declining. I suppose this is the last time I shall come to a burial *en amateur.*"

By the summer of 1864, his was a solitary, resigned existence of reading, meditating, struggling against spiritual weariness, and waiting for death.

FIGURE 14.1 Daniel F.-E. Auber.

FIGURE 14.2 Funeral homage paid to Meyerbeer in the Gare du Nord. *L'Illustration*, 14 May 1864.

"He was an old man at sixty," writes Cairns. Berlioz simply shrugged at the spectre of death: "'When you will.' Why does he delay?"[8]

Meyerbeer died on 2 May, a fortnight after having finished *L'Africaine*. His body was borne by rail away from the Gare du Nord to Berlin after a magnificent cortège and ceremony in the station, a grand *tableau final* which can be likened in size and pomposity only to the arrival in France of Napoleon's remains. The one subtle thing about it was the way it confirmed much of what Berlioz had said of Parisian taste.

The Institute awarded its *prix de Rome* that year to a young composer named Sieg, over the candidacy of Saint-Saëns. Berlioz felt some anguish at not having supported his twenty-eight-year-old disciple; on the other hand, he told himself, he could look with satisfaction on Saint-Saëns's well-established career, on a brilliant future all but assured.

Louis arrived for a sojourn of several weeks on 25 July and was in Paris when his father was named an *officier* of the Legion of Honor on 12 August. Berlioz was decorated, simultaneously with Legouvé and Mme Massart, on 15 August, in celebration of the *fête de l'Empereur*.

*O*therwise he was alone and bored that summer. Most of his friends were away on holiday, and he was adrift in the deserted Parisian

FIGURE 14.3 Louis Berlioz, c. 1864.

August without, for the first time in many years, Plombières or Baden-Baden to look forward to. "Rarely have I known such mortal weariness," he says of those weeks. He and Louis and Stephen Heller dined together most of those evenings, often wandering to Asnières or some other suburb, talking endlessly of Beethoven and Shakespeare. In late September, after Louis had left, Berlioz was so lonely that he gratefully accepted the invitation of his nieces to come for a visit to the Dauphiné and the Isère.

He wired his brother-in-law Suat of his impending arrival and was soon enjoying two blissful weeks with his nieces and their father at their country house in Estressin, near Vienne. They talked not of Beethoven and Marie but of Adèle and family happinesses since vanished. Out of a sense of obligation he called on his cousins and other family members in Vienne, but his thoughts were dominated by Estelle Fornier, just as they had been in 1848 after his father died. With frenzied excitement he sent Suat to discover her address and, learning that she lived in nearby Lyon, bid his family farewell and set forth to follow those yearnings to whatever conclusion might lie in store. He began by traveling to Meylan to find the spot where first he had set eyes on her.

He had tried to find her vetch-covered rock in 1848, without success. This time, on 22 September, he discovered it (or at least imagined that he did) easily enough, though the vetch was gone. He filled his pockets with souvenirs—bark from the cherry tree, for example, and a bit of granite from her rock. Then he went back toward Lyon, determined, this time, to pay her a personal visit. He was there by nightfall and the next morning, 23 September, wrote a brief note asking to meet her. Too excited to wait for the post, he took the letter to her house on the avenue de Noailles, rang the bell, and presented the maid his calling card and the letter. Presently Mme Fornier appeared.

Estelle was seventy years of age. The untimely deaths of her husband and more than one of her children had left her saddened and resigned to her uneventful life. She received Berlioz with bemused indifference and quiet dignity; she had read of his exploits and knew him to be famous. She was flattered by his attention and, in her softspoken way, grateful for it. He kissed her hand, trying to stifle a tearful outburst; they bade each other farewell, Mme Fornier naively imagining she had seen the last of him. Her son Charles was soon to be married, and she would be moving with the bride and groom to Geneva, well off Berlioz's customary routes of travel.

Returning to his hotel, he ran into the manager of Adelina Patti, the celebrated soprano on her way to becoming the next Jenny Lind. Patti was singing in *The Barber of Seville* at the municipal theater, and nothing would do but that he dine with her that evening. Berlioz toyed with the idea of staying another day to take Estelle to Patti's opera and went so far as to go back to her house to beg his answer in person. She declined this invitation: she was going to the country. He returned to the hotel, in a swivet, for his dinner with Patti. She was delighted to see him and fawned on him "as if some marvelous glittering bird with eyes like diamonds were humming around my head, alighting on my shoulder, pecking at my hair and, with a

FIGURE 14.4 Estelle Fornier, c. 1864.

flutter of brilliant wings, whistling me its gayest, sweetest tunes."[9] Afterward she and her entourage took him to the station and waved farewell as his train pulled away.

He spent more time than he should have, that fall, writing Estelle intimate, passionate, and very long letters. "One word from you, dear lady, one word," he wrote, and she responded, "You are still young at heart; it is not so for me: I am simply old." He was courteous but insistent in demanding to be allowed to visit her: "Your address [in Geneva]! your address!"[10] He sent her copies of his books. At length she came around to his way of thinking, largely, it seems, to avoid being disagreeable. She made certain that her son, Charles Fornier, and his new Javanese-Creole wife, Suzanne, called on Berlioz during their wedding trip to Paris in October.

Liszt passed through Paris in October on his way back to Rome, where in a few weeks he would take his minor holy orders. (There was no longer any talk of his marrying Carolyne Sayn-Wittgenstein, but they stayed in close touch in Rome, and Berlioz's warm correspondence with the princess continued through 1867.) He and Berlioz dined together twice that October. Writing at the end of his life to Berlioz's biographer Hippeau, Liszt summarized the new turn of their friendship:

> From 1829 until 1864, my relationship with Berlioz was of the simplest sort: complete admiration on my part, cordiality on his. This was so in Paris, Prague, and Weimar, where I had the honor to produce and conduct his *Benvenuto Cellini*—an admirable work, magnificent, of the liveliest colors and rhythm, overflowing with bright melodies, and for which I await the *glorious* revival in Paris, when there is a tenor; *Cellini* of rare occasion and manner . . .
>
> After '64, without personal estrangement, the question of Wagner, burning then but much cooler now, caused a chill to come between Berlioz and me. He could not imagine that Wagner might be the future of music drama in Germany, surpassing Beethoven and Weber.[11]

Thus they avoided discussing musical issues in 1864. On the whole their brief encounter must have seemed melancholy to both of them.

Berlioz took care to send Estelle a copy of the libretto of *Les Troyens à Carthage* for her to read on Sunday, 18 December, when the great act IV (act II in the shortened version) was to be given by the Société des Concerts. He marked the place with leaves gathered in Meylan. Estelle's daughter-in-law, Suzanne, was in Paris on business, and he invited her to the concert. But in a last squabble with the Société des Concerts, Berlioz withdrew the excerpts from *Les Troyens* when the governing committee insisted on one too many cuts. Suzanne Fornier had to be satisfied with a performance of Donizetti's *Poliuto,* which she watched with Berlioz from a box offered by the leading lady, Mme Charton-Demeur.

He continued to write Estelle something on the order of a letter a month, some forty-three letters altogether, and they exchanged photographs. He visited her annually as long as he was able. Pursuing Estelle helped him

FIGURE 14.5 Adelina Patti, c. 1865.

through his worst loneliness after Marie's death, and the long letters gave vent to his pent-up resignations. In sum the affair probably prolonged his life.

His birthday on 11 December was observed in Vienna with a performance of the chorus of soldiers and students from *Faust* during a concert by the Männersingverein, whose conductor thought to send him a birthday telegram. Louis, now the lieutenant commander of a troop ship called the *Louisiana,* had returned from Mexico to the port of St. Nazaire, at the mouth of the Loire near Nantes, for only a few days. Berlioz went to see him off again, and over the next few years would make several such trips.

On his return he attacked the *Mémoires* one last time, adding to the 1856 postscript a postface on the production of *Les Troyens à Carthage* and a chapter called "Travels in Dauphiné," mostly the letters to Estelle. The last line, "Stella! I can die now without anger or bitterness," is followed by the date 1 January 1865. This time he was done for certain, so he took the manuscript directly to his publisher, Michel Lévy.

*C*he idea of a new romantic attachment, if not the speed with which it was progressing, was bracing, and for a time between his return to Paris in the fall of 1864 and the spring of 1865, his health in fact seemed much better. During the six months he read proofs of the *Mémoires* and made meticulous corrections and adjustments, some of which reflect events after 1 January. Buoyed by the goal of carrying Estelle a copy of the *Mémoires* on his forthcoming visit to Geneva, he urged the printers on to breakneck speed. It occurred to him to ask if he might use Estelle's real name in the postface, but this dubious honor she refused.

The winter became spring, during which his life was still dominated by the proofs, a few outings, and above all the promise of the trip to Geneva. Louis urged his father to come again to St. Nazaire. Spring was an ideal time for such a journey, and Berlioz set out with a light heart, only to be seized in his railway coach at Nantes with the worst attack of intestinal neuralgia he had yet sustained. He was violently ill for his three days in St. Nazaire, terrifying Louis, then had to return to Paris for three weeks of recuperation. In his confusion he mistakenly congratulated Janin on his election to the Institute, just after he had in fact been defeated.

Because of his illness he attended only the dress rehearsal of *L'Africaine.* Meyerbeer's opera was nearly six hours long—at least in the early weeks— and the rehearsal kept Berlioz out until 1:30 A.M., so exhausting him that he was unable to leave his bed for the premiere.

Aside from an albumleaf here and there[12]—the inevitable demands on a composer of his standing and a member of the Institute—he composed no more. In all probability his last work was a series of three short pieces for women's voices destined to appear in a collection called *Le Livre choral,* compiled by an acquaintance of his named Prosper Sain d'Arod and not so different from many another venture intended for marketing to provincial church choirs. The last of the three pieces is not even an original work, but rather a setting of a harpsichord piece by Couperin, the text by an anonymous author of the eighteenth century. Documentation on this project is scarce; no edition prior to 1885 has been preserved. Carolyne Sayn-Wittgenstein suggested that Berlioz harness the energy of his romantic attachment with a work on Estelle, but that of course had already been done, with the first movement of the *Fantastique.*

The *Mémoires* came off the press in July. He had perhaps fifty copies printed on special paper, handsomely bound, and otherwise readied for presentation to his circle: Louis, his mother-in-law, his uncles and nieces, Ferrand, the princess, his Parisian admirers, and the closest of his friends elsewhere in Europe. The subsequent commercial run of 1,200 copies he left, unbound, at the Conservatoire, pending the death he thought imminent. When Louis suddenly appeared in late July, Berlioz reluctantly delayed for two weeks his planned departure to visit Estelle. He could not, then, deliver her the *Mémoires* in person. Rather, on 29 July he put her copy on a train bound for Geneva, along with a second copy for her son Charles. Inside the first was a bookmark to which was attached a chip from her granite rock.

On 15 August he went by rail to Geneva, where he took rooms in a hotel near the Fornier house. The Alpine air and the tranquil lake rejuvenated him; the Forniers received him warmly. He cradled the infant child of Charles and Suzanne Fornier on his lap, went to the baptism, and joined the family in lakeside promenades and carriage rides in the country. But he and Estelle were never by themselves, and the talk was always of "other things." To the Damckes he complained that she simply did not comprehend.

Finally, they were alone, and, guessing that his thoughts were turning in that direction, she took the opportunity to disabuse him of the notion of a third marriage. She set rigid guidelines for the romance: they might correspond, and he might visit from time to time to "nourish" her attentions. That was all. Berlioz took it well. What he could not do without, he told her, was the occasional trip "to see you, to hear your voice and to breathe your air. Then I shall hasten back to Paris, proud and happy as a bee taking home his spoils, and—better off than a bee—full of tender gratitude."[13]

On 22 August he inscribed her copy of the *Mémoires* "to Estelle Fornier from her devoted H. B." She kept his letters in it. On his way to Paris he visited the Pals and his cousins in Grenoble and the Suats in Vienne, leaving copies of the *Mémoires* as he went, then was back in Paris by the end of September. He had been gone three weeks.

In the fall he undertook to help Carvalho and Saint-Saëns present Gluck's *Armide* at the Théâtre-Lyrique, his third Gluck production in recent years. Saint-Saëns, Berlioz's heir apparent in Gluck study, came with Mme Charton-Demeur to his apartment daily to rehearse, an obligation that forced him from his bed each day, "like everybody else,"[14] his faculties now lively once again.

By the spring he was fully active, swept up in the events of a Paris season that had grown to nearly two hundred significant concerts annually. On 1 March he led a concerto by Léon Kreutzer at a concert of Massart—his last public appearance in Paris—and on 7 March he was cheered as Pasdeloup played the magnificent septet from *Les Troyens*. Between Pasdeloup's giant concerts in the Cirque-Napoléon and George-Hainl's with the Société des Concerts, he was now assured of several performances a year at home, albeit of his shorter, more accessible excerpts and single-movement works. George-Hainl, for example, announced *La Fuite en Egypte* for the *concert spirituel* on 1 April, two Sundays before Easter; Pasdeloup programmed Berlioz for both 25 March and 1 April.

The *abbé* Liszt came again to Paris in March, this time to offer the revised version of his *Missa solemnis* of the late 1850s, called the "Gran" Mass after the Austro-Hungarian city for whose basilica it was first written. Berlioz, who found Liszt's dallying with religious faith difficult to endure, was unimpressed and found the Mass, given at St.-Eustache on 5 and 16 March with a splendor that must have reminded him of his own Requiem there, to be "the negation of art."[15] Its modernisms shocked the public. He went to a party at Kreutzer's with what remained of the Old Guard—Liszt, d'Ortigue, and Damcke—but fell into an access of depression and went home early. It was the last time he saw Liszt.

When Clapisson died on 19 March 1866, Berlioz was named to succeed him as curator of musical instruments at the Conservatoire, an appointment worth 2,000 francs of further annual stipend. Much to Berlioz's satisfaction, Gounod was elected in May to fill Clapisson's chair, and he and Legouvé offered the new *membre de l'Institut* his celebratory dinner. Berlioz was vivacious and talkative for the first part of the evening, babbling about Estelle, then became disoriented and had to be led home. Before they had reached the last corner, unable to go farther, he sat down on the curb and cried.

He managed to go to performances, in Italian, of *Othello* and *Hamlet,* then for three days in mid-July journeyed by rail to Louvain, in Belgium, to join Samuel, d'Ortigue, Saint-Saëns, and the organist Batiste on the jury for a music competition there. They heard sixty entries in a few days, rating masses in the same way that, in 1855, he had listened to and rated pianos.

As the autumn holiday with Estelle approached, he took care to muster what was left of his strength, the better to be in excellent form by his departure date of 15 September. An account book for this trip has been preserved;[16] it shows the cost of a first-class railway ticket (70 francs each way), a book, and a haircut and shave. He stayed in Switzerland for two weeks and returned, as had become his habit, through Vienne to call upon his nieces. He was due in Paris by early October, when a revival of his 1861 production of *Alceste* was to take place. This opened on 12 October and made a few new converts, among them Stephen Heller; in general, however, the Gluck fever was subsiding, and the revival lasted for only eight performances.

Perhaps the most interesting result of the 1866 *Alceste* was that it led to a final reconciliation with Fétis. Fétis, overwhelmed by the work, immediately wrote to Berlioz to "pay homage to your perfect sentiment for the beauties of this score . . . Accept the thanks of a sincere and devoted lover of art, as well as the expression of high regard that I profess for you personally. I would have come to see you had I not gone back to Brussels today." Berlioz responded by return mail on 14 October: "You are still a lance, I am but a shield."[17] Their relationship had begun to ease with their amiable encounter in Brussels in 1855; in the interim, Berlioz had further quelled the old hostilities by sending Fétis a complimentary letter on the appearance of the second edition of his *Biographie universelle* in 1860.

A complete *Roméo et Juliette* was being readied for performance in Basel in early December 1866, and for a time Berlioz firmly intended to be there to conduct it. That trip was preempted by a more demanding call, the renewal of the long-standing invitation to appear in Vienna before the orchestra of the Gesellschaft der Musikfreunde. This season it was not a question of the early symphonies but rather of the full *Damnation de Faust*. He left for Vienna during the first week of December and was there in time to lead several rehearsals.

Infirmity and his poor knowledge of German conspired to keep him from conducting well. Both these circumstances, combined with exasperation at his inability to remember the score and frustration at the slow progress of the players, put him in a volatile frame of mind. He rebuked a cellist for a false entry—"Taisez-vous donc"—and hurled his baton at the unsuspecting English horn player for some blunder in the breathtaking (though physically grueling) introduction to Marguerite's aria. Johann Herbeck, who had invited him, gracefully returned the baton, but Berlioz walked out of the rehearsal and went to bed.[18]

He was able to conduct the concert on 16 December, and though his conducting was flawed, the results were good enough to provoke a brilliant public reception, surely the best he had had in Vienna. He was called back to the podium ten times; his letters describing the event pant with the excitement of earlier times. I am sure it was one of those bittersweet occasions when an audience, accepting the inevitability of an artist's decline, suddenly grasps that it is bidding a legend *adieu*. The press accounts are mixed, for the critics of Vienna, spurred on by Hanslick, were embroiled in a bitter controversy over the matter of modernism. And there was still the problem of a French *Faust*. Hanslick did not like what he heard, writing "regretfully" that

> Of all the great works of this composer, *Faust* seems to us the weakest . . . I confess candidly to the subjective view that Berlioz's composition no longer exercises a vital, direct hold on the musical world, that the public enthusiasm for it will not increase but rather subside. For historians of art Berlioz will be one of the most remarkable and estimable of personalities, for musicians an inexhaustible source of study. But public opinion, as I see it, is more apt to conclude that a work like Berlioz's *Faust* is not music, not true music, at all. And I suspect I am right to say that Schumann's *Faust's Verklärung* will delight every ear and stir every heart long after nothing is left of *La Damnation de Faust* but the name and the memory.[19]

At a huge banquet on 17 December, on the other hand, Herbeck and Cornelius outdid themselves to lionize him. Herbeck's toast, in verse, talked of new paths in art and of Berlioz's succession to Beethovenian ideals. Berlioz burst into tears at his moment to respond.

*T*he Seine was frozen over when he reached Paris at the end of December to face a cruel winter. As though it had been an engraved announcement of his availability, his appearance in Vienna unleashed dozens of calls to conduct from all over Europe. Adolphe Samuel, for example, who was regularly programming Berlioz's music with great success in the theretofore uncomprehending city of Brussels, tendered yet another in his long series of offers. There was nothing much to attract Berlioz to Brussels, but he could scarcely decline the invitation from Ferdinand Hiller, one of his earliest and most intimate foreign friends, to lead *Harold en Italie* in Cologne, where Hiller had been Kapellmeister since 1850. Berlioz left on 23 February and for that concert conducted *Harold* and the Duo-Nocturne. Hiller had prepared the orchestra well, and this time there was no unpleasantness.

The latest of the century's many exhibitions, an Exposition Universelle des Beaux-Arts to be held simultaneously with an Exposition Agricole et Industrielle, was opening in Paris on 1 April, and Berlioz was again appointed to provide the music for the ceremonial events. There could not have been a more embarrassing moment to have a fair purporting to celebrate international harmony through progress. The ominous new military power of the Prussian empire lent grave definition to the sorry state of Franco-Prussian diplomacy, and the French experience in Mexico had just reached its tawdry end. (The French abandoned Mexico in February 1867.) The Paris Exposition, however, had been decreed two years before, in February 1865; handsome new iron-and-glass buildings had been erected in the Champ de Mars (where, in 1889, the Eiffel Tower was erected for the Centennial Exposition). There was no turning back from it, whatever the political implications.

Berlioz assembled forces for a typical program: the *Hymne à la France;* magnificent scenes from the operas of Gluck, Rossini, and Auber; and patriotic ceremonial choruses of Méhul and David. D'Ortigue had urged that Berlioz be commissioned for a ceremonial work on the order of the *Symphonie funèbre et triomphale,* hoping that the "sadness, discontent, and illness" that Berlioz had nourished for so long might thus be combatted, that the project "might recall him to his art, and perhaps even to his health."[20] But d'Ortigue died of a stroke on 20 November 1866, just after writing those words, and the pressure on the government ceased. It may be that Berlioz revised his *Temple universel* of 1860 for the ceremony, but there is little direct evidence to support that hypothesis.

He used his professional obligation to the government as an excuse to overlook the first performance of Gounod's *Roméo et Juliette* on 27 April. The idea of another musical setting of a work so close to his heart troubled him, and Gounod knew better than to invite him to the rehearsals or first performance. Yet just afterward, at the Institute, the young composer took Berlioz in his arms and embraced him; "I don't know why," Berlioz remarked.[21]

On 8 May the thirty-two-year-old American conductor Theodore Thomas came to call, brimming with a disciple's admiration. He was in Paris for several days and determined to meet the composer of the many works he had himself introduced to American audiences. The entry in Thomas's diary for that day reads as follows:

Spent a delightful hour with Berlioz, in which we talked over all his larger compositions. It seems he had heard already that I played his music, and, as I was leaving, he asked me if there was anything of his that I would like which I did not already have in my library. I told him yes, there was one thing that I wanted very much, and that was his great "requiem Mass." Hearing this Berlioz went to the music case, took down his own copy of the score, and inscribed it, "To Theodore Thomas in remembrance of the grateful author, Hector Berlioz," and presented it to me.[22]

He gave Thomas a copy of the newly revised edition just published by Ricordi.

In June he suddenly slipped into a melancholy mood, worried mostly over the safety of his son, somewhere in the troubled waters of the Mexican gulf. "Dearest Louis," he writes, "what would I do if I didn't have you?" His friends contrived to cheer him up; on the morning of 29 June, for example, Theodore Ritter, the Massarts, Reyer, and Heller planned to give a reception in his honor in the *atelier* of Marquis Arconati Visconti. They decorated the

FIGURE 14.6
Grande Messe des morts (Milan: Ricordi, [1867]). Theodore Thomas's copy, with legend by Rose Fay Thomas.

studio with bright fabrics, flowers, posters bearing the titles of his works, and, dominating all this, a portrait wreathed in palm branches—the whole affair rather too suggestive of Wagner's saccharine birthday parties. Berlioz, troubled with his gloomy premonitions, did not want to go, but Berthold Damcke came to fetch him and walk him to the party.

In the boulevard Rochechouart a friend stopped them to offer Berlioz condolences on his cruel loss. Louis Berlioz, at the age of thirty-two, had died on 5 June of yellow fever on board his ship, the *Louisiana,* anchored in Havana harbor. The news was just reaching the Paris papers.

Berlioz fled home in shock, turning first of all to write Estelle of "the most frightful affliction of my life." "It was to me to die."[23] The unthinkable had happened. For days he refused to receive calls or even to speak at all. After a time he rose one morning, went to the Conservatoire, and, with the help of a porter who later described the event in some detail, burned all his mementos: the letters, cards, souvenirs, and laurel crowns commemorating his triumphs, his newspaper cuttings, and all the rest. There was no one to leave them to. "I am alone."[24]

A month later, on 29 July 1867, Berlioz prepared his last will and testament. The bulk of his estate would pass to his nieces, Mathilde Masclet, née Pal, and Josephine and Nanci Suat. There was an annual stipend of 2,900 francs for Mme Martin, his mother-in-law, an increase over the amount ceded to her in legal acts of 24 July and 13 October 1862, after Marie's death. She was left all the furnishings of their house that were not hers already. The Swiss maid, Caroline Seheur, was left an annual stipend of 300 francs, and there was another stipend of 1,600 francs for Estelle. His goods and properties were to be sold to guarantee such income.

The four opera scores (that is, *Benvenuto Cellini, Béatrice et Bénédict,* and the two halves of *Les Troyens*) were left to the Conservatoire library, with the direction that *Les Troyens* should be translated into German by Peter Cornelius. He reminded Choudens of his unmet contracts:

> M. Choudens *never fulfilled* this obligation, but I did not want to sue him. My executors must do whatever they see fit to oblige him to do so, but I absolutely require . . . that the score be published without cuts, without modifications, without the least suppression of the text—in sum, exactly as it stands.[25]

The 1,200 copies of the *Mémoires,* in his office at the Conservatoire, were left to Lévy or Hachette or anyone else interested in marketing them. The German translation, in which the Leipzig publisher Gustav Heinze had already expressed interest, was to be done by Mlle Cornelius, sister of Peter Cornelius, and not, by inference, Richard Pohl.

He named as his executors Edouard Alexandre, who was to take for himself the batons in gilt, silver, and wood, and Berthold Damcke, who was to have all the other contents of his cupboard, apparently including the fragmentary autographs of *Les Francs-Juges* and *La Nonne sanglante,* which later passed down through Damcke's estate. He was too poor, he said, to leave them anything of value. His copy of *Paul et Virginie* he left to Ernest Reyer, his (and d'Ortigue's) successor at the *Journal des Débats*, "who will soon be famous"; to his lawyer, Nogent Saint-Laurent, he bequeathed his one-volume Latin Virgil; to Mme Massart, who adored his dramatic readings, he left his one-volume English Shakespeare.

The following 12 June 1868 he appended a codicil to the will adding a further 1,800 francs to his legacy for his mother-in-law.

*W*ith Berlioz in mourning, it fell to George-Hainl to conduct the closing ceremonies for the 1867 Exposition. The prizegiving was on 1 July, and the festival concerts were offered on 8 and 11 July, with, as announced, Berlioz's *Hymne à la France* and scenes from Gluck's *Armide*. An Orphéon of six thousand sang that week, and there was a competition of four thousand bandsmen. Those ten days, in short, constituted a true Berliozian festivity, but with Berlioz nowhere to be seen.

The doctors were alarmed by the gravity of his reaction to Louis's demise and insisted that he go at once to take a cure. Following their instructions, he went on 5 August for two weeks to Néris, a spa northeast of Vichy and Clermont-Ferrand, after which, somewhat revived, he established himself with his family in Vienne. Estelle had moved to St. Symphorien d'Ozon, between Lyon and Vienne, and during those weeks Berlioz made the short trip three times. There they walked and talked of death: Estelle, too, had lost a son. They met for the last time on 9 September.

The next day offered something more festive: the wedding of his niece Joséphine to the young army officer Marc-Antoine Chapot. Thirty-two family members were there, including Uncle Félix Marmion, and though many of these were seeing him for the last time and must have known it, their merrymaking left him in a much improved frame of mind.

He was nevertheless quite weak and very thin, finding warmth only during his extended walks along the sunny boulevards. His abdominal pains were relieved only by hot weather; otherwise he was lethargic and disinclined to work at all, complaining that "I feel as if I have spent all my life in bed."[26] For a time he maintained his disinclination to accept further engagements, notably refusing the invitation of "a rich American piano manufacturer"— Steinway—who offered him 100,000 francs to come to the United States. (Instead, Steinway had a bust of Berlioz sculpted by Perraud and drew three bronze copies; one each for Paris, New York, and St. Petersburg.[27] Berlioz, for his part, managed to praise the Steinway piano, in a testimonial of 25 September.)

By contrast he could not turn down the Grand Duchess Elena Pavlovna, in Paris for the Exposition, who took him unaware when she called, rich with flattery and financial incentive, to insist that he undertake a second journey to Russia. On 17 September he reluctantly signed a contract to give a series of six concerts in St. Petersburg over a three-month period during the winter. Five of these would consist of classical music by Beethoven and his predecessors, and the last would be devoted to his own compositions. (Later, the celebrated violinist Wieniawski made known his desire to play *Harold en Italie* and *Rêverie et Caprice* and was accommodated.) He was promised residence in the palace, a carriage at his disposal, and an income of perhaps 15,000 francs plus 1,000 francs of travel money. They would arrange for all the rehearsals he required. He had enough sense to decline Hiller's invitation to stop, en route, for another concert in Cologne.

He was manifestly in no health to make such a long journey to so forbidding a winter climate; he knew he would suffer cruelly. He knew, too, that the trip would represent his last farewell to one of his favorite and most faithful publics. He feared he would find all his acquaintances in Russia dead, and that the Italian singers there would not suit. But he had been charmed by the grand duchess, as his letters make clear: she had literally begged him to come. The money was already attractive, he says to the Princess Sayn-Wittgenstein, for the grand duchess had left 6,000 francs behind. It fatigued him merely to write the necessary letter to Auber begging a three-month leave from his position at the Conservatoire.

On 12 November he left Paris, arriving the next day in Berlin, where he rested in his hotel room for the better part of three days. Together with Mlle Regan, the singer, and Alfred Dörffel, the pianist, both of whom were to appear in his concerts, he left Berlin on the 15th, arriving in St. Petersburg on the 17th. It was thus a journey of five days, superior in every respect to the many-staged trip of 1847 that had ended in the bitter cold with the long, Napoleonic journey by sledge.

His concerts extended from late November to early February, with a repertoire chosen almost entirely from the masterpieces of his musical Olympus: Beethoven's Third, Fourth, Fifth, and Sixth Symphonies and works of Mozart, Gluck, and Weber. The Russians were not happy with the small selection of his own works to which he and the grand duchess had agreed—perhaps he was afraid of repeating his Vienna experience, where he had forgotten the music. Little by little, therefore, his orchestral works were added to the programs. At the first concert, on Thursday, 28 November, Beethoven's Sixth Symphony was presented, and the second, on 7 December, featured the *Symphonie fantastique* and excerpts from *Iphigénie en Tauride*. As he had hoped, the experience of conducting his favorite composers proved a great tonic. In fact, this substantial dose of the Beethoven symphonies, one on the heels of the next, occasioned a valedictory outburst to Félix Marmion: "I have so profoundly adored this poor hero, who was somehow able to create such a thunderous musical poetry."[28] He introduced the Russians to the *Scène du Temple* from Gluck's *Alceste* and conducted the *Fantastique* for the first time since the 1855 Weimar concert.

He was approached early on by the Russian Grand Opera for a full score of *Les Troyens,* and he wrote forthwith to Choudens in Paris to try to secure it. Choudens had made no progress, of course, on the engraved full score; instead the opera company was granted the privilege of copying it, for which they offered Berlioz an honorarium of 500 francs.

The Russians treated him regally. For his birthday on 11 December, they threw a party for 150 noteworthy guests. The grand duchess sent him a magnificent photograph album, graced at the front with her own portrait. His state of health precluded much socializing, but according to the critic Vladimir Stasov, he read the grand duchess long excerpts from Virgil and Byron and Shakespeare in French, and one evening he shared a box with Balakirev and Stasov at *A Life for the Tsar.* He left after the first act—it was past his bedtime—commenting only on his joy at hearing understated orchestration in light of the modern excesses.

The third concert, on Saturday, 14 December, offered Beethoven's Fifth and act II of *Orphée,* with Wieniawski playing a concerto of his own and Berlioz's *Rêverie et Caprice.* The fourth, on 28 December, included Beethoven's *Eroica* Symphony, excerpts from *Alceste,* and the *Francs-Juges* overture.

Despite the excitement the concerts stirred up among the younger Russian composers, Berlioz did not cultivate their acquaintance, spending his time rather with Balakirev, who had engineered the visit and led the preliminary rehearsals. Berlioz apparently showed little interest in the new Russian music, and there is no evidence of his meeting Mussorgsky, Borodin, or Rimsky-Korsakov. (Stravinsky's description of Rimsky-Korsakov's encountering the master shivering by a hot-water pipe, wearing a *pince-nez*—"so you compose music, too," Berlioz supposedly said—is probably apocryphal, as is Stasov's remark that Berlioz "was in frequent contact with all the musicians of the new Russian school.")[29] Yet the younger Russians, including both Cui and Rimsky-Korsakov, agreed that Berlioz, otherwise so feeble, came to life at the concerts and was a valiant conductor. They particularly admired his simple, small gestures and austere style, both of these surely attributes of his frailty. (A few years before, a journalist had noted that "he is as thin as his baton, and no one ever knows which of the two is beating time.")[30] Cui, indeed, preferred Berlioz's conducting to the affected sentimentality of Wagner: "How well he understands Beethoven! What severity, what austerity of performance! What effects, with never a concession to tinsel-showiness or poor taste!"[31] Berlioz's very celebrity animated the Russians, now musically and philosophically prepared to understand what he had been about. Rimsky-Korsakov turned straight to writing a programmatic symphony (*Antar,* 1868) and from thence tried purposefully to be a worthy rival to Berlioz in matters regarding orchestration. The new Russians saw that "we were brothers-in-arms of Berlioz."[32]

Once again Berlioz went to Moscow. As opposed to the situation he found there in 1847, this time they were expecting him and had arranged concerts for him on 8 and 11 January. He gave *Le Carnaval romain,* the Offertoire from the Requiem, the *Fête chez Capulet,* and Beethoven's Fifth on the first concert; on the second were programmed *Le Roi Lear* and, with Ferdinand Laub as soloist, *Harold en Italie* and the Beethoven Violin Concerto. Both concerts were on a grand scale, with an orchestra of five hundred, a chorus of two hundred, and thousands in the audience.

His remaining concerts in St. Petersburg were on 18 January and 8 February. The fifth concert lacked any of his music: Wieniawski played a Paganini concerto and Dörffel, with whom Berlioz had worked in Brussels a quarter century before, appeared in the "Emperor" Concerto. His season drew to a close with excerpts from *Roméo et Juliette* and *La Damnation de Faust* and a full performance of *Harold en Italie* with Weichmann as soloist (Wieniawski having left St. Petersburg). This was the last concert he ever conducted.

At some point in St. Petersburg he posed for the wonderful portrait that shows him standing, with raised baton (fig. 14.7). He looks pale and old and ill; there is defeat in his eyes. His hair is as white as if it had been

FIGURE 14.7
Berlioz as conductor,
St. Petersburg, 1867.

bleached; his features are deep set. But the overall effect is one of great dignity, and one can begin to sense, from even this fading souvenir, something of his aura on the podium in the 1840s and 1850s. Much the same can be said of what is probably his last photograph, taken by Reutlinger sometime in 1867 or 1868 (fig. 14.8).

*O*n 15 February 1868 Berlioz left St. Petersburg by train. He dined a day later in Berlin and arrived in Paris on the 17th, exhausted from the three days of virtually uninterrupted rail travel. There he discovered his niece Josephine and her new husband, who deserved to be attended to and taken out to dinner. It took him several days to finish a round of enthusiastic letters on his trip and take account of his finances. He returned with 34,449 francs; while he was gone he had earned 6,260 francs on his properties.[33]

It had been a rigorous trip, the cold taking its toll on his health. For several weeks he had been looking forward to the warmth and tranquility of Nice, where he could collect himself, rest, smell the violets, and greet the sea. He paused in Paris only long enough to attend to his affairs, then went by train to the southern coast. He went directly to Nice and registered at the Hôtel des Etrangers, overlooking the Mediterranean.

The vacation began uneventfully, fulfilling his visions of Elysian rest. Later that week he went to Monaco, a journey of four hours by omnibus, where he endeavored to work his way down through the rocks from the road to the sea. During the descent he lost his footing, almost surely as a consequence of the first of a pair of mild strokes, and fell forward down the cliff, opening a large cut on his face. Two railway workers saw him and helped him back to the Hôtel de Paris, where he stayed the night. The next day he took the tiring ride back to Nice. In the afternoon he went walking on the terraces to find a better view of the sea and lost consciousness again, falling on his face a second time. Some young men carried him to his hotel, where he stayed—possibly near death—for eight days. Obstinately refusing the attention of the local physicians, he had himself delivered to the train to Paris, where he arrived in the third week of March. Both his mother-in-law and the manservant now engaged to look after him, one Pierre-Guillaume Schumann, were shocked by the apparition at their door.

Finally he saw his own doctor, who ordered complete bed rest. This advice he was happy enough to take, as his face was in any case not presentable to the public. In his waking hours he wrote a few letters, including a long description of his accident to Dörffel and preliminary suggestions for the Breitkopf Gluck edition. His inability to hold a pen, of which he complained, must have been the result of partial paralysis. Dr. Nélaton asked him: "Are you a philosopher?" "Yes," replied Berlioz. "Well, take courage in philosophy, because you will never get entirely well."[34]

FIGURE 14.8 Berlioz c. 1868, his last portrait.

He convalesced through the spring and summer. By August, overconfident, he felt up to a journey to Grenoble to judge a festival of the local choral society. He arrived on 13 August for the performances scheduled from the 15th to the 18th. He required support from friends on either side to reach the formal banquet on 16 August—this had evolved into a homecoming and testimonial dinner honoring the region's favorite son. They put wreaths of laurel on his head and listened as he tried to deliver his toast. But he could not summon his power of speech and had to be escorted from the room. Bazin read his speech; his brother-in-law Pal took him home to his hotel during a driving rainstorm.

The result of this episode is that Berlioz resolved never again to leave Paris, but rather to live the life of a hermit, venturing out only to meetings of the Institute or for an occasional evening with his friends. He amused himself by feeding the birds outside his window, or by walking in the parc Monceau and in the cemetery where his wives rested and where he, too, soon would rest.

There were nevertheless occasions when his former enthusiasm and lucidity returned. He enjoyed offering his friends pâté from Strasbourg and *vol-au-vent,* and took great pleasure in showing off souvenirs from his princely

German-speaking patrons. One evening, after d'Ortigue and Kreutzer were gone, Heller was with him as he lay on his sofa complaining of his ills. Suddenly he leapt up, kissed Heller on both cheeks, and invited him to the Restaurant Bignon for supper. They would eat a dozen oysters, several slices of *foie gras,* and drink the best wine available. Damcke was not invited: he should be left at home with his "charming wife," for it was after 11:00 P.M.

Arm in arm they went, down the rue Blanche to the Chaussée d'Antin, and reached the restaurant at 11:30. They ordered the promised victuals as well as a cold fowl, salad, fruit, champagne, and Bordeaux. They dined until the waiters extinguished the gas lights, then lingered by candlelight until 2:00 A.M., drinking coffee and smoking cigars, talking of Shakespeare, Byron, and the rest. Then Berlioz stood up suddenly to go home, delighted at the notion of disturbing his mother-in-law.

On 25 November Berlioz ventured to the Left Bank for perhaps the last time in order to vote for Charles Blanc's candidacy at the Institute. Blanc was an art critic; a former director of Fine Arts, he had aided Berlioz materially in 1848 by preserving his sinecure at the Conservatoire. When Blanc had paid the customary (and in this case unnecessary) call on Berlioz to ask for his support, Berlioz had told him, "My days are numbered—my doctor told me so—he's even told me how long. But the election is on 25

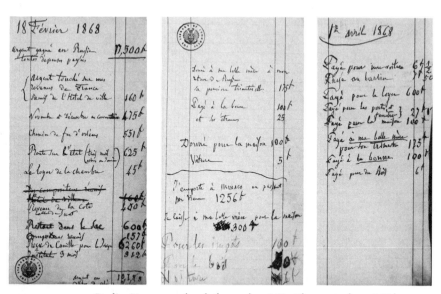

FIGURE 14.9 Berlioz's account book for early 1868. The entry for 18 February shows 17,500 francs profit from Russia and his other income. The next two pages record pensions paid his mother-in-law and the maid's wages, the monies he took to Monaco, taxes, and on 1 April the expense of a haircut.

November, and I have at least that long."[35] The servant Schumann offered him bodily support as he went to cast his ballot.

The strokes had taken their toll. His speech was slurred and often unintelligible; his manservant had to feed him. One evening Ernest Reyer asked him to autograph a copy of *Cellini,* but Berlioz could not: "I've forgotten your name," he sobbed.[36] Blaze de Bury described him as a ghost-like apparition: "Even his eyes, those great, vital eyes, had lost their spark."[37] The medicine succeeded only in stupefying him. A musical idea came to him from time to time, but he could not write it down. He wrote his last letter on 3 January 1869: there is nothing more in his own hand. The documentation from late 1868 until the end is thus largely from eyewitnesses, careful to record their observations of the man they all knew to be dying.

Berlioz's mantle as music critic at the *Débats* had already fallen on Ernest Reyer; soon he would become in turn librarian of the Conservatoire and successor, after Félicien David, to Berlioz's chair at the Institute. He took care, after Berlioz's death, to secure the servant Schumann a position as porter with the city government, and Schumann returned the favor on the day after Reyer was elected to the Institute in 1876, bringing him Berlioz's ceremonial uniform, bonnet, and sword for the inauguration.

In December, January, and February Berlioz withered away. His look became vacant; his capacity for speech vanished, but for rare outbursts. In March he passed into a restless state bordering on a coma, though he was still able to smile at his intimates. The ladies—Mme Damcke, Mme Charton-Demeur, and Mme Delaroche of St.-Germain (who had been there for Marie's death)—stood vigil at the deathbed, organized into shifts by Mme Martin. The men assembled when they could, and it appears that Reyer, Damcke, and Alexandre were there for the final hours. There was also a foreigner present, possibly Schumann, who scribbled an account in garbled French beneath a photograph of the master.[38] Berlioz babbled deliriously about *Roméo et Juliette* and *Béatrice et Bénédict* and once cried "O mère Recio, consummatum est!" On 8 March it was obvious that he had only moments left. Reyer finally sent for Dr. Nélaton, who would have to certify the death: "Please come at once to Berlioz's house—4 rue de Calais; he is dying."[39] At half past noon, he slipped away.

*M*me Martin contacted the undertakers and arranged for the funeral. Lithographed death notices of but medium quality were sent to his friends and associates (fig. 14-10). Reyer stayed with the body as Damcke went about collecting Berlioz's guitar—the Vuillaume instrument, once lent to Paganini and signed by them both—the batons, and the other valuables and took them to the Conservatoire for safekeeping from souvenir hunters.

The services on Thursday 11 March, though understated, were proper for a man of distinction and a member of the Institute and officer of the Legion

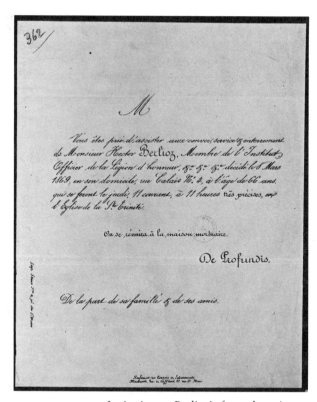

FIGURE 14.10 Invitation to Berlioz's funeral services.

of Honor. After appropriate blessings were administered in the mortuary, his coffin was brought into the street, where it was greeted with the *Symphonie funèbre*, played by a National Guard band led by Sax. His golden crowns lay atop the bier, as did the decorations he so treasured: the White Falcon and Red Eagle and the orders and crosses of the other German princes. Uniformed members of the Institute followed the casket to the Eglise de la Trinité for the funeral at 11:00 A.M. The view from the church was down the Chaussée d'Antin, toward the boulevards and the quarters where he had spent so much of his life.

Among the canopy bearers were Ambroise Thomas as director of the Conservatoire; Auber, Gounod, Reyer; the lawyer Nogent-St.-Laurent; Camille Doucet; the sculptor Guillaume as president of the Académie des Beaux-Arts of the Institute; Emile Perrin for the Opéra; and Baron Taylor, who had performed similar duties for Harriet and Marie. The just-finished Trinité, Haussmann and Ballu's "cathedral of the Second Empire," with its covered carriage entrance and wooden floors and ceilings, was architecturally fitting for a paragon of the century. Waiting in the church were an orchestra of his colleagues from the Société des Concerts and elsewhere, the choirs of the Trinité, and a double octet from the Opéra, conducted by George-Hainl; Pasdeloup's orchestra; and the *fanfare Sax,* under the direction of the faithful Litolff, of piston cornets and tubas. The chosen repertoire included the march from *Alceste,* the second movement of Beethoven's Seventh, the Hostias from the Requiem, and excerpts from the Requiems of Cherubini and Mozart. The organist Chauvet had intended to offer what would have been the most appropriate selection, the septet from *Les Troyens* ("All is at peace around us"), before the Office for the Dead, but a cue was somehow missed and the organ playing was interrupted by the Sax instruments playing Litolff's funeral march for Meyerbeer. The organ postlude was the *Marche des pèlerins* from *Harold.*

The cortège then proceeded to the Montmartre cemetery and assembled around the family plot Alexandre had given Berlioz. (Later the executors and the architect Duc would see to a monument; in a year's time there would be an important festival concert at the Opéra as well.) Guillaume spoke for the Institute, Frédéric Thomas for the Society of Men of Letters, Gounod for the Society of Authors and Composers, and Elwart for the Conservatoire. The orations were formulaic and pale. ("If you must make a speech," Berlioz had said to Elwart, "I'd rather not die.") Bizet was annoyed that Elwart called Berlioz, on behalf of the Conservatoire, "our colleague," and he was not the only one to cry uncontrollably over the open coffin before the day-long ceremonies reached their altogether grey conclusion.[40]

I have not been able to discover how long Mme Martin survived him. Two of the nieces bore children whose heirs prosper today, although the name Berlioz had long since disappeared from the direct lineage. A century later Berlioz, along with Harriet and Marie, was moved to a handsome site near the entrance to the cimetière Montmartre, and the path there was renamed the Avenue Hector Berlioz.

Abbreviations · Appendixes · Bibliography
Notes · List of Illustrations · Indexes

Abbreviations Used in Appendixes, Bibliography, and Notes

LIBRARY SIGLA

A-Wgn Vienna: Gesellschaft der Musikfreunde in Wien.

B-Bc Brussels: Conservatoire Royale de Musique, Bibliothèque.

CH-Bkoch Basel: private collection of Louis Koch (property of the family).

CH-G Geneva: Bibliothèque du Conservatoire de Musique.

D-Bds Berlin: Deutsche Staatsbibliothek.

F-CSA La Côte-St.-André: Musée Hector Berlioz.

F-G Grenoble: Bibliothèque Municipale.

F-Pan Paris: Archives Nationales.

F-Pc Paris: Bibliothèque du Conservatoire (Bibliothèque Nationale, Département de la Musique).

F-Pn Paris: Bibliothèque Nationale.

F-Po Paris: Bibliothèque de l'Opéra.

F-Psoc Paris: Library of the Société des Concerts (Orchestre de Paris).

GB-En Edinburgh: National Library of Scotland (Cecil Hopkinson Berlioz Collection).

GB-WImacnutt Withyham (Sussex): private collection of Richard Macnutt.

H-Bn Budapest: Országos Széchényi Könyvtár (National Széchényi Library).

I-Nc Naples: Biblioteca del Conservatorio.

J-Tmc Tokyo: Musashino College of Music Library.

S-Smf Stockholm: Stiftelsen Musikkulturens Främjande.

US-NYcu New York: Columbia University Library.

US-NYkallir New York: private collection of R. F. Kallir.

US-NYpm New York: The Pierpont Morgan Library.

US-Pwannemacher Philadelphia: private collection of Edward H. Wannemacher.

US-STu Stanford: Stanford University Library.

USSR-Lsc Leningrad: M. E. Saltykov-Shchedrin State Public Library.

BOOKS AND ARTICLES

ATC Berlioz, *A Travers Chants* (Paris, 1862). Page references are to edn. of Léon Guichard (Paris: Gründ, 1971).

Barzun Jacques Barzun, *Berlioz and the Romantic Century,* 2 vols. (3rd edn., New York, 1969).

Berlioziana Julien Tiersot, *Berlioziana*, serialized in *Le Ménestrel*, vols. 70–72 (1904–6) and 75–77 (1909–11). A complete index to the work is found in Holoman, *Autographs*, pp. 365–67.

Boschot Adolphe Boschot, *L'Histoire d'un romantique*. Vol. 1, *La Jeunesse d'un romantique: Hector Berlioz, 1803–1831* (Paris, 1906); vol. 2, *Un Romantique sous Louis-Philippe: Hector Berlioz, 1831–1842* (Paris, 1908); vol. 3, *Le Crépuscule d'un romantique: Hector Berlioz, 1842–1869* (Paris, 1913). Citations refer to this first edition; subsequent editions were abbreviated and repaginated.

Cairns *The Memoirs of Hector Berlioz*, trans. and ed. David Cairns (Norton paperback edn., revised, corrected, and enlarged; 3rd edn; New York, 1969).

CG *Correspondance générale*, gen. ed. Pierre Citron, to be 7 vols. (Paris, 1975–).

CI *Correspondance inédite de Hector Berlioz, 1819–1868*, ed. Daniel Bernard (Paris, 1879).

Condé *Hector Berlioz: Cauchemars et passions*, ed. Gérard Condé (Paris, 1981).

Cone:SF *Hector Berlioz: Fantastic Symphony; An Authoritative Score, Historical Background, Analysis, Views and Comments*, Norton Critical Score (New York, 1971).

Dwight's *Dwight's Journal of Music and Musicians*.

Est. *Une Page d'amour romantique: Lettres inédites à Madame Estelle F.* (Paris, 1903).

Ganz A. W. Ganz, *Berlioz in London* (London, 1950; rpt. edn., New York, 1981).

GM *Gazette musicale*.

Grotesques Berlioz, *Les Grotesques de la musique* (Paris, 1859). Page references are to edn. of Léon Guichard (Paris: Gründ, 1969).

Hallé *Life and Letters of Charles Hallé*, ed. C. E. and Marie Hallé (London, 1896).

Hiller Ferdinand Hiller, *Kunstlerleben* (Cologne, 1880).

Holoman, *Autographs* D. Kern Holoman, *The Creative Process in the Autograph Musical Documents of Hector Berlioz, c. 1818–1840* (2nd edn., rev. and corr.; Ann Arbor, 1980).

Holoman, *Catalogue* D. Kern Holoman, *Catalogue of the Works of Hector Berlioz*, New Berlioz Edition, vol. 25 (Kassel, 1987).

Holoman, "Sketchbook" D. Kern Holoman, "The Berlioz Sketchbook Recovered," *19th-Century Music* 7 (1984), 282–317, with a *separatum* facsimile.

JD *Journal des Débats*.

Legouvé Ernest Legouvé, *Soixante Ans de souvenirs*, 2 vols. (Paris, 1886). For convenience I cite page references to the more readily accessible English translation: *Sixty Years of Recollections*, trans. Albert D. Vandam, 2 vols. (London and Sydney, 1893).

LEF *Lettres de musiciens écrites en français du XVe au XXe siècle*, ed. Julien Tiersot (Turin, 1924), II, 154–218. For convenience I cite page references to the more readily accessible edition serialized in the *Rivista musicale italiana;* the Berlioz chapter appears in vols. 36 (1929), pp. 1–25, 408–29 and 37 (1930), pp. 1–20.

LI *Hector Berlioz: Lettres intimes* [to Humbert Ferrand] (Paris, 1882).

Locke Ralph P. Locke, *Music, Musicians, and the Saint-Simonians* (Chicago, 1986).

Macdonald Hugh Macdonald, *Berlioz* (London, 1982).

Malherbe and Weingartner *Hector Berlioz: Werke*, ed. Charles Malherbe and Felix Weingartner, 20 vols. (Leipzig, 1900–7). An index to the series is found in Holoman, *Autographs*, pp. 359–61.

Mémoires *Mémoires de Hector Berlioz, . . .* (Paris, 1870). Unless otherwise noted, all translations are from Cairns.

MM *Hector Berlioz: Les Musiciens et la musique*, intro. by André Hallays (Paris, [1903]; rpt. edn., Westmead, Farnborough, Hants.: Gregg Press, 1969).

NBE *Hector Berlioz: New Edition of the Complete Works,* gen. ed. Hugh Macdonald, 25 vols. planned (Kassel: Bärenreiter-Verlag, 1967–).

The New Grove *The New Grove Dictionary of Music and Musicians,* 6th edn. ed. Stanley Sadie (London, 1980).

NL *New Letters of Berlioz, 1830–1868,* trans. and ed. Jacques Barzun (2nd edn.; Westport, Conn., 1974).

Raby Peter Raby, *"Fair Ophelia": A Life of Harriet Smithson Berlioz* (Cambridge, 1982).

R&GM *Revue et Gazette musicale.*

Roger Gustave Roger, *Le Carnet d'un ténor* (Paris, 1880).

Sauzay "La Vie musicale à Paris à travers les *Mémoires* d'Eugène Sauzay (1809–1901)," ed. Brigitte François-Sappey, *Revue de musicologie* 60 (1974), 159–210.

Soirées Berlioz, *Les Soirées de l'orchestre* (Paris, 1852). Citations include the relevant evening (*Soirées,* XIII = the thirteenth evening); page references are to edn. of Léon Guichard (Paris: Gründ, 1968). Unless otherwise noted, all translations are from *Evenings with the Orchestra,* ed. and trans. Jacques Barzun (New York, 1956; rpt. edn., Chicago, 1973).

SW *Briefe von Hector Berlioz an die Fürstin Carolyne Sayn-Wittgenstein,* ed. La Mara (Leipzig, 1903).

Traité Berlioz, *Grand Traité d'instrumentation et d'orchestration modernes* (Paris, [1843]); references are to revised Lemoine rpt. edn. of c. 1860 (Westmead, Farnborough, Hants.: Gregg Press, 1970).

V&A *Berlioz and the Romantic Imagination,* catalogue of the exhibition at the Victoria and Albert Museum (London, 1969).

VM Berlioz, *Voyage musical en Allemagne et en Italie; Etudes sur Beethoven, Gluck et Weber; Mélanges et nouvelles* (Paris, 1844; rpt. edn., Westmead, Farnborough, Hants.: Gregg Press, 1970). Vol. 1 composed of "Voyage musical en Allemagne" and "Etude analytique des symphonies de Beethoven"; vol. 2 composed of "Voyage musical en Italie" and "Astronomie musicale."

Appendix A

Compositions

This appendix lists Berlioz's compositions in chronological order. Entries include date of composition, author of text, and primary source. Numbers in the left column refer to entries in Holoman, *Catalogue;* numbers in lightface indicate subsequent versions of a particular work. In text of entry, numbers in boldface are cross-references to other entries. Following the library siglum, where appropriate, is the shelfmark of the document cited. (**F-Pn** Rés. Vm^2 177, for example, indicates a source in the reserve section of the Bibliothèque Nationale, Paris.) Dates in square brackets indicate deductions of the author or other Berlioz scholars.

1   *Potpourri concertant sur des thèmes italiens,* for flute, horn, two violins, viola, and bass (1817–18). Lost.

2–3   Two quintets for flute and string quartet (late 1818–early 1819). Lost.

4   *Romances* for voice and piano (late 1818–early 1819). Lost.

5   Guitar accompaniment to *Fleuve du Tage* (c. 1819). Text by J. H. Demeun. Manuscript: **F-CSA**.

6   *Je vais donc quitter pour jamais* (c. 1819). Text by Florian. Lost.

7   *Le Dépit de la bergère* (c. 1819). Text anonymous. Source: published edition (Paris, [c. 1819]).

8   Manuscript anthology of thirty-five songs with guitar accompaniments by Berlioz: *Recueil de romances* (c. 1819–22). Various composers, various texts. Autograph: **F-CSA**.

9A   *L'Arabe jaloux,* version I (autograph), for voice and piano (c. 1819–21). Text by Florian. Autograph: **F-CSA**.

10A   *Invocation à l'amitié,* version I (autograph), for three voices and piano (c. 1819–21). Text by Florian. Autograph: **F-CSA**.

11   *Pleure, pauvre Colette* (March 1822). Text by Bourgerie. Source: published edition (Paris, [1822]).

9B   *Le Maure jaloux,* version II, published for voice and piano (before April 1822). Source: published edition (Paris, [1822]).

12   *Le Cheval arabe* (autumn 1822). Text by Millevoye. Lost.

13   *Canon à trois voix* (autumn 1822). Lost.

14   *Canon libre à la quinte* (before December 1822). Text by Bourgerie. Source: published edition (Paris, [1822]).

15   *Le Montagnard exilé* (before February 1823). Text by du Boys. Source: published edition (Paris, [1823]).

16   *Toi qui l'aimas, verse des pleurs* (before February 1823). Text by du Boys. Source: published edition (Paris, [1823]).

10B *Amitié, reprends ton empire,* version II (before February 1823). Source: published edition (Paris, [1823]).

17 *Estelle et Némorin* (mid 1823). Text by Gerono. Lost.

18 *Le Passage de la mer rouge* (winter 1823–24). Biblical text. Lost.

19 *Beverley, ou Le Joueur* (late 1823–early 1824). Text by Saurin. Lost.

20A *Messe solennelle* (spring–December 1824). Traditional text. Lost, for the most part.

21A *Scène héroïque (La Révolution grecque),* version I, for soloists, chorus, and orchestra (winter 1825–26). Text by Ferrand. Manuscript: **F-Pc** D 944.

22 Fugue (July 1826). Autograph: **F-Pn** W 33 (10).

23A *Les Francs-Juges* (May–October 1826). Text by Ferrand. Fragmentary autograph: **F-Pn** Rés. Vm² 177.

23D *Grande Ouverture des Francs-Juges* (September–October 1826). Source: published parts (1833) and score (1836).

24 Fugue (July 1827). Lost.

25 *La Mort d'Orphée* (July 1827). Text by Berton. Manuscript: **F-Pn** Rés. Vma ms 1.

26 *Grande Ouverture de Waverley* (c. October 1826–February 1828). Autograph: **F-Pc** ms 1507.

27 *Marche religieuse des mages* (before May 1828). Text anonymous. Lost.

20B *Resurrexit,* version II, revised (May 1828). Manuscript scores: **F-G** Rés. 90665, **F-Pc** ms 1510.

23B *Mélodie pastorale,* version II, for three soloists, chorus, piano (May 1828). Text by Ferrand. Autograph: **F-Pn** Rés. Vm² 177, item 1.

28 Fugue (July 1828). Lost.

29 *Herminie* (July 1829). Text by Vieillard. Autograph: **F-Pc** ms 1185.

30 Variations on *Là-ci darem la mano* (c. 1828). Lost.

31 *Nocturne à deux voix* (c. 1828). Text anonymous. Lost.

32 *Salutaris* (winter 1828–29). Lost.

33 *Huit Scènes de Faust* (September 1828–January 1829). Text by Goethe, as translated by Gerard de Nerval. Source: published edition (Paris, [1829]).

33A *Le Roi de Thulé,* version for piano and voice (September 1828). Autograph: **US-NYpm.**

34 *Chanson des pirates* (early 1829). Text by Hugo. Lost.

35 *Fugue à trois sujets* (July 1829). Autograph: **F-Pc** ms 1506.

36 *Cléopâtre* (July 1829). Text by Vieillard. Autograph: **F-Pc** ms 1505.

37 *Le Ballet des ombres* (April–December 1829). Text by du Boys after Herder. Source: published edition (Paris, [1829]).

38 *Neuf Mélodies irlandaises* (May–December 1829). Texts by Thomas Moore, translated by Thomas Gounet (no. 9 translated by Louise Sw. Belloc). Source: published edition (Paris, [1830]).

39 *Le Coucher du soleil: Rêverie* (May–December 1829).

40A *Hélène: Ballade à deux voix,* version I, for two voices and piano (May–December 1829).

41 *Chant guerrier* (May–December 1829).

42A *La Belle Voyageuse: Ballade,* version I, for voice and piano (May–December 1829).

43 *Chanson à boire* (May–December 1829).

44A *Chant sacré,* version I, for tenor or soprano solo, chorus, and piano (May–December 1829).

45 *L'Origine de la harpe: Ballade* (May–December 1829).

46A *Adieu, Bessy: Romance anglaise et française,* version I, in A♭ (May–December 1829).

47 *Elégie en prose* (c. December 1829).

48 *Episode de la vie d'un artiste: Symphonie fantastique en cinq parties* (January–April 1830). Autograph: **F-Pc** ms 1188.

49 *Fugue* (July 1830). Lost.

50 *Sardanapale* (July 1830). Text by Gail. Fragmentary autograph: **F-Pn** Rés. Vm² 178 (with fragments of *La Nonne sanglante*).

51A *Hymne des Marseillais*, arrangement of the patriotic song with text and music by Rouget de Lisle, version I, for chorus and large orchestra (July–August 1830). Source: published edition (Paris, [1830]).

51bis *Chant du neuf Thermidor*, arrangement of the patriotic song with text and music by Rouget de Lisle (c. late 1830). Autograph: **CH-G** R 268.

52 *Grande Fantaisie dramatique sur La Tempête, drame de Shakespeare* (August–October 1830). Text possibly by Berlioz. Autograph: **F-Pc** ms 1192.

53 *Grande Ouverture du roi Lear* (April–May 1831). Autograph: **US-NYpm** Koch Foundation Deposit 250.

54 *Intrata di Rob-Roy MacGregor* (May–July 1831). Manuscript: **F-Pc** ms 1512.

55A *Le Retour à la vie*, version I, later revised and called *Lélio* (May–July 1831). Text by Berlioz. Autograph: **F-Pc** ms 1511.

56A *Méditation religieuse*, version I, for chorus and wind instruments (August 1831). Text by Thomas Moore, translated by Louise Sw. Belloc. Lost.

57 *Chœur* (late September 1831). Text by Berlioz. Lost.

58 *Chœur d'anges* (late 1831). Text anonymous. Lost.

59 *Quartetto e Coro dei Maggi* (early 1832). Text anonymous. Manuscript: F-Pc ms 1512*bis*.

60A *La Captive*, version I, for voice and piano (February 1832). Text by Hugo. Autographs: **F-Pc** ms 1173, **US-NYcu**, **US-NYkallir**.

61 *Le Dernier Jour du monde* (April 1831–August 1832). Scenario by Berlioz; text to have been by Ferrand. Music, if any, lost.

60B *La Captive*, version II, a revision for voice and piano (c. 1832). Autograph: **F-G** Rés. R 10759.

60C *La Captive*, version III, first published version, with cello obbligato (c. December 1832). Source: published edition (Paris, [1833]).

62 Sketchbook of c. 1832–36, with sketches for *Dans l'alcôve sombre* (text by Hugo) and *Le Retour de l'armée d'Italie*. Autograph: **F-CSA**.

63 *La Chasse de Lützow*, arranged from Weber (before June 1833). Text by Körner, translated (possibly) by Ferrand. Lost.

21B *Scène héroïque*, version II, for chorus and military band (July 1833). Manuscript parts: **F-Pc** L 17239.

64 *Sur les Alpes, quel délice!*, arrangement of a traditional Alpine melody (before June 1833). Text anonymous. Autograph vocal score and part: **F-Pc** ms 1188 (in the autograph of the *Symphonie fantastique*).

65A *Le Paysan breton*, version I, for voice and piano (before December 1833). Text by Brizeux. Autographs: **F-Pc** ms 1175, **GB-En** H. B. 5/4.

23C *Le Cri de guerre du Brisgaw*, intermezzo drawn from *Les Francs-Juges* and including *Le Paysan breton* (November 1833–January 1834). Autograph libretto: **F-Pn** Rés. Vm² 177, item 2.

66 *Romance de Marie Tudor* (December 1833). Text by Hugo. Lost.

67A *Les Champs*, version I (April 1834). Text by Béranger. Source: published edition (Paris, 1834).

68 *Harold en Italie* (January–c. June/July 1834). Autograph: **F-Pc** ms 1189.

69A *Sara la baigneuse*, version I, for male quartet and orchestra (summer 1834). Text by Hugo. Lost.

70 *Je crois en vous* (before September 1834). Text by Guérin. Source: published edition (Paris, 1834).

60D *La Captive*, version IV, for soprano and orchestra (November 1834). Lost.

65B *Le Jeune Pâtre breton*, version II, for soprano and orchestra (November 1834). Lost.

65C *Le Jeune Pâtre breton*, version III, for voice, piano, and horn *ad libitum* (late 1834). Source: published edition (Paris, [1835]).

42B *La Belle Voyageuse*, version II, for male quartet and orchestra (November 1834). Lost.

71A *Le Chant des bretons*, version I, for tenor solo or male chorus and piano (early 1835). Text by Brizeux. Source: published edition (Paris, [1835]).

72 *Fête musicale funèbre* (summer 1835), incomplete. Lost.

73 *Chansonette de M. Léon de Wailly* (c. 1831–November 1835). Text by de Wailly. Autographs: **S-Smf** collection Rudolf Nydahl, sketchbook at **F-CSA**.

74 *Le Cinq Mai* (c. 1831–November 1835). Text by Béranger. Sources: manuscript parts, **F-Pc** D 17532–33; published edition (Paris, [1844]).

65D *Le Jeune Pâtre breton*, version IV, for voice and orchestra (November 1835). Sources: manuscript parts, **F-Pn** Vma ms 866; published edition (Paris, [c. 1839]).

75 *Grande Messe des morts* (Requiem) (late March–June 1837). Traditional text. Autograph: **F-Pc** ms 1509.

76A *Benvenuto Cellini* (May 1834–September 1838, revised 1852–56). Text by de Wailly and Barbier, assisted by Vigny. Autograph: **F-Pc** ms 1508.

76B *Grande Ouverture de Benvenuto Cellini* (February 1838). Source: published edition (Paris, [1839]).

69B *Sara la baigneuse*, version II, for vocal quartet, chorus, and orchestra (before March 1838). Lost.

77 *Erigone* (c. 1835–39), incomplete. Text after Ballanche. Sources: manuscript libretto and fragmentary autograph score, **F-Pc** ms 1186 (a, b).

78A *Aubade*, version I, for voice and two horns (May 1839). Text by Musset. Autograph: **GB-WImacnutt**.

78B *Aubade*, version II, for voice, four horns, and two cornets *à pistons*, is undatable and may be from the 1850s. Autograph: **F-CSA**.

79 *Roméo et Juliette* (January–September 1839). Text by Emile Deschamps. Autograph: **F-Pc** ms 1165.

80A *Symphonie funèbre et triomphale*, version I, for military band (June–July 1840). No text. Manuscript score (partly autograph): **F-Pc** ms 1164.

81A *Les Nuits d'été*, version I, for voice and piano (1840–September 1841). Texts by Gautier. For autographs see individual songs below.

82A *Villanelle*. Autograph: **F-Pc** ms 1179.

83A *Le Spectre de la rose*. Autograph: **F-Pc** ms 1181.

84A *Sur les Lagunes. Lamento*. Autograph lost.

85A *Absence*. Autograph: **F-Pc** ms 1180.

86A *Au Cimetière. Clair de lune*. Autograph: **F-Pc** ms 1183.

87A *L'Ile inconnue*. Autograph: **F-Pc** ms 1182.

88 *Rêverie et Caprice* (March 1841). Source: published edition (Paris, [1841]).

89 Recitatives for Weber's *Le Freyschutz* (March–June 1841). Libretto translated by E. Pacini. Autograph: **I-Nc** Rari 4.5.10.

90 Orchestration of Weber's *L'Invitation à la valse* for the *ballet-divertissement* in *Le Freyschutz* (May 1841). Autograph: **F-Pn** Rés. Vm^7 664.

91 *La Nonne sanglante*, opera to a libretto by Scribe, after M. G. Lewis (begun 1841, abandoned after 1847), incomplete. Fragmentary autograph score: **F-Pn** Rés. Vm^2 178.

92A   *La Mort d'Ophélie*, version I, for voice and piano (May 1842). Text by Legouvé. Autograph: **A-Wgn** A 170.

80B   *Symphonie funèbre et triomphale*, version II, with strings and chorus *ad libitum* (February, September 1842). Text by Antoni Deschamps. Autograph: **F-Pc** ms 1164.

42C   *La Belle Voyageuse*, version III, for mezzo-soprano and orchestra (December 1842). Sources: manuscript parts, **F-Pc** D 16486; published edition (Paris, [c. 1844]).

93   Souvenir album of 1842–43 tour: *Souvenirs—Bêtises—Improvisations*. Autograph: **F-CSA**.

94   *La Belle Isabeau,* for voice and piano (late 1843). Text by Alexandre Dumas père. Autograph: **F-Pc** ms 1515.

85B   *Absence*, version II, for soprano and orchestra (February 1843). Autographs: **D-Bds** mus ms H. Berlioz 1, **F-Pn** Rés. Vma ms 496.

44B   *Chant sacré*, version II, for chorus and orchestra (November 1843). Sources: manuscript parts, **F-Pc** D 17821; published edition (Paris, [1844]).

95   *Le Carnaval romain* (June 1843–January 1844). Source: published edition (Paris, [1844]).

40B   *Hélène*, version II, for male quartet and orchestra (January 1844). Autograph: **F-Pc** ms 1172.

96   Albumleaf of sixteen bars (January 1844). Autograph: **F-Pc** ms 1169.

44C   *Chant sacré,* version III, for six wind instruments and orchestra (February 1844). Lost.

97   *Hymne à la France* (June–July 1844). Text by Barbier. Sources: fragmentary manuscript score, **F-Pc** ms 1517; manuscript parts, **F-Pc** D 16457; published score.

Three short pieces for Alexandre's *Orgue mélodium:*

98   *Sérénade agreste à la madone sur le thème des pifferari romains* (November 1844). Autograph: **F-Pc** ms 1166.

99   *Toccata* (November 1844). Autograph: **F-Pc** ms 1168.

100   *Hymne pour l'élévation* (November 1844). Autograph: **F-Pc** ms 1167.

101A   *La Tour de Nice*, first version of *Le Corsaire* (August–November 1844). Autograph: **F-Pc** ms 1159 and 1519 (another fascicle).

Pieces for a production of *Hamlet* (November 1844–1845):

102   *Scène de la comédie* (c. November 1844–1845). Lost.

103   *Marche funèbre pour la dernière scène d'Hamlet* (possibly c. November 1844–1845). Autograph: **F-Pc** ms 1187 (score of *Tristia*).

104A   *Le Chasseur danois*, version I, for voice and piano (before December 1844). Text by de Leuven. Source: published edition (Paris, 1844).

105   *Marche marocaine*, setting of a piano work by Léopold de Meyer (before April 1845). Sources: ms. parts, **F-Po** ♮ 3102; published edition (Vienna, [1846]).

106   *Le Vent gémit*, albumleaf (June 1845). Autograph: **J-Tmc** A-M-0103.

107A   *Zaïde*, version I for voice and piano (November 1845). Text by de Beauvoir. Autograph: **F-Pc** ms 1176.

107B   *Zaïde*, version II, orchestrated (November 1845). Autograph: **F-Pn** Rés. Vm^7 665.

104B   *Le Chasseur danois*, version II, orchestrated (November 1845). Autograph: **F-Pn** Rés. Vm^7 661.

108   *Marche d'Isly*, arrangement of a work by Léopold de Meyer (before December 1845). Lost.

109 *Marche de Rákóczy* (February 1846). Autograph: **H-Bn** ms mus 29.

110 *Chant des chemins de fer* (June 1846). Text by Janin. Autograph: **F-Pn** Rés. Vm^7 666.

111 *La Damnation de Faust* (November 1845–October 1846). Text by Berlioz, Gandonnière, and Nerval, after Goethe. Autograph: **F-Pc** ms 1190.

112 *Prière du matin* (before November 1846). Text by Lamartine. Source: published edition (Paris, 1848).

113 *Le Trébuchet* (before November 1846). Text by Antoine de Bertin and Emile Deschamps. Source: published edition (Paris, [1850]).

101B *Ouverture du Corsaire*, version II, revised and retitled (1846–51). Autograph: **F-Pc** ms 1159.

114 *Nessun maggior piacere*, albumleaf (November 1847). Text a parody of Dante. Autograph: **F-Pc** W 6, 11.

115 *Chant du départ* (March 1848). Arrangement; music by Méhul, text by M.-J. Chénier. Lost.

116 *Mourons pour la patrie* (March 1848). Arrangement; music and text by Rouget de Lisle. Lost.

80C *Apothéose* from *Symphonie funèbre*, version III, for voices and piano in E♭ (March 1848). Source: published edition (London, [1848]).

51B *La Marseillaise*, version II, for piano and voices (March 1848). Source: published edition (London, [1848]).

117 *Le Menace des francs* (before April 1848). Text anonymous. Sources: manuscript parts, **F-Pc** 17545; published edition (Paris, [1851]).

60E *La Captive*, version V, for contralto or mezzo-soprano and orchestra, in E major (before June 1848). Autograph parts: **F-Pc** ms 17667.

92B *La Mort d'Ophélie*, version II, for women's chorus and orchestra (July 1848). Autograph: **F-Pc** ms 1187 (*Tristia*).

60F *La Captive*, version VI, for contralto or mezzo-soprano and orchestra, in D major (before October 1848). Autograph: **F-Pc** ms 1189 (2).

118 Te Deum (October 1848–1849; revised 1852 and 1855). Traditional Latin text. Autograph: **USSR-Lsc**.

56B *Méditation religieuse*, version II, for chorus and orchestra (late 1848–1849).

119A *Tristia*, version I, for piano and voice (October 1849), collection of two works: *Méditation religieuse*, reduced for piano and voice (**56**), and *La Mort d'Ophélie* (**92A**).

120 *Vox Populi* (before November 1849), collection of two works for orchestra and chorus: *Le Menace des francs* (**117**) and *Hymne à la France* (**97**). Sources: published full and piano-vocal editions (Paris, [1851, 1850]).

46B *Adieu, Bessy*, version II, transposed to G. Source: published edition (Paris, [1849]).

121 *Feuillets d'album* (September 1850), collection of three works issued as *œuvre* 19 in piano-vocal score: *Zaïde* (**107**), *Les Champs* (**67B**), and *Chant des chemins de fer* (**110**). Source: published editions (Paris, [1850]).

67B *Les Champs*, version II, for tenor and piano (September 1850). Source: published edition (Paris, [1850]).

122 *Chant des cherubins* (before September 1850). Arrangement; music by Bortniansky, Latin text overlain by Berlioz. Source: published edition (Paris, [1851]).

123 *Pater noster* (before September 1850). Arrangement; music by Bortniansky, Latin text overlain by Berlioz. Source: published edition (Paris, [1851]).

69C *Sara la baigneuse*, version III, for three choruses and orchestra (October 1850). Sources: manuscript parts, **F-Pc** D 16468; vocal score, **F-Pn** Vma ms 872; published edition (Paris, [1851]).

124 *Fleurs des landes* (November 1850), publisher's collection of five *mélodies* issued as *œuvre* 13: *Le Matin* (125), *Petit Oiseau* (126), *Le Trébuchet* (113), *Le Jeune Pâtre breton* (65C), and *Le Chant des bretons* (71B).

71B *Le Chant des bretons*, version II (November 1850). Source: published edition (Paris, [1850]).

125 *Le Matin* (November 1850). Text by Bouclon. Source: published edition (Paris, [1850]).

126 *Petit Oiseau* (November 1850). Text by Bouclon. Source: published edition (Paris, [1850]).

42D *La Belle Voyageuse*, version IV, for female chorus and orchestra (March 1851). Sources: manuscript parts and published score with ms. revisions, **F-Pc** D 16486 (1–2).

119B *Tristia*, version II, for chorus and orchestra (1851), collection of three works, issued as *œuvre* 18: *Méditation religieuse* (56B), *La Mort d'Ophélie* (92B), and *Marche funèbre pour la dernière scène d'Hamlet* (103).

127 Albumleaf for Eduard Silas (March 1852). Autograph: Silas's album, in a private collection.

128 *La Fuite en Egypte* (begun October 1850; completed prior to 1852), incorporated whole into *L'Enfance du Christ* (130). Text by Berlioz. Autograph: **F-Pc** ms 1160.

129 *L'Impériale* (before July 1854). Text by Capitaine Lafont. Autograph: **F-Pc** ms 1191.

130 *L'Enfance du Christ* (October 1850–June, July 1854). Text by Berlioz. Autograph: **F-Pn** Rés. Vm¹ 241.

55B *Lélio*, version II of *Le Retour à la vie*, slightly revised and retitled (January 1855). Source: published edition (Paris, [1857]).

131 *Valse chantée par le vent dans les cheminées d'un de mes châteaux en Espagne*, albumleaf for Marie Sayn-Wittgenstein (February 1855). Autograph: **CH-Bkoch**.

81B *Les Nuits d'été*, version II, orchestrated (February 1843 for *Absence*, then late 1855–March 1856). For autographs see individual songs below.

83B *Le Spectre de la rose*, version II (late 1855–January 1856). Autograph: **F-CSA**.

82B *Villanelle*, version II (March 1856). Manuscript score: **GB-En** H. B. 5/7.

84B *Sur les Lagunes. Lamento*, version II (March 1856). Autograph: **F-CSA**.

86B *Au Cimetière. Clair de lune*, version II (March 1856). Autograph: **F-CSA**.

87B *L'Ile inconnue*, version II (March 1856). Autograph: **F-CSA**.

132 *Au bord d'une rivière*, sketch (1855–56). Autograph: **US-NYcu**.

133A *Les Troyens* (April 1856–1858). Text by Berlioz. Autographs: **F-Pc** mss 1161 (*La Prise de Troie*) and 1162 (*Les Troyens à Carthage*).

134 *Plaisir d'amour*, arrangement of Martini's popular song (June 1859). Text by Florian. Autograph: **F-Pc** ms 17687.

135 *Hymne pour la consecration du nouveau tabernacle* (before October 1859). Text anonymous. Source: published edition (Paris, [1859]).

136 *Le Roi des aulnes*, an orchestration of Schubert's *Erlkönig* (August 1860). Text by Goethe, translated by Bouscatel. Sources: manuscript parts, **F-Psoc**: published edition (Paris, [1860]).

137A *Le Temple universel*, version I, for two choruses and organ (before February 1861). Text by J.-F. Vaudin. Fragmentary autographs: **GB-En** H. B. 5/3, **US-STu** MLM 78, **US-NYpm** Koch 913.

138 *Béatrice et Bénédict* (c. August 1860–February 1862). Text by Berlioz after Shakespeare. Autograph: **F-Pc** ms 1513.

139 *Collection de 32 Mélodies,* publisher's collection of earlier works incorporating several revisions to previous editions (November 1863). Source: published edition (Paris, [1863]).

133B *Marche troyenne,* concert version (early 1864). Autograph score: **F-Pn** Rés. Vm² 174.

140 *Salut matinal,* an albumleaf for Mr Mendès (c. 1865 or possibly earlier), "improvised in Kanaque music and text." Autograph score: formerly **US-Pwannemacher.**

Compositions for Sain d'Arod's *Livre choral:*

141 *Veni Creator* (c. 1861–68). Traditional text. Source: published edition (Paris, [c. 1885]; posthumous.).

142 *Tantum ergo* (c. 1861–68). Traditional text. Source: published edition (Paris, [c. 1885]; posthumous.).

143 *Invitation à louer Dieu,* after Couperin (c. 1861–68). Text by Berlioz. Source: published edition (Paris, [c. 1885]; posthumous.).

137B *Le Temple universel,* version II, abbreviated, for unaccompanied male chorus (c. 1867–68). Source: published edition (Paris, [1868]).

Appendix B

Prose Writings

This appendix summarizes the most significant of Berlioz's thousand or so *feuilletons* and cites his books and contributions to such collaborative publications as jury reports. Within the entries, boldface citations beginning with **A** or **B** are to the relevant listing in Holoman, *Catalogue*.

12 August 1823. First contribution to a newspaper: "Polémique musicale" (letter to the editor), in *Le Corsaire.*

11 January 1824. Second "Polémique musicale" for *Le Corsaire.*

19 December 1825. Third "Polémique musicale" for *Le Corsaire.*

7 February 1829. First article for *Berliner allgemeine musikalische Zeitung:* "Auber's neuste Oper, 'La Fiancée' (Die Braut)" (continuing series throughout 1829).

21 April 1829. First article for *Le Correspondant:* "Considérations sur la musique religieuse."

4 August 1829. "Biographie étrangère: Beethoven" (*Le Correspondant;* also 11 August, 6 October).

15 March 1832. "Lettre d'un enthousiaste sur l'état de la musique en Italie" (*Revue européene*). Extracted and reprinted in the *Revue musicale* (31 March, 9 April); a major portion later included in *Voyage musical* and *Mémoires.*

23 December 1832. Joseph d'Ortigue's biography of Berlioz, prepared with the composer's assistance (*Revue de Paris*).

12 June 1833. "Concours annuel de composition musicale" (*L'Europe littéraire;* also 19 July).

16 March 1834. "*Don Juan,* musique de Mozart" (*Le Rénovateur;* also 23 March).

1 June 1834. "Gluck" (*GM;* also 8 June).

20 July 1834. "Le Suicide par enthousiasme: Nouvelle" (*GM;* also 27 July, 3, 10 August).

12 October 1834. "*Guillaume Tell* de Rossini" (*GM;* also 19, 26 October, 2 November).

9 November 1834. "*Iphigénie en Tauride*" (*GM;* also 16, 23 November, 7 December).

2 October 1835. "Du Système de Gluck en musique dramatique" (*JD*).

16 October 1835 "Des Deux Alcestes de Gluck" (*JD;* also 23 October).

1836. Essays on Italy, for *Italie pittoresque.*

6 March 1836. "*Les Huguenots*" (*R&GM;* also 13, 20 March).

10 November 1836. "*Les Huguenots:* La Partition" (*JD;* also 10 December).

1 January 1837. "De l'Imitation musicale" (*R&GM;* also 8 January).

1 October 1837. "Le Premier Opéra: Nouvelle" (*R&GM;* also 8 October).

15 October 1837. "Nécrologie: Jean-François Lesueur" (*R&GM;* also *JD,* 15 October).

28 January 1838. "Symphonies de Beethoven" (*R&GM;* also 4, 11, 18 February, 4 March).

11 March 1838. *"Guido et Ginévra, ou La Peste de Florence"* (*R&GM;* also 18 March, 1 April).

15 July 1838. "Biographies: Reicha" (*R&GM*).

29 July 1838 "Biographies: Spontini" (*R&GM*).

4 November 1838. "Vogel et ses opéras" (*R&GM;* also 10 November).

13 June 1841. "Premiere Représentation du *Freyschutz,* opéra en trois actes de Carl Maria de Weber" (*JD*).

21 November 1841. "De l'Instrumentation" (*R&GM;* also 21, 28 November, 5, 12, 19 December, 2, 9, 16, 23 January 1842, 6, 13 March, 24 April, 26 June, 3, 10, 17 July).

20 March 1842. Obituary of Cherubini (*JD*).

7 August 1842. "De Rameau et de quelques uns de ses ouvrages" (*R&GM;* also 14 August, 4, 13 September [*Castor et Pollux*]).

1843. *Grand Traité d'instrumentation et d'orchestration modernes* (Paris: Schonenberger; **A2**).

13 August 1843 "Voyage musical en Allemagne" (*R&GM;* also 20, 28 August, 3, 12, 23 September, 8, 21 October, 8 November, 9 January 1844).

18 February 1844. *"Euphonia, ou La Ville musicale:* Nouvelle" (*R&GM;* also 25 February, 3, 17, 24 March, 28 April, 2 June, 28 July).

15 December 1844. "Concert de M. Félicien David" [*Le Désert*] (*JD*).

1844. *Notice sur les orgues mélodium d'Alexandre et fils* (collaborative report **B1**).

1844. *Voyage musical en Allemagne et en Italie; Etudes sur Beethoven, Gluck et Weber; Mélanges et nouvelles,* 2 vols. (Paris: Jules Labitte; readied and serially published in *R&GM,* 1843).

16 April 1845. "Michel de Glinka" [*La Vie pour le czar; Russlane et Ludmila*] (*JD*).

22 August 1845. "Des Fêtes musicales de Bonn" (*JD;* also 3 September).

24 August 1847. "Voyage musical en Autriche, en Russie et en Prusse" (*JD;* also 5 September, 19 October; reprinted in *R&GM*).

23 July 1848. "Voyage musical en Bohème" (*R&GM;* also 30 July, 6, 20, 27 August).

10 September 1848. "Voyage musical en France" (*R&GM;* also 15 October, 19 November).

20 April 1849. "Première Représentation du *Prophète,* opéra en cinq actes, de MM. Scribe et Meyerbeer" (*JD*).

17 March 1850. "L'*Alceste* de Gluck" (*R&GM*).

c. 1850. *Statuts et règlement de la Société fondée en 1850* (collaborative report **B2**).

12 February 1851. "Spontini, sa vie, ses œuvres" (*JD*).

31 May 1851. "Au Rédacteur" (letters from London on the Crystal Palace Exhibition) (*JD;* also 20 June, 1, 29 July, 12 August).

1852. *Exhibition of the Works of Industry of All Nations* (collaborative report **B3**).

December 1852. *Les Soirées de l'orchestre* (Paris: Michel Lévy frères; **A3**).

6 February 1853. "Première Représentation de *Louise Miller,* opéra en quatre actes, musique de M. Verdi" (*JD*).

21 February 1854. "Première Représentation de *L'Etoile du Nord,* opéra en trois actes, de MM. Scribe et Meyerbeer" (*JD*).

6 September 1854. *Feuilleton de silence* (*JD*). No mention of the Opéra or of Mme Stoltz.

24 October 1854. "Première Représentation de *La Nonne sanglante*, opéra en cinq actes, de MM. Scribe et Germain Delavigne, musique de M. Gounod" (*JD*).

1854. *Rapport sur les instruments de musique . . . Exposition universelle de Londres* (Paris: Imperial printshop; collaborative report **B4**).

25 November 1855. "Voyage en Russie (1847)" (*Magasin des Demoiselles*; also 25 December, 25 January 1856, 25 March, 25 April).

Late 1855. *Grand Traité d'instrumentation et d'orchestration modernes*, 2nd edn., including *Le Chef d'orchestre: Théorie de son art* (Paris: Schonenberger).

1855. *Travaux de la Commission française; Exposition universelle de 1851* (Paris: Imperial printshop; collaborative report **B5**).

9 January 1856. "Les Instrumens de musique à l'Exposition universelle" (*JD*; also 12, 15 January).

4 September 1856. "Plombières et Bade" (*JD*; also 8 September).

6 March 1857. "Première Représentation d'*Obéron*, opéra fantastique de Ch.-M. Weber" (*JD*).

8 September 1857. "Première Représentation d'*Euryanthe*, opéra fantastique de Weber" (*JD*).

March 1859. *Les Grotesques de la musique* (Paris: A. Bourdilliat; **A4**).

20 August 1859. Excerpts from *Les Troyens* (*JD*, before the concert of 29 August).

October 1859. *Mémoires* serialized in *Le Monde illustré*.

22 November 1859. "Première Représentation d'*Orphée*, opéra de Gluck.—Mme Pauline Viardot" (*JD*).

9 February 1860. "Concerts de Richard Wagner. La Musique de l'avenir" (*JD*).

19 May 1860. "Première Représentation de *Fidelio*, opéra en trois actes et quatre tableaux, musique de Beethoven" (*JD*; also 22 May).

1860. *Observations de quelques amateurs sur la "Méthode de musique de M. le Docteur Emile Chevé"* (Paris: Claye; collaborative report **B6**).

11 September 1861. "A MM. les membres des l'Académie des Beaux-Arts de l'Institut" (report on Baden-Baden) (*JD*; also 12 September).

12 October 1861. L'*Alceste* d'Euripide, celles de Quinault et de Calsabigi; les partitions de Lulli, de Gluck, de Schweitzer et de Guglielmi sur ce sujet." (*JD*; also 15, 20 October, 6, 23 November, 8 December).

24 October 1861. "Première Représentation de la reprise d'*Alceste*, tragédie lyrique en trois actes, musique de Gluck" (*JD*).

September 1862. *A Travers Chants: études musicales, adorations, boutades et critiques* (Paris: Michel Lévy frères; **A5**).

8 October 1863. "Première Représentation des *Pêcheurs de perles*, opéra en trois actes, de MM. Michel Carré et Cormon, musique de M. Bizet" (*JD*).

July 1865. *Mémoires* (**A6**); printed, not published.

Appendix C

Concerts

This appendix summarizes what is known of the major performances of Berlioz's works, or the concerts at which Berlioz conducted, including date, venue, principal performers, and repertoire presented. The name of the conductor is given in the right-hand column.

27 December 1824   Paris, Church of St.-Roch
Rehearsal of Mass, but the performance set for 28 December was canceled.

10 July 1825   Paris, Church of St.-Roch   Valentino
Mass (Prévost, bass).

22 November 1827   Paris, Church of St.-Eustache   Berlioz
St. Cecilia's Day. Mass (with Prévost [?] and the orchestra and chorus of the Odéon).

26 May 1828   Paris, Salle du Conservatoire   Bloc
Pentecost. *Scène héroïque. Waverley* ov. Credo and Resurrexit of Mass. *Marche religieuse des mages.* Excerpts from *Les Francs-Juges* (movts. 3, 7, and ov.). *La Mort d'Orphée* (with Dupont, tenor, who canceled; Mme Lebrun, soprano; Duprez, tenor; Prévost, bass).

25 February 1829   Paris, Opéra-Comique
Waverley ov.

1 August 1829   Paris, Institut de France
Cléopâtre (Mme Dabadie's sister, soloist, with piano accompaniment).

1 November 1829   Paris, Salle du Conservatoire   Habeneck
Waverley ov. *Le Jugement dernier. Francs-Juges* ov. *Grand Air de Conrad* from *Les Francs-Juges* (canceled). *Concert des sylphes* from *Huit Scènes de Faust.* Beethoven's Emperor Concerto (Hiller) and vocal selections by Mlle Marioni.

18 February 1830   Paris, Athénée Musical concerts
Le Coucher du soleil and *Chant sacré* from *Neuf Mélodies.*

16 May 1830   Paris, Salle du Conservatoire
Rehearsal of *Symphonie fantastique* (performance canceled).

30 October 1830   Paris, Institut de France
Sardanapale.

7 November 1830   Paris, Opéra
La Tempête.

5 December 1830   Paris, Salle du Conservatoire
Francs-Juges ov. *Chant guerrier* and *Chant sacré* from *Neuf Mélodies. Symphonie fantastique. Sardanapale.* The program of the *Symphonie fantastique* was printed and distributed at the concert.

9 December 1832 Paris, Salle du Conservatoire Habeneck
Symphonie fantastique with *Mélologue* (Bocage, récitant; Dupont, tenor; Hébert, bass; Fessy, piano). The program, printed on pink paper, and a libretto were distributed at the concert.

30 December 1832 Paris, Salle du Conservatoire Habeneck
Repeat of 9 December, with *La Captive* (Mme Kunzé-Boulanger; Fessy, piano; Desmarest, cello) and *Francs-Juges* ov. The program, printed on pink paper, was distributed at the concert; presumably the full libretto was also available.

12 March 1833 Paris, Salle du Vauxhall Girard
Francs-Juges ov.

2 April 1833 Paris, Salle Favart
Benefit for Harriet Smithson. No Berlioz played. Appearances by Liszt, Chopin, Urhan, Rubini, and by French and English actors.

14 April 1833 Paris, Salle du Conservatoire Habeneck
Société des Concerts subscription concert. *Rob-Roy* (only performance). Works by Beethoven, Meyerbeer, Cherubini, and Franchomme.

2 May 1833 Paris, Hôtel de *L'Europe littéraire* Girard
Waverley ov. Movts. II–IV of *Symphonie fantastique*. *Le Pêcheur* (Boulanger, tenor). *Francs-Juges* ov. Guitar solo by Huerta, and a quintet for brasses by Strons [Struntz]. An edition of *La Captive* and excerpts from *Le Retour à la vie* were published in conjunction with this concert and the next.

6 June 1833 Paris, Hôtel de *L'Europe littéraire* Girard
Le Pêcheur (Boulanger, tenor). *Sur les Alpes,* called *Le Chasseur des chamois* (only performance, with ten [male] singers from the Opéra). *La Captive* (Boulanger, tenor; Desmarest, cello; Bertini, piano). Weber's *Chasse de Lützow,* called *Chanson des Hussards de la mort,* arranged by Berlioz (first performance, with ten singers from the Opéra, string quintet, and piano). Works by Bertini and Sor.

22 July 1833 Paris, studio of the painter Ciceri Habeneck
Rehearsal of the *Scéne héroïque*, version II. (Performances planned for 28 July in the Place Vendôme and 9 August at the Opéra canceled.)

24 November 1833 Paris, Théâtre-Italien Berlioz
Benefit for Harriet Smithson Berlioz. *Sardanapale.* Weber's *Chasse de Lützow,* arranged by Berlioz, and *Konzertstück* (with Liszt, piano). *Hamlet,* act IV (with Smithson as Ophelia). Dumas's *Antony,* act I (Mmes Dorval and Firmin). *Francs-Juges* ov. and *Symphonie fantastique* scheduled, but not played.

22 December 1833 Paris, Salle du Conservatoire Girard
Le Roi Lear (first performance). *Le Jeune Pâtre breton,* probably with piano (first performance; Boulanger, tenor). *Romance de Marie Tudor* (only performance; Boulanger, tenor). *Symphonie fantastique.* Works of Hausmann and Weber (Liszt, piano). Program for the *Symphonie fantastique* printed on pink paper and distributed at the concert.

9 November 1834 Paris, Salle du Conservatoire Girard
First 1834 concert. *Le Roi Lear* ov. *Sara la baigneuse* (first performance of version I, for male quartet and orchestra). *La Belle Voyageuse* (first performance of version II, for male quartet and orchestra). *Symphonie fantastique.* Works of Panofka (Panofka, violin) and Rossini.

23 November 1834 Paris, Salle du Conservatoire Girard
Second 1834 concert. *Harold en Italie* (first performance; Urhan, viola). *La Captive* (first performance of version IV, for soprano and orchestra; Mlle Falcon, soprano). *Waverley* ov. *Le Jeune Pâtre breton* (first performance of version II, for soprano and orchestra; Mlle Falcon). *Symphonie fantastique,* movt. IV. Liszt's fantasia on themes from *Mélologue* announced but not played. Ernst announced as soloist but did not appear. *Mélodie pastorale* from *Les Francs-Juges* and a *Chœur des ciseleurs* announced but canceled.

14 December 1834   Paris, Salle du Conservatoire   Girard
Third 1834 concert. *Harold en Italie* (second performance; Urhan). *Les Francs-Juges* ov. *Sardanapale* (Puig). *Le Pêcheur. Le Roi Lear* ov.

28 December 1834   Paris, Salle du Consevatoire   Girard
Fourth 1834 concert. *Harold en Italie* (third performance; Urhan). *Symphonie fantastique.* Works of Handel and Liszt, including excerpts from Liszt's arrangement of the *Symphonie fantastique.*

9 April 1835   Paris, Hôtel de Ville, Salle St. Jean   Girard
Le Pêcheur (Boulanger). *Symphonie fantastique. Harold en Italie,* movt. II (Urhan). Liszt's fantasia on *Mélologue* themes (Liszt).

3 May 1835   Paris, Salle du Conservatoire   Girard
Symphonie fantastique and *Mélologue* (Geoffroy, récitant; Boulanger, tenor). Work by Moscheles (Liszt). Program for the *Symphonie fantastique* printed on pink paper and distributed at the concert.

4 June 1835   Paris, Gymnase Musicale   Tilmant *aîné*
Harold en Italie (Urhan). *Le Roi Lear* ov. *Le Jeune Pâtre breton* (voice and orchestra; Ponchard, tenor). Air from Gluck's *Telemacco.*

25 June 1835   Paris, Gymnase Musicale   Tilmant *aîné*
Harold en Italie (Urhan). *Francs-Juges* ov. *Waverley* ov. Solos for piano and violin.

22 November 1835   Paris, Salle du Conservatoire   Girard
First 1835 concert. *Le Cinq Mai* (first performance; ten basses sang the solo). *Le Jeune Pâtre breton* (Mlle Falcon). *Harold en Italie* (Urhan). Girard's overture to *Antigone* and his arrangement for orchestra of Beethoven's C♯-Minor Sonata. Air from *Crociato* (Mlle Falcon).

13 December 1835   Paris, Salle du Conservatoire   Berlioz
Second 1835 concert. *Le Roi Lear. Le Cinq Mai* (with ten basses). *Symphonie fantastique.* Movt. II of *Harold en Italie* (Urhan). Songs for Mlle Falcon, unnamed but presumably including songs of Berlioz. Works of Meyerbeer and Gluck.

4 December 1836   Paris, Salle du Conservatoire   Berlioz
First 1836 concert. *Harold en Italie* (Urhan). *Symphonie fantastique.* Works by Hasse and Louise Bertin. Program for the *Symphonie fantastique* printed on pink paper and distributed at the concert.

18 December 1836   Paris, Salle du Conservatoire   Berlioz
Berlioz / Liszt concert; second 1836 concert. *Francs-Juges* ov. Movts. I and II of *Harold en Italie* (Urhan). Liszt's symphonic fantasia on themes from *Mélologue,* and movts. II and IV of his transcription of the *Symphonie fantastique.* Works by Mercadante, Pacini, and Bellini.

5 December 1837   Paris, Eglise des Invalides   Habeneck
Requiem (first performance; with Duprez, tenor).

10 September 1838   Paris, Opéra   Habeneck
Benvenuto Cellini (first performance; Duprez: Cellini; Dérivis: Balducci; Massol: Fieramosca; Serda: Cardinal; Mme Dorus-Gras: Teresa; Mme Stoltz: Ascanio; Duprez replaced by Dupont). Then 12 and 14 September, and 11 January 1839. Act I only, together with a ballet, 20 February and 8 and 17 March 1839. Total of four complete and three partial performances. A libretto and a revised libretto, to which was added "La gloire était ma seule idole," were published along with a printed synopsis.

25 November 1838   Paris, Salle du Conservatoire   Habeneck
First 1838 concert. *Le Roi Lear.* Ascanio's air from *Benvenuto Cellini* (Mme Stoltz). *Symphonie fantastique.* Teresa's *cavatine* from *Benvenuto Cellini* (Mme Dorus-Gras). *Waverley.* Clari's *Cantando un dì.* Berlioz was ill. Program for the *Symphonie fantastique* printed on pink paper and distributed at both this concert and the next.

16 December 1838   Paris, Salle du Conservatoire   Berlioz
Second 1838 concert. *Harold en Italie* (Urhan). *Le Jeune Pâtre breton* (Mme Stoltz). *Symphonie fantastique*. Works of Donizetti, Clari, and Gluck.
24 November 1839   Paris, Salle du Conservatoire   Berlioz
Roméo et Juliette (first performance; Alizard, bass: Père Laurence; Mme Widemann, contralto; Dupont, tenor). A libretto was published, and a vocal score of the strophes was ready shortly afterward.
1 December 1839   Paris, Salle du Conservatoire   Berlioz
Roméo et Juliette, second performance.
15 December 1839   Paris, Salle du Conservatoire   Berlioz
Roméo et Juliette, third performance (possibly abridged), with *Harold en Italie* (Urhan) and Teresa's *cavatine* from *Benvenuto Cellini* (Mme Dorus-Gras).
6 February 1840   Paris, Salle du Vauxhall   Berlioz
Seventh *Revue et Gazette musicale* concert. *Harold en Italie* (Urhan). *Benvenuto Cellini* ov. Works of Grétry, Méhul, Cherubini, and others.
28 July 1840   Paris, open air   Berlioz
Symphonie funèbre et triomphale, first performance (Dieppo, solo trombone). Place de la Concorde to Place de la Bastille via the boulevards.
7 August 1840   Paris, Salle Vivienne   Berlioz
First of four Salle Vivienne concerts (see also 1842). *Benvenuto Cellini* ov. Movts. I–III of *Harold en Italie* (Urhan). Movts. II–IV of *Symphonie fantastique*. *Symphonie funèbre* (Dieppo).
14 August 1840   Paris, Salle Vivienne   Berlioz
Second of four Salle Vivienne concerts (see also 1842). Repeat of 7 August, with *Fête chez Capulet* from *Roméo et Juliette.*
1 November 1840   Paris, Opéra   Berlioz
Festival de M. Berlioz. Dies irae, Tuba mirum, Quid sum miser, and Lacrymosa from Requiem. Movts. II, III, and VII from *Roméo et Juliette. Apothéose* from *Symphonie funèbre* (Dieppo). Works of Palestrina and Handel and act I of Gluck's *Iphigénie en Tauride.*
8 November 1840   Paris, Salle du Conservatoire   Berlioz
Eighth *Revue et Gazette musicale* concert. *Absence* and *Le Spectre de la rose* announced, not performed (Wartel, tenor; Collignon, piano).
13 December 1840   Paris, Salle du Conservatoire   Berlioz
Movts. I–IV of *Roméo et Juliette. Sara la baigneuse* (first performance of version II, for vocal quartet, chorus, and orchestra; Mlle Elian, Boulanger, Prévôt, Alizard). *Le Cinq Mai,* called *Chant sur la mort de l'Empereur Napoléon* (Alizard). *Symphonie fantastique.*
25 April 1841   Paris, Salle du Conservatoire   Berlioz
Festival Berlioz / Liszt, the proceeds to support construction of the Beethoven monument in Bonn. All Beethoven program with Liszt at the piano. Berlioz conducted the Sixth Symphony and the Emperor Concerto.
7 June 1841   Paris, Opéra   Pantaléon Battu
Weber's *Le Freyschutz,* with recitatives by Berlioz and his orchestration of *L'Invitation à la valse* as *ballet-divertissement.* Thereafter performed thirteen times in 1841. A libretto was published and, a year later, the vocal score.
1 February 1842   Paris, Salle Vivienne   Berlioz
Third of four Salle Vivienne concerts (see also 1840). *Harold en Italie* (Alard). *L'Invitation à la valse. Rêverie et Caprice* (first performance; Alard, violin). *Symphonie funèbre,* first performance of version II, with strings, but without chorus. Possibly an excerpt from *Roméo et Juliette.* Beethoven's Triple Concerto (Alard, Desmarest, Hallé).

15 February 1842   Paris, Salle Vivienne   Berlioz
Fourth of four Salle Vivienne concerts (see also 1840). *Symphonie fantastique.*
Movt. II of *Harold en Italie* (Alard). *Rêverie et Caprice* (Alard). *Symphonie funèbre*, version II, no chorus. A *Grande Caprice* for piano by Heller (Hallé).

24 April 1842   Paris, Salle du Conservatoire   Berlioz
Concert of M. and Mme Mortier de Fontaine. *Les Francs-Juges* ov. *Absence* (Mme Mortier). Works by Arcadelt, Mozart, L'Abbé Roch, Beethoven, Mendelssohn, and Mortier de Fontaine.

26 September 1842   Brussels, Concert Hall of the Royal   Berlioz
                     Brussels Military Band
Strophes from *Roméo et Juliette* (Mme Widemann; Demunck, cello). *Le Jeune Pâtre breton* (Marie Recio). Movt. II of *Harold en Italie* (Ernst). *Symphonie funèbre* (Schmidt), first performance with chorus. Works by Snel and Ernst.

9 October 1842   Brussels, Temple des Augustins   Berlioz
Les Francs-Juges ov. *L'Invitation à la valse.* Movt. II of *Harold en Italie* (Singelée). *Romances* (Recio; Döhler, piano). *Symphonie fantastique.* Works by Meyerbeer, Masini, and Döhler.

7 November 1842   Paris, Opéra   Habeneck
Symphonie funèbre, first performance with both strings and chorus. Works of Adam and Auber. Berlioz conducted the chorus and wind band.

29 December 1842   Stuttgart, Redoutensaal   Berlioz
Les Francs-Juges ov. Movts. II and III of *Harold en Italie* (Barnbeck). *Romances* (Recio). Movts. II–IV of *Symphonie fantastique.* Air from *Robert le diable* (Recio).

2 January 1843   Hechingen, Prince's Concert Room   Berlioz
Court concert for the prince of Hohenzollern-Hechingen. *Le Roi Lear.* Movt. II of *Harold en Italie* (Täglichsbeck). Movt. II of *Symphonie fantastique. Le Jeune Pâtre breton* (Recio).

13 January 1843   Mannheim, Theater   Berlioz
Les Francs-Juges ov. *Le Jeune Pâtre breton* (Recio). Movts. I–III of *Harold en Italie. Le Roi Lear.* Vocal works by Meyerbeer and Masini (Recio).

25 January 1843   Weimar, Grand-Ducal Theater   Berlioz
Symphonie fantastique. Le Jeune Pâtre breton (Recio). Movt. II of *Harold en Italie. La Belle Voyageuse,* version III, with orchestra (possibly first performance; Recio). *Absence,* with piano (Recio). *Les Francs-Juges* ov.

4 February 1843   Leipzig, Gewandhaus   Berlioz
First Leipzig concert. *Le Roi Lear. Le Jeune Pâtre breton* (Recio). *Rêverie et Caprice* (Ferdinand David). *Symphonie fantastique. La Belle Voyageuse,* version III; *Absence,* with piano (Recio). Offertoire from Requiem. *Les Francs-Juges* ov. The program note was printed in German and was given also in the *Signale für die musikalische Welt* 1 (1843), 54–55.

10 February 1843   Dresden, Royal Theater   Berlioz
First Dresden concert. *Le Roi Lear. Symphonie fantastique.* Excerpts from Requiem, including Sanctus (Tichatschek). Movts. II and III of *Symphonie funèbre* (Reissiger conducting the strings in the pit). *Absence* and other songs, with piano (Recio). *Cavatine* from *Benvenuto Cellini* (Mme Schubert).

17 February 1843   Dresden, Royal Theater   Berlioz
Second Dresden concert. *Benvenuto Cellini* ov. Offertoire and Sanctus from Requiem. *Rêverie et Caprice* (Lipinski). *Le Cinq Mai* (Wächter). *Harold en Italie* (Lipinski). Strophes (Mme Schubert) and movt. II of *Roméo et Juliette. La Belle Voyageuse,* with orchestra; *Absence,* with piano (Recio). *Apothéose* from *Symphonie funèbre.*

23 February 1843   Leipzig, Gewandhaus   Berlioz
Second Leipzig concert: benefit for the poor. *Absence* (first performance of the orchestrated version; Recio). Offertoire from Requiem. *Le Roi Lear.*

9 March 1843   Brunswick, Ducal Theater   Berlioz
Absence and *La Belle Voyageuse* (Recio). *Harold en Italie* (Carl Müller). Movts. IV and II from *Roméo et Juliette*. *Benvenuto Cellini* ov. Offertoire and Quaerens me from Requiem. *Rêverie et Caprice* (Müller).

22 March 1843   Hamburg, Municipal Theater   Berlioz
Harold en Italie (Spars). Offertoire and Quaerens me from Requiem. *L'Invitation à la valse. Le Jeune Pâtre breton. Absence* (Recio). *Le Cinq Mai* (Reichel). *Rêverie et Caprice* (Lindemann). *Cavatine* from *Benvenuto Cellini* (Mme Cornet). *Les Francs-Juges* ov.

8 April 1843   Berlin, Royal Opera House   Berlioz
First Berlin concert. *Benvenuto Cellini* ov. *Harold en Italie* (Leopold Ganz). *Le Cinq Mai* (Boetticher). Excerpts from Requiem. *L'Invitation à la valse. Cavatine* from *Benvenuto Cellini* (Fräulein Marx).

23 April 1843   Berlin, Royal Opera House   Berlioz
Second Berlin concert. *Le Roi Lear.* Movts. I–IV of *Roméo et Juliette* (Fräulein Hähnel). *Absence. Le Jeune Pâtre breton* (Recio). Movts. II and III of *Harold en Italie.* Lacrymosa from Requiem.

6 May 1843   Hanover, Royal Theater   Berlioz
Le Cinq Mai (Steinmüller). *L'Invitation à la valse. Harold en Italie* (Anton Bohrer). *Waverley* ov. *Le Jeune Pâtre breton. Cavatine* from *Benvenuto Cellini. Absence* (Recio).

23 May 1843   Darmstadt   Berlioz
Le Roi Lear. Le Cinq Mai (Reichel). Movts. II–IV of *Roméo et Juliette. Le Jeune Pâtre breton* (Recio). *Harold en Italie. Cavatine* from *Benvenuto Cellini* (Recio). *L'Invitation à la valse.* Reichel sang *Non più andrai* as an encore.

19 November 1843   Paris, Salle du Conservatoire   Berlioz
Le Roi Lear. Rêverie et Caprice (Alard). Trio and *Cavatine* from *Benvenuto Cellini* (Mme Dorus-Gras, Duprez, Massol). *Harold en Italie* (Urhan). Movt. IV of *Roméo et Juliette. Absence* (first Paris performance; Duprez). Movts. II and III of *Symphonie funèbre* (Dieppo). Last concert in Salle du Conservatoire.

3 February 1844   Paris, Salle Herz   Berlioz
L'Invitation à la valse. Hélène (first performance of version II, for male quartet and orchestra). *Chant sacré,* for six Sax instruments (Dauverné, Arban, Dufresne, Lepers, Duprez, and Sax). *Le Carnaval romain* (first performance). Three excerpts from *Roméo et Juliette. Absence* (Recio). A scene from *Faust* and act III of Gluck's *Alceste* announced, but not performed.

6 April 1844   Paris, Opéra-Comique   Berlioz
Concert spirituel for Palm Sunday. *Le Roi Lear. Cavatine* from *Benvenuto Cellini* (Recio). *Le Cinq Mai. Le Carnaval romain.* Sanctus from Requiem (Roger and Recio). *Apothéose* from *Symphonie funèbre* (Dieppo). Works by Le Sueur, Meyerbeer, and Sivori (Alard, violin).

4 May 1844   Paris, Théâtre-Italien   Berlioz
Berlioz / Liszt concert. *Symphonie fantastique.* Liszt's arrangement of *Un Bal* from *Symphonie fantastique* (Liszt). *Les Francs-Juges* ov. *Le Carnaval romain. Harold en Italie* (Urhan). *Waverley.* Virtuoso piano works by Weber and Liszt (Liszt).

1 August 1844   Paris, Palais de l'Industrie   Berlioz, with
                                                  Tilmant assisting
Festival de l'Industrie; approximately one thousand musicians participating. *Hymne à la France* (first performance). Movt. IV of *Symphonie fantastique.*

Apothéose from *Symphonie funèbre*. Works by Gluck, Beethoven, Spontini, Auber, Halévy, Rossini, Mendelssohn, Meyerbeer, and Méreaux. A published handbill gave text of the *Hymne à la France* and the *Apothéose*.

19 January 1845   Paris, Cirque Olympique   Berlioz
First festival-concert. *Le Carnaval romain*. Excerpts from Requiem. *La Tour de Nice* (first performance). Works by Piccini and Gluck (Eugénie Garcia, Ponchard) and Beethoven's "Emperor" Concerto (Hallé).

16 February 1845   Paris, Cirque Olympique   Berlioz
Second festival-concert: *séance orientale*. *Les Francs-Juges* ov. Excerpts from Requiem. Félicien David's *Le Désert* and *Choeur des Janissaires*. De Meyer's *Marche marocaine* (de Meyer, piano).

16 March 1845   Paris, Cirque Olympique   Berlioz
Third festival-concert: *séance russe*. *L'Invitation à la valse*. Excerpts from Requiem. Félicien David's *Le Désert* and *Chœur des Janissaires*. De Meyer's *Marche marocaine* (de Meyer, piano).

6 April 1845   Paris, Cirque Olympique   Berlioz
Fourth and last festival-concert. *Marche marocaine* (first performance of Berlioz's orchestration). Movt. II of *Harold en Italie*. Movts. IV and VII of *Roméo et Juliette*. Excerpts from Requiem. Works by Weber, Rossini, Louise Bertin, Glinka, and Félicien David.

19 June 1845   Marseille, Theater   Berlioz
First Marseille concert. *Le Cinq Mai* (Alizard). *Apothéose* from *Symphonie funèbre*. *Hymne à la France*.

25 June 1845   Marseille, Theater   Berlioz
Second Marseille concert. Repeat of concert of 19 June.

20 July 1845   Lyon, Grand Theater   Berlioz
First Lyon concert. *Le Carnaval romain*. Movts. II–IV of *Symphonie fantastique*. *Hymne à la France*. *L'Invitation à la valse*. Movt. II of *Harold en Italie* (Cherblanc). *Apothéose* from *Symphonie funèbre*. Works of Gluck and Weber.

24 July 1845   Lyon, Grand Theater   Berlioz
Second Lyon concert. Repeat of concert of 20 July.

16 November 1845   Vienna, Theater an der Wien   Berlioz
First Vienna concert. *Le Carnaval romain*. *Chant sacré* (first performance of orchestrated version; Behringer, tenor). *Cavatine* from *Benvenuto Cellini* (Fräulein von Marra). *Harold en Italie* (Heissler). *Le Cinq Mai* (Staudigl). *Apothéose* from *Symphonie funèbre*.

23 November 1845   Vienna, Theater an der Wien   Berlioz
Second Vienna concert. Movts. I–IV of *Symphonie fantastique*. *Le Carnaval romain*. Movt. II of *Harold en Italie*. *Le Roi Lear*. *Marche marocaine*. Aria from *Benvenuto Cellini* (Graufeld). *Scène de brigands* from *Le Retour à la vie* (Staudigl).

29 November 1845   Vienna, Theater an der Wien   Berlioz
Third Vienna concert. *Les Francs-Juges* ov. *Le Jeune Pâtre breton*. *Zaïde* (first performance of orchestrated version; Henriette Treffz). Movt. II of *Harold en Italie*. *Le Chasseur danois* (first performance of orchestrated version, encored; Staudigl). *Le Carnaval romain*. Movts. I–IV of *Symphonie fantastique*. A printed program note was distributed at the concert.

17 December 1845   Vienna   Dreyschock and
                                                Berlioz
Dreyschock's concert of the Kärntnerthor Orchestra. Berlioz conducted *Le Carnaval romain*, *Le Jeune Pâtre breton*, and possibly *Zaïde* (Fräulein Treffz).

2 January 1846   Vienna, Theater an der Wien   Groidl
Fourth Vienna concert. *Roméo et Juliette* complete (Staudigl, bass: Père Laurence; Mlle Bury, contralto; Behringer, tenor).

11 January 1846   Vienna, Redoutensaal   Berlioz
Fifth Vienna concert (*d'adieu*). *Le Carnaval romain*. Movts. III and IV of *Roméo et Juliette*. *Harold en Italie* (Ernst). Works by Ernst (Ernst), Schiff, and Esser (Pischek, baritone).

19 January 1846   Prague, Sofia Hall   Berlioz
First Prague concert. *Le Carnaval romain*. *Le Chasseur danois* (Strakaty). Movt. II of *Harold en Italie*. *Zaïde* (Mme Podhorska). *Symphonie fantastique*.

25 January 1846   Prague, Sofia Hall   Berlioz
Second Prague concert. Movts. IV and III of *Roméo et Juliette*. Movts. II–IV of *Symphonie fantastique*. *Le Carnaval romain*. Movt. II of *Harold en Italie*.

27 January 1846   Prague, State Theater   Berlioz
Third Prague concert. *Le Carnaval romain*. *Le Chasseur danois* (Strakaty). Movt. II of *Harold en Italie*. *Zaïde* (Mme Podhorska). Movts. I and II of *Symphonie fantastique*. Movts. II–IV of *Roméo et Juliette*.

1 February 1846   Vienna, Redoutensaal   Berlioz
Sixth Vienna concert. *Le Carnaval romain*. Movts. I–IV of *Symphonie fantastique*. Movt. II of *Harold en Italie*. Excerpts from *Roméo et Juliette*, with prologue spoken by Lowe, the *regisseur*. Works by Speyer and Krenzer (Pischek).

15 February 1846   Pest, National Theater   Berlioz
First Pest concert. *Le Carnaval romain*. Movts. II–IV of *Symphonie fantastique*. Movt. II of *Harold en Italie*. *Marche de Rákóczy*.

20 February 1846   Pest, National Theater   Berlioz
Second Pest concert. Repeat of concert of 15 February, with *Le Jeune Pâtre breton* and *Zaïde* (Mme Schodel, who had not arrived in time for the first concert).

20 March 1846   Breslau, University Concert Hall Berlioz
Le Carnaval romain. *Zaïde* (Mme Seidelmann). Movt. II of *Harold en Italie*. Movts. I–IV of *Symphonie fantastique*. Mendelssohn's *Capriccio brillant* for piano and orchestra (Hesse).

31 March 1846   Prague, State Theater   Berlioz
Fourth Prague concert. *Le Carnaval romain*. *Rêverie et Caprice* (Mildner). *La Belle Voyageuse* (Mme Podhorska). *Symphonie fantastique*.

7 April 1846   Prague, Sofia Hall   Berlioz
Fifth Prague concert: benefit for monastery of Mount Carmel in the Holy Land. *Invitation à la valse*. *Le Roi Lear*. *Rêverie et Caprice* (Mildner). Movt. II of *Harold en Italie*. Movts. II–IV of *Symphonie fantastique*. Aria from Mendelssohn's *St. Paul* (Mlle Soukupová).

17 April 1846   Prague, Sofia Hall   Berlioz
Sixth and last Prague concert. *Roméo et Juliette* complete (Strakaty, bass: Père Laurence; Frau Rzepka, contralto).

24 April 1846   Brunswick, Ducal Theater   Berlioz
Le Carnaval romain. *Zaïde* (Frau Fischer-Achten). Movt. II of *Harold en Italie*. *Le Chasseur danois* (Fischer). *Symphonie fantastique*.

9 May 1846   Paris, Théâtre-Italien   Berlioz
Concert in honor of Ibrāhīm Pasha. *Marche marocaine*. Egyptian works and David's *Le Désert*.

14 June 1846   Lille, public promenade and   Berlioz
                     Hôtel de Ville
Apothéose from *Symphonie funèbre* (on the public promenade). *Chant des chemins de fer* (first and only performance, in the Hôtel de Ville).

20 August 1846   Paris, Church of St.-Eustache   Berlioz, Baron
                                                       Taylor assisting
Requiem (Roger, tenor).

6 December 1846   Paris, Opéra-Comique   Berlioz
La Damnation de Faust (first performance; Roger: Faust; Herman-Léon: Méph-istophélès; Mme Maillard: Marguerite; Henri: Brander). A published libretto, which includes the "Labitte catalogue" of Berlioz's works, was circulated before the concerts.

20 December 1846   Paris, Opéra-Comique   Berlioz
La Damnation de Faust (second performance).

15 March 1847   St. Petersburg, Assembly of the Nobility   Berlioz
First St. Petersburg concert. *Le Carnaval romain.* Parts I and II of *La Damnation de Faust* (Ricciardi: Faust, in French; Versing: Méphistophélès, in German). Movts. IV and V of *Roméo et Juliette. Apothéose* from *Symphonie funèbre.*

25 March 1847   St. Petersburg, Assembly of the Nobility   Berlioz
Second St. Petersburg concert. Repeat of concert of 15 March.

27 March 1847   St. Petersburg   Berlioz
Benefit for invalids. *Apothéose* from *Symphonie funèbre* included on program.

10 April 1847   Moscow, Assembly of the Nobility   Berlioz
Parts I and II of *La Damnation de Faust* (Leonov: Faust; Slavik: Méphistophélès).

5 May 1847   St. Petersburg, Imperial Theater   Berlioz
Third St. Petersburg concert. *Roméo et Juliette,* complete, in German (Versing: Père Laurence; Mme Walker, contralto; Holland, tenor). Movts. I and II of *Harold en Italie* (Ernst). *Le Carnaval romain.*

12 May 1847   St. Petersburg, Imperial Theater   Berlioz
Fourth St. Petersburg concert. *Roméo et Juliette,* complete (same cast as before). Part II of *La Damnation de Faust.*

20 May 1847   St. Petersburg   Berlioz
Fifth St. Petersburg concert: farewell of Versing, bass, and of Berlioz. *Symphonie fantastique.*

29 May 1847   Riga   Berlioz
Harold en Italie (Löbmann). *Le Carnaval romain. Concert des sylphes* (no chorus) and *Marche hongroise* from *La Damnation de Faust.* Mlle Bamberg sang two songs with orchestra.

19 June 1847   Berlin, Royal Opera House   Berlioz
La Damnation de Faust, complete (Krause: Faust; Boetticher: Méphistophélès; Fräulein Brexendorf: Marguerite; Haas: Brander).

6 December 1847   London, Drury Lane Theatre   Berlioz
Donizetti's *Lucia di Lammermoor.* Thereafter performed several times.

20 December 1847   London, Drury Lane Theatre
Balfe's *Maid of Honour.* The composer apparently conducted at first; Berlioz conducted after January 1.

10 January 1848   London, Dury Lane Theatre   Berlioz
Donizetti's *Linda di Chamounix.* Thereafter performed several times.

7 February 1848   London, Drury Lane Theatre   Berlioz
"Mr. Berlioz's First Grand Instrumental and Vocal Concert." *Le Carnaval romain. Le Jeune Pâtre breton* (Miss Miran). *Harold en Italie* (Hill). Parts I and II of *La Damnation de Faust,* in English (Sims Reeves: Faust; Weiss: Méphistophélès; Gregg: Brander). *Cavatine* from *Benvenuto Cellini* (Mme Dorus-Gras). Offertoire from Requiem ("Chorus of Souls in Purgatory"). Movts. II and III of *Symphonie funèbre* (König).

9 February 1848   London, Drury Lane Theatre   Berlioz
Benefit for Sims Reeves. *Le Carnaval romain.* Movt. II of *Harold en Italie.* Donizetti's *Lucia di Lammermoor.*

11 February 1848   London, Drury Lane Theatre   Berlioz
Mozart's *Marriage of Figaro.*

18 February 1848   London, Buckingham Palace   Godfrey
Symphonie funèbre (movt. I only?).

16 June 1848   London, Covent Garden   Berlioz
Marche hongroise from *La Damnation de Faust.*

29 June 1848   London, Hanover Square Rooms   Berlioz
Le Carnaval romain. Le Chasseur danois (Bouché). Movts. I and II of *Harold en Italie* (Hill). *Zaïde* (Mme Sabatier). *Choeur et Ballet des sylphes* and *Air de Méphistophélès* from *La Damnation de Faust. La Captive* and another selection (Mme Viardot). Works by Mendelssohn and Glinka(?).

29 October 1848   Versailles, Opera House   Berlioz
Benefit for Association of Artist-Musicians; Armand Marrast, presiding. *La Captive* (Mme Widemann). *Marche hongroise* from *La Damnation de Faust.* Movt. II of *Roméo et Juliette. L'Invitation à la valse.* Works by Gluck, Mozart, Beethoven, Bellini, Rossini, and Meyerbeer.

15 April 1849   Paris, Salle du Conservatoire   Girard
Société des Concerts subscription concert. *Choeur et Ballet de gnomes et des sylphes* and *Marche hongroise* from *La Damnation de Faust* (Dupont: Faust; Depassio: Méphistophélès). Works by Spontini and Cherubini and Beethoven's Sixth Symphony.

19 February 1850   Paris, Salle Ste.-Cécile   Berlioz
First Société Philharmonique concert. Parts I and II of *La Damnation de Faust.* Works by Gluck (Mme Viardot), Méhul (Roger), Beethoven, Meyerbeer, Ernst (Joachim), and Demuth (Demuth, cello).

19 March 1850   Paris, Salle Ste.-Cécile   Berlioz
Second Société Philharmonique concert. *Harold en Italie* (Massart). Works of Palestrina, Gluck, Weber, Rossini, and Herman.

30 March 1850   Paris, Salle Ste.-Cécile   Berlioz
Third Société Philharmonique concert. Movt. II of *Harold en Italie* (Wieniawski? Massart?). Works of Palestrina, Vogel, Spontini, Weber (Mme Massart, piano), Niedermeyer, Gastinel, Dietsch, and Wieniawski (Wieniawski, violin).

23 April 1850   Paris, Salle Ste.-Cécile   Berlioz
Fourth Société Philharmonique concert. Part I of *La Damnation de Faust* (Roger: Faust). *L'Invitation à la valse.* Works by Méhul, Rossini, Mendelssohn, Meyerbeer, Apollinaire de Kontski, Cadaux, Servais, and David (David, conducting).

3 May 1850   Paris, Church of St.-Eustache   Berlioz
Société Philharmonique, extra concert in memory of the victims of the tragedy at Angers. Requiem (Roger, tenor).

22 October 1850   Paris, Salle Ste.-Cécile   Berlioz
First Société Philharmonique concert of the second season. *Sara la baigneuse* (first performance of version III, for three choruses and orchestra). *Chant des cherubins* (first performance of Berlioz's arrangement of the work of Bortniansky). *Francs-Juges* ov. *Le Cinq Mai* (Barroilhet). Works of Le Sueur, Beethoven, Weber, Halévy, Donizetti, Schubert, and Bellini.

12 November 1850   Paris, Salle Ste.-Cécile   Berlioz
Second Société Philharmonique concert. *Symphonie fantastique. Sara la baigneuse. L'Invitation à la valse. L'Adieu des bergers* (first performance). *Chant des cherubins.* Works by Piccini, Donizetti, and Verdi.

17 December 1850   Paris, Salle Ste.-Cécile   Berlioz
Third Société Philharmonique concert. Possibly *L'Adieu des bergers.* Other works.

28 January 1851   Paris, Salle Ste.-Cécile   Berlioz
Fourth Société Philharmonique concert. Movts. I–IV of *Roméo et Juliette* (Mme Maillard, contralto; Roger, tenor). Bortniansky's *Pater noster,* arranged by Berlioz (first performance). Works by Gluck, Stradella, and others.

25 February 1851   Paris, Salle Ste.-Cécile   Berlioz
Fifth Société Philharmonique concert. Movts. I–IV of *Roméo et Juliette* (Mme Maillard, contralto; Roger, tenor). *Marche hongroise* from *La Damnation de Faust*. Works of Dalayrac, Mlle de Reyset, and Willmes.

25 March 1851   Paris, Salle Ste.-Cécile   Berlioz
Sixth Société Philharmonique concert. *Symphonie fantastique. Cavatine* from *Benvenuto Cellini* (Mme Dorus-Gras). *La Belle Voyageuse* (first performance of version IV, for female chorus and orchestra). *Le Menace des francs* (first performance). Other works.

29 April 1851   Paris, Salle Ste.-Cécile   Berlioz
Seventh Société Philharmonique concert. Works of Cohen and Morel; no Berlioz.

30 June 1851   Lille
Third Festival du Nord. *Chant des cherubins*. Lacrymosa from Requiem. Works of many others.

20 March 1852   Weimar, Grand-Ducal Theater   Liszt
Benvenuto Cellini (first performance of the Weimar version). Berlioz not there. Performed again on 24 March.

24 March 1852   London, Exeter Hall   Berlioz
First concert (ever) of the New Philharmonic Society. Movts. I–IV of *Roméo et Juliette* (Miss Dolby, contralto; Lockey, tenor). Works by Mozart, Gluck, Beethoven, Weber, Rossini, and Bottesini.

14 April 1852   London, Exeter Hall   Berlioz
Second New Philharmonic Society concert. *Chant des cherubins*. Works by Mozart, Gluck, Beethoven, Cherubini, Wylde, Loder, and Gambert.

28 April 1852   London, Exeter Hall   Berlioz
Third New Philharmonic Society concert. Movt. I of *Roméo et Juliette*. Works by Gluck, Spontini, Beethoven, Weber, and Mendelssohn.

29 April 1852   London, Hanover Square Rooms   Berlioz
Absence (Reichardt). Works of Beethoven, Schubert, Mendelssohn, and Auber.

12 May 1852   London, Exeter Hall   Berlioz and Dr. Wylde
Fourth New Philharmonic Society concert. Berlioz conducted Beethoven's Ninth Symphony.

29 May 1852   London, Exeter Hall   Berlioz
Fifth New Philharmonic Society concert. *Francs-Juges* ov. *L'Invitation à la valse*. Works of Mercadante, Handel, Beethoven, Mendelssohn, Silas, and Smart.

9 June 1852   London, Exeter Hall   Berlioz
Sixth and last New Philharmonic Society concert. *Ballet des sylphes* and *Marche hongroise* from *La Damnation de Faust* (Staudigl). Works of Weber, Liszt (Mme Pleyel, piano), Wylde, and Benedict and Beethoven's Ninth Symphony.

22 October 1852   Paris, Church of St.-Eustache   Berlioz
Services in memory of Baron de Trémont. Requiem, complete (Roger advertised as tenor; part actually sung by ten basses).

17 November 1852   Weimar, Grand-Ducal Theater   Liszt
Berlioz Week performance. *Benvenuto Cellini,* Weimar version. Performed again on 23 November.

20 November 1852   Weimar, Grand-Ducal Theater   Berlioz
Berlioz Week performance. *Roméo et Juliette,* complete. Parts I and II of *La Damnation de Faust*.

30 May 1853   London, Hanover Square Rooms
Philharmonic Society, sixth subscription concert. *Le Repos de la Sainte Famille* (first performance; Gardoni, tenor). *Harold en Italie. Le Carnaval romain*. Berlioz conducted half the concert.

25 June 1853   London, Covent Garden   Berlioz
Benvenuto Cellini, London version (only performance, in an Italian translation by J. Nicodemo; Tamberlick: Cellini; Mme Julienne-Dejean: Teresa; Mme Nantier-Didiée: Ascanio; Formès: Cardinal; Tagliafico: Fieramosca).

11 August 1853   Baden, Salon de Conversation   Berlioz
Parts I and II of *La Damnation de Faust* (Eberius: Faust; Oberhoffer: Méphistophélès; Bregenzer: Brander). *Le Carnaval romain*. Works of Ernst and Rossini.

24 August 1853   Frankfurt, Municipal Theater   Berlioz
Harold en Italie (Ernst). Parts I and II of *La Damnation de Faust*. *Le Repos de la Sainte-Famille*.

29 August 1853   Frankfurt, Municipal Theater   Berlioz
Repeat of concert of 24 August.

22 October 1853   Brunswick, Ducal Theater   Berlioz
Benefit for widows and orphans of the musicians. Excerpts from *La Damnation de Faust*. Excerpts from *Roméo et Juliette*. Excerpts from *Harold en Italie* (Joachim). *Le Roi Lear*. *Le Repos de la Sainte-Famille* (Schmetzer, tenor).

25 October 1853   Brunswick, Ducal Theater   Berlioz
Repeat of concert of 22 October.

8 November 1853   Hanover, Royal Theater   Berlioz
Le Repos de la Sainte-Famille. *Le Roi Lear*. Excerpts from *La Damnation de Faust*.

15 November 1853   Hanover, Royal Theater   Berlioz
Repeat of concert of 8 November.

22 November 1853   Bremen   Berlioz
Harold en Italie (Joachim). *Le Repos de la Sainte-Famille*. *Le Carnaval romain*.

1 December 1853   Leipzig, Gewandhaus   Berlioz
Eighth subscription concert. *La Fuite en Egypte* (first performances of all three movts.). Movts. I–III of *Harold en Italie* (David). *Le Jeune Pâtre breton*. *La Reine Mab* from *Roméo et Juliette*. Air de Méphistophélès ("Voici des roses"; Behr: Méphistophélès). *Le Carnaval romain*. Schneider was tenor for *La Fuite en Egypte*, the song, and *Faust*.

10 December 1853   Leipzig, Gewandhaus   Berlioz
Movts. I–IV of *Roméo et Juliette* (Frau Dreyschock, alto; Schneider, tenor; Jeanette Pohl, harp). *La Fuite en Egypte* (Schneider, tenor). Parts I and II of *La Damnation de Faust* (Schneider: Faust; Behr: Méphistophélès; Cramer: Brander).

18 December 1853   Paris, Salle Ste.-Cécile   Seghers
La Fuite en Egypte (first Paris performance; Chaperon, tenor).

1 April 1854   Hanover, Royal Theater   Berlioz
Subscription concert. *Le Roi Lear* ov. *Absence* (Frau Noltes). *Tendresse et Caprice* [sic] (Joachim). Movts. IV and III of *Roméo et Juliette*. *Le Jeune Pâtre breton* (Bernard). Movts. I–IV of *Symphonie fantastique*.

8 April 1854   Brunswick, Ducal Theater   Carl Müller
Le Corsaire (first performance of revised version). Berlioz conducted his piece during a concert otherwise led by the regular Kapellmeister.

22 April 1854   Dresden, Royal Theater   Berlioz
First of four Dresden concerts. *La Damnation de Faust*, complete (Weixlstorfer: Faust; Mitterwurzer: Méphistophélès; Abiger: Brander; Agnes Bunke: Marguerite).

25 April 1854   Dresden, Royal Theater   Berlioz
Second Dresden concert. Repeat of concert of 22 April.

29 April 1854   Dresden, Royal Theater   Berlioz
Third Dresden concert. Excerpts from *Roméo et Juliette* (Conradi: Père Laurence). *La Fuite en Egypte*. *Benvenuto Cellini* ov. *Le Carnaval romain*.

1 May 1854   Dresden, Royal Theater   Berlioz
Fourth Dresden concert. Repeat of concert of 29 April.
10 December 1854   Paris, Salle Herz   Berlioz
First of three *Enfance du Christ* concerts. *L'Enfance du Christ* (first performance;
Mme Meillet: Ste. Marie; Meillet: St. Joseph; Depassio: Hérode; Jourdan, *récitant*;
Bataille: *père de famille*). *Tendresse et Caprice* [*sic*] (Maurin).
24 December 1854   Paris, Salle Herz   Berlioz
Second *Enfance du Christ* concert. *La Captive* (orchestral version; Mme Stoltz).
L'Enfance du Christ (same cast as before).
28 January 1855   Paris, Salle Herz   Berlioz
Third *Enfance du Christ* concert. Repeat of concert of 24 December.
17 February 1855   Weimar, Court   Berlioz
First of two Weimar concerts. Excerpts from *Roméo et Juliette*. *La Captive*. *Chœur
des ciseleurs* from *Benvenuto Cellini*. *Concert des sylphes* from *La Damnation de
Faust*. Liszt's E♭ Concerto (Liszt, piano).
21 February 1855   Weimar, Grand-Ducal Theater   Berlioz
Second Weimar concert benefiting musicians' pension fund. *L'Enfance du Christ*
(Fräulein Genast: Ste. Marie; von Milde: St. Joseph; Hermanns: Hérode; Caspari:
récitant). *Symphonie fantastique*. *Lélio* (Grans, declamation; Caspari, tenor; von
Milde, baritone; Liszt, piano; Jeanette Pohl, harp).
17 March 1855   Brussels, Théâtre du Cirque   Berlioz
First of three *Enfance du Christ* concerts. *L'Enfance du Christ*, complete (Mlle
Dobré: Ste. Marie; Carman: St. Joseph; Depoitier: Hérode; Audran: *récitant;*
Barielle: *père de famille*). *Le Carnaval romain*. *La Captive* (Mlle Elmire). *Fête
chez Capulet* from *Roméo et Juliette*.
22 March 1855   Brussels, Théâtre du Cirque   Berlioz
Second *Enfance du Christ* concert. *L'Enfance du Christ*.
27 March 1855   Brussels, Théâtre du Cirque   Berlioz
Third *Enfance du Christ* concert. *L'Enfance du Christ*.
7 April 1855   Paris, Opéra-Comique   Berlioz
Part I of *L'Enfance du Christ*. Works of Clari and Haydn.
30 April 1855   Paris, Church of St.-Eustache   Berlioz
Te Deum, first performance (Perrier, tenor; Edouard Batiste, organ).
13 June 1855   London, Exeter Hall   Berlioz
Fifth concert of the New Philharmonic Society. Movts. II, IV, and III of *Roméo
et Juliette*.
4 July 1855   London, Exeter Hall   Berlioz
Sixth concert of the New Philharmonic Society. *Harold en Italie* (Ernst).
6 July 1855   London, Covent Garden   Berlioz
Mrs. Anderson's Annual Grand Morning Concert. *La Captive* (Mme Viardot).
Air from *Benvenuto Cellini* (Mme Nantier-Didiée). Works by Mozart, Beethoven
(Mrs. Anderson, piano), Weber, Rossini, and Ernst.
15 November 1855   Paris, Palais de l'Industrie   Berlioz with five
                                                      assistants
Award ceremony. *L'Impériale* (first performance). Mozart's *Ave verum corpus*.
16 November 1855   Paris, Palais de l'Industrie   Berlioz with five
                                                      assistants
L'Impériale. *Apothéose* from *Symphonie funèbre*. Movts I, II, VI, and VII of Te
Deum. Works by Handel, Mozart, Gluck, Beethoven, Weber, Rossini, and Mey-
erbeer.
18 November 1855   Paris, Palais de l'Industrie   Berlioz, Gounod,
                                                      and Delaporte
Works by Gounod, Auber, Clapisson, Dugue, and de Rille.

24 November 1855   Paris, Palais de l'Industrie
Repeat of concert of 16 November.
25 November 1855   Paris, Palais de l'Industrie
Repeat of concert of 18 November.
25 January 1856   Paris, Salle Herz   Berlioz
L'Enfance du Christ.
6 February 1856   Gotha, Ducal Theater   Berlioz
L'Enfance du Christ. Le Spectre de la rose (Mme Falconi).
16 February 1856   Weimar, Grand-Ducal Theater   Liszt
Benvenuto Cellini.
17 February 1856   Weimar, Grand-Ducal Palace   Berlioz
Le Corsaire. L'Adieu des bergers and *Le Repos de la Sainte-Famille* from *L'Enfance du Christ. Evocation et menuet des follets* from *La Damnation de Faust.*
18 February 1856   Weimar, Grand-Ducal Theater   Liszt
Benvenuto Cellini.
28 February 1856   Weimar, Grand-Ducal Theater   Berlioz
Benefit for widows and orphans of the musicians. *La Damnation de Faust,* complete (Caspari: Faust; von Milde: Méphistophélès; Roth: Brander; Frau von Milde: Marguerite).
15 August 1856   Baden, Salon de Conversation   Berlioz
Excerpts from *L'Enfance du Christ* (Greminger, tenor). *L'Invitation à la valse.* Works by Victoria, Grandi, Gluck, Mozart, Beethoven, Bellini, and Verdi (vocal works sung by Greminger, Mlle Duprez, and Mme Viardot).
18 August 1857   Baden, Salon de Conversation   Berlioz
Les Francs-Juges ov. *Le Spectre de la rose* (Mme Widemann). Judex crederis from Te Deum. *Marche hongroise* from *La Damnation de Faust.* Works by Handel, Mozart, Gluck, Beethoven, Rossini, and Verdi.
2 May 1858   Paris, Salle du Conservatoire   Berlioz
Third Henry Litolff concert. *La Captive* (orchestra, with Mme Falconi). Movt. II of *Roméo et Juliette.* Works of Handel, Rossi, and Litolff.
27 August 1858   Baden, Salon de Conversation   Berlioz
Movts. I–IV of *Roméo et Juliette* (Mme Charton-Demeur). *Sara la baigneuse,* with three choruses. Works by Victoria, Mozart, Beethoven, Weber, Rossini, and Litolff (Roger, tenor; Litolff, piano; Vivier, horn).
23 April 1859   Paris, Opéra-Comique   Berlioz
L'Enfance du Christ (Mme Meillet: Ste. Marie; Meillet: St. Joseph; Jourdan: récitant). *Hymne à la France.* Excerpts from *La Damnation de Faust.* Works of Bach/Gounod, Beethoven, Weber, and Ritter.
8 June 1859   Bordeaux, Municipal Theater   Berlioz
Le Carnaval romain. Excerpts from *L'Enfance du Christ.* Excerpts from *Roméo et Juliette.*
29 August 1859   Baden, Salon de Conversation   Berlioz
Movts. I–IV of *Roméo et Juliette.* Duo of Chorèbe and Cassandre from act I of *Les Troyens* (Mme Viardot: Cassandre; Jules Lefort: Chorèbe). Duo of Didon and Enée from act IV of *Les Troyens* (Mme Viardot, Lefort). *Plaisir d'amour* (?). Works by Rossini, Meyerbeer, and Ritter (Ritter, piano; Alexandre, organ; Schwab, clarinet).
27 August 1860   Baden, Salon de Conversation   Berlioz
Francs-Juges ov. *Cavatine* from *Benvenuto Cellini* (Mme Carvalho). Excerpts from *Faust* (Eberius: Faust; Oberhofer: Méphistophélès). *Le Roi des aulnes* (Roger, tenor). Works of Gluck (with Mme Viardot), Weber, Molique, Vieuxtemps, and Bach/Gounod.

26 August 1861   Baden, Salon de Conversation   Berlioz
Harold en Italie (Grodvolle). Dies irae and Offertoire from Requiem. Works by Beethoven, Méhul, Donizetti, Mendelssohn, Halévy, and Verdi.

9, 13 August 1862   Baden, New Theater   Berlioz
Béatrice et Bénédict (first performances; Mme Charton-Demeur: Béatrice; Montaubry: Bénédict; Mlle Montrose: Héro).

8 February 1863   Paris, Salle Martinet   Berlioz
Concert of Félicien David's Société Musicale. *La Fuite en Egypte* from *L'Enfance du Christ* (Wartôt, tenor). *Le Carnaval romain. L'Invitation à la valse.* Works of David and Bizet.

22 February 1863   Paris, Salle Martinet   Berlioz
Concert of Félicien David's Société Musicale. Berlioz's portion of the concert repeated from 8 February. David's *Christophe Colomb.*

8, 10 April 1863   Weimar, Grand-Ducal Theater   Berlioz
Béatrice et Bénédict, with two new movements (Mme Milde: Béatrice; Knop: Bénédict). Also performed on 30 April, conductor unknown.

19 April 1863   Löwenberg, Court Theater   Berlioz
Le Roi Lear. Harold en Italie. Le Carnaval romain. Movts. III and II of *Roméo et Juliette.*

22 June 1863   Strasbourg, Place Kleber   Berlioz
Lower Rhine Music Festival; opening of Kehl bridge. *L'Enfance du Christ.* Works of other composers.

14, 18 August 1863   Baden Theater   Berlioz
Béatrice et Bénédict, revival of 1862 production, with the new movements first heard in Weimar.

4 November 1863   Paris, Théâtre-Lyrique   Delloffre
Les Troyens à Carthage (first performance; Mme Charton-Demeur: Didon; Monjauze: Enée; Mme Dubois: Anna; Petit: Narbal; De Quercy: Iopas; Rhapsode: Jouanny). Then performed 6, 9, 11, 13, 16, 18, 20, 23, 25, 27, 30 November, 2, 4, 7, 9, 11, 14, 16, 18, 20 December: a total of twenty-one performances.

16 December 1866   Vienna, Redoutensaal   Berlioz
La Damnation de Faust (first Vienna performance; Wolter: Faust; Mayerhofer: Méphistophélès; Mlle Bettelheim: Marguerite).

26 February 1867   Cologne   Berlioz
Harold en Italie. Duo-Nocturne from *Béatrice et Bénédict.*

8 July 1867   Paris, Palais de l'Industrie   George-Hainl
A festival program with *Hymne à la France* and works of Gluck, Beethoven, Méhul, Rossini, Auber, and David. Because of Louis's death, Berlioz did not conduct.

28 November 1867   St. Petersburg   Berlioz
First St. Petersburg concert. *Absence* (Mlle Regan). *Benvenuto Cellini* ov. Works by Mozart, Beethoven (Sixth Symphony), and Weber (*Oberon* ov.).

7 December 1867   St. Petersburg   Berlioz
Second St. Petersburg concert. *Symphonie fantastique.* Excerpts from Gluck's *Iphigénie et Tauride.* Beethoven's *Leonora* overture No. 3.

14 December 1867   St. Petersburg   Berlioz
Third St. Petersburg concert. *Le Carnaval romain. Rêverie et Caprice* (Wieniawski). Act II of Gluck's *Orphée.* Beethoven's Fifth Symphony. A Wieniawski concerto.

28 December 1867   St. Petersburg   Berlioz
Fourth St. Petersburg concert. *Francs-Juges* ov. Offertoire from Requiem. Excerpts from Gluck's *Alceste* and Beethoven's Third Symphony.

8 January 1868   Moscow, Assembly of the Nobility   Berlioz
   Le Carnaval romain. Offertoire from Requiem. Movt. II of *Roméo et Juliette*.
   Works by Handel, Mozart, Beethoven, and Glinka.
11 January 1868   Moscow, Assembly of the Nobility   Berlioz
   Le Roi Lear. Offertoire from Requiem. *Harold en Italie* (Laub). Beethoven's Violin
   Concerto (Laub).
25 January 1868   St. Petersburg   Berlioz
   Fifth St. Petersburg concert. No Berlioz. Works by Bach, Haydn, Weber, and
   Paganini. Beethoven's Emperor Concerto (Dörffel) and Fourth Symphony.
8 February 1868   St. Petersburg   Berlioz
   Sixth and last St. Petersburg concert. Excerpts from *Roméo et Juliette*. Excerpts
   from *Faust*. *Harold en Italie* (Weickmann).

Bibliography

GENERAL

Scores. Berlioz's scores are available in two critical editions. The New Berlioz Edition (*Hector Berlioz: New Edition of the Complete Works*), under the general editorship of Hugh Macdonald, is published by Bärenreiter-Verlag of Kassel in association with the Berlioz Centenary Committee and the Calouste Gulbenkian Foundation of Lisbon. To date the following volumes have been published:

2. *Les Troyens,* ed. Hugh Macdonald, three fascicles (1969–70).
3. *Béatrice et Bénédict,* ed. Hugh Macdonald (1980).
5. *Huit Scènes de Faust,* ed. Julian Rushton (1970).
8. *La Damnation de Faust,* ed. Julian Rushton (1979; vol. 8b, Supplement, 1986).
9. *Grande Messe des morts* (Requiem), ed. Jürgen Kindermann (1978).
10. Te Deum, ed. Denis McCaldin (1973).
13. *Songs for Solo Voice and Orchestra,* ed. Ian Kemp (1975).
16. *Symphonie fantastique,* ed. Nicholas Temperley (1972).
18. *Roméo et Juliette,* ed. D. Kern Holoman (1989).
19. *Grande Symphonie funèbre et triomphale,* ed. Hugh Macdonald (1967).
25. D. Kern Holoman, *Catalogue of the Works of Hector Berlioz* (1987).

Benvenuto Cellini, vol. 1, ed. Hugh Macdonald, is in the final stages of preparation. All the volumes of the New Berlioz Edition include facsimiles of sources.

The numeration scheme for musical compositions adopted in my *Catalogue of the Works of Hector Berlioz* is summarized in Appendix A. The *Catalogue* also documents work envisaged but not composed, books, and all the newspaper articles.

Edition Eulenburg has issued miniature reprints of the NBE *Symphonie fantastique* (no. 422), the *Grande Symphonie funèbre et triomphale* (no. 599), the Te Deum (no. 1095), *Les Troyens* (no. 925), and the *Chasse royale et orage* (no. 1371) drawn from that opera. Eulenburg has also reprinted a number of earlier editions with new introductions by Hugh Macdonald.

The first Berlioz edition (*Hector Berlioz: Werke,* 20 vols.) was prepared by Charles Malherbe and Felix Weingartner between 1900 and 1907 (Leipzig: Breitkopf & Härtel). It appears that Malherbe, an archivist at the Opéra and distinguished collector of musical autographs, did most of the scholarly work, while Weingartner modernized the scores according to his notions of proper orchestral practice. (Most notable of the changes were the revoicing of the bassoon parts and the rewriting of ophicleide parts for the modern tuba, this latter practice sometimes involving octave transpositions. His most vexing change.was the insertion of the horn lines above the bassoon lines. Texted works were presented in three languages, of which the English is especially poor.) The enterprise collapsed, apparently the victim of Malherbe's deteriorating health and the strained political relationship between France and Germany, before it could offer full scores of *Benvenuto Cellini* and *Les Troyens*.

Despite Jacques Barzun's savage attack on Malherbe and Weingartner's work ("Errors in the 'Complete' Edition of the Scores," *Berlioz and the Romantic Century*, vol. 2 [New York, 1969], pp. 358–81), the old edition provided reasonably accurate, if not definitive, texts of the great majority of Berlioz's works and encouraged serious and informed performances of his compositions all over the world. Edwin F. Kalmus reprinted the old edition in both conventional and miniature formats, including in the reprinted series French scores of the two operas lacking from Malherbe and Weingartner as well as a reprint of Schlesinger's edition of the Weber-Berlioz *Freischütz* (Paris, 1842).

The original French editions of the scores, published for the most part by Maurice Schlesinger, Schlesinger's successor Gemmy Brandus, or Simon Richault, are of excellent quality and are still available in various reprints. (Berlioz's own copies, carefully bound and titled, are in **F-Pc**.) Several of the modern pocket scores are modeled directly on the French originals.

The published editions of Berlioz's works are copiously documented by Cecil Hopkinson in *A Bibliography of the Musical and Literary Works of Hector Berlioz, 1803–1869, with Histories of the French Music Publishers Concerned* (Edinburgh, 1951; 2nd edn., incorporating the author's additions and corrections, ed. Richard Macnutt, Tunbridge Wells; Richard Macnutt, 1980). The order of publication of Berlioz's works, which Hopkinson generally follows, has, however, little to do with the chronology of their composition.

Edward T. Cone's edition of the *Symphonie fantastique*, a Norton Critical Score (New York, 1971), is a useful source, particularly for its analysis of the work. In the United States, several of the larger works for orchestra and chorus have been published in handsome editions by Broude Brothers: *Lélio*, the Requiem, *Roméo et Juliette*, *La Damnation de Faust*, and *L'Enfance du Christ*.

Recordings: The Colin Davis Berlioz Cycle. Conceived as a definitive recording project, the Colin Davis Berlioz cycle has immortalized performances based on reliable sources and using proper instrumentation. Excellent jacket notes and translations are provided. The recordings include the overtures (Philips recording number 6570031); *La Mort de Cléopâtre* and *Herminie* (9500683); the *Symphonie fantastique* (6500774; a later recording with Davis and the Amsterdam Concertgebouw is 835188); *Harold en Italie* (9500026); the Requiem (670019); *Benvenuto Cellini* (6707019); *Roméo et Juliette* (839716/7); *Nuits d'été*, using the voice parts Berlioz suggests, and several of the other important orchestral songs (6500009; a later recording of the *Nuits d'été* with Jessye Norman is 9500783); the *Symphonie funèbre et triomphale*, prologue to *Les Troyens à Carthage*, and *Marche funèbre pour la dernière scène d'Hamlet* (802913); *La Damnation de Faust* (6703042); the Te Deum, though without the concluding *Marche pour la présentation des drapeaux* (839770); *L'Enfance du Christ* (6700106; a later recording is 9500342); *Les Troyens* (6709002), and *Béatrice et Bénédict* (6700121). Davis describes the project on p. 5 of the booklet accompanying *Les Troyens*.

Colin Davis also recorded several Berlioz works (*L'Enfance du Christ*, *Béatrice et Bénédict*, *Cléopâtre*) for Oiseau-Lyre, a firm that released the *Neuf Mélodies* in their original settings (SOL 305). Charles Munch conducted the Boston Symphony Orchestra in a much earlier series of Berlioz recordings.

Prose Writings. Berlioz's *Mémoires* were written in several installments. The final pages were penned in 1865, just before the book went to the engraver; a few copies were drawn at that time and distributed by Berlioz to his friends. He left several hundred copies in his office at the library of the Conservatoire to be bound and released after his death; thus the publication was ultimately dated 1870. Ernest Newman's revision (New York, 1932) of a translation by Rachel and Eleanor Holmes (London, 1884) is still available in a Dover reprint. The more exceptional accomplishment is David Cairns's translation and scholarly annotation of the work (various edns., notably New York: W. W. Norton, 1975), critical to modern Berlioz scholarship. The Cairns edition includes, on pp. 613–14, a summary of "Sources of the Memoirs." A two-volume paperback edition of the French text is published by Garnier-Flammarion (ed. Pierre Citron, Paris, 1969). Joseph-Marc Ballbé entitles his assessment of the autobiography *Berlioz, artiste et écrivain dans les "Mémoires"* (Paris, 1972).

Berlioz's most engaging prose was collected during his lifetime in three books, each offered in a scholarly edition during the Berlioz centenary (ed. Léon Guichard, Paris: Gründ): *Les Soirées de l'orchestre* (1852; 1968); *Les Grotesques de la musique* (1859; 1969); and *A Travers Chants* (1862; 1971). Jacques Barzun has translated *Evenings with the Orchestra* (New York, 1956; reprinted by University of Chicago Press, 1973); except where noted, I have used Barzun's translations when citing excerpts from the *Soirées*. English translations of six of the major articles from *A Travers Chants* are found in *Hector Berlioz: Selections from His Letters and Writings* (New York, 1879). The complete work was published as three little books translated by Edwin Evans: *A Critical Study of Beethoven's Nine Symphonies* (London, 1913); *Gluck and His Operas* (London, 1915); and *Mozart, Weber and Wagner, with Various Essays on Musical Subjects* (London, 1918). These have been reprinted several times.

The complete literary works—that is to say, the books published during Berlioz's lifetime—have been reprinted from early French editions by Gregg Press (7 vols.: Westmead, Farnborough, Hants., 1973). This set includes, in addition to the three collections and the *Mémoires*, both the orchestration treatise of 1843 and the *Voyage musical en Allemagne et en Italie* (2 vols., Paris, 1844).

The *Grand Traité d'instrumentation et d'orchestration modernes* appeared in 1843, published by Schonenberger. It had been written in sixteen installments for the *R&GM*, 21 November 1841 to 17 July 1842. A second edition was published in 1855, to which was added a section on conducting (*L'Art du chef d'orchestre*) and descriptions of certain instruments recently invented. The Gregg Press edition of Berlioz's literary works includes as vol. 5 the 1860 Lemoine reprint of the 1855 revised edition. The treatise was translated into most of the European languages; the English translation was by Mary Cowden Clarke (London, 1856). A new English translation is being prepared by Hugh Macdonald. Berlioz's treatise was revised and expanded by both Felix Weingartner (1904) and Richard Strauss (1904–5).

Feuilletons. The monumental series of newspaper articles written by Berlioz is presently being prepared for publication by H. Robert Cohen and a team of assisting scholars. André Hallays selected important *feuilletons* from the *Journal des Débats*, mostly concerning the great opening nights at the Opéra, for a collection he called *Les Musiciens et la musique* (Paris, [1903]), reprinted in the Gregg Press series cited above. An interesting selection of articles not included in the familiar sources appears in a recent book called *Hector Berlioz: Cauchemars et Passions* (Nightmares and Passions), ed. Gérard Condé (Paris, 1981).

I catalogue Berlioz's *feuilletons* and their subsequent reprintings in part II of my *Catalogue*, pp. 435–88. Earlier attempts at chronicling this huge *œuvre* were made by J.-G. Prod'homme in his "Bibliographie berliozienne," *Sammelbände der Internationalen Musikgesellschaft* 5 (1903–4), 622–59 (reprinted in *Revue musicale* 233 [1956]: 97–147), and by Julius Kapp in his *Berlioz: eine Biographie* (Berlin, 1917), pp. 226–56.

Berlioz's critical writings have drawn much scholarly attention. H. Robert Cohen's doctoral dissertation on the criticism, titled "Berlioz on the Opéra (1829–1849)" (New York University, 1973), lists a great deal of the previous work on the subject. See also Cohen's article "Hector Berlioz critique musical: ses écrits sur l'Opéra de Paris de 1829 à 1849," *Revue de musicologie* 63 (1977), 17–34. Katherine Kolb-Reeve's doctoral dissertation was titled "The Poetics of the Orchestra in the Writings of Hector Berlioz," (Yale University, 1978); her superb treatment of Berlioz as a writer, "Hector Berlioz (1803–1869)," appears in *The Romantic Century (European Writers*, vol. 6) (New York, 1985), pp. 771–812. The Australian musicologist Kerry Murphy has done interesting work on the question of the authenticity of unsigned articles; see her "Attribution of Some Unsigned Articles of Berlioz in the *Revue et Gazette musicale de Paris* (1834–1837)," *Musicology Australia* 8 (1985), 39–49.

Correspondence. Berlioz's correspondence is collected in the excellent *Correspondance générale*, edited by a group of scholars led by Pierre Citron of the Université de la Sorbonne Nouvelle (vol. I: 1803–32 [1972]; vol. II: 1832–42 [1975]; vol. III: 1842–50 [1978]; vol. IV: 1851–55 [1983]; vol. V: 1855–59 [1989]; two volumes are yet to be published). None of the earlier editions or translations of the letters compares in scope and accuracy with the *Correspondance générale*.

Volume II (1832–42) of the *Correspondance générale*, ed. Frédéric Robert (Paris, 1975), must be used with caution, however, for it makes quite a number of errors of date and fact; I have noted these where they affect the information presented here. (To give a single example, nothing could be clearer than that the loan of 2,000 francs from Legouvé to allow the composer to finish *Benvenuto Cellini*, mentioned in chapter 48 of the *Mémoires*, is but an exaggerated version of the 1,000 francs mentioned in CG 558, 559, 561, and 563, all of July 1838; yet Robert [p. 271] dates the incident as occurring in 1836—an error perpetuated in Macdonald's *Berlioz;* see p. 32.)

The *Correspondance générale* succeeds a perplexing jumble of editions, the first of which were an abridged and inaccurate *Correspondance inédite de Hector Berlioz, 1819–1868*, ed. Daniel Bernard (Paris, 1879), and the 141 *Lettres intimes* to Humbert Ferrand (Paris, 1882). These were succeeded by Julien Tiersot's multivolume, but unfinished, attempt to collect the complete correspondence: *Les Années romantiques, 1819–1842* (Paris, 1904); *Le Musicien errant, 1842–1852* (Paris, 1915); and *Au milieu du chemin, 1852–1855* (Paris, 1930). Tiersot's project continued in bits and pieces (though no further book-length collections appeared); the most useful of these is "Lettres de Berlioz sur 'Les Troyens'," *Revue de Paris* 28, no. 4 (1921), 449–73, 749–70; no. 5 (1921), 146–71. The letters, mostly to Mme Viardot and to Berlioz's family, go from 11 June 1856 to 24 June 1863. A selection of letters to, from, and about Berlioz is included in Tiersot's *Lettres de musiciens écrites en français du XVe au XXe siècle* (2 vols., Turin, 1924–36), II, 154–218; the Berlioz section appears also in *Rivista musicale italiana* 36 (1929), 1–25, 408–29; 37 (1930), 1–20.

Volume V of the *Correspondance générale* concludes with a letter to Adèle of 26 August 1859; Tiersot's third volume of collected corespondence, *Au milieu du chemin, 1852–1855*, has thus been superseded. Pending publication of volumes VI and VII of the *Correspondance générale*, the reader must be content with the array of editions of the correspondence that existed before *CG*. These include the *Briefe von Hector Berlioz an die Fürstin Carolyne Sayn-Wittgenstein*, ed. La Mara (a pseudonym of Marie Lipsius) (Leipzig, 1902), the most important collection of his later correspondence, and Berlioz's letters to Estelle Fornier, found in *Une Page d'amour romantique: Lettres à Mme Estelle F.* (Paris, 1903). Another important collection is Jacques Barzun's *New Letters of Berlioz, 1830–1868,* with text in French and English (translated by Barzun) (New York, 1954; reprinted by Greenwood Press).

In his review of the *Correspondance générale,* vol. II, Ralph Locke transcribes and translates a cache of letters from the collection of Rudolf Nydahl, now in the Stiftelsen Musikkulturens Främjande, Stockholm; most of them are from the 1830s. See his "New Letters of Berlioz," *19th-Century Music* I (1977), 71–84.

Biographies. The first book-length biography of Berlioz was Eugène de Mirecourt's study of 1856, sympathetic if somewhat anecdotal and flawed. (The author's true name was C. J. B. Jacquot.) Chief among the great biographies of Berlioz are the three volumes of Adolphe Boschot: *La Jeunesse d'un romantique: Hector Berlioz, 1803–1831* (Paris, 1906; rev. 1946); *Un Romantique sous Louis-Philippe: Hector Berlioz, 1831–1842* (Paris, 1908; rev. 1948); and *Le Crépuscule d'un romantique: Hector Berlioz, 1842–1869* (Paris, 1913; rev. 1950). (Note that the pagination differs in the revised editions.) Other biographies in French include Adolphe Jullien, *Hector Berlioz: Sa Vie et ses œuvres* (Paris, 1888); Edmond Hippeau, *Berlioz intime* (Paris, 1883) and *Berlioz et son temps* (Paris, 1890); Julien Tiersot, *Hector Berlioz et la sociéte de son temps* (Paris, 1904); and J.-G. Prod'homme, *Hector Berlioz (1803–1869): Sa Vie et ses œuvres* (Paris, 1904). Tiersot (1857–1936), Boschot (1871–1955), and Prod'homme (1871–1956) were a formidable trio, who "preferred to work on their own and only come together when special circumstances demanded an entente" (see Hugh Macdonald, "Hector Berlioz 1969: A Centenary Assessment," *ADAM* 331–33 [1969], 38). Their work constitutes the first wave of Berlioz scholarship.

In German, Louise Pohl's *Hector Berlioz' Leben und Werke* (Leipzig, 1900) incorporates the significant research and first-person reminiscences of her husband Richard Pohl, whose second wife she was. (The first Mme Pohl was the harpist who often played for Berlioz in Germany.) The most interesting recent book in German is by Wolfgang Dömling, *Hector Berlioz und seine Zeit* (Regensburg, 1986), a collection of various critical and biographical essays with substantial scholarly apparatus (texts of libretti, pictures, index of works, bibliography).

For a grand biography in English, see Jacques Barzun, *Berlioz and the Romantic Century* (Boston, 1950; reprinted as a third edition, with some changes, New York, 1969). Barzun's two volumes conclude with a comprehensive bibliography, for all intents and purposes the definitive listing of work through 1950. A "second edition," abridged and widely available in paperback, was titled *Berlioz and His Century* (New York, 1956; reprinted by University of Chicago Press). Barzun's table of "Berlioz' Domiciles" (II, 356–57), has largely been superseded. (His remark "This and other differences are usually due to the renumbering of the street, and occasionally to the writer's careless haste" must be disregarded altogether, as must his implication that the rue de Calais and the rue Vintimille—which in fact intersect—are the same street.) Barzun's most recent commentary on Berlioz appears in his collected essays, *Critical Questions on Music and Letters, Culture and Biography, 1940–80* (Chicago, 1982). Hugh Macdonald's *Berlioz* (London, 1982) is a relatively short but formidable life-and-works in the Master Musicians series. Finally, vol. I of David Cairn's two-volume biography, *Hector Berlioz, 1803–1832: The Making of an Artist,* has recently been published (London, 1989).

Exhibition Catalogues. Of the several very interesting published catalogues of centenary exhibitions, the most useful is *Berlioz and the Romantic Imagination,* the catalogue of an Arts Council exhibition at the Victoria and Albert Museum (London, 1969). See also *Hector Berlioz,* the catalogue of an exhibition at the Bibliothèque

Nationale (Paris, 1969), and the catalogue of the Gulbenkian Foundation's *Exposição commemorativa de centençentrio da morte de Hector Berlioz* (Lisbon, 1969).

Miscellaneous. Most of the important musicians and literary figures of the century included passages on Berlioz in their recollections. Among these contemporaries were Ferdinand Hiller, Auguste Barbier, Antoine Etex, Eugène Sauzay, Ernest Legouvé, Joseph d'Ortigue, Gilbert Duprez, Max Maretzek, Francis Hueffer, J. W. Davison, Gustave Roger, Peter Cornelius, Gounod, Saint-Saëns, Stasov, Rimsky-Korsakov, and Ernest Reyer. Their works are cited in the following pages.

Many of the original sources for Berlioz study were described by Tiersot in *Berlioziana,* which was serialized weekly in *Le Ménestrel,* 1904–6 and (for brief runs) 1909–11. I discussed much of the Berlioz literature to 1975 in my article "The Present State of Berlioz Research," *Acta musicologica* 47 (1975), 31–67. More recently Michael G. H. Wright, in *A Berlioz Bibliography: Critical Writing on Hector Berlioz from 1825 to 1986* (Farnborough, Hants., [1988]) has indexed nearly 2,500 books and articles.

The Berlioz Style. The most accomplished book-length study of the Berlioz style is Julian Rushton's *The Musical Language of Berlioz* (Cambridge, England, 1983); for reviews, see Hugh Macdonald in the [London] *Times Literary Supplement,* no. 4221 (24 February 1984), 187, and Charles Rosen, "Battle over Berlioz," in the *New York Review of Books* 31, no. 7 (26 April 1984), 40–43. Briefer but no less excellent is the treatment of Edward T. Cone, "Inside the Saint's Head" (the reference is to an incident recounted in the *Mémoires), Musical Newsletter* 1 (1971), 3–12, 16–20; 2 (1972), 19–22 (reprinted in *The Garland Library of the History of Western Music,* vol. 9 [New York, 1985], pp. 1–19). Cone's other critical remarks on Berlioz include his analysis of the *Symphonie fantastique* in the Norton Score, cited later, and "A Lesson from Berlioz," in *The Composer's Voice* (Berkeley, 1974), pp. 81–114.

Other general studies of the Berlioz style include Hugh Macdonald's *Berlioz Orchestral Music,* a BBC Music Guide (London, 1969; reprinted 1974); Brian Primmer, *The Berlioz Style* (London, 1973); and John Crabbe, *Hector Berlioz: Rational Romantic* (London, 1980), which is devoted to "the spiritual and intellectual framework" for Berlioz's ideas. Philip Friedheim provides a significant consideration of Berlioz's musical grammar in "Radical Harmonic Procedures in Berlioz," *Music Review* 21 (1960), 282–96. Rudolf Bockholdt's *Berlioz-Studien* (Tutzing, 1979) consists of essays on Berlioz's instrumental style, notably in *Roméo et Juliette,* and on the works (including the *Freischütz* recitatives) with French and German texts. See also Bockholdt's "Eigenschaften des Rhythmus im instrumentalen Satz bei Beethoven und Berlioz," *Bericht über des internationalen musikwissenschaflichen Kongress, Bonn 1970,* ed. Carl Dalhaus et al. (Kassel, 1971), pp. 29–33. I cite quite a number of earlier analytical and critical studies in "The Present State of Berlioz Research," pp. 61–65. Rushton's *Musical Language of Berlioz* has a comprehensive bibliography of analytical studies, pp. 293–96.

On the matter of self-borrowings, see Hugh Macdonald "Berlioz's Self-Borrowings," *Proceedings of the Royal Musical Association* 92 (1965–66), 27–44 (reprinted in *The Garland Library of the History of Western Music,* vol. 9 [New York, 1985], pp. 79–96).

1 8 0 3 – 4 0

The La Côte Period. The acknowledged master of the La Côte period in Berlioz's life is David Cairns. See, especially, the entry on "The Berlioz Family" in his edition of the *Memoirs,* pp. 529–30; the discussion of the family tree, p. 531; the entry on "La Côte-St.-André," p. 537; and the notes on pp. 573–75. A comprehensive tree of the Berlioz side of the family appears as a foldout plate at the beginning of the *Livre d'or du centenaire d'Hector Berlioz* (Paris, 1907); a good chronology of the Berlioz ancestors, 1747–1815, is found in the *Correspondance générale*, I, 21–22.

The La Côte period is described in French in Edmond Hippeau's *Berlioz intime* (Paris, 1889), pp. 1–190, which includes Joseph Favre's recollections; see also the opening chapter of Tiersot's *Berlioziana*, "Au Musée Berlioz." *Berlioz and the Romantic Imagination,* the Victoria and Albert catalogue, opens with a splendid evocation of La Côte-St.-André. Dr. Berlioz's *livre de raison* and the contracts with the music masters are in the Berlioz Museum in La Côte-St.-André. The contracts are transcribed in *Berlioziana* 1904, p. 84. The passport, now lost, was formerly in the Collection Maignien, Grenoble. It was described by most of the early biographers, including Tiersot (*Berlioziana* 1904, p. 4) and Boschot (I, 29 and 81); see also *Memoirs*, ed. Cairns, p. 519. The *Recueil de romances* was published as 25 *Romances for Voice & Guitar*, ed. M. Henke and M. Stegemann (Heidelberg: Chanterelle, 1986).

Paris. The most useful treatment of Paris in the nineteenth century is a compendium of 4,000 illustrations, diverse documents of all sorts, and an annual chronology of events, titled *Paris de 1800 à 1900, d'après les estampes et les mémoires du temps,* ed. Charles Simond (3 vols.; Paris, 1900). An excellent general work on French history and culture is *France: A Companion to French Studies,* 2nd edn., ed. D. G. Charlton (New York, 1979). On the sort of street life Berlioz probably led, see the engaging work of Paul d'Ariste, *La Vie et le monde du boulevard (1830–70): Un Dandy (Nestor Roqueplan)* (Paris, 1930); Georges Cain, *Anciens Théâtres de Paris* (Paris, 1920); and Jacques Boulenger, *Sous Louis-Philippe: Le Boulevard* (Paris, 1933). A more recent, specialized work on *La Musique à Paris en 1830–31,* prepared by a seminar of French scholars under the direction of François Lesure (Paris, 1983), is essentially an almanac documenting every detail of musical life in those two years. Lesure's introduction (pp. 1–11) is an especially penetrating overview of the artistic climate in Paris at the time.

The look of Paris music-making is encyclopedically captured in *Les Gravures musicales dans L'Illustration (1843–1899),* ed. H. Robert Cohen, with Sylvia L'Ecuyer Lacroix and Jacques Léveillé (3 vols.; Quebec, 1983). Concerning productions at the Opéra, see also Nicole Wild, *Décors et costumes du XIXe siècle,* vol. 1, *Opéra de Paris* (Paris, 1987).

Concerning the holdings and movement of various archives of documents in Paris, see *French Archives,* a special issue of *19th-Century Music* (VII [1983], 99–142), with contributions by M. Elizabeth C. Bartlet, Elisabeth Bernard, Peter Bloom, H. Robert Cohen, D. Kern Holoman, and Jean-Michel Nectoux.

For more on Parisian musical life, see three recent books: William Weber, *Music and the Middle Class: Social Structure of Concert Life in London, Paris, and Vienna, 1830–1848* (London, 1975); Jeffrey Cooper, *The Rise of Instrumental Music and Concert Series in Paris, 1828–1871* (Ann Arbor, 1983); and Jane F. Fulcher, *The Nation's Image: French Grand Opera as Politics and Politicized Art* (Cambridge, Mass., 1987). On Weber in Paris, see John Warrack, *Carl Maria von Weber,* 2nd edn. (Cambridge, 1976), pp. 345–49.

Le Sueur. For biographical information on Le Sueur, see Octave Fouque, *Les Révolutionnaires de la musique* (Paris, 1882), pp. 1–184, and Jean Mongrédien, *Jean-François Le Sueur: Contribution à l'étude d'un demi-siècle de musique française (1780–1830)* (2 vols.; Berne, 1980). Mongrédien simultaneously published a thematic catalogue of Le Sueur's works. This remarkable trilogy was reviewed and summarized in English by me (*Journal of the American Musicological Society* 34 [1981], 566–73) and by David Charlton (*19th-Century Music* 6 [1982], 166–70). Berlioz's obituary articles on Le Sueur for the *R&GM* and the *JD* are conflated, with a few other lines about Le Sueur from other articles, in Condé, pp. 150–61. See also *MM*, pp. 59–79.

The Conservatoire and the prix de Rome. On Cherubini's notebooks, see Holoman, "Berlioz au Conservatoire: Notes biographiques," *Revue de musicologie* 62 (1976), 289–92. Eugène Sauzay's memoirs are transcribed by Brigitte François-Sappey in "La Vie musicale à Paris à travers les *Mémoires* d'Eugène Sauzay (1809–1901)," *Revue de musicologie* 60 (1974), 159–210. Sauzay's memoirs were compiled between 1889 and 1891.

On Berlioz and his encounters with the Institute and the government, see the excellent work of Peter Bloom: "Orpheus' Lyre Resurrected: A *Tableau Musical* by Berlioz," *Musical Quarterly* 61 (1975), 189–211 (on *La Mort d'Orphée*); "Berlioz and Officialdom: Unpublished Correspondence," *19th-Century Music* 4 (1980), 134–46 (a series of letters mostly from 1833–36); "Berlioz and the *Prix de Rome* of 1830," *Journal of the American Musicological Society* 34 (1981), 279–304; and the more general study, dealing mostly with later developments, "Berlioz à l'Institut Revisited," *Acta musicologica* 53 (1981), 171–99. See also Bloom's "Berlioz and the Critic: *La Damnation de Fétis*," in *Studies in Musicology in Honor of Otto E. Albrecht* (Kassel, 1980; written 1973), pp. 240–65, wherein most of Fétis's assessments of Berlioz are translated into English.

A facsimile of the scribal copy of Berlioz's 1827 prize cantata, *La Mort d'Orphée* (Paris: Réunion des Bibliothèques nationales, 1930) has been made from **F-Pn** Rés. Vma ms 1. See also Adolphe Boschot, "Berlioz: Une Cantate perdue pendant un siècle," in *Chez les musiciens*, 2ᵉ série (Paris, 1924), pp. 50–56.

Harriet Smithson, the English Shakespeare troupe. Peter Raby filled a long-acknowledged gap in Berlioz studies with his *Fair Ophelia: Harriet Smithson Berlioz* (Cambridge, 1982), an altogether scintillating biography. My review for the *Musical Times* (124, no. 1690 [December 1983], 749–50) is largely incorporated in this book; see also Cosette Thompson's review in *19th-Century Music* 8 (1984), 69–71. Concerning Shakespeare in Paris, see (in addition to Raby) John R. Elliott, Jr., "The Shakespeare Berlioz Saw," *Music and Letters* 57 (1976), 292–308, and a dissertation by Dale Cockrell, "Hector Berlioz and 'Le Système Shakespearien'" (Ph.D. diss., University of Illinois, 1978), summarized in "A Study in French Romanticism: Berlioz and Shakespeare," *Journal of Musicological Research* 4 (1982), 85–113. Emile Deschamps's recollections of the genesis of *Roméo et Juliette* are found in the preface to *Macbeth et Roméo et Juliette: Tragédies de Shakespeare, traduites en vers français, avec une préface, des notes et des commentaires* (Paris, 1844), reprinted in *Œuvres complètes*, vol. 6, pt. 1 (Paris, 1874) and widely available in a Geneva reprint of 1973.

The Société des Concerts. Antoine Elwart provided the best chronicle of the *Histoire de la Société des Concerts du Conservatoire Impérial de Musique*, . . . (Paris, 1860). See also E.-M.-E. Deldevez, *La Société des Concerts, 1860 à 1885* (Paris, 1887) and A. Dandelot, *La Société des Concerts du Conservatoire de 1828 à 1897* (Paris, 1898, with illustrations; 2nd edn., without illustrations, Paris, 1923). I treat one significant chapter of the relationship between Berlioz and the Société in "Orchestral Material from the Library of the Société des Concerts," *19th-Century Music* 7 (1983), 106–18.

Rouget de Lisle. See Ernest Newman, "Rouget de L'Isle, 'La Marseillaise,' and Berlioz," *Musical Times* 56 (1915), 461–63 (originally in the Birmingham *Daily Post*, 19 July 1915; see also letters of response from Tom Wotton, pp. 551–52, and Arnold Dolmetsch, p. 605), and Cecil Hopkinson, "Berlioz and the 'Marseillaise'," *Music and Letters* 51 (1970), 435–39. The recently recovered arrangement of a second patriotic work by Rouget is described by Jacques Tchamkerten, "Un Autographe inédit de Berlioz: *Le Chant du neuf Thermidor,*" *Revue musicale de Suisse romande* 37 (1984), 22–39; the article includes a complete facsimile of the autograph.

Gluck, Spontini, Beethoven. Berlioz's important essay on Gluck's *Iphigénie en Tauride* (1834) is given by Condé, pp. 186–99. On Berlioz and Spontini, see David Cairns, "Spontini's Influence on Berlioz," in *From Parnassus: Essays in Honor of Jacques Barzun* (New York, 1976), pp. 25–41. The classic treatment on the advent of Beethoven is Leo Schrade's *Beethoven in France* (New Haven, 1942). Berlioz's analyses of the Beethoven symphonies, some chamber music, and *Fidelio* are found most conveniently in *ATC,* pp. 35–103.

Les Francs-Juges. On *Les Francs-Juges,* see my article "Les Fragments de l'opéra 'perdu' de Berlioz: *Les Francs-Juges,*" *Revue de musicologie* 63 (1977), 78–88, and *Autographs,* pp. 215–36 (a subchapter on the opera and its sources) and pp. 219–325 (a transcription of the libretto). I give bibliographical references to the squabble between Boschot and Tiersot in "The Present State of Berlioz Research," p. 44 and n. 35. Macdonald treats the incident in "A Berlioz Controversy and Its Aftermath," a subchapter (pp. 38–43) of "Hector Berlioz 1969: A Centenary Assessment," *ADAM* 331–33 (1969), 35–47. Both autograph title pages of the *Marche au supplice* are given in facsimile in vol. 5 of the New Berlioz Edition, pp. 183–84.

For more on *Les Francs-Juges,* see Michel Brenet (a pseudonym of Marie Bobillier), "Berlioz inédit: *Les Francs-Juges, La Nonne sanglante,*" *Le Guide musical* 42 (1896), 63–67; Brenet offers some hints on the transmission of the manuscript fragments from Berlioz's estate to the Bibliothèque Nationale.

On the overture to *Les Francs-Juges,* see some venerable treatments: Schumann, "Ouvertüre zur 'Heimlichen Feme' (in F)," *Neue Zeitschrift für Musik* 4 (1836), 101–2 and *Gesammelte Schriften,* 5th edn. (Leipzig, 1914; reprinted Westmead, Farnborough, Hants., 1969), I, 146–47; J. L. de Casembroot, "L'Ouverture des Francs-Juges: Opinions de Mendelssohn, Schumann, et Moscheles," *Revue internationale de musique* 21 (1899), 1327–33; and the literature from the German press summarized by Theodor Müller-Reuter in *Lexikon der deutschen Konzertliteratur* (Leipzig, 1909), pp. 227–29.

The prix de Rome cantatas. The fragment of *Sardanapale* was rounded off and performed by the Springfield (Massachusetts) Symphony in connection with the Smith College colloquium of 1982. Peter Bloom's program booklet describes the work and the reconstruction.

Huit Scènes de Faust. The *Huit Scènes de Faust* constitute vol. 5 of the New Berlioz Edition, ed. Julian Rushton. See also Rushton's articles "Berlioz's 'Huit Scènes de Faust': New Source Material," *Musical Times* 155 (1974), 471–73, and "The Genesis of Berlioz's 'La Damnation de Faust'," *Music and Letters* 56 (1975), 129–46.

The Symphonie fantastique. The *Symphonie fantastique* is vol. 16 of the New Berlioz Edition, ed. Nicholas Temperley; this edition gives comprehensive citations of the literary sources for the work. See also Nicholas Temperley, "The *Symphonie fantastique* and Its Program," *Musical Quarterly* 57 (1971), 593–608. Edward T. Cone's edition for the Norton Critical Scores (New York, 1971) is an indispensable source, both for the criticism of Fétis and Schumann and for Cone's own analysis. (Note that Cone assigns measure numbers to both endings in the first movement, unlike the New Berlioz Edition; I follow the practice of the NBE.) I consider some aspects of the genesis of the *Fantastique* in chapter 4 of *Autographs,* pp. 262–82. Paul Banks treats "Coherence and Diversity in the *Symphonie fantastique*" in *19th-Century Music* 8 (1984), 37–43. See also Wolfgang Dömling's handbook, *Hector Berlioz: Symphonie fantastique* (Munich, 1985), which includes a useful bibliography for further study.

Schumann's analysis of the *Fantastique,* "Sinfonie von H. Berlioz," first appeared in the *Neue Zeitschrift für Musik* 3 (1835), 1–2, 33–35, 37–38, 41–44, 45–46, 49–51; see also Schumann's *Gesammelte Schriften* 5th edn. (Leipzig, 1914; reprinted Westmead, Farnborough, Hants., 1969), I, 69–90.

Italy. Berlioz's collected essays on his Italian journey appear, of course, in the *Mémoires*, chaps. 32–43, headed "Travels in Italy." These chapters were adopted—with a few notable changes—from the second volume of *Voyage musical en Allemagne et en Italie* (Paris, 1844; reprinted by Gregg Press, 1970). The collection *Voyage musical ... en Italie* was in turn drawn from essays of the 1830s, most notably the contributions to *Italie pittoresque* (1836) and the *Revue européene* 3, no. 7 (March–May 1832). The sad and sentimental story of Gibert's mistress Vincenza is told on the first night of the *Soirées de l'orchestre;* it originally appeared in *L'Europe littéraire* of 8 May 1833.

Berlioz's earliest and in some respects most stirring account of life in Rome is contained in his many-paged epistle from Nice of 6 May 1831 to Gounet, Girard, Hiller, and the others (*CG* 223). The memoirs of Antoine Etex are called *Les Souvenirs d'un artiste* (Paris, 1877).

I trace Berlioz's return from Rome as documented by the 1832 sketchbook in "The Berlioz Sketchbook Recovered," *19th-Century Music* 7 (1984), 282–317. Earlier descriptions of the sketchbook are in Tiersot's *Berlioziana* 1906, pp. 351–52, 361–62, 367–68, 375–76, and Boschot, II, 46n, and 86–96.

The St.-Simonians. On Berlioz's flirtation with St.-Simonism, see Ralph P. Locke, *Music, Musicians, and the St.-Simonians* (Chicago, 1986); my review appears in *Journal of the American Musicological Society* 41 (1988), 539–47. Locke's study was preceded by André Espiau de la Maestre's "Hector Berlioz und Metternich," *Oesterreichische Musikzeitschrift* 8 (1953), 365–71, which was published in French, with more commentary, as "Berlioz, Metternich, et le Saint-Simonisme," *Revue musicale* 233 (1956), 65–78.

The Return to Paris. Peter Bloom treats the composition and first performance of the *Mélologue* in "Berlioz and the Critic," cited above. The original texts of Fétis's review of the 9 December 1832 concert and of his hostile analysis of the published *Fantastique* (as transcribed by Liszt) are given by Albert Vander Linden in "En marge du centième anniversaire de la mort d'Hector Berlioz (8 mars 1869)," *Académie Royale de Belgique: Bulletin de la classe des beaux-arts* 51 (1969), 55–60.

The autograph of the sketch Berlioz prepared for d'Ortigue's 1832 article is no. 38 of the *Papiers divers de Berlioz* in F-Pn; it is transcribed in Tiersot, *Lettres de musiciens écrites en français du XVᵉ au XXᵉ siècle* (Turin, 1936), II, 172–78. See also Charles Malherbe, "Une Autobiographie de Berlioz," *Rivista musicologica italiana* 13 (1906), 506–21. D'Ortigue's biography is incorporated into his book *Le Balcon de l'Opéra* (Paris, 1833); Edward Lockspeiser translated it into English in his *The Literary Clef* (London, 1958), pp. 7–13.

Ernest Legouvé's reminiscences of Berlioz are found in his *Soixante Ans de souvenirs* (2 vols.; Paris, 1886); the English translation is by Albert D. Vandam (London, 1893), I, 203–62. Ferdinand Hiller considers Berlioz in his *Künstlerleben* (Cologne, 1879), pp. 63–143. Stephen Heller writes about Berlioz in his *Lettres d'un musicien romantique à Paris*, ed. Jean-Jacques Eigeldinger (Paris, 1981); Berlioz's own assessments of Heller appear in the *Mémoires* (ed. Cairns, p. 498) and in the last paragraph of his article for the *JD* of 23 July 1861, reprinted in *ATC* (ed. Guichard, pp. 347–48).

On the patronage offered Berlioz and Harriet by Crown Prince Ferdinand-Philippe, Duc d'Orléans, see Peter Bloom, "Berlioz and Officialdom," *19th-Century Music* 4 (1980), 134–46, which includes French and English texts of fourteen unpublished letters, largely from the 1830s.

The concerts of May and June 1833 are the subject of an article Peter Bloom and I wrote, "Berlioz's Music for *L'Europe littéraire*," *Music Review* 39 (1978), 100–9. The libretto of *Le Cri de guerre du Brisgaw* is transcribed from the autograph in *Autographs*, pp. 327–35.

Berlioz's long analysis of *Guillaume Tell* for the *Revue et Gazette musicale* of 1834 is translated by Oliver Strunk in *Source Readings in Music History* (New York, 1950), pp. 809–26.

Courtship and Marriage. Uncle Félix Marmion's reactions to Harriet, as conveyed to the family in La Côte-St.-André, can be traced in the footnotes of CG II, pp. 70ff., as can the flurry of outraged, self-indulgent correspondence among the other family members. The documentation concerning the wedding of Berlioz and Harriet Smithson is treated by Léon Guichard in "Quel furent les témoins du premier marriage de Berlioz?" *Revue de musicologie* 52 (1966), 211–24, which includes a facsimile of the marriage deed.

On the Théâtre-Nautique, see Octave Fouque, *Histoire du Théâtre Ventadour* (Paris, 1881).

La Captive. *La Captive* is one of the compositions treated by Tom S. Wotton in *Berlioz: Four Works* (London, 1929), pp. 40–44.

Harold en Italie. The best score of *Harold en Italie* remains the Malherbe and Weingartner edition (1900). Liszt began a planned series on Berlioz's works with "Berlioz und seine Harold-Symphonie," *Neue Zeitschrift für Musik* 43 (1855), 25–32, 37–46, 49–55, 77–84, 89–97; the article also appears in *Gesammelte Schriften*, vol. 4 (Leipzig, 1882), pp. 1–102.

The Requiem. The *Grande Messe des morts* is vol. 9 of the New Berlioz Edition (ed. Jürgen Kindermann, 1978).

Edward T. Cone's fine treatment of the Requiem, called "Berlioz's Divine Comedy," appears in *19th-Century Music* 4 (1980), 1–16. See also Henry Barraud's "La Spiritualité du *Requiem*," *Revue de musicologie* 63 (1977), 121–31.

On Habeneck and his problems, see David Cairns, "The Pinch of Snuff," *Berlioz Society Bulletin* 40 (October 1962), 3–7; 41 (January 1963), 3–10. See also Julien Tiersot's long digression from the main matter of *Berlioziana*: "Lettres et documents inédits sur le *Requiem* de Berlioz" in *Le Ménestrel* 70 (1904), 19–20, 27–28, 36–37, 44–45.

Benvenuto Cellini. Hugh Macdonald is in the final stages of preparing a comprehensive score embracing the many stages of *Benvenuto Cellini* for the New Berlioz Edition (vol. 1, forthcoming). There have been any number of attempts to sort out the versions of *Benvenuto Cellini*; see J.-G. Prod'homme, "Les Deux 'Benvenuto Cellini' de Berlioz," *Sammelbände der Internationalen Musikgesellschaft* 14 (1912–13), 449–60; Macdonald, "The Original 'Benvenuto Cellini'," *Musical Times* 107 (1966), 1042–45; Macdonald, "Benvenuto Cellini," *Revue de musicologie* 63 (1977), 107–14; and Thomasin K. LaMay, "A New Look at the Weimar Versions of *Benvenuto Cellini*," *Musical Quarterly* 65 (1979), 559–72 (though in this last there are a number of factual errors). Tiersot, too, examined the original performance material for *Cellini* and treats it briefly in *Berlioziana* 1905, pp. 43–44. Auguste Barbier's 1872 discussion of the genesis of *Benvenuto Cellini* appears in his *Etudes dramatiques: Jules César, Benvenuto Cellini*, rev. edn. (Paris, 1874), pp. 203–8. The memoirs of the tenor Duprez are called *Souvenirs d'un chanteur* (Paris, [1880]); he talks of Berlioz on pp. 153–54.

Joseph d'Ortigue's study of the vicissitudes of *Cellini* was published in the early days of 1839: *De l'Ecole musicale italienne et de l'administration de l'Académie royale de musique, à l'occasion de l'opéra de M. Hector Berlioz;* it was reviewed by Léon Escudier in *La France musicale*, 30 December 1838, and by Adolphe Gueroult in the *JD*, 10 February 1839. In the handout accompanying her unpublished paper read before the American Musicological Society in 1979, Laurie Shulman lists fourteen major reviews of the 1838 performances and three related articles; these include pieces by Mainzer (*La France musicale*, 16 September 1838); Janin (*JD*, 15 September); Berlioz's friend Morel (*Journal de Paris*, 11 and 15 September), Gautier (*La Presse*, 10 and 17 September); Blaze de Bury (*Revue des deux mondes*, October); and Boisselot (*R&GM*, 16 September).

Eric Gräbner's "Some Aspects of Rhythm in Berlioz," *Soundings* 2 (1971–72), 18–28, concerns metric ambiguities in the overture.

I transcribe the *Chansonnette de M*ͬ*. de Wailly* in *Autographs*, pp. 186–88; there are sketches for that song, and for *Je crois en vous*, in the 1832 sketchbook. (Both these songs are incorporated into *Cellini*.) It was Ralph Locke who called my attention to an error in my first transcription of the text of the *Chansonette;* he gives the correct full text in his "New Letters of Berlioz," *19th-Century Music* 1 (1977), 76–77.

Roméo et Juliette. *Roméo et Juliette* is vol. 18 of the New Berlioz Edition (ed. D. Kern Holoman, 1989). On the genesis of *Roméo et Juliette*, see Barbier's *Souvenirs personnels et silhouettes contemporaines* (Paris, 1883 [posthumous]), pp. 230–33. Stephen Heller's long review is titled "A Robert Schumann, à Leipzig," *R&GM* (1839), 546–49, 560–62.

Compositional Process. A major portion of my study of *Autograph Musical Documents* (pp. 111–213) concerns Berlioz's methods of work, with particular attention to the sketches for the compositions before 1840 and their implications. Illustrating the commentary are transcriptions of many sketches and perhaps two dozen facsimiles. Additional facsimiles appear in my articles on "The Present State of Berlioz Research," *Acta musicologica* 47 (1975), 31–67; "Reconstructing a Berlioz Sketch," *Journal of the American Musicological Society* 28 (1975), 125–30; and especially "The Berlioz Sketchbook Recovered" (Holoman, "Sketchbook"). I touch on the matter of sketches and give further facsimiles in my study of "Orchestral Material from the Library of the Société des Concerts," *19th-Century Music* 7 (1983), 106–18.

1840–52

Le Freyschutz. Wagner's 1841 essays on the Paris *Freyschutz*, written for the *R&GM* and for the Dresden *Abendzeitung*, are given in English in *Richard Wagner's Prose Works*, translated by William Ashton Ellis (London, 1898; reprinted New York, 1966), VII, 169–204.

The First Journeys. Berlioz's trips to Brussels, the first of which was in October, 1842, are discussed exhaustively by Albert Vander Linden in "En marge du centième anniversaire de la mort d'Hector Berlioz (8 Mars 1869)," *Académie Royale de Belgique: Bulletin de la classe des beaux-arts* 51 (1969), 36–75.

The first German journey of 1842–43 was the subject of Berlioz's letters "Voyage musical en Allemagne" in the *JD*, 13 August 1843 to 9 January 1844. These were collected, with the essays on Italy, for the *Voyage musical en Allemagne et en Italie* (Paris, 1844). They were then retouched and included in the *Mémoires*, between chapters 51 and 52, as the major account of his trip.

On the 1843 visit to Brunswick, see W. J. Griepenkerl's *Ritter Berlioz in Braunschweig* (Brunswick, 1843), one of the first foreign assessments of Berlioz.

Peter Bloom, in "La Mission de Berlioz en Allemagne: Un Document inédit," *Revue de musicologie* 66 (1980), 70–85, offers a document of 28 December 1843, in which Berlioz reported to the minister of the Interior on what he had discovered of the state of music in Germany.

Euphonia, Berlioz's novel about musical utopia, appeared first in the *R&GM* of 1844 (18 February to 28 July). The work occupies the attention of Corsino and his cronies in the twenty-fourth of the *Soirées de l'orchestre*, pp. 331–78. Hugh Macdonald treats it in an article entitled "Un Pays où tous sont musiciens . . ." in *From Parnassus: Essays in Honor of Jacques Barzun* (New York, 1976), pp. 285–94.

Léopold de Meyer. On the *Marche marocaine* and *Marche d'Isly*, see R. Allen Lott, "A Berlioz Premiere in America: Leopold De Meyer and the *Marche d'Isly,*" *19th-Century Music* 8 (1985), 226–30. Lott's doctoral dissertation, "The American Concert Tours of Léopold de Meyer, Henri Herz, and Sigismond Thalberg" (City University of New York, 1986) treats his American journey in considerable detail.

The Concerts in Provincial France. The 1845 trips to Marseille and Lyon are the subject of "Voyages en France: Correspondance académique," first published in the *R&GM* under the title "Voyage musical en France" (10 September and 15 October 1848, addressed to M. [Edouard] M[onnais]), and included in the *Grotesques,* pp. 274–96.

Bonn. Berlioz describes his 1845 trip to the Beethoven festivities in Bonn in "Fête musicale de Bonn," first published in the *JD* (22 August and 3 September 1845) and found in the second epilogue of the *Soirées,* pp. 411–32.

Vienna. The trip to Vienna and outlying capitals was reported to Paris in open letters first published in 1847 as "Voyage musical en Autriche, en Russie, et en Prusse" (*R&GM,* 3 October to 7 November); despite the title, the letters cover only the 1845 trip to Vienna. These became the second batch of letters from Germany in the *Mémoires,* after chapter 53.

The orchestral versions of *Zaïde* and *Le Chassseur danois,* both prepared in conjuction with the Vienna trip, are found in vol. 13 of the NBE (ed. Ian Kemp) (on pp. 100–2 and 91–99, respectively). Concerning the orchestral material prepared for this journey and related issues, see Holoman, "Orchestral Material from the Library of the Société des Concerts," *19th-Century Music* 7 (1983), 106–18, with facsimiles. The state of the collection of Berlioz's orchestral parts, now mostly at the Bibliothèque Nationale, largely reflects the readings of the 1840s and 1850s.

On Berlioz in Prague, see Katinka Emingerova, "Hector Berlioz à Prague," *Revue française de Prague* (15 October 1933), 167–86. On Berlioz in Hungary, see Emile Haraszti, *Berlioz et la Marche hongroise* (Paris, 1946).

Lille. The story of the inauguration of the railroad line in Lille is the third letter of the *Correspondance académique* cited above (*R&GM,* 19 November 1848; *Grotesques,* pp. 301–10). The third festival in Lille is described in a little program book published at the time: *Ville de Lille: Troisième Festival du Nord, 1851.*

Russia. The Russian letters were first published in the *Magasin des Demoiselles,* a monthly magazine that appeared on the 25th of each month, from November 1855 to April 1856. On Berlioz's Russian journeys see Michel Hofmann, "Berlioz en Russie," *Musica: Journal musical français* 179 (April 1969), 28–30. Stasov's general remarks on Berlioz (from an 1879 review of the *CI*) are to be found in his *Selected Essays on Music,* translated by Florence Jonas (London, 1968), pp. 52–61; Stasov's reactions to the 1847 visit are on pp. 146–61.

London. The best treatment of Berlioz's five trips to England is A[lbert] W. Ganz's *Berlioz in London* (London, 1950; reprinted New York, 1981). Ganz was the son of William (Wilhelm) Ganz, a violinist and conductor who settled permanently in London in 1850 and who, among other things, served as Jenny Lind's accompanist. This Anglicized Ganz was second violinist in the New Philharmonic Society (and after Berlioz's time, its conductor; indeed it was he who finally did offer the first London performance of the *Fantastique*). A. W. Ganz's grandfather and William's father was Adolf, a violinist; Adolf's brothers were the cellist Moritz and the violinist Leopold Ganz. Berlioz met at least two of the brothers Ganz in Berlin in 1843 and admired all of them. A. W. Ganz, a lawyer, wrote a delightful and engaging work filled with correspondence, citations from newspapers, memoirs of the London elite, and the personal recollections of his own family. On Vincent Wallace, see Berlioz's essay in the second epilogue of the *Soirées*, "V. Wallace, compositeur anglais: ses aventures à la Nouvelle-Zélande."

On the piano-vocal editions published by Cramer & Beale in London during Berlioz's first visit, see Cecil Hopkinson, "Berlioz and the 'Marseillaise'," *Music and Letters* 51 (1970), 435–39.

The bibliography on the Great Exhibition is enormous. The most official of the documents is the 867-page volume called *Reports of the Juries* (London, 1852); the contributions of the music jury are found on pp. 324–35, wherein Berlioz is clearly the author of several of the remarks "contributed by a Juror." There is also a three-volume *Official Descriptive and Illustrated Catalogue* of the exhibition (London, 1852), along with such popular guides as the serial *Illustrated Exhibitor* (London, 1851) and *Hunt's Hand-Book to the Official Catalogues: An Explaining Guide, . . .* (2 vols.; London, [1851]). In 1950, the Victoria and Albert Museum published a centennial picture book, *The Great Exhibition of 1851: A Commemorative Album* (London, 1950; revised and reprinted 1964).

Gustave Roger's diary, which begins in March 1847, was published as *Le Carnet d'un ténor*, 3rd edn. (Paris, 1880; preface by Philippe Gille, biographical notice by Charles Chincolle). Roger's experiences as a vagabond closely parallel Berlioz's: he, too, was lavishly welcomed at Sans Souci and was fawned over by the prince of Hohenzollern-Hechingen. His greatest successes outside Paris were in the British Isles.

On the later London visits, 1852–59, see Max Maretzek, *Sharps and Flats* (New York, 1890; reprinted New York, 1968) and *Life and Letters of Sir Charles Hallé* (London, 1896; portions reprinted as *The Autobiography of Charles Hallé*, ed. Michael Kennedy [London, 1972]).

Weimar. On the 1852 and 1856 Weimar performances of *Benvenuto Cellini*, see von Bülow in the *Neue Zeitschrift für Musik* 66 (2 April 1852), 156–69; (30 April 1852), 204–8 (reprinted in *Ausgewählte Schriften, 1850–92* [Leipzig, 1911], pp. 61–78); note especially the references cited for *Cellini*.

La Nonne sanglante. See Michel Brenet, "Berlioz inédit: *Les Francs-Juges, La Nonne sanglante*," *Le Guide musical* 42 (1896), 83–85; J.-G. Prod'homme, "Wagner, Berlioz and Monsieur Scribe: Two Collaborations That Miscarried," *Musical Quarterly* 12 (1926), 359–75; Mina Curtiss, "Gounod before *Faust*," *Musical Quarterly* 38 (1952), 48–67; and A. E. F. Dickinson, "Berlioz's 'Bleeding Nun'," *Musical Times* 107 (1966), 584–88.

La Damnation de Faust. *La Damnation de Faust* is vol. 8a of the New Berlioz Edition; the Supplement, vol. 8b, contains the critical apparatus. Julian Rushton, editor of these volumes, is author of the related article "The Genesis of Berlioz's 'La Damnation de Faust'," *Music and Letters* 56 (1975), 129–46. The genesis of *Faust* is also the subject of Kent Werth's doctoral dissertation "Berlioz's *La Damnation de Faust*: A Manuscript Study" (University of California, Berkeley, 1979). See also J.-G. Prod'homme's *La Damnation de Faust*, part of his *cycle Berlioz* (Paris, 1896).

On the Labitte catalogue of Berlioz's works, see Werth, "Dating the 'Labitte Catalogue' of Berlioz's Works," *19th-Century Music* 1 (1977), 137–41, which includes a transcription of the catalogue. On the catalogue's implications with respect to the question of unknown and unfinished works, most of them from this period, see Hugh Macdonald, "The Labitte Catalogue: Some Unexplored Evidence," *Berlioz Society Bulletin* 69 (1970), 5–7, and "The Labitte Catalogue: More Evidence," *Berlioz Society Bulletin* 70 (1971), 7–8.

Songs. On the genesis of *La Belle Isabeau*, see Cecil Hopkinson, "Berlioz: A Recent Discovery," *Brio* 7 (1970), 32–33, and David Charlton, "A Berlioz Footnote," *Music* *and Letters* 52 (1971), 157–58. On *Le Trébuchet,* see Macdonald, "Le Trébuchet: A Misattribution," *Berlioz Society Bulletin* 54 (April 1968), 4–7.

Conducting. On Berlioz as conductor, see Tiersot, "Berlioz, directeur des concerts symphoniques," part of *Berlioziana,* in *Le Ménestrel* 75–76 (1909–1910), from 16 October 1909 (p. 332) to 30 July 1910 (p. 244); Elliott W. Galkin, "Hector Berlioz chef d'orchestre," *Revue de musicologie* 63 (1977), 41–54; and my own "The Emergence of the Orchestral Conductor in Paris in the 1830s," in *Music in Paris in the Eighteen-Thirties / La Musique à Paris dans les années mil huit cent trente,* ed. Peter Bloom (Stuyvesant, New York, 1987), pp. 387–430. See also Adam Carse, "Conducting" and "Conductors," pp. 289–390 of *The Orchestra from Beethoven to Berlioz* (London, 1948).

Berlioz's *Le Chef d'orchestre: Théorie de son art* was appended (pp. 299–312) to the 1855 edition of the *Traité* and was also issued separately, as the second pagination (pp. 1–14) shows. Kastner's remarks on conducting are found in "Des qualités à exiger des artistes d'un orchestre, et du chef lui-même," the supplement (pp. 12–15) to his *Cours d'instrumentation . . . ,* 2nd edn. (Paris, 1844). See also E.-M.-E. Deldevez, *L'Art du chef d'orchestre* (Paris, 1879). On one aspect of Berlioz's other entrepreneurial activities, see Joël-Marie Fauquet, "Notes et documents: Hector Berlioz et l'Association des Artistes-musiciens," *Revue de musicologie* 67 (1981), 211–36.

Orchestration. Important studies of Berlioz's orchestrational practice include Hans Bartenstein, *Hector Berlioz' Instrumentationskunst und ihre geschichtlichen Grundlagen* (Strassburg, 1939; reprinted Baden-Baden, 1974). Macdonald offers some interesting observations on problems of orchestrational practice in "Berlioz's Orchestration: Human or Divine?" *Musical Times* 110 (1969), 255–58. I cite further, more detailed studies in "The Present State of Berlioz Research," pp. 64–65. On orchestration treatises see Adam Carse, "Text-books on Orchestration before Berlioz," *Music and Letters* 22 (1941), 26–31.

1852–69

Tyskiewicz, Gounod. On the 1853 Tyskiewicz scandal, see the *Mémoires,* chapter 52. On the 1854 opening of Gounod's *La Nonne sanglante,* see Mina Curtiss, "Gounod before *Faust,*" *Musical Quarterly* 38 (1952), 48–67 (titled "Gounod and Berlioz" on the title page) with a facsimile of Berlioz's letter. Curtiss has a rambling though lighthearted style of considerable charm and gives splendid evocations of Mme Viardot and Nestor Roqueplan.

Brussels. The 1855 Brussels performances of *L'Enfance du Christ* are as elegantly treated by Vander Linden as the 1842 concerts were, with illustrations and ample transcriptions of the documentation. See "En marge du centième anniversaire de la mort d'Hector Berlioz (8 mars 1869)," in *Académie Royale de Belgique: Bulletin de la classe des beaux-arts* 51 (1969), 36–75, especially pp. 46–51 and the documents on pp. 70–75. The letters to Adolphe Samuel are in "Vingt Lettres inédites d'Hector Berlioz [à M Adolphe Samuel]," ed. Victor Wilder, *Le Ménestrel* 45 (1879), in six installments beginning on p. 217 and ending on p. 259.

Weimar. On *Lélio* in Weimar, see Peter Bloom, "Orpheus's Lyre Resurrected: A Tableau Musical by Berlioz," *Musical Quarterly* 61 (1975), 189–211; "Une Lecture de *Lélio ou le Retour à la Vie,*" *Revue de musicologie* 63 (1977), 89–106; and "A Return to Berlioz's *Retour à la Vie,*" *Musical Quarterly* 64 (1978), 354–85. A central source for all this is Cornelius's "Hector Berlioz à Weimar," *R&GM* 22 (1855): 27 May 1855, 163–64; 3 June 1855, 169–70. See also *Briefe hervorragender Zeitgenossen an Franz Liszt,* ed. La Mara (3 vols.; Leipzig, 1895–1904); vols. 1 and 2 contain sixty-one letters to Berlioz.

On Berlioz's relationship with Rieter-Biedermann, see "Achtzehn Briefe von Hector Berlioz an der Winterthurer Verleger J. Rieter-Biedermann," ed. Max Fehr, *Schweizerisches Jahrbüch für Musikwissenschaft* 2 (1927), 90–106. These letters go from 1 April 1856 to 1 January 1859.

The Paris Exhibition of 1855. The article "Instruments de musique à l'Exposition Universelle," in the *Grotesques* (pp. 71–80), and some of the following vignettes concern the 1855 exhibition, not the London Great Exhibition of 1851 (as Barzun incorrectly alleges in his translation of *Soirées*, p. 228n, and in *NL*, p. 95, n. 75.)

The Gluck Revival. Berlioz reviewed the Théâtre-Lyrique production of Gluck's *Orphée* in the *JD* of 22 November 1859; this review is included in *ATC*, pp. 133–46.

Last Years. For Ernest Reyer's recollections of Berlioz in his last years, see his *Notes de musique* (Paris, 1875). On the Pasdeloup concerts, see Elisabeth Bernard, "Jules Pasdeloup et les Concerts Populaires," *Revue de musicologie* 57 (1971), 150–78. John W. Freeman, in "Berlioz and Verdi," *Atti del III° Congresso internazionale di studi Verdiani* (Milan, 1972; Parma, 1974), makes an initial attempt to trace junctures of the two composers' lives and works.

Russia. A summary of Berlioz's 1867 journey to Russia, with his letters to Kologrivov planning the venture, is found in Octave Fouque, *Les Revolutionaires de la musique* (Paris, 1882), pp. 233–56. The obscure and often conflicting recollections of Berlioz in Russia are found in Rimsky-Korsakov, *My Musical Life,* translated by Judah A. Joffe, rev. edn. (New York, 1942), pp. 82–83; in Stasov, *Selected Essays on Music,* translated by Florence Jonas (London, 1968), pp. 161–69; and in Stravinsky/Craft, *Conversations with Igor Stravinsky* (New York, 1959), p. 29.

Berlioz's Will. François Lesure transcribes Berlioz's will in "Le Testament d'Hector Berlioz," *Revue de musicologie* 55 (1969), 219–23. A facsimile of the will is in the collection of the Bibliothèque Nationale, under the shelfmark F. S. 276. On Berlioz's estate, see Bernadette Gérard, "L'Inventaire après décès de Louis-Hector Berlioz," *Bulletin de la Société de l'histoire de Paris* (1979), 185–91.

The Choudens full scores of *Les Troyens* and *Benvenuto Cellini,* not yet published when Berlioz prepared his will in 1867, were finally published in 1885 and 1889 because of a lawsuit brought by the composer's heirs and executors. Even then, it was *Les Troyens à Carthage* that appeared, rather than the entire *Les Troyens.*

The Te Deum. The Te Deum is vol. 10 of the New Berlioz Edition, ed. Denis McCaldin (1973). See Hugh Macdonald, "The Colossal Nightingale," *Music and Musicians* 17, no. 11 (July 1969), 24–25, on the genesis of the Te Deum in incomplete early works.

L'Enfance du Christ. See J.-G. Prod'homme, *L'Enfance du Christ* (Paris, 1898), which is part of his *cycle Berlioz.*

Les Troyens. *Les Troyens* is vol. 2 of the New Berlioz Edition, ed. Hugh Macdonald (1969–70). Macdonald's doctoral dissertation is entitled "A Critical Edition of Berlioz's Les Troyens" (Cambridge University, 1968). Cairns treats the relation of the opera to its Classical source in "Les Troyens and the Aeneid," in *Responses: Musical Essays and Reviews* (New York, 1973; reprinted New York, 1980), pp. 88–110. An earlier version appears as "Berlioz and Virgil: A Consideration of *Les Troyens* as a Virgilian Opera," *Proceedings of the Royal Musical Association* 95 (1968–69), 97–110; see also "Les Troyens et L'Enéide," *Romantisme* 12 (1976), 43–50. Chapter 1 of Peter Conrad's book *Romantic Opera and Literary Form* (Berkeley, 1977), entitled "Operatic Epic and Romance," treats that subject with regard to *Les Troyens* in some detail. Patrick J. Smith, in *The Tenth Muse: A Historical Study of the Opera Libretto* (New York, 1970), begins chapter 19, "The French Libretto of the Late Nineteenth and Early Twentieth Centuries," from the perspective of *Les Troyens* as the culmination of the *tragédie-lyrique*. For more on Berlioz and the lyric theater, see Joseph-Marc Bailbé, *Berlioz et l'art lyrique: Essai d'interpretation à l'usage de notre temps* (Berne, 1980).

Sketches for the opera are found in three collections: **F-Pn** (formerly part of the collection of André Meyer), **F-CSA**, and **F-G**. The genesis of the work is best followed in the letters to Carolyne Sayn-Wittgenstein and, to a lesser extent, those to Pauline Viardot.

Jeffrey Langford, in "Berlioz, Cassandre, and the French Operatic Tradition," *Music and Letters* 62 (1981), 310–17, considers the role of Cassandre as an outgrowth of dramatic necessity and Berlioz's personal affection for that sort of character. He also notes the striking parallels between *Les Troyens* and the final tableau of Rossini's *Le Siège de Corinthe*. Concerning organizational principles in *Les Troyens*, see Julian Rushton, "The Overture to *Les Troyens*," *Musical Analysis* 4 (1985), 119–44.

Hugh Macdonald has summarized "*Les Troyens* at the Théâtre-Lyrique," in *MT* 110 (1969), 919–21. The critical reception and later performances are treated by Louise Goldberg in "A Hundred Years of Berlioz's 'Les Troyens'" (Ph.D. diss., University of Rochester, 1973).

The splendid and comprehensive Cambridge Opera Handbook on *Les Troyens*, ed. Ian Kemp (Cambridge, 1988), written collaboratively by the best specialists in the field, will serve as cornerstone of future Berlioz research and criticism.

Béatrice et Bénédict. *Béatrice et Bénédict* is vol. 3 of the New Berlioz edition, ed. Hugh Macdonald (1980). *Béatrice et Bénédict* first appeared in full score in Malherbe & Weingartner's complete edition (1907). One of the few analytical looks at the opera is by Julian Rushton, "Berlioz's Swan-Song: Towards a Criticism of *Béatrice et Bénédict*," *Proceedings of the Royal Musical Association* 109 (1982–83), 105–18.

Notes

References to the letters of Berlioz are by serial number in the published volumes of the *Correspondance générale (CG)* and in the other books of letters cited herein; volume and page citations to these works indicate material in the critical commentary.

1. "THE REAL BERLIOZ"

1. Legouvé, p. 224 (my translation).
2. "Love of my art": CG 240; "religion of beauty": CG 752; "love of beauty and of truth": CG 1691.
3. CG 981.

2. LA CÔTE-ST.-ANDRÉ

1. Cairns, p. 573; V&A, p. 4, item 2, is incorrect on the time of birth.
2. In his new book, *Hector Berlioz, 1803–1832: The Making of an Artist* (London, 1988), David Cairns illuminates Mme Berlioz's character quite considerably, drawing especially on Dr. Berlioz's letters to her.
3. CG 236 gives the text of such a song.
4. *R&GM*, 11 March 1849; cited in *Grotesques*, p. 395.
5. F-CSA; transcribed in *Berlioziana* 1904, pp. 83–84.
6. CG 3, 4.
7. F-CSA; transcribed in *Berlioziana* 1904, p. 84.
8. CG 5; translation after Cairns, p. 575.
9. F-CSA; see Holoman, *Catalogue*, 7 and 9.
10. F-CSA; see Holoman, *Catalogue*, 8.
11. The passport, now lost, was formerly in the Collection Maignien, Grenoble. It was described by most of the early biographers, including Tiersot in *Berlioziana* 1904, p. 4, and Boschot, I, 29 and 81. See also Cairns, p. 519.

3. THE LATIN QUARTER AND THE BOULEVARDS

1. Charles Simond gives a population figure of 890,000 citizens in 1826, in *Paris de 1800 à 1900* (Paris, 1900), I, 568; the *New Encyclopaedia Britannica* (15th edn., Chicago, 1978) XIII, 1006, says 786,000 in 1831.
2. CG, vol. I, p. 25.
3. *Mémoires,* chap. 5.

4. *CG* 10.
5. *CG* 11.
6. *GM*, 9 November 1834; French in Condé, pp. 187–88; English in Cairns, p. 576.
7. See *CG* 16D; see also *Mémoires*, chap. 5: "I actually wrote off then and there to my father."
8. *Livre de raison:* "Le 21 [Oct.] Hector est parti pour Paris et je lui ai remis cinq cent fr 500."
9. V&A, p. 22, item 57, in **GB-WImacnutt**; facsimile of the first page of the excerpts from *Iphigénie en Aulide* in V&A, p. 2. In his 1834 article on *Iphigénie en Tauride*, Berlioz suggests that he discovered the scores *before* witnessing a live production; see Condé, p. 188.
10. *Le Reveil*, 16 December 1822; French in NBE 24, no. 14.
11. Title headings of *Canon libre*, *Le Montagnard exilé*, and *Toi qui l'aimas*, Holoman, *Catalogue*, 14, 15, 16.
12. *Mémoires*, chap. 20.
13. See *CG*, vol. I, pp. 47–49n.
14. *CG*, vol. I, pp. 47–48n.
15. *Livre de raison:* "Le 11 mai remise à Hector à son départ pour Paris 400."
16. *CG* 105 and vol. I, p. 219n3.
17. "Keen and lofty": *Mémoires*, "Travels in Germany II," letter 1; "insouciance": *CG* 77.
18. *CG* 24.
19. *CG* 26.
20. Marmion to Dr. Berlioz: see *CG* 29D and 30D; Berlioz to his father: *CG* 31.
21. Malherbe and Weingartner edn., VII, 10–11. Just how much this movement was revised for each of its several performances is not clear; this is surely the passage referred to in 1829 (*CG* 140) as a new recitative.
22. "O génie": *CG* 34; "Ah, foutre": *CG* 33.
23. Castil-Blaze apparently did most of his work after the first performance, which was nearly complete; see Cairns, pp. 86–87n.
24. *Mémoires,* chap. 7, dated 31 December 1824.
25. *CG* 36.
26. See *CG* 37D.
27. *CG* 32.
28. "You'll not be doctor": *CG* 48; "Damn, my boy": *Grotesques*, p. 216; "Here the first step": *CG* 47.
29. "Everyone came away": *Revue musicale*, 1 February 1835, translated in Cone:*SF*, p. 216; "the devout old ladies": *Soirées*, VII, p. 110.
30. *CG*, vol. I, pp. 99–100n.
31. This is to accept the chronology of the *Mémoires*, which may be out of order at this point; the malediction at Le Chuzeau may well have taken place earlier.
32. *Mémoires,* chap. 11.
33. *Irish Melodies* (London and Dublin, 1807–34); Berlioz probably knew the Paris edition of Moore in English (1827).
34. Condé, p. 11.
35. *CG* 61; see also *Mémoires*, chap. 11.
36. *CG* 76.
37. *Mémoires*, chap. 10, suggests he entered in 1825 and failed the preliminaries, but there are in the early chapters many examples of his being mistaken on dates by a year or more; in fact, a comparison of the fugues and fugue subjects preserved from the period strongly suggests that his first experience with the *prix de Rome* was in 1826.

38. *Mémoires*, chap. 12; *CI*, p. 17; Cairns, p. 72n. The account book can no longer be located.
39. Le Sueur to Boucher, 11 February 1828, given by Tiersot in *Lettres de musiciens écrites en français du XVe au XXe siècle*, vol. 1 (Turin, 1924), pp. 535–36.
40. Sauzay, p. 170. In his obituary of Cherubini, Berlioz tells a rather different story with the same punch line; *JD*, 20 March 1842; see Condé, p. 143.
41. *JD*, 20 March 1842; see Condé, pp. 141–44.
42. **F-Pan** AJ^{37} 207^4 and 208$^{1-4}$; see Holoman, "Berlioz au Conservatoire: Notes biographiques," *Revue de musicologie* 62 (1976), 289–92.
43. *CG* 76.
44. Peter Bloom, "Academic Music: The Archives of the Académie des Beaux-Arts," *19th-Century Music* 7 (1983), 129–35; see pp. 132–33.
45. Archives of the Académie des Beaux-Arts, Paris; minutes of 1 November 1827.
46. "The part of Ophelia was nothing": Raby, p. 55; "Do they like it—or hate it?": idem, p. 66; "inconsequential walking-lady": idem, p. 67.
47. *CG*, vol. I, p. 162n.
48. The story is denied by Berlioz in *Mémoires* (chap. 18); but see Cairns, p. 97n and pp. 582–83. It must be noted, however, that at this juncture Berlioz can have had little idea of what was meant by "symphony."
49. Quoted in *Mémoires*, chap. 59.
50. *CG* 77.
51. "Beethoven alone": Sauzay, pp. 190–91; "valiant and diligent": Sauzay, p. 184.
52. *CG* 83.
53. Fétis in *Revue musicale*, 1 February 1835, translated in Cone:*SF*, p. 217; *Mémoires*, chap. 19. See also Cairns, p. 103n.
54. Fétis in *Revue musicale*, [June] 1828, cited by Cairns, p. 103n.
55. See Deschamps's *Préface* to *Macbeth et Roméo et Juliette. Tragédies de Shakespeare, traduites en vers français, avec une préface, des notes et des commentaires* (Paris 1844). Reprinted in *Œuvres complètes*, VI/1 (Paris, 1874; reprinted in Geneva, 1973).
56. *CG* 100.
57. "For some years now": *CG* 122; "sneezing, croaking, vomiting": Zelter to Goethe, 21 June 1829, cited in *CG*, vol. I, pp. 247–48n.
58. *Mémoires*, chap. 24.
59. *CG* 117; see also *CG* 121.
60. *CG* 117.
61. *Mémoires*, chap. 21, the chapter title.
62. "Prize in hand": *CG* 134; "volcanic" (*volcanisée*): *CG* 133.
63. "Littered with emendations": *Mémoires*, chap. 44; Fétis's defense: *Revue musicale*, March 1829, p. 136, cited by Peter Bloom in "Berlioz and the Critic: La Dammation de Fétis," *Studies in Musicology in Honor of Otto E. Albrecht* (Kassel, 1980), pp. 240–65; see pp. 244–45.
64. *CG* 145.
65. See *CG*, vol. I, pp. 305–6n; for more on his tooth problems see *CG* 152 and 155.
66. *CG* 158.
67. *CG* 219, 323.
68. See *CG* 206, 219, 223.
69. *CG* 167.
70. *CG* 166.
71. Given by François Lesure in a review of *CG*, vol. I, *Revue de musicologie* 58 (1972), 274–76.
72. *CG* 187.

73. *Journal du Commerce,* 31 October 1830, cited in *CG,* vol. I, p. 380n.
74. *CG* 189.
75. **F-Pan** O⁴ 1327; given by Marie-Noëlle Colette, "Le Cour," in *La Musique à Paris en 1830–1831,* ed. François Lesure (Paris, 1983), pp. 17–38; see p. 38.
76. Fétis in *Revue musicale,* 1 February 1835, translated in Cone:*SF,* p. 217.
77. *CG* 190.
78. *CG* 194.
79. *Mémoires,* chap. 29; I have slightly amended the translation.

4. THE EMERGENCE OF A STYLE

1. *Mémoires,* postscript. Edward T. Cone considers this summary the appropriate place from which to begin a criticism of Berlioz's style; see "Inside the Saint's Head," *Musical Newsletter* 1 (1971), 3–12, 16–20, and 2 (1972), 19–22 (reprinted in *The Garland Library of the History of Western Music* [New York and London, 1985], IX, 1–19).
2. *Mémoires,* chap. 15.
3. Preface to *Alceste* (1769), translated by Eric Blom, in Alfred Einstein, *Gluck* (London, 1936), pp. 98–100 (reprinted London, 1962, p. 113); also given by Oliver Strunk, in *Source Readings in Music History* (New York, 1950), pp. 673–75.
4. *GM,* 9 November 1834; reprinted in Condé, p. 186.
5. *Traité,* p. 34.
6. David Cairns, "Spontini's Influence on Berlioz," in *From Parnassus: Essay in Honor of Jacques Barzun,* ed. Dora B. Weiner and William R. Keylor (New York, 1976), pp. 25–41; see p. 27.
7. "Inexpressible admiration": *CG* 178; "it is true": *CG* 752 (concerning *Cortez*).
8. *Soirées,* XIII, p. 206.
9. Jean Mongrédien, *Catalogue thématique de l'œuvre complète du compositeur Jean-François Le Sueur, 1760–1837* (New York, 1980), pp. xxvii–xxviii of the preface. More generally see Montgrédien, *Jean-François Le Sueur: Contribution à l'étude d'un demi-siècle de musique française (1780–1830),* 2 vols. (Berne, Frankfurt, and Las Vegas, 1980), pp. 998–1002.
10. Fétis in *Revue musicale,* 1 February 1835, translated in Cone:*SF,* p. 216.
11. **F-Pn** Rés. Vm² 178, fol. 41ʳ (autograph of *La Nonne sanglante*).
12. *Mémoires,* chap. 11 (my translation).
13. *CG* 93.
14. *CG* 472 refers to this melody as a *prière,* and Lenor's invocation is the only "prayer" in the opera.
15. A point made by Macdonald, pp. 80–81.
16. *CG* 926.
17. *CG* 111.
18. *ATC,* p. 38.
19. *ATC,* p. 41.
20. *ATC,* p. 41.
21. *ATC,* pp. 42–43.
22. *ATC,* p. 53.
23. *ATC,* p. 65.
24. *ATC,* p. 58.
25. *ATC,* pp. 57–58.
26. *CG* 107.
27. *CG* 100.

28. *CG* 182. This is the first of several times he uses this phrase to describe his better works.
29. *CG* 153.
30. The formulation is, I believe, Barzun's.
31. *King Lear,* IV, 1, 36.
32. *CG* 151.
33. Cone considers the implications of the repeat signs in some detail in "Schumann Amplified," pp. 268–69 of Cone:*SF.*
34. "Schumann Amplified," pp. 249–77 of Cone:*SF.*
35. See Paul Banks, "Coherence and Diversity in the *Symphonie fantastique,*" *19th-Century Music* 8 (1984), 37–43.
36. See David Cairns, "Berlioz, the Cornet, and the Symphonie Fantastique," *Berlioz Society Bulletin* 47 (July 1964), 2–6.
37. *Mémoires,* chap. 49.
38. See Holoman, *Autographs,* p. 206.
39. See, for example, V&A, p. 90, item 265.
40. *Revue musicale* (December 1830), p. 151; cited in NBE, XVI, xii.
41. Schumann, "Konzertovertüren für Orchester: J. J. H. Verhulst, W. Sterndale Bennett, H. Berlioz," *Neue Zeitschrift für Musik* 10 (1839), 185–87; and *Gesammelte Schriften* (5th edn. Leipzig, 1914) I, 419–24; see p. 422. Translated as "Overture to Waverley, opus 1," in *Robert Schumann: On Music and Musicians,* ed. Konrad Wolff, translated by Paul Rosenfeld (Norton edn. New York, 1969), pp. 188–91; see p. 188.

5. A SOJOURN—A COURTSHIP—A BIRTH

1. *CG,* vol. I, p. 410n4.
2. Hiller in Cologne to Hippeau, 10 June 18[82], in *LEF* 37 (1930), p. 6.
3. *CG* 211.
4. George Sand, "Lettre d'un voyageur" (to Liszt), *Revue des deux mondes,* 1 September 1835. The translation is Charles Suttoni's.
5. *Mémoires,* chap. 42.
6. *Mémoires,* chap. 32.
7. *CG* 217.
8. NBE, XVI, 171–72; *Autograph Musical Documents,* 265–66; see also *Mémoires,* chap. 34.
9. *CG* 223.
10. *CG* 230; see also *Mémoires,* chap. 35. Corpus Christi, if my figures are correct, would have been on Thursday, 2 June 1831; thus Berlioz arrived again in Rome four, not three, days before this letter of 6 June.
11. See the subentry "Self-Borrowings" in Holoman, *Catalogue,* entry 55.
12. *Mémoires,* chap. 44.
13. *Mémoires,* chap. 33.
14. *CG* 231.
15. See *CG* 223 and *Mémoires,* chap. 33, on meeting Mendelssohn. For more on Mendelssohn in Rome, see *Mémoires,* "Travels in Germany I," letter 4.
16. Mendelssohn to his mother, 29 March 1831, first published in *Reisebriefe aus den Jahren 1830 bis 1832,* ed. Paul Mendelssohn (Leipzig, 1861), in English as *Letters from Italy and Switzerland,* translated by Lady Wallace (London, 1864). For the complete German text, see the modern edn., *Eine Reise durch Deutschland, Italien und die Schweiz,* ed. Peter Sutermeister (Tübingen, 1979), pp. 123–25. To capture the color of nineteenth-century English, I have transcribed the

version that appeared in *Dwight's Journal of Music*, 15 February 1861, pp. 261–62. See also Mendelssohn's letter of 15 March 1831, edn. Sutermeister, pp. 119–20; in English in Cone:*SF*, pp. 281–82, translated by Sam Morgenstern.

17. *Mémoires*, "Travels in Germany I," letter 4 (a footnote dated 25 May 1864).
18. CG 257.
19. CG 234.
20. CG 257.
21. He was in Tivoli by midday; see CG 235.
22. CG 236.
23. Enfantin to Fournel, 26 October 1830, in *Œuvres de Saint-Simon et d'Enfantin* (47 vols.; Paris, 1865–78; reprinted Aalen, 1963–64); III, 49; cited by Locke, p. 98.
24. CG 237.
25. Locke, pp. 118–19.
26. *Grotesques*, p. 25; translation after Locke, p. 120.
27. Given by André Espiau de la Maëstre, "Berlioz, Metternich et le St.-Simonisme," *Revue musicale* 233 (1956; special Berlioz issue), 65–78; see p. 66.
28. The date is found in an 1848 autograph of *Tristia*, **F-Pc** ms 1187, suggesting that Berlioz was then working from a much earlier manuscript.
29. I have reconstructed the itinerary according to my reading of CG 244–47; the chronology is clearly out of sequence in the *Mémoires*, chap. 41.
30. CG 244.
31. CG 247.
32. CG 268.
33. *VM*, II, 125n1 (see also *Soirées*, p. 608). For more on Gibert, see CG 1158.
34. CG 262.
35. To judge from sentiments expressed in CG 282; see also the entry on Mme Horace Vernet in CG, vol. II, p. 759.
36. CG 264; see also *Mémoires*, chap. 37.
37. Holoman, "Sketchbook," includes a facsimile and transcriptions.
38. Sketchbook (**F-CSA**), back flyleaf^v; the phrase is "delicieux pays poussinnien."
39. CG 271.
40. I do not believe, *pace* Tiersot, that any of the other music in the sketchbook is intended for the military symphony; see Holoman, "Sketchbook," pp. 290–91.
41. CG 1061.
42. *R&GM*, 6 May 1855; my translation follows that of NBE, X, viii.
43. Unpublished letter of 1 June 1832 from Nanci Berlioz Pal to her sister, Adèle. I am grateful to David Cairns for drawing my attention to this letter.
44. CG 284.
45. CG, vol. II, p. 19n2.
46. CG 284.
47. CG 282.
48. Cited by Cosette Thompson in a review of Raby's *Fair Ophelia*, in *19th-Century Music* 8 (1984), 69–71.
49. CG 293.
50. *Mémoires*, chap. 45.
51. D'Ortigue, *Le Balcon de l'Opéra* (Paris, 1833), pp. 318–19. In the *Mémoires* 45, Berlioz conflates the concerts of 9 December 1832 and 22 December 1833.
52. "In the name of pity": CG 296; "je vous aime": CG 307; "a constant love": CG 307.
53. In *Correspondance de Liszt et de la Comtesse d'Agoult*, ed. Daniel Ollivier (Paris, 1934); cited in CG, vol. II, p. 42n1.

54. CG 303.
55. CG 307; see also CG 338 ("ma vie est un roman qui m'interesse beaucoup") and 607 (a happy incident in "mon roman"); the sentiment is prefigured in CG 262, which refers to the most recent episodes in his life as "un triste roman."
56. F-Pc *papiers divers de Berlioz*, no. 38.
57. "The name Berlioz": d'Ortigue, *Le Balcon de l'Opéra* (Paris, 1833), p. 296, cited in Boschot, II, 304; "average height": d'Ortigue, pp. 322–23 (translated by Cairns).
58. D'Ortigue, *Balcon*, p. 304.
59. *Les Feuilles d'automne* (Paris, 1831) (my translation). Berlioz inverts two words and two lines in the last quatrain.
60. CG 308.
61. See *CG*, vol. II, p. 67n1.
62. CG 314; the quote is from a letter to Joseph d'Ortigue of two days later, CG 315.
63. "Remarkable traits": Marmion to Nanci, 10 February 1833, in CG, vol. II, p. 75n5; "it would be folly": Marmion to Mme Berlioz, 6 March [1833], in CG, vol. II, p. 82n1.
64. See CG 323.
65. See Raby, p. 22.
66. CG 330.
67. CG 335.
68. Marmion to Mme Berlioz, 6 March [1833], in CG, vol. II, pp. 82–83n1.
69. CG 327.
70. Nanci to Adèle, 20 March [1833], in CG, vol. II, p. 90n1.
71. CG 285; the 1833 letters to Adèle almost invariably refer to her as "chère et bonne sœur."
72. See CG 311 and 312. In 1852 he prepared an autograph scenario titled *Bénédict et Beatrix* (F-Pc *papiers divers de Berlioz*, 44); the libretto was apparently to have been by Legouvé. It is transcribed in NBE, III, 299–300.
73. "Curiosities of the musical season": Boschot, II, 154; "mon cher sublime": d'Ortigue in *La Quotidienne*, cited in Boschot, II, 154; see also Legouvé, pp. 225–26.
74. *L'Europe littéraire*, 19 April 1833; cited in *CG*, vol. II, p. 97n2.
75. In George Thomson's *Select Collection of Original Scotish Airs* (London, 1801 edn.), p. 74; see James C. Dick, *The Songs of Robert Burns* (London, 1903; reprinted New York, 1973), pp. 231 (music) and 448–51 (notes). Note that it is this collection of Thomson's for which the instrumental accompaniments were prepared by Pleyel, Kozeluch, Haydn, and Beethoven.
76. *Mémoires*, chap. 39.
77. Peter Bloom and I made this point in "Berlioz's Music for *L'Europe littéraire*," *Music Review* 39 (1978), 100–9; see p. 102.
78. The scenario is described in the *Catalogue Charavay*, no. 697 (June 1957), lot 26,325, item 2; see CG, vol. I, pp. 543–44n3.
79. CG 341.
80. CG 342.
81. Hiller, pp. 88–89.
82. CG 348.
83. *Séance publique annuelle*, 12 October 1833; see Boschot, II, 200–201.
84. "Messieurs, ayez pitié": d'Ortigue in *La Quotidienne*, cited in Boschot, II, 205; "Au Conservatoire!": CG 363.
85. My account of the finances follows CG 363; this differs from the 7,000 francs mentioned in *Mémoires*, chap. 45. On the dressmaker's note, see CG 407.

86. D'Ortigue, in *La Quotidienne* (17 January 1834), cited in *CG*, vol. II, p. 158n1.
87. *Le Rénovateur*, 21 January 1834; text given in *CG*, vol. II, p. 159n4; and in Holoman *Catalogue*, note to entry 68.
88. Now the rue du Mont-Cenis. Utrillo, who is said to have lived there, painted a half-dozen or so views of the *maison de Berlioz à Montmartre;* two of these, from the Collection Walter-Guillaume, are now on permanent display at the Musée de l'Orangérie, Paris.
89. See *CG* 378 and 384.
90. Charter of the Théâtre Nautique, 12 August 1833, published widely in the press.
91. I am grateful to Peter Bloom for clarifying this point.
92. *CG* 408.
93. *CG* 409.

6. AFFAIRS OF STATE

1. *CG* 409.
2. *Galignani's Messenger*, 29 November 1834; cited by Raby, p. 154.
3. See, in *Soirées*, XVI, "Paganini" (pp. 245–52), as well as Guichard's commentary, pp. 544–47. Janin's hostile *feuilletons* appeared in the *JD* of 22 April 1833 and 15 and 22 September 1834.
4. Letter of 17 October 1834, cited in full and translated by Peter Bloom in "Berlioz and Officialdom: Unpublished Correspondence," *19th-Century Music* 4 (1980), 134–46; see pp. 138–39.
5. *GM*, 7 December 1834, p. 395; cited by Bloom, "Berlioz and Officialdom," p. 139n17. Robert, in *CG*, vol. II, p. 191n1, is incorrect: it was the orchestral *La Captive* that was performed that Sunday afternoon.
6. *R&GM*, 12 May 1844, pp. 167–69, a review by Berlioz of his own concert of 4 May; reprinted in Condé, pp. 78–81; see p. 80.
7. *Revue de Paris*, 15 November 1834; complete text in *CG*, vol. II, pp. 204–5n1.
8. *GM*, 5 October 1834, pp. 317–19; *JD*, 10 October 1834; reprinted in Condé, pp. 73–76.
9. Cited in Boschot, II, 288.
10. **F-Pc** *papiers divers de Berlioz*, no. 10.
11. *CG* 449. This letter is inaccurately dated; it is from 22 October 1850, before the concert that evening.
12. *R&GM*, 29 November 1835.
13. *CG* 454.
14. George Sand, *Lettres d'un voyageur* (Paris, 1857; reprinted Geneva, 1980), no. 11 (Sand in Geneva to Meyerbeer, September 1836), p. 385.
15. *Agenda musical ou indicateur des amateurs, artistes et commerçans en musique pour 1836, par Planque, musicien et accordeur de pianos* (Paris, 1836; reprinted Geneva, 1981), p. 55.
16. Charter of the Gymnase, cited by Georges Cain, *Anciens Théâtres de Paris*, p. 260.
17. *CG* 457.
18. *CG* 462.
19. *CG* 464.
20. *La Quotidienne*, 24 March 1836; cited in *CG*, vol. II, p. 289n1.
21. *CG* 472.
22. *Œuvres complètes de Hector Berlioz, 1852*, a broadside published by Richault. Copy in **F-Pn** Rés. Vma 22.

23. "Miserable skeleton": "Hector Berlioz, Ouvert. zur Heimlichen Feme (Ouv. des Francs-Juges), in F," *Neue Zeitschrift für Musik* 4 (1836), p. 101. "No idea": Schumann to Zuccalmaglio, 20 August 1837; cited in *CG*, vol. II, p. 327n1.

24. Moscheles to Sigismond Neukomm, 10 February 1834 (collection of Richard Macnutt); cited in *CG*, vol. II, p. 328n1, where the text should read "philharmonic *trial*."

25. *R&GM*, 12 February 1837, p. 55; cited in *CG*, vol. II, p. 327n2.

26. *CG* 486.

27. *CG* 470.

28. Heine, "Lettres confidentielles II," *R&GM*, 4 February 1838; reprinted in *Heinrich Heine: Historisch-kritische Gesamtausgabe der Werke*, ed. Jean-René Derré and Christiane Giesen, vol. 12/1 (Hamburg, 1980), p. 497. Heine wrote in the spring of 1837 about the previous winter season.

29. *JD*, 19 December 1836.

30. *CG* 490.

31. The account in *CG* 490 differs in some details from the version in the beginning of chap. 46 of the *Mémoires*.

32. *CG* 492.

33. "Explode:" *Mémoires*, chap. 46; "dominated:" *CG* 493.

34. See Edward T. Cone, "Berlioz's Divine Comedy: The *Grande Messe des morts*," *19th-Century Music* 4 (1980), 3–16.

35. Autograph of the Requiem (F-Pc ms 1509), p. 21.

36. *Le National*, [July 1837]; cited in *CG*, vol. II, p. 354n1.

37. *CG* 506.

38. "Not be able to breathe": *CG* 502; "hard head": *CG* 504.

39. See *CG* 511, with the new address and a reference to "un déménagement."

40. *R&GM*, 1 and 8 October 1837; reprinted in *VM*, II, 229–62, and in *Soirées*, I.

41. *CG* 523.

42. *CG* 522.

43. Eduard Devrient, *Meine Erinnerungen an Felix Mendelssohn Bartholdy und dessen Briefe an mich* (Leipzig, 1869), p. 64; translated by Natalia MacFarren as *My Recollections of Felix Mendelssohn-Bartholdy, and His Letters to Me* (London, 1869), pp. 58–60.

44. See *Mémoires*, chap. 48.

45. *JD*, 8 December 1837; cited in *CG*, vol. II, p. 385n1.

46. *CG* 521.

47. See *CG* 534, doubtless misdated by Berlioz; it was probably written on 18 January 1838, though possibly as late as 16 February.

48. *CG* 535.

49. *CG* 543; for Berlioz's response to his father's letter, see *CG* 547.

50. *Mémoires*, chap. 47.

51. *CG* 561; see also *CG* 626.

52. *CG* 565.

53. Gilbert Duprez, *Souvenirs d'un chanteur* (Paris, n.d. [1880]), pp. 153–54; see p. 153.

54. Liszt to Ferdinand Denis, September 1838, cited in *CG*, vol. II, p. 457n4.

55. Auguste Barbier, *Etudes dramatiques: Jules César, Benvenuto Cellini* (rev. edn. Paris, 1874), pp. 205–6.

56. *CG* 588.

57. *CG* 602.

58. *CG* 616.

59. *CG* 600.

60. *CG* 608.

61. *Journal de Paris,* 18 January 1839; cited by Cairns, p. 598, where an excellent summary of the Paganini affair may be found.

62. *R&GM,* 2 December 1838, pp. 491–92, a review of the concert of 25 November.

63. *ATC,* p. 347.

64. See Cairns, pp. 597–98.

65. F-Pc *papiers divers de Berlioz,* no. 35: "Fête musicale donnée au Théâtre de la Renaissance."

66. *CG* 671.

67. *CG* 688.

68. *CG* 697.

69. *CG* 683.

70. See the letter from Paganini to Berlioz of 20 January 1840 (*CG* 699), and the accompanying commentary (*CG,* vol. II, pp. 624–25n2).

71. Spleen: *CG* 703; "110 years old": *CG* 700.

72. Formerly in the collection of Léon Constantin and his heirs; now in The Pierpont Morgan Library, New York; letter of dedication: *CG* 702.

73. *Mémoires,* chap. 50.

74. Dresden *Abendzeitung,* 14–17 June 1841, reprinted in *Richard Wagner's Prose Works,* ed. William Ashton Ellis (London, 1899; reprinted New York, 1966), VIII, 131–37; see p. 136 (my translation).

7. PORTRAIT IN 1839–40

1. Long excerpts from Legouvé's chapter on Berlioz are cited by Cairns, pp. 520–25.

2. Legouvé, p. 234; I use Cairns's translation, pp. 521–22. The impact on Guizot is cited by Cairns, p. 521.

3. See Macdonald, illustration 4, between pp. 70 and 71.

4. Fol. 28[r]; see Holoman, "Sketchbook," p. 311.

5. *CG* 549; I use a translation by Ralph P. Locke.

6. Felix Boisson in *Léon Gastinel* (Paris, 1893), cited in *CG,* vol. II, p. 200n1.

7. Sketches for *Nuit d'ivresse;* formerly in the collection of André Meyer, these have been acquired by F-Pn ms 20627.

8. Sketchbook, fols. 17[v]–18[r]; transcribed in Holoman, "Sketchbook," pp. 300–1. The *Cellini* sketches are treated on pp. 297–304.

9. Sketchbook: the pencil sketch is on fol. 31[v]; ink sketches are on (in order of composition) fols. 32[v], 30[v], and 31[r]. Transcribed in Holoman, "Sketchbook," pp. 308–9, with commentary on p. 307.

10. F-Pc ms 17998.

11. NBE, X, 147–50.

12. Further on the *Faust* sketches, see Julian Rushton, "The Genesis of Berlioz's 'La Damnation de Faust'," *Music and Letters* 56 (1975), 129–46.

13. *CG* 256.

14. *Mémoires,* chap. 49.

15. *CG* 472.

16. F-Pc ms 1165.

17. *Mémoires,* chap. 53.

18. See, for example, V&A, p. 102, items 307–8. Near the beginning of *Mémoires,* chap. 53, Berlioz compares these tasks favorably to those of the *feuilletoniste.*

19. Berlioz to Prosper Sainton, 16 January 1856, *NL* 52.

20. Liszt, *Pages romantiques* (Paris, 1918), p. 28, cited by Elisabeth Bernard, "Jules Pasdeloup et les Concerts Populaires," *Revue de musicologie* 57 (1971), 150–78; see p. 154.
21. *Mémoires*, chap. 59.
22. *GM*, 31 May 1835.
23. "The pale work of criticism": *CG* 887; "dog-work": *CG* 1260.
24. Sketchbook, fols. (reading backward) 26ʳ–22ʳ; transcribed in Holoman, "Sketchbook," pp. 312–14.
25. *Mémoires*, chap. 16.
26. *CG* 1707; translation after Locke, "New Letters of Berlioz," *19th-Century Music* 1 (1977), 71–84; see p. 81.
27. Ms. letter to Baron Donop, 2 October 1858.
28. *Revue musicale*, November 1830, pp. 367–69; *Courrier des théâtres*, 6 November 1830.
29. *Mémoires*, chap. 38.
30. *Mémoires*, chap. 37.
31. *CG* 570.
32. The performance material at **F-Po**; the dossier at **F-Pan** AJ XIII, 203, item 54.
33. E.-M.-E. Deldevez, *L'Art du chef d'orchestre* (Paris, 1878), pp. 140–41.
34. *Mémoires*, chap. 48.
35. Notably "Berlioz's Divine Comedy," *19th-Century Music* 4 (1980), 1–16.
36. *LI* 132.
37. "Lettre d'un enthousiaste sur l'état de la musique en Italie," *Revue européene*, 15 March 1832, p. 48, reprinted, virtually in its entirety, in *Mémoires*, chap. 35.
38. "Avant-Propos de l'auteur," p. i of Rieter-Biedermann's vocal score (Winterthur, [1858]).
39. Footnote to NBE versions 10–11 of the published program leaflet; see NBE, XVI, 167–68 and the transcription on p. 170, col. 2.
40. Macdonald, *Berlioz* (London, 1982), p. 122.
41. Adam to Spiker, 12 August 1840, cited in *CG*, vol. II, p. 647n1.
42. *CG* 721.
43. "De l'avenir de rhythme," *JD*, 10 November 1837, reprinted in Condé, pp. 124–28.
44. Ibid.; see Condé, p. 127. My translation slightly paraphrases Berlioz's original.

8. VAGABONDAGE

1. *Charivari*, 1 November 1840; cited by Boschot (II, 552) and Cairns (p. 258). The *Mémoires* conflate the festival performance of 1840 with the farewell performance before he goes abroad in 1842—the occasion for which the *Symphonie funèbre* was revised. Later biographers perpetuate the error.
2. See *Mémoires*, chap. 51, and Cairns's clarification on p. 261.
3. *CG* 736 mentions 9,551 francs taken in at the box office, and *CG* 746 mentions Berlioz's having contributed the balance lacking, 130 francs. The *Mémoires*, chap. 51, give the figures as 8,500 francs of income and 360 francs lacking.
4. *CG* 737.
5. *CG* 736.
6. *CG* 739.
7. A[ntoine] E[lwart] in *Le Ménestrel*, 20 December 1840; cited in *CG*, vol. II, p. 671n2.
8. Contractual note of 26 March 1841, transcribed in *CG*, vol. II, p. 735.
9. See *Berlioziana* (1905), pp. 355–56.

10. *CG* 751*bis*.
11. Théodore de Lajarte, in *Bibliothèque musicale du Théâtre de l'Opéra: Catalogue historique, chronologique, anecdotique* (Paris, 1878), II, 167, gives a total of 114 performances.
12. *CG* 750.
13. *Œuvres complètes de Hector Berlioz, 1852*, a broadside published by Richault. Copy in **F-Pn** Rés. Vma 22.
14. *CG* 755.
15. *CG* 746, and surrounding letters to Nanci and the family.
16. *CG* 765.
17. *CG* 765.
18. *CG* 1060.
19. See, for example, *CG* 761, 763.
20. Heller to Eugénie de Froberville, [16 February 1842], letter no. 6 of *Stephen Heller: Lettres d'un musicien romantique à Paris*, ed. Jean-Jacques Eigeldinger (Paris, 1981), pp. 102–4; see p. 102.
21. *CG* 765.
22. Félix Marmion to Nanci Berlioz, 26 May 18[42], collection of Mme Reboul-Berlioz, Paris, cited in *CG,* vol. I, p. 726n1.
23. *CG* 786.
24. See Holoman, *Catalogue,* pp. 504–8.
25. Ernst in The Hague to Liszt, 4 October 1842, in *Briefe hervorragender Zeitgenossen an Franz Liszt,* ed. La Mara (Leipzig, 1895), I, 52–53; see p. 52.
26. "The compositions of M. Berlioz": *L'Observateur* (Brussels), 27–28 September 1842 (translation after V&A, p. 107); cited by Vander Linden, "En marge du centième anniversaire de la mort d'Hector Berlioz (8 Mars 1969)," in *Académie Royale de Belgique: Bulletin de la classe des beaux-arts* 51 (1969), 36–75; see pp. 63–64.
27. "There is little to be said": *L'Observateur,* 27–28 September 1842; "Mlle Recio, of somewhat frail soprano voice": Charles Hanssens, in *La Belgique musicale,* 29 September 1842; both cited by Vander Linden, pp. 63–64. Vander Linden, pp. 67–69, quotes extensively from the 1842 press.
28. **B-Bc** ms 55,833.
29. *CG* 820.
30. Lobe to Berlioz: *CG* 793; Mendelssohn to Berlioz: *CG* 805.
31. *CG* 867.
32. *Mémoires,* "Travels in Germany I," letter 1.
33. Hiller, p. 90.
34. Hiller, p. 91.
35. *CG* 813 (my translation). See the version given in the *Mémoires,* "Travels in Germany I," letter 4. This incident was vehemently denied by "Anti-Puff," who claimed to be a friend of Mendelssohn, in *Dwight's,* 21 March 1857, p. 196. But the batons did indeed change hands: Berlioz's is in the Mendelssohn collection at the Bodleian Library, Oxford, and Mendelssohn's is preserved with several of Berlioz's effects at the Musée Instrumental du Conservatoire, Paris.
36. See *CG,* vol. III, p. 69n1.
37. Wagner to Lehrs, 7 April 1843, cited by Ernest Newman in *The Life of Richard Wagner,* vol. 1, 1813–1848 (London, 1945; reprinted, Cambridge, 1976), p. 355.
38. *CG* 816 and *Mémoires,* "Travels in Germany I," letter 4 (fn.).
39. *Mémoires,* "Travels in Germany I," letter 4 (fn.).
40. *CG* 719; see also *CG* 815, 831, 832.

41. *CG*, vol. III, p. 81n1.
42. *VM*, II, p. 96.
43. *Mémoires,* "Travels in Germany I," letter 6.
44. The baton is at **F-CSA.**
45. **F-CSA.**
46. *CG* 830.
47. *CG* 838.
48. *CG*, vol. III, p. 99n1.
49. *CG* 864, Chélard in Weimar to Berlioz in Paris, 15 November 1843.
50. *Panthéon musical, par J. Traviès: Les Principaux Compositeurs en 1843* (lithograph Paris: Bureau Central de Musique, 1843), reprinted in Adolphe Jullien, *Hector Berlioz: Sa Vie et ses œuvres* (Paris, 1888), between pp. 166 and 167.
51. *CG*, vol. III, p. 118n2.
52. *CG* 866, Spontini to Berlioz, 20 November 1843. See also Louis to his aunt: *CG*, vol. III, p. 138n2. Rapture two days later: *CG* 867 to Lecourt.
53. *CG* 902.
54. *CG* 887.
55. David Cairns, "Berlioz, the Cornet, and the Symphonie Fantastique," *Berlioz Society Bulletin* 47 (July 1964), 2–6.
56. *CG* 876.
57. *CG* 910.
58. The climax to the Harriet situation can be traced in the following letters: *CG* 920–924, 926, and Citron's accompanying notes.
59. *CG* 914 and a document of July 5, 1844: *Projet de rédaction du privilège du 3ᵉ Théâtre Lyrique,* **F-Pan** F²¹ 1119², given in *CG*, vol. III, pp. 759–63.
60. *CG* 1038.
61. *CG*, vol. III, p. 200n2.
62. *Notice sur les orgues mélodium d'Alexandre et fils* (Paris, 1844), 18 pp., no. **B1** of Holoman, *Catalogue; JD,* 23 June 1844.
63. "A great composer": *JD,* 15 December 1844, reprinted in *MM,* pp. 219–37; see pp. 219–20 and 236. "By the way": *CG* 928, Charles Duveyrier to Berlioz, 17 December 1844.
64. *CG* 953.
65. *JD,* 16 April 1845, reprinted in *MM,* pp. 205–15.
66. *R&GM,* 13 April 1845, cited by R. Allen Lott in "A Berlioz Premiere in America: Leopold De Meyer and the *Marche d'Isly,*" *19th-Century Music* 8 (1985), 226–30; see p. 228.
67. "As instrumented": New York *Herald,* 10 November 1845, cited by Lott, p. 228, and by Vera Brodsky Lawrence in *Strong on Music* (New York, 1988), chap. 7; "expressly arranged": New York *Herald,* 2 October 1846, cited by Lott, p. 230.
68. *La Clochette* [Dijon], 27 July 1845, cited in *CG*, vol. III, p. 272n2; see also *CG* 987.
69. *Soirées* (2ᵐᵉ Epilogue: "Fêtes musicales de Bonn"), pp. 411–20; see p. 416.
70. See Locke, pp. 210–11.
71. Jelen, in *Květy,* 3 February 1846, cited in *CG*, vol. III, p. 307n4. This note summarizes the reactions of the press.
72. "Population of antiquarian pedants": *CG* 1017; "Charming young man": *CG* 1030.
73. For a picture of the University Aula, see *The New Grove,* XX, 544 (article "Wrocław," Zygmunt M. Szweykowski).
74. *CG* 1033.

75. CG 1027.
76. CG 1045.
77. *Grotesques*, p. 382.
78. *Grotesques*, p. 302.
79. *Grotesques*, pp. 302–3.
80. CG 1045.
81. CG, vol. III, pp. 368–69n4.
82. *JD*, 29 July 1846, cited by Boschot (III, 118), whose formulation I follow.
83. Boschot's short chronological index at this point (III, 674) is incorrect.
84. CG 1057.
85. CG 1061.
86. *Le Tintamarre*, 29 November–5 December 1846; cited in *CG*, vol. III, p. 377n1.
87. *Mémoires*, chap. 54.

9. PORTRAIT IN 1846

1. Legouvé, p. 217.
2. He bought his shirts, according to their archives, at the shop of Charles Charvet, established in 1838 and still thriving. I am grateful to John M. Anderson for providing me with this information.
3. I adduce this from the inventory of Berlioz's estate taken just after his death; see Chapter 11, note 72.
4. CG 1361.
5. Hallé in *Life and Letters of Charles Hallé* (London, 1896), cited by Cairns, p. 611.
6. CG 1060.
7. CG 1029.
8. CG 1093.
9. This section of the text summarizes my article "The Emergence of the Orchestral Conductor in Paris in the 1830s," in *Music in Paris in the Eighteen-Thirties,* ed. Peter Bloom (Stuyvesant, New York, 1987), pp. 387–430.
10. *Mémoires*, chap. 48.
11. *Mémoires*, chap. 8.
12. Hallé, *Life and Letters of Charles Hallé* (London, 1896), p. 68.
13. Chap. 2, article 11 of the *Réglement* adopted 24 March 1828, given in full in A. Elwart, *Histoire de la Société des Concerts du Conservatoire Impérial de Musique*, etc. (Paris, 1860), pp. 69–82.
14. Seidl, "On Conducting," in *The Music of the Modern World* (New York, 1895–97); later in German on p. 306 of "Ueber das Dirigiren," *Bayreuther Blätter* 23 (1900), pp. 291–308. It is not clear where or when Seidl (who was born in 1850 in Pest) could have heard Belioz conduct late enough in his own childhood to have remembered it; he seems to be basing his remarks for the most part on accounts of "those who heard [Berlioz] or who played under his direction."
15. Spontini: *CG* 866; Rimsky-Korsakov: *My Musical Life*, translated by Judah A. Joffe (rev. edn. New York, 1942), p. 83; Deldevez: *L'Art du chef d'orchestre* (Paris, 1878), p. 76. The Rimsky-Korsakov citation actually continues in a less positive vein: "No vagaries at all in shading. And yet (I repeat from Balakirev's account) at a rehearsal of his own piece Berlioz would lose himself and beat three instead of two or vice versa. The orchestra tried not to look at him and kept on playing, and all would go well."
16. Hallé, *Life and Letters of Charles Hallé* (London, 1896), p. 64. On the question of taking bows, see CG 729.

17. *CG* 1106.
18. Metronome: *Traité,* p. 300; Moscheles: in chap. 32 of Charlotte Moscheles, ed., *Aus Moscheles' Leben nach Briefen und Tagebüchern,* 2 vols. (Leipzig, 1872), II, 235, translated as *Recent Music and Musicians As Described in the Diaries and Correspondence of Ignaz Moscheles, Edited by His Wife,* by A. D. Coleridge, 2 vols. (London, 1873; reprinted, New York, 1970), II, 229.
19. *New Letters,* pp. 140–43, letter of [3 July] 1855 to Théodore Ritter. The source of this letter is an English translation given for the first time in book form in Ganz, p. 204. This may not be an entirely fair assessment of Wagner, for Berlioz had had a difficult time with Klindworth at a rehearsal the day before, and, in any case, his visit to London had not so far gone particularly well. The two references to Klindworth have most often been conflated in the Berlioz literature, following Barzun, II, 111. After seeing the 1843 performances of Wagner's opera in Dresden, Berlioz originally praised the "uncommon energy and precision" of Wagner's conducting (*VM,* II, 102), but this observation was removed when the letter was redacted for the *Mémoires.*
20. *Mémoires,* chap. 8.
21. *CI* 149.
22. *Mémoires,* chap. 59.
23. E.-M.-E. Deldevez, *L'Art du chef d'orchestre* (Paris, 1876), p. 76.
24. *Traité,* pp. 293–94 and 310 (conducting treatise).
25. *Traité,* p. 310; I conflate two successive thoughts.
26. The successors to Berlioz's orchestration treatise were those of Gevaert (1863) and Ebenezer Prout (1876). Richard Strauss's revision of Berlioz's works, incorporating examples from later German masters including Wagner, is from 1904–5. Rimsky-Korsakov's long-delayed project for an orchestration text, on which he was at work from his deathbed, bears in overall concept several close affinities to Berlioz's study. Maximilian Steinberg's completion of the treatise was published in 1912.
27. Macdonald, p. 79, suggests that one of the unidentified passages in the *Traité* comes from the *Messe solennelle* of 1824.
28. *Traité,* p. 54; I use the translation of Mary Cowden Clarke (London, 1856), p. 25.
29. *JD,* 2 October 1835, cited by H. Robert Cohen, "Berlioz on the Opéra (1829–1849): A Study in Music Criticism" (Ph.D. diss., New York University, 1973), p. 35 (my translation).
30. *ATC,* p. 120.
31. *Rénovateur,* 3 December 1835; see also *Mémoires,* postscript.
32. **F-Pc** ms 1187, the full score of *Tristia.*
33. See Raby's closing chapter, "Romantic Image," pp. 176–93.
34. Copy in the Bibliothèque municipale, Versailles.
35. Julian Rushton, *The Musical Language of Berlioz* (Cambridge, 1983), pp. 97–98.
36. Macdonald, pp. 130–31.
37. On the sources for *Faust,* see NBE, VIIIb, 455–56; see also Berlioz's preface VIIIa, 2.
38. See Rushton, "Tonality in *La Damnation,*" in *The Musical Language of Berlioz,* pp. 253–56.
39. On D and B♭, see Cone, "Inside the Saint's Head," pt. x.
40. See, for example, Julian Rushton, "The Genesis of Berlioz's *La Damnation de Faust,*" *Music and Letters* 56 (1975), 129–46.

10. THE PARIS PROBLEM

1. *CG* 1101.
2. *CG* 1089.
3. *LEF* 37 (1930), 11.
4. *CG* 1097.
5. The *Mémoires*, chap. 55, talk of a gross receipt of 18,000 francs with a net profit of 12,000; in *CG* 1100, Berlioz mentions to his father a net profit of about 15,000 francs; in *CG* 1102, he mentions what is clearly a gross receipt of 30,000 francs.
6. Here the *Mémoires*, chap. 55, speak of a profit of 8,000 francs, whereas *CG* 1102 mentions 15,000—clearly, again, a gross receipt.
7. *CG* 1105.
8. *CG* 1135 and 1158.
9. *Soirées*, XXI, 306–7.
10. *Correspondance de Liszt et de la Comtesse d'Agoult,* ed. Daniel Ollivier, vol. 2 (Paris, 1934), p. 383; cited in *CG*, vol. III, p. 425n3.
11. *CG* 1123; compare with the account in the *Mémoires*, chap. 57. See also *CG* 1124, 1125.
12. Collection of François Lang, Royaumont; transcribed in *CG*, vol. III, pp. 765–67.
13. *CG* 1130.
14. Letter from Holmes to Clara Novello, given in *Clara Novello's Reminiscences, compiled by her daughter Contessa Valeria Gigliucci* (London, 1910), p. 213.
15. London *Morning Herald*, [7?] December 1847, cited by Ganz, p. 29.
16. See *CG* 1137 (12 November 1847), 1148 (Gautier to Berlioz, December 1847), 1153 (13 December 1847), and 1155 (22 December).
17. Sims Reeves, in *My Jubilee* (London, 1889), cited by Ganz, p. 33.
18. London *Morning Post*, [8?] February 1848, cited by Ganz, p. 43.
19. *Illustrated London News,* 12 February 1848, treated by Ganz, p. 44; compare with *Mémoires*, chap. 18.
20. Douglas Johnson, "French History and Society from the Revolution to the Fifth Republic," pp. 119–221 in *France: A Companion to French Studies,* ed. D. G. Charlton (2nd edn. London, 1979); see p. 168. I have reversed the clauses in the citation.
21. *CG* 1200.
22. See Ganz, p. 69.
23. Roger, p. 58.
24. Also in the *Musical World* of July and the *Athenaeum* of 15 July; given in English in Ganz, pp. 72–73, and in French in *CG* 1209.
25. *JD*, 26 July 1848. "Ouverture du Théâtre de la Nation ou du Théâtre National ou de l'Opéra (vieux style)."
26. *Mémoires*, chap. 58 (wrongly dated 5 December); see *CG* 1225.
27. An observation of Citron in *CG*, vol. III, p. 582n2.
28. Roger, pp. 184–86.
29. *CG* 1256; see also 1258.
30. Berlioz's draft: *CG* 1256; Janin's article: *Journal des Débats*, 23 April 1849.
31. *CG* 1253–55, Meyerbeer to Berlioz, 9, 12, and 15 April 1849.
32. *CG* 1255.
33. *CG* 1258.
34. Ibid.
35. *JD*, 20 April 1849; reprinted in *MM*, pp. 106–17; see pp. 115–16.
36. *CG* 1271.

37. The vignette is reproduced as plates IVA and IVB in Hopkinson.

38. *CG*, vol. III, p. 689n1.

39. Berlioz's notebook of minutes of the Société Philharmonique, 27 April 1850, collection of Mme Reboul-Berlioz, Paris; cited in Boschot, III, 239.

40. *CG* 1343.

41. *CG* 1265 (21 May 1849); see also Macdonald, "Le Trébuchet: A Misattribution," *Berlioz Society Bulletin* 54 (April 1968), 4–7.

42. Program note for the Lille concert of 30 June 1851 (*Ville de Lille: Troisième Festival du Nord, 1851*), p. 23.

43. *CG* 1357.

44. Berlioz mentions two performances of *L'Adieu des bergers* (see, for example, *Mémoires*, postscript, and *CG* 1471); the first was clearly on 12 November 1850, and the most likely date for the second is 17 December 1850, the date of a second Berlioz concert in the Salle Ste.-Cécile. On this second occasion, it would have been the only work by Berlioz on the program—though of course it was at the time said to be by Ducré.

45. *CG* 1388.

46. *CG* 1379.

47. *CG* 1389.

48. *CG* 1395.

49. See, for example, *CG* 1395, 1415, 1417, 1433.

50. *CG* 1415.

51. Cited in "Industrial Design," an unsigned article in the *New Encyclopaedia Britannica* (15th edn., Chicago, 1978), IX, 514.

52. *Hunt's Handbook to the Official Catalogues* [of the Crystal Palace Exhibition], 2 vols. (London, 1851); see II, 776–77.

53. *CG* 1417.

54. Barzun, in his translation of *Soirées* (p. 228n1) and *NL* (pp. 94–95), conflates the London exhibition of 1851 with the Paris exhibition of 1855. What is in *Grotesques*, pp. 71–80, under the title "Les Instruments de musique à l'Exposition universelle" concerns the Paris exhibition; see *Grotesques*, p. 325.

55. George Eliot to Mr. and Mrs. Charles Bray, 5 June 1852, cited by Barzun in his translation of *Soirées*, p. 232n6.

56. *CG* 1455.

57. *Œuvres complètes de Hector Berlioz*, 1852, a broadside published by Richault. Copy in **F-Pn** Rés. Vma 22.

58. New Philharmonic Society prospectus, cited in *The New Grove*, XI, 195 (article "London," §VI,4).

59. Ganz, p. 121; see illustration opposite p. 97.

60. "Pyramidal": *CG* 1461; poetical look of satisfaction: a recollection of John Francis Barnett, cited by Ganz, p. 128.

61. *CG* 1459.

62. Open letter to Loder in *The Musical World*, 8 May 1852.

63. Cited by Ganz, p. 132.

64. *CG* 1476.

65. *CG* 1491.

66. *CG* 1479.

67. Cited by Charles Simond in *Paris de 1800 à 1900* (Paris, 1900), II, 423.

68. *CG* 1530.

69. *CG* 1499.

70. *Recent Music and Musicians As Described in the Diaries and Correspondence of Ignaz Moscheles, Edited by His Wife* [Charlotte Moscheles], translated by A. D. Coleridge (London, 1873), II, 229.

1. "Notes pour l'organisation d'une chapelle impériale à Paris," transcribed in *CG*, vol. IV, pp. 727–29; see p. 729.
2. Guichard, in *Soirées*, p. 629.
3. *La Presse*, 28 December 1854, cited by Guichard in *Soirées*, p. 16; see also pp. 633–34.
4. *La France musicale*, 9 January 1853; cited by Guichard in *Soirées*, p. 631.
5. *CG* 1562.
6. *CG* 1562.
7. Ganz, p. 154.
8. *CG* 1566.
9. If my notes and documentation are correct, the New Berlioz Edition is in error in implying that the deletions in movts. V and VII were incorporated in the Ricordi edn. of 1853 (see NBE, X, 170–72). On the contrary, it was necessary for Ricordi to reengrave the plates for pp. 64 and 109–13 in 1867 to accommodate the changes.
10. *CG* 1581.
11. *CG* 1601.
12. Cited by Ganz, p. 162.
13. Edward Holmes to Clara Novello, January 1857, in *Clara Novello's Reminiscences, compiled by her daughter Contessa Valeria Gigliucci* (London, 1910), p. 213.
14. Berlioz to Gye, published in the *Illustrated London News*, 2 July 1853; see Ganz, p. 167; in French as *CG* 1607.
15. Cairns, p. 611, is incorrect: the first Baden concert was in 1853.
16. *CG* 1619.
17. *CG* 1627.
18. Ibid.
19. "Occasionally in port": *CG* 1631; "city of gaming and gamblers": *CI* 114.
20. *CG*, vol. IV, p. 256, in part following Boschot (III, 685), gives dates of 20 and 24 August for the Frankfurt concerts of 1853. But for a variety of reasons having to do with Berlioz's faulty dating of his letters, I think it clear the concerts were on 24 and 29 August.
21. *CG* 1631.
22. Janin to his wife, 14 October 1853, in *Jules Janin: 735 Lettres à sa femme*, ed. Mergier-Bourdeix, vol. 2 (Paris, 1975), pp. 379–80; see p. 379.
23. Ibid., p. 380. It is evident from this letter, despite Citron's assertion to the contrary (*CG*, vol. IV, pp. 372–73n2), that Berlioz did go to Meyerbeer's dinner party, which appears to have been on the 11th (as Berlioz implies in *CG* 1633) or possibly even the 12th (as Janin says), Berlioz's presumed departure date.
24. *CG* 1636.
25. The baton is now at **F-CSA**.
26. *Mémoires*, postscript.
27. *CG* 1648.
28. Brahms to Joachim, 7 December 1853, in *Johannes Brahms im Briefwechsel mit Joseph Joachim* (Berlin 1908; reprinted by Tutzing, 1974), I, 21–23; see p. 22; cited by Ganz, p. 171.
29. *CG* 1650.
30. *JD*, 22 December 1853; see *CG* 1674; reprinted in the *Revue et Gazette musicale*, 25 December 1853, and in various other periodicals of those weeks.
31. *CG* 1684; facs. in V&A, p. 85.
32. *Mémoires*, chap. 59, say Cherbourg, but Berlioz's letter to Adèle of 6 March 1854, *CG* 1701, suggests Calais.

33. Harriet's death warrant, cited by Cosette Thompson in her review of Raby's *Fair Ophelia*, *19th-Century Music* 8 (1984), 69–71; see p. 69.
34. *Mémoires*, chap. 59.
35. *JD*, 20 March 1854, quoted in *Mémoires*, chap. 59; translation slightly amended.
36. *Mémoires*, chap. 59; see *CG* 1711.
37. *CG* 1726.
38. *Mémoires*, chap. 59.
39. "Daring and impulsive": *Mémoires*, "Travels in Germany II," letter 2; "elevation and profundity": *CG* 1726.
40. Von Bülow in Dresden to Liszt, 30 April 1854, cited by Cairns, p. 476, n. 8.
41. "What love of art": *CG* 1768; von Bülow to Liszt, 30 April 1854, in *Briefe und ausgewählte Schriften* (Leipzig, 1936), II, 200.
42. "Rascals": *CG* 1756; bulletin: *CG* 1747.
43. F-Pn Rés. Vm^7 521.
44. *CG* 1771 (to Morel, 26 June 1854); compare with Malherbe and Weingartner edn., I, ix.
45. *CG* 1901.
46. *CG* 1908.
47. *CG* 2115.
48. *CG* 1773.
49. *CG* 1781.
50. *CG* 1798.
51. Adam: *CG* 1849; Heine: *CG* 1850; see also in *CG* quite a number of similar letters from these weeks.
52. *CG* 1899.
53. *Valse chantée par le vent dans les cheminées d'un de mes châteaux en Espagne*, Holoman, *Catalogue*, no. 131, in the collection of Louis Koch, Basel; see Georg Kinsky, *Manuskripte, Briefe, Dokumente: . . . Katalog der Musikautographen-Sammlung Louis Koch* (Stuttgart, 1953), pp. 199 and 338–39.
54. *Mémoires*, chap. 59 (my translation).
55. On Barielle's getting lost, see J. Isnardon, *Le Théâtre de la Monnaie depuis sa fondation* (Brussels, 1890), p. 407, cited by Vander Linden, "En marge du centième anniversaire de la mort d'Hector Berlioz (8 Mars 1969)," *Académie Royale de Belgique: Bulletin de la classe des beaux-arts* 51 (1969), 36–75; see p. 48. "Spanish cowherds": *CG* 1924.
56. Fétis to Liszt, 1 April 1855, cited as a note to *CG* 1924, in vol. V (forthcoming).
57. Edgar Quinet to Bernard Lavergne, 5 April 1855, in *Lettres d'exil* (Paris, 1885), cited as a note to *CG* 1930, in vol. V.
58. *La France musicale*, 15 April 1855, p. 116.
59. Verdi to Escudier, February 1860, in *Carteggi Verdiani*, ed. Alessandro Luzio, vol. 2 (Rome, 1935), p. 194.
60. *The Musical World*, 30 June 1855 (Berlioz's letter dated 26 June); cited in Ganz, p. 191.
61. See the remarks of Frédéric Robert, given by Yves Gérard in his "Avant-Propos" to the proceedings of the 1975 Colloque Hector Berlioz, *Revue de musicologie* 63 (1977), 5–16; see p. 9.
62. Diary entry of 4 July 1855; cited in Ganz, p. 207.
63. F-Pc *papiers divers de Berlioz*, no. 38*bis*; transcribed in the appendix of Holoman, *Catalogue*.
64. See *CG* 2128 (23 May 1856, to Morel): "a German publisher was so taken with it . . ."
65. *CG* 2380 (20 June [1859], to Carolyne Sayn-Wittgenstein).
66. Letter to Adèle of June 1856; see NBE, IIc, 755n4.

67. Peter Bloom, in "Berlioz à l'Institut Revisited," *Acta musicologica* 53 (1981), 171–99, says just the opposite, however; see p. 180.

68. **F-Pan F**^{17} 3578, the imperial decree of 25 June 1856, transcribed by Bloom in "Berlioz à l'Institut Revisited," p. 182.

69. *JD*, 4 and 9 September 1856; reprinted in *Grotesques*, pp. 157–82; see p. 159.

70. *Dwight's Journal of Music*, 23 September 1854, p. 196, on a concert of 25 August 1854 that featured Miss Anabella Goddard, Vivier, and Bazzini.

71. *Grotesques*, p. 182.

72. See Bernadette Gérard, "L'inventaire après décès de Louis-Hector Berlioz," *Bulletin de la société de l'histoire de Paris* (1979), 185–91.

73. See NBE, XIII, xii and n. 53. At Théodore Ritter's concert in the Salle Herz on 19 April 1857, Berlioz had conducted the only Paris performance of *Le Spectre de la rose*, with Mme Falconi as the singer.

74. *Mémoires*, postface, where the letter is dated 28 March 1858.

75. Letter to Baron Donop of 2 October 1858; see NBE, IIc, 756n16.

76. Cited by Tiersot in *Berlioziana* 1910, p. 92.

77. *Mémoires*, postface.

78. Entry in the Goncourt brothers' journal of 15 November 1862, cited by Cairns, p. 456.

79. Ms. letter to his brother-in-law Pal, collection of Sarah C. Fenderson, Cambridge, Massachusetts; see also *CI* 95.

80. Note in Berlioz's ms. account book for June 1859, in the collection of Richard Macnutt, Withyham, Sussex.

81. Letter to Pauline Viardot, 13 September 1859, published by Tiersot in the *Revue musicale* (1903), p. 428.

82. Pauline Viardot to Julius Rietz, 22 September 1859, cited in "Pauline Viardot-Garcia to Julius Rietz, Letters of Friendship," *Musical Quarterly* 2 (1916), 42–45 (French and facing English translation by Theodore Baker); see p. 43. The present translation follows Macdonald, p. 62.

83. The feuilleton: *JD*, 17 March 1839; "pretended talent; *diva manquée*": CG 628.

84. *ATC*, pp. 137–38.

12. PORTRAIT IN 1859

1. Letter to Richard Pohl, 7 June 1863, given by Tiersot in "Lettres de Berlioz sur 'Les Troyens'," *Revue de Paris* 28 (1921), no. v, pp. 165–66.

2. Judith Gautier, *Le Second Rang du collier* (Paris, 1903), cited by Macdonald in "Hector Berlioz 1969—A Centenary Assessment," *ADAM* 331–33 (1969), 35–47; see pp. 44–45.

3. Liszt to Carolyne Sayn-Wittgenstein, May 1861, cited by Macdonald in "Hector Berlioz 1969," p. 46.

4. Harry Schraemli, *Von Lucullus zu Escoffier* (Zurich, 1949), pp. 132–33.

5. *CG*, vol. IV, pp. 474–75n1.

6. An anecdote given by several authors; see, for example, Daniel Bernard in *CI*, p. 56.

7. *Mémoires*, chap. 59.

8. Letter to Cornelius, 9 April 1862.

9. Proofs with manuscript annotations in the collection of Frederic V. Grunfeld; facsimile and transcription in Grunfeld, "Not Two Flutes, You Scoundrels," *Horizon* XII/4 (Autumn, 1970), 103–11; see pp. 106–7.

10. *NL*, pp. 189–91.

11. *NL*, pp. 205–7.

12. *Mémoires*, chap. 59.
13. CG 1783.
14. NBE, XIII, xii–xiii.
15. Macdonald, pp. 122–23.
16. Macdonald, p. 177.
17. CG 1552.
18. Ibid.
19. *La France musicale*, 20 April 1855; transcribed in NBE, X, 194.
20. CG 2012.
21. CG 2115.
22. See Cairns, "Spontini's Influence," cited in full in the Bibliography.
23. See Patrick J. Smith, in *The Tenth Muse: A Historical Study of the Opera Libretto* (New York, 1970), p. 152.
24. CI 84.
25. Macdonald, in NBE, IIc, 935, calls this a sketch for Aeneas's *récit*, no. 7, presumably on the basis of key similarity, contour, and proximity to other sketches for the *récit*. But the *Combat de ceste* is in the same scene, is as closely related in key to the sketch, and does after all have a significant section in $\frac{5}{8}$.

The sketches for *Les Troyens* are found, in large and roughly equal measure, in **F-G** R 9028 and in the collection of the late André Meyer, recently acquired by **F-Pn** and given the shelfmark ms 20627.
26. Rushton, "The Overture to *Les Troyens*," *Music Analysis* 4 (1985), 105–18, treats these and other organizational relationships.
27. Gounod, in the preface to *LI*, p. vii.

13. PARNASSUS

1. Ms. letter to Adèle of 2 February 1860.
2. *LT* 5, p. 161, letter to Mme Viardot of [February 1860].
3. *ATC*, p. 327.
4. Excerpted from *ATC*, pp. 328–32.
5. Ms. letter, 23 May 1860; excerpts in *NL*, pp. 206–9.
6. "Like twins": ms. letter of 9 March 1860 to Morel; "Poor Adèle": *Mémoires*, "Travels in Dauphiné."
7. "My opera is finished" and "I wait with quasi-indifference": ms. letter of 4 April 1860, collection of Sarah C. Fenderson, Cambridge, Massachusetts.
8. *JD*, 19 and 22 May 1860; reprinted in *ATC*, pp. 87–103; see p. 91.
9. Ms. letter of 27 November 1860 to Cornelius in Cornelius, *Literarische Werke*, vol. 2 (Leipzig, 1905), pp. 756–57.
10. CI 100.
11. Boschot, III, 542, cites performances of *Le Temple universel* at an Orphéon festival in the Palais de l'Industrie, 13 and 17 September 1861. I can find no confirmation of this festival elsewhere.
12. "Cold in nature": Fauré, "Souvenirs," *Revue musicale* 10 (1922), 8; "most asinine": von Bülow to Raff in von Bülow, *Briefe* (Leipzig, 1989), III, 386, cited by Ernest Newman in *The Life of Richard Wagner* (London, 1945; reprinted Cambridge, 1976), III, 103.
13. Judith Gautier, *Le Second Rang du collier* (Paris, 1903), cited by Macdonald in "Hector Berlioz 1969—A Centenary Assessment," *ADAM* 331–33 (1969), 35–47; see pp. 44–45.
14. Ms. letter to Janin, 8 April 1861, in the collection of François Lang, Royaumont.
15. *JD*, 19 June 1861.

16. Report by Royer of 8 June 1861, archives of the Opéra, cited by Boschot, III, 539–40; see p. 540.
17. I combine phrases from *SW* 34 and *LI* 86.
18. Ms. letter of 28 August 1861, from a facsimile in Louise Pohl, *Hector Berlioz' Leben und Werke* (Leipzig, 1900), p. 276.
19. Ms. letter to the minister of State, 4 September 1861, **F-Pan** F²¹ 1069, dossier *Alceste*.
20. See *CI* 111, letter to Louis of 28 October 1861, which dwells on the matter of wives and children; and *CI* 112, letter to Morel of 3 March 1862, where Louis's behavior is said to have caused Berlioz "a chagrin more poignant than any I have experienced."
21. See ms. letter to Mutée, director of the Strasbourg theater, of 6 April 1862, **F-Pn** Berlioz letter 49, which lists the various properties required.
22. **F-Pc** Rés. 1791.
23. Berlioz was *not* with Marie when she died, as Boschot (III, 555) and Barzun (II, 212) say; the circumstances recounted here are from a ms. letter to Félix Marmion, 18 June [1862], now in the National Library of Scotland, Edinburgh.
24. Berlioz's financial accounts for the funeral and for Louis's subsequent visit are in the collection of Richard Macnutt, Withyham, Sussex; see V&A, p. 134, item 397. See also *CI* 114, letter to Louis of 17 June 1862.
25. **F-Pc** Rés. 1790.
26. "Brusque and violent separation": *LI* 91; "most profound chagrin": ms. letter to Freudenthal of Friday, 27 June 1862.
27. Some leaves from the manuscript sent to the printer are in the collection of Richard Macnutt, Withyham, Sussex; see V&A, p. 101, item 306, and facsimile on p. 100.
28. See Holoman, "Orchestral Material from the Library of the Société des Concerts," *19th-Century Music* 7 (1983), 106–18, esp. p. 108 and n. 11.
29. *CI* 113; see also *SW* 36 and a ms. letter to Mme Viardot, both of 21 September.
30. *SW* 36.
31. *LEM* 38 (1931), 210–13 (Carolyne Sayn-Wittgenstein in Rome to Berlioz, 27 September 1862); see p. 213.
32. "Lettres de Berlioz sur 'Les Troyens'," *Revue de Paris* 28, no. 5 (1921), 163.
33. Ms. letter to the Société des Concerts of 25 March 1863, draft in the **F-CSA**; transcribed in Holoman, "Orchestral Material from the Library of the Société des Concerts," p. 106.
34. Minutes of the governing committee, **F-Pc** D 17345 (6); cited by Holoman, "Orchestral Material," p. 108 and n. 8.
35. *NL*, p. 235.
36. "Dove-like beauty": ms. letter of 9 April 1863 to Mme Viardot, in the collection of François Lang, Royaumont; "Sicilian lioness": *CI* 119. The images of the German dove and the Sicilian lioness recur in the correspondence of this week.
37. *Mémoires*, postface.
38. Ms. letter of 3 May 1863 to the prince of Hohenzollern-Hechingen, collection of Alexander Meyer Cohn, Berlin.
39. Ms. letter of 29 April 1863 to Schwab ("It was impossible for me to stop in Strasbourg as I had hoped; they kept me too long in Löwenberg"), **F-Pc**. Boschot (III, 579 and 704) is incorrect: Berlioz did not stop in Strasbourg.
40. Cited, from an autograph draft of the toast then in the collection of Charles Malherbe, by Boschot III, 582.
41. *The New Grove*, IV, 358 (article "Choudens") offers the misleading implication that Choudens published "most of Berlioz's works." In fact Choudens acquired rights, in 1863, only to *Benvenuto Cellini* and *Les Troyens*.

42. *JD*, 9 November and 10 December 1863, cited in part in Macdonald, "Les Troyens at the Théâtre-Lyrique," *Musical Times* 110 (1969), 919–21; see p. 920.
43. *LEF* 37 (1930), p. 14.
44. *Mémoires*, postface.
45. Ms. letter of candidacy in the *Livre d'or* of the Société des Concerts, **F-Pc** ms. 17698.

14. *MARCHE FUNÈBRE*

1. Ms. letter of 20 March 1864, collection of Mme Reboul-Berlioz, Paris; given in *Clés de la musique*, February 1969, p. 8.
2. Bizet: *JD*, 8 October 1863; reprinted in Condé, pp. 274–75; see p. 275. Slavery: *Mémoires*, postface.
3. Boschot (III, 598) gives the date of the exhumation as 3 February; Berlioz does not describe it in his letter to Louis of 1 March, however, but rather in the letter of 17 March. It seems likely that the event took place in early March.
4. Cairns, p. 495, following Boschot (III, 600), gives 10 April as the concert date, however, and it seems possible the work was offered again at an extra concert on 17 April. If there was a delay not mentioned on the printed program (which carries the date 3 April), I do not know the reason.
5. Massarts as "personification of order and propriety": Stephen Heller [and Camille Saint-Saëns], "Anecdotes sur Berlioz," *Revue musicale* 3 (1903), 421–26; see p. 422. Hiller's anecdotes were first written in a letter to Hanslick, dated Paris, 1 February 1879; then published in the *Neue freie Presse*, and reprinted in the *Guide musical* of 20 February 1879.
6. "Ten years": journal of Ludovic Halévy, entry for 5 November 1863 (V, 891), collection of Mina Curtiss; cited in *NL*, p. 243.
7. *LI* 92.
8. "Old man": Cairns, p. 11; "When you will": *Mémoires*, postface, a sentiment repeated in a number of letters of the period.
9. *Mémoires*, "Travels in Dauphiné."
10. *Mémoires*, "Travels in Dauphiné," letter 2.
11. *LEF* 39 (1931), 463–64 (Liszt in Weimar to Hippeau, 15 May 1882).
12. See, for example, the facsimile of a leaf in the album of a M. Mendès, *NL*, opposite p. 43, estimated by Barzun to be from 1865; this is number 140 in Holoman, *Catalogue*.
13. To Estelle, 30 August 1865, *Est.* 12; translation after Macdonald in "One Hundred Years Ago," *Berlioz Society Bulletin* 52 (October 1965), pp. 18–19; see p. 19.
14. "Like everybody else": *LI* 125.
15. *LI* 128.
16. Collection of Richard Macnutt, Withyham, Sussex.
17. Fétis to Berlioz, 13 October 1866, cited by Vander Linden, "En marge du centième anniversaire de la mort d'Hector Berlioz (8 Mars 1969)," *Académie Royale de Belgique: Bulletin de la classe des beaux-arts* 51 (1969), 36–75; see p. 53; Berlioz to Fétis, 14 October 1866, cited by Locke, "New Letters of Berlioz," *19th-Century Music* 1 (1977), 71–84; see p. 84.
18. A recollection of Oscar Berggruen to Adolphe Jullien, cited in Jullien's *Hector Berlioz: Sa Vie et ses œuvres* (Paris, 1888), p. 301.
19. "'Faust's Verdammung,' dramatische Legende von H. Berlioz," a report to the Gesellschaft der Musikfreunde, 16 December 1866, in *Geschichte des Concert-*

wesens in Wien, vol. 2: *Aus dem Concertsaal* (Vienna, 1870; reprinted Westmead, Farnborough, Hants., 1971), pp. 411–16; see pp. 412–13.

20. Cited in Boschot, III, 637–38.
21. Ms. letter to Morel, 12 May 1867.
22. Originally in German. See Rose Fay Thomas, *Memoirs of Theodore Thomas* (New York, 1911), p. 37. The copy of the Requiem is in the Newberry Library, Chicago.
23. "The most frightful affliction": *Est.* 25; "it was to me to die": this phrase and the circumstances in which Berlioz was told of Louis's death were first recorded by Jullien, *Hector Berlioz,* p. 301, presumably on the basis of conversations with the Damckes and Reyer.
24. *Mémoires,* postface.
25. Berlioz's will, facsimile in **F-Pn**, F. S. 276.
26. Ms. letter to Marmion, 5 September 1867; I paraphrase Berlioz's remarks.
27. "Rich American": *Est.* 26.
28. Ms. letter to Marmion, 8 December 1867.
29. "So you compose music, too": Stravinksy, in Stravinsky and Robert Craft, *Conversations with Igor Stravinsky* (New York and London, 1959), p. 29, cited by Cairns, p. 525; "in frequent contact": Stasov, *Selected Essays on Music,* translated by Florence Jonas (New York, 1968), p. 166.
30. *Le Nain jaune,* November 1863, cited by Macdonald in "Les Troyens at the Théâtre-Lyrique," *Musical Times* 110 (1969), 919–21; see p. 921.
31. Cited by Fouque, *Les Révolutionnaires de la musique* (Paris, 1882), p. 252.
32. Rimsky-Korsakov, *My Musical Life,* translated by Judah A. Joffe (rev. edn. New York, 1942), p. 71; my translation is after Gerald Abraham, in his *Rimsky-Korsakov: A Short Biography* (London, 1945), p. 35.
33. Ms. letter to Camille Pal, 19 February 1868, **GB-WImacnutt.**
34. Berlioz to Daniel Bernard, see *CI,* p. 58.
35. Legouvé, p. 243 (date corrected).
36. The anecdote told by Jullien, in *Hector Berlioz: Sa Vie et ses œuvres* (Paris, 1888), p. 312, presumably on the basis of conversations with Reyer; facsimile of the inscription in ibid., p. 309.
37. Blaze de Bury, in *Musiciens d'hier et d'aujourd-hui* (Paris, 1880); cited by Cairns, p. 518.
38. V&A, pp. 138–40, item 416, and facsimile, p. 139.
39. Ms. letter to a doctor, collection of André Meyer, Paris; cited in V&A, p. 138, item 415.
40. My account of Berlioz's funeral is assembled from newspaper accounts, notably Oscar Commetant, "Hector Berlioz," *Le Ménestrel,* 14 March 1869, p. 115; [Escudier], "Funérailles de Berlioz," *La France musicale,* 14 March 1869, p. 79; Pierre Lascombe, "Obsèques de Berlioz," *L'Art musical,* 18 March 1869, p. 125; Em. Mathieu de Monter, "Mort et obsèques d'Hector Berlioz," *R&GM,* 14 March 1869, pp. 85–86.

List of Illustrations

Index of Compositions

General Index

Berlioz, Louis-Hector (*continued*)
early musical efforts of, 11–12, 13–14,
17; early musical influences on, 12, 20,
23, 26–27; evolution of musical style of,
3–4, 27, 39, 52, 53, 72–110, 128, 131,
144, 211, 213, 226, 243, 247, 251–252,
257, 262, 268–270, 367–370, 375, 377,
380, 516–517, 520–521, 523; family
background of, 6, 8; *feuilleton de silence*
of, 464; four compositional periods of, 3–
4; funeral services for, 593–594; in Germany, 447–449, 450–453, 457–460; and
the guitar, 13–14, 15, 102, 215, 239;
health of, 3, 41, 44, 58, 114, 126, 190,
195–196, 197, 203, 210, 283, 297, 301,
311–312, 353, 396, 407, 434, 457, 464,
469, 483, 484, 485–486, 492, 495, 501,
543, 553, 566, 567, 572, 577–578, 585,
589, 592; influence on younger composers
of, 510–511; in Italy, 67, 112–130, 131,
238; last will and testament of, 584–585;
in London, 393–402, 423–427, 429, 430–
433, 443–446, 472–475; monetary situation of, 33, 41, 137, 155, 164–165, 170,
183, 189, 197, 203, 229–230, 277, 278,
279, 305, 311, 313, 340, 383, 386, 399,
415, 416, 466, 472, 478, 501–502, 505,
569, 586, 591; in Montmartre, 158–159,
170; as musical director of the Gymnase-
Musical, 172, 173; as musical journalist
and critic, 56, 126, 144, 149, 155–156,
157, 160, 165, 170, 176, 181, 187, 198,
235–238, 282, 323, 361, 362–363, 385–
386, 387–388, 408–409, 425, 426, 476,
543, 545, 568–569; musical shorthand of,
182, 215; in National Guard, 181, 274;
orchestral effects of, 95, 102–103, 528;
and orchestral placement, 354–355; orchestral songs of, 364–366; physical appearance of, 17, 59, 72, 137, 206, 342,
352, 499–501, 549, 588–589, 592 (*see
also* Berlioz, portraits and caricatures of);
and the piano, 102, 126, 214, 215, 585;
polémiques musicales of, 29, 38; portraits
and caricatures of, 73, 112, 115, 121,
127, 207, 208, 209, 210, 302, 303, 317,
318–319, 320, 327, 328, 333, 342, 343,
405, 413, 426, 430, 460, 469, 476, 483,
498–501, 502, 503, 507, 508, 509, 588,
590 (*see also* Berlioz, physical appearance
of); preliminary musical sketches of, 215–
223; printed musical programs of, 101;
production of concerts by, 231–235, 272,
412; public perceptions of, 4, 58, 159,
161, 196, 207, 271, 301, 311, 343, 347,

385, 506–507; publication of works of,
24, 137, 229–231, 301, 345, 399–400,
410, 429, 461–462, 470, 512–514; and
relationship with his family, 27, 31, 33,
40, 138, 139, 140, 141, 142, 151, 155,
158, 173, 271, 403–404; retirement of,
568–571; revisions to compositions by,
512; rhythm in music of, 97, 268–270;
romantic liaisons of, 150–151, 388, 555–
556, 577; in Russia, 383, 384–389, 586–
589; self-borrowing by, 36, 82, 83, 85,
88, 144, 205, 237, 527, 546; and study of
medicine, 17, 19–20, 23–24; suicide attempt by, 150; travels abroad of, 286–
301, 326–334, 346, 347, 429, 430, 447–
453, 457–460, 469–470, 581; turning
points in life of, 344; understanding of
musical history by, 362; use of drugs by,
100, 572; use of instruments by, 95, 102–
103, 233, 291, 357–359, 361, 528; in
Weimar, 294, 347, 435–438, 467–469,
480–481, 514, 560–562; work habits of,
211–214, 223–229
Berlioz, Louise-Julie-Virginie (sister), 9
Berlioz, Louis-Joseph (father), 6–7, 139,
141, 142, 173, 271, 313, 403; *livre de raison* of, 9, 151
Berlioz, Louis-Jules (brother), 9, 17
Berlioz, Marie-Antoinette-Joséphine Marmion (mother), 7–8, 133, 188
Berlioz, Nanci (Marguerite-Anne-Louise; sister), 9, 13, 23, 125, 131, 132, 139, 141,
142, 173, 180, 239, 279, 408, 413, 505
Berlioz, Prosper (brother), 9, 132, 133, 173,
179, 194–195, 199
Berlioz, Victor (uncle), 6
Berry, Duc de, 18
Bert, Charles, 11
Bertin, Armand, 165, 166, 203, 227, 313
Bertin, François-Edouard, 156, 165, 166,
486, 550
Bertin, Louise-Angélique, 157, 165, 178
Bertin, Louis-François, 165, 166
Berton, Henri-Montan, 80–81, 166
Bloc, Nathan (conductor), 51
Bocage, Pierre, 134, 135
Bockholtz-Falconi, Anna, 474, 478, 515
Bohain, Victor, 144
Boieldieu, François-Adrien (composer), 15,
20, 57
Boieldieu, *jeune* (publisher), 24
Boschot, Adolphe (biographer of B), 343
Bottée de Toulmon. *See* Toulmon, Auguste
Bottée de
Bourgery, Jean-Marc, 24

Legouvé, Ernest, 1, 118, 134, 185, 189, 197, 208–209, 344, 364, 486
Le Sueur, Jean-François, 26, 40, 65, 166, 184, 433; as B's mentor, 25–27, 80, 362; B's only existing letter to, 30–31
Lévy, Michel (publisher), 439–440, 577
Lévy, Michel-Maurice (singing teacher), 315, 337
Lind, Jenny, 306, 324, 400, 475
Lipinski, Karl, 296
Liszt, Blandine, 306, 558
Liszt, Cosima, 449
Liszt, Franz, 1, 2, 4, 71, 134, 166, 192, 234, 327, 329, 332, 412, 428, 436, 437, 449, 480, 489, 508, 543, 558; and Beethoven monument, 276, 323–324; musical efforts of, 142, 149, 153, 154, 167, 180, 306–307, 453, 509, 517; production of *Cellini* by, 427, 428, 431, 435; relationship with B of, 69, 136–137, 142, 151, 156, 209, 294, 389, 393, 459–460, 461, 501, 520, 576, 579–580; and works of B, 110, 144, 164, 333, 433, 435
London Philharmonic Society, 198, 401
Louis XVIII, 18
Louis-Napoléon ("prince-president"), 219, 255, 399, 427–428, 435, 439, 440, 483, 485, 487, 488, 490, 491, 511
Louis-Philippe ("citizen-king"), 64–65, 342–343, 398, 399; attempted assassination of, 168; support of the arts by, 68
Lvov, Alexei Feodorovich (master, Russian Imperial Chapel), 323, 384

Macdonald, Hugh, 210, 266
Madelaine. *See* Stéphen de La Madelaine
Malherbe and Weingartner (editors of B's works), 99, 219, 262, 276
Malvenuto Cellini, 192, 193
Marmion, Félix (uncle), 6, 139–140, 141, 142, 181, 184, 284, 456, 464, 585; as intermediary for B, 27–28, 31, 33
Marmion, Nicolas (grandfather), 11, 181
Marrast, Armand, 363, 398, 405
Martin, Adolf (German publisher), 181
Martin, Mme Solera Villa-Récio (mother-in-law), 465, 481, 484–485, 504–505, 554–555, 592, 594
Martini, Giovanni Battista, 15
Massart, Lambert, 323, 406, 412, 570, 571
Massart, Louise, 412, 570, 571
Massol, J.-E.-A., 190, 401
Méhul, Etienne, 20, 80
Mémoires, 5, 13, 41, 42, 102, 124, 138, 149, 169, 185–186, 234–235, 245, 343, 349, 363, 391, 400, 408, 429, 453, 457,

465, 488, 490, 506, 511–512, 546, 569, 577–578, 579. *See also* Berlioz, autobiographies of
Mendelssohn, Félix, 4, 118, 119, 121, 289, 290, 294, 295, 296, 323, 332, 393, 512
Le Ménestrel, 149, 301
Meyer, Léopold de, 315, 316, 317, 319–320
Meyerbeer, Giacomo, 20, 54, 75, 80, 142, 166, 171, 174, 175, 180, 199, 279, 289, 300, 305, 324, 362, 390, 408–409, 412, 474, 525, 573
Millevoye, Charles Hubert, 25
Moke, Camille (later Pleyel), 60–61, 62, 67, 68, 69, 111, 114–116, 432
Le Monde dramatique, 171
Le Monde illustré, 490
Le Monde musical, 302
Moore, Thomas, 35, 38, 55, 94, 123
Morel, Auguste, 227, 290
Moscheles, Ignaz, 177, 199, 352, 436, 571
Mozart, Wolfgang Amadeus, 155, 160, 215, 330, 362
Müller, Carl, 299
Müller, Georg, 299
Musard, Philippe, 233, 234, 235
Musical World (London), 192, 473
Musikalische Reise in Deutschland, 302

Nadar, Félix, 498
Napoleon, 6, 18, 19, 149–150, 203, 206, 274, 275; Italian campaign of, 130; Russian campaign of, 384, 387
Napoleon III, Emperor. *See* Louis-Napoléon
Nathan-Treillet, Mme, 292, 305
Neue Zeitschrift für Musik, 177, 282
New Philharmonic Society, 427, 430–433, 441, 473, 474
Nicholas, Czar of Russia, 302, 334, 383, 386, 468
Nourrit, Adolphe (tenor), 23, 60, 134, 180, 199
Novello (London publisher), 513

Onslow, George, 285, 451
Opéra (Académie Royale de musique), 20, 21, 74, 166, 171, 174, 179, 181, 235, 271, 278, 279, 281, 390–391, 464, 490, 492, 527, 528, 542, 548–549, 550, 559
Opéra-Comique, 157, 235, 340
Orgue melodium, 314, 357
Orléans, Duc d', 164, 183, 185, 285
Orphéon movement, 547

Paganini, Niccolò, 1, 134, 143, 155, 161, 163, 196, 197, 198, 202, 203